RESEARCH HANDBOOK ON INTERNATIONAL CRIMINAL LAW

RESEARCH HANDBOOKS IN INTERNATIONAL LAW

This highly original series offers a unique appraisal of the state-of-the-art of research and thinking in international law. Taking a thematic approach, each volume, edited by a prominent expert, covers a specific aspect of international law or examines the international legal dimension of a particular strand of the law. A wide range of sub-disciplines in the spheres of both public and private law are considered; from international environmental law to international criminal law, from international economic law to the law of international organisations, and from international commercial law to international human rights law. The *Research Handbooks* comprise carefully commissioned chapters from leading academics as well as those with an emerging reputation. Taking a genuinely international approach to the law, and addressing current and sometimes controversial legal issues, as well as affording a clear substantive analysis of the law, these *Handbooks* are designed to inform as well as to contribute to current debates.

Equally useful as reference tools or introductions to specific topics, issues and debates, the *Handbooks* will be used by academic researchers, postgraduate students, practising lawyers and lawyers in policy circles.

Titles in this series include:

Research Handbook on International Human Rights Law
Edited by Sarah Joseph and Adam McBeth

Handbook of Research on International Consumer Law
Edited by Geraint Howells, Iain Ramsay and Thomas Wilhelmsson with David Kraft

Research Handbook on International Environmental Law
Edited by Malgosia Fitzmaurice, David M. Ong and Panos Merkouris

Research Handbook on International Criminal Law
Edited by Bartram S. Brown

Research Handbook on International Criminal Law

Edited by

Bartram S. Brown

Professor of Law and Co-Director, Program in International and Comparative Law, IIT Chicago–Kent College of Law, Illinois Institute of Technology, USA

RESEARCH HANDBOOKS IN INTERNATIONAL LAW

Edward Elgar
Cheltenham, UK • Northampton, MA, USA

Published by
Edward Elgar Publishing Limited
The Lypiatts
15 Lansdown Road
Cheltenham
Glos GL50 2JA
UK

Edward Elgar Publishing, Inc.
William Pratt House
9 Dewey Court
Northampton
Massachusetts 01060
USA

A catalogue record for this book is available from the British Library

Library of Congress Control Number: 2010927653

ISBN 978 1 84720 278 9 (cased)

Typeset by Cambrian Typesetters, Camberley, Surrey
Printed and bound by MPG Books Group, UK

Contents

Contributors

Kai Ambos is Professor and Chair of Criminal Law, Criminal Procedure, Comparative Law and International Criminal Law at the Georg-August-Universität Göttingen, Germany. Head of the Department of 'Foreign and International Criminal Law,' Institute of Criminal Law and Justice at the University of Göttingen. Judge at the Provincial Court (*Landgericht*) of Lower Saxony in Göttingen. Former Dean of Students of the Faculty of Law at the University of Göttingen (April 2008–2010). Former senior research fellow at the Max-Planck Institute for Foreign and International Criminal Law, Freiburg im Breisgau, Germany, in charge of the sections 'International Criminal Law' and 'Spanish-speaking Latin America' (1991–2003). Member of the German Delegation to the Diplomatic Conference on the Establishment of an International Criminal Court (Rome, 15 June–17 July, 1998). Member of the expert working group established by the Federal Ministry of Justice for the elaboration of the German 'International Criminal Law Act,' implementing the Rome Statute for an ICC. Referee of the European Research Council in peer review evaluations (appointment from 13 October 2010–31 December 2013).

Kelly D. Askin, BS, JD, PhD (law) is senior legal officer for the International Justice Program of the Open Society Justice Initiative. She was also 2004-2005 Fulbright New Century Scholar on the Global Empowerment of Women. Since 1995, Askin has taught and served as a visiting scholar at Notre Dame, Washington College of Law, Harvard, Yale and Oxford. She also served as Executive Director of the International Criminal Justice Institute and American University's War Crimes Research Office. Askin served as a legal adviser to the judges of the International Criminal Tribunal for the Former Yugoslavia and for Rwanda from 2000–2002, and has also served as an expert consultant, legal adviser, and international law trainer to prosecutors, judges and registry at the International Criminal Tribunal for the Former Yugoslavia, the International Criminal Tribunal for Rwanda, the Serious Crimes Unit in East Timor, the International Criminal Court, the Special Court for Sierra Leone, and the Extraordinary Chambers in the Courts of Cambodia. Her books include *War Crimes Against Women: Prosecution in International War Crimes Tribunals* (1997) and the three volume treatise *Women and International Human Rights Law* (1999, 2001, 2002, co-editor). She serves on the board of several organizations, including the Executive Board of the American Branch of the International Law Association, the International Judicial Academy and International Criminal Law Services.

M. Cherif Bassiouni, Distinguished Research Professor of Law Emeritus; President Emeritus, International Human Rights Law Institute, DePaul University, United States; President, International Institute of Higher Studies in Criminal Sciences (ISISC), Italy; Honorary President, Association Internationale de Droit Pénal (AIDP). He has served in the following United Nations' positions: Independent Expert Human Rights in Afghanistan, (2004–2006); Independent Expert on the Rights to Restitution, Compensation and Rehabilitation for Victims of Grave Violations of Human Rights and Fundamental Freedoms

(1998–2000); Chairman, Drafting Committee, Diplomatic Conference on the Establishment of an International Criminal Court (1998); Vice-Chairman, General Assembly's Ad Hoc and Preparatory Committees on the Establishment of an International Criminal Court (1995 and 1996–1998); Member, then Chairman, of the Security Council's Commission to Investigate Violations of International Humanitarian Law in the Former Yugoslavia (1993), and the Commission's Special Rapporteur on Gathering and Analysis of the Facts (1992–1993); Co-chairman of the Committee of Experts to Draft the Convention on the Prevention and Suppression of Torture (1977).

Bartram S. Brown is Professor of Law and Co-Director, Program in International and Comparative Law, at the Chicago-Kent College of Law of the Illinois Institute of Technology, United States. He received his BA from Harvard University, his JD from Columbia University, and his Ph.D from the Graduate Institute of International Studies in Geneva, Switzerland. He has published a book on the law and politics of the World Bank, as well as articles on international human rights law, international humanitarian law, international criminal tribunals and international trade law. Professor Brown is a member of the Council on Foreign Relations (New York) and has served on the Board of Directors of Amnesty International, United States. He served as a law clerk to Judge Gabrielle Kirk McDonald at the International Criminal Tribunal for the Former Yugoslavia, and participated in the 1998 Rome Diplomatic Conference on the Establishment of an International Criminal Court as legal adviser to the Republic of Trinidad and Tobago.

John Cerone is Professor of Law and Director of the Center for International Law and Policy, New England Law, Boston, United States. He teaches Public International Law, Human Rights Law, the International Law of Armed Conflict and International Prosecution. He has served as a confidential legal adviser to international criminal courts and was involved in the establishment of the Special Court for Sierra Leone and the Extraordinary Chambers in the Courts of Cambodia.

David M. Crane is Professor of Practice at the Syracuse University College of Law, New York, United States. From 2002–2005 he served as the founding Chief Prosecutor of the Special Court for Sierra Leone, the world's first hybrid national/international war crimes tribunal located in Freetown, Sierra Leone. With the rank of Undersecretary General, Professor Crane's mandate was to prosecute those who bear the greatest responsibility for war crimes, crimes against humanity and other atrocities committed during the civil war in Sierra Leone. Among those he indicted for those horrific crimes was the President of Liberia, Charles Taylor, the first sitting African Head of State in history to be held accountable.

Clare da Silva worked at the Special Court for Sierra Leone between 2004 and 2008. She was defence legal assistant at the trial of Norman and others and defence legal counsel in the appeal of Kondewa and Fofana.

Margaret M. deGuzman is Assistant Professor of Law, Temple University, Beasley School of Law, Philadelphia, United States. She teaches International Criminal Law and Transitional Justice. Professor deGuzman served as a legal adviser to the Senegal delegation at the Rome Conference on the International Criminal Court. She is currently participating in the work of expert groups drafting a convention on crimes against humanity and general rules and principles of international criminal procedure.

Mark A. Drumbl is the Class of 1975 Alumni Professor of Law at the School of Law, Washington and Lee University, Virginia, United States, where he also serves as Director of the Transnational Law Institute.

Mark S. Ellis is Executive Director, International Bar Association, London. Prior to joining the IBA, he spent ten years as the first Executive Director of the Central European and Eurasian Law Initiative (CEELI), a project of the American Bar Association (ABA), providing technical legal assistance to 28 countries in Central Europe and the former Soviet Union, and to the International Criminal Tribunal for the Former Yugoslavia in The Hague. Twice a Fulbright Scholar at the Economic Institute in Zagreb, Croatia, he earned his J.D. and economics degrees from Florida State University and his PhD in international criminal law from King's College, London.

Ved P. Nanda is Evans University Professor and Thompson G. Marsh Professor of Law at the Sturm College of Law, University of Denver, Colorado, United States. He is Past President of the World Jurist Association and now its Honorary President, former honorary Vice-President of the American Society of International Law and now its counselor, and a member of the advisory council of the United States Institute of Human Rights. He was formerly the United States Delegate to the World Federation of the United Nations Associations, Geneva, and Vice-Chair of its Executive Council, and also served on the Board of Directors of the United Nations Association (United States). He also serves as an elected member of the American Law Institute and as a council member for the American Bar Association Section of International Law.

Sarah M.H. Nouwen is the Mayer Brown Research Fellow in Public International at the Lauterpacht Centre for International Law and Pembroke College, University of Cambridge. Her forthcoming book *Complementarity in the Line of Fire: The Catalysing Effect of the International Criminal Court in Uganda and Sudan*, based on months of fieldwork in both countries, examines the effects of the complementarity principle on the Ugandan and Sudanese legal systems. She has worked as a transitional-justice and rule-of-law consultant to Ministries of Foreign Affairs and non-governmental organisations, and holds Masters degrees in Law (Utrecht, with specialisation in Cape Town) and International Relations (Cambridge) and a PhD in Law (Cambridge).

Faiza Patel King is Director of Planning and Counsel in the Liberty and National Security Project at the Brennan Center for Justice, New York University School of Law, New York, United States. She works on civil liberties issues affecting Muslims in the United States, focusing particularly on domestic radicalization. Before joining the Brennan Center, Ms Patel worked as a senior policy officer at the Organization for the Prohibition of Chemical Weapons in The Hague. She clerked for Judge Sidhwa at the International Criminal Tribunal for the Former Yugoslavia, and previously worked as an associate at Debevoise & Plimpton in Washington, DC. Born and raised in Pakistan, Ms Patel graduated *magna cum laude* from Harvard College and *cum laude* from NYU School of Law.

Katharina Peschke has worked as a lawyer with hybrid courts in Bosnia and Herzegovina and Kosovo and in various positions on issues of rule of law, international law and human rights with the United Nations in Sudan (DPKO), Vienna (UNODC) and Geneva HCHR). In 2004, she was a Visiting Fellow in International Law at Cambridge University. She holds Master degrees in Law (University College London) and in International Relations (Cambridge University).

Naomi Roht-Arriaza is Professor of Law at the Hastings College of Law of the University of California, United States. She is the author of *The Pinochet Effect: Transnational Justice in the Age of Human Rights* (2005) and *Impunity and Human Rights in International Law and Practice* (1995), and co-editor of *Transitional Justice in the Twenty-First Century: Beyond Truth versus Justice*. She is an associate editor of the *Yearbook on International Environmental Law*. She continues to write on accountability, both state and corporate, for human rights violations as well as on other human rights, international criminal law and global environmental issues. Her co-author, **Menaka Fernando**, will graduate from the University of California, Hastings College of Law, in 2011.

William A. Schabas, OC, MRIA, is Professor of Human Rights Law, National University of Ireland, Galway and Director, Irish Centre for Human Rights; Global Legal Scholar, University of Warwick School of Law; Visiting Professor, Queen's University Belfast School of Law; Visiting Professor, LUISS Guido Carli University, Rome (2008).

Michael P. Scharf is the John Deaver Drinko/Baker and Hostetler Professor of Law and Director of the Frederick K. Cox International Law Center at Case Western Reserve University School of Law, United States. In 2004–2005, Scharf served as a member of the international team of experts that provided training to the judges of the Iraqi High Tribunal; in 2006 he led the first training session for the investigative judges and prosecutors of the newly established UN Cambodia Genocide Tribunal, and in November 2008 he served as Special Assistant to the Prosecutor of the Cambodia Tribunal. In February 2005, Scharf and the Public International Law and Policy Group, an NGO he co-founded, were nominated for the Nobel Peace Prize by six governments and the Prosecutor of an International Criminal Tribunal for the work they have done to help in the prosecution of major war criminals, such as Slobodan Milosevic, Charles Taylor and Saddam Hussein. During the elder Bush and Clinton administrations, Scharf served in the Office of the Legal Adviser of the US Department of State, where he held the positions of Attorney-Adviser for Law Enforcement and Intelligence, Attorney-Adviser for United Nations Affairs, and delegate to the United Nations Human Rights Commission. Scharf is the author of over 70 scholarly articles and 13 books, including three that have won National Book of the Year Awards.

David Weissbrodt is Regents Professor of Law and Fredrikson and Byron Professor of Law, University of Minnesota Law School, United States. His co-author, **Kristin K. Zinsmaster**, is Editor-in-Chief of vol. 94, *Minnesota Law Review*; JD 2010, University of Minnesota Law School.

Preface

Since the 1993 creation of the International Criminal Tribunal for the Former Yugoslavia (ICTY) international law has been applied, as rarely before, to hold individuals directly accountable for their criminal acts. The ICTY and its sister institution the International Criminal Tribunal for Rwanda (ICTR) have brought perpetrators of genocide, war crimes and crimes against humanity to justice, and a permanent International Criminal Court (ICC), recently established by treaty, is working on its first cases.

Some, including many West European governments, trumpet these developments as inevitable and long overdue in today's increasingly globalized and inter-dependent world. Others, especially within the US government, are concerned that independent and effective norms and institutions of international criminal law could undermine both state sovereignty and national security. The United States has never accepted the ICC Treaty, and for that reason alone the appropriate balance between the jurisdiction of national courts and of international criminal courts remains a matter of some controversy.

Although the ICC has been successfully established, its fate has not been fully determined. It faces cross-cutting pressures. It is expected to act effectively and yet to be scrupulously fair and impartial with regard both to the individuals being investigated and also concerning any countries whose legitimate interests may be implicated. The practice and experience of the next several years should define the direction of things to come. The ICC may grow into a strong pillar of the international community, or it may wither into ineffectiveness.

Whatever the fate of the ICC, new alternative mechanisms of international criminal law are developing in parallel, such as the mixed national/international criminal courts established in Sierra Leone and Cambodia. Universal jurisdiction prosecutions by national courts, on the *Pinochet* case model, provide another alternative. The very existence of these relatively exotic mechanisms of criminal accountability challenges national courts to strengthen their traditional role in investigating and prosecuting those within the national jurisdiction who commit serious international crimes.

All these stunning developments affect the practice of law as well as the geopolitical landscape. An international criminal bar is taking shape bringing together criminal lawyers and international lawyers and opening up new career possibilities for legal professionals.

This *Research Handbook of International Criminal Law* describes the legal processes and institutional mechanisms of international criminal law, exploring how they have developed and operated in a variety of contexts.

I am indebted to the contributing authors without whom this *Handbook* would obviously not have been possible. From the beginning our shared objective was to break down complicated issues of international criminal law in clear and concise language. This can be a difficult challenge even for talented scholars and practitioners such as those contributing to this volume. In the event, their efforts have produced a work which should be useful and accessible even to those without legal training or prior experience relating to international criminal law. Many thanks as well to students Tiffany Carey, Victoria Hayes and Brian Langs for their invaluable assistance in editing this volume.

Bartram S. Brown
Chicago

Abbreviations

AAAS	American Association for the Advancement of Science (NGO)
ABA	American Bar Association
ABA/CEELI	American Bar Association's Central European and Eurasia Initiative
AFRC	Armed Forces Revolutionary Council
ALI	American Law Institute
AMICC	American NGO Coalition for the ICC (NGO)
APC	All People's Congress
ASF	Avocats sans frontières (NGO)
ATS	Alien Tort Statute (US)
BAB	Bridges Across Borders (NGO)
BBC	British Broadcasting Corporation
CAT	Convention Against Torture
CCL10	Control Council Law No. 10 (Nuremburg)
CCR	Centre for Constitutional Rights
CDF	Civil Defence Forces
CICC	Coalition for an International Criminal Court
CIJ	Coalition for International Justice (NGO)
CPTJ	Center for Peace Through Justice (NGO)
CSD	Center for Social Development (NGO)
CSRT	Combatant Status Review Tribunal
CWHRCS	Coalition for Women's Human Rights in Conflict Situations (NGO)
CWRACS	Coalition for Women's Rights in Armed Conflict Situations (NGO)
DC-Cam	Documentation Centre of Cambodia (NGO)
DRC	Democratic Republic of Congo
EAW	European Arrest Warrant
ECCC	Extraordinary Chambers in the Courts of Cambodia
ECHR	European Convention on Human Rights
ECJ	European Court of Justice
ECOMOG	Economic Community Cease-Fire Monitoring Group
ECOWAS	Economic Community of West African States
ECtHR	European Court of Human Rights
FARDC	Armed Forces of the Democratic Republic of Congo
FIDH	Fédération Internationale des Ligues des Droits de l'Homme (NGO)
FRY	Federal Republic of Yugoslavia
GoSS	Government of South Sudan
HAI	humanitarian armed intervention
HLC	Humanitarian Law Center
HRF	Human Rights First (NGO)
HRW	Human Rights Watch
IBA	International Bar Association

ICC	International Criminal Court
ICCPR	International Covenant on Civil and Political Rights
ICDAA	International Criminal Defence Attorneys Association (NGO)
ICG	International Crisis Group (NGO)
ICJ	International Court of Justice
ICL	international criminal law
ICRC	International Committee of the Red Cross (NGO)
ICTJ	International Center for Transitional Justice (NGO)
ICTR	International Criminal Tribunal for Rwanda
ICTY	International Criminal Tribunal for the Former Yugoslavia
IDP	internally displaced person
IHF	International Helsinki Federation (NGO)
IHL	international humanitarian law
ILC	International Law Commission
IMT	International Military Tribunal at Nuremberg
IMTFE	International Military Tribunal for the Far East
IOM	International Organisation for Migration
IST	Iraqi Special Tribunal
IWHRLC	International Women's Human Rights Law Clinic (NGO)
IWPR	Institute for War and Peace Reporting
JCE	joint criminal enterprise (theory of liability)
KID	Khmer Institute for Democracy (NGO)
LICADHO	Cambodian League for the Promotion and Defence of Human Rights
LRA	Lord's Resistance Army
MCA	Military Commissions Act of 2006
MCRE	Military Commission Rules of Evidence
MLAT	mutual legal assistance treaty
MONUC	United Nations Mission to the Democratic Republic of Congo
NATO	North Atlantic Treaty Organization
NAWO	National Alliance of Women's Organizations (NGO)
NGO	non-governmental organization
NORMA	Kosovar Association of Women Lawyers (NGO)
NPFL	National Patriotic Front of Liberia
NPRC	National Provisional Ruling Council
NPWJ	No Peace Without Justice (NGO)
NSA	non-state actor
OAS	Organization of American States
OHCHR	United Nations Office of the High Commissioner for Human Rights
OPCV	Office of Public Counsel for Victims
OSJI	Open Society Justice Initiative
OTP	Office of the Prosecutor
PGA	Parliamentarians for Global Action (NGO)
PHR	Physicians for Human Rights (NGO)
POW	prisoner of war
PSC	private security contractor
REMJA	Meeting of Ministers of Justice of the Americas

RMC	Rules for Military Commissions
RUF	Revolutionary United Front
SCSL	Special Court for Sierra Leone
SCWG	Special Court (of Sierra Leone) Working Group
SLA	Sierra Leone Army
SLCMP	Sierra Leone Court Monitoring Program
SLPP	Sierra Leone People's Party
SOAT	Sudan Organisation Against Torture (NGO)
SPLM/A	Sudanese People's Liberation Movement/Army
TRC	Sierra Leone Truth and Reconciliation Commission
UDHR	Universal Declaration of Human Rights
UN	United Nations
UNAMSIL	United Nations Mission in Sierra Leone
UNCTOC	UN Convention Against Transnational Organized Crime
UNDP	United Nations Development Programme
UNMIS	United Nations Mission to Sudan
UPDF	Ugandan People's Defense Forces
VRWG	Victims' Rights Working Group (formed by the NGO Redress)
VTF	Victim Trust Fund
VWS	Victims and Witness Section (ICTY)
VWSU	Victims and Witness Support Unit (Sierra Leone)
VWU	Victims and Witnesses Unit
WIGJ	Women's Initiatives for Gender Justice (NGO)
WSU	Witness Support Unit (Cambodia)
WVS	Witness and Victims Support Unit

PART I

INDIVIDUAL CRIMINAL RESPONSIBILITY UNDER INTERNATIONAL LAW

1 International criminal law: nature, origins and a few key issues

Bartram S. Brown

The purpose of international criminal law is to establish the criminal responsibility of individuals for international crimes. Public international law is traditionally focused on the rights and obligations of states, and thus is not particularly well suited to this task. It has adapted through a long and slow historical process, drawing upon multiple sources. Many of the chapters in this *Handbook* explore to some extent the historical development of international criminal law. I will not attempt to summarize that history in detail, but a few historical observations here will help to explain how international criminal law emerged from its sources in public international law, comparative law, international humanitarian law and international human rights law. This will set the stage for an introductory discussion of some key issues in contemporary international criminal law.

ORIGINS AND SOURCES

Public International Law

International criminal law has developed and grown as part of a broader system of public international law which, since 1648, has been based on state sovereignty, including each state's jurisdiction over its own territory and citizens. A basic system of international law, defining the rights and obligations of states, was needed to recognize and validate this sovereignty, but this decentralized system has no legislature. Instead, international law must be based on the consent of states, arising from one or more of three formal sources: i.e. treaties, customary international law, or general principles of law. Treaties make binding law for those states that agree to accept them. Rules of customary international law develop when the actions of states, their general and consistent practices, demonstrate their implied consent to those rules. General principles of law, especially when common to the laws of many nations, can also be applied at the international level. Judicial decisions and scholarly writings are recognized as secondary sources of international law, and are especially useful as indicators of changes in customary international law. International crimes, and the other substantive aspects of international criminal law, emerge from these same sources.

Public international law is predominantly state-centric both in the sense that it is based on the consent of states and also because its central focus has always been the rights and obligations of states. According to the well-established and recently codified law of state responsibility,[1] any state's violation of its international legal obligations entails legal consequences.

---

[1] For the Articles on Responsibility of States for Internationally Wrongful Acts and the ILC

But the law of state responsibility says nothing about the legal responsibility of individual persons for international crimes,[2] therefore the progress of international criminal law has required the development of a whole new field of public international law. International criminal law is largely unconcerned with state responsibility, focusing instead on the criminal responsibility of those individuals who commit international crimes.[3]

It is impossible to introduce the development of individual criminal responsibility in international law without referring, at least briefly, to the unique 1474 precedent of Peter von Hagenbach, Governor of Breisach, in southern Germany. In that year he was charged with 'trampling under foot the laws of God and man' for acts including murder, rape, and 'orders to his non-German mercenaries to kill the men in the houses where they were quartered so that the women and children would be completely at their mercy'.[4] He was tried by an international panel of 28 judges, and after his conviction for multiple crimes, stripped of his knighthood and executed. This singular historical example nonetheless illustrates that an international criminal trial for atrocities was viewed as an appropriate option well prior to the formal birth of the nation-state system circa 1648. It would be centuries before the states at the center of that new system would once again resort to an international criminal trial.

Traditionally, international law has defined very few crimes, proscribing only acts generally viewed as a serious threat to the interests of the international community as a whole. For centuries, piracy has been recognized as an international crime under customary international law. Slave trading joined the list at the end of the nineteenth century when that practice was outlawed by treaty.

Comparative Law

Criminal law developed first at the national level. Its principles emerged from philosophy and government, grew through practice and experience and were spread by forces ranging from violent revolution to their peaceable incorporation into constitutions and legislation. The US Constitution's Bill of Rights and France's 1789 Declaration of the Rights of Man and of the Citizen are examples of this. Each reflects philosophical notions of justice which were

---

Commentary to the Articles, see Report of the International Law Commission on the Work of Its Fifty-third Session, UN GAOR, 56th Sess., Supp. No. 10, at 43, UN Doc. A/56/10 (2001), reprinted in James Crawford, THE INTERNATIONAL LAW COMMISSION'S ARTICLES ON STATE RESPONSIBILITY: INTRODUCTION, TEXT AND COMMENTARIES (2002) (hereinafter 'ILC Articles on State Responsibility').

   [2]   With regard to individual criminal responsibility, the International Law Commission (ILC) has merely observed as follows: 'The term "individual responsibility" has acquired an accepted meaning in light of the Rome Statute and other instruments; it refers to the responsibility of individual persons, including State officials, under certain rules of international law for conduct such as genocide, war crimes and crimes against humanity.' ILC Commentary on the Draft Articles on Responsibility of States for Internationally Wrongful Acts, UN Doc. A/56/10 (2001) (hereinafter 'ILC Commentary') Commentary on Article 58, para. 3.

   [3]   In the course of its attempts to codify the law of state responsibility the International Law Commission (ILC) did explore the possibility of defining state crimes under international law. The attempt was controversial and was omitted from the final version of the Articles on State Responsibility adopted by the ILC. This matter is briefly discussed in notes 38 and 39 *infra* and the associated text.

   [4]   For more on this case and for a good discussion of the development of individual criminal responsibility under international law, see Edoardo Greppi, *The Evolution of Individual Criminal Responsibility under International Law*, 835 INT'L REV. RED CROSS 531 (1999), available at www.icrc.org/web/eng/siteeng0.nsf/html/57JQ2X.

invoked to justify political and social revolution before being enshrined in a new constitutional framework of laws, notably including criminal law. From their national origins, basic principles of criminal law have percolated up into the international legal arena via their incorporation into treaties and their acceptance, based on state practice, as general principles of law or even as part of customary international law.

Inevitably, international criminal law has borrowed from the rules, principles and ideas to be found within the domestic legal systems of states, adapting the best of these as the basis of individual criminal responsibility under international law. This method of borrowing from another legal system is the essence of comparative law.[5] The Statute of the International Court of Justice identifies 'the general principles of law recognized by civilized nations' as a formal source of international law.[6] Thus, comparative law is a source of international law at least insofar as it facilitates the identification of legal principles common to national legal systems.[7] It is important to keep in mind that, beyond this formal source, an ultimate material source of the general principles of law lies in philosophical notions of right and justice.

National systems of criminal justice can be divided into at least two very different models, that is the Anglo-American common law model or the civil law model familiar on the continent of Europe. National criminal law can vary widely even among states both following the same one of these two models. The fact is that national legal systems of criminal law do not necessarily share the same general principles, and this complicates the task of building a system of international criminal law which is truly international.

Two overarching principles of criminal law, both deeply rooted in comparative law and philosophy, are the principle of culpability and the principle of legality.[8] These principles underlie most of the general principles of criminal law codified into the Rome Statute of the International Criminal Court (ICC), but even they are not universally recognized as general principles of national, or international, criminal law.

Principle of legality

The principle of legality, considered to be fundamental to the rule of law on the European

---

5   'The utility of comparative law … The only serious answer, it seems to me, is that the utility is the improvement which is made possible in one legal system as a result of knowledge of the rules and structures in another system. This improvement may occur in various sways … What these ways all have in common is that they concern borrowing. Comparative law as a practical study is therefore about legal transplants, the desirability and practicality of borrowing from another legal system.' Alan Watson, *Comparative Law and Legal Change*, 37 CAMBRIDGE LJ 313, 317–18 (1978).

6   Statute of the International Court of Justice, 26 June 1945, art. 38(1)(b), (c), 59 Stat. 1055, 1060, 3 Bevans 1153, 1187.

7   'The basic notion is that a general principle of international law is some proposition of law so fundamental that it will be found in virtually every legal system. When treaties and customary international law fail to offer a needed international rule, a search may be launched in comparative law to discover if national legal systems use a common legal principle. If such a common legal principle is found, then it is presumed that a comparable principle should be attributed to fill the gap in international law.' MARK JANIS, AN INTRODUCTION TO INTERNATIONAL LAW 56 (4th edn, Aspen Publishers, 2003).

8   See Nils Jareborg, *Criminal Reponsibility: Criminalization as Last Resort (Ultima Ratio)*, 2 OHIO ST. J CRIM. L 521, 522 (2005): 'The principle of legality (*nulla poena sine lege*) and the principle of culpability (*nulla poena sine culpa*) are often mentioned as the basic pillars of modern criminal law, but usually only the first of these is given any legally binding status in relation to the legislator.'

continent,[9] is rarely referred to as such in the United States.[10] Nonetheless, the underlying concept is as well known in that country as it is in Western Europe. A rare US district court decision that does directly refer to the principle of legality observes that it 'has historically found expression in the [US] criminal law rule of strict construction of criminal statutes, and in the [US] constitutional principles forbidding *ex post facto* operation of the criminal law, [and] vague criminal statutes'. [11]

The ICC Statute does not refer to the principle of legality by name, but that principle is reflected in both article 22 of the ICC Statute, *nullum crimen sine lege* (no crime without law), and in article 23, *nulla poena sine lege* (no penalty without law). These are two different expressions of the principle of legality.

Principle of culpability

The principle of culpability expresses a moral theory of responsibility and punishment which essentially holds that '[t]he equation of criminal responsibility with moral blameworthiness is the primary justification for imposing criminal sanctions'.[12] This notion is broadly, but not universally,[13] accepted as the basis of criminal law. In many countries the principle of culpability is seen as a fundamental precept of criminal law, requiring that moral culpability be the basis for the imposition of individual criminal liability and that the severity of any sentence imposed be likewise based on the moral culpability of the actor concerned.[14]

---

9   Stanislaw Pomorski notes that the principle of legality, '*nullum crimen, nulla poena sine lege* is considered as fundamental to the rule of law by all penal systems of continental Europe. It is commonly understood as including at least four requirements: 1) making statutory law the exclusive source of criminalization; 2) prohibition of criminalization by analogy; 3) prohibition of ex post facto laws; and 4) a requirement of definiteness of criminal statutes.' Stanislaw Pomorski, *Review Essay: Reflections on the First Criminal Code of Post-Communist Russia*, 46 AM. J COMP. L 375, 384 (citing a work by Hans-Heinrich Jescheck in Polish).   LEGALITY

10   See Jordan J. Paust, *Conceptualizing Violence: Present and Future Developments in International Law: Panel II: Adjudicating Violence: Problems Confronting International Law and Policy on War Crimes and Crimes Against Humanity: It's No Defense: Nullum Crimen, International Crime and the Gingerbread Man*, 60 ALB. L REV. 657, 669 (1997) (noting that US court cases have hardly ever referred to *nullum crimen sine lege, nulla poena sine lege* or to the principle of legality).

11   *United States* v. *Walker*, 514 F. Supp. 294, 316–17 (E.D. La. 1981).

12   See John T. Parry, *Culpability, Mistake, and Official Interpretations of Law*, 25 AM. J CRIM. L 1, 21 (1997): 'The equation of criminal responsibility with moral blameworthiness is the primary justification for imposing criminal sanctions', citing H.L.A. Hart's statement that 'it is necessary to be able to say on good conscience in each instance in which a criminal sanction is imposed for a violation of law that the violation was blameworthy and, hence, deserving of the moral condemnation of the community'. Henry M. Hart, Jr, *The Aims of the Criminal Law*, 23 LAW & CONTEMP. PROBS 401, 412 (1958).

13   See John L. Diamond, *The Myth of Morality and Fault in Criminal Law Doctrine*, 34 AM. CRIM. L REV. 111, 112 (1996), 'criminal law is not explained by moral individual culpability'.

14   See Pomorski, note 9 *supra*, at 385. ('The principle of culpability is recognized in European democracies as a fundamental precept of criminal law. Since criminal sanction expresses social condemnation, it must be personally deserved by an actor. Consequently, not only must the ascription of responsibility be contingent upon a finding of personal culpability, but the severity of punishment must not exceed the limits of actor's culpability. Preventive goals of criminal punishment may be pursued only within the limits marked by culpability of an actor. This way the culpability principle works as a restraint on the government, as a safeguard against inflicting punishment on undeserving individuals for some purely pragmatic reasons.')

The ICC Statute does not mention the principle of culpability by name, much less identify it as a general principle of criminal law. Nonetheless, the principle is reflected in many articles of the Statute, perhaps most clearly in article 30 on the mental element, or *mens rea*. This article restricts criminal responsibility before the ICC to those who have intentionally committed the material elements of a crime, with knowledge or awareness of the likely consequences.[15] These, of course, are basic elements of culpability.

International Humanitarian Law

International humanitarian law originated in the nineteenth century, a time when a 'state-centric'[16] concept of international law prevailed. The law of nations[17] of that era was generally believed to define rights and duties for states but not for individuals, and so the law of armed conflict, as it first emerged, did not formally recognize the rights of individuals or directly provide for individual criminal responsibility for any violations.

An international humanitarian law defining and regulating individual criminal responsibility differs substantially from one which merely defines the legal obligations of states *inter se*. In order to develop, international criminal law has often needed to bridge this conceptual gap through a functional adaptation of the norms of international humanitarian law.

In 1863, President Abraham Lincoln signed the Lieber Code, the first real codification of the customary laws of war. It set out a broad range of rules formulated as Instructions for the Government of Armies of the United States in the Field.[18] Among other things, the Lieber Code called for the humane and ethical treatment of populations in occupied areas, forbade the use of poisons and the use of torture, described the rights and duties of prisoners of war, and distinguished between the permissible and impermissible means to attain the ends of warfare. The substance of the Lieber Code was incorporated into treaty in the 1907 Hague

---

15   See Rome Statute of the International Criminal Court, 17 July 1998, 2187 UNTS 90, UN Doc. A/CONF 183/9*, 37 ILM 1002 (1998), corrected up to 16 January 2002, available at www.icc-cpi.int/. ICC Statute, art. 30, on the mental element provides: '1. Unless otherwise provided, a person shall be criminally responsible and liable for punishment for a crime within the jurisdiction of the Court only if the material elements are committed with intent and knowledge. 2. For the purposes of this article, a person has intent where: (a) in relation to conduct, that person means to engage in the conduct; (b) in relation to a consequence, that person means to cause that consequence or is aware that it will occur in the ordinary course of events.'

16   See Bartram S. Brown, *The Protection of Human Rights in Disintegrating States: A New Challenge*, 68 Chicago-Kent L Rev. 203, 204 (1992) (discussing the 'state-centric' nature of international law).

17   Mark Janis argues that 'the law of nations of the seventeenth and eighteenth centuries [was] a law common to individuals as well as to states' which developed into an international law of narrower scope in the era of nineteenth-century positivism. Janis notes that in 1789, when Jeremy Bentham invented the expression 'international law' in his Introduction to the Principles of Morals and Legislation, he offered the term as a replacement for the older term 'law of nations' and that Bentham incorrectly assumed that, under either name, the scope of that law was limited to the relations between states. This contributed to the narrow scope of international law which prevailed in the nineteenth century. Mark W. Janis, An Introduction to International Law 228–34 (2nd edn, 1993).

18   Instructions for the Government of Armies of the United States in the Field (Lieber Code of 1863), prepared by Francis Lieber, Correspondence, Orders, Reports and Returns of the Union Authorities from January 1 to December 31, 1863 #7, OR Series III, vol. III [S# 124], General Orders No. 100.

Regulations, which still did not address the issue of individual criminal responsibility under international law.

The essential purpose of international humanitarian law is to protect individuals in time of war.[19] To do so effectively, it should be applied as international criminal law to the broadest possible range of international and internal armed conflicts. Thus, as notions of natural and inalienable rights unfolded in the nineteenth century, subjecting even the conduct of devastating wars to civilizing rules of humanity, it was inevitable that there would eventually have to be a criminal law aspect. International law is still largely state-centric, but since individuals commit international crimes, international criminal responsibility is essential if these crimes are to be addressed effectively. Without it the system of international law would on its face seem to be incomplete. The 1474 prosecution of Peter von Hagenbach presaged this truth.

International Human Rights Law

International human rights law is a relatively new part of international law, and its focus upon individual rights makes it less state-centric than general international law. The idea of universal human rights has its origins in concepts of natural rights and the inherent dignity of the human being, but the international law of human rights has developed well beyond its philosophical origins.

The horrors of the Nazi holocaust brought home to many the need for an international law of human rights. When concerned people and governments abroad protested the treatment of Jews and other oppressed groups in Germany, apologists for the Nazi regime could reject these protestations by characterizing the issue as a matter within the domestic jurisdiction and national sovereignty of the German state. Although the genocidal 'Final Solution' was morally abhorrent and unmistakably wrong, its illegality under positive international law was less clear. The inadequacy of the existing positive international law became apparent, and this provided the impetus for changes to come.

Since the Second World War there has been a major thrust toward the enactment of a positive international law of human rights. By articulating human rights norms in treaties and other international normative instruments, states and international organizations have done more than simply create a few more rules of positive international law. They have begun to transform the nature of the international system.

The United Nations Charter represented a major advance in the codification of the international political order, and it did much to develop the international legal order as well. Promoting and encouraging respect for human rights and fundamental freedoms for all is explicitly mentioned as one of that organization's purposes,[20] and thus human rights were for the first time definitively declared to be a matter of international concern. On the other hand, the Charter is not very specific about the human rights and freedoms to be promoted, or about any specific obligations of states relating to human rights.

---

[19]   'It is the object of international humanitarian law to regulate hostilities in order to attenuate their hardships. Humanitarian law is that considerable portion of international law which is inspired by a feeling for humanity and is centered on the protection of the individual in time of war.' JEAN PICTET, DEVELOPMENT AND PRINCIPLES OF INTERNATIONAL HUMANITARIAN LAW 1 (1985).

[20]   See the Preamble to the UN Charter, and art. 1(3).

Another problem is that the Charter also expresses principles which can be invoked against international action to protect human rights. It reaffirms the 'sovereign equality' of UN member states,[21] and the United Nations's lack of authority to intervene in the domestic jurisdiction of its members.[22] The latter two provisions serve to reinforce the argument that state sovereignty should preclude any intrusive international action for the protection of human rights.

Some of these deficiencies were remedied when the Universal Declaration of Human Rights[23] was adopted by the UN General Assembly in 1948, and the post-Charter evolution of international human rights norms and procedures began. The Universal Declaration proclaims itself 'as a common standard of achievement for all peoples and all nations'[24] in the field of human rights, and it is, in fact, the most frequently cited standard of international human rights. But as a resolution of the UN General Assembly, it is formally non-binding, and this raises the question of its effect upon the development of international human rights law.

Georges Abi-Saab has noted that the normative effect of UN General Assembly resolutions depends upon three factors, i.e. the degree of consensus behind the resolution, the degree of concreteness of the normative language in the resolution, and the extent to which mechanisms of implementation have been provided for.[25] The Universal Declaration was adopted by the General Assembly with no negative votes (although there were eight abstentions); thus, the consensus behind that resolution was very strong. Today, more than 60 years after the adoption of the Declaration, the international consensus on the international human rights standards it sets out remains strong. As far as concreteness is concerned, the Universal Declaration represents a vast improvement over the general human rights language found in the UN Charter.

A large number of international human rights treaties, such as the International Covenant on Civil and Political Rights,[26] the International Covenant on Economic, Social and Cultural Rights,[27] and the Convention Against Torture,[28] have expanded and clarified the scope of international human rights law. Unfortunately, this progress in the normative development of

---

21   UN Charter, art. 2, para. 1, states that 'The Organization is based on the principle of sovereign equality of all its Members.'
22   UN Charter, art. 2, para. 7 states that 'Nothing contained in the present Charter shall authorize the United Nations to intervene in matters which are essentially within the domestic jurisdiction of any state, or shall require the Members to submit such matters to settlement under the present Charter.'
23   General Assembly Res. 217A (III), 10 December 1948, UN Doc. A/810/71 (1948).
24   *Ibid*. Preamble.
25   See Georges Abi-Saab, *Introduction*, in LES RESOLUTIONS DANS LA FORMATION DU DROIT INTERNATIONAL DU DÉVELOPMENT, Etudes et Travaux de l'IUHEI No. 13 9–10. Geneva, Institut Universitaire de Hautes Etudes Internationales, 1971).
26   International Covenant on Civil and Political Rights (ICCPR), General Assembly Res. 2200A (XXI), 21 UN GAOR Supp. (No. 16) 52, UN Doc. A/6316 (1966), 999 UNTS 171, entered into force 23 March 1976.
27   International Covenant on Economic, Social and Cultural Rights, General Assembly Res. 2200A (XXI), 21 UN GAOR Supp. (No. 16) 49, UN Doc. A/6316 (1966), 993 UNTS 3, entered into force 3 January 1976.
28   Convention Against Torture and Other Cruel, Inhuman or Degrading Treatment or Punishment, General Assembly Res. 39/46, 39 UN GAOR Supp. (No. 51) 197, UN Doc. A/39/51 (1984), entered into force 26 June 1987.

human rights has not been matched by the development of truly effective mechanisms of implementation.

International human rights law is relevant to international criminal law in a number of ways. First and foremost, international human rights law defines international fair-trial standards[29] that apply throughout international criminal law and which have been incorporated into the Rome Statute of the International Criminal Court.[30] These rules reflect a broad international consensus on the principles of legality and culpability referred to in the discussion of comparative law above. As a matter of substantive criminal law, the Convention Against Torture (CAT) requires states parties to make torture a crime under their domestic law[31] and to prosecute or extradite those suspected of committing acts of torture as defined in that treaty.[32] For the most part, the basic rules of the CAT have been accepted by states as part of customary international law, and therefore bind all states. Similar rules apply to the crime of genocide, which is also defined by treaty.[33]

A FEW KEY THEMES IN CONTEMPORARY INTERNATIONAL CRIMINAL LAW

Development of General Principles of International Criminal Law

The identification and clarification of the general principles of international criminal law is an important goal,[34] but making progress towards that goal has not been easy. While it is clear that general principles of law recognized by civilized nations may be a source of international law, it is far less clear what general principles of *criminal* law have been recognized by the major legal systems of the world. Identifying them is an exercise in comparative law. The task is complicated by the fact that general principles of criminal law have developed in national systems which vary a great deal. In addition to the differences between the two best-known models, i.e. common law and civil law, there are also legal systems reflecting Islamic law and many other variations. International criminal law has had very little time to develop independently of that diverse array of national legal systems, as most of that development has come during the past 20 years. In general, there is a lack of clarity and consensus about the relationship between general principles of law, general principles of international law, general principles of criminal law, and general principles of international criminal law.

---

29   See ICCPR, art. 14, for the most generally accepted codification of international fair trial rights.

30   See David Weisssbrodt and Kristin K. Zinsmaste, Chapter 11.

31   'Each State Party shall ensure that all acts of torture are offences under its criminal law.' Convention Against Torture, art. 4(1).

32   *Ibid.* art. 5.

33   See Mark Drumbl, Chapter 3.

34   See Kai Ambos, *Remarks on the General Part of International Criminal Law*, 4 J INT'L CRIM. JUSTICE 660 (2006), calling for more focus upon the identification and application of the general principles of international criminal law, in order to ensure consistency with fundamental principles of criminal law including the principles of legality and culpability.

General principles of law recognized by civilized nations are, as noted above,[35] a source of international law, whereas general principles of international law are, at least arguably, 'the principles inherent in the international legal system'.[36] What Cassese refers to as 'general principles of criminal law recognized by the community of nations'[37] is presumably a subset of the general principles of law mentioned above which can be identified by comparative analysis, but it seems clear that there is as yet no consensus on a complete set of such principles. The general principles of international criminal law will therefore need to be built and agreed upon over time. The 'general principles of criminal law' set out in the Rome Statute of the International Criminal Court were the subject of diplomatic negotiations and will provide the basis for further development of relevant general principles in the future.

State Responsibility Versus Individual Criminal Responsibility: The State or Entity Behind International Crimes

As noted above, the focus of international criminal law is establishing the criminal responsibility of individuals for their violations of international law which constitute international crimes. Since international crimes are committed by and attributed to individuals and not states, international criminal law is not a matter of state responsibility. In the course of its decades-long effort to codify the international law of state responsibility, the International Law Commission considered the notion that states themselves could face penal, as well as delictual, responsibility for certain especially serious violations of international law. [38] The concept of so-called 'crimes of state' was ultimately so sensitive and controversial that no consensus could be achieved on the subject.[39] But the International Law Commission's decision to exclude language about state crimes from the final version of its articles on state responsibility did not resolve the underlying tensions.

The fact is that governments may feel threatened by the criminal prosecutions of their officials or other nationals even if this does not entail a formal determination of state responsibility. At the conclusion of the Rome diplomatic conference, the US government was highly critical of the Rome Statute which had just been adopted. At one point, US officials argued that if the ICC could try a US national without the consent of the US government, the treaty would effectively be imposing obligations upon the United States as a non-party state.[40]

---

35 See the discussion of general principles of law as referred to in Article 38 of the Statute of the International Court of Justice, art. 38 note 6 *supra* and the accompanying text.

36 Cassese states that '[g]eneral principles of international law consist of principles inherent in the international legal system'. ANTONIO CASSESE, INTERNATIONAL CRIMINAL LAW 31 (2003).

37 *Ibid*. 32.

38 Compare 'crimes of state' in the meaning of art. 19 of the International Law Commission's Draft Articles on State Responsibility (Part 1), adopted by the ILC on first reading. [1976] 2 YB Int'l L Comm'n, Pt 2, 73, 95–6, UN Doc. A/CN.4/SER.A/1976/Add.1 (Pt 2).

39 See ILC Commentary, note 2 *supra*, at 279–81.

40 Compare comments by US Ambassador David Scheffer that 'I can tell you that it would be bizarre, utterly bizarre consequence for governments to think that this treaty can be adopted and brought into force with the presumption that it will cover governments that have not joined the treaty regime. That is bizarre. That's weird. That is unheard of in treaty law.' Davod Scheffer, Ambassador-at-Large For War Crimes Issues, On-the-Record Briefing at the Foreign Press Center, 31 July 1998, available at www.amicc.org/docs/Scheffer7_31_98.pdf.

Equating potential ICC jurisdiction over individuals with the idea that non-party states are being inappropriately 'bound' is a clever rhetorical device, but as legal reasoning it is completely untenable. This argument conflated the potential individual criminal responsibility of a US national with a legal obligation of the United States under the Rome Statute. Like any treaty, the Statute creates obligations for states parties: these include the obligations to comply with requests for the surrender and transfer of suspects to the Court,[41] to provide requested evidence,[42] to give effect to fines or forfeitures ordered by the Court,[43] and to pay assessments for the regular budget of the Court.[44] None of these obligations applies to any non-party state, nor does the exercise of criminal jurisdiction against an individual accused formally bind or condemn the state of his nationality.

Recent codification efforts have been careful to distinguish state responsibility from individual criminal responsibility. The Rome Statute of the ICC clarifies that '[n]o provision in this Statute relating to individual criminal responsibility shall affect the responsibility of States under international law',[45] while the ILC Articles on State Responsibility affirm that '[t]hese articles are without prejudice to any question of the individual responsibility under international law of any person acting on behalf of a State'.[46]

Despite the clear legal distinction between individual criminal responsibility, on the one hand, and state obligations and state responsibility, on the other, in some situations both types of responsibility/accountability may indeed be involved.[47] In one example of this 'duality of responsibility'[48] the International Court of Justice (ICJ) concurred with the judgment of the International Criminal Tribunal for the Former Yugoslavia (ICTY) that the 1995 massacre of Muslim men by Bosnian Serbs in Srebrenica was genocide,[49] in the course of ruling that the Serbian state had breached international law by failing to prevent and punish that genocide.[50] The court's decision acknowledged a link between state responsibility and individual responsibility when it affirmed that 'a State can be held responsible for breaching the obligation to

---

[41]   ICC Statute, art. 89(1).

[42]   *Ibid.* art. 93.

[43]   *Ibid.* art. 109(1).

[44]   *Ibid.* art. 117.

[45]   *Ibid.* art. 25(4(.

[46]   ILC Articles on State Responsibility, *supra* note 1, art. 58.

[47]   As the International Law Commission has observed: 'Where crimes against international law are committed by State officials, it will often be the case that the State itself is responsible for the acts in question or for failure to prevent or punish them. In certain cases, in particular aggression, the State will by definition be involved. Even so, the question of individual responsibility is in principle distinct from the question of State responsibility. The State is not exempted from its own responsibility for internationally wrongful conduct by the prosecution and punishment of the State officials who carried it out.' ILC Commentary, note 2 *supra*, Commentary on Article 58, para. 3.

[48]   'The Court observes that that duality of responsibility continues to be a constant feature of international law.' *Application of the Convention on the Prevention and Punishment of the Crime of Genocide (Bosnia and Herzegovina v. Serbia and Montenegro),* ICJ, Judgment of 26 February 2007, 65, para. 173 (hereinafter 'Genocide Case'), available at www.icj-cij.org/docket/files/91/13685.pdf.

[49]   'The Court concludes that the acts committed at Srebrenica falling within Article II(a) and (b) of the Convention were committed with the specific intent to destroy in part the group of the Muslims of Bosnia and Herzegovina as such; and accordingly that these were acts of genocide, committed by members of the VRS in and around Srebrenica from about 13 July 1995.' *Ibid.* 108, para. 297.

[50]   *Ibid.* 158, para. 438, and 161, para. 450.

prevent genocide only if genocide was actually committed'.[51] A similar logic will no doubt apply if and when the ICC decides to apply its recently agreed definition of aggression. Thus, an individual will be subject to prosecution for the international crime of aggression only if the state linked to him bears responsibility for prohibited acts of aggression.[52] Any government would be likely to resist the prosecution of its national leader or leaders for a crime implicating the responsibility of the state itself.

CONCLUSIONS

International criminal law is a relatively young area of law that has developed rapidly since the ICTY was created in 1994. Looking ahead, it is likely that the law, practice and institutions of international criminal law will continue to develop well into the future. No particular result, however, is inevitable. It is possible that the ICC will evolve into a stronger, more independent and effective institution of international justice; less beholden to states, and to the UN Security Council, than international criminal tribunals have proved to be so far. It is also possible that the ICC will fail to survive as a viable and credible institution.

The dynamic development and continuing uncertainty that together characterize the present state of international criminal law present both challenges and opportunities for individuals, NGOs and states. The opportunity lies in the chance to participate in shaping a key aspect of the future international order and hopefully in making it better. The challenge is to do so in a principled way consistent not only with the requirements of criminal justice, but also with agreed limits on international authority.

Advancing the Rule of Law Within the Agreed Limits of International Authority

So long as notorious impunity for international crimes endures, considerations of justice will argue for greater and stronger international institutions to remedy the situation. Although it is essential, moral theory alone cannot be the basis of effective and authoritative international institutions of justice. A certain degree of international consensus is necessary as well. The ICC Statute has been accepted by more than 114 countries, and thus its legitimacy extends to over half the states in the international community. But what of the many states not accepting the ICC Statute, a group including the United States, China, India and Russia? These countries represent most of the world's population, possess most of its military force and hold three vetoes within the UN Security Council as presently constituted. Their reluctance to endorse the ICC is significant and cannot be ignored. The ICC was established based on a broad but limited consensus of states. It must now operate within the jurisdictional constraints that result from these limits.

The ICC Statute establishes an institution with extremely restricted jurisdiction, limited only to specified criminal acts committed on the territory of, or by a national of, a state party and in situations where there is no state willing or able genuinely to prosecute the case.[53] In

---

51   *Ibid*. 154, para. 431.
52   See Faiza Patel King, Chapter 6
53   See ICC Statute, art. 17. For an in-depth discussion of how this system of 'complementary jurisdiction' is supposed to work and of how it is working in practice, see Sarah Nouwen, Chapter 9.

many situations, such as that involving the atrocities in Darfur, this will not be enough juris-diction to permit effective action.[54] The UN Security Council ultimately referred the situation in Darfur to the ICC, thereby granting it extraordinary jurisdiction based on the Council's authority under Chapter VII of the UN Charter.[55] The experience of the ad hoc tribunals for the Former Yugoslavia and Rwanda has already shown that international criminal courts can function with the full support and authority of the UN Security Council. It remains to be seen how effectively the ICC can operate in situations where that support is not forthcoming.

Institutions and officials involved in international criminal law should strive to advance the rule of law and to be effective, but without exceeding the agreed limits of their authority. Judge Georges Abi-Saab, writing in a separate opinion of the ICTY Appeals Chamber in 1995, briefly opined that the international judges of the ICTY 'are ... afforded a unique opportunity to assume the responsibility for the further rationalisation' of the various categories of international crimes 'from the perspective of the evolving international legal order'.[56] His point is that, at times, international judges should use their authority to build, develop and reorganize international law. Our international legal order provides few opportunities for such a reasoned assessment because it is decentralized and chaotic in that there is no international legislature, no international executive, and the existing international courts have little effective jurisdiction.

But while international judges may rightly promote more effective international institutions, it is important for international judges, prosecutors and other officials to act within the agreed limits of their authority. This is another aspect of the principle of legality discussed above. Respect for this principle does not preclude judges from occasionally advancing the development of international law through 'teleological interpretation' of treaties in the light of their object and purpose. Inevitably, however, there must be limits on the discretion of judges, especially when used to extend their own authority. In fact, recent developments regarding the ICC Statute demonstrate that teleological interpretation may sometimes require a more restrictive, rather than a more expansive, interpretation of a treaty text. The ICC's radical redefinition of its own complementary jurisdiction is a case in point.

The text of the Rome Statute of the ICC was agreed only after extended negotiations involving a careful balance between the jurisdiction of the ICC and the national criminal jurisdiction of states. If the practice of the ICC does not scrupulously respect this balance, the ability to reach compromise in future international negotiations will be undermined. There is ample reason for concern in this regard.

---

54   In the case of Darfur, the same state, Sudan, is both the territorial state where the alleged crimes were committed, and the state of nationality of those accused. Sudan is not a party to the ICC Statute, therefore under the ICC Statute, the only possible basis for ICC jurisdiction over crimes in Darfur is a referral by the UN Security Council.

55   See UN Security Council Res. 1593, 31 March 2005, UN Doc. S/RES/1593 (2005), referring the situation in Darfur to the ICC.

56   *Prosecutor* v. *Tadic*, Case IT-94-1-AR72, ICTY, Separate Opinion of Judge Abi-Saab on the Defence Motion for Interlocutory Appeal on Jurisdiction, 2 October 1995, 2–3. Judge Abi-Saab also argued (at 5) that 'with a view to introducing a modicum of order among the categories of crimes falling within the substantive jurisdiction of the Tribunal' the Appeals Chamber should have followed 'a teleological interpretation of the Conventions in the light of their object and purpose to the effect of including internal conflicts within the regime of "grave breaches".'

Perhaps the most fundamental compromise leading to agreement on the ICC Statute concerned the relationship between the criminal jurisdiction of states and the so-called 'complementary' jurisdiction of the ICC. During the Rome negotiations, complementary jurisdiction was understood to mean that the Court can exercise its jurisdiction over a case only if the case is not being and has not been genuinely investigated or prosecuted by any state.[57] But thus far, the jurisprudence of the ICC suggests that its judges are taking an approach to complementary jurisdiction which could deprive states of any real possibility of challenging ICC jurisdiction by exercising their own criminal jurisdiction. The Court has ruled that the complementarity assessment is case, and not situation, specific. In practice this means that even if national courts genuinely and effectively pursue a full range of cases within the context of a specific 'situation', to preclude ICC jurisdiction, those national proceedings must be found by the ICC to concern the same 'conduct', the same 'person' and perhaps even the same 'incident'. Since it is difficult for any state to anticipate exactly which cases the ICC Prosecutor will ultimately choose to bring regarding a given overall situation, states may find it difficult, or even impossible, to exclude ICC jurisdiction by exercising their national criminal jurisdiction under the principle of complementarity.[58]

Sarah Nouwen argues persuasively, based on the text of the ICC Statute, that popular notions of complementarity are simplistic and misleading.[59] Her technical argument is quite sound, as is that of the ICC judges who have so far fleshed out the application of ICC admissibility/complementarity in practice. From a broader perspective, however, the degree of legal hair-splitting involved in that argument seems to betray the true intent of the parties at the Rome ICC Conference.[60] International criminal courts, like national courts, should exercise judicial restraint where appropriate. An appropriate time to do so may be now, with regard to the sensitive issue of balancing national and international criminal jurisdiction. 'Popular notions of complementarity' may appear simplistic in light of the actual text of the ICC Statute, but it was on the basis of just these popular notions that states were persuaded to adopt the Statute in Rome and then subsequently to ratify it. The arguments that effectively carried the day in bringing the ICC into existence cannot be irrelevant to the interpretation and application of the ICC Statute.

The relevant object and purpose of the ICC Statute, for purposes of its teleological interpretation, should include not only advancing international justice, but also ensuring effective ICC deference to the national jurisdiction of those states genuinely willing and able to prosecute serious international crimes. In general, these goals are not incompatible. Prioritizing the former over the latter, even when there is no evidence of a clear conflict between them, could have unintended negative consequences, not only for international justice, but for international law and institutions in general.

---

57   See ICC Statute, art. 17(1)(a)(b)(c), (2) and (3).

58   Sarah Nouwen, Chapter 9, discusses this possibility in much greater detail.

59   Nouwen argues that 'shorthand definitions of complementarity according to which 'the Court may assume jurisdiction only when national jurisdictions are unwilling or unable to exercise it' are misleading' (citing and critiquing the definition of complementarity set out in M.H. Arsanjani and W.M. Reisman, *Developments at the International Criminal Court: The Law-in-Action of the International Criminal Court*, 99 AMERICAN JIL 385, 396 (2005)).

60   Nouwen notes that '[t]he definition of "case" was not elaborated upon during the negotiations nor in the first commentaries on the Statute'.

International Justice Depends Primarily upon the National Jurisdiction of States

The pioneering work of international criminal tribunals has kick-started the cause of international justice, but it has also exposed the limits of these same institutions. International trials are slow, expensive and ultimately they depend upon the cooperation of states. National courts must be a big part of any general strategy for the enforcement of international criminal law, and a proper balance must be found between national and international criminal jurisdiction.

The establishment and functioning of international criminal courts and tribunals is certainly an important historic accomplishment, but this success should not blind us to the fact that these international institutions have only limited economic and political resources which should be used wisely. International prosecutors, in particular, need to be strategic in focusing upon the most important cases.

In most cases the only way to enforce international criminal law is through the use of national courts. International criminal courts are needed to complement this mechanism, not to replace it. The essays in this volume highlight the astonishing pace of development of international criminal law over the past two decades, as well as the many contentious issues yet to be resolved. Answers to all these questions will not come overnight. One can only hope that the best way forward will eventually emerge from the practice of states and that of the evolving institutions of international criminal law.

2 The vanishing relevance of state affiliation in international criminal law: private security contractors and other non-state actors

John Cerone

INTRODUCTION

Much has been made recently of international law's deficiencies in grappling with violence perpetrated by non-state actors. From transnational terrorist networks to private security contractors (PSCs), organizations that are not officially part of the apparatus of any state are increasingly engaged in protracted episodes of intense violence, giving rise to questions of accountability under international law. Does international law provide rules applicable to such conduct?

While the repression of crime, especially that perpetrated by non-state actors, has traditionally been left to the internal law of states, most international jurists will point to the ancient rules of international law pertaining to piracy in support of the proposition that international law has always governed criminal activity by non-state actors. Today, these same jurists can point to article 25(2) of the Rome Statute of the International Criminal Court (ICC) which provides for individual criminal responsibility of perpetrators without any reference to state affiliation. In light of the correspondence between these ancient and modern rules of international law, why is there such controversy over the responsibility of non-state actors under international criminal law?

In order to understand the controversy, it is essential first to recognize that Grotius' condemnation of pirates as guilty of violating the law of nations had a very different legal character from the concept of individual criminal responsibility under the Rome Statute. For Grotius, the pirate was guilty of violating natural law,[1] a body of law that bound individuals in the first place, and only by extension from this central case formed part of the law of nations applicable to states. Once the foundation of international law shifted from natural law to positivism (that is, law based on the consent of states), the focus of the international rules concerning piracy shifted from the individual to the state. Rather than focusing on individual responsibility, the rules of international law were understood to afford jurisdiction to all states to repress piracy.

By the early twentieth century, the natural law conception of the international legal system had receded to the vanishing point, so much so that delegates to the League of Nations could take the view that 'inasmuch as only States were subjects of international law, individuals could only be punished in accordance with their national law'.[2] The significance of the

---

[1]   H. Grotius, *De Jure Belli Ac Pacis* (1615), Book II, Chapter XX, para. XL.
[2]   *Report on the Question of International Criminal Jurisdiction* (Richard J. Alfaro, Special Rapporteur), A/CN.4/15, II YEARBOOK OF THE INTERNATIONAL LAW COMMISSION (1950), at para. 17.

Nuremberg Tribunal's revival of individual criminal responsibility can be fully appreciated only when seen against this state-centric backdrop.

THE POSITIVIST CONCEPTION OF THE INTERNATIONAL LEGAL SYSTEM AND THE SCOPE OF THE TERM 'NON-STATE ACTOR'

From the inception of the Westphalian system, the sovereign equality of states and the related principle of non-intervention were paramount. As the positivist conception of the international legal system came to prevail, only states could be deemed true subjects of international law. Individuals were generally relegated to the status of mere objects,[3] and the substantive norms of international law were conceived as a network of consent-based, reciprocal obligations that focused almost exclusively on inter-state relations.

According to this traditional model, international law had no direct application to individuals. At the same time, states, as abstract entities, are incapable of acting as such. The conduct of states is the conduct of individuals whose acts or omissions are attributable to the state.[4]

'State Actors' and 'Non-State Actors'

The term 'state actor' is traditionally employed to describe those who are officially part of the machinery of the state. The conduct of these individuals is generally attributable to the state. In contrast, the term 'non-state actor' (NSA) is employed to describe those who are not officially part of the machinery of the state, and whose conduct is not generally attributable to the state. However, as a brief survey of the rules of attribution will demonstrate, there is no category of individuals whose conduct is always attributable to the state. Nor is there a category of individuals whose conduct is never attributable to the state.[5]

The first rule of attribution is that the conduct of an organ of a state, including that of any individual who is an official part of the machinery of the state,[6] or of an entity legally empowered by a state to exercise elements of governmental authority[7] is considered to be an act of that state. This would also include situations in which an organ is placed at the disposal of a

---

[3]   The legal status of the individual in the pre-Second World War international legal system is a matter of some debate. The individual was regarded as a subject of natural law, and was thus regulated by international law to the extent the Westphalian system was superimposed onto a pre-existing natural law system. See J. Cerone, *The Status of the Individual in International Law*, PROCEEDINGS OF THE 100TH ANNUAL MEETING OF THE ASIL (2006). The scope of the present chapter is limited to rules of positive international law, and includes natural law only to the extent it has been incorporated into the positive law.

[4]   Responsibility of States for Internationally Wrongful Acts, General Assembly Res. 56/83, art. 2, UN GAOR, 56th Sess., Supp. No. 10, UN Doc. A/RES/56/83 (28 January 2002). J. Cerone, *Human Dignity in the Line of Fire: The Application of International Human Rights Law During Armed Conflict, Occupation, and Peace Operations*, 39 VAND. J TRANSNAT'L L 1447, 1455 (2006).

[5]   JAMES CRAWFORD, THE INTERNATIONAL LAW COMMISSION'S ARTICLES ON STATE RESPONSIBILITY: INTRODUCTION, TEXT AND COMMENTARIES (2002). The Rules of Attribution are reprinted at *ibid.* 61 *et seq.*

[6]   See ILC Articles on State Responsibility, art. 4.

[7]   *Ibid.* art. 5.

state by another state and the organ is acting in the exercise of elements of the governmental authority of the former state.[8] The conduct of such actors is attributable to the state even where an actor's conduct is ultra vires, or beyond the scope of his or her authority, so long as he or she was acting in an official capacity.[9]

The conduct of non-state actors may also be attributed to a state under certain circumstances. The conduct of a non-state actor may be imputed to a state when the actor is in fact acting on the instructions of, or under the direction or control of, a state in carrying out the conduct;[10] when the actor is exercising elements of governmental authority in the absence or default of official authorities;[11] when the conduct is subsequently adopted by a state;[12] or when the conduct is that of an insurrectional movement that becomes the new government of a state.[13]

Use of Private Contractors Within the Framework of State Responsibility

The use of private contractors in the recent conflicts in Iraq and Afghanistan has drawn increased attention to the relationship between the conduct of non-state actors and state responsibility. The rules of attribution contemplate two situations in which the conduct of private contractors may be attributable to the state.

The first is where the contractor is *de jure* acting on behalf of the state. This situation is covered by article 5 of the Articles on State Responsibility, which applies to entities that are empowered by the law of the state to exercise elements of governmental authority. Thus, the conduct of private contractors that are legally authorized to carry out public functions on behalf of the state will be attributable to the state. These entities essentially become assimilated to organs of the state when they are acting in their public capacity. Thus, their ultra vires conduct remains attributable to the state so long as they are acting in that capacity.

The second situation is where the contractor is in fact instructed to act on behalf of the state, without the official imprimatur of legal empowerment. In such situations, it does not matter whether the contractor is carrying out a public function. However, this situation would be governed by article 8 of the Articles, which, as noted above,[14] sets a fairly high threshold for attribution. In addition, as there is not necessarily any 'official' capacity in such situations,

---

[8]   *Ibid.* art. 6. This rule is limited to situations in which 'the organ, originally that of one State, acts *exclusively* for the purposes of and on behalf of another State and its conduct is attributed to *the latter State alone*'. ILC Commentary on Articles on State Responsibility, Report of the International Law Commission on the Work of its Fifty-third Session, UN Doc. A/56/10 at 95 (emphasis added).

[9]   ILC Articles on State Responsibility, art. 7. See also *Velasquez-Rodriguez* case, Judgment, 29 July 1988, Inter-Am. CtHR (Ser. C) No. 4 (1988), paras 169–70.

[10]   ILC Articles on State Responsibility, art. 8. In the absence of specific instructions, a fairly high degree of control has been required to attribute the conduct to the state. According to the ILC Commentary, note 7 *supra* at 104, 'Such conduct will be attributable to the State only if it directed or controlled the specific operation and the conduct complained of was an integral part of that operation. The principle does not extend to conduct which was only incidentally or peripherally associated with an operation and which escaped from the State's direction or control.'

[11]   ILC Articles on State Responsibility, art. 9.

[12]   *Ibid.* art. 11. See also *United States* v. *Iran*, discussed below.

[13]   ILC Articles on State Responsibility, art. 10.

[14]   See note 10 *supra*.

the entity's conduct will not be attributable to the state if such conduct was contrary to the state's instructions.[15]

The legal position of such NSAs whose conduct in a given instance is attributable to the state is essentially the same as that of state actors. In any event, the rules of international law, as traditionally understood, would not directly bind even state actors. It was the state as such that was the subject of legal obligation.

However, the events of the Second World War spurred a number of developments in international law, the most significant of which went to the very structure of the system. The two most important developments for present purposes were the emergence of the individual as a subject of international law and the erosion of the non-intervention principle.

BEYOND THE STATE-CENTRIC MODEL: THE EMERGENCE OF INDIVIDUAL CRIMINAL RESPONSIBILITY AND THE EROSION OF THE NON-INTERVENTION PRINCIPLE

While the state-centric model of the international legal system persists even to this day, it was significantly eroded by the events of the Second World War. One feature of this transformation was the emergence[16] of the principle that violation of certain norms of international law could give rise to individual criminal responsibility. According to this principle, certain serious violations of international law would engage not only the classical form of responsibility in international law, that is, the responsibility of the state, but also that of the individuals perpetrating the violation. Such perpetrators could be criminally prosecuted and punished for these violations of international law.

The emergence of this principle was driven by the need to develop effective means of enforcement. As reasoned by the International Military Tribunal at Nuremberg (IMT),

---

15   But see *Prosecutor v. Tadic*, 38 ILM 1518 (1999). In *Tadic*, the ICTY Appeals Chamber took the position that overall control of a hierarchically-organized non-state entity may be sufficient to assimilate that entity to a state organ, rendering all of its conduct attributable to the state. For a comprehensive overview of these developments, see Cerone, note 4 *supra*.

16   As noted above, this principle was not generally accepted among international lawyers in the decades prior to the Second World War. Early in its existence, the Council of the League of Nations had before it a proposal to create an international criminal court. An Advisory Committee of Jurists, appointed by the Council in February 1920, recommended the creation of a 'High Court of International Justice', which would be competent to criminally prosecute individuals for violations of the 'universal law of nations'. *Report on the Question of International Criminal Jurisdiction* (Richard J. Alfaro, Special Rapporteur), A/CN.4/15, II YEARBOOK OF THE INTERNATIONAL LAW COMMISSION (1950) at para. 15. This proposal was rejected by the League. According to the Third Committee of the League Assembly, it was 'best to entrust criminal cases to the ordinary tribunals as is at present the custom in international procedure'. While recognizing that 'crimes of this kind' might 'in future be brought within the scope of international penal law', consideration of the issue was, 'at the moment, premature'' *Ibid.* para. 16. According to UN Special Rapporteur Richard Alfaro, this rejection 'reflected the views of those who had opposed the establishment of an international jurisdiction for the trial of the First World War criminals, for certain legal reasons, to wit: that there was no defined notion of international crimes; that there was no international penal law, that the principle *nulla poena sine lege* would be disregarded; that the different proposals were not clear; and that inasmuch as only States were subjects of international law, individuals could only be punished in accordance with their national law'. *Ibid.* para. 17.

'Crimes against international law are committed by men, not by abstract entities, and only by punishing individuals who commit such crimes can the provisions of international law be enforced.'[17] While the IMT lacked a solid juridical basis for espousing the principle of individual criminal responsibility, subsequent acceptance of the principle by the international community arguably cured any defect in its legal foundation, at least prospectively.

The IMT had at least two potential paths to deriving individual criminal liability for violations of international law. One possible path contemplated that individual criminal responsibility was predicated on a violation of international law by the state. Once a violation was established, it could then inquire as to whether the violation was serious enough to give rise to the criminal responsibility of the individual as well as that of the state. The other jurisprudential strand drew upon remnants of the natural law system, positing that some of the rules of the 'law of nations' were addressed directly to individuals. Under this latter theory, it would not be necessary to first establish that a violation of international law had been committed by a state. While this approach would seem to have a weaker foundation in the positive law of the time,[18] it appears to be the position adopted by the Tribunal.[19]

Once the link between state responsibility and individual responsibility is severed, the significance of the distinction between state and non-state actors greatly diminishes. Much of this significance had related to a conception of international law in which the state was the exclusive subject of legal obligation. In that context, the distinction mattered because the conduct of state actors was generally attributable to the state, and the conduct of non-state actors was generally not. Once the individual is deemed capable of being directly bound by rules of international law, it essentially becomes a policy choice of those creating the law

---

[17]   1 Trial of the Major War Criminals Before the International Military Tribunal 223 (1947), available at www.yale.edu/lawweb/avalon/imt/proc/judlawch.htm.

[18]   As noted above, earlier conceptions of individual responsibility for violations of the 'law of nations' rested on a conception of the latter as consisting primarily of natural law. Even this pre-existing doctrine was unclear and not without controversy. For example, the traditional prohibition of piracy in international law is often cited as an example of the regulation of non-state actors by international law. Yet it remains unclear whether the rules of international law were directly binding on the pirates or whether these rules merely provided to states a jurisdictional basis to prosecute them. In common law jurisdictions, as customary international law was applied through the vehicle of the common law, it is difficult to tell whether individual criminal responsibility arose through international law itself or through the common law. To further confuse matters, customary international law and the common law were both rooted, traditionally, in natural law, which was primarily addressed to individuals. In any event, the principle of individual criminal responsibility for violations of international law was not universally embraced as positive law until after the Second World War. Today, of course, the principle of individual criminal responsibility is clearly regarded as positive law. See the ICC Statute, art. 25(2).

[19]   The IMT's peculiar legal posture makes it difficult to draw definite conclusions as to the nature of its jurisdiction. While the IMT purported to sit as an international tribunal applying international law directly to individuals, it simultaneously relied on the fact that, in constituting the tribunal, the Allies had 'done together what any one of them might have done singly'. 1 Trial of the Major War Criminals Before the International Military Tribunal 223 (1947), available at www.yale.edu/lawweb/avalon/imt/proc/judlawch.htm. The Judgment also refers to the creation of the Charter as 'the exercise of the sovereign legislative power by the countries to which the German Reich unconditionally surrendered; and the undoubted right of these countries to legislate for the occupied territories has been recognised by the civilised world'. *Ibid.* Taken together, these propositions blur the line between an international tribunal and a domestic court. The attendant uncertainty may have facilitated the Tribunal's invocation of the principle of individual responsibility.

whether they wish to address rules of international law to all individuals or only to individuals falling within certain categories or operating within certain contexts. The issue was no longer one of legal coherence, but the more discretionary matter of why certain criminal activity should be regulated by international law.

The IMT Charter primarily adopts a context-based approach. Although the Charter recognized the individual as a subject of international obligations, it still largely reflected the existing substance of international law as a body of rules concerned almost exclusively with inter-state transactions. In addition, the Charter restricted the Tribunal's personal jurisdiction to those who were 'acting in the interests of the European Axis countries'.[20] As such, several aspects of the IMT's jurisdiction narrowed the scope of possible defendants to those who had some connection to the state.

The subject matter jurisdiction of the IMT was largely concerned with state-sponsored violence. The IMT was given jurisdiction to prosecute three categories of crimes: crimes against peace, war crimes, and crimes against humanity.[21] The inclusion of crimes against peace and war crimes was not particularly controversial, as each entailed a substantial transnational dimension, either the use of armed force by one state against another or abuses committed by someone acting on behalf of one state against the citizen of another. This transnational dimension placed these acts within the traditional inter-state framework of international law.

However, the inclusion of crimes against humanity, which comprised certain inhumane acts committed in the course of an attack against any civilian population, was a watershed event in international law. Use of the term 'any' made clear that such crimes could be committed even within a single state. In addition, the definition did not require that the perpetrator have any connection to the state. The boldness of including this crime, however, was tempered by the insertion of a jurisdictional element.

Recognizing that they were breaking new ground, the drafters expressed a degree of caution by including a nexus requirement. Crimes against humanity could only be prosecuted if they were committed 'in execution of or in connection with any crime within the jurisdiction of the Tribunal' (i.e., crimes against peace or war crimes).[22] Thus, there had to be a connection to a violation of a traditional inter-state rule of international law for the IMT to exercise jurisdiction over this newly defined category of crimes.

Each of the categories of crimes thus required some connection to state-sponsored violence, either as a substantive element or as a jurisdictional requirement. This was only reinforced by the Charter's restriction of personal jurisdiction to those who were 'acting in the interests of the European Axis countries'.[23]

Thus, even though individual non-state actors could be prosecuted for their participation in violations of international law, it was still necessary to show some link[24] to the state in

---

20   Charter of the International Military Tribunal, 6 October 1945, 59 Stat. 1544, 82 UNTS 279, art. 6, available at www.yale.edu/lawweb/avalon/imt/proc/imtconst.htm.
21   *Ibid.*
22   *Ibid.* art. 6(C).
23   *Ibid.* art. 6.
24   This link, of course, need not rise to the level required by the rules of attribution. As the concern here was not state responsibility, the rules of international criminal law were not constrained by the law of state responsibility.

determining whether they fell within the Tribunal's jurisdiction.[25] Subsequent developments, however, lessened the significance of whether a given perpetrator had any connection to a state.

THE POST-NUREMBERG EVOLUTION OF INTERNATIONAL CRIMINAL LAW

International criminal law continued to evolve in the post-war period. This evolution occurred, in part, through the further development of humanitarian law (that is, the law of armed conflict).

The 1949 Geneva Conventions and Non-State Actors

International criminal law, born as it was in the cauldron of armed conflict, evolved primarily from international humanitarian law (IHL), resulting in a dynamic relationship between these two bodies of law. It was the establishment of the International Military Tribunals in the aftermath of the Second World War that spurred the development of international criminal law. As a result, the overwhelming majority of international crimes that were given cognizance by the international community at that time were those relating to war; that is, criminal violations of humanitarian law. As such, the work of the IMTs in turn facilitated the further development of IHL.

This development is manifest in the 1949 Geneva Conventions, which contain a number of advances over earlier IHL treaties. One advance was the inclusion of a regime of mandatory criminal sanctions for certain serious violations.

In the course of its judgment, the IMT at Nuremberg relied heavily on the rules of humanitarian law set forth in the Hague Conventions of 1907.[26] While those treaties were not

---

25   A number of cases involving non-state actors were prosecuted by the occupying powers in post-Second World War Germany. See, for example, Trials of War Criminals Before the Nuernberg Military Tribunals under Control Council Law No. 10 (1949), the *Krupp* case, the *Flick* case, the *Farben* case, and the *Zyklon-B* case. The *Flick* tribunal saw no difficulty in prosecuting private citizens for violations of international law. Perhaps overstating the position of the individual in international law, the *Flick* tribunal held that '[i]nternational law, as such, binds every citizen just as does ordinary municipal law'. See *Flick* case at vol. VI, 1192 ('[I]t is argued that individuals holding no public offices and not representing the State do not, and should not, come within the class of persons criminally responsible for a breach of international law. It is asserted that international law is a matter wholly outside the work, interest, and knowledge of private individuals. The distinction in unsound. International law, as such, binds every citizen just as does ordinary municipal law. Acts adjudged criminal when done by an officer of the government are criminal also when done by a private individual. The guilt differs only in magnitude, not in quality. The offender in either case is charged with personal wrong and punishment falls on the offender in *propria persona*. The application of international law is no novelty. There is no justification for a limitation of responsibility to public officials.') However, it should be noted that, notwithstanding its protestations to the contrary, the *Flick* tribunal was essentially sitting as a domestic, and not an international, court. As such, it is more difficult to discern whether the law being applied by the tribunal was international law as such, or rules of domestic law that had been derived from international norms.

26   Convention Respecting the Laws and Customs of War on Land, 18 October 1907, 36 Stat. 2277, 1 Bevans 631 (hereinafter 'Hague Convention'), art. 3, available at www.yale.edu/lawweb/avalon/lawofwar/hague04.htm.

applicable to the Second World War because several of the belligerents were not parties to those treaties, the IMT found that the rules set forth therein had acquired the status of customary law and that their breach gave rise to individual criminal responsibility.[27]

Part of what made this finding so extraordinary is that the Hague Conventions do not require criminal punishment of violations. Indeed, the exclusive remedy provided for in those treaties is compensation by the violating state.

The 1949 Geneva Conventions, building on the achievements of the IMTs, include a special penal regime for certain violations – the so-called 'grave breaches'. When a grave breach is committed, all states parties are obliged to seek out the perpetrators and to bring them to justice through prosecution or extradition.[28] While these rules do not purport to directly bind individuals, they clearly show the drafters' intent that their violation entail criminal consequences for individual perpetrators. Nothing in the text of the Conventions limits application of the grave breaches regime to state actors.

Another major development of the 1949 Geneva Conventions was the inclusion of provisions expressly regulating non-international armed conflicts, and consequently, directly binding non-state organized, armed groups.

As noted above, at the time of the IMT judgment, existing IHL treaties were embedded in the traditional structure of the international legal system and thus regulated only international (that is, inter-state) armed conflicts. Prior to the Second World War, internal conflicts were generally regarded as an internal matter. However, by providing that crimes against humanity could be committed against *any* civilian population, the drafters of the IMT Charter heralded a continuing erosion of the non-intervention principle that led to the development of the law of non-international armed conflict.

Common article 3 of the 1949 Geneva Conventions sets forth standards regulating armed conflicts 'not of an international character'.[29] Thus, even purely internal armed conflicts were now regulated by express treaty provisions. Even more significantly, the text of the article makes clear that it binds all parties to the conflict, including non-state organized, armed groups. This was the first time that a multilateral IHL treaty expressly asserted that a non-state entity was bound by international law.

In light of the dynamic relationship between IHL and international criminal law, as humanitarian law expanded to regulate the conduct of non-state actors, so did international criminal law increasingly provide for their individual responsibility.[30]

---

[27]   Trial of German Major War Criminals, 1946, The Law of the Charter, available at www.yale.edu/lawweb/avalon/imt/proc/judlawch.htm

[28]   See for example, Geneva Convention for the Amelioration of the Condition of the Wounded and Sick in Armed Forces in the Field (First Geneva Convention), 75 UNTS 31 (1949), art. 50 ('Grave breaches to which the preceding Article relates shall be those involving any of the following acts, if committed against persons or property protected by the Convention: willful killing, torture or inhuman treatment, including biological experiments, willfully causing great suffering or serious injury to body or health, and extensive destruction and appropriation of property, not justified by military necessity and carried out unlawfully and wantonly.').

[29]   Geneva Convention Relative to the Protection of Civilian Persons in Time of War (1949), art. 3, available at www.unhchr.ch/html/menu3/b/92.htm.

[30]   While it was initially unclear whether violations of common article 3 gave rise to individual criminal responsibility, it has now been accepted by a number of international criminal courts. See below.

The Genocide Convention

In 1948, the UN General Assembly adopted the Convention on the Prevention and Punishment of the Crime of Genocide.[31] The Genocide Convention provides a definition for the crime of genocide and asserts that it is a crime under international law.

The Convention provides that genocide may be committed in peacetime, thus making clear that the existence of armed conflict is not required as a contextual element for genocide. Even more significantly, the Convention expressly states that genocide may be committed by a non-state actor. According to article 4 of the Convention, 'Persons committing genocide or any of the other acts enumerated in article III shall be punished, whether they are constitutionally responsible rulers, public officials or private individuals.'

Crimes Against Humanity

The legal content of crimes against humanity continued to evolve in the decades following the Second World War. Severing the link between this category of crimes and a state of armed conflict, the 1968 Convention on the Non-Applicability of Statutory Limitations to war crimes and crimes against humanity provides that statutes of limitations shall not apply to crimes against humanity 'whether committed in time of war or in time of peace'.[32]

Draft code of crimes against the peace and security of mankind

The notion of crimes against humanity continued to evolve through the work of the International Law Commission, which had been charged with developing a draft code of international criminal law. In its final incarnation, the Code defined crimes against humanity as including acts 'instigated or directed by a Government *or by any organization or group*', affirming that crimes against humanity need not be committed on behalf of a state.[33]

Other crimes included in the Draft Code were genocide, war crimes, crimes against the United Nations and associated personnel, and aggression. Only one of these categories of crimes was expressly limited to individuals having some connection to a state. The crime of aggression, derived from the IMT category of 'crimes against peace', was limited to individuals who participate in 'the planning, preparation, initiation or waging of aggression *committed by a State*'.[34]

Torture

In apparent contrast to the trend in favor of extending international criminal law to reach the conduct of non-state actors, the 1984 Convention Against Torture and Other Cruel, Inhuman

---

[31]   Genocide Convention (1948), 78 UNTS 277 (1951), art. II, available at www.unhchr.ch/html/menu3/b/p_genoci.htm.

[32]   See Convention on the Non-Applicability of Statutory Limitations to War Crimes and Crimes Against Humanity, General Asssembly Res. 2391 (XXIII), Annex, 23 UN GAOR Supp. (No. 18) 40, UN Doc. A/7218 (1968), entered into force 11 November 1970, art. 1(b).

[33]   *Draft Code of Crimes Against the Peace and Security of Mankind* (1996), II Yearbook of the International Law Commission (1996), Pt 2, art. 2 (emphasis added).

[34]   *Ibid.* art. 16 (emphasis added).

or Degrading Treatment or Punishment (CAT) defines torture so as to exclude purely private conduct. Article 1 defines torture as:

> any act by which severe pain or suffering, whether physical or mental, is intentionally inflicted on a person for such purposes as obtaining from him or a third person information or a confession, punishing him for an act he or a third person has committed or is suspected of having committed, or intimidating or coercing him or a third person, or for any reason based on discrimination of any kind, *when such pain or suffering is inflicted by or at the instigation of or with the consent or acquiescence of a public official or other person acting in an official capacity.*[35]

This would seem to preclude purely private conduct from the scope of the Convention. However, this does not mean that the conduct of non-state actors is entirely excluded from its scope. Indeed, the language of the definition makes clear that the perpetrator need not be a state actor. There need only be some level of state involvement; even mere acquiescence will suffice.[36]

Perhaps of even greater significance is that CAT does not purport to apply directly to individuals. It operates through the modality of domestic legislation. All parties must 'ensure that all acts of torture are offences under its criminal law'. The Convention does not assert that acts of torture as defined therein give rise to individual criminal responsibility in international law. As will be demonstrated below, international criminal courts have been granted jurisdiction to prosecute torture only when committed as a war crime or a crime against humanity. These courts have found that the act of torture does not require any state involvement when committed as a war crime or crime against humanity.[37]

FURTHER DEVELOPMENT OF INTERNATIONAL CRIMINAL LAW BY INTERNATIONAL CRIMINAL COURTS

International criminal law has evolved rapidly in recent years. This evolution was spurred in large part by the development of a number of international criminal courts since the early 1990s. The International Criminal Tribunal for the Former Yugoslavia (ICTY), the International Criminal Tribunal for Rwanda (ICTR), and the International Criminal Court (ICC) are competent to prosecute all individuals, including non-state actors, who commit crimes falling within their jurisdictions.

---

[35]   Convention Against Torture and Other Cruel, Inhuman or Degrading Treatment or Punishment, 1465 UNTS 113 (10 December 1984), art.1 (emphasis added) available at www.unhchr.ch/html/menu3/b/h_cat39.htm

[36]   In addition, the obligation to criminalize applies also to 'attempt to commit torture and to an act *by any person* which constitutes complicity or participation in torture'. CAT, art. 4(1) (emphasis added). Thus, once the minimum level of state involvement to constitute torture is established, the status of the individuals perpetrating the crime or participating in it is irrelevant.

[37]   See, for example, *Prosecutor v. Kuranac et al.*, Case Nos. ICTY IT-96-23-T, IT-96-23/1-T, ICTY Trial Chamber, 22 February 2001).

International Criminal Tribunal for the Former Yugoslavia

The subject matter jurisdiction of the ICTY includes war crimes, genocide and crimes against humanity. As noted above, each category of crimes is capable of being committed by a non-state actor, and the Tribunal has convicted a number of such individuals.[38]

By the time of ICTY's establishment, it was clear that genocide and crimes against humanity could occur within a single state[39] and could be perpetrated by a non-state actor,[40] and this was reflected in the Tribunal's Statute. The definition of genocide was taken directly from the text of the 1948 Genocide Convention. The definition of crimes against humanity drew upon the work of the post-Second World War International Military Tribunals, as well as that of the International Law Commission.

The contextual elements for crimes against humanity are set forth in the chapeau of article 5 of the ICTY Statute. It defines crimes against humanity as certain inhumane acts 'committed in armed conflict, whether international or internal in character, and directed against any civilian population'. The ICTY has interpreted this language as requiring a nexus between an individual's inhumane act and this broader attack.[41] Thus, crimes against humanity consist of individual 'acts' that, on some essential level, form part of the attack.[42]

It is this nexus requirement that distinguishes crimes against humanity from ordinary crimes, just as war crimes are distinguished from ordinary crimes by virtue of their connection to an armed conflict and genocidal acts are distinguished from ordinary crimes by the special intent required for their commission (that is, the intent to destroy a racial, ethnical, national or religious group in whole or in part).

The war crimes provisions of the ICTY Statute retain a bit more of the traditional inter-state structure of international law. When the drafters of the Statute began to develop the subject matter jurisdiction of the Tribunal, they were faced with the challenge of determining

---

38   See,for example, *Prosecutor* v. *Limaj et al.*, Case No. IT-03-66-A, Appeal Judgment, 27 September 2007); *Prosecutor* v. *Vasiljevic*, Case No. IT-98-32-A, Appeal Judgment, 25 February 2004); *Prosecutor* v. *Haradinaj et al.*, Case No. IT-04-84-T, Judgment, 3 April 2008). See also, *Prosecutor* v. *Kunarac*, Case No. IT-96-23-T, IT-96-23/1-T, Judgment, 22 February 2001, para. 419 (abandoning the state involvement requirement for torture as a war crime).

39   The definition of the crimes against humanity in the ICTY Statute includes an armed conflict requirement as a jurisdictional element. Statute of the International Tribunal for the Prosecution of Persons Responsible for Serious Violations of International Humanitarian Law Committed in the Territory of the Former Yugoslavia since 1991, Security Council Res. 827, 25 May 1991, UN Doc. S/RES/827. However, the definition makes clear that the armed conflict may be international or internal. The ICTY has also opined that this requirement is a purely jurisdictional element, and is not part of the definition of crimes against humanity in customary international law. See, for example, *Prosecutor* v. *Dusko Tadic*, Case No. IT-94-1-T, Judgment, 7 May 1997, para. 572; *Prosecutor* v. *Rajic*, Case No. IT-95-12-R61, Review of the Indictment, 13 September, 1996, para. 7); *Prosecutor* v. *Blaskic*, Case No. IT-95-14-T, Judgment, 3 March 2000, para. 66.

40   While an early decision of the ICTY seemed to indicate that a policy was a necessary element in sustaining a prosecution for crimes against humanity, the Appeals Chamber rejected this. *Prosecutor* v. *Blaskic*, Case No. IT-95-14-T, Judgment, 3 March 2000, paras 69–70. To the extent a policy was required, it would have been easier to establish in a governmental context.

41   This requirement is separate from the jurisdictional element, also set forth in the chapeau, that an armed conflict exist at the relevant time.

42   *Prosecutor* v. *Tadic*, Case No. IT-94-1-A, Appeal Judgment, 15 July 1999, para. 251, available at www.un.org/icty/tadic/appeal/judgement/tad-aj990715e.pdf.

which violations of IHL gave rise to individual criminal responsibility. The first category of war crimes they included in the Statute was the category of 'grave breaches' as set forth in the 1949 Geneva Conventions. Because such breaches were the subject of a mandatory penal regime in the Conventions, the drafters of those Conventions had clearly intended that the breach of these norms should attract criminal sanctions.

Early on, the ICTY Appeals Chamber held that grave breaches could only be committed in international armed conflict.[43] In order to determine whether a conflict was international or non-international, the Appeals Chamber relied on the law of state responsibility. It thus made more relevant the nature of the actor and his or her relationship to the state. At the same time, the Appeals Chamber seemed to lower the threshold for attributing the conduct of certain non-state actors to the state. In a departure from the rules of attribution as formulated by the International Law Commission, the Appeals Chamber held that overall control of a hierarchically-organized non-state entity may be sufficient to assimilate that entity to a state organ, rendering all of its conduct attributable to the state.[44]

The other category of war crimes included in the ICTY Statute is described simply as '[v]iolations of the laws or customs of war',[45] essentially leaving to the judges the question of which violations of IHL would constitute war crimes. In the *Tadic* decision, the Appeals Chamber developed a framework for analyzing which norms of IHL gave rise to individual criminal responsibility, and could thus be prosecuted before the ICTY. The primary criteria set forth were the character of the norm itself, the severity of the violation, and the interest of the international community in its repression.[46]

In that same decision, the Appeals Chamber also made clear that the rubric '[v]iolations of the laws and customs of war' under article 3 of the ICTY Statute potentially encompassed all of humanitarian law, including the law of non-international armed conflict. It thus found that serious violations of common article 3 of the 1949 Geneva Conventions could also be prosecuted under the ICTY Statute.

Whether an individual is prosecuted under article 2 or article 3 of the Statute, the Prosecutor must demonstrate not only the existence of the requisite type of armed conflict (that is, either international or non-international), but also a nexus between the alleged offence and the armed conflict which gives rise to the applicability of international humanitarian law.[47] The ICTY has determined that such a nexus exists where an act is closely related to an armed conflict, that is, if the act was committed in furtherance of an armed conflict, or under the guise of an armed conflict. It has cited as factors in this determination: the fact that the perpetrator is a combatant; the fact that the victim is a member of the opposing party; the fact that the act may be said to serve the ultimate goal of a military campaign; and the fact that the crime is committed as part of or in the context of the perpetrator's official duties.

In light of these contextual elements, an individual's status as a state official may be relevant in establishing the commission of crimes within the Tribunal's jurisdiction. However it

---

43   *Tadic*, Decision on the Defence Motion for Interlocutory Appeal on Jurisdiction, para. 71.
44   *Tadic* Appeal Judgment, note 41 *supra*, para. 121.
45   ICTY Statute, art. 3.
46   *Tadic* Appeal Judgment, note 41 *supra*, para. 128.
47   It should be noted, however, that unlike crimes against humanity, war crimes need not be committed as part of a broader pattern of crimes. A single act may constitute a war crime so long as it has the requisite nexus to an armed conflict.

is not strictly required. Effectively, the question of whether an individual is a state actor has been replaced with the question of whether an individual's act is sufficiently connected with a context that justifies international regulation. State affiliation is just one factor among many that may enter into that calculation.

International Criminal Tribunal for Rwanda

The subject matter jurisdiction of the Rwanda Tribunal encompasses the same three categories – war crimes, genocide and crimes against humanity.[48] Significantly, however, the ICTR was established in the context of a conflict that was deemed to be internal in nature. Thus, the war crimes provisions of the ICTR Statute were limited to violations of the law of non-international armed conflict – to wit, common article 3 and Additional Protocol II to the 1949 Geneva Conventions. Tailored as it was to the context of an internal conflict, the subject matter jurisdiction of the Rwanda Tribunal is even less concerned with the issue of state affiliation.

At the same time, the ICTR has further elaborated on the nexus requirements for war crimes and crimes against humanity and has made a number of valuable contributions to the evolving international jurisprudence on genocide. Providing guidance as to what sort of nexus is required for crimes against humanity, the Semanza Trial Chamber held that while the act does not need to be committed at the same time or place as the attack, or share the same features as the actual attack, the act must, on some essential level, form part of the attack.[49] The act does not even have to be committed against the same population as the broader attack of which it is a part.[50] However, the act 'must, by its characteristics, aims, nature, or consequence objectively form part of the discriminatory attack'.[51]

Another dimension of this nexus is found in the *mens rea* requirement for crimes against humanity. Again, it is the association with a widespread or systematic overarching attack that elevates these offenses to matters subject to international regulation. This requirement was made express by the Bagilishema Trial Chamber:

> A mental factor specific to crimes against humanity is required to create the nexus between an underlying offence and the broader criminal context, thus transforming an ordinary crime into an attack on humanity itself.
>
> [T]he Accused mentally must include his act within the greater dimension of criminal conduct. This means that the accused must know that his offence forms part of the broader attack. By making his criminal act part of the attack, the perpetrator necessarily participates in the broader attack.[52]

---

[48] Statute of the International Criminal Tribunal for Rwanda, Security Council. Res. 955, 8 November 1994, UN Doc. S/RES/955, arts 2–4.

[49] *Semanza,*ICTR-97-20-T, Judgment and Sentence, para. 326 ('Although the act need not be committed at the same time and place as the attack or share all of the features of the attack, it must, by its characteristics, aims, nature, or consequence objectively form part of the discriminatory attack.'); compare *Tadic*, IT-94-1-A, Judgment, para. 251.

[50] See *Semanza*, note 48 *supra*, para. 330 (although the act does not have to be committed against the same population, if it is committed against the same population, that characteristic may be used to demonstrate the nexus between the act and the attack).

[51] See *ibid.* para. 326. Note that, unlike the ICTY and ICC Statutes, the ICTR Statute requires as a jurisdictional element for prosecuting Crimes Against Humanity that the 'attack' against a civilian population be discriminatory.

[52] *Prosecutor* v. *Bagilishema*, Case No. ICTR-95-1A-T, Trial Chamber, 7 June 2001, paras 93–4 (citations and paragraph numbers omitted).

To satisfy this *mens rea* element, the defendant must be aware of the attack that makes his or her act a crime against humanity. In practice, this means that the perpetrator must have knowledge of the attack, either actual or constructive, and some understanding of the relationship between his or her acts and the attack.[53]

While proving the requisite nexus may be assisted by demonstrating a policy, the existence of a policy is not required. In any event, all a prosecutor need ultimately prove in this regard is that, given the context and circumstances surrounding an act, the act cannot reasonably be seen as random or isolated.

With respect to the *mens rea,* the nexus between an act and an attack is partly established through showing that the perpetrator had knowledge of the attack. It need not be proven, however, that by the time the accused committed the act at issue, he or she had made the legal determination that the attack was indeed a crime against humanity.

International Criminal Court

The Rome Statute of the International Criminal Court sets forth the most comprehensive codification of international criminal law to date.[54] While the ICC, similar to the ad hoc tribunals, has jurisdiction to prosecute war crimes, genocide and crimes against humanity, it also has jurisdiction to prosecute the crime of aggression, a crime that had not been included within the jurisdiction of an international court since the IMTs. The crime of aggression, however, was left undefined, and the ICC cannot prosecute this crime until the Assembly of States Parties (to the ICC Statute) settles upon a definition and jurisdictional regime.[55]

As with the ad hoc tribunals for the Former Yugoslavia and Rwanda, the crimes are addressed to all individuals, but their scope is limited by contextual elements. For war crimes, the contextual element is armed conflict. Some of the war crimes provisions require a nexus to international armed conflict. The others require a nexus to non-international armed conflict. In addition, the Statute stipulates that the 'Court shall have jurisdiction in respect of war crimes in particular when committed as part of a plan or policy or as part of a large-scale commission of such crimes',[56] perhaps raising the contextual bar.

The contextual elements for crimes against humanity are found in the requirement that they be committed 'as part of a widespread or systematic attack directed against any civilian population, with knowledge of the attack'.[57] This definition is a bit broader than the defini-

---

[53]   *Semanza*, ICTR-97-20-T, Judgment and Sentence, para. 332; *Prosecutor* v. *Kayishema*, Case No. ICTR-95-1-T, Judgment, Trial Chamber II, 21 May 1999, paras 133–4 ('The perpetrator must knowingly commit crimes against humanity in the sense that he must understand the overall context of his act.'). Under ICTY jurisprudence, the requisite *mens rea* is satisfied if the perpetrator 'took the risk that his acts were part of the attack'. *Prosecutor* v. *Kunarac*, Case No. IT-96-23/1-A, Judgment, Appeals Chamber, 12 June 2002, para. 102). The Appeals Chamber in *Kunarac* made clear that the perpetrator need not know the details of the attack. *Ibid.*

[54]   Rome Statute of the International Criminal Court, 37 ILM 999 (1998).

[55]   See, for example, Reports of the ICC Working Group on the Crime of Aggression. In June 2010, the ICC Assembly of States Parties adopted a definition for aggression, as well as a package of jurisdictional triggers. However these amendments were made subject to delayed entry into force provisions, and will not become operational until some time after 2017.

[56]   ICC Statute, art. 8.

[57]   *Ibid.* art. 7(1).

tions in the ICTY and ICTR statutes in that it does not include the jurisdictional elements of armed conflict (ICTY) or that the attack be discriminatory (ICTR). However, the ICC Statute does narrow the definition a bit by requiring the existence of a policy. It defines '[a]ttack directed against any civilian population' as 'a course of conduct involving the multiple commission of acts … against any civilian population, pursuant to or in furtherance of a State or organizational policy to commit such attack'.[58]

While the definition of genocide in the ICC Statute does not expressly set forth contextual elements, they are arguably implicit in the *mens rea* requirement for the crime. In addition, the ICC Elements of the Crimes sets forth as an element of the crime of genocide that the 'conduct took place in the context of a manifest pattern of similar conduct directed against that group or was conduct that could itself effect such destruction'.[59]

Thus, each category of crimes entails contextual elements linking the particular act to a larger context that is deemed to warrant international regulation. Arguably, the commission of any of these crimes requires some connection to an organized power structure. In a sense, the focus on the state has been replaced with a more realistic focus on power.

At the same time, the jurisprudence of these courts continues to evolve in a way that broadens the reach of international criminal law. For example, in light of the broad nexus tests formulated for war crimes and crimes against humanity, individual perpetrators need not even be part of a particular power structure. Their conduct need only be in some way related to that power structure or its activities.

APPLICATION TO PRIVATE SECURITY CONTRACTORS

In light of the foregoing, it becomes clear that the situation of individuals working for PSCs is no different from that of any other individual. The key task is to identify whether the contextual elements of an international crime are met and then to examine whether there is a sufficient link between the individual perpetrator and that context. If the individual perpetrator commits an act in the context of and associated with an armed conflict and that act constitutes a serious violation of the law of armed conflict, such conduct will constitute a war crime. If an individual perpetrator commits an inhumane act as part of a widespread or systematic attack directed against a civilian population, such conduct will constitute a crime against humanity.

The fact that an individual is a member of a PSC may be relevant in linking the individual to the requisite context. For example, where a PSC is engaged in hostilities, this will suffice to link the conduct of the personnel to an ongoing armed conflict. If the PSC is working in furtherance of a policy to commit a widespread or systematic attack directed against a civilian population, this would be sufficient to link the conduct of its personnel to that attack.

Another issue that may arise in this context is command or superior responsibility. Depending upon the structure of authority within the PSC, superiors within that structure may be liable for the crimes of their subordinates where they fail to take steps to prevent or respond to these crimes.[60] Whether or not command or superior responsibility may extend upward beyond the

---

[58]   *Ibid.* art. 7(2)(a).
[59]   See ICC Elements of the Crimes at 2, available at www.icc-cpi.int/library/about/official journal/Element_of_Crimes_English.pdf.
[60]   See ICC Statute, art. 28: 'In addition to other grounds of criminal responsibility under this

internal command structure of the PSC will depend on the relationship between the PSC and the hiring authority. Where the hiring authority does not exercise command and control over the PSC, that authority may not be liable on the basis of command responsibility. Nonetheless, other forms of accomplice liability may apply depending upon the circumstances.[61]

The analysis is complicated by the varied roles typically accorded to PSCs in practice. The resulting ambiguities were evident in the legal controversy surrounding the conduct of Blackwater contractors operating in Iraq.[62] Blackwater was hired by the United States to carry out public functions, and as such its conduct was attributable to the United States. However, Blackwater personnel were not incorporated into the US armed forces or otherwise engaged as combatants. Nonetheless, the conduct of Blackwater personnel seemed to blur at times into combat functions. This ambiguity of function and status can have an impact on the application of international criminal law – in particular, those rules of international criminal law derived from the law of armed conflict.[63]

In an effort to clarify rules of international law as they apply to the activities of PSCs in the context of armed conflict, a number of states participated in a gathering convened by Switzerland and the International Committee of the Red Cross in the fall of 2008. This gathering produced the Montreux Document on Pertinent International Legal Obligations and Good Practices for States related to Operations of Private Military and Security Companies during Armed Conflict.[64] In addition to recalling pertinent rules of international law,[65] the Montreux Document contains a compilation of good practices designed to assist states in implementing their obligations under international law. Some of these practices are directed toward clarifying the functions of PSCs, as well as toward ensuring adequate supervision and accountability for their conduct.

Statute for crimes within the jurisdiction of the Court: (a) A military commander or person effectively acting as a military commander shall be criminally responsible for crimes within the jurisdiction of the Court committed by forces under his or her effective command and control, or effective authority and control as the case may be, as a result of his or her failure to exercise control properly over such forces, where: (i) that military commander or person either knew or, owing to the circumstances at the time, should have known that the forces were committing or about to commit such crimes; and (ii) that military commander or person failed to take all necessary and reasonable measures within his or her power to prevent or repress their commission or to submit the matter to the competent authorities for investigation and prosecution. (b) With respect to superior and subordinate relationships not described in paragraph (a), a superior shall be criminally responsible for crimes within the jurisdiction of the Court committed by subordinates under his or her effective authority and control, as a result of his or her failure to exercise control properly over such subordinates, where: (i) the superior either knew, or consciously disregarded information which clearly indicated, that the subordinates were committing or about to commit such crimes; (ii) the crimes concerned activities that were within the effective responsibility and control of the superior; and (iii) the superior failed to take all necessary and reasonable measures within his or her power to prevent or repress their commission or to submit the matter to the competent authorities for investigation and prosecution.

[61]   And of course, as noted above, even in the absence of individual responsibility on the part of the hiring authorities, the state would still bear responsibility for the wrongful conduct of the PSC where the relevant attribution standards have been met.

[62]   See, for example, BBC News, *Blackwater 'hired for CIA plan'*, 20 August 2009, available at http://news.bbc.co.uk/2/hi/americas/8211088.stm.

[63]   See G. Corn, *Murky 'Blackwater' and the Direct Participation Dilemma*, THE JURIST, 2 October 2007, available at http://jurist.law.pitt.edu/forumy/2007/10/murky-blackwater-and-the-direct.php.

[64]   UN Doc. A/63/467–S/2008/636 (6 October 2008).

[65]   The Montreux Document does not purport to create any new international legal obligations.

CONCLUSION

The IMT, through its revival of a natural law concept in a positivist era, facilitated the transformation of the principle of individual criminal responsibility into positive law. The necessary consent of the international community was made clear in the UN General Assembly affirmation of the Nuremberg principles[66] and codified in the ICC Statute.

Once the individual has been deemed a subject of positive international law, the requirement of state affiliation is no longer essential to analytical coherence. The issue becomes simply whether international law should directly regulate the conduct of non-state actors – something that was traditionally left to the internal law of states.

As the non-intervention principle continues to erode and as international law penetrates more deeply into the internal sphere, the international community is faced with the question of what sorts of activities should be regulated by international criminal law. The international community and the IMT's progeny have adopted a primarily context-based approach. Thus, most of the rules of international criminal law in the strict sense are addressed to all individuals, but the scope of these crimes is limited by contextual elements.

There is no requirement in modern international criminal law that a perpetrator be a state actor. However, the status of an individual is not necessarily irrelevant. While rules of international criminal law are not addressed exclusively to state actors, whether or not a perpetrator is a state actor may be relevant in establishing contextual elements, such as whether a conflict is international for purposes of prosecuting grave breaches, or to establish the existence of a policy for the prosecution of crimes against humanity under the ICC Statute. It could also be relevant for crimes that are based on the status of the victim, for example, crimes against prisoners of war, or in establishing certain modes of liability, such as command responsibility, which is predicated on a superior-subordinate relationship.[67]

Ultimately, all individual non-state actors, including those working for PSCs, are bound by the rules of international criminal law. The question is simply whether the elements of a particular crime are present – a question which may turn in part on the role and structure of a given PSC, as well as its relationship to the state.

---

[66]   General Assembly Res. 95(I) (1946).

[67]   This type of relationship may be more easily established in the *de jure* hierarchy of a state's official machinery.

PART II

CRIMES UNDER
INTERNATIONAL LAW

3 The crime of genocide

Mark A. Drumbl*

OVERVIEW AND DEFINITION

The Convention on the Prevention and Punishment of the Crime of Genocide ('Genocide Convention', adopted in 1948) defines genocide as:

> [A]ny of the following acts committed with intent to destroy, in whole or in part, a national, ethnical, racial or religious group, as such:
> (a) killing members of the group;
> (b) causing serious bodily or mental harm to members of the group;
> (c) deliberately inflicting on the group conditions of life calculated to bring about its physical destruction in whole or in part;
> (d) imposing measures intended to prevent births within the group;
> (e) forcibly transferring children of the group to another group.[1]

The Genocide Convention's definition reappears in other international legal instruments, such as article 2(2) of the Statute of the ad hoc International Criminal Tribunal for Rwanda (1994) (ICTR),[2] article 4(2) of the Statute of the ad hoc International Criminal Tribunal for the former Yugoslavia (1993) (ICTY),[3] and article 6 of the Rome Statute of the International Criminal Court (ICC) (entered into force in 2002).[4] In the case of the ICC Statute, additional elaborative content is provided by the Elements of the Crimes (under article 9 of the ICC Statute, the Elements of the Crimes assist judges and parties before the ICC in interpreting and applying the proscribed crimes). As Cherif Bassiouni observes, genocide 'remains a single instrument crime' owing to the influence of the Genocide Convention.[5]

Looking beyond the treaty framework, the prohibition of genocide is a *jus cogens* (peremptory) norm;[6] this obligation is owed to the international community as a whole and, consequently, is also of an *erga omnes* nature.[7] Genocide is, therefore, a crime under customary international law.[8]

---

*   Thanks to Andrew Finnicum for research assistance.
1   Convention on the Prevention and Punishment of the Crime of Genocide (1948), 78 UNTS 277, art. 2.
2   Statute of the International Criminal Tribunal for Rwanda, Security Council Res. 955 (1994).
3   Statute of the International Criminal Tribunal for the Former Yugoslavia, Security Council Res. 827 (1993).
4   Rome Statute of the International Criminal Court, 2187 UNTS 90 (1998).
5   M.C. BASSIOUNI, INTRODUCTION TO INTERNATIONAL CRIMINAL LAW 139 (2003).
6   Ibid. 507; *Prosecutor* v. *Kayishema and Ruzindana*, Case No. ICTR-95-1-T, Judgment, 21 May 1999, para. 88.
7   *Reservations to the Convention on the Prevention and Punishment of the Crime of Genocide*, Advisory Opinion, 1951 ICJ Rep. 15, 23.
8   *Prosecutor* v. *Musema*, Case No. ICTR-96-13-T, Judgment, 27 January 2000.

By virtue of article I of the Genocide Convention, 'genocide, whether committed in time of peace or in time of war, is a crime under international law which [contracting parties] undertake to prevent and to punish'.[9] Genocide 'is a crime simultaneously directed against individual victims, the group to which they belong, and human diversity'.[10] Along with crimes against humanity, war crimes and the crime of aggression, genocide takes its place among the core international crimes. That said, the ICTR has identified genocide as the 'crime of crimes'.[11] Although there is no formally explicit normative or punitive hierarchy among extraordinary international crimes, genocide is perceived to be of particular gravity.[12]

Genocide also may give rise to individual civil liability. For example, survivors, acting as *parties civiles*, have brought civil damage claims in Rwandan courts against persons accused of genocide.[13] Victims of atrocity have filed civil damage claims under the Alien Tort Claims Act in US district courts for a variety of international crimes, including genocide.[14] Genocide may also give rise to state responsibility. In 2007, the International Court of Justice ruled that states (in that particular case, Serbia) can be responsible for failing to prevent or punish genocide.[15]

The crime of genocide can be prosecuted and punished by international or national tribunals.[16] Three elements must be found in order for an individual to be convicted for genocide. One is the special mental intent to destroy a protected group in whole or in part. Another is the mental intent to commit the underlying offense (for example, killing, causing serious bodily harm). Third, the physical element – namely, the specified underlying offense committed in a manner that entails individual penal responsibility – also must be established.

Archetypically, genocide is a collective crime. The victim is signaled out not because of her conduct as an individual, but because of her membership in a despised group. The victim may be unknown to the attacker; the victim may be a neighbor; or the victim may even be a family member. In all cases, however, she faces attack not because of a grievance the attacker has with her individually, but because of a grievance the attacker has with the group to which she belongs. Genocide is a crime involving 'a denial of the right of existence of entire human

---

[9]   Genocide Convention, art. 1.

[10]   R. Cryer, H. Friman, D. Robinson and E. Wilmshurst, An Introduction to International Criminal Law and Procedure 165 (2007).

[11]   *Prosecutor* v. *Kambanda*, Case No. ICTR-97-23-S, Judgment, 4 September 1998, para. 16; W. Schabas, Genocide in International Law 9 (2000).

[12]   The International Military Tribunal at Nuremberg identified aggression (crimes against the peace) as the 'supreme international crime'.

[13]   M. Drumbl, Atrocity, Punishment, and International Law 80–3 (2007).

[14]   See, for example, *Kadić* v. *Karadzić*, 70 F.3d 232 (2[d] Cir. 1995); *Almog* v. *Arab Bank PLC*, 471 F.Supp.2d 257, 287 (EDNY 2007).

[15]   *Application of the Convention on the Prevention and Punishment of the Crime of Genocide (Bosnia and Herzegovina* v. *Serbia and Montenegro)*, Judgment, 26 February 2007, available at www.icj-cij.org/docket/files/91/13685.pdf?PHPSESSID=4035476c6c7926d1026c168e28d194cc. Insofar as Montenegro seceded from Serbia in June 2006, the ICJ no longer considered it a party to the case. See also M. Milanović, *State Responsibility for Genocide*, 17 European J International Law 553 (2006).

[16]   Genocide Convention, art. 6 ('Persons charged with genocide or any of the other acts enumerated in Article III shall be tried by a competent tribunal of the State in the territory of which the act was committed, or by such international penal tribunal as may have jurisdiction with respect to those Contracting Parties which shall have accepted its jurisdiction.').

groups'.[17] Although some social science evidence suggests that perpetrators may also be motivated to eliminate 'the other' for private material gain or out of social coercion,[18] the perpetrators of genocide largely remain ideologically motivated agents. The instantiation of genocide often is preceded by years of hate propaganda, which baptizes the perpetrator group with infallibility and supremacy, and denigrates the target group as vermin, maggots and scum. As a result, many low-level perpetrators may see the commission of genocide as a day's labor in service to the state, and intermediary and even senior officials may see the crime as discharge of bureaucratic and professional duties. For this reason, Hannah Arendt has described crimes like genocide as epitomizing the 'banality of evil'.[19]

ORIGINS, PROSECUTING INSTITUTIONS AND CONVICTIONS

Genocide originated as a legal term in response to the Holocaust. Raphael Lemkin, a Polish lawyer, initially 'coined' the word in his 1944 work, *Axis Rule in Occupied Europe*.[20] As William Schabas notes, Lemkin created the term genocide from 'two words, *genos*, which means race, nation or tribe in ancient Greek, and *caedere*, meaning to kill in Latin'.[21] Genocide first formally became an international crime in January 1951, when the Genocide Convention (adopted on 9 December 1948) came into force. That said, genocide had been recognized as an international crime as early as December 1946, when the United Nations General Assembly adopted Resolution 96(1). In any event, although the Holocaust constituted genocide and would today be prosecuted as such, genocide 'was not a crime within the jurisdiction of the Nuremberg Tribunal, and the term was not mentioned in its judgment'.[22] The term genocide was not included in the London Charter and, hence, could not be punished by the International Military Tribunal (IMT) at Nuremberg; however, the Prosecutor's indictment did include the term 'genocide'.[23] Assuredly, Nazis were pursued for genocide in proceedings subsequent to the IMT, whether held by military tribunals or by national courts.[24] In 1961–1962, Israeli courts convicted and executed Adolf Eichmann, the architect of the Final Solution, for crimes against the Jewish people. Still, the first *international* convictions for genocide occurred in the 1990s at the ICTR; specifically, the convictions of Jean-Paul Akayesu (a Rwandan mayor) and Jean Kambanda (former Rwandan Prime

---

17   *Reservations to the Convention on the Prevention and Punishment of the Crime of Genocide*, note 7 *supra*, at 23.

18   P. Verwimp, An Economic Profile of Peasant Perpetrators of Genocide: Micro-level Evidence from Rwanda, 77 J DEVELOPMENT ECONOMICS 297 (2005). See also, S. Straus, THE ORDER OF GENOCIDE: RACE, POWER, AND WAR IN RWANDA (2006).

19   H. Arendt, EICHMANN IN JERUSALEM: A REPORT ON THE BANALITY OF EVIL (1965).

20   R. LEMPKIN, AXIS RULE IN OCCUPIED EUROPE 79 (1944); Cryer *et al.*, note 10 *supra*, at 166; Schabas, note 11 *supra*, at 14 (noting that '[r]arely has a neologism had such rapid success').

21   Schabas, note 11 *supra*, at 25.

22   Cryer *et al.*, note 10 *supra*, at 166.

23   G. METTRAUX, INTERNATIONAL CRIMES AND THE AD HOC TRIBUNALS 194 (2005). Paradoxically, as Mettraux notes, 'the very absence of any reference to "genocide" in the Nuremberg Judgment may have prompted states to establish such a prohibition via an international treaty and may have facilitated the adoption of the Genocide Convention'. *Ibid.* 198.

24   Schabas, note 11 *supra*, at 48–9; A. CASSESE, INTERNATIONAL CRIMINAL LAW 96 (2003).

Minister) in 1998. To date, three atrocities have been identified by international tribunals as genocide: the Holocaust, Rwanda and Srebrenica. National courts have gone further in identifying other tragedies as genocide. For example, the Iraqi High Tribunal has held that the Anfal campaign undertaken by Saddam Hussein in northern Iraq constituted acts of genocide against the Kurds.

Colloquially, the term 'genocide' has been 'used for any large-scale killings'.[25] Furthermore, the phrase 'cultural genocide' appears in the popular lexicon despite the fact that the drafters of the Genocide Convention rejected the notion of cultural genocide.[26] Thus, the legal meaning of genocide is much more circumscribed than the colloquial or popular meaning. The hallmark of genocide, as a crime, is the intended destruction in whole or in part of a national, racial, religious or ethnic group. The destruction must be of the biological or physical existence of the target group, although attacks upon cultural characteristics of the group could support the finding that the group was being targeted for physical or biological destruction.[27] The requirement of this very high level of intention gives genocide its special intent, or *dolus specialis*.

Insofar as this *Handbook* is one of international criminal *law*, from this point forward this chapter will address the *legal* definition of genocide. At this juncture, it is important to underscore that just because conduct falls short of the legal elements of genocide does not mean that it is not punishable at the international level – such conduct readily can amount to war crimes or crimes against humanity (including extermination or persecution). As Antonio Cassese notes, 'genocide was first recognized in international law as a subclass of the category of crimes against humanity', but has since become 'a category of crimes *per se*, with its own specific *actus reus* and *mens rea*'.[28]

Following codification in the 1948 Genocide Convention, there was little formal international law-making activity involving the crime of genocide. All this changed with the tragedies in the Balkans in the 1990s and in Rwanda in 1994. Responding to these tragedies, and unencumbered from the sclerosis of the Cold War, the UN Security Council in 1993 and 1994 created the ICTY and ICTR, respectively. Both tribunals were given authority to prosecute genocide, and both have done so – though the ICTR has done so much more frequently and successfully than the ICTY. The ICC has jurisdiction over genocide; at the time of writing, an ICC Pre-Trial Chamber has granted the ICC Prosecutor's request for an arrest warrant for Sudanese President al-Bashir, although not on charges of genocide (the matter remains under litigation). In each of the other situations in which indictments have been issued by the ICC Prosecutor, genocide is not among the crimes charged. In terms of internationalized institutions, the Special Court for Sierra Leone is not empowered to prosecute genocide. The Special Panels for Serious Crimes with jurisdiction over serious criminal offenses in Timor-Leste, which ceased operations in May 2005, had jurisdiction to prosecute genocide, though in practice did not issue genocide convictions (in one case, a genocide conviction was entered

---

25   Cryer *et al.*, note 10 *supra*, at 165.
26   Schabas, note 11 *supra*, at 179–85.
27   *Prosecutor* v. *Krstić*, Case No. IT-98-33-T, Judgment, 2 August 2001, para. 580; see also *Prosecutor* v. *Krstić*, Case No. IT-98-33-A, Judgment, 19 April 2004, para. 26; C. Kress, *The International Court of Justice and the Elements of Genocide* (2007) 18 EUROPEAN J INTERNATIONAL LAW 619, 626–7 (2007).
28   Cassese, note 24 *supra*, at 106.

by the East Timor Court of Appeal). The Extraordinary Chambers in the Court of Cambodia (ECCC) also have jurisdiction to prosecute genocide. Article 4 of the Law on the Establishment of the Extraordinary Chambers once again borrows from article II of the Genocide Convention.[29]

Mettraux notes that the codification of genocide in the ICTR and ICTY Statutes, as well as the tribunals' jurisprudence, has 'done a great deal to liberate genocide from the historical and sociological environment in which it was born'.[30] In other words, the judicial determination that the atrocity in Bosnia and Rwanda was genocide applied the crime – as a generally applicable legal norm – to tragedies other than the Holocaust. As Mettraux notes, this jurisprudence has given 'some welcome precision and foreseeability to a body of law characterized by a high degree of uncertainty and generalization', thereby moving the field of international criminal law 'from paper into reality'.[31] Assuredly, the extension of genocide to cover atrocities in other places has not been without controversy. Examples of elasticity in the legal interpretation of genocide include the Srebrenica massacre in Bosnia[32] and the ECCC's judicial mandate, where the factual circumstances leave it unclear whether genocide actually occurred.[33]

In accordance with article V of the Genocide Convention,[34] and consonant with the complementary framework established by article 17 of the ICC Statute, many states have criminalized genocide in their national laws and have empowered their national courts to convict offenders. As Schabas notes, the vast majority of states 'have borrowed the [Genocide] Convention definition, … but occasionally they have contributed their own innovations'.[35] The involvement of national courts in the accountability matrix means that, in some jurisdictions, prosecutions for genocide can occur at multiple levels. Rwanda is an example. Senior leaders of the Rwandan genocide appear before the ICTR (which has, at the time of writing, convicted around 30 offenders and has acquitted six). Roughly 10,000 individuals have been convicted by Special Chambers of Rwanda's national courts[36] while the Rwandan government maintains that one million individuals have appeared before neo-traditional *gacaca* courts. Genocide trials can also occur within the national courts of states removed from the atrocity. In some instances, cases may be transferred to distant national courts from international institutions; in other cases, these foreign national courts may have

---

29   See www.eccc.gov.kh/english/cabinet/law/4/KR_Law_as_amended_27_Oct_2004_Eng.pdf.
30   Mettraux, note 23 *supra*, at 199.
31   *Ibid.*
32   *Prosecutor* v. *Krstić*, Case No. IT-98-33-T, Judgment, 2 August 2001; *Prosecutor* v. *Krstić*, Case No. IT-98-33-A, Judgment, 19 April 2004; see *Bosnia* v. *Serbia*, note 15 *supra*. For early discussion of this controversy prior to the *Krstić* judgments, see W. Schabas, *Was Genocide Committed in Bosnia and Herzegovina? First Judgments of the International Criminal Tribunal for the Former Yugoslavia*, 25 FORDHAM INTERNATIONAL LJ 23 (2001).
33   For an argument in favor of the existence of auto-genocide (namely that the perpetrator group can also be the target group) in Cambodia, see H. Hannum, *International Law and Cambodian Genocide: The Sounds of Silence*, 11 HUMAN RIGHTS QUARTERLY 82 (1989).
34   Genocide Convention, art. 5 states: 'The Contracting Parties undertake to enact, in accordance with their respective Constitutions, the necessary legislation to give effect to the provisions of the present Convention and, in particular, to provide effective penalties for persons guilty of genocide or any of the other acts enumerated in Article III.'
35   Schabas, note 11 *supra*, at 5.
36   Drumbl, note 13 *supra*, 72, 91 (citing the work of Schabas).

taken offenders located within their jurisdictions into custody. In still other cases, foreign national courts may elect to exercise universal jurisdiction[37] over the crime of genocide.[38] The interactions between international institutions, on the one hand, and national and local institutions, on the other, in the prosecution of extraordinary international crimes has been the subject of considerable academic research and commentary.[39] National juridical institutions that have convicted for genocide include the Iraqi High Tribunal for the Anfal campaign,[40] Germany in regard to atrocity in the Balkans, Ethiopia, and Israel in regard to crimes against the Jewish people. Also, the Brazilian courts have treated the Helmet massacre of the Tikuna people in 1988 as genocide.

Pursuant to article VII of the Genocide Convention, genocide is not to be considered as a political crime for the purpose of extradition. This means that the requested state may not refuse extradition of a genocide suspect on the grounds that the crime is determined to be political in nature.

The International Court of Justice (ICJ) has ruled that state responsibility can issue from a breach of the Genocide Convention, which accords the ICJ jurisdiction under article IX.[41] The ICJ adjudges contentious disputes between states and also renders advisory opinions. Although states cannot commit crimes per se, they can be held responsible for breaches of their international obligations, including their obligations to prevent and punish genocide. On 26 February 2007, the ICJ held that, although Serbia was not directly responsible for committing genocide in Bosnia and Herzegovina, it was responsible for having failed to prevent genocide at Srebrenica, where 7,000 Bosnian Muslim men and boys were massacred in July 1995.[42] The ICJ also found that Serbia breached the Genocide Convention for its failure, in the wake of genocide at Srebrenica, to fully cooperate with the ICTY. However, the ICJ did not award damages against Serbia. Instead, it ruled that the issuance of the judgment alone constituted satisfaction for Bosnia.

---

[37]   See Naomi Roht-Arriaza and Menaka Fernando, Chapter 15, for more on the concept of universal jurisdiction.

[38]   When foreign courts exercise jurisdiction, controversy may ensue. In April 2007, Rwanda submitted an application to the ICJ in a dispute that has arisen between it and France with regard to the issuance by French courts of international arrest warrants in November 2006. France issued arrest warrants for nine Rwandan officials. France alleged they played a role in the shooting down of then Rwandan President Habyarimana's airplane, the event that precipitated the genocide. France separately requested the UN Security Council to call on Rwandan President Paul Kagame to stand trial at the ICTR. The diplomatic feud between the two countries continues. Rwanda alleges that France supports these indictments to cover up its own role in training Rwandan forces that ended up participating in the execution of the 1994 genocide. 'Rwanda has long said France shares blame for the genocide.' Reuters, *Rwanda Files World Court Case Against France* (18 April 2007) (document on file with the author). France denies any responsibility. *Ibid.*

[39]   See generally Drumbl, note 13 *supra*; W. Burke-White, *Proactive Complementarity: The International Criminal Court and National Courts in the Rome System of International Justice*, 49(1) HARVARD INTERNATIONAL LJ 53 (2008).

[40]   Article 11 of the Statute of the Iraqi High Tribunal proscribes genocide.

[41]   Genocide Convention, art. 9 ('Disputes between the Contracting Parties relating to the interpretation, application or fulfillment of the present Convention, including those relating to the responsibility of a State for genocide or any of the other acts enumerated in Article III, shall be submitted to the International Court of Justice at the request of any of the parties to the dispute.').

[42]   See *Bosnia* v. *Serbia*, note 15 *supra*.

Although the ICJ is not a criminal court, this judgment is of considerable importance for criminal lawyers and political scientists concerned with transitional justice. *Bosnia* v. *Serbia* is the first time a state has sued under, and another state has been found responsible for breaching, the Genocide Convention. Though the ultimate finding and remedy were anemic, it is important not to underestimate the relevance of the fact that Bosnia's application actually led to a judgment. After more than a decade of jurisdictional wrangling, counterclaims, and an application for revision by Serbia, the ICJ found that states can be responsible for genocide, meaning that the prospect of accountability for genocide extends beyond individual culpability. Accordingly, and in line with the arguments that Bosnia had raised, individual penal responsibility does not extinguish collective state responsibility. Assuredly, awarding damages against an entire state also gives rise to difficult questions. Who ends up paying? Are all citizens of that state on the hook? Is that fair? Although prosecuting a small number of criminal defendants undercaptures the many layers of public complicity that makes an atrocity truly massive, sanctioning an entire state may lead to overcapture in that individuals who resisted or were themselves victimized could indirectly be held responsible. How is the international community to strike the balance? Does collective state responsibility so dehumanize citizens that it impedes reconciliation efforts? Might the legal fiction of collective innocence serve reconstitutive purposes? Notwithstanding the legal and moral complexities, collective responsibility schemes may more truthfully reflect the broad societal forces that often are a condition precedent to wide-scale genocide.

LEGAL ISSUES

Under international criminal procedure, genocide must be proven beyond reasonable doubt.[43] This part considers several complex interpretive questions that have arisen regarding the application of the crime of genocide. These questions are: (1) Which groups, exactly, are protected groups? (2) What is the requisite physical element (*actus reus*)? (3) How can individual penal responsibility for genocide be established? (4) What is the requisite mental element (*mens rea*)? (5) What are possible defenses to genocide? (6) How are perpetrators sentenced?

Protected Groups

By protecting only national, religious, racial and ethnical groups, the Genocide Convention affirms the international community's sense that the destruction of groups based on these characteristics is particularly heinous. Violence directed against groups because of their political views, gender, class, social characteristics, profession or occupation has tragically been commonplace and extensive in scope. However, such violence does not constitute genocide per se, although it could well constitute crimes against humanity. According to Cryer *et al.*, the prohibition of genocide 'protects the rights of certain groups to survival, and thus human

---

[43]   ICC Statute, art. 66; ICTR Rules of Procedure and Evidence, rule 87(A), available at http://69.94.11.53/ENGLISH/rules/150607/rop-150607.pdf; ICTY Rules of Rules of Procedure and Evidence, rule 87(A), available at www.un.org/icty/legaldoc-e/index-t.htm.

diversity'.[44] Many believe that diversity of race, ethnicity, religion and nationality is a value to be cherished beyond that of political viewpoints or occupational activities and, accordingly, the international community repeatedly, and deliberately, has chosen to limit genocide to these characteristics. Schabas carefully documents how attempts to increase the number of enumerated groups during the negotiation of the Genocide Conventions were unsuccessful.[45] Additionally, attempts to expand the list of protected groups during the Rome Statute negotiations similarly failed.[46]

The settled nature of the law does not extinguish the controversies that continue to arise regarding the typology of protected groups. For example, due to questions about the protected class concerned, it is unclear how the ECCC may find, or the Prosecutor may allege, that genocide has occurred in Cambodia. This is because the Khmer Rouge violence, in which 1.7 million people perished, was not materially mobilized along oppositional racial, ethnic, national or religious lines. The only way to generally construct it along these lines would be to present the violence as auto-genocide, which is 'mass killing of members of the group to which the perpetrators themselves belong'.[47] Whether a political group can be the target of genocide has also arisen in Spanish courts in litigation involving politically motivated violence in Chile, Guatemala and Argentina.[48] That said, certain national jurisdictions explicitly permit the prosecution of genocide in regard to attacks against groups other than national, religious, racial or ethnic ones. Schabas reports that national legislation in Ethiopia permitted prosecution of former leaders of the Derg regime for genocide committed against political opponents.[49] Schabas also notes that the 'domestic penal codes of Bangladesh, Panama, Costa Rica, Peru, Slovenia, and Lithuania also recognize genocide of political groups'.[50] That said, these states are outliers insofar as a large majority of states stick by the Genocide Convention's list of protected groups.

Perhaps more importantly, the settled nature of the typology of protected groups does not extinguish controversy regarding exactly what a racial, religious, ethnic or national group is. The Genocide Convention does not provide definitions. Mettraux, surveying the jurisprudence of the ICTY and ICTR, defines the four protected groups as follows:[51]

---

[44]   Cryer *et al.*, note 10 *supra*, at 167–8.
[45]   Schabas, note 11 *supra*, at 130–50.
[46]   Cryer *et al.*, note 10 *supra*, at 169.
[47]   Schabas, note 11 *supra*, at 118; see also Hannum, note 33 *supra*.
[48]   Much of this litigation has involved charges of torture and crimes against humanity. A case involving alleged genocide in Guatemala is moving forward; genocide charges in the case of Argentinian Adolfo Scilingo did not result in an actual conviction (though the Spanish Supreme Court Criminal Chamber did convict the former naval officer on charges of crimes against humanity under international law and sentenced him to 25 years' imprisonment). R. Wilson, *Spanish Supreme Court Affirms Conviction of Argentine Former Naval Officer for Crimes Against Humanity*, 12(1) ASIL INSIGHT, (2008) at nn. 23–4. In the *Scilingo* case, the Spanish Supreme Court Criminal Chamber explicitly held that political groups 'are not within the groups defined under the Genocide Convention', stating that 'the doctrine is practically unanimous on the subject'. *Ibid.* (citations omitted).
[49]   Schabas, note 11 *supra*, at 141.
[50]   *Ibid.*
[51]   Mettraux, note 23 *supra*, at 227–8 (for each definition, the citations from the actual tribunal judgments are omitted).

1. National group: 'a collection of people who are perceived to share a legal bond based on common citizenship'.
2. Ethnic group: 'a group whose members share a common language or culture'.
3. Racial group: 'is based on the hereditary physical traits often identified with a geographical region, irrespective of linguistic, cultural, national or religious factors'.
4. Religious group: 'one whose members share the same religion, denomination or mode of worship'.

Matters get even trickier when courts and tribunals are called upon to determine, on the facts, whether a targeted group meets one or more of the definitions of a protected group. For example, the ICTR's early jurisprudence was concerned with determining to which protected group the targeted population in Rwanda, the Tutsi, corresponded. Both Hutu and Tutsi share Rwandan nationality and similar racial categorization. Moreover, religious identification in Rwanda manifests independently of the status of an individual as Tutsi or Hutu. That left the question of whether the Tutsi were an ethnic group. On this note, Tutsi and Hutu speak the same language and share similar culture. They 'attended the same schools and churches, worked in the same offices, and drank in the same bars ... celebrated the same heroes: even during the genocide, the killers and their intended victims sang of some of the same heroes from the Rwandan past.'[52] The ICTR transcended these traditional objective markers of ethnicity and engaged in analysis that focused on the social construction and identification of ethnicity. One example which the ICTR cited was the fact that, from 1933 and owing to Belgian colonial policy, Rwandans were obliged to carry ethnic identity cards. These cards weighed heavily in the materiality of ethnicity to the sociology of Rwanda. In 1994, individuals unable to produce an ethnic identity card marking the bearer as a Hutu were signaled out for eradication. The ICTR also noted that Rwandan laws identified Rwandans by reference to their ethnic group. These two factors, although identified by the ICTR as objective, enter into the realm of positivist construction of ethnicity. Some ICTR Trial Chambers also incorporated subjective elements, noting in the *Akayesu* judgment that 'the Tutsis were conceived of as an ethnic group by those who targeted them for killing'[53] and in *Kayishema and Ruzindana* that an ethnic group can be one 'identified as such by others, including perpetrators of the crime'.[54]

Although there may be some subjectivity in determining whether a target group is in fact a protected group, 'the group must have some form of objective existence in the first place; otherwise the Convention could be used to protect entirely fictitious national, ethnic, racial or religious groups'.[55] Accordingly, the best approach may be a blended one. As the ICJ opined in *Bosnia* v. *Serbia*, 'international jurisprudence accepts a combined subjective-objective approach'.[56] Similarly, the Report of the International Commission of Inquiry on Darfur, in

---

52   A. Des Forges, Human Rights Watch, 'LEAVE NONE TO TELL THE STORY': GENOCIDE IN RWANDA 4, 31 (1999). It was possible to 'transform' oneself from Tutsi to Hutu and from Hutu to Tutsi. T. Cruvellier, *Le Tribunal des Vaincus* 29 (2006).

53   *Prosecutor* v. *Akayesu*, Case No. CTR-96-4-T, Judgment, 2 September 1998, para. 171.

54   See, for example, *Prosecutor* v. *Kayishema and Ruzindana*, Case No. ICTR-95-1-T, Judgment and Sentence, 21 May 1999, para. 98.

55   Cryer *et al.*, note 10 *supra*, at 173.

56   *Bosnia* v. *Serbia*, note 15 *supra*, at para. 191.

assessing whether genocide is occurring in Darfur, adopted a combined approach, concluding:

> [The] process of formation of a perception and self-perception of another group as distinct ... may begin as a subjective view, as a way of regarding the others as making up a different or opposed group, it gradually hardens and crystallizes into a real and factual opposition. It thus leads to an objective contrast. The conflict, thus, from subjective becomes objective. It ultimately brings about the formation of two conflicting groups, one of them intent on destroying the other.[57]

The Commission of Inquiry concluded that tribes subject to attack in Darfur (the Fur, Massalit and Zaghawa) were protected groups even though they spoke the same language (Arabic) and shared the same religion (Muslim) as their attackers. Genocide, however, was not found to exist in Darfur insofar as the attackers did not have the intent to destroy the targeted group in whole or in part. What is more, in 2009 an ICC Pre-Trial Chamber found there were no reasonable grounds to charge Sudanese President al-Bashir with genocide (though this remains subject to litigation). However, that is a different question than whether or not the target group constitutes a *prima facie* protected group.

A targeted group can fit into more than one type of protected group. For example, identifying Bosnian Muslims as a protected group draws from the religious, national and ethnic categories. Schabas remarks: 'The four terms in the [Genocide] Convention not only overlap, they also help to define each other, operating much as four corner posts that delimit an area within which a myriad of groups covered by the Convention find protection.'[58]

Actus Reus

A conviction for genocide requires proof of the commission of one of a number of physical acts against one or – much more likely the case – many members of the target group. These acts are often referred to as the 'underlying offenses'. These offenses include killing, causing serious bodily or mental harm, deliberately inflicting on the group conditions of life calculated to bring about its physical destruction in whole or in part, imposing measures intended to prevent births within the group, and forcibly transferring children of the group to another group.

Certain acts of genocide, such as sexual violence, can constitute multiple underlying offenses. For example, rape and sexual violence cause serious bodily or mental harm, or even death; sexual torture and mutilation can amount to the imposition of measures intended to prevent births (as can sterilization). Torture generally can amount to serious bodily harm for the purposes of constituting an act of genocide; the harm need not, however, be permanent.[59]

As to the scope of deliberately inflicting conditions of life calculated to bring about the physical destruction of the group, the ICC Elements of the Crimes include among the conditions the 'deliberate deprivation of resources indispensable for survival, such as food or

---

57   *Report of the International Commission of Inquiry on Darfur to the United Nations Secretary-General* (25 January 2005), pursuant to Security Council Res. 1564, 18 September 2004, para. 500.

58   Schabas, note 11 *supra*, at 111.

59   *Ibid.* 162.

medical services, or systematic expulsion from homes'.[60] The Guatemalan Commission for Historical Clarification concluded that governmental practices of razing villages and food supplies constituted an act of genocide. Although in principle the *actus reus* of genocide 'may be either an act of commission or an act of omission',[61] in practice genocide by omission appears most likely to attach only to deliberately inflicting on the group conditions of life calculated to bring about its physical destruction in whole or in part.

As a general matter of settled international criminal law, the act of 'ethnic cleansing' is not equivalent to genocide. Ethnic cleansing aims at changing the ethnic composition of a territory by displacing or expelling a given population; it does not aim at destroying that population in whole or in part.[62] Such was the approach of the District Court of Jerusalem in the trial of Adolf Eichmann. It acquitted Eichmann for acts prior to mid-1941, the point at which the Final Solution was adopted. The Final Solution was geared to the elimination of Jews, not their expulsion and marginalization. The ICJ has similarly distinguished between forcible deportation and expulsion, on the one hand, and the infliction of conditions designed to induce a group's physical or biological destruction, on the other, with genocide being limited to the latter conduct.[63] Assuredly, persecution of Bosnian Muslims and Bosnian Croats in the Balkans colloquially described as 'ethnic cleansing' qualifies as a crime against humanity; as would Nazi violence prior to the Final Solution. Moreover, ethnic cleansing is often a precursor to genocide. As William Schabas wryly remarks: 'Genocide is the last resort of the frustrated ethnic cleanser.'[64]

There is no formal requirement that many people be killed or attacked in order for there to be genocide. This contrasts with crimes against humanity, which can only occur 'as part of a widespread or systematic attack directed against any civilian population, with knowledge of the attack'.[65] Genocide also contrasts with war crimes, for which a nexus to armed conflict, whether international or non-international, is required. That said, in practice genocides involve large-scale, organized, often state-sponsored attacks laced with the ideology of

---

[60]   International Criminal Court, Elements of the Crimes, article 6(c), element 4, note 4 (document on file with the author). See also Nikolai Jorgić, BVerfG, 2 BvR 1290/99, 12 December 2000, available at www.bverfg.de/entscheidungen/rk20001212_2bvr129099en.html, para. 2 (German Constitutional Court upholding that prohibited acts of genocide could include property damage or expulsion). But see Kress, note 27 *supra*, at 624 (viewing the ICC Elements of the Crimes on this issue as 'lamentable' and in conflict with the requirement for physical or biological destruction).

[61]   Schabas, note 11 *supra*, at 156.

[62]   If the goal of the ethnic cleansing is expulsion from a given territory, that falls short of genocide. *Prosecutor* v. *Stakić*, Case No. IT-97-24-T, Judgment, 31 July 2003, paras 519, 554. This position, although operational at the ICTY, is not universally shared. See Jorgić case, note 60 *supra*.

[63]   *Bosnia* v. *Serbia*, note 15 *supra*, para. 190. That said, national courts may push the frontiers on this point. In the *Jorgić* case, the German Constitutional Court upheld lower court decisions that the intent to destroy the group is not limited to physical-biological annihilation but also extends to the 'group as a social unit with its special qualities, uniqueness and its feeling of togetherness'. *Jorgić* case, note 59 *supra*, para. 2. In 2007, the European Court of Human Rights ruled that the German approach in *Jorgić*, which the German Constitutional Court itself acknowledged was within, but expanded the margins of, settled international law, was a foreseeable and reasonable exercise of national judicial discretion. The German Constitutional Court had held that the lower courts' decisions it was upholding lay 'within the margins of the possible interpretation of the international law elements of the crime of genocide and conforms to the relevant jurisprudence and practice of the United Nations'. *Ibid.* para. 2.

[64]   Schabas, note 11 *supra*, at 201.

[65]   ICC Statute, art. 7.

massive eliminationist propaganda. Certainly, the special heinousness of genocide would be undermined by including isolated crimes within the proscription.

Establishing Individual Criminal Responsibility

The Genocide Convention criminalizes much more than just the conduct of the so-called principal offender, namely the person who actually kills or causes serious bodily or mental harm. The Genocide Convention actively extends its reach to other acts beyond those of principal offenders. Under article III, the following acts are punishable:

(a)   genocide;
(b)   conspiracy to commit genocide;
(c)   direct and public incitement to commit genocide;
(d)   attempt to commit genocide;
(e)   complicity in genocide.

Article III therefore provides for individual penal liability for accomplices and persons other than principal offenders. Now, it is important to recognize that the term 'principal offender' often is a misnomer. After all, the actual killers tend to be low-level soldiers, militia members and brain-washed believers. The ability to prosecute their superiors, leaders, organizers and financiers – who often have killed no one personally – based on these putatively secondary theories of criminal liability does not mean that those individuals bear only a secondary moral responsibility for genocide: quite the contrary. Assuredly, extensive recourse to these theories of secondary liability to prosecute other lower-level offenders may raise concerns of vicarious liability in situations where it may be difficult to establish convincing evidence of the onerous *mens rea* of genocide.[66]

Article III also establishes individual criminal responsibility for certain incomplete or inchoate offenses where the ultimate crime may or may not take place. Responsibility for direct and public incitement to commit genocide and for conspiracy to commit genocide stand out as examples. In theory, aggressive pursuit of inchoate offenses might deter genocides from actually occurring. This, however, heavily assumes the deterrent value of criminal prosecutions as preventative measures.

Although conspiracy is an inchoate offense that at common law technically does not require that the agreed upon crimes in fact are carried out, in practice and as a matter of international legality the agreed upon crimes probably will have been committed in order for the prosecuting tribunal to invest itself in the matter. The ICTR, acting on its statutory authority, has convicted defendants for conspiracy to commit genocide (for example, the *Kambanda* case).[67] In contrast, conspiracy does not explicitly appear in the Rome Statute. This is not surprising, given that, starting with Nuremberg, conspiracy remains a somewhat controversial crime under international criminal law. Whereas the law of conspiracy is robust in

---

[66]   See the discussion of *mens rea*, below.
[67]   *Prosecutor* v. *Kambanda*, Case No. ICTR-97-23-S, Judgment, 4 September 1998; see also *Nahimana, Barayagwiza and Ngeze* v. *The Prosecutor*, Case No. ICTR-99-52-A, summary of the Judgment, 28 November 2007, at 16 ('the *actus reus* of conspiracy to commit genocide is the agreement to act with a view to committing genocide').

common law legal systems, it remains an outlier in civil law legal systems. The ICC Statute does include co-perpetration as a form of individual criminal responsibility. Co-perpetration serves as the liability theory on which charges of war crimes were confirmed in the ICC's first case, involving Congolese rebel leader Thomas Lubanga Dyilo.[68]

The criminalization of direct and public incitement to commit genocide can address the use of propaganda and the responsibility of leaders and media officials in disseminating genocidal vitriol. An early example is Julius Streicher, publisher of the virulently anti-Semitic Nazi newspaper *Der Stürmer*, who was convicted by the IMT and executed. His publishing firm released anti-Semitic children's books, including *Der Giftpilz* (*The Poisonous Mushroom*). Another IMT defendant, Hans Fritzsche, who was head of the radio section of the Nazi propaganda ministry, was acquitted because he was not in control of the policies but was merely a conduit for them. There was no evidence of his genocidal intent. Fritzsche later was charged with other crimes and imprisoned. The ICTR has convicted for incitement. On 28 November 2007, in the cases of *Nahimana*, *Barayagwiza* and *Ngeze*, the ICTR Appeals Chamber affirmed some of the convictions of three Rwandan media leaders (newspaper and radio) for genocide that an ICTR Trial Chamber had entered in 2003.[69] On the question of direct and public incitement to commit genocide, the Appeals Chamber took a more reserved position than the Trial Chamber whose judgment was under review.[70] The Appeals Chamber ruled that only statements made during the ICTR's temporal jurisdiction (the calendar year 1994) could lead to a conviction for incitement, insofar as incitement is an inchoate crime that is committed once the words in question are uttered, broadcast or published – it is not a continuing crime.[71] However, statements made prior to 1994 could 'be taken into account as contextual factors that would permit a better understanding of the broadcasts or newspapers published in 1994'.[72] '[T]he Appeals Chamber considers that an approach whereby incitement to commit genocide is considered direct only when it is explicit and whereby the Judge can in no circumstance consider the contextual elements in determining if a speech constitutes direct incitement to genocide is too restrictive.'[73] The Appeals Chamber also reined in the scope of command responsibility for corporate and bureaucratic superiors for the inciting acts of journalists and employees.

As for attempt, as a matter of law-in-practice, it is unlikely that the resources of international and national courts will be directed to this offense.

The Statutes of the ICTR and ICTY incorporate the other acts listed in article III within the definition of the crime of genocide. The ICC Statute, on the other hand, only makes specific mention of incitement to genocide (article 25(3)(e)). Instead. the ICC Statute subjects

---

68   *Situation in the Congo, Prosecutor* v. *Thomas Lubanga*, Case No. ICC-01/04-01/06, Pre-Trial Chamber I, Decision on the Confirmation of Charges, 29 January 2007.

69   *Nahimana, Barayagwiza and Ngeze* v. *The Prosecutor*, Case No. ICTR-99-52-A, summary of the Judgment, 28 November 2007. The Appeals Chamber lowered the sentences from life, life, and 35 years to 30, 35 and 32 years, respectively. In addition to exhorting violence against the Tutsi as a group, these media (especially the radio) also targeted specific individual Tutsis for attack.

70   *Prosecutor* v. *Nahimana, Barayagwiza and Ngeze*, Case No. ICTR-99-52-T, Judgment and Sentence, 3 December 2003.

71   *Nahimana, Barayagwiza and Ngeze* v. *Prosecutor*, Case No. ICTR-99-52-A, summary of the Judgment, 28 November 2007, at 13.

72   *Ibid.* 13–14.

73   *Ibid.* 13.

genocide to the general principles of criminal responsibility enumerated in article 25, which include co-perpetration; ordering, soliciting or inducing; aiding and abetting; contributing to the commission or attempted commission of the crime by a group of persons acting with a common purpose; and attempting to commit the crime by taking action that commences its execution by means of a substantial step, but the crime does not occur because of circumstances independent of the person's intentions. For Mettraux, the ICC Statute's approach is a positive development, in that it 'contains the implicit message that this crime may be committed in just the same manner and under the same conditions as any other crime within the [ICC's] jurisdiction'.[74] Schabas distinguishes the approach of the ad hoc tribunals from the ICC in the following manner: '[U]nder the Rome Statute, the "secondary" offender commits the crime of genocide, whilst under the Genocide Convention and the statutes of the ad hoc tribunals he or she is guilty of an "other act" '.[75] Most national jurisdictions proceed in a manner similar to the ICC Statute.[76]

All that said, although the Statutes of the ICTR and ICTY specifically list the other acts in regard to genocide, they also contain a general provision on criminal participation.[77] Consequently, ICTR and ICTY Prosecutors have charged, and when considered jointly these tribunals in some cases have convicted for, genocide (and crimes against humanity) based on these general species or principles of liability. Examples include joint criminal enterprise (JCE),[78] command/superior responsibility,[79] and aiding and abetting.[80] These constitute 'mode[s] of liability through which an accused may be individually criminally responsible despite not being the direct perpetrator of the offence'.[81]

With joint criminal enterprise, crimes must actually have been committed in furtherance of the enterprise. Three forms of enterprise participation have been pursued under JCE theories. These are 'a shared intent to bring about a certain offense, organized systems of repres-

---

[74]   Mettraux, note 23 *supra*, at 203.

[75]   Schabas, note 11 *supra*, at 258.

[76]   *Ibid.*

[77]   ICTR Statute, art.. 6; ICTY Statute, art. 7.

[78]   For discussion of JCE in the context of genocide, see *Prosecutor* v. *Brdjanin*, Case No. IT-99-36-A, Decision on Interlocutory Appeal, 19 March 2004. paras 5-10 (finding third category of JCE as being potentially applicable to genocide, though in this case ultimately no convictions for genocide were entered); E. van Sliedregt, *Joint Criminal Enterprise as a Pathway to Convicting Individuals for Genocide* J International Criminal Justice (2006), available at http://jicj.oxfordjournals.org/cgi/content/full/mql042v2 ('Can JCE be a basis for genocide convictions? The answer would be: yes, but a conditional yes. JCE and genocide can only be reconciled when JCE is applied as a form of criminal participation.'); *Prosecutor* v. *Simba*, Case No. ICTR-01-76-A, Judgment, 27 November 2007, on this point affirming Case No. ICTR-01-76-T, Judgment, 13 December 2005. For discussion of JCE generally, see *Prosecutor* v. *Tadić*, Case No. IT-94-1-A, Judgment, 15 July 1999, paras 185–229.

[79]   ICTY Statute, art. 7(3); ICTR Statute, art. 6(3); *Prosecutor* v. *Musema*, Case No. ICTR-96-13-T, Judgment and Sentence, 27 January 2000 (Trial Chamber finding Musema bore superior responsibility for those acts carried out by employees of the tea factory over whom he had control; he also incurred individual criminal responsibility for genocide for having ordered and, by his presence and participation, aided and abetted in the murder of members of the Tutsi ethnic group).

[80]   ICTY Statute, art .7(1); ICTR Statute, art, 6(1); *Prosecutor* v. *Krstić*, Case No. IT-98-33-A, Judgment, 19 April 2004 (convicting for genocide); *Prosecutor* v. *Ntakirutimana*, Case No. ICTR 96-17-A, Judgment, 13 December 2004 (convicting for genocide).

[81]   *Prosecutor* v. *Brdjanin*, Case No. IT-99-36-A, Decision on Interlocutory Appeal, 19 March 2004, para. 5.

sion and ill-treatment, and criminal acts beyond the common design but which are "a natural and foreseeable consequence" of the actions taken'.[82] The ICC Statute does not mention JCE, referring instead to common purpose liability (article 25(3)(d)).

In the jurisprudence of the ad hoc tribunals, the line between aiding and abetting, on the one hand, and complicity, on the other, is fuzzy.[83] In the *Blagojević* case, the ICTY Appeals Chamber reversed a conviction for complicity that the Trial Chamber had entered.[84]

At the ad hoc tribunals, commander/superior responsibility may lead to individual criminal responsibility for the superior if 'he or she knew or had reason to know that the subordinate was about to commit such acts or had done so and the superior failed to take the necessary and reasonable measures to prevent such acts or to punish the perpetrators thereof'.[85] The ICC Statute also contains a detailed provision (article 28) on command responsibility in both the military and non-military context, which provides as follows:

(a) A military commander or person effectively acting as a military commander shall be criminally responsible for crimes within the jurisdiction of the Court committed by forces under his or her effective command and control, or effective authority and control as the case may be, as a result of his or her failure to exercise control properly over such forces, where:
  (i) that military commander or person either knew or, owing to the circumstances at the time, should have known that the forces were committing or about to commit such crimes; and
  (ii) that military commander or person failed to take all necessary and reasonable measures within his or her power to prevent or repress their commission or to submit the matter to the competent authorities for investigation and prosecution.
(b) With respect to superior and subordinate relationships not described in paragraph (a), a superior shall be criminally responsible for crimes within the jurisdiction of the Court committed by subordinates under his or her effective authority and control, as a result of his or her failure to exercise control properly over such subordinates, where:
  (i) the superior either knew, or consciously disregarded information which clearly indicated, that the subordinates were committing or about to commit such crimes;
  (ii) the crimes concerned activities that were within the effective responsibility and control of the superior; and
  (iii) the superior failed to take all necessary and reasonable measures within his or her power to prevent or repress their commission or to submit the matter to the competent authorities for investigation and prosecution.

Unlike the case with the crime of aggression, there is no leadership or policy-making requirement for the crime of genocide. Although leaders often face international justice, many low-level killers also face the same (for example, in Rwanda).

Mens Rea

A conviction for genocide requires proof of the intent to commit the underlying crime (for example, killing, causing severe harm) and the *dolus specialis* (special intent) of genocide,

---

82   N. Weisbord, *Prosecuting Aggression* 49 Harvard International LJ 161, 213 (2008) (footnotes and citations omitted).

83   Mettraux, note 23 *supra*, at 257–8. See also *Prosecutor v. Niyitegeka*, Case No. ICTR-1996-14-A, Judgment, 9 July 2004 (convicting for complicity in genocide).

84   *Prosecutor v. Blagojević and Jokić*, Case No. IT-02-60-A, Judgment, 9 May 2007.

85   ICTY Statute, art. 7(3); ICTR Statute, art. 6(3).

namely to destroy a protected group in whole or in part, as such. The remainder of this section focuses on the *dolus specialis* for genocide (also called the chapeau intent because it textually precedes the listing of the enumerated offenses).[86] Even if there is proof of a protected group and the requisite acts committed against that group, genocide may not be found if the special eliminationist intent is absent. Such was the case with the Report of the International Commission of Inquiry on Darfur, which found that the government of the Sudan did not have the requisite genocidal intent but, instead, was animated by goals of counter-insurgency warfare.

The special intent of genocide can be proved through direct evidence supporting the perpetrator's mindset at the relevant time. This might include explicit recorded statements or authored publications in which the perpetrator exhorts the destruction of the targeted group. Alternatively, the special intent can be established circumstantially from the statements or behavior of the accused, or even of others; the special intent also may be inferred from the massive and systematic nature of the atrocity.[87] A failure to establish the special intent for genocide does not mean that the accused lacks the requisite intent to be convicted of a crime against humanity, a war crime, or a crime under ordinary national penal law.

Although there is no formal requirement (as an element of the crime) for an organized plan or a specific number of leaders in order for genocide to occur, in practice it would be very difficult to imagine genocide without these elements.[88] Moreover, as Claus Kress notes, 'categorizing the conduct of a lone individual as genocide would disconnect the crime of genocide from its historical roots as a crime against humanity'.[89] In this vein, the ICC's Elements of the Crimes on genocide explicitly add a 'contextual element', which mandates that the 'conduct took place in the context of a manifest pattern of similar conduct directed against that group or was conduct that could itself effect such destruction'.[90] Cryer *et al.* note that this does not entirely exclude the possibility of a 'lone' perpetrator,[91] but it does seem to make such a finding unlikely.[92] This 'contextual element' establishes a link between genocide and crimes against humanity.

The *mens rea* for genocide is to destroy the group in whole or in part. This does not mean that the destruction needs to be totalizing. The Nazis may not have intended to destroy all Jews everywhere, but certainly intended to destroy European Jewry. In 1994, the Rwandan Hutu leadership did not intend to destroy all Tutsis everywhere, but to destroy Rwandan Tutsis. In both cases, the aggressors still committed genocide. Moreover, just because an indi-

---

[86]   The choice to limit the discussion in this fashion does not reflect lack of academic interest in the elements of the individual *mens rea* for each underlying act. Rather, this choice reflects the reality that this topic is heavily informed by domestic criminal law and comparative criminal law and, hence, outside the scope of this chapter. For details on this issue, see Mettraux, note 23 *supra*, ch. 15 and Schabas, note 11 *supra*, at 241–5.

[87]   Cryer *et al.*, note 10 *supra*, at 183–4; *Prosecutor* v. *Kayishema and Ruzindana*, Case No. ICTR-95-1-A, Judgment, 1 June 2001, para. 159; *Prosecutor* v. *Akayesu*, Case No. ICTR-96-4-T, Judgment, 2 September 1998, para. 478.

[88]   *Prosecutor* v. *Jelisić*, Case No. IT-95-10-T, Judgment, 14 December 1999, para. 100.

[89]   Kress, note 27 *supra*, at 621.

[90]   ICC Elements of the Crime, art. 6, available at www.icc-cpi.int/library/about/officialjournal/ Element_of_Crimes_English.pdf.

[91]   Cryer *et al.*, note 10 *supra*, at 169.

[92]   Kress, note 27 *supra*, at 620.

vidual Rwandan Hutu may have spared some Tutsi, actively saved some, or hidden some in his home does not necessarily negate his genocidal intent, though this may be a factor considered in mitigation of sentence.

The ICTY and ICJ have included a significance or substantiality requirement in terms of the relationship of the targeted part to the protected group.[93] In *Krstić*, the ICTY Appeals Chamber suggested some guidelines it found useful in defining substantiality, including the numeric size of the targeted part in relation to the overall size of the entire group, the prominence of the targeted part within the overall group, and the area of the perpetrators' activity and control. In the case of the Srebrenica atrocity,[94] the Bosnian Serb army did not kill all the Bosnian Muslims of Srebrenica. Killing was limited to Bosnian Muslim men and boys, largely of military age. The ICTY Appeals Chamber upheld the ICTY Trial Chamber's conclusion that the intent to kill these men constituted the intent to destroy a substantial part of the Srebrenica Bosnian Muslim group. The Appeals Chamber turned to several facts to support this conclusion, including the long-term relational impact and procreative implications between the murders of the men and the survival of the community. The Appeals Chamber affirmed the finding that, given the 'patriarchal character of the Bosnian Muslim society in Srebrenica, the destruction of such a sizeable number of men would "inevitably result in the physical disappearance of the Bosnian Muslim population at Srebrenica" '.[95] In an earlier work, I opined:

> The [*Krstić*] Appeals Chamber adopted [a] dynamic and fluid approach to the construction of genocidal intent, the categorisation of the target group, and the manner in which the killing of a demographic subset of a group can bear upon the extinction of the group as a whole. It found a causal connection between the murder of 7,000 men and the intent to destroy the Srebrenica Bosnian Muslims; it then found a further causal link between the intended destruction of the Srebrenica Bosnian Muslims as a target group and the intended destruction of the protected group, namely Bosnian Muslims as a national whole. This methodology places limited priority on stringent quantitative criteria (how many people need to have been killed) and complex value judgments (how important may one or another strata be to the survival of the entire group).[96]

One area of controversy involves the intersection between accessorial or accomplice liability and the existence of genocidal *mens rea*. As a system crime, genocide involves a large number of people. In response to the group-based nature of mass atrocity and the diffusion of responsibility for the actual mechanics of the violence, international criminal law permits defendants to be convicted on a variety of theories of criminal responsibility (discussed in greater detail in the preceding section). The intersection of certain broader accessorial forms of responsibility (in particular joint criminal enterprise, common purpose liability, aiding and abetting, and command responsibility) with the *dolus specialis* of genocide remains an unsettled area of law and penal theory. If proof of the special intent of genocide is what differentiates this

---

93   *Prosecutor* v. *Krstić*, Case No. IT-98-33-A, Judgment, 19 April 2004; *Bosnia* v. *Serbia*, note 15 *supra*, para. 198 ('the part targeted must be significant enough to have an impact on the group as a whole').

94   Which the ICTY and ICJ have authenticated as genocide.

95   *Prosecutor* v. *Krstić*, Case No. IT-98-33-A, Judgment, 19 April 2004, para. 28.

96   M. Drumbl, *Prosecutor* v. *Radislav Krstić: ICTY Authenticates Genocide at Srebrenica and Convicts for Aiding and Abetting*, 5 MELBOURNE J INTERNATIONAL LAW 434, 440 (2004) (footnotes omitted).

crime from others, as a matter of penal theory does it properly follow that this intent can be inferred when a participant in a common plan or criminal enterprise knows of the genocidal goal, knows of the genocidal intent of the principal (or other) offenders, and knows that his involvement will further that goal? Does knowledge of the principal offender's intent, or of the intent of co-perpetrators, mean the defendant himself has the requisite genocidal intent? One response would be to substitute the purpose-based approach to genocidal intent with a knowledge-based approach. Looking beyond actual knowledge, however, what if the accused simply was reckless or willfully blind to the intent of the principals or of the co-perpetrators? What if a subordinate is ordered to kill by a superior with genocidal intent – does it necessarily follow that he also has the requisite genocidal intent?

Among all of these theories of liability, JCE probably is the most controversial on the question of the existence of the requisite *mens rea*. JCE has the potential to implicate a broad variety of defendants outside formal chains of command, including contractors, industrialists, those who supply weapons, financiers, militias and civilians. The ICTY Appeals Chamber has observed that a conviction for genocide based on joint criminal enterprise can be found where genocide is a natural and foreseeable consequence of the defendant's acts.[97] That said, this position on joint criminal enterprise is not without contradiction, even within the ICTY's own jurisprudence.[98]

On the topic of aiding and abetting, van Sliedregt (writing in 2006) observes:

> In *Krstić*, the ICTY Appeals Chamber found *Krstić* guilty of aiding and abetting genocide. The Appeals Chamber was of the view that an aider/abettor does not need to share the specific intent to commit genocide, it is sufficient that the accused rendered substantial assistance to the commission of the crime *knowing* the intent behind the crime. In *Blagojević & Jokić* this ruling was endorsed. The Trial Chamber held that aiding and abetting genocide requires that the accused (i) carried out an act which consisted of practical assistance, encouragement or moral support to the principal that had 'substantial effect' on the commission of the crime; (ii) had knowledge that his or her own acts assisted in the commission of the specific crime by the principal offender and (iii) knew that the crime was committed with specific intent.[99]

In May 2007, the ICTY Appeals Chamber in *Blagojević and Jokić* acquitted Blagojević of the conviction that had been entered by the Trial Chamber for complicity in genocide. The Appeals Chamber based the acquittal on the determination that 'no reasonable trier of fact could find beyond reasonable doubt that, without knowledge of the mass killings, Mr. Blagojevic's awareness of the other facts related to the forcible transfer operation shows that he had knowledge of the principal perpetrators' genocidal intent'.[100]

Some ICTR jurisprudence supports the position that knowledge is a sufficient basis for a commander to be held responsible for genocide based on the actions of subordinates.[101] Assuredly, inciting and ordering genocide involves direct action by a superior. However, when stripped to its essence, command responsibility is a crime of omission, often times

---

[97]   *Prosecutor v. Brdjanin*, Case No. IT-99-36-A, Decision on Interlocutory Appeal, 19 March 2004, paras 6, 9.
[98]   *Prosecutor v. Stakić*, Case No. IT-97-24-T Judgment, 31 July 2003, paras 530, 558.
[99]   van Sliedregt, note 78 *supra*.
[100]   ICTY Press Release, 9 May 2007, available at www.un.org/icty/pressreal/2007/pr1158e-summary.htm.
[101]   Mettraux, note 23 *supra*, at 262–63 (criticizing this approach).

negligence. Can this conduct satisfy the onerous special intent requirement? Might this raise the prospect that a commander be held criminally responsible without actually possessing genocidal intent?

Another related area of controversy on the topic of the *dolus specialis* of genocide is whether judicial notice can be taken of the existence of a genocide and, once such notice is taken, whether the defendant's special intent can be inferred (for example, by dint of status, position or relationships). In the *Karemera et al.* decision, an ICTR Trial Chamber took judicial notice of genocide in Rwanda.[102] Kevin Jon Heller expresses concern about the intersection of this judicial notice with JCE as a mode of liability. Heller begins by noting that establishment of joint criminal enterprise liability hinges on proof of '(1) a common plan to commit genocide; (2) the defendant participated in the common plan by assisting, encouraging, or lending moral support to it; and (3) the defendant intended to further the common plan through his actions'.[103] If judicial notice can be taken of (1), then according to Heller:

> [T]he only live question will be whether the defendant participated in the nationwide common plan with the intent to further it … [I]f a trial chamber can infer a defendant's specific intent to commit genocide solely from the existence of a nationwide campaign of genocide, it can certainly use even the most ambiguous act … to infer a defendant's membership in, and support for, that campaign.[104]

On the other hand, it would be undesirable for offenders to escape responsibility for genocide simply because the diffusion of responsibility for a group crime permits individuals to remain consciously ignorant of the outcome or because there is no recorded or authenticated evidence in which they affirmed their special eliminationist intent. Perhaps inevitably, these complications arise when genocide is prosecuted through liberal legalist criminal process with its presumption of individual agency and focus on individual responsibility. These complications have prompted (and should continue to prompt) discussion of alternate yet synergistic modalities of accountability for genocide, such as truth commissions, reparations and group-based remedies.

Finally, the destructive acts must be undertaken to wipe out a group, in whole or in part, *as such.* There is some debate whether 'as such' refers to the motive of the accused, or simply refers to the requirement that the crimes be directed against the victims in their collective character or capacity.[105] Mettraux defines 'as such' in the following manner: 'the physical victim of the crime must have been selected because he or she was a member of the targeted group and that, through his or her victimization, the perpetrator intended to inflict suffering (and ultimately destruction) upon this group'.[106]

---

[102]   *Prosecutor* v. *Karemera, Ngirumpatse and Nzirorera*, Case No. ICTR-98-44-AR73(C), Decision on Interlocutory Appeal, 16 June 2006.

[103]   K.J. Heller, *Case Note, Prosecutor* v. *Karemera et al*, 101 American JInternational Law 157, 162 (2007) (citing *Tadić* judgment).

[104]   *Ibid.* See also Mettraux, note 23 *supra*, at 212–14 (evoking similar concerns); Schabas, note 11 *supra*, at 259 ('considerations concerning the mens rea of genocide … should also apply mutatis mutandis to the other acts listed in article III [of the Genocide Convention]').

[105]   For more discussion, see Schabas, note 11 *supra*, at 245–6.

[106]   Mettraux, note 23 *supra*, at 231.

Defenses to Genocide

A defendant can present defenses to genocide.[107] Unlike factors considered in mitigation of sentence, a defense goes to the question of guilt and, if successfully pleaded, excuses criminal responsibility.

Article 31 of the ICC Statute permits the following defenses: (a) mental disease or defect; (b) intoxication; (c) self-defense; and (d) duress resulting from a threat of imminent death or of continuing or imminent serious bodily harm against that person or another person. On the topic of duress, even though the ICTY Appeals Chamber held in *Erdemović* that duress could not be a defense to violations of international humanitarian law, the drafters of the ICC Statute explicitly included it (thereby following the dissenting judgments in that case).[108] By virtue of the drafting of article 31, the ICC Statute also permits the closely related defense of necessity as a form of duress.

The ICC Statute also permits the introduction of general defenses, such as mistake of fact and mistake of law (article 32), if these negate the mental element required by the crime. Minors (under 18 years of age) incur no criminal responsibility by virtue of article 26 of the ICC Statute. The Special Court for Sierra Leone has jurisdiction over defendants above 15 years of age, though it creates a different sentencing schematic for juvenile offenders and there is no will in the Prosecutor's office to try any minor.[109] The Rwandan national courts have convicted minors between the ages of 14 and 18 of genocide, though minority can serve as a mitigating factor reducing sentence.[110]

Some defenses are no longer permissible before international criminal tribunals. These include the following.

> *Immunities.* Article IV of the Genocide Convention eliminates immunities as a defense: 'Persons committing genocide or any of the other acts enumerated in Article III shall be punished, whether they are constitutionally responsible rulers, public officials or private individuals.' The ICTY Statute,[111] ICTR Statute,[112] Statute of the Special Court for Sierra Leone,[113] and the ICC Statute[114] eliminate immunities. That head of state, ministerial and diplomatic immunities cannot be raised in international courts to charges of genocide does not foreclose the possibility that, depending on the details of the accusations and the

---

[107]   See Kai Ambos, Chapter 13, for more on defences in international criminal law.

[108]   *Prosecutor* v. *Erdemović*, Case No. IT-96-22-A, Judgment, 7 October 1997, para. 89.

[109]   Statute of the Special Court for Sierra Leone, art. 7(1), available at www.sc-sl.org/ Documents/scsl-statute.html ('The Special Court shall have no jurisdiction over any person who was under the age of 15 at the time of the alleged commission of the crime. Should any person who was at the time of the alleged commission of the crime between 15 and 18 years of age come before the Court, he or she shall be treated with dignity and a sense of worth, taking into account his or her young age and the desirability of promoting his or her rehabilitation, reintegration into and assumption of a constructive role in society, and in accordance with international human rights standards, in particular the rights of the child.').

[110]   Drumbl, note 13 *supra*, at 79–80.

[111]   ICTY Statute, art. 7(2) ('The official position of any accused person, whether as Head of State or Government or as a responsible Government official, shall not relieve such person of criminal responsibility nor mitigate punishment').

[112]   ICTR Statute, art. 6(2).

[113]   Statute of the Special Court for Sierra Leone, art. 6(2).

[114]   ICC Statute, art. 27.

accused, as a matter of customary international law immunities may be raised as defenses in foreign national courts to prosecutions conducted under assertions of universal jurisdiction.[115]

Following orders. Article 8 of the Nuremberg Charter restricted obedience to superior orders as a defense, but permitted it to be raised in mitigation of sentence. The ICTR and ICTY Statutes similarly preclude following orders as a defense, but allow judges to consider it in mitigation of sentence.[116] Under the ICC Statute, orders to commit genocide and crimes against humanity are determined to be 'manifestly unlawful',[117] and a subordinate cannot claim that following them relieved him or her of criminal responsibility. However, the ICC Statute leaves open the possibility that following orders can serve as a defense to war crimes and, in this regard, formally takes a different approach than the ad hoc tribunals.[118] Following orders differs from duress in that, for a duress defense to be successful, an absence of moral choice would likely have to be found.

Tu quoque. This defense, which 'is a plea that the adversary committed similar atrocities', has been rejected by the ICTY in its applicability to *erga omnes* obligations.[119]

Sentencing

Although not involving genocide charges, by way of illustrative starting-point, the IMT sentenced 12 prominent Nazis to death, three to life imprisonment, and four to fixed terms (ranging between 10 and 20 years). In proceedings conducted by military tribunals held subsequent to the IMT, many defendants were sentenced to death as well. For a variety of political reasons, many of the perpetrators sentenced to death eventually had their sentences commuted, while others who had been sentenced to terms of imprisonment were released before they had served their full sentence.

Defendants convicted of genocide by contemporary international or internationalized tribunals are sentenced to imprisonment, in accordance with the classic penitentiary model. At the ad hoc tribunals, there are no statutory sentencing guidelines. The only explicit guidance the ad hoc tribunals receive is to take into account 'the gravity of the offense and the individual circumstances of the convicted person'.[120] The ICTR and ICTY Rules of Procedure and Evidence do not provide for a minimum sentence, but they provide for a maximum sentence of life imprisonment. 'Therefore, ICTR and ICTY judges have the power to impose any sentence ranging from one-day imprisonment to life imprisonment for any crime over which the tribunal has jurisdiction.'[121] ICTY and ICTR judges acknowledge that they

---

[115]   *Case Concerning the Arrest Warrant of 11 April 2000 (Democratic Republic of the Congo* v. *Belgium)*, 14 February 2002, ICJ 3, 41 ILM 536.

[116]   ICTY Statute, art. 7(4); ICTR Statute, art. 6(4).

[117]   ICC Statute, art. 33(2).

[118]   *Ibid.* art. 33(1) ('The fact that a crime within the jurisdiction of the Court has been committed by a person pursuant to an order of a Government or of a superior, whether military or civilian, shall not relieve that person of criminal responsibility unless: (a) the person was under a legal obligation to obey orders of the Government or the superior in question; (b) the person did not know that the order was unlawful; and (c) the order was not manifestly unlawful.').

[119]   Schabas, note 11 *supra*, at 341–2.

[120]   ICTY Statute, art. 24(2); ICTR Statute, art. 23(2).

[121]   Drumbl, note 13 *supra*, at 51.

have considerable discretion in fashioning sentences.[122] The ICC Statute does not provide for a minimum sentence either. The maximum sentence it stipulates is 30 years but, in extreme cases, a sentence of life can be imposed.[123] The ECCC is mandated to award a minimum sentence of five years and a maximum sentence of life imprisonment.

International judges evoke a number of aggravating and mitigating factors in establishing the quantum of the sentence. These factors help funnel the considerable judicial discretion to sentence. Unlike the case with the ad hoc tribunals, where aggravating and mitigating factors have been developed jurisprudentially, ICC judges receive some official guidance concerning aggravating and mitigating factors from rule 145 of the ICC Rules of Procedure and Evidence. Overall, regardless of their textual or jurisprudential provenance, aggravating factors – namely factors that suggest imposing a more severe sentence – include: the gravity of the crime; the breadth of the crimes and the suffering inflicted; vulnerability of the victims; nature of the perpetrator's involvement; abuse of superior position; and behavior of the accused during trial.[124] Mitigating factors, which suggest imposing a more lenient sentence, include: whether and when the accused pled guilty; substantial cooperation on the part of the accused; remorse; personal circumstances of the offender; extent to which the offender was subject to duress, superior orders or coercion; character of the offender; absence of a prior criminal record; and any human rights abuses suffered by the offender during pre-trial detention.[125]

The ICTR routinely issues life sentences for genocide convictions. The ICTY has been considerably more stinting in convicting for genocide. The ICTY imposed a sentence of 35 years on Radislav Krstić for aiding and abetting genocide. The ICTY Appeals Chamber overturned a Trial Chamber conviction for complicity to commit genocide imposed on Vidoje Blagojević, resulting in a diminution of his cumulative sentence from 18 years to 15 years. Blagojević is presently serving his sentence in Norway.

ICTY and ICTR defendants are entitled to benefit from the national laws regarding early release (parole) of the states in which they actually serve sentence. Thus far, most ICTR convicts serve their sentences in Mali. For the ICTY, whose convicts serve their sentences in correctional facilities located in Western European countries, these national schemes on average permit convicts to apply for early release after two-thirds of the sentence has been served. Many ICTY defendants have thus far benefited from early release. The East Timor Special Panels also accorded convicts the right to be released from prison after two-thirds of the sentence had been served, so long as they behaved well while in custody and their release would not threaten public safety and security.[126] The ICC Statute also contemplates early release.[127]

---

[122]   *Prosecutor* v. *Rutaganda*, Case No. ICTR-96-3, Judgment and Sentence, 6 December 1999, para. 458 (affirmed on appeal *Prosecutor* v. *Rutaganda*, Case No. ICTR-96-3-A, Judgment, 26 May 2003); *Prosecutor* v. *Delalić*, Case No. IT-96-21-A, Judgment, 20 February 2001, paras 717–18; *Prosecutor* v. *Momir Nikolić*, Case No. IT-02-60/1-A, Judgment, 8 March 2006, para. 8.

[123]   ICC Statute, arts 77(1), 78(3).

[124]   Drumbl, note 13 *supra*, at 64–5.

[125]   *Ibid.*

[126]   *Prosecutor* v. *Mau*, Case No. 08/C.G./2003/TD.DIL (Dili Dist. Ct Serious Crimes Spec. Panel, 23 February 2004); UNTAET Regulation 2000/30 as amended by UNTAET Regulation 2001/25, para. 43.1.

[127]   ICC Statute, art. 110.

At the national level, there is a greater diversity of sentence for convicted genocide offenders, though imprisonment remains the preferred remedy. National courts have issued death sentences for genocide. In April 1998, the Rwandan government executed 22 persons convicted of genocide in Rwandan national courts. Rwandan courts have sentenced a much larger number of defendants to death, but there have been no executions in Rwanda since April 1998. Moreover, in 2007, Rwanda repealed the death penalty for domestic genocide convictions.[128] Rwandan courts also have sentenced large numbers of perpetrators to fixed terms of imprisonment and, in the neo-traditional *gacaca* process, there is a possibility of community service (*travaux d'intérêt général*) for convicts. At the national level in Rwanda, survivors can claim civil damages awards against perpetrators. Many claims have been filed and some have been adjudicated in great detail. Overwhelmingly, the survivors cannot collect upon these awards, even if ordered by the court, because most of the defendants are impecunious. Although the Statutes of the ad hoc tribunals permit restitutionary awards, none have yet been made. The ICC Statute creates a Trust Fund for Victims, capitalized by some states parties.

Courts and tribunals offer several rationales with regard to how and why they sentence genocide perpetrators. Retribution and general deterrence are frequently cited;[129] a secondary rationale is expressivism. Other rationales include rehabilitation, reintegration, promotion of peace and reconciliation, and restoration. Although some international jurisprudence could be read to suggest that sentencing of genocide might be harsher than other extraordinary international crimes insofar as genocide is the 'crime of crimes', other jurisprudence, for example the 2006 *Stakić* judgment by the ICTY Appeals Chamber, flatly ruled that 'there is no hierarchy of crimes within the jurisdiction of the Tribunal'.[130]

CONCLUSION: FROM PUNISHING TO PREVENTING GENOCIDE?

Article I of the Genocide Convention mandates both the punishment and prevention of genocide. There is limited cause to believe that retrospective criminal punishment serves much of a preventative function.[131] However, this subject remains a topic of debate among scholars and greater empirical research, if obtainable, would be of significant value. Although the Genocide Convention explicitly invests states with a preventative duty, states have not taken effective anticipatory measures to prevent genocide. This gap exists despite article VIII of the Genocide Convention, which states, 'Any Contracting Party may call upon the competent organs of the United Nations to take such action under the Charter of the United Nations as they consider appropriate for the prevention and suppression of acts of genocide or any of the other acts enumerated in Article III.'

---

[128]   A. Boctor, *Impact of the ICTR? International Law, the Death Penalty and Rwanda's Reconstruction* (unpublished manuscript on file with the author, June 2007) at 9 (noting also that Rwanda is abolishing the death penalty completely from Rwandan law).

[129]   Drumbl, note 13 *supra*, at 60–63. For a discussion of how well the sentences fare in attaining these penological goals, see *ibid*. ch. 6. See also *ibid*. 60 ('retribution and deterrence are very difficult to operationalize in the context of mass atrocity through the tools of punishment currently available').

[130]   *Prosecutor* v. *Stakić*, Case No. T-97-24-A, Judgment, 22 March 2006, para. 375.

[131]   Drumbl, note 13 *supra*, at 149.

Assuredly, as Schabas details, United Nations organs have discussed, investigated and identified (or not identified) genocide when atrocity rages in certain regions. Furthermore, these organs have created institutions to punish individual perpetrators or determine state responsibility retrospectively.[132] This engagement serves an important dialogic and expressive function. Conceptually, serious violations by states of the human rights of their own citizens are no longer shielded by doctrines of sovereignty. Instead, these violations remain of concern to the international community at large.

However, the more nettlesome question remains: How to prevent genocide? One response is to use military force. Classic international law recognizes two justifications for the use of force. The first is through UN Security Council authorization after the Security Council determines the existence of a threat to the peace, breach of the peace or act of aggression.[133] The second justification for the use of force is when such force is necessary in self-defense.[134] Peace-keeping is another response available to UN institutions (as opposed to peace enforcement involving the use of force).

Regardless of the type of intervention, when it comes to preventing genocide the track record of the Security Council, and of the United Nations generally, is far from compelling. Rwanda is a bitter example.[135] The slow-moving nature of Security Council decision-making, the possibility for political gridlock, and the fact that past Security Council interventions have been too-little-too-late in genocidal situations have conspired to seed the notion that perhaps ad hoc coalitions of willing states could intervene militarily on their own to avert massive human rights abuses.[136] This notion has been called 'humanitarian armed intervention' (HAI). HAI came to the forefront in 1999, when NATO bombed the former Federal Republic of Yugoslavia (FRY). Prior to this use of force, the FRY government, then led by Slobodan Milošević, inflicted massive human rights abuses and ethnic cleansing on Albanians in Kosovo, which at that point formed part of the FRY. Although technically illegal, NATO's use of force was deemed to be legitimate. A United States-led coalition cited HAI (namely, to topple Saddam Hussein, bring him and other Ba'ath officials to justice, and to protect the Iraqi people) as a third justification for the invasion of Iraq in 2003.[137] HAI also links to the concept of the state's 'responsibility' or 'duty' to 'protect' its own citizens from systematic human rights abuses. Should the state fail to reasonably exercise this duty, the Security Council or, subsequently, other states, may intercede to uphold this obligation. On the one hand, the odiousness of genocide seems to make it a particularly meritorious candidate for HAI, thereby justifying the use of violence that otherwise would be condemned as aggression or, at least, as unlawful use of force.[138] On the other hand, although HAI may provide some

---

132   Schabas, note 11 *supra*, at 453–79.

133   Charter of the United Nations, 59 Stat. 1031 (26 June 1945), arts 39, 42.

134   *Ibid*. art. 51; Letter of Secretary of State Daniel Webster to Special Minister Ashburton, dated 27 July 1842, available at www.yale.edu/lawweb/avalon/diplomacy/britain/br-1842d.htm (the *Caroline* case).

135   R. DALLAIRE, SHAKE HANDS WITH THE DEVIL: THE FAILURE OF HUMANITY IN RWANDA (2004); S. POWER, A PROBLEM FROM HELL: AMERICA AND THE AGE OF GENOCIDE (2003).

136   There is a voluminous literature on this topic. See for example, J. DONNELLY, UNIVERSAL HUMAN RIGHTS IN THEORY AND PRACTICE ch. 14 (2003).

137   The other two cited justifications were self-defense and Security Council authorization.

138   For more discussion, see L. May, Genocide, Social Groups, and Criminal Trials (book manuscript on file with the author, 2008) at ch. 12.

flexibility, if recourse thereto became too available, it could be used to provide cover or justification for military invasions actually based on ulterior motives.

Amending the Genocide Convention to require military intervention when a series of warning signals of incipient genocide are found to exist might give more teeth to prevention. Alternatively, it might not. Fundamentally, states will only prevent genocide if they have the will to do so; they will only commit forces if they want to do so; they will only put their citizens in harm's way if there is political consensus to do so. Although amending the Genocide Convention in this manner might serve an important expressive function, it also might create a chilling effect if states become concerned about taking on too much in the way of legal obligation. As a result, in an international order where commitment to international law is largely based on consent, states may simply agree not to assume that obligation. As legal scholars have noted in the human rights context, over-legalization may lead to backlash and retrenchment.[139]

There also are less intrusive forms of prevention, for example non-forcible measures under article 41 of the United Nations Charter. After all, genocide archetypically starts out with smaller discriminatory measures, moves toward persecution, and then ends up in an eliminationist context. What if it were possible to discredit, limit and impose sanctions on a state when the warning signs of genocide begin to emerge? Might that go some way toward prevention? Humanitarian communications intervention, such as radio jamming, is another non-forcible option. During the Rwandan atrocity, authorities used the radio extensively to broadcast genocidal vitriol and even identify the location of targeted Tutsis. Instead of punishing radio executives after the genocide, it might have been much more effective to block radio transmissions before the fact.

Regardless of methodology, one concluding lesson is clear. Retrospective judicial interventions, whether undertaken by criminal prosecutions, civil liability or communal and indigenous forms of justice, can only do so much. In order for 'never again' truly to mean 'never again', some sort of effective emergency interventions, whether forcible or non-forcible, would have to take place.

---

[139] L. Helfer, *Overlegalizing Human Rights: International Relations Theory and the Commonwealth Caribbean Backlash Against Human Rights Regimes*, 102 COLUMBIA LAW REVIEW 1832 (2002).

4 Crimes against humanity

Margaret M. deGuzman

INTRODUCTION

The modern concept of crimes against humanity is a product of the scale and horror of the crimes committed in the two world wars as well as a growing consensus in the international community that certain crimes committed within national borders are legitimate subjects of international law and adjudication. At its inception, the notion of crimes against humanity was essentially an extension of the laws of war. Those laws have deep historic roots and aim to limit the devastation wrought by armed conflict by, among other things, criminalizing certain conduct by nationals of one state against nationals of another. In contrast, crimes committed within national borders were, until quite recently, considered outside the purview of international law. The Holocaust proved a tipping point in international law, spurring the rapid development of international human rights law and the concomitant evolution of international criminal law. The Nuremberg Charter thus provided for jurisdiction not only over war crimes, but also over 'crimes against humanity' and 'crimes against peace'.[1]

Unlike war crimes and genocide, crimes against humanity are not codified in an international convention. Instead, the law of crimes against humanity has primarily developed through the evolution of customary international law. Although the statutes of most international and internationalized[2] tribunals contain definitions of these crimes, there are significant differences among those definitions. For example, the Nuremberg Charter and the Statute of the International Criminal Tribunal for Former Yugoslavia (ICTY) require that crimes against humanity be committed in the context of an armed conflict, while the Statute of the International Criminal Tribunal for Rwanda (ICTR) and the law of the Extraordinary Chambers in the Courts of Cambodia (ECCC) require no nexus with armed conflict but do require an element of discrimination that is lacking in the other definitions.[3] Furthermore, the evolution of the defin-

---

[1]   Agreement for the Prosecution and Punishment of the Major War Criminals of the European Axis, art. 6, 8 August 1945, Annex, 59 Stat. 1544, 82 UNTS 279, reprinted in 39 AM. J INT'L L 257 (Supp. 1945) (hereinafter 'Nuremberg Charter').

[2]   Internationalized tribunals, sometimes called 'hybrid' tribunals, employ both national and international laws and judges. The Special Court for Sierra Leone and the Extraordinary Chambers in the Courts of Cambodia are examples. See Clare da Silva, on the hybrid experience of the Special Court for Sierra Leone.

[3]   Compare Nuremberg Charter, note 1 *supra*, art. 6(c) and Statute of the International Tribunal for the Prosecution of Persons Responsible for Serious Violations of International Humanitarian Law in the Territory of the Former Yugoslavia Since 1991, art. 5, UN SCOR, Annex, UN Doc. S/25704 (1993), reprinted in 32 ILM 1159, 1192 (1994) (ICTY Statute) with Statute of the International Criminal Tribunal for the Prosecution of Persons Responsible for Genocide and Other Serious Violations of International Humanitarian Law Committed in the Territory of Rwanda and Rwandan Citizens Responsible for Genocide and Other Such Violations Committed in the Territory of Neighbouring States Between 1 January 1994 and 31 December 1994, art. 3, Security Council Res. 955, UN SCOR,

ition of crimes against humanity in these international instruments has not been entirely linear; later definitions are sometimes more expansive and sometimes narrower than their predecessors. As a result, the content of the norm prohibiting crimes against humanity remains subject to greater controversy than the norms proscribing genocide and war crimes.

The definition in the Rome Statute of the International Criminal Court provides an appropriate starting point for a discussion of crimes against humanity. Although the ICC Statute does not purport to codify customary international law and explicitly rejects the notion that it crystallizes such law for the future,[4] the Statute nonetheless represents the agreement of the majority of the world's states concerning the definition of crimes against humanity as of July 1998.[5] The ICC Statute defines crimes against humanity as follows:

1. For the purpose of this Statute, 'crime against humanity' means any of the following acts when committed as part of a widespread or systematic attack directed against any civilian population, with knowledge of the attack:
  (a) murder;
  (b) extermination;
  (c) enslavement;
  (d) deportation or forcible transfer of population;
  (e) imprisonment or other severe deprivation of physical liberty in violation of fundamental rules of international law;
  (f) torture;
  (g) rape, sexual slavery, enforced prostitution, forced pregnancy, enforced sterilization, or any other form of sexual violence of comparable gravity;
  (h) persecution against any identifiable group or collectivity on political, racial, national, ethnic, cultural, religious, gender as defined in paragraph 3, or other grounds that are universally recognized as impermissible under international law, in connection with any act referred to in this paragraph or any crime within the jurisdiction of the Court;
  (i) enforced disappearance of persons;
  (j) the crime of apartheid;
  (k) other inhumane acts of a similar character intentionally causing great suffering, or serious injury to body or to mental or physical health.
2. For the purpose of paragraph 1:
  (a) 'attack directed against any civilian population' means a course of conduct involving the multiple commission of acts referred to in paragraph 1 against any civilian population, pursuant to or in furtherance of a State or organizational policy to commit such attack;[6] ...

This definition resulted from a series of intense negotiations and reflects a number of political compromises.[7] In some respects, the ICC's definition is more expansive than previous

---

49th Sess., 3453d mtg., Annex, UN Doc. S/RES/955 (1994), reprinted in 33 ILM 1598, 1602 (1994) (ICTR Statute) and Law on the Establishment of the Extraordinary Chambers in the Courts of Cambodia for the Prosecution of Crimes Committed During the Period of Democratic Kampuchea, art. 5, 27 October 2004, NS/RKM/1004/006 (ECCC Statute).

   [4]   See Rome Statute of the International Criminal Court, art. 10, 17 July 1998, 2187 UNTS 90 (ICC Statute) ('Nothing in this Part shall be interpreted as limiting or prejudicing in any way existing or developing rules of international law for purposes other than this Statute.').

   [5]   The ICC Statute was adopted on 17 July 1998 by a vote of 120 states in favor, seven against and 21 abstentions.

   [6]   ICC Statute, art. 7.

   [7]   See generally Herman von Hebel and Darryl Robinson, *Crimes Within the Jurisdiction of the Court*, in The International Criminal Court: The Making of the Rome Statute 79, 90–103 (Roy S. Lee ed., 1999).

and subsequent formulations and in others it is narrower. Nonetheless, the definition reflects the fundamental structure and content of these crimes. Essentially, crimes against humanity are inhumane acts of a serious nature committed as part of a widespread or systematic attack against civilians. Each of the inhumane acts constitutes a crime in most of the world's criminal law systems, but their commission as part of a broader attack justifies their characterization as crimes against humanity and the exercise of international criminal jurisdiction. The definition thus comprises the elements of the 'constitutive crimes' (murder, extermination, etc.) as well as those of the 'chapeau' or 'contextual' aspect of the crimes reflected in the opening paragraph above. In other words, to be guilty of a crime against humanity, a defendant must commit the underlying inhumane act knowing that he or she is contributing to a widespread or systematic attack against civilians.

The primary challenge in defining crimes against humanity is to identify the precise elements that distinguish these offenses from crimes subject exclusively to national laws. The contours of the definition not only determine the scope of international jurisdiction, but also give rise to a number of additional important consequences. First, unlike most domestic crimes, crimes against humanity are generally considered outside the purview of statutes of limitations.[8] Second, the immunities that often shield state representatives from criminal responsibility are not available for crimes against humanity, at least when trials are held before international tribunals.[9] Third, although the concept of universal jurisdiction – the theory that certain crimes are subject to the jurisdiction of all states – remains controversial, proponents of universal jurisdiction invariably include crimes against humanity within its scope. This means, for example, that while the crime of murder generally can only be tried in a court with a jurisdictional link to the act, a murder committed as a crime against humanity arguably can be tried in any criminal court in the world. Finally, the prohibition of crimes against humanity is a *jus cogens* norm of international law, which means that derogation is not permitted under any circumstances. As a result of this status, some authorities assert that states have an international law obligation either to prosecute perpetrators of crimes against humanity or to extradite them to states intending to pursue prosecutions.[10]

---

[8]   There are two conventions on this question, although neither is widely ratified. See Convention on the Non-Applicability of Statutory Limitations to War Crimes and Crimes Against Humanity, adopted 26 November 1968, 754 UNTS 73 (entered into force 11 November 1970), reprinted in 8 ILM. 68 (1969); European Convention on the Non-applicability of Statutory Limitations to Crimes Against Humanity and War Crimes, 25 January 1974, Europ. TS No. 82. Additionally, many states have eschewed statutes of limitations for crimes against humanity in their domestic laws and an argument can be made that customary international law at least permits, if not requires, that limitations be inapplicable to such crimes. See STEVEN R. RATNER AND JASON S. ABRAMS, ACCOUNTABILITY FOR HUMAN RIGHTS ATROCITIES IN INTERNATIONAL LAW: BEYOND THE NUREMBERG LEGACY 143–4 (2nd edn, 2001).

[9]   *Case Concerning the Arrest Warrant of 11 April 2000 (Congo v. Belgium)*, 2002 ICJ 121, para. 61 (holding that Congo's incumbent Minister of Foreign Affairs was immune from prosecution for crimes against humanity in Belgian courts, but stating that he could be prosecuted by an international court with jurisdiction); Adam Day, *Crimes Against Humanity as a Nexus of Individual and State Responsibility: Why the ICJ Got Belgium v. Congo Wrong*, 22 BERKELEY J INT'L L 489, 491 (2004) (arguing that customary international law does not allow immunity for crimes against humanity even before national courts).

[10]   M. CHERIF BASSIOUNI, CRIMES AGAINST HUMANITY IN INTERNATIONAL CRIMINAL LAW 224 (2nd edn, 1999) ('The duty to prosecute or extradite whether alternative or co-existent is clearly established in conventional and customary international criminal law with respect to "crimes against humanity".').

In light of the very serious legal consequences of designating an offense a crime against humanity, as well as the heightened moral condemnation the label entails, the importance of understanding the exact contours of these offenses cannot be underestimated. The remainder of this chapter provides a brief historical sketch of the evolution of the norm prohibiting crimes against humanity, assesses the current state of the definition with respect to each potential element of the *chapeau* and some of the constitutive crimes, and argues that a normative framework should be adopted to resolve the remaining uncertainties surrounding this category of international crimes.

HISTORICAL EVOLUTION

The origins of the international law prohibition of crimes against humanity lie in humanitarian principles regulating armed conflict.[11] The concept of 'laws of humanity' first found expression in conventional international law in the Hague Conventions of 1899 and 1907. In a preambular paragraph that became known as the 'Martens Clause' after its drafter, the 1907 Convention declares that, in cases not otherwise covered therein, 'the inhabitants and the belligerents remain under the protection and the rule of the principles of the law of nations, as they result from the usages established among civilized peoples, *from the laws of humanity*, and the dictates of the public conscience'.[12]

The first official use of the term 'crimes against humanity' was in a 1915 declaration by the governments of Great Britain, France and Russia describing the Turkish massacres of Armenians as 'crimes against humanity and civilization for which all the members of the Turkish Government will be held responsible together with its agents implicated in the massacres'.[13] Although no prosecutions ensued, the term resonated and the prospect of imposing criminal liability for crimes against humanity was raised again in a report of the commission tasked with assigning responsibility for violations committed during the First World War.[14] This effort also failed to yield prosecutions for these crimes. This time failure was largely due to concerns expressed by the delegation from the United States that crimes against humanity were not cognizable in a criminal court.[15]

Although significant state practice appears to contradict such assertions, one author argues that most amnesties should be viewed as derogations from the duty rather than contrary state practice. See Miles M. Jackson, *The Customary International Law Duty to Prosecute Crimes Against Humanity: A New Framework*, 16 TUL. J INT'L & COMP. L 117 (2007).

[11]   For a description of the evolution of humanitarian law as it pertains to crimes against humanity see Bassiouni, note 10 *supra*, at 41–88.

[12]   Convention Respecting the Laws and Customs of War on Land, pmbl., 18 October 1907, 36 Stat. 2277, 1 Bevans 631 (emphasis added). The Hague Convention of 1899 contains similar language. See Convention with Respect to the Laws and Customs of War on Land, pmbl., 29 July 1899, 32 Stat. 1803, 1 Bevans 247.

[13]   Egon Schwelb, *Crimes Against Humanity*, 23 BRIT. YB INT'L L 178, 181 (1946) (quoting Armenian Memorandum Presented by the Greek Delegation to the Commission of Fifteen on 14 March 1919).

[14]   Commission on the Responsibility of the Authors of the War and on Enforcement of Penalties, *Report Presented to the Preliminary Peace Conference*, reprinted in 14 AM. J INT'L L 95, 117 (1920) (proposing criminal prosecutions of persons 'guilty of offenses against the laws and customs of war or the laws of humanity').

[15]   Memorandum of Reservations Presented by the Representatives of the United States to the

Thus, it was not until after the Second World War that the first prosecutions for crimes against humanity occurred. The Charter of the International Military Tribunal for the Trial of the Major War Criminals ('Nuremberg Charter') included crimes against humanity within the Tribunal's jurisdiction, defining these crimes as:

> murder, extermination, enslavement, deportation, and other inhumane acts committed against any civilian population, before or during the war, or persecutions on political, racial or religious grounds in execution of or in connection with any crime within the jurisdiction of the Tribunal, whether or not in violation of the domestic law of the country where perpetrated.[16]

Similar definitions were included in the laws enacted to prosecute Nazi perpetrators in the various Allied occupied zones in Germany[17] and to prosecute Japanese war criminals.[18]

The post-Second World War prosecutions for crimes against humanity were widely criticized on the grounds that they violated the principle of legality or *nullum crimen sine lege*, which holds that there can be no conviction for a crime without prior law. When defendants raised the principle as a defense, however, courts universally rejected their arguments, although one judge in the Tokyo proceedings issued a scathing dissent charging the tribunal with engaging in 'a sham employment of legal process for the satisfaction of a thirst for revenge'.[19] The debate about whether the Nuremberg Charter's inclusion of crimes against humanity was an appropriate articulation of pre-existing legal principles or an illegal assertion of 'victor's justice' continues today. There is little question in light of subsequent developments, however, that if these crimes were not enshrined in customary international law when the Nuremberg Charter was drafted, they gained that status shortly thereafter.

Although it would be almost half a century after Nuremberg before another international criminal tribunal was created, the intervening years saw the development of the law of crimes against humanity through the work of the International Law Commission (ILC). In 1947, the United Nations General Assembly tasked the ILC with formulating the principles of international law recognized in the Nuremberg Charter and judgment and preparing a draft code of offenses against the peace and security of mankind.[20] The ILC's consideration of the definition of crimes against humanity spanned nearly five decades. The final draft code, submitted to the General Assembly in 1996, contributed greatly to the process that resulted in the Rome Statute of the ICC. The 1996 draft code defined crimes against humanity as encompassing various inhumane acts 'when committed in a systematic manner or on a large scale and insti-

---

Report of the Commission on Responsibilities (4 April 1919), Annex II, reprinted in Commission on the Responsibility of the Authors of the War and on Enforcement of Penalties, *Report Presented to the Preliminary Peace Conference* (29 March 1919), 14 Aм. J Int'l L 95, 134 (1920).

   [16]   Nuremberg Charter, *supra* note 1, art. 6(c).

   [17]   Control Council Law No. 10, Punishment of Persons Guilty of War Crimes, Crimes Against Peace and Against Humanity, art. 2(1)(c), 20 December 1945, available at http://avalon.law.yale.edu/imt/imt10.asp.

   [18]   Charter of the International Military Tribunal for the Far East, art. 5(c), 19 January 1946, 4 Bevans 20, TIAS No. 1589.

   [19]   *United States* v. *Araki et al.*, Dissenting Opinion of Justice Pal, in 21 The Tokyo Major War Crimes Trial 37 (R. John Pritchard and Sonia Magbanua Zaide eds, 1981). For a thorough discussion of *nullum crimen sine lege* in international criminal law see Beth Van Schaack, *Crimen Sine Lege: Judicial Lawmaking at the Intersection of Law and Morals*, 97 Geo. LJ 119 (2008).

   [20]   General Assembly Res. 177(II), UN GAOR, 2d Sess., 123d mtg., UN Doc. A/519 (1947).

gated or directed by a Government or by any organization or group'.[21] In addition to these international efforts, the post-war years saw a few states codify crimes against humanity in their national laws, and Canada, France and Israel conducted domestic prosecutions for crimes against humanity committed during the war.[22]

The second milestone in the development of the law of crimes against humanity occurred in 1993 when the UN Security Council established the International Criminal Tribunal for the Former Yugoslavia (ICTY) to prosecute those crimes as well as genocide and war crimes committed in former Yugoslavia. The ICTY Statute defines crimes against humanity as any of the listed inhumane acts 'when committed in armed conflict, whether international or internal in character, and directed against any civilian population'.[23] This definition revived the Nuremberg Charter's required nexus with armed conflict, but also expanded the listed inhumane acts to include imprisonment, torture and rape. The following year, the Security Council established the International Criminal Tribunal for Rwanda (ICTR), this time dropping the linkage to armed conflict but adding a separate requirement that the enumerated inhumane acts be 'committed as part of a widespread or systematic attack against any civilian population on national, political, ethnic, racial or religious grounds'.[24] The establishment of these two tribunals greatly spurred the development of the law of crimes against humanity, both through the elaboration of these statutory definitions and, perhaps more importantly, through the extensive production of case law addressing these crimes.

It was in this newly active legal and jurisprudential context that the definition of crimes against humanity in the ICC Statute was negotiated. Among the most contentious issues in the negotiations were: (1) whether a nexus with armed conflict should be required; (2) whether the definition should require discrimination generally or only for persecution; and (3) whether the contextual elements of 'widespread' and 'systematic' should be conjunctive ('widespread and systematic') or disjunctive ('widespread or systematic').[25] With regard to each of these issues, the delegates ultimately settled on the more expansive alternative. The ICC Statute also enlarges the list of inhumane acts to include all forms of grave sexual violence, enforced disappearance and apartheid, and expands the grounds on which persecution can be committed. At the same time, however, the ICC Statute's definition appears to limit the circumstances under which convictions for crimes against humanity are possible by defining the 'attack directed against any civilian population' to require multiple acts committed pursuant to a state or organizational policy. Critics charge that this effectively turned the disjunctive 'widespread or systematic' into a conjunctive requirement of both elements.[26]

---

21   ILC, Draft Code of Crimes Against the Peace and Security of Mankind, in *Report of the International Law Commission on the Work of its Forty-Eighth Session*, 51 UN GAOR Supp. (No. 10), art. 19, at 47, UN Doc. A/51/10 (1996), reprinted in 2 YB ILC Pt. 2 (1992), UN Doc. A/CN.4/SER.A/1996/Add.1 (Pt 2).

22   See Bassiouni, note 10 *supra*, at 5 n. 9 (citing cases).

23   ICTY Statute, note 3 *supra*, art. 5.

24   ICTR Statute, art. 3.

25   For detailed discussions of the negotiations in Rome concerning the definition of crimes against humanity see Margaret M. deGuzman, *The Road From Rome: The Developing Law of Crimes Against Humanity*, 22 HUM. RTS Q 335 (2000); Darryl Robinson, *Defining 'Crimes Against Humanity' at the Rome Conference*, 93 AM. J INT'L L 43 (1999).

26   See, for example, Phyllis Hwang, *Defining Crimes Against Humanity in the Rome Statute of the International Criminal Court*, 22 FORDHAM INT'L LJ 457, 499 (1998) ('While welcoming the treat-

This and other remaining ambiguities in the ICC's definition will have to be clarified in the Court's case law.[27]

Interestingly, the internationalized courts that have been established after the ICC have not simply adopted the latter's definition of crimes against humanity. The Special Court for Sierra Leone (SCSL) eschewed the ICC Statute's policy element, defining crimes against humanity broadly to include inhumane acts committed 'as part of a widespread or systematic attack against any civilian population'.[28] The policy element is also absent from the laws of the ECCC and the special panels established to adjudicate crimes committed in East Timor.[29] The ECCC law, however, narrows the definition by reintroducing the contextual discrimination requirement articulated in the ICTR Statute.[30] Furthermore, domestic laws criminalizing crimes against humanity do not necessarily track the ICC Statute's definition.[31] In sum, the various definitions of crimes against humanity in national and international laws contain inconsistencies that complicate the task of determining the elements of these crimes under customary international law.

CONTEXTUAL ELEMENTS

The contextual or 'chapeau' elements in the definition provide the moral basis for labeling particular inhumane acts crimes against humanity and justify the exercise of international jurisdiction. As the historical evolution of these crimes demonstrates, the contextual elements have differed significantly in various international and national definitions. It remains important, however, to establish the elements of these crimes under customary international law in order to comply with the mandates of *nullum crimen sine lege*, particularly with respect to the retrospective application of newly codified definitions. This section therefore discusses the current state of customary international law with respect to each of the potential contextual elements.

---

ment of "widespread" and "systematic" as alternative criteria in paragraph 1, NGOs viewed the explanatory definition of "attack directed against any civilian population" in the second paragraph as an ill-disguised attempt to reintroduce these criteria as cumulative.').

[27]   The ICC has already begun this process. For example, in confirming charges against two defendants a pre-trial chamber elaborated the content of the definition's 'widespread or systematic' and 'policy' elements. See *Prosecutor* v. *Katanga and Chui*, Case No. ICC-01/04-01/07, Decision on the Confirmation of Charges, 30 September 2008, paras 389–98, n. 545.

[28]   Statute of the Special Court for Sierra Leone, art. 2, 16 January 2002, 2178 UNT 138, available at www.sc-sl.org/scsl-statute.html (SCSL Statute).

[29]   ECCC Statute, UNTAET Regulation 15/2000, available at www.un.org/peace/etimor/untaetR/r-2000.htm; see also Kai Ambos and Steffen Wirth, *The Current Law of Crimes Against Humanity: An Analysis of UNTAET Regulation 15/2000*, 13 CRIM. L FORUM 1, 3 (2002) (the UNTAET Regulation generally reflects the ICC Statute definition but deliberately omits the policy requirement).

[30]   ECCC Statute, art. 5.

[31]   See Stuart Ford, *Crimes Against Humanity in the Extraordinary Chambers in the Courts of Cambodia: Is a Connection with Armed Conflict Required?*, 24 UCLA PAC. BASIN LJ 125, 184–92 (discussing definitions in various national laws).

War Nexus

As noted above, the Nuremberg Charter required that there be a connection to war before that tribunal could exercise jurisdiction over crimes against humanity. This same restriction was subsequently included in the ICTY's definition, although the latter allowed that requirement to be fulfilled by internal armed conflict as well as by the international armed conflict that brings into play the more traditional laws of war. Nonetheless, there is little doubt that the nexus with armed conflict – whether international or internal – is no longer part of the customary international law definition of crimes against humanity.[32] As early as 1995, an appellate decision of the ICTY found that it was a 'settled rule of customary international law that crimes against humanity do not require a connection to international armed conflict' and 'may not require a connection [to] any conflict at all'.[33] In fact, although the matter was debated at the Rome Conference on the ICC,[34] none of the definitions adopted since the ICTY Statute has required a nexus with armed conflict.

Nonetheless, the question of when customary international law evolved to exclude the nexus with armed conflict retains significance in some contexts. For example, the ECCC was established to prosecute crimes committed between 1975 and 1979. Although the ECCC's definition of crimes against humanity does not require a nexus with armed conflict, defendants before the ECCC will likely argue that application of that definition violates the principle of *nullum crimen sine lege*. To convict the defendants, the court will have to determine either (1) that the customary law definition of crimes against humanity did not require a nexus with armed conflict in 1975 (which will be difficult in light of the ICTY's inclusion of the nexus), or (2) that it was reasonably foreseeable at that time that the nexus would be eliminated.[35]

Widespread or Systematic Attack

The essential element that distinguishes crimes against humanity from domestic crimes is that the constitutive inhumane acts are committed as part of a broader criminal attack. In fact, all definitions of crimes against humanity adopted since the ICTR Statute require a nexus between the individual crime and a widespread or systematic attack against a civilian population.[36] Furthermore, the ICTY has interpreted its Statute to require this element even though

---

[32]   See deGuzman, note 25 *supra*, at 355–60; Beth Van Schaack, *The Definition of Crimes Against Humanity: Resolving the Incoherence*, 37 COLUM. J. TRANSNAT'L L 787 (1999).

[33]   *Prosecutor* v. *Tadic*, Case No. IT-94-1, Decision on the Defense Motion for Interlocutory Appeal on Jurisdiction, 2 October 1995, para.141. In a subsequent decision in the *Tadic* case, the Trial Chamber reaffirmed this conclusion, stating that 'the inclusion of the requirement of an armed conflict deviates from the development of the doctrine after the Nürnberg Charter, beginning with Control Council Law No. 10, which no longer links the concept of crimes against humanity with an armed conflict'. *Prosecutor* v. *Tadic*, Case No. IT-94-1, Opinion and Judgment, 7 May 1997, para. 627.

[34]   See deGuzman, note 25 *supra*, at 358–9.

[35]   Ford, note 31 *supra*, at 199. Compare Antonio Cassese, *Balancing the Prosecution of Crimes Against Humanity and Non-Retroactivity of Criminal law*, 4 J INT'L CRIM. JUST. 410, 413–14 (2006) (arguing the European Court of Human Rights failed properly to apply the principle of non-retroactivity to an Estonian case involving crimes against humanity committed in 1949).

[36]   Even the earlier definitions that did not explicitly reference a widespread or systematic attack were interpreted to require this element. See deGuzman, note 25 *supra*, at 375.

it is not explicitly stated therein.[37] In other words, the perpetrator of an inhumane act is only guilty of a crime against humanity if he or she commits the act knowing it is part of a widespread or systematic attack against a civilian population.

While the ICC Statute defines 'attack' to require multiple acts and a state or organizational policy, it is not clear that customary international law mandates either of these elements. The case law of the ad hoc tribunals has been inconsistent with regard to the 'attack' requirement. For example, a Trial Chamber of the ICTY defined 'attack' to mean 'a course of conduct involving the commission of acts of violence'.[38] In contrast, an ICTR Trial Chamber stated that 'attack' simply means an 'unlawful act of the kind enumerated' in the court's Statute, which can be 'non violent in nature, like imposing a system of apartheid'.[39] Another Chamber of the same tribunal stated that '[t]he elements of the attack effectively exclude from crimes against humanity, acts carried out for purely personal motives and those outside of a broader policy or plan'.[40] The SCSL has declared that an attack can be a '"campaign, operation, or course of conduct" … not limited to the use of armed force, but also encompass[ing] any mistreatment of the civilian population'.[41]

This case law suggests that the ICC's requirements of multiple inhumane acts in furtherance of a state or organizational policy do not reflect customary international law. Rather, the meaning of 'attack' in the definition remains unclear for the purposes of customary law. Certainly, the attack need not involve violence that rises to the level of an armed conflict since that nexus has been eliminated from the definition. In fact, as the case law of the ICTR and SCSL reflects, an attack may not require any violence at all. Furthermore, the attack need not cover a very large geographic area.[42] Nonetheless, at a minimum, the concept of 'attack' requires an underlying connectivity that excludes isolated crimes against unconnected victims from the definition of crimes against humanity.[43]

Additionally, the debate about whether the attack (or the constitutive act) must be committed on discriminatory grounds appears to have been resolved in favor of the exclusion of that requirement. Among the proponents of a discrimination requirement at the Rome Conference was the French delegation,[44] reflecting the provision in French law that crimes against humanity are 'inspirées par des motifs politiques, philosophiques, raciaux ou religieux'.[45]

---

[37]   See *Prosecutor v. Blaskic*, Case No. IT-95-14-T, Judgment, 3 March 2000, para. 202.

[38]   *Prosecutor v. Kunarac*, Case No. IT-96-23, Judgment, 22 February 2001, para. 415.

[39]   *Prosecutor v. Akayesu*, Case No. ICTR-96-4, Judgment, 2 September 1998, para. 581.

[40]   *Prosecutor v. Kayishema*, Case No. ICTR-95-1-T, Judgment, 21 May 1999, para. 122).

[41]   *Prosecutor v. Fofana and Kondewa*, Case No. SCSL-04-14-T, Judgment, 2 August 2007, para.111).

[42]   Guénaël Mettraux, *Crimes Against Humanity in the Jurisprudence of the International Criminal Tribunals for the Former Yugoslavia and for Rwanda*, 43 HARV. INT'L LJ 237, 250, n. 56 (2002) (citing ICTY and ICTR cases involving attacks alleged to have taken place in relatively small geographic areas).

[43]   See for example, *Prosecutor v. Akayesu*, Case No. ICTR-96-4, Judgment, 2 September 1998, para. 579 ('The Chamber considers that it is a prerequisite that the act must be committed as part of a widespread or systematic attack and not just a random act of violence.').

[44]   See von Hebel and Robinson, note 7 *supra*, at 93. In fact, the French delegation made a similar proposal with respect to the Nuremberg Charter. *See* Matthew Lippman, *Crimes Against Humanity*, 17 BC THIRD WORLD LJ 171, 181 (1997).

[45]   See Code Penal, art. 212-1, available at www.legifrance.gouv.fr/affichCodeArticle. do?cidTexte=LEGITEXT000006070719&idArticle=LEGIARTI000006417535&dateTexte=

The definitions of crimes against humanity at the ICTR and ECCC also require that the attack be committed on discriminatory grounds. This contextual discrimination requirement was broadly opposed at the Rome Conference,[46] however, and has been excluded from all international definitions of these crimes other than those of the ICTR and ECCC.

As noted above, there were contentious discussions at the Rome Conference about whether the attack should be both widespread and systematic or whether the disjunctive formulation was preferable. A strong minority, which included permanent members of the Security Council, supported the conjunctive requirement, arguing that a widespread crime wave should not constitute a crime against humanity.[47] The compromise that emerged is reflected in the second paragraph's definition of 'attack directed against any civilian population' as encompassing multiple acts pursuant to a policy. Some commentators argue that this provision essentially changes the 'or' into 'and' because multiple acts can be equated with widespread, and systematic is synonymous with policy.[48] However, Darryl Robinson, a member of the Canadian delegation who helped draft the provision, counters that the requirements of multiple acts and a policy are lower thresholds than 'widespread and systematic'.[49]

As a matter of customary international law it is not clear that qualification as 'widespread' requires multiple acts or that 'systematicity' requires a policy. In fact, the requirement that the attack be 'widespread' arguably refers to the scale of victimization rather than the number of acts perpetrated as part of the attack. Thus, for example, the ICTY has held that the 'widespread' element 'refers to the scale of the acts perpetrated and to the number of victims' and that a single inhumane act of extraordinary magnitude can fulfill the requirement.[50] In other words, the 'widespread' criterion appears primarily to require a substantial number of victims, although the geographic scope of the crimes may also be taken into account.[51] In fact, some commentators have suggested that the ICC Statute's reference to 'multiple acts' should be interpreted to include singular acts resulting in multiple victims.[52]

Furthermore, even after the adoption of the ICC Statute, the ICTY Appeals Chamber held that the 'systematic' alternative does not necessarily require a policy.[53] According to that

---

20081122 ('La déportation, la réduction en esclavage ou la pratique massive et systématique d'exécutions sommaires, d'enlèvements de personnes suivis de leur disparition, de la torture ou d'actes inhumains, et organisées en exécution d'un plan concerté à l'encontre d'un groupe de population civile sont punies de la réclusion criminelle à perpétuité.') ('The deportation, enslavement, or the massive and systematic practice of summary executions, kidnappings followed by disappearance, torture or inhuman acts inspired by political, philosophical, racial or religious groups and organized in pursuance of a concerted plan against a group of civilians is punishable by imprisonment for life.').

[46]   See von Hebel and Robinson, note 7 *supra*, at 94.

[47]   *Ibid.* 94.

[48]   MACHTELD BOOT, GENOCIDE, CRIMES AGAINST HUMANITY, WAR CRIMES: NULLUM CRIMEN SINE LEGE AND THE SUBJECT MATTER JURISDICTION OF THE INTERNATIONAL CRIMINAL COURT 482–3 (2002).

[49]   See Robinson, note 25 *supra*, at 48.

[50]   *Prosecutor* v. *Blaskic*, Case No. IT-95-14-T, Trial Chamber Judgment, 3 March 2000, para. 206. The ICTR and SCSL have followed a similar approach. See *Prosecutor* v. *Akayesu*, note 39 *supra*, para. 580 (defining 'widespread' as 'massive, frequent, large scale action, carried out collectively with considerable seriousness and directed against a multiplicity of victims'); *Fofana*, note 41 *supra*, para. 112 ('the term "widespread" refers to the large-scale nature of the attack and the number of victims').

[51]   GERHARD WERLE, PRINCIPLES OF INTERNATIONAL CRIMINAL LAW 225 (2005).

[52]   Ambos and Wirth, note 29 *supra*, at 17.

[53]   *Prosecutor* v. *Kunarac*, Case No. IT-96-23/1-A, Judgment, 12 June 2002, para. 98. But see

court, the requirement of systematicity entails 'the organised nature of the acts of violence and the improbability of their random occurrence'.[54] The court noted that proof of a policy may be useful in establishing the existence of an attack against a civilian population – particularly a systematic attack – but that 'it may be possible to prove these things by reference to other matters'.[55] The SCSL has also rejected the policy requirement.[56] Nonetheless, judicial and academic opinions on the need for a policy remain mixed.[57] Thus, it is unclear whether, outside the context of the ICC Statute, courts adjudicating crimes against humanity must require proof of a policy or whether other forms of organization, such as less formal discussions or coordination, suffice.

For the ICC, the introduction of the policy requirement raises a number of questions regarding the required levels and methods of proof. The ICC's Elements of the Crimes specify that the policy criterion requires that a state or organization 'actively promote or encourage' the attack.[58] It remains unclear whether the Court can infer such promotion or encouragement from the manner in which crimes are committed, as the ad hoc tribunals have sometimes done,[59] or will instead require testimonial or documentary evidence establishing the state or organizational policy. A recent ICC Pre-Trial Chamber decision suggests the latter approach, although this may simply reflect the availability of documentary evidence in that case.[60] Furthermore, the Statute does not specify whether the policy must be adopted at the highest levels of authority or whether lower-level state or organizational actors can form the requisite policy. Finally, although the ICC Statute specifies that the policy need not be that of a state,[61] uncertainty

---

William A. Schabas, *State Policy as an Element of International Crimes*, 98 J CRIM. L & CRIMINOLOGY 953, 959 (2008) (arguing that the authorities cited in the *Kunarac* decision do not necessarily support the conclusion that a state plan or policy is not an element of crimes against humanity and that the court appears to have reached a 'results-oriented political decision').

[54]   *Prosecutor* v. *Kunarac*, note 53 supra, para. 93.

[55]   *Ibid.* para. 98.

[56]   *Fofana*, note 41 *supra*, para. 113.

[57]   See for example, Werle, note 51 *supra*, at 229 (opining that customary international law does not require a policy element); Ambos and Wirth, note 29 *supra*, at 31–2 (a policy element is required even under the 'widespread' alternative and can be fulfilled by a government policy of tolerating unorganized widespread violence); Schabas, note 53 *supra* (arguing for a policy element); *Prosecutor* v. *Kayishema*, Case No. ICTR-95-1-T, Judgment, 21 May 1999, para. 124 ('For an act of mass victimisation to be a crime against humanity, it must include a policy element.'); *Prosecutor* v. *Kunarac*, note 53 *supra*, para. 98 ('[N]either the attack nor the acts of the accused needs to be supported by any form of "policy" or "plan".').

[58]   Assembly of State Parties to the Rome Statute of the ICC (ICC-ASP), Elements of Crimes, art. 7, ICC-ASP/1/3 (Pt II-B) (9 September 2002).

[59]   See, for example, *Prosecutor* v. *Tadic*, Opinion and Judgement, note 53 *supra*, para. 653 ('Notably, if the acts occur on a widespread or systematic basis that demonstrates a policy to commit those acts, whether formalized or not').

[60]   *Prosecutor* v. *Katanga and Chui*, Case No. ICC-01/04-01/07, Decision on the Confirmation of Charges, 30 September 2008, para. 413, n. 545 (referencing a letter allegedly sent by one of the defendants discussing the details of a plan of attack).

[61]   But see M. BASSIOUNI, I THE LEGISLATIVE HISTORY OF THE INTERNATIONAL CRIMINAL COURT 151–2 (2005) (arguing that 'organizational policy' in the ICC Statute means 'policy of an organ of the state'); BASSIOUNI, note 10 *supra*, at 257 ('"Crimes against humanity" requires the use of the state's institutions, personnel and resources in order to commit, or refrain from preventing the commission of, the specific crimes described in [the various definitions of crimes against humanity].').

remains as to what kind of 'organization' is required. The ICC's case law will thus largely determine the content of the policy criterion.[62]

In practice, the ICC may find, like the ad hoc tribunals, that the existence of a widespread or systematic attack is reasonably easy to establish.[63] Although the concept of 'attack' in the definition of crimes against humanity does not require an armed conflict, as a practical matter most such attacks are part of armed conflicts. In other words, crimes against humanity generally involve leaders of armed conflicts illegally directing their attacks at civilians. These illegal attacks are often highly visible and notorious. As a result, in the practice of the ICTY, the existence of the contextual elements of crimes against humanity have often been stipulated by the parties or proven through expert testimony.[64] In fact, the ICTR has been willing simply to take judicial notice of the existence of a widespread or systematic attack against civilians during the Rwandan genocide.[65]

Directed Against Any Civilian Population

The contextual attack must be 'directed against' a civilian population, that is, the civilian population must be the primary target of the attack.[66] The term 'any' is used to highlight the inclusion within the definition of crimes committed by nationals of a state against fellow nationals, which was the original impetus for the formulation of this category of crimes after the Second World War. The ad hoc international criminal tribunals have adopted broad interpretations of the 'civilian' and 'population' criteria.[67] The latter has been interpreted simply to connote broad-based victimization, excluding small-scale crimes against isolated victims.[68] It is not necessary that the entire population of a particular geographic area be attacked,[69] but rather there must be a number of victims and some connection among them. In essence, the term 'population' seems simply to reiterate the requirement of a 'widespread or systematic attack'.[70]

The definition's restriction of the attack to a 'civilian' population has given rise to some controversy. Professor Cassese, a judge and eminent scholar of international criminal law, argues that the exclusion of military personnel from the class of victims of crimes against

---

[62]   Werle suggests that the ICC should interpret its Statute's policy element broadly so that it becomes 'essentially nothing more than an illustration of the requirements for the contextual element of a widespread or systematic attack on a civilian population'. Werle, note 51 *supra*, at 230.

[63]   Patricia M. Wald, *Genocide and Crimes Against Humanity*, 6 WASH. U GLOBAL STUD. L REV. 621, 630 (2007) (former ICTY judge notes that 'the "systematic or widespread" chapeau of crimes against humanity presents no great obstacle to prosecution').

[64]   *Ibid.* 630.

[65]   See *Semanza* v. *Prosecutor*, Case No. ICTR-97-20-A, Judgment, 20 May 2005, para. 192.

[66]   *Prosecutor* v. *Kunarac*, Case No. IT-96-23, Judgment, 22 February 2001, para. 421.

[67]   See, for example, *Prosecutor* v. *Kupreskic*, Case No. IT-95-16, Judgment, 14 January 2000, para. 547 ('It would seem that a wide definition of "civilian" and "population" is intended.').

[68]   See for example, *Prosecutor* v. *Kunarac*, Case No. IT-96-23/1-A, Judgment, 12 June 2002, para. 90 ('It is sufficient to show that enough individuals were targeted in the course of the attack, or that they were targeted in such a way as to satisfy the Chamber that the attack was in fact directed against a civilian "population", rather than against a limited and randomly selected number of individuals.').

[69]   *Prosecutor* v. *Kamuhanda*, Case No. ICTR-95-54A-T, Judgment, 22 January 2004, para. 669.

[70]   Ambos and Wirth, note 29 *supra*, at 21–2.

humanity does not comport with customary international law.[71] He points out that in times of peace, in particular, this limitation runs counter to the purposes of international human rights and humanitarian laws.[72] Nonetheless, this limitation is included in virtually every definition of crimes against humanity, including that of the ICC Statute, which tends to suggest it is required under customary international law.

In determining who qualifies as 'civilian', international tribunals tend to refer to analogous provisions in international humanitarian law, which protect those not actively engaged in hostilities.[73] They have thus broadly interpreted this criterion to include members of resistance movements and former combatants who are no longer participating in the conflict.[74] The categorization of targeted persons is made not simply according to their status, but rather by reference to the situation in which they find themselves when the crimes are committed.[75] Finally, the presence of combatants within a predominantly civilian population does not change the character of the population.[76]

Since most crimes against humanity are committed during armed conflicts, there is little jurisprudence concerning the content of 'civilian population' when such crimes are committed in peacetime. Only the ICTR has ruled on this question, holding that in the absence of armed conflict, all persons are civilians 'except those who have the duty to maintain public order and have the legitimate means to exercise force'.[77] This ruling appears to conflict with the principles underlying the law of crimes against humanity.[78] The purpose of the 'civilian' restriction is to exclude legal attacks on combatants from the purview of crimes against humanity. In peacetime, this restriction is irrelevant and all persons who have not taken up arms against the perpetrator should arguably be considered 'civilians' for the purposes of crimes against humanity even if they are tasked with maintaining public order.[79]

Nexus Between Individual Act and Attack

To constitute a crime against humanity, an individual's act must be 'part of' a widespread or systematic attack. This requirement comprises objective and subjective components.[80] First, the act must objectively – 'by its nature or consequences' – be part of the attack.[81] The objective component does not require, however, that the act was committed in the midst of the

---

[71]   Antonio Cassese, *Crimes Against Humanity*, in I THE ROME STATUTE OF THE INTERNATIONAL CRIMINAL COURT: A COMMENTARY 353, 375 (2002).

[72]   Antonio Cassese, *The Multifaceted Criminal Notion of Terrorism in International Law*, 4 J INT'L CRIM. JUST. 933, 949 (2006) ('Generally speaking, it would be contrary to the whole spirit and logic of modern international human rights law and humanitarian law to limit to civilians (especially in time of peace) the international protection of individuals against horrendous and large-scale atrocities.').

[73]   See for example, *Prosecutor* v. *Rutaganda*, Case No. ICTR-96-3, Judgment and Sentence, 6 December 1999, para. 72, n. 18.

[74]   See for example, *Prosecutor* v. *Blaskic*, Case No. IT-95-14-T, Trial Chamber Judgment, 3 March 2000, para. 214.

[75]   *Ibid.*

[76]   *Ibid.*

[77]   *Prosecutor* v. *Kayishema*, Case No. ICTR-95-1-T, Judgment, 21 May 1999, para. 128.

[78]   See Ambos and Wirth, note 29 *supra*, at 25.

[79]   See *ibid.* at 26.

[80]   *Prosecutor* v. *Kunarac*, Case No. IT-96-23/1-A, Judgment, 12 June 2002, para. 99.

[81]   *Ibid.*

attack. A crime can be part of an attack even if it is geographically or temporally distant from the attack as long as it is connected in some manner.[82] Judges take into account the particular circumstances involved in determining whether an act can 'reasonably be said to have been part of the attack'.[83]

It remains an open question whether the individual's act may itself be sufficient to constitute the attack on a civilian population. For example, can a single terrorist act that kills hundreds constitute a crime against humanity? The ICC's Elements of Crimes for genocide provide that the conduct must have taken place in the context of a pattern of similar conduct against a group or must itself constitute conduct that could effect the destruction of the group.[84] In contrast, the Elements of crimes against humanity do not provide the alternative that the defendant's conduct might itself constitute a widespread or systematic attack.[85] Nonetheless, it is at least arguable that a single act that causes massive harm should qualify as a crime against humanity.[86]

Second, the subjective or mental element of crimes against humanity requires that the perpetrator act with knowledge that his act is part of a widespread or systematic attack against a civilian population. Although an early decision of the ICTY suggested that the perpetrator must act with the specific intent or purpose to contribute to the attack,[87] subsequent decisions of all of the ad hoc tribunals, as well as the ICC Statute, confirm the knowledge standard.[88] In fact, the ad hoc tribunals have adopted a broad approach to this requirement, holding that the mental element is satisfied if the defendant knew, had reason to know,[89] or took the risk[90] that his or her act was part of the broader attack. The ICC Statute, on the other hand, includes a more restrictive understanding of 'knowledge', requiring 'awareness that a circumstance exists or a consequence will occur in the ordinary course of events'.[91] Thus, a question remains whether, under customary international law, crimes against humanity require actual knowledge that one's act is part of a widespread or systematic attack or, instead, it is sufficient to have assumed the risk of such a connection. Finally, the ICC Statute's Elements of Crimes specify a more stringent mental element '[i]n the case of an emerging widespread or systematic attack against a civilian population'.[92] When the defendant's acts are part of such an emerging attack, knowledge of the attack is not sufficient; instead, the perpetrator must

---

[82]   *Ibid.* para. 100.

[83]   *Ibid.*

[84]   Elements of Crimes, note 58 *supra*, art. 6.

[85]   *Ibid.* art. 7.

[86]   Compare Wald, note 63 *supra*, at 629 ('Granted, a loner can't commit a crime against humanity all by himself as in genocide, without a wider campaign against civilians in the background.') with Ambos and Wirth, note 29 *supra*, at 17 (stating that a single perpetrator acting once can commit a crime against humanity by, for example, poisoning the water supply for a large population).

[87]   See *Prosecutor* v. *Tadic*, Case No. IT-94-1-T, Judgment, 7 May 1997, para. 659.

[88]   See for example, *Prosecutor* v. *Blaskic*, Case No. IT-95-14-T, Judgment, 3 March 2000, paras 251–7; ICC Statute, note 4 *supra*, art. 7(1). For additional discussion of the mental element see deGuzman, note 25 *supra*, at 381–402; Ambos and Wirth, note 29 *supra*, at 36–42.

[89]   *Prosecutor* v. *Fofana and Kondewa*, Case No. SCSL-04-14-T, Judgment, 2 August 2007, para. 254.

[90]   *Prosecutor* v. *Kunarac*, Case No. IT-96-23, Judgment, 22 February 2001, para. 434; *Prosecutor* v. *Blaskic*, Case No. IT-95-14-T, Judgment, 3 March 2000, para. 254.

[91]   ICC Statute, art. 30(3).

[92]   Elements of Crimes, *supra* note 58, art. 7.

intend to further the attack.[93] It remains unclear when an attack should be considered 'emerging'.

The perpetrator's motive is irrelevant to the mental element – a crime committed for purely personal reasons nonetheless constitutes a crime against humanity if the perpetrator knows the act is part of the broader attack.[94] As such, unlike genocide, there is no requirement for crimes against humanity that the perpetrator act with discriminatory intent except with regard to the constitutive crime of persecution.[95] Furthermore, the perpetrator need not have detailed knowledge of the nature of the attack. The ICC Statute's Elements of Crimes note that the knowledge requirement 'should not be interpreted as requiring proof that the perpetrator had knowledge of all characteristics of the attack or the precise details of the plan or policy of the State or organization'.[96] This provision implies, however, contrary to what this author had suggested prior to its adoption, that the perpetrator must have *some* knowledge of the policy behind the attack.[97] The precise contours of this requirement remain to be determined. Of course, to the extent tribunals other than the ICC have rejected the policy element, they do not require the perpetrator to have any such knowledge.[98]

ENUMERATED ACTS

The elements of a crime against humanity include not only the contextual elements discussed above, but also the physical (*actus reus*) and mental (*mens rea*) elements associated with one or more of the underlying inhumane acts. Thus, for example, murder as a crime against humanity requires that the perpetrator (1) caused the death of another through act or omission (physical element); and (2) intended to kill or inflict grievous bodily harm on the victim knowing that death would likely result or, for the purposes of the ad hoc tribunals, acted in reckless disregard of such a possible result (mental element).[99]

Aside from the addition of apartheid and enforced disappearance, the ICC Statute's list of inhumane acts mirrors that of other international instruments and thus generally appears to reflect customary international law. Nonetheless, the negotiations surrounding the enumerated acts of 'persecution' and the catch-all reference to 'other inhumane acts' were particularly contentious due to concerns about the need for precision in criminal law.[100] Persecution

---

[93]   *Ibid.*

[94]   See *Prosecutor* v. *Tadic*, Case No. IT-94-1-A, Judgment, 15 July 1999, paras 271–2.

[95]   *Ibid.* at para. 305.

[96]   Elements of the Crimes, note 58 *supra*, art. 7. Note that the Elements' inclusion of 'plan' in addition to 'policy' is overridden by the Statute's exclusion of the plan alternative. See ICC Statute, art. 9(3) (stating that the Elements of the Crimes must be consistent with the Statute).

[97]   See deGuzman, note 25 *supra*, at 380. Compare Ambos and Wirth, note 29 *supra*, at 42 (arguing the existence of a policy is a necessary element of crimes against humanity and therefore the perpetrator must at least take the risk that the attack is pursuant to a policy).

[98]   *Prosecutor* v. *Kunarac*, Case No. IT-96-23/1-A, Judgment, 12 June 2002, para. 104.

[99]   See *Prosecutor* v. *Akayesu*, Case No. ICTR-96-4, Judgment, 2 September 1998, para. 589. The ICC Statute excludes the possibility of recklessness. For a discussion of the mental element of crimes against humanity under the ICC Statute see John D. Van der Vyver, *The International Criminal Court and the Concept of Mens Rea in International Criminal Law*, 12 U Miami Int'l & Comp. L Rev. 57, 94–109 (2004).

[100]   See von Hebel and Robinson, note 7 *supra*, at 101, 102.

is among the most widely charged of the inhumane acts which may constitute crimes against humanity, but courts have struggled to identify the requirements for this crime.[101] International tribunals have found a wide range of acts and omissions can constitute persecution when committed with discriminatory intent, including harassment, humiliation, psychological abuse,[102] destruction of property[103] and even hate speech.[104] In order to limit the range of acts subject to prosecution as persecution, the drafters of the ICC Statute defined it as 'the intentional and severe deprivation of fundamental rights contrary to international law by reason of the identity of the group or collectivity'.[105] The drafters further ensured that acts of persecution as crimes against humanity would reach a certain level of gravity by requiring that they be committed in connection with other crimes within the Court's jurisdiction.[106] Finally, the drafters constrained the ICC's ability to elaborate additional grounds of discrimination by mandating that any grounds of persecution other than those listed (political, racial, national, ethnic, cultural, religious and gender) must be 'universally recognized as impermissible under international law'.[107] Similarly, the residual category of 'other inhumane' acts was limited to those 'intentionally causing great suffering, or serious injury to body or to mental or physical health'.[108] In light of these restrictions, it remains for the ICC and other international tribunals to determine what acts constitute 'persecution' as well as when the standard for 'other inhumane acts' is satisfied.

NEED FOR A NORMATIVE FRAMEWORK

As the foregoing discussion demonstrates, a significant number of uncertainties remain with regard to the definition of crimes against humanity under customary international law and even under the ICC Statute. Thus, the call Professor Bassiouni issued 15 years ago for the international community to adopt a specialized convention addressing these crimes remains important today.[109] Such a convention would assist states in incorporating the prohibition of crimes against humanity into their national laws and encourage states to prosecute these crimes.

Ideally, a convention addressing crimes against humanity would reflect an international consensus on the underlying normative framework for this category of crimes. Much of the scholarly and judicial discussion of crimes against humanity has focused on the doctrine as it

---

[101]   Wald, note 63 *supra*, at 630.

[102]   See *Prosecutor* v. *Kvocka*, Case No. IT-98-30/1-T, Judgment, 2 November 2001, paras 1186–92.

[103]   See *Prosecutor* v. *Blaskic*, Case No. IT-95-14-T, Judgment, 3 March 2000, para. 227.

[104]   See *Prosecutor* v. *Nahimana*, Case No. ICTR-99-52-T, 3 December 2003, para. 1072.

[105]   ICC Statute, art. 7(2)(g).

[106]   *Ibid.* art. 7(1)(h).

[107]   *Ibid.*

[108]   *Ibid.* art. 7(1)(k).

[109]   M. Cherif Bassiouni, *'Crimes Against Humanity': The Need for a Specialized Convention*, 31 COLUM. J TRANSNAT'L L 457 (1994). Professor Bassiouni is currently leading a group of experts in the task of drafting such a convention. See *Harris World Law Institute Kicks Off Landmark Crimes Against Humanity Project*, Washington University in St. Louis News & Information, available at http://news-info.wustl.edu/news/page/normal/11641.html (last visited 25 November 2008).

has evolved since Nuremberg, with little attention paid to the normative underpinnings of these crimes. Definitions such as the one contained in the ICC Statute were crafted mostly by reference to prior definitions and case law rather than through critical analysis of the norms undergirding the international prohibition of crimes against humanity. As the international community continues to shape the definitions of these crimes for both existing and future international tribunals, as well as with respect to their implementation in national courts, additional focus should be placed on the philosophical justifications for these crimes. Such an orientation would help to bring normative and doctrinal coherence to this body of international criminal law. This section therefore suggests a number of possible normative lenses through which the law of crimes against humanity can be viewed.

As discussed above, the concept of crimes against humanity evolved out of the criminal prohibitions contained in the laws of war. The theoretical justification for international jurisdiction over war crimes was that the criminal conduct 'crossed borders' because it was committed during international armed conflict.[110] Thus, states had a direct interest in prosecuting the crimes even when they were committed outside their territories and by non-nationals. Crimes against humanity, on the other hand, were developed to capture crimes that did not cross borders – initially, Nazi crimes committed within German territory. The international community's interest in such crimes stems less from the presence of concrete international harm than from a moral conviction that such crimes must be punished. This normative difference between the justifications for the two types of crimes helps to explain the 'war nexus' discussed above. Since there was no precedent for the exercise of international criminal jurisdiction based solely on a moral interest, the Nuremberg Tribunal found it necessary to link crimes against humanity to war crimes for which there was an established basis of jurisdiction. Thus, the Nuremberg Tribunal refused jurisdiction over crimes – 'revolting and horrible' as they were – that were committed before the outbreak of the war.[111]

The ICTY Statute maintained the jurisdictional linkage to armed conflict, but included internal armed conflict within its scope. This moved the normative justification for such jurisdiction away from the cross-border harm of war toward a more general moral concern for the way conflicts are conducted, even within states. Ultimately, of course, the nexus with armed conflict was abandoned entirely, placing the theoretical justification for jurisdiction over these crimes squarely in the realm of moral principles. Thus, over time, crimes against humanity have become more closely associated with the moral norms at the heart of international human rights law than with their original progenitor, war crimes.

The term 'crimes against humanity' suggests that the *raison d'etre* of this category of crimes is that they harm or threaten harm to 'humanity' in addition to their more immediate victims. The relevant question, therefore, is what harm do these crimes inflict on 'humanity?' One view is that they threaten the peace and security of the world and therefore present a possibility of direct harm to each of its inhabitants. This rationale provided the impetus for the ILC's efforts to codify 'offenses against the peace and security of mankind'. However, the ILC found it quite difficult to identify a principled basis on which to determine which

---

[110]   See LARRY MAY, WAR CRIMES AND JUST WAR 14 (2007) ('In war crimes, borders have normally already been crossed; and because both offending and defending States are sovereign, there is no presumption that priority should be given to the exclusive jurisdiction of one State over another.').

[111]   International Military Tribunal (Nuremberg), Judgment and Sentences, reprinted in 41 AM. J INT'L L 172, 249 (1947).

crimes pose such a threat. In fact, a Special Rapporteur to the ILC struggling with this question lamented that 'the distinction between crimes under internal law and crimes under international law is relative and at times arbitrary'.[112] Initially, the ILC focused on whether the crimes had a 'political element'[113] and later on the 'seriousness' of the crimes.[114] As discussed below, however, the seriousness of the crimes can itself serve as an independent normative basis for jurisdiction. As such, it became unclear in the ILC's deliberations whether 'seriousness' was serving as a proxy for a threat to peace and security or instead had become an independent rationale for international criminalization.

The 'seriousness' or 'gravity' rationale for international crimes is sometimes expressed by describing the crimes as 'shocking the conscience of humanity'.[115] This expression mirrors the Martens Clause's invocation of 'the laws of humanity and the requirements of the public conscience' as a basis for legal protections.[116] In fact, there is often an assumption that crimes that shock the conscience of humanity also threaten the peace and security of the world. Thus, the ICC Statute's preamble equates 'unimaginable atrocities that deeply shock the conscience of humanity' with crimes that 'threatened the peace, security, and well-being of the world'.[117] The UN Security Council has invoked the common conscience on multiple occasions to justify using its Chapter VII powers, thereby linking the world's shock at atrocities to the maintenance of peace and security.[118] In such cases, the rationale for action often rests more on the moral repugnance of the harm occurring within borders than on the imminence of concrete cross-border harm.

Despite this linkage between the collective conscience and peace/security rationales, over time the former has acquired independent force as a normative basis for crimes against humanity.[119] There is little consensus, however, about what makes crimes sufficiently shocking or grave to merit international adjudication. Certainly, there is a tendency to focus on the scale of the crimes as reflected in the 'widespread' criterion in the definition. At the same time, many commentators are reluctant to ground the rationale for crimes against humanity in a quantitative analysis because of the implausibility of drawing a line: do crimes against humanity require ten victims, one hundred, or one thousand?[120] The systematic nature of the

---

112   Doudou Thiam, *First Report on the Draft Code of Offences Against the Peace and Security of Mankind*, UN Doc. A/CN.4/364, para. 35, reprinted in 2 YB ILC Pt 1 (1983), UN Doc. A/CN.4/SER.A/1994/Add.1.

113   ILC, *Report of the International Law Commission Covering Its Second Session*, 5 UN GAOR Supp. (No. 12), para. 149, UN Doc. A/1316 (1950), reprinted in 2 YB ILC 1, 379–80 (1950), UN Doc. A/CN.4/SER.A/1950/Add.1.

114   ILC, *Report of the International Law Commission on the Work of Its Thirty-fifth Session*, 38 UN GAOR Supp. (No. 10), paras 47–8, UN Doc. A/38/10 (1983), reprinted in 2 YB ICFL Pt 2, 1, 13–14 (1983), UN Doc. A/CN.4/SER.A/1983/Add.1 (Pt 2) (noting that the Commission 'unanimously agreed' that the Draft Code should cover 'the most serious of the most serious offenses').

115   See BRUCE BROOMHALL, INTERNATIONAL JUSTICE AND THE INTERNATIONAL CRIMINAL COURT: BETWEEN SOVEREIGNTY AND THE RULE OF LAW 49 (2003) (positing 'collective conscience' as the primary normative rationale for crimes against humanity).

116   Convention Respecting the Laws and Customs of War on Land, note 12 *supra*, pmbl.

117   ICC Statute, pmbl.

118   See BROOMHALL, note 115 *supra*, at 46, n. 80 (providing examples).

119   BROOMHALL, note 115 *supra*, at 46.

120   See for example, Richard Vernon, *What is a Crime Against Humanity?*, 10 J POLITICAL PHILOSOPHY 237–8 (2002); David Luban, *A Theory of Crimes Against Humanity*, 29 YALE J INT'L L 85, 108 (2004).

crimes, including perhaps their commission pursuant to a policy, presents an alternate basis on which to find them particularly grave. Here, the concern is that crimes committed systematically have a strongly increased potential for harm compared to random crimes. The ICC Statute's inclusion of a gravity threshold for admissibility[121] is stimulating scholarly interest in these questions.[122] The ICC Prosecutor has suggested a number of factors that might impact gravity for the purposes of admissibility before that Court, including the scale of the crimes, the nature of the crimes, the manner of commission of the crimes, and the impact of the crimes.[123] Such factors would also seem relevant to the determination whether one or more acts rises to the level of a crime against humanity.

A third normative rationale for international jurisdiction over crimes against humanity posits that these crimes capture the particular evil of the abuse of state power to harm rather than protect.[124] Sometimes, non-state organizations are included in this rationale as expressed in the ICC Statute's requirement of a state *or organizational* policy.[125] Although this approach certainly describes how crimes against humanity tend to be committed, it appears both over- and underinclusive as a normative explanation for these crimes. Not all inhumane state policies qualify as crimes against humanity. For example, much of the world considers the US policy of executing persons convicted of certain crimes inhumane and yet few would claim American executioners are committing crimes against humanity. Furthermore, there would seem to be no normative basis for excluding from the category of crimes against humanity an act committed by an individual non-state actor that causes extremely widespread harm. Why should an individual who spreads a deadly agent to destroy an ethnic group be guilty of genocide, but not a crime against humanity?[126]

Finally, some commentators focus on 'group-based harm' as the normative justification for crimes against humanity. According to David Luban, the international interest protected by crimes against humanity is the interest 'all human beings share ... in ensuring people are not killed solely because of their group affiliation'.[127] Similarly, for Larry May, international jurisdiction over crimes against humanity is justified because they harm groups, or in the alternative, are perpetrated by groups such as states.[128] May thus considers the group-based

---

[121]   ICC Statute, art. 17(d).

[122]   See for example, Margaret M. deGuzman, *Gravity and the Legitimacy of the International Criminal Court*, 32 FORDHAM INT'L LJ 1400 (2009); Kevin Jon Heller, *Situational Gravity Under the Rome Statute*, in FUTURE DIRECTIONS IN INTERNATIONAL CRIMINAL JUSTICE (Carsten Stahn and Larissa van den Herik eds, 2009). See also Sarah Nouwen, Chapter 9 on fine-tuning complementarity *infra*.

[123]   ICC Office of the Prosecutor, *Report on Prosecutorial Strategy* 5 (14 September 2006).

[124]   See for example, Vernon, note 120 *supra*, at 242 (arguing that crimes against humanity represent the abuse of state power through the systematic inversion of the jurisdictional resources of the state); BASSIOUNI, note 61 *supra*; JOSEPH B. KEENAN and BRENDAN FRANCIS BROWN, CRIMES AGAINST INTERNATIONAL LAW 117 (Washington, DC, 1950) ('[Crimes against humanity] are inhumanities which result from policy decisions made at the highest plane of civil or military authority. They are the effects of a definitely criminal State policy.'); Schabas, note 53 *supra*, at 982 ('Mainly, it is when perpetrators commit heinous acts precisely because they are acting on behalf of a State, and in pursuit of its policies that we require international justice to step in.').

[125]   ICC Statute, art. 7(2)(a). But see Bassiouni, note 61 *supra*, at 151–2 (arguing that 'organizational policy' in the ICC Statute means 'policy of an organ of the State').

[126]   Luban, note 120 *supra*, at 98.

[127]   *Ibid.* at 139.

[128]   LARRY MAY, CRIMES AGAINST HUMANITY 86 (2005).

nature of the crimes and the state action ground discussed above to be alternative rationales for these crimes, although in his 'ideal model' both are present.[129] Like the focus on state action, the notion that crimes against humanity target groups is descriptively accurate. Group-on-group harm, in particular harm committed on the basis of ethnicity and religion, remains the dominant modality of mass violence. Nonetheless, the notion of group-based harm does not seem to capture completely the moral impulse behind the prohibition of crimes against humanity. As Adil Haque notes, 'it is ... quite unlikely that the international community could justifiably remain indifferent to mass violence were it not for the special harm involved in non-individualized treatment'.[130] Here again, the question of scale seems pertinent. If a single perpetrator killed 1,000 victims who were not joined together in a particular group, why should that not constitute a crime against humanity?

The current definitions of crimes against humanity in various international instruments and decisions fail to address adequately these normative questions. Instead, they reflect a rather incoherent combination of normative perspectives. The Nuremberg and ICTY definitions view crimes against humanity through the lens of peace and security by linking these crimes to armed conflict. The ICC Statute and some of the jurisprudence of the ad hoc tribunals incorporate the focus on state action or policy, while other statutes and cases, such as those of the SCSL, place significant reliance on the gravity of the crimes. Finally, the ICTR and ECCC emphasize group-based harm by incorporating a discrimination requirement among the contextual elements. In sum, the failure of the international community to adopt a more coherent normative framework for crimes against humanity has led to significant inconsistencies in this body of international criminal law.

CONCLUSION

The law of crimes against humanity has developed largely in reaction to specific, horrific historical circumstances, in particular, the Holocaust, ethnic cleansing in the former Yugoslavia, and genocide in Rwanda. Definitions were crafted to enable the international community to prosecute such crimes while attempting to respect the principle of legality. Even the ICC Statute's definition, although theoretically crafted to respond to unforeseen future circumstances, reflects political compromises rather than a consistent and integrated normative framework. Thus, the norm prescribing crimes against humanity remains unclear in a number of respects. For example: Is a policy required? If so, must it be a state policy? What must the perpetrator know about the policy, if anything? Must the perpetrator have actual knowledge of the connection between his act and the broader attack or is recklessness sufficient? Can crimes against humanity target military personnel in peacetime? Can a single act with many victims qualify as a crime against humanity? What acts of persecution and 'other inhumane acts' rise to the level of crimes against humanity?

Furthermore, the relationship between crimes against humanity and genocide remains uncertain. The Genocide Convention proscribes substantially the same underlying conduct as

---

[129] *Ibid.* at 89.
[130] Adil Ahmad Haque, *Group Violence and Group Vengeance: Toward a Retributivist Theory of International Criminal Law*, 9 BUFF. CRIM. L REV. 273, 308 (2005).

the law of crimes against humanity, but instead of requiring a nexus with a broader attack on a civilian population, the indispensable element for genocide is the perpetrator's intent to destroy, in whole or in part, a national, ethnic, racial or religious group.[131] The ILC's early discussions of crimes against humanity reveal differing opinions among governments about the relationship between these crimes.[132] Judges and commentators continue to disagree about whether genocide is more serious than crimes against humanity.[133] Defendants, on the other hand, have clearly demonstrated that they would rather plead guilty to crimes against humanity,[134] as genocide carries a significantly greater stigma in the popular imagination.[135] Furthermore, the Genocide Convention arguably contains a serious 'blind spot' in excluding political groups from the list of groups targeted by that crime.[136] This means that, despite the supreme moral stigma associated with that crime, some of the world's greatest tragedies may not fit within the technical definition of genocide.[137] Future efforts to clarify the definition of crimes against humanity should therefore also address the relationship between these two crimes.

Now, more than ever, it is important for the international community to resolve the uncertainties and 'schizophrenias'[138] in the law governing crimes against humanity. Increasingly, states are incorporating crimes against humanity into their domestic law and prosecuting these crimes in their national courts. Thus, ambiguities in the definition of crimes against humanity affect not only international tribunals, but also the law applied in individual states. Furthermore, states are increasingly seeking to exercise universal jurisdiction over crimes against humanity and to require states harboring persons accused of these crimes to extradite or prosecute them. If states are to understand and fully implement their international legal

---

[131]   Convention on the Prevention and Punishment of the Crime of Genocide, art. II, 9 December 1948, 102 Stat. 3045, 78 UNTS 277.

[132]   See Boot, note 48 *supra*, at 461–3.

[133]   See for example, Steven R. Ratner, *Can We Compare Evils? The Enduring Debate on Crimes Against Humanity and Genocide*, 6 WASH. U GLOBAL STUD. L REV. 583 (2007); *Prosecutor v. Kambanda*, Case No. ICTR-97-23-S, Judgment and Sentencing, 14 September 1998, para. 14 (stating that although crimes against humanity are more serious than war crimes 'it seems more difficult for the Chamber to rank genocide and crimes against humanity in terms of their respective gravity'); *Prosecutor v. Serushago*, Case No. ICTR-98-39-S, Sentence, 5 February 1999, para. 15 ('[T]he Chamber is of the opinion that genocide constitutes the "crime of crimes", which must be taken into account when deciding the sentence.').

[134]   Wald, note 63 *supra*, at 627.

[135]   See Ratner, note 133 *supra*, at 583.

[136]   See Beth Van Schaack, *The Crime of Political Genocide: Repairing the Genocide Convention's Blind Spot*, 106 YALE LJ 2259 (1997).

[137]   For the debate on whether the recent atrocities in Darfur constitute genocide, compare David Luban, *Calling Genocide By Its Rightful Name: Lemkin's Word, Darfur, and the UN Report*, 7 CHI. J INT'L L 303 (2007) (arguing that crimes in Darfur should constitute genocide and that the definition of genocide should be amended to include the crime against humanity of extermination) with William A. Schabas, *Genocide, Crimes Against Humanity, and Darfur: The Commission of Inquiry's Findings of Genocide*, 27 CARDOZO L REV. 1703, 1720 (2006) (supporting the conclusion of the Darfur Commission that genocide had not been committed and arguing that 'genocide is reserved for the arguably most heinous crime against humanity, namely the intentional physical destruction of an ethnic group').

[138]   See Steven R. Ratner, *The Schizophrenias of International Criminal Law*, 33 TEX. INT'L LJ 237 (1998).

obligations with respect to crimes against humanity, a clear and generally-accepted definition of these crimes will be essential. Such a definition, in customary or treaty law, would be an essential piece in the development of a consistent and coherent normative framework of international criminal law.

5 Crimes against women under international criminal law

Kelly D. Askin

Since time immemorial, women have endured a number of abuses, particularly ones of a sexual nature, committed exclusively or disproportionately against them because of their gender. Over the centuries, women and girls have been treated as subservient to men, for it was they who ruled the world. Women's primary purposes were to serve man, bring him pleasure, bear him children, and take care of his children and household. That custom and attitude remains in some parts of the world, but in the twenty-first century, much of the globe now recognizes, at least in law, equality between men and women, notwithstanding some physical and anatomical differences between these two sexes.

As women have struggled for equality and autonomy domestically, they have also struggled internationally. Ironically, it has been in international courts where women have made the greatest progress in both clarifying international laws and in redressing international crimes.

The past 16 years in particular have witnessed unprecedented advancement in ending impunity for some of the most serious international crimes, such as war crimes, crimes against humanity and genocide. This improvement has been achieved through criminal trials of individuals by international or hybrid (mixed international and domestic) courts seated in Europe, Africa and Asia. In these courts, enormous – yet nonetheless grossly insufficient – progress has been made in holding some political and military leaders and others accountable for sex crimes. The prosecution of gender-related crimes (crimes committed primarily against women as a result of socially constructed norms and power imbalances) in these courts has been unparalleled in history. Crimes such as rape, sexual slavery, enforced prostitution, forced pregnancy, enforced sterilization, forced nudity, forced marriage, sexual mutilation, forced abortion, gendered persecution, and trafficking of women and children, are increasingly recognized and prosecuted as some of the most heinous of all crimes anyone could commit. When committed in the context of war, as part of a widespread or systematic attack, or with an intent to destroy a protected group, they are considered crimes so serious that they may threaten international peace and security.

While much of international criminal law doctrine has remained unchanged in the past 16 years, the existing rules are being tested, interpreted and enforced more than ever before. Jurisprudence from international criminal tribunals has recognized various forms of gender - related crimes constituting instruments of genocide, crimes of war, crimes against humanity, and forms of torture, persecution and slavery, among other crimes. These courts have confirmed that in addition to the deaths, injuries, destruction of homes, forced displacement, and other abuses inflicted on civilians during periods of war and mass oppression, women and girls are the primary (but not exclusive) targets of sexual violence. Particularly during wartime, sexual atrocities are inflicted both intentionally, as weapons of war, terror and destruction designed to harm an extended group, and opportunistically, because the atmosphere of war and the breakdown of law and order creates the opportunity.

The international criminal laws having the most direct relevance to gender-related crimes are the international conventions focused on genocide, torture, sex trafficking and slavery, the laws of armed conflict, and the proscription of crimes against humanity. Each of these will be examined below insofar as they relate to gender crimes. There is significant overlap between international humanitarian law, international criminal law and international human rights law, and more than one may be simultaneously applicable in a specific context. International humanitarian law applies only when armed conflict exists, whereas the crime of genocide and, generally speaking, crimes against humanity may be prosecuted regardless of any connection to war or armed conflict.

The focus in this chapter is on (1) international laws having the most impact on crimes committed against women and girls, and (2) how international criminal courts and tribunals have enforced these laws by prosecuting some of the crimes and developing the international jurisprudence.

The past 65 years have seen a variety of international war crimes tribunals, beginning with the two post-Second World War tribunals set up by the victorious Allied powers to prosecute German and Japanese war crime suspects: the International Military Tribunal at Nuremberg (IMT or Nuremberg Tribunal)[1] and the International Military Tribunal for the Far East (IMTFE or Tokyo Tribunal).[2] The next big step was the setting up of the two ad hoc tribunals by the UN Security Council, in 1993 and 1994 respectively, to prosecute atrocities in the former Yugoslavia (International Criminal Tribunal for the Former Yugoslavia, ICTY)[3] and in Rwanda (International Criminal Tribunal for Rwanda, ICTR).[4] These, in turn, foreshadowed the creation of the permanent International Criminal Court (ICC)[5] set up by an international treaty in Rome in 1998 and which came into force in July 2002. A parallel development has been the ad hoc hybrid courts set up by agreement between the respective countries and the United Nations to prosecute atrocities in Sierra Leone (Special Court for Sierra Leone, SCSL)[6] and in Cambodia (Extraordinary Chambers in the Courts of Cambodia, ECCC).[7] All of these courts are mandated to adjudicate cases of war crimes and crimes

---

[1]   Charter of the International Military Tribunal, (IMT Charter) 82 UNTS 279; 3 Bevans 1238; (1945). For the official record of the trial see, Trial of the Major War Criminals Before the International Military tribunal, Nov. 14, 1945 to Oct. 1, 1946 (1947), (IMT Docs) available at http://www.loc.gov/rr/frd/Military_Law/NT_major-war-criminals.html

[2]   Special Proclamation by the Supreme Commander for the Allied Powers at Tokyo, 19 January 1946, TIAS No. 1589, 4 Bevans 20. The Annex to the Special Proclamation contains the Charter of the International Military Tribunal for the Far East, 19 January 1946, 4 Bevans 21, as amended 26 April 1946, 4 Bevans 27 (IMTFE Charter). Documents of the Tokyo Trial are reproduced in THE TOKYO WAR CRIMES TRIAL: THE COMPLETE TRANSCRIPTS OF THE PROCEEDINGS OF THE INTERNATIONAL MILITARY TRIBUNAL FOR THE FAR EAST (R. Pritchard and S. Zaide eds, 1981) ('IMTFE Docs').

[3]   International Criminal Tribunal for the Former Yugoslavia, Security Council Res. 827, UN SCOR, 48th Sess., 3217th mtg at 29, UN Doc. S/827/1993 (1993) (ICTY).

[4]   International Criminal Tribunal for Rwanda, Security Council Res. 955, UN SCOR, 49th Sess., 3453d mtg at 15, UN Doc. S/INF/50 Annex (1994) (ICTR).

[5]   Rome Statute of the International Criminal Court, UN Doc. A/CONF.183/9 (1998), entered into force 1 July 2002.

[6]   Special Court for Sierra Leone, UN Doc. S/2002/246 (8 March 2002) (SCSL).

[7]   Law on the Establishment of Extraordinary Chambers in the Courts of Cambodia, General

against humanity, and all except the SCSL, also have the authority to prosecute genocide. Each court is mandated to prosecute rape crimes, as well as other gender-related crimes.

All of these institutions will be discussed in this chapter, but because the Yugoslav and Rwanda Tribunals have been around the longest, some 15 to 16 years, and they have set most of the precedents on gender-related crimes, these courts will be examined in the greatest detail.

INTERNATIONAL LAWS AND GENDER RELATED CRIMES

International Criminal Law Instruments

Four international instruments having criminal sanction, and which can have significant impact on gender crimes, are the Slavery Convention, the Genocide Convention, the Trafficking Protocol, and the Torture Convention. Enforcement of crimes proscribed in these treaties has been largely through international war crimes courts following, or even in the midst of, mass atrocities.

1926 Slavery Convention[8]

The 1926 Slavery Convention, which is designed to prevent and suppress the slave trade and to lead to the abolition of all forms of slavery, is supplemented by a subsequent treaty signed in 1953. These two international instruments make slavery an international crime and impose a duty on states parties to punish slavery. While not explicitly recognized in the treaties, sexual slavery and other forms of gender-related slave practices are common worldwide.

Article 1 of the Slavery Convention defines slavery as 'the status or condition of a person over whom any or all of the powers attaching to the right of ownership are exercised'. It makes explicit that:

> [The] slave trade includes all acts involved in the capture, acquisition or disposal of a person with intent to reduce him to slavery; all acts involved in the acquisition of a slave with a view to selling or exchanging him; all acts of disposal by sale or exchange of a slave acquired with a view to being sold or exchanged, and, in general, every act of trade or transport in slaves.

Article 6 of the Convention requires that states parties without adequate provisions to punish slavery must adopt measures imposing 'severe penalties' for the crime.

1956 Supplemental Slavery Convention[9]

In its Preamble, the Supplementary Convention on the Abolition of Slavery, the Slave Trade, and Institutions and Practices Similar to Slavery stresses that the 1926 Slavery Convention

---

Asssembly Res. 57/228, UN Doc. A/RES/57/228 (18 December 2002) (ECCC). The ECCC is also known as the Khmer Rouge Tribunal or KRT.

[8]   Slavery Convention, signed at Geneva on 25 September 1926, entered into force 9 March 1927, in accordance with art. 12.

[9]   Supplementary Convention on the Abolition of Slavery, the Slave Trade, and Institutions and Practices Similar to Slavery, 226 UNTS 3, entered into force 30 April 1957) ('Supplemental Slavery Convention').

needs to be augmented in order to 'intensify national as well as international efforts towards the abolition of slavery, the slave trade and institutions and practices similar to slavery'. This Convention adopted the same definition of slavery as in the 1926 Treaty, and among other things, obliges states parties to 'take all practicable and necessary legislative and other measures to bring about progressively and as soon as possible the complete abolition or abandonment' of any institution or practice under which:

(i)   A woman, without the right to refuse, is promised or given in marriage on payment of a consideration in money or in kind to her parents, guardian, family or any other person or group; or

(ii)   The husband of a woman, his family, or his clan, has the right to transfer her to another person for value received or otherwise; or

(iii)   A woman on the death of her husband is liable to be inherited by another person.[10]

Article 5 makes clear that attempts, conspiracies, accessories and other acts are also covered by the Convention, and states that 'mutilating, branding or otherwise marking a slave or a person of servile status in order to indicate his status, or as a punishment, or for any other reason' also incurs criminal penalties. Article 6 emphasizes that slavery and slavery-like practices 'shall be a criminal offence' and the individuals convicted of the crime 'liable to punishment'.

As examined below, rape and enslavement have been jointly prosecuted in the ICTY for acts constituting sexual slavery. Sexual slavery is expressly listed as a crime in the Statutes of the ICC and the SCSL and both of these courts have indicted for the crime.

1949 Genocide Convention[11]

The Convention on the Prevention and Punishment of the Crime of Genocide was adopted by the UN General Assembly in 1949, following horrific crimes committed against targeted groups, particularly Jews, during the Second World War. Its Preamble considers that 'genocide is a crime under international law, contrary to the spirit and aims of the United Nations and condemned by the civilized world', it recognizes that 'at all periods of history genocide has inflicted great losses on humanity', and notes that international cooperation in needed 'in order to liberate mankind from such an odious scourge'.

Article I of the Genocide Convention confirms that genocide is an international crime, whether committed in wartime or peacetime, and obliges states parties to prevent and punish the crime. In article II, genocide is defined as:

[A]ny of the following acts committed with intent to destroy, in whole or in part, a national, ethnical, racial or religious group, as such:
(a)   killing members of the group;
(b)   causing serious bodily or mental harm to members of the group;
(c)   deliberately inflicting on the group conditions of life calculated to bring about its physical destruction in whole or in part;
(d)   imposing measures intended to prevent births within the group;
(e)   forcibly transferring children of the group to another group.

---

[10]   Supplemental Slavery Convention, art. 1.
[11]   Convention on the Prevention and Punishment of the Crime of Genocide, 3 December 1948, 78 UNTS 277, entered into force 12 January 1951) ('Genocide Convention').

Articles III and IV make not only genocide, but also conspiracy to commit genocide, direct and public incitement to genocide, attempt to commit genocide, and complicity in genocide, all punishable crimes, regardless of whether the person responsible is a leader, public official, or private individual. Article V obliges states parties to enact legislation which provides effective penalties for the crime, and article VI specifies that anyone charged with genocide must be tried by a competent domestic or international criminal tribunal.

As discussed later in this chapter, the Rwanda and Yugoslav Tribunals have successfully prosecuted sexual violence as an instrument of genocide used in Rwanda and Bosnia. The ICC is poised to follow suit. In July 2008, the ICC Prosecutor presented evidence of crimes committed in Darfur, Sudan, to the judges of the ICC, requesting that an arrest warrant be issued against the President of Sudan for genocide, including for crimes of sexual violence as part of the genocide. The Pre-Trial Chamber issued an arrest warrant in March 2009. Although it did not charge the President with genocide, it did specifically charge him with rape as a crime against humanity.

Convention Against Torture[12]
The Preamble to the Convention against Torture and Other Cruel, Inhuman or Degrading Treatment or Punishment (CAT), adopted in 1984, invokes the principles contained in the Charter of the United Nations and the inalienable rights enshrined in the Universal Declaration for Human Rights and International Covenant on Civil and Political Rights, in declaring its opposition to torture and torture-like practices which disrespect human dignity.

In article 1, torture is defined, for the purposes of the treaty, as:

> [A]ny act by which severe pain or suffering, whether physical or mental, is intentionally inflicted on a person for such purposes as obtaining from him or a third person information or a confession, punishing him for an act he or a third person has committed or is suspected of having committed, or intimidating or coercing him or a third person, or for any reason based on discrimination of any kind, when such pain or suffering is inflicted by or at the instigation of or with the consent or acquiescence of a public official or other person acting in an official capacity. It does not include pain or suffering arising only from, inherent in or incidental to lawful sanctions.

The Convention requires parties to criminalize torture and to take extra measures to prevent the crime. It also obliges states to investigate torture and to either prosecute or extradite offenders, so that there is harsh punishment when it occurs. The Convention Against Torture prohibits torture at all times and in all situations, emphasizing that 'no exceptional circumstances whatsoever, whether a state of war or a threat of war, internal political instability or any other public emergency, may be invoked as a justification of torture'.[13]

The Yugoslav and Rwanda Tribunals have recognized various forms of sexual violence against both males and females as torture, including torture by means of rape.

---

    [12]   Convention Against Torture and Other Cruel, Inhuman or Degrading Treatment or Punishment, General Assembly Res. 39/46, Annex, 39 UN GAOR Supp. (No. 51) 197, UN Doc. A/39/51 (1984), entered into force 26 June 1987 (CAT.
    [13]   CAT, arts 2, 4–9, 12 and 16.

Trafficking Protocol[14]

The Protocol to Prevent, Suppress and Punish Trafficking in Persons, Especially Women and Children was adopted in 2001 as a separate instrument designed to supplement the UN Convention Against Transnational Organized Crime. Article 2 of the Protocol recognizes that effective action is needed in order to prevent and combat trafficking, especially that of women and children. Article 4 focuses not only on prevention, but on investigation and prosecution of certain trafficking offenses, and article 5 focuses on criminalizing trafficking through legislation and other appropriate measures.

In February 2009, the UN Office on Drugs and Crime published its *Global Report on Trafficking in Persons*. Its Preface states: 'The term *trafficking in persons* can be misleading: it places emphasis on the *transaction* aspects of a crime that is more accurately described as *enslavement*. Exploitation of people, day after day. For years on end.' It further notes that 'sexual exploitation is by far the most commonly identified form of human trafficking (79%)'.[15]

The ICC incorporates 'trafficking in persons, in particular women and children' into its definition of enslavement, which can be prosecuted as a crime against humanity under article 7(1)(c) of its Statute.

International Humanitarian Law

International humanitarian law, the law of war, strives to lessen the horrors of war on combatants and non-combatants and insists upon humane treatment. Fundamental principles of humanitarian law are that combatants may never target civilians for attack and that robust efforts must be made to protect them from even collateral (incidental or accidental) harm. All individuals, civilian or combatant, must be treated as humanely as possible under the circumstances. Failing to honor these principles may constitute a war crime.

Historically, and indeed until a few hundred years ago, wartime sexual violence was not necessarily a crime. In domestic laws and practices, women were long (and sometimes still) regarded as men's (typically, fathers', then husbands' or sons') 'property'. The rape of a woman was viewed as an offense against the man, not the woman, for violating something (the woman) that the man owned or had entitlement to. During periods of war, women were considered booty, rightfully belonging to the victors as legitimate spoils of war. By the Middle Ages, the right to rape or enslave captured women was used by military leaders as an incentive or reward to their men for taking a village. Once customary international law began prohibiting rape, sexual violence was less blatantly encouraged, but military commanders regularly turned a blind eye to its commission. As rape became explicitly prohibited, it was still largely considered a mere inevitable by-product of war, not a serious crime.[16]

---

14   Protocol to Prevent, Suppress and Punish Trafficking in Persons, Especially Women and Children, Supplementing the United Nations Convention Against Transnational Organized Crime, General Asssembly Res. 25, Annex II, UN GAOR, 55th Sess., Supp. No. 49, 60, UN Doc. A/45/49 (2001), entered into force 9 September 2003.

15   UNODC, *Global Report on Trafficking in Persons* 6 (February, 2009) (emphasis in original).

16   For a detailed analysis of the development of gender crimes under customary law, see KELLY DAWN ASKIN, WAR CRIMES AGAINST WOMEN: PROSECUTION IN INTERNATIONAL WAR CRIMES TRIBUNALS 1–48 (1997).

Serious violations of humanitarian law entail the criminal responsibility of the individual perpetrator or of others responsible for the crimes, including military or political leaders who fail to take appropriate measures to prevent or halt the crimes, or to punish subordinates responsible.[17] The principal international humanitarian law treaties that regulate contemporary armed conflicts are the 1907 Hague Conventions and Regulations, the four 1949 Geneva Conventions along with annexes to these Conventions, and the two 1977 Additional Protocols to the Geneva Conventions. All or parts of these instruments are recognized as customary international law. The Hague treaties regulating warfare can be said to prohibit rape by their provision insisting that 'family honour and rights, the lives of persons … must be respected'.[18]

Prior to the mid-1800s, before the first treaties on the laws of war were signed in Geneva and in The Hague, customary law, along with domestic military codes, regulated armed conflict. Rape had been prohibited by customs of war on some continents since at least the fourteenth century.[19] In 1863, the United States surveyed customary laws of war and codified these laws into a US Army military manual regulating the laws of land warfare. This US military code listed rape by a combatant as one of the most serious war crimes, warranting the death penalty. Article 44 stated that 'all rape … is prohibited under the penalty of death'.[20]

All international war crimes courts have prosecuted rape, either implicitly or explicitly. The first ad hoc international military court trial, held by the Holy Roman Empire in 1474, tried Sir Peter Hagenbach for a series of crimes, including rape crimes, committed by his subordinates during the occupation of Breisach. He was found guilty of war crimes and sentenced to death.[21]

The post-Second World War international war crimes trials were set up by the victorious Allied powers and were held in Nuremberg and Tokyo to prosecute senior Nazi and Japanese leaders accused of war crimes, crimes against peace, and crimes against humanity. At the International Military Tribunal held in Nuremberg,[22] rape and other forms of sexual violence were prosecuted to a limited extent. Although sex crimes were not explicitly listed in the IMT indictment or cited in the judgment, a sordid variety of sex offences entered into evidence at

---

[17]   ICC Statute, arts 25 and 28.

[18]   Convention Concerning the Laws and Customs of War on Land, 18 October 1907, 36 Stat. 2277, 3 Martens Nouveau Recueil (ser. 3) (Hague Convention IV), Annex to the Convention, Regulations Respecting the Laws and Customs of War on Land, art. 46.

[19]   See discussion in Askin, note 16 *supra*, at 18–35.

[20]   Instructions for the Government of the United States in the Field by Order of the Secretary of War, Washington, DC (24 April 1863); Rules of Land Warfare, War Dept Doc. No. 467, Office of the Chief of Staff (GPO 1917) (approved 25 April 1914), known as the Lieber Code or as General Orders No. 100. Article 47 dictated that 'crimes punishable by all penal codes, such as … rape … are not only punishable as at home, but in all cases in which death is not inflicted, the severer punishment shall be preferred'.

[21]   See discussion in William Parks, COMMAND RESPONSIBILITY FOR WAR CRIMES, 62 MIL. L REV. 1 (1973); M. CHERIF BASSIOUNI, INTERNATIONAL CRIMINAL LAW: A DRAFT INTERNATIONAL CRIMINAL CODE 8 (1980); TELFORD TAYLOR, NUREMBERG AND VIETNAM: AN AMERICAN TRAGEDY 81–2 (1970); Theodor Meron, *Shakespeare's Henry the Fifth and the Law of War*, 86 AM. J INT'L L 1 (1992).

[22]   Charter of the International Military Tribunal, Annexed to the Agreement for the Prosecution and Punishment of the Major War Criminals of the European Axis ('London Agreement'), 8 August 1945, 82 UNTS 59; 279 Stat. 1544.

trial and can be considered subsumed within the persecution charge.[23] Before the International Military Tribunal for the Far East held in Tokyo, gender crimes were indicted as war crimes charges of 'inhumane treatment', 'mistreatment', 'ill-treatment', and 'failure to respect family honour and rights'.[24] As a result of these charges, the IMTFE held General Matsui, Commander Hata and Foreign Minister Hirota criminally responsible for a series of crimes, including rape crimes, committed by subordinates.[25]

In another post-Second World War war crimes trial held in Asia by the US military commission, General Yamashita, commander of the Fourteenth Area Army of Japan, was charged with failing to exercise adequate control over his troops, who had devastated Manila, Philippines through a campaign of rape, murder and pillage. At his trial, Yamashita was found guilty of failing in his command responsibility to prevent these atrocities and sentenced to death for these crimes.[26]

The atrocities committed during the Second World War came on the heels of horrific crimes committed during the First World War. As a result, after the war ended in 1945, the international community joined to strengthen international laws of war. In 1949, the Geneva Conventions were amended, and a new treaty protecting civilians was added. The 1949 Geneva Conventions are now the principal international humanitarian law treaties governing the treatment of combatants and non-combatants during wartime. Article 27 of the Fourth Geneva Convention, which protects the civilian population, states:

> Protected persons are entitled, in all circumstances, to respect for their persons, their honour, their family rights, their religious convictions and practices, and their manners and customs. They shall at all times be humanely treated, and shall be protected especially against all acts of violence or threats thereof and against insults and public curiosity. Women shall be especially protected against any attack on their honour, in particular against rape, enforced prostitution, or any form of indecent assault.[27]

In 1977, the 1949 Geneva Conventions were supplemented by two Additional Protocols, the first Protocol regulating international armed conflicts and the second regulating non-international armed conflicts. Article 76(1) of Protocol I states: 'Women shall be the object of special respect and shall be protected in particular against rape, forced prostitution and any other form of indecent assault'.[28] Article 4(2)(e) of Protocol II similarly prohibits 'outrages

---

23   See IMT Docs, note 1 *supra*. For some examples of documentation of sexual violence by the IMT, see, for example, vol. 2, transcript at 139; vol. 6, transcript at 211–14, 404–7; vol. 7, transcript at 449–67; vol. 10, transcript at 381.

24   For some examples of documentation of sexual violence by the tribunal, see IMTFE Docs, note 2 *supra*, vol. 2, transcript at 2568–73, 2584, 2593–5, 3904–4, 4463–79, 4496–8, 4501–36, 4544, 4559, 4572–3, 4594, 4602, 4615, 4638, 4642, 4647; vol. 6, transcript at 12521–48, 12995, 13117, 13189, 13641–2, 13652.

25   THE TOKYO JUDGMENT: THE INTERNATIONAL MILITARY TRIBUNAL FOR THE FAR EAST 446–54 (B.V.A. Roling and C.F. Ruter eds, 1977).

26   *In re Yamashita*, 327 US 1 (1946).

27   Geneva Convention (IV) Relative to the Protection of Civilian Persons in Time of War, 6 UST 3516, 75 UNTS 287 (Fourth Geneva Convention), art. 27. The 1949 Geneva Conventions supersede the 1864, 1906 and 1929 Geneva Conventions.

28   Protocol Additional to the Geneva Conventions of 12 August 1949, and Relating to the Protection of Victims of International Armed Conflicts, 8 June 1977, 1125 UNTS 3, 16 ILM 1331, entered into force 7 December 1978) ('Additional Protocol I').

upon personal dignity, in particular humiliating and degrading treatment, rape, enforced prostitution and any form of indecent assault'.[29] While the provisions expressly include rape and enforced prostitution, they regrettably identify rape as a violation of honor or dignity, disregarding its violent nature and perpetuating gendered stereotypes. The ICC Statute, on the other hand, disconnects rape and other forms of sexual violence from crimes of dignity or honor.[30]

International Human Rights Instruments

Most international human rights laws remain applicable during war and upheaval. The Universal Declaration of Human Rights (UDHR) and the International Covenant on Civil and Political Rights (ICCPR) denounce all forms of slavery, torture, and inhuman or degrading treatment. The right to be free from such abuses is non-derogable.[31] The Convention on the Rights of the Child obliges states to protect children from sexual assault and torture and to respect rules of humanitarian law.[32] The core provisions of the Convention on the Elimination of All Forms of Discrimination against Women ('Women's Convention')[33] remain applicable during wartime. International human rights law thus supplements and strengthens international criminal law.

In addition to treaties, customary international law is also of relevance to gender-related crimes. Customary international law is grounded in the notion of tacit agreement or consent. It is based on the general and consistent practice of states which, when motivated by a sense of legal obligation (*opinio juris*), is evidence of acceptance of or acquiescence to such an obligation. Some international crimes, including genocide, war crimes, torture, slavery and crimes against humanity, have achieved *jus cogens* status, meaning that those crimes are prohibited at all times and in all places. Peremptory norms supersede any treaty or custom to the contrary. Except for war crimes, these crimes do not need a nexus to a war or require ratification of a treaty; they are crimes that are so grave they can be prosecuted by any state on the basis of universal jurisdiction.[34]

---

[29]   Protocol Additional to the Geneva Conventions of 12 August 1949, and Relating to the Protection of Victims of Non-International Armed Conflicts, 8 June 1977, S. Treaty Doc. No. 100-2, 1125 UNTS 609, entered into force 7 December 1978) ('Additional Protocol II').

[30]   ICC Statute, art. 9 on war crimes, lists 'committing outrages upon personal dignity, in particular humiliating and degrading treatment' under art. 9(2)(b)(xxi) and 9(2)(c)(ii), whereas various forms of sexual violence are listed under art. 9(2)(b)(xxii) and 9(2)(e)(vi).

[31]   Universal Declaration of Human Rights, arts. 1, 2, 3, 4, 5, 7, 12,UN GAOR, 3d Sess. Pt I, UN Doc. A/810/171 (1948) (UDHR); International Covenant on Civil and Political Rights, arts 4(2), 6–8, 16 December 1966, 999 UNTS 171, 6 ILM 368 (1967), entered into force on 23 March 1976 (ICCPR).

[32]   Convention on the Rights of the Child, arts 34, 37, 38, 20 November 1989, 28 ILM 1448, entered into force on 2 September 1990.

[33]   Convention on the Elimination of all Forms of Discrimination Sgainst Women, 18 December 1979, 1249 UNTS 13, 19 ILM 33, entered into force 3 September 1981, as interpreted by the Committee on the Elimination of Discrimination of Violence Against Women, General Recommendation No. 19, UN GAOR, 49th Sess., Supp. No. 38, 1, UN Doc A/47/38 (1993) (adopted on 29 January 1992).

[34]   See Naomi Roht-Arriaza and Menaka Fernando, Chapter 15 for more information on *jus cogens* crimes and on universal jurisdiction.

Grave breaches of the Geneva Conventions

Each of the 1949 Geneva Conventions provides a list of acts considered 'grave breaches' which incur criminal penalties when committed against persons or property protected by the Convention. Article 147 of the Fourth Geneva Convention, which protects the civilian population, enumerates the grave breaches as: 'willful killing, torture or inhuman treatment, including biological experiments, willfully causing great suffering or serious injury to body or health, unlawful deportation or unlawful confinement of a protected person'.

Although forms of sexual violence are not explicitly listed as grave breaches, sex crimes are covered by several provisions, particularly torture, inhuman treatment, willfully causing great suffering, and serious injury to body or health.

Violations of common article 3 of the Geneva Conventions

The term 'common article 3' refers to the identical language found in article 3 of each of the four 1949 Geneva Conventions. Common article 3 is regarded as a 'mini convention' within the Geneva Conventions as it was originally intended to be the provision regulating the treatment of persons in internal conflicts. However, common article 3 is now recognized as part of customary international law, applicable to both internal and international armed conflicts alike. Additional Protocol II, which governs internal conflicts, and which is also included within the jurisdiction of the Rwanda Tribunal, in Article 4 of its Statute, uses similar language. Common article 3 requires that humane treatment be afforded to 'persons taking no active part in the hostilities, including members of armed forces who have laid down their arms and those placed *hors de combat* by sickness, wounds, detention, or any other cause'. Among other things, it prohibits: '(a) Violence to life and person, in particular murder of all kinds, mutilation, cruel treatment and torture' and '(c) Outrages upon personal dignity, in particular humiliating and degrading treatment'.

The jurisprudence of the tribunals, as discussed below, confirms that common article 3 encompasses various forms of sexual violence. The ICTY Appeals Chamber has recognized that violations of common article 3 may qualify as violations of the laws or customs of war.[35]

Violations of the laws or customs of war

Serious violations of the laws or the customs of war, such as murder, torture and rape, may be prosecuted as war crimes. The ICTY authorizes prosecutions of violations of the laws or customs of war under article 3 of its Statute, which has been interpreted as having a 'catch-all' residual function with regard to war crimes.[36] The ICTY Appeals Chamber has detailed the requirements for when an act constitutes a serious violation of the laws or customs of war:

(i) the violation must constitute an infringement of a rule of international humanitarian law;

(ii) the rule must be customary in nature or, if it belongs to treaty law, the required conditions must be met ...;

(iii) the violation must be 'serious', that is to say, it must constitute a breach of a rule protecting important values, and the breach must involve grave consequences for the victim...;

(iv) the violation of the rule must entail, under customary or conventional law, the individual criminal responsibility of the person breaching the rule.[37]

---

[35] *Prosecutor* v. *Tadic,* Case No. IT-94-1-AR72, Decision on the Defense Motion for Interlocutory Appeal on Jurisdiction, 2 October 1995, reprinted in 35 ILM 32 (1996), paras 87–98.

[36] *Ibid.* para. 91.

[37] *Ibid.* para. 94.

The Yugoslav and Rwanda Tribunals have prosecuted gender-related crimes as grave breaches, as violations of common article 3, and most often, as violations of the laws or customs of war. This latter rubric allows the prosecution of war crimes without requiring proof of an armed conflict. Many of the charges for rape crimes, as well as other crimes, are pled under multiple articles, and in the alternative.

PROSECUTING INTERNATIONAL GENDER CRIMES IN WAR CRIMES TRIBUNALS

Prosecuting Sexual Violence as War Crimes

Rape as a war crime
The *Akayesu* Trial Chamber judgment[38] of the ICTR was the first court decision in history to define rape and sexual violence under international law. In this September 1998 judgment, the first judgment handed down by the ICTR, the Trial Chamber noted that while national jurisdictions have historically defined rape as 'non-consensual sexual intercourse', a broader definition was warranted to include 'acts which involve the insertion of objects and/or the use of bodily orifices not considered to be intrinsically sexual'.[39] It thus *defined* rape under international law as 'a physical invasion of a sexual nature, committed on a person under circumstances which are coercive'. Sexual violence, which is broader than rape, is defined by the Trial Chamber as 'any act of a sexual nature which is committed on a person under circumstances which are coercive. Sexual violence is not limited to physical invasion of the human body and may include acts which do not involve penetration or even physical contact'.[40] These definitions apply regardless of whether rape is being charged as a war crime or a crime against humanity.

Further, the *Akayesu* Trial Chamber emphasized that the amount of coercion required does not need to amount to physical force, as 'threats, intimidation, extortion and other forms of duress which prey on fear or desperation may constitute coercion' and it stressed that coercion may be 'inherent' in armed conflict situations or when military personnel, such as militia, are present.[41]

In the *Kunarac* trial before the ICTY, four men were charged with various forms of sexual violence committed in Foca municipality in Bosnia. The *Kunarac* Trial Chamber set out the *elements* of rape under international law:

> [T]he *actus reus* of the crime of rape in international law is constituted by: the sexual penetration, however slight: (a) of the vagina or anus of the victim by the penis of the perpetrator or any other object used by the perpetrator; or (b) the mouth of the victim by the penis of the perpetrator; where such sexual penetration occurs without the consent of the victim. Consent for this purpose must be consent given voluntarily, as a result of the victim's free will, assessed in the context of the surrounding circumstances. The *mens rea* is the intention to effect this sexual penetration, and the knowledge that it occurs without the consent of the victim.[42]

---

[38] *Prosecutor* v. *Akayesu*, Case No. ICTR-96-4-T, Judgment, 2 September 1998.
[39] *Ibid*. para. 686.
[40] *Ibid*. para. 688.
[41] *Ibid*. para. 688.
[42] *Prosecutor* v. *Kunarac et al.*, Case Nos IT-96-23-T and IT-96-23/1-T, Judgment 22 February 2001, paras 127–9.

By adding a lack of consent or free will into the elements of the crime, the *Kunarac* Trial Chamber modified the elements of rape which had been articulated by a previous Trial Chamber, stating that 'the *Furundzija* definition does not refer to other factors which would render an act of sexual penetration non-consensual or non-voluntary on the part of the victim'.[43] It emphasized that while force, threat of force or coercion are relevant, these factors are not exhaustive and the emphasis must be placed on violations of sexual autonomy, since 'the true common denominator which unifies the various systems may be a wider or more basic principle of penalising violations of sexual autonomy'.[44]

The *Kunarac* Trial Chamber held that sexual autonomy is violated 'wherever the person subjected to the act has not freely agreed to it or is otherwise not a voluntary participant'.[45] Concluding that most common law systems define rape by the absence of free will or genuine consent, the Trial Chamber identified three broad categories of factors to be used to determine when sexual activity should be classified as rape:

(i)   the sexual activity is accompanied by force or threat of force to the victim or a third party;
(ii)   the sexual activity is accompanied by force or a variety of other specified circumstances which made the victim particularly vulnerable or negated her ability to make an informed refusal; or
(iii) the sexual activity occurs without the consent of the victim.[46]

The ICC Statute imposes an additional jurisdictional requirement which is that war crimes must be 'committed as part of a plan or policy or as part of a large-scale commission of such crimes'.[47] The effect upon customary international law is limited by the fact that the Statute is a treaty which explicitly notes that it should not be 'interpreted as limiting or prejudicing in any way existing or developing rules of international law for purposes other than this Statute'.[48] The ICC's Elements of the Crimes, articulates the elements of the war crime of rape under article 8(2)(b)(xxii) of the ICC Statute to be:

1. The perpetrator invaded the body of a person by conduct resulting in penetration, however slight, of any part of the body of the victim or of the perpetrator with a sexual organ, or of the anal or genital opening of the victim with any object or any other part of the body.
2. The invasion was committed by force, or by threat of force or coercion, such as that caused by fear of violence, duress, detention, psychological oppression or abuse of power, against such person or another person, or by taking advantage of a coercive environment, or the invasion was committed against a person incapable of giving genuine consent.
3. The conduct took place in the context of and was associated with an international armed conflict.
4. The perpetrator was aware of factual circumstances that established the existence of an armed conflict.[49]

---

[43]   *Ibid.* para. 438.
[44]   *Ibid.* para. 440.
[45]   *Ibid.* para. 457.
[46]   *Ibid.* para. 442.
[47]   ICC Statute, art. 8.
[48]   *Ibid.* art. 10.
[49]   ICC Elements of the Crimes, ICC-ASP/1/3(Pt II-B), adopted on 9 September 2002, entered into force 9 September 2002).

Because 'rape' is not explicitly listed as a war crime in the ICTY Statute, it has primarily been prosecuted under other war crimes language of that Statute (that is, as torture or other specifically enumerated crimes). 'Rape' is listed as a war crime under article 4 of the ICTR Statute, under the rubric 'Violations of Common Article 3', which allows for the prosecution of '[o]utrages upon personal dignity, in particular humiliating and degrading treatment, rape, enforced prostitution and any form of indecent assault'.[50] Yet, in part because the ICTR has focused largely on the crime of genocide, and in part due to poor pleading, there have been no war crime convictions for rape in the Rwanda Tribunal's 15-year history.

Torture as a war crime for sexual violence
The *Celebici* Trial Chamber judgment of the ICTY, handed down on 16 November 1998, was the first instance of contemporary international tribunals prosecuting gender crimes as the war crime of torture.[51] In this case, four suspects were on trial for various war crimes charged as grave breaches of the 1949 Geneva Conventions and as violations of common article 3 of the Geneva Conventions constituting violations of the laws or customs of war. They were charged with an assortment of abuses, including sexual violence, committed against both female and male detainees in Celebici prison camp in Bosnia. Most of the charges were for superior responsibility, for crimes committed by subordinates in the camp which those on trial failed to prevent, halt or punish, although direct individual responsibility was also charged for an incident in which one of the accused (Delic) physically perpetrated rapes. The war crimes were charged as unlawful confinement of civilians, willfully causing great suffering, cruel treatment, willful killing, murder, torture, inhuman treatment and plunder. The indictment alleged that detainees in Celebici camp were 'killed, tortured, sexually assaulted, beaten, and otherwise subjected to cruel and inhuman treatment'.[52]

The sexual nature of crimes committed against both male and female detainees is not immediately obvious due to the non-gendered language of the charges as expressed in the indictment. For example, Delic was charged with torture as a grave breach of the 1949 Geneva Conventions and as a violation of the laws or customs of war for the *actus reus* of forcible sexual penetration. He was also charged in the alternative with cruel treatment for these same acts.[53]

In considering torture charges for the sexual violence, the Trial Chamber stated that 'in order for rape to be included within the offence of torture it must meet each of the elements of this offence'.[54] The elements of torture for purposes of the war crimes provisions of the ICTY Statute were held by the *Celebici* Trial Chamber to be:

(i)   there must be an act or omission that causes severe pain or suffering, whether physical or mental;
(ii)   which is inflicted intentionally; and
(iii) for such purposes as obtaining information or a confession from the victim, or a third person, punishing the victim for an act he or she or a third person has committed or is

---

50   ICTR Statute, art. 4(e).
51   *Prosecutor* v. *Delalic et al.*, Case No. IT-96-21-T, Judgment, 16 November 1998.
52   *Ibid.* Indictment, 19 March 1996), para. 2.
53   *Ibid.*, paras 18 and 19.
54   *Prosecutor* v. *Delalic*, note 51 *supra*, at para. 480.

suspected of having committed, intimidating or coercing the victim or a third person, or for any reason based on discrimination of any kind; and

(iv) such act or omission being committed by, or at the instigation of, or with the consent or acquiescence of, an official or other person acting in an official capacity.[55]

The Trial Chamber thus adopted the elements of torture contained in the Convention Against Torture, which have a 'state actor' requirement, and stipulated that when any form of sexual violence satisfies these elements, it may constitute torture.[56] However, a subsequent Trial Chamber eliminated the state actor requirement for war crimes, holding that:

[T]he definition of torture under international humanitarian law does not comprise the same elements as the definition of torture generally applied under human rights law. In particular, the Trial Chamber is of the view that the presence of a state official or of any other authority-wielding person in the torture process is not necessary for the offence to be regarded as torture under international humanitarian law.[57]

More recent decisions have also eliminated the state action element.

Interpreting the elements of torture vis-à-vis the rapes, the *Celebici* Trial Chamber stressed:

The Trial Chamber considers the rape of any person to be a despicable act which strikes at the very core of human dignity and physical integrity. The condemnation and punishment of rape becomes all the more urgent where it is committed by, or at the instigation of, a public official, or with the consent or acquiescence of such an official. Rape causes severe pain and suffering, both physical and psychological. The psychological suffering of persons upon whom rape is inflicted may be exacerbated by the social and cultural conditions and can be particularly acute and long lasting.[58]

According to the evidence established at trial, the defendant Delic repeatedly raped a woman while interrogating her. The Chamber found that the rapes committed by Delic caused severe pain and suffering and were committed for the purpose of obtaining information, to punish her for not providing the information, to punish her for the acts of her husband, and to coerce and intimidate her into cooperating. Furthermore, the Trial Chamber found that she was raped for discriminatory purposes, concluding that discrimination on the basis of 'sex' was another purpose behind the torture. It emphasized that sexual violence was used as an instrument of terror and subordination, since rapes were committed with an aim of 'intimidating not only the victim but also other inmates, by creating an atmosphere of fear and powerlessness'.[59] The Trial Chamber also found that Delic had repeatedly raped another victim in order to intimidate, coerce and punish her, and that these rapes caused severe mental and physical pain and suffering. For these acts, Delic was convicted of torture for the *actus reus* of forcible sexual penetration.[60]

---

55   *Ibid.* para. 494.
56   *Ibid.* para. 496.
57   *Prosecutor* v. *Kunarac* Trial Chamber Judgment, note 42 *supra*, para. 496.
58   *Prosecutor* v. *Delalic*, note 51 *supra*, para. 495.
59   *Ibid.* para. 941.
60   *Ibid.* paras 475–96 and 965.

In another ICTY war crimes trial, the *Furundzija* case, the prosecution charged the defendant with two counts of violating the laws or customs of war for the sexual violence inflicted upon a woman in detention. The charges were for torture and 'outrages upon personal dignity, including rape'.[61] Furundzija was not accused of raping the woman himself; he was charged for his role in verbally interrogating the woman while a colleague repeatedly raped her.

Noting that a large number of persons typically participate in the torture process by performing different tasks, the *Furundzija* Trial Chamber stressed that under international law, all of these individuals are 'equally accountable' and the relative differences in their roles should be taken into account in sentencing.[62] It expands the list of prohibited purposes behind the CAT's definition of torture to include humiliation, stating that 'among the possible purposes of torture one must also include that of humiliating the victim. This proposition is warranted by the general spirit of international humanitarian law: the primary purpose of this body of law is to safeguard human dignity'.[63] Finding that the victim was raped by means of torture in an effort to 'degrade and humiliate her', and stressing that 'the [sexual] attacks were particularly horrifying', cruel and barbaric, the Trial Chamber found Furundzija guilty of sexual violence as a co-perpetrator of torture and as an aider and abettor of outrages upon personal dignity including rape.[64]

Significantly, the *Furundzija* Trial Chamber also found that being forced to witness rape may constitute torture. The judgment states that '[t]he physical attacks upon Witness D, as well as the fact that he was forced to watch sexual attacks on a woman, in particular, a woman whom he knew as a friend, caused him severe physical and mental suffering'.[65] Expanding upon this, another ICTY Trial Chamber concluded that the threat of rape may constitute torture, finding sexual violence among the most common acts which constitute torture, along with 'threats to torture, rape, or kill relatives'.[66]

The *Kunarac* Appeals Chamber held, in considering rape as torture, that 'some acts establish per se the suffering of those upon whom they were inflicted. Rape is ... such an act. Sexual violence necessarily gives rise to severe pain or suffering, whether physical or mental, and in this way justifies its characterization as an act of torture.'[67] The Appeals Chamber emphasized that 'the act of rape necessarily implies such pain or suffering' thus that element of the crime of torture is established when rape is established.[68] Similarly, the *Furundzija* Appeals Chamber found it 'inconceivable' that sexual violence could be considered not serious enough to amount to torture.[69] This finding applies regardless of whether the sexual violence is being charged as a war crime or a crime against humanity.

---

[61]   *Prosecutor v. Furundzija*, Case No. IT-95-17/1-PT, Indictment, Amended-Redacted, 2 June 1998, counts 13 and 14.

[62]   *Prosecutor v. Furundzija*, Case No. IT-95-17/1-T, Judgment, 10 December 1998, paras 254 and 257.

[63]   *Ibid.* para. 162.

[64]   *Ibid.* paras 124, 130, 269, 275 and 282–3.

[65]   *Ibid.* para. 267.

[66]   *Prosecutor v. Kvocka*, Case No. IT-98-30-T, Judgment, 2 November 2001, para. 144.

[67]   *Prosecutor v. Kunarac et al.*, Case Nos IT-96-23-A and IT-96-23/1-A, Appeals Chamber Judgment, 12 June 2002, paras 150–1.

[68]   *Ibid.* para. 151.

[69]   *Prosecutor v. Furundzija*, Case No. IT-95-17/1-A, Appeals Chamber Judgment, 21 July 2000, paras 113–14.

Outrages upon personal dignity as a war crime

The *Furundzija* Trial Chamber before the ICTY analyzed the 'outrages upon personal dignity including rape' charge and considered that a rape victim 'suffered severe physical and mental pain, along with public humiliation', committed by the accused, and that this 'amounted to outrages upon her personal dignity and sexual integrity'.[70]

The *Alexovski* Trial Chamber, in a case not involving sexual violence, held that an outrage upon personal dignity:

> is an act which is animated by contempt for the human dignity of another person. The corollary is that the act must cause serious humiliation or degradation to the victim …While the perpetrator need not have had the specific intent to humiliate or degrade the victim, he must have been able to perceive this to be the foreseeable and reasonable consequence of his actions.[71]

It is clearly foreseeable that rape violates a person's dignity, as the act is committed through intruding upon some of the most private, intimate parts of one's body.

In the *Kunarac* case, the ICTY prosecution charged one of the three defendants, Kovac, with 'outrages upon personal dignity' for sexual violence committed against women and girls he held in conditions of enslavement. In convicting Kovac of outrages upon personal dignity for instances in which girls were made to dance nude on a table, together or individually, while he and others gawked and laughed at them, the Trial Chamber emphasized:

> [Kovac] certainly knew that, having to stand naked on a table, while the accused watched them, was a painful and humiliating experience for the three women involved, even more so because of their young age. The Trial Chamber is satisfied that Kovac must have been aware of that fact, but he nevertheless ordered them to gratify him by dancing naked for him. The Statute does not require that the perpetrator must intend to humiliate his victim, that is that he perpetrated the act for that very reason. It is sufficient that he knew that his act or omission could have that effect.[72]

The *Kunarac* Trial Chamber further emphasized that the suffering need not necessarily be long lasting:

> So long as the humiliation or degradation is real and serious, the Trial Chamber can see no reason why it would also have to be 'lasting'. In the view of the Trial Chamber, it is not open to regard the fact that a victim has recovered or is overcoming the effects of such an offence as indicating of itself that the relevant acts did not constitute an outrage upon personal dignity.[73]

Thus, whether the accused forced these young girls to dance nude for his own gratification or for the sexual degradation of the victims, the Tribunal held criminal responsibility ensues for the war crime of outrages upon personal dignity if the effect was serious humiliation. The Trial Chamber recognized that serious humiliation is a clearly foreseeable consequence of forced nudity. The *Kvocka* Trial Chamber also found that enduring 'the constant fear of being subjected to physical, mental, or sexual violence' in detention camps constitutes the crime of outrages upon personal dignity.[74]

---

[70] *Ibid.* para. 273.
[71] *Prosecutor* v. *Aleksovski*, Case No. IT-95-14/1-T, Judgment, 25 June 1999, para. 56.
[72] *Prosecutor* v. *Kunarac*, note 42 *supra*, paras 773–4.
[73] *Ibid.* para. 501.
[74] *Prosecutor* v. *Kvocka* note 66 *supra*, para. 173.

Other war crimes charges for sexual violence

Rape and other forms of sexual violence have also been charged under other provisions as both grave breaches and violations of the laws or customs of war. In charges such as torture, enslavement and persecution, the sexual nature of the crime is not necessarily obvious without details of the acts supporting the charge.

In the *Celebici* case, defendants were tried and convicted for superior responsibility for the crimes of 'willfully causing great suffering or serious injury to body or health' as a grave breach, and with cruel treatment as a violation of the laws or customs of war, for sexual assault committed by their subordinates. Such acts included subjecting two male detainees to abusive treatment by having a burning fuse cord placed around their genitals.[75] Three accused were also charged with superior responsibility for the grave breach of inhuman treatment, and for cruel treatment as a violation of the laws or customs of war, when subordinates forced two male detainees to perform fellatio on each other.[76]

When considering the crime of inhuman treatment, which is a grave breach of the Geneva Conventions, the *Celebici* Trial Chamber surveyed the term's usage in the Commentary to the Geneva Conventions, human rights instruments and jurisprudence of human rights bodies. The Trial Chamber defines inhuman treatment as 'an intentional act or omission, that is an act which, judged objectively, is deliberate and not accidental, which causes serious mental or physical suffering or injury or constitutes a serious attack on human dignity'.[77] As intentional mistreatment is inconsistent with the fundamental principle of humanity, inhuman treatment thus 'forms the umbrella' covering all other 'grave breaches' listed in the Geneva Conventions.[78]

The Trial Chamber also found that the crime of cruel treatment as a violation of common article 3 to the Geneva Conventions shares an identical definition with inhuman treatment. As such, cruel treatment has the 'equivalent meaning and therefore the same residual function for the purposes of common article 3 ... as inhuman treatment does in relation to grave breaches'.[79]

Convictions were entered for inhuman treatment and cruel treatment when subordinates forced two brothers to publicly perform fellatio on each other. The Trial Chamber notes that the forced fellatio 'could constitute rape for which liability could have been found if pleaded in the appropriate manner'.[80] If the forced fellatio had been pleaded as rape, the Trial Chamber would have convicted the defendants of rape instead of the more general and obscure crimes of inhuman and cruel treatment.

Further, the *Cesic* Trial Chamber stated:

[H]umiliation is clearly an element of the crime of humiliating and degrading treatment, as a violation of the laws or customs of war, while it is not explicitly an element of the crime of rape. However, it is uncontested that rape is an inherently humiliating offence and that humiliation is always taken into account when appreciating the inherent gravity of this crime.[81]

---

75   *Prosecutor v. Delalic*, note 51 *supra*, para. 24.
76   *Ibid.* para. 26.
77   *Ibid.* para. 543.
78   *Ibid.* para. 543.
79   *Ibid.* para. 552.
80   *Ibid.* para. 1066.
81   *Prosecutor v. Cesic*, Case No. IT-95-10/1-T, Judgment, 11 March 2004, para. 53.

Crimes Against Humanity for Sexual Violence

The term 'crimes against humanity' first appeared in an international instrument in the Nuremberg Charter, when it was included as a means of prosecuting the German Nazi leaders before the International Military Tribunal for the horrific crimes committed against select members of the civilian population, including German citizens, during the Second World War.[82] While rape was not explicitly listed as a crime against humanity in the IMT Charter, as noted above, there was a fair amount of sexual violence included in the evidence admitted at trial and offences of sexual violence can be considered subsumed in the IMT judgment.

Subsequent Nuremberg trials also held in Germany by the Allied forces under the auspices of Control Council Law No. 10 (CCL10), did specifically list rape as a crime against humanity.[83] In some of these trials of war criminals who were not senior military and political leaders, such as medical doctors and concentration camp guards, the crimes of forced sterilization, forced abortion and sexual mutilation were mentioned but given only cursory treatment.[84]

Rape is prosecutable as a crime against humanity under article 5 of the ICTY Statute, article 3 of the ICTR Statute, article 7 of the ICC Statute, article 2 of the SCSL Statute, and article 5 of the Law of the ECCC. The ICC and SCSL Statutes additionally enumerate as crimes against humanity not only rape, but enforced prosecution, sexual slavery, forced pregnancy, enforced sterilization and 'other forms of sexual violence of comparable gravity'. (Note, however, that the SCSL Statute eliminates enforced sterilization from this list).

The *Kvocka* Trial Chamber of the ICTY noted that sexual violence covers a broad range of acts and includes such crimes as rape, molestation, sexual slavery, sexual mutilation, forced marriage, forced abortion, enforced prostitution, forced pregnancy and forced sterilization.[85]

Sex crimes constitute a crime against humanity when committed as part of a widespread or a systematic attack against a civilian population. It is the attack that must be widespread or systematic, not each persecuting or criminal act forming part of the attack, such as rape.[86] Nonetheless, practice of rape itself is often both widespread and systematic.

Sex crimes, including rape, may also be prosecuted as a crime against humanity under the persecution, torture, enslavement and inhumane acts provisions. Some cases have also included rape crimes under the extermination charges, particularly when rape is but a prelude

---

[82]   IMT Charter, *supra* note 1.

[83]   Punishment of Persons Guilty of War Crimes, Crimes Against Peace and Against Humanity, Allied Control Council Law No. 10, 20 December 1945, Official Gazette of the Control Council for Germany, No. 3, (31 January 1946), art. II(1)(c).

[84]   See, for example, *United States* v. *Brandt*, in 2 Trials of War Criminals Before the Nuremberg Military Tribunal Under Control Council Law No. 10 (1946) (forced sterilization and castration); *United States* v. *Pohl*, in 5 Trials of War Criminals Before the Nuremberg Military Tribunal Under Control Council Law No. 10 (1947) (evidence of forced abortion and concentration camp 'brothels'); *United States* v. *Greifelt*, in 4_5 Trials of War Criminals Before the Nuremberg Military Tribunal Under Control Council Law No. 10 (1947) (forced abortion, gender/ethnic persecutions, genocide and reproductive crimes).

[85]   *Prosecutor* v. *Kvocka*, note 66 *supra*, para. 180, n. 343.

[86]   See, for example, *Prosecutor* v. *Kunarac*, note 42 *supra*, para. 419 ('It is sufficient to show that the act took place in the context of an accumulation of acts of violence which, individually, may vary greatly in nature and gravity.').

to death.[87] The ICC Statute also recognizes 'gender' as one of the discriminatory grounds for the crime of persecution.[88]

The ICTY Appeals Chamber has confirmed that under customary international law, and as applied by the Yugoslav Tribunal, the general (chapeau) requirements for crimes against humanity are:

> (i) there must be an attack; (ii) the acts of the perpetrator must be part of the attack; (iii) the attack must be directed against any civilian population; (iv) the attack must be widespread or systematic; and (v) the perpetrator must know that his acts constitute part of a pattern of widespread or systematic crimes directed against a civilian population and know that his acts fit into such a pattern.[89]

The ICC Elements of the Crimes for crimes against humanity under article 7 of the ICC Statute stipulate:

> 1. Since article 7 pertains to international criminal law, its provisions, consistent with article 22, must be strictly construed, taking into account that crimes against humanity as defined in article 7 are among the most serious crimes of concern to the international community as a whole, warrant and entail individual criminal responsibility, and require conduct which is impermissible under generally applicable international law, as recognized by the principal legal systems of the world.
> 2. The last two elements for each crime against humanity describe the context in which the conduct must take place. These elements clarify the requisite participation in and knowledge of a widespread or systematic attack against a civilian population. However, the last element should not be interpreted as requiring proof that the perpetrator had knowledge of all characteristics of the attack or the precise details of the plan or policy of the State or organization. In the case of an emerging widespread or systematic attack against a civilian population, the intent clause of the last element indicates that this mental element is satisfied if the perpetrator intended to further such an attack.
> 3. 'Attack directed against a civilian population' in these context elements is understood to mean a course of conduct involving the multiple commission of acts referred to in article 7, paragraph 1, of the Statute against any civilian population, pursuant to or in furtherance of a State or organizational policy to commit such attack. The acts need not constitute a military attack. It is understood that 'policy to commit such attack' requires that the State or organization actively promote or encourage such an attack against a civilian population.[90]

These provisions underlay the specific elements required under each particular act which may be prosecuted as a crime against humanity. The ICC Elements of the Crimes for adjudicating rape and sexual slavery at the ICC are articulated below. The addition of sex crimes listed as war crimes and crimes against humanity in the ICC Statute are a major advancement. They will not be given separate treatment below because they have not been prosecuted yet before any of the international courts, including the ICC.

---

87   See, for example, the *Kanyabashi*, *Semanza* and *Bikindi* Indictments of the ICTR, available at www.ictr.org.
88   ICC Statute, art. 7(h).
89   *Prosecutor* v. *Kunarac*, Appeals Chamber, note 67 *supra* , paras 85 and 105.
90   ICC Elements of the Crimes, note 49 *supra*, art. 7.

Prosecuting Gender Crimes as Crimes Against Humanity in Contemporary International War Crimes Tribunals

Rape as a crime against humanity

The *Akayesu* Trial Chamber Judgment in the ICTR was the first time in history that an accused was convicted for rape as a crime against humanity. The Trial Chamber held that the accused, a bourgmestre (mayor), could be held accountable for sexual violence because of the role he played in facilitating, by his presence, words or acquiescence, the rapes, forced public nudity and sexual mutilation committed in his commune.[91] The Trial Chamber determined that 'by virtue of his authority', his presence and words of encouragement 'sent a clear signal of official tolerance' for the acts of sexual violence.[92] In finding Akayesu guilty of rape as a crime against humanity, the Trial Chamber indicated that while only the attack need be widespread or systematic, here the rapes were themselves both widespread and systematic.

The *Kunarac* Trial Chamber judgment was the first trial involving rape as a crime against humanity before the ICTY.[93] All three defendants on trial were charged with rape as a crime against humanity for the sexual violence inflicted on women and girls in Foca in Bosnia, where dozens of women and young girls were raped and sexually enslaved for weeks and months at a time. They all physically committed rapes, and two held victims in detention or loaned them out with the full knowledge that they would be raped by others. As noted above, the *Kunarac* Trial Chamber articulated elements of rape under international law. It further found that the rape crimes formed part of a widespread and systematic attack on the civilian population in the town of Foca, constituting rape as a crime against humanity.

In the *Kvocka* Trial Chamber judgment before the ICTY, there was no evidence admitted at trial that indicated that four of the five accused even knew about the rapes or other forms of sexual violence committed in the Omarska prison camp in Bosnia. However, the Trial Chamber found that by knowingly working in the camp where persecution, murders, tortures and other criminal activity were rampant, the participants assumed the risk of incurring criminal responsibility for all natural or foreseeable crimes, including rape crimes, committed therein. Holding that sexual violence in the camp was patently foreseeable and virtually inevitable under the circumstances, the *Kvocka* Trial Chamber reasoned:

> In Omarska camp, approximately 36 women were held in detention, guarded by men with weapons who were often drunk, violent, and physically and mentally abusive and who were allowed to act with virtual impunity. Indeed, it would be unrealistic and contrary to all rational logic to expect that none of the women held in Omarska, placed in circumstances rendering them especially vulnerable, would be subjected to rape or other forms of sexual violence. This is particularly true in light of the clear intent of the criminal enterprise to subject the targeted group to persecution through such means as violence and humiliation.[94]

The most recent rape as a crime against humanity case before the ICTR was handed down in December 2008. Colonel Bagosora, alleged mastermind of the genocide in Rwanda, was convicted of, among other crimes, rape as a crime against humanity. The Trial Chamber stated:

---

[91]   *Prosecutor* v. *Akayesu*, note 38 *supra*, paras 692–4.
[92]   *Ibid.* para. 693.
[93]   *Prosecutor* v. *Kunarac*, note 42 *supra*.
[94]   *Prosecutor* v. *Kvocka*, note 66 *supra*, para. 327.

Rape as a crime against humanity requires proof of the non-consensual penetration, however slight, of the vagina or anus of the victim by the penis of the perpetrator or by any other object used by the perpetrator, or of the mouth of the victim by the penis of the perpetrator. Consent for this purpose must be consent given voluntarily and freely and is assessed within the context of the surrounding circumstances. Force or threat of force provides clear evidence of non-consent, but force is not an element per se of rape.[95]

After recognizing the *mens rea* for rape as a crime against humanity as 'the intention to effect the prohibited sexual penetration with the knowledge that it occurs without the consent of the victim', the Trial Chamber then specified that '[i]t is clear that, given the circumstances surrounding these attacks, there could have been no consent for these acts of sexual violence and that the perpetrators would have known this fact'.[96] It is indicative of the horrific nature of the sexual violence that the lack of consent or the violation of the sexual autonomy of the victims was inferred, as no rape victims were called to give testimony before the Trial Chamber in this case.

The first judgment delivered by the Special Court for Sierra Leone handed down convictions for rape as a crime against humanity against three rebel leaders of the Armed Forces Revolutionary Council (AFRC).[97] The *AFRC* Trial Chamber cited rape crime jurisprudence of the ICTY and ICTR, and adopted the same elements of rape as found in the *Kunarac* judgment of the ICTY.[98] It further recognized that:

Consent of the victim must be given voluntarily, as a result of the victim's free will, assessed in the context of the surrounding circumstances. Force or threat of force provides clear evidence of non-consent, but force is not an element per se of rape and there are factors other than force which would render an act of sexual penetration non-consensual or non-voluntary on the part of the victim. This is necessarily a contextual assessment. However, in situations of armed conflict or detention, coercion is almost universal. 'Continuous resistance' by the victim, and physical force, or even threat of force by the perpetrator are not required to establish coercion. Children below the age of 14 cannot give valid consent.[99]

The *AFRC* Trial Chamber also acknowledged the very real difficulty of applying the elements of rape, particularly in situations of massive violence:

[T]he very specific circumstances of an armed conflict where rapes on a large scale are alleged to have occurred, coupled with the social stigma which is borne by victims of rape in certain societies, render the restrictive test set out in the elements of the crime difficult to satisfy. Circumstantial evidence may therefore be used to demonstrate the actus reus of rape.[100]

---

[95]   *Prosecutor* v. *Bagosora et al.*, Case No. ICTR-96-7-T, Judgment and Sentence, 18 December 2008, para. 2199.

[96]   *Ibid.* paras 2200–1.

[97]   *Prosecutor* v. *Brima et al.*, Case No. SCSL-04-16-T, Judgment, 20 June 2007 ('AFRC Judgment').

[98]   *Ibid.* para. 693: 'In addition to the chapeau requirements of Crimes against Humanity pursuant to Article 2 of the Statute, the Trial Chamber adopts the following elements of the crime of rape: 1. The non-consensual penetration, however slight, of the vagina or anus of the victim by the penis of the perpetrator or by any other object used by the perpetrator, or of the mouth of the victim by the penis of the perpetrator; and 2. The intent to effect this sexual penetration, and the knowledge that it occurs without the consent of the victim.'

[99]   *Ibid.* para. 694.

[100]   *Ibid.* para. 695.

Sexual violence as torture constituting a crime against humanity

Although rape crimes were not charged as torture in the amended indictment in the *Akayesu* case before the ICTR, in *dicta*, the judgment of the Trial Chamber analogizes aspects of the crimes of rape and torture, noting that rape 'is a form of aggression' and the elements of the crime 'cannot be captured in a mechanical description of objects and body parts'. It stresses that 'like torture, rape is used for such purposes as intimidation, degradation, humiliation, discrimination, punishment, control or destruction of a person. Like torture, rape is a violation of personal dignity, and rape in fact constitutes torture' when all of the elements of torture are satisfied.[101]

In the *Kunarac* case before the ICTY, defendant Kunarac was found to have raped and sexually tortured several women and girls, selecting them for abuse because they were Muslim and female. The Trial Chamber stated:

> The treatment reserved by Dragoljub Kunarac for his victims was motivated by their being Muslims, as is evidenced by the occasions when the accused told women, that they would give birth to Serb babies, or that they should 'enjoy being fucked by a Serb'.[102]

The Trial Chamber stipulated that discrimination need not be the sole purpose for which the crime is committed. Thus, the Trial Chamber concluded that discriminating against the women and girls was part of the reason they were singled out for the rape but it need not be the exclusive reason. [103]

In the *Kunarac* case, another defendant, Vukovic, was also jointly charged with rape and torture as crimes against humanity for several instances of sexual violence committed against women and girls in Foca. In contesting allegations of sexual torture, Vukovic argued that even if it were proved that he had committed rape, he 'would have done so out of a sexual urge, not out of hatred' and claimed that he did not commit the rape for a prohibited purpose necessary for establishing torture. However, the Trial Chamber explained that 'all that matters in this context is his awareness of an attack against the Muslim civilian population of which his victim was a member and, for the purpose of torture, that he intended to discriminate between the group of which he is a member and the group of his victim'.[104] The Trial Chamber stressed that torture can be committed for any number of reasons, and one of the prohibited purposes need merely be part of the motivation behind the act, not necessarily even the principal motivation:

> There is no requirement under international customary law that the conduct must be solely perpetrated for one of the prohibited purposes of torture, such as discrimination. The prohibited purpose need only be part of the motivation behind the conduct and need not be the predominant or sole purpose.[105]

The Tribunal convicted Vukovic for torture as a war crime and a crime against humanity for the sexual torture he inflicted upon his victims.

---

[101]   *Prosecutor* v. *Akayesu*, note 38 *supra*, para. 687.
[102]   *Prosecutor* v. *Kunarac*, note 42 *supra* , para. 654.
[103]   *Ibid.*
[104]   *Ibid.* para. 816.
[105]   *Ibid.* para. 816.

The *Kvocka* Trial Chamber before the ICTY considered rape and torture charges alleged against Radic, one of the five accused, for torture by means of rape, as well as for other forms of sexual violence. Allegations of sexual violence committed by Radic ranged from groping women to raping them. In concluding that he committed sexual violence against women held in Omarska prison camp in Bosnia, the Chamber recalled the definition of sexual violence set out in the *Akayesu* judgment as 'any act of a sexual nature, which is committed on a person under circumstances which are coercive' and found that 'the sexual intimidations, harassment, and assaults committed by Radic ... clearly fall within this definition, and thus [found] that Radic committed sexual violence against these survivors'.[106] The *Kvocka* Trial Chamber also stated that:

> The fear was pervasive and the threat was always real that they [the women in the camp] could be subjected to sexual violence at the whim of Radic. Under these circumstances, the Trial Chamber finds that the threat of rape or other forms of sexual violence undoubtedly caused severe pain and suffering ... and thus, the elements of torture are also satisfied in relation to these survivors.[107]

Sexual slavery (rape and enslavement) as a crime against humanity

A particularly groundbreaking aspect of the *Kunarac* judgment of the ICTY is in its elaboration on the crime of enslavement in conjunction with gender-related crimes. The Trial Chamber made extensive findings related to enslavement, articulated indicia of enslavement present in the case, and found two of the accused guilty of rape and enslavement as crimes against humanity for acts essentially amounting to sexual slavery. Unlike the ICC and SCSL Statutes, the ICTY Statute does not specifically list sexual slavery as a crime, so the prosecution charged rape and enslavement jointly. Noting that international law, including the Slavery Convention, has consistently defined slavery as 'the status or condition of a person over whom any or all of the powers attaching to the right of ownership are exercised', the *Kunarac* Trial Chamber held that the *actus reus* of the crime of enslavement is 'the exercise of any or all of the powers attaching to the right of ownership over a person'. The *mens rea* is the intentional exercise of such powers.[108]

The *Kunarac* Trial Chamber found that indicia of enslavement can include sub-elements of control and ownership, such as restricting or controlling an individual's autonomy, free choice or free movement, absence of consent or free will, exploitation, forced or compulsory labor, sex, prostitution, trafficking in persons, assertions of exclusivity, cruel treatment and abuse or control of sexuality. The Trial Chamber stressed that it may be appropriate to consider duration as a factor when determining whether someone has been enslaved, but that duration is not an element of the crime.[109]

In this case, most of the women and girls had been held enslaved for extended periods, where they were repeatedly raped during their captivity. They were not always physically prevented from escaping, for example, the door to their room may not always have been locked. The Trial Chamber deemed the absence of physical barriers irrelevant in light of the psychological or logistical barriers present and found that neither physical restraint nor deten-

---

[106]   *Prosecutor v. Kvocka*, note 66 *supra*, para. 559.
[107]   *Ibid*. para. 561.
[108]   *Prosecutor v. Kunarac*, note 42 *supra*, para. 540.
[109]   *Ibid*. paras 542–3.

tion is a required element of enslavement. The Chamber accepted fear of retribution if they escaped and were recaptured as a reason that the women were psychologically prevented from escaping. Further, it was dangerous to leave while the conflict was ongoing, and hostile military forces were present in the area.[110]

The facts of the *Kunarac* case demonstrated that the enslavement and rapes were inseparably linked: the defendants enslaved the women and girls as a means to effectuate continuous rape and for the purpose of having women and girls available for sexual access at will and with ease. In convicting Kunarac of both rape and enslavement as crimes against humanity, the Trial Chamber held that Kunarac held women and girls against their will, treated them as his personal property, and forced them to provide sexual and domestic services at his whim. The Trial Chamber emphasized that controlling a person's sexual autonomy or obliging someone to provide sexual services may be indicia of enslavement, but such indicia are not elements of the crime.[111]

Sexual slavery was prosecuted in the Special Court for Sierra Leone, and there is extensive discussion of rape, sexual slavery and 'forced marriage' in the *AFRC* Trial and Appeals Chamber judgments, but sexual slavery in this case will not be discussed here.[112] The SCSL has repeatedly lauded its historic conviction for sexual slavery, but the crime was not actually the basis of a distinct conviction by either the Trial or Appeals Chambers.[113]

In the ICC Elements of the Crimes, the elements of sexual slavery (in addition to the general or 'chapeau' elements of crimes against humanity) under article 7(1)(g) of the ICC Statute are:

1. The perpetrator exercised any or all of the powers attaching to the right of ownership over one or more persons, such as by purchasing, selling, lending or bartering such a person or persons, or by imposing on them a similar deprivation of liberty.
2. The perpetrator caused such person or persons to engage in one or more acts of a sexual nature.
3. The conduct was committed as part of a widespread or systematic attack directed against a civilian population.
4. The perpetrator knew that the conduct was part of or intended the conduct to be part of a widespread or systematic attack directed against a civilian population.[114]

The ICC Statute further specifies that 'enslavement' under the Statute means 'the exercise of any or all of the powers attaching to the right of ownership over a person and includes the exercise of such power in the course of trafficking in persons, in particular women and children'.[115]

---

[110]   *Ibid.* paras 741–2 and 750.

[111]   *Ibid.* paras 750–80.

[112]   The prosecution essentially bundled the charge of sexual slavery under broad charges of 'outrages upon personal dignity', as well as under a separate charge of 'forced marriage' pled under inhumane acts instead of 'other forms of sexual violence'. *AFRC* Judgment, note 97 *supra*. *Prosecutor v. Brima*, Case No., SCSL-2004-16-A, Appeals Chamber Judgment, 28 February 2008 ('*AFRC* Appeals Chamber Judgment').

[113]   See *AFRC* Judgment, note 97 *supra*; AFRC Appeals Chamber Judgment, note 112 *supra*.

[114]   ICC Elements of the Crimes, note 49 *supra*, regarding crimes against humanity and sexual slavery.

[115]   ICC Statute, art. 7(2)(c).

Persecution as a crime against humanity for sexual violence

The ICC Statute recognized for the first time that 'gender' is a basis of persecution deserving of prosecution under the persecution prong of crimes against humanity. Article 7(1)(h) of the Statute allows for the prosecution of:

> persecution against any identifiable group or collectivity on political, racial, national, ethnic, cultural, religious, gender as defined in paragraph 3, or other grounds that are universally recognized as impermissible under international law, in connection with any act referred to in this paragraph or any crime within the jurisdiction of the court.

In defining 'gender', paragraph 3 explains, 'it is understood that the term "gender" refers to the two sexes male and female, within the context of society. The term "gender" does not indicate any meaning different from the above.'[116] The ICTY and ICTR Statutes do not include gender within the context of persecution (or anywhere else for that matter.)

Rape and other forms of sexual violence are increasingly prosecuted under the persecution count of crimes against humanity. The *Brdjanin* Trial Chamber of the ICTY concluded that 'Any sexual assault falling short of rape may be punishable as persecution under international criminal law, provided that it reaches the same level of gravity as the other crimes against humanity enumerated in Article 5 of the Statute.'[117]

In the *Kvocka* case before the ICTY, five defendants who worked in or regularly visited Omarska prison camp in Bosnia were charged with a series of crimes committed in the camp. A central charge was for persecution as a crime against humanity for the murder, torture, beatings, sexual assaults, humiliation, psychological abuse and inhuman conditions of confinement in the camp. The *Kvocka* Trial Chamber recognized that persecution takes many forms and is not limited to physical violence:

> Just as rape and forced nudity are recognized as crimes against humanity or genocide if they form part of an attack directed against a civilian population or if used as an instrument of the genocide, humiliating treatment that forms part of a discriminatory attack against a civilian population may, in combination with other crimes or, in extreme cases alone, similarly constitute persecution.[118]

The five defendants in *Kvocka* were convicted of rape and other forms of sexual violence on formal charges of persecution as a crime against humanity.

The crimes committed in the *Kvocka* case, including persecution and sexual violence, were all prosecuted under the joint criminal enterprise (JCE) theory of liability, which was developed in the Yugoslav Tribunal's first trial, the *Tadic* case,[119] based largely upon jurisprudence from the post-Second World War Nuremberg trials. Essentially, they held that under international law, individual criminal liability for participation in a JCE may exist when there is (1) a plurality of persons, (2) a common objective which amounts to or involves the commission of a crime within the Statute, and (3) the accused participated in the crimes or the objective's implementation.[120] JCE is widely recognized as having three forms: JCE I,

---

116   *Ibid.* art. 7(1)(h) and (3).
117   *Prosecutor* v. *Brdjanin*, Case No. IT-99-36, Judgment 1 September 2004, para. 1012.
118   *Prosecutor* v. *Kvocka*, note 66 *supra*, para. 190.
119   *Prosecutor* v. *Tadic*, Case No. 1T-94-1-A, Judgment, 15 July 1999, paras 185–229.
120   See, for example, *Prosecutor* v. *Krajisnik*, Case No. IT-00-39-T, Judgment, 27 September 2006, para. 883.

which is the basic form where participants agree on a common objective; JCE II, which is the systemic form, mostly but not exclusively applying to concentration camp situations, as well as other cases where there is a system of persecution; and JCE III, which is the extended form for crimes outside the intended crimes which were natural or foreseeable consequences of implementing the common objectives.

The *Kvocka* Trial Chamber judgment has considerable implications for securing criminal responsibility for gender crimes committed either as part of a persecution scheme or as part of a joint criminal enterprise. This is especially important given the increasing trend in most war crime tribunals to indict suspects under the JCE theory and to use persecution as a catch-all category that captures a range of crimes (that is, murder, torture, rape, deportation, pillage) without indicting each crime separately.

Using the joint criminal enterprise theory of liability for prosecuting sexual violence
Building upon the development of the JCE theory of liability contained in the *Tadic* Appeals Chamber judgment and other decisions, the *Kvocka* Trial Chamber recognized JCE as particularly pertinent to situations of mass atrocities and noted that a joint criminal enterprise may exist:

> whenever two or more people participate in a common criminal endeavor. This criminal endeavor can range anywhere along a continuum from two persons conspiring to rob a bank to the systematic slaughter of millions during a vast criminal regime comprising thousands of participants. Within a joint criminal enterprise there may be other subsidiary criminal enterprises ... [where] the criminal purpose may be more particularized: one subset may be established for purposes of forced labor, another for purposes of systematic rape for forced impregnation, another for purposes of extermination, etc.[121]

Implicit in the *Kvocka* Trial Chamber judgment is that such detention, whether in a large facility where many women are formally detained or in a house where a small group or even one woman is unlawfully kept, may constitute a criminal enterprise if individuals knowingly participate with others in criminal activity. The Trial Chamber specified that extra measures may be necessary in order to protect women from rape crimes in such situations: 'If a superior has prior knowledge that women detained by male guards in detention facilities are likely to be subjected to sexual violence, that would put him on sufficient notice that extra measures are demanded in order to prevent such crimes.'[122] The decision can be interpreted as imposing a burden on those detaining females to ensure that adequate protections are in place to prevent sexual abuse and monitor the facilities to guarantee compliance with the preventative measures.

In the *Krstic* Trial Chamber judgment, finding General Krstic guilty of crimes against humanity and genocide for the slaughter of over 7,700 men and boys in Srebrenica, rape crimes were included in the crimes for which Krstic was convicted of under the JCE theory of liability. Although the Trial Chamber was not convinced that many crimes, including rape, committed against refugees were 'an agreed upon objective among the members of the joint criminal enterprise', nonetheless, the crimes were 'natural and foreseeable consequences of

---

121   *Prosecutor* v. *Kvocka*, note 66 *supra*, para. 307.
122   *Ibid.* para. 318.

the ethnic cleansing campaign'.[123] Indeed, the *Krstic* Trial Chamber found that not only were the crimes of murder, rape, beatings and other abuses foreseeable, the circumstances made the crimes virtually 'inevitable' due to the 'lack of shelter, the density of the crowds, the vulnerable condition of the refugees, the presence of many regular and irregular military and paramilitary units in the area and the sheer lack of sufficient numbers of UN soldiers to provide protection'.[124] As a consequence, General Krstic was held criminally liable for the foreseeable rapes committed by his subordinates during the persecution of non-Serbs leading up to and during the Srebrenica massacres.

The *Krajišnik* Trial Chamber judgment of the ICTY was particularly groundbreaking in recognizing gender crimes under the JCE theory of liability by recognizing that political or military leaders far from the battlefield may be held responsible for rape crimes when they are well known and continuous and no effort is made by leadership to disassociate these crimes from the other acts committed as part of a criminal campaign. It essentially made leaders responsible for repeated and known crimes, including rape, for which they fail to object. Krajišnik, a member of the Presidency of the Bosnian-Serb Republic and a colleague of Slobodan Milošević, Radovan Karadžić and Ratko Mladić, is the most senior person yet convicted by the ICTY. He was charged with genocide and crimes against humanity. Sexual violence was included in a charge of persecution as a crime against humanity, and the case was prosecuted under the JCE theory of liability.

The *Krajišnik* Trial Chamber found that originally the common criminal plan was to deport and forcibly transfer non-Serbs out of the territory. However, additional crimes, including rape, became frequent, and once the Serb leadership, including Krajišnik, had information available about these other crimes and not only made no attempt to prevent or halt them, but continued their same discriminatory policies and practices, these additional crimes were deemed by the Trial Chamber to have become just as much a part of the joint criminal enterprise as the originally intended crimes.[125] Thus, eventually they were no longer merely foreseeable crimes (JCE III); they formed part of the common criminal plan agreed upon by participants in the plan (JCE I).

The *Krajišnik* judgment has major implications for holding senior leaders, whether military or civilian, responsible for sex crimes when committed during the course of a scheme of persecution or other criminal endeavor. If sex crimes are notorious or widespread, and leaders make no effort to prevent or halt the crimes, an inference can be made that the leaders sanction the crimes. Responsibility under JCE constitutes individual responsibility, not superior or command responsibility, as leaders are held criminally liable for their own role in facilitating crimes, including sex crimes, by their tacit approval through silence or acquiescence when there is common knowledge of the crimes.

Prior to the *Krajišnik* decision, in most other JCE cases, rape crimes were prosecuted as JCE II as part of a concentration camp effort to persecute a targeted group, or as JCE III as a foreseeable crime incidental to the criminal campaign. In the *Krajišnik* case, the Trial Chamber recognized rape and other forms of violence as JCE I, crimes intentionally committed to terrorize and harm, even when the leader was far from the crime scene. It is unfortu-

---

123   *Prosecutor v. Krstic*, Case No. IT-98-33-T, Judgment, 2 August 2001, para. 616.
124   *Ibid.* para. 616.
125   *Prosecutor v. Krajisnik*, note 120 *supra*, paras 1096–1119.

nate that, soon after this chapter was written, the *Krajišnik* Appeal Chamber judgment[126] largely undid the progress discussed above.

Genocide and Sexual Violence

Article II of the Genocide Convention, as reproduced in the Statutes of the ICTY, ICTR, ICC, and ECCC defines genocide as follows:

> [G]enocide means any of the following acts committed with intent to destroy, in whole or in part, a national, ethnical, racial or religious group, as such:
> (a)   killing, members of the group;
> (b)   causing serious bodily or mental harm to members of the group;
> (c)   deliberately inflicting on the group conditions of life calculated to bring about its physical destruction in whole or in part;
> (d)   imposing measures intended to prevent births within the group;
> (e)   forcibly transferring children of the group to another group.[127]

As noted previously, genocide is an international crime imposing individual criminal responsibility upon those committing or facilitating the commission of the crime. It is predominately defined by intent. Four of the sub-elements do not necessarily result in death, although sub-element (c) is committed with a desire that at least partial physical destruction of the group be the result. These sub-elements acknowledge that there are many ways to inflict devastating harm on a group, and even to exterminate a group, aside from outright killing them. Negatively impacting reproduction within a group or negatively impacting the identity of a group through a variety of means, including sexual violence, has great potential to inflict enormous harm on the targeted group. Sexual violence can fall under each of the sub-elements of genocide.[128] The most common means of using sex crimes as instruments of genocide, as recognized in the jurisprudence of contemporary war crimes tribunals, is sub-element (b): 'causing serious bodily or mental harm to members of the group' (by means such as by raping or otherwise violating women).

The ICTR has extensively developed the law on genocide over the past 15 years. In contrast, only a small percentage of ICTY cases allege genocide. As noted above, however, General Krstic was convicted for genocide by the ICTY for his responsibility in the Srebrenica massacres.[129] He was convicted under the JCE theory of responsibility, and the rape crimes can be considered to be subsumed within the genocide conviction. In considering the elements of genocide, the *Krstic* Trial Chamber emphasized that 'inhuman treatment, torture, rape, sexual abuse and deportation are among the acts which may cause serious bodily or mental injury'.[130] Similarly, the *Brdjanin* Trial Chamber emphasized that '"[c]ausing serious bodily or mental harm" in sub-paragraph (b) is understood to mean, *inter alia*, acts of torture, inhumane or degrading treatment, [and] sexual violence including rape'.[131]

---

126   *Prosecutor* v. *Krajisnik*, Case No. IT-00-39-A, Apepals Chamber Judgment, 17 March 2009.
127   Genocide Convention, note 11 *supra*, art. II.
128   Kelly D. Askin, *Women and International Humanitarian Law*, in 1 Women and International Human Rights Law 41, 71–6 (Kelly D. Askin and Dorean M. Koenig eds, 1999).
129   *Prosecutor* v. *Krstic*, note 123 *supra*.
130   *Ibid*. para. 513.
131   *Prosecutor* v. *Brdjanin*, note 116 *supra*, para. 690.

The *Akayesu* case before the ICTR was the first international trial in history to hold an accused responsible for genocide, and this landmark case found that the sexual violence in Rwanda was used as an instrument of the genocide. The *Akayesu* Trial Chamber recognized that sexual violence causes extensive harm and is intentionally used as a weapon to subjugate and destroy a collective enemy group. The Trial Chamber recognized that rape crimes were perpetrated by Hutus as 'an integral part of the process of destruction' of the Tutsi group.[132] It explained that 'sexual violence was a step in the process of destruction of the Tutsi group – destruction of the spirit, of the will to live, and of life itself'.[133] As an element of genocide, the Trial Chamber concluded that the:

> acts of rape and sexual violence, as other acts of serious bodily and mental harm committed against the Tutsi, reflected the determination to make Tutsi women suffer and to mutilate them even before killing them, the intent being to destroy the Tutsi group while inflicting acute suffering on its members in the process.[134]

The *Akayesu* Chamber thus acknowledged that the injury and suffering inflicted by sexual violence extends far beyond the individual to the collective targeted group, in this case, the Tutsis.

The *Akayesu* Trial Chamber held that rape crimes 'constitute genocide in the same way as any other act as long as they were committed with the specific intent to destroy, in whole or in part, a particular group, targeted as such'.[135] It found that rape was used as an instrument of the genocide in Taba and that Akayesu's acts and omissions rendered him individually criminally responsible for these crimes.

In 2008, the Prosecutor of the ICC charged President Bashir of Sudan for war crimes, crimes against humanity and genocide, including for sexual violence, for the atrocities committed in Darfur.[136] The ICC later issued an arrest warrant charging him only with war crimes and crimes against humanity, but including a specific charge of rape as a crime against humanity.[137]

FINAL NOTE

The international criminal laws, cases and jurisprudence mentioned above are not the only ones applicable to gender crimes under international law, but they are the principal ones or the ones which have set the leading precedent. The ICC has indicted for sex crimes committed in Uganda, the Democratic Republic of Congo (DRC), Darfur and Central African Republic. The only ICC trial to have started as of the time of writing, the *Lubanga* trial for

---

[132]   *Prosecutor* v. *Akayesu*, note 38 *supra*, para. 731.
[133]   *Ibid.* para. 732.
[134]   *Ibid.* para. 733.
[135]   *Ibid.* para. 731.
[136]   *Prosecutor* v. *Bashir*, Case No. ICC-02/05, Public Redacted Version of the Prosecutor's Application under Article 58, ICC-02/05-157-AnxA 12-09-2008 1/113 SL PT, 14 July 2008.
[137]   *Prosecutor* v. *Bashir*, Warrant of Arrest for Omar Hassan Ahmad Al Bashir, ICC-02/05-01/09, Pre-Trial Chamber I, 4 March 2009.

crimes in the DRC, does not explicitly charge sexual violence and is focused primarily on the war crime of conscripting child soldiers.[138]

Regional courts in Europe, Africa and Inter-America have also used (and can increasingly use) international law to enforce human rights proscriptions against rape and other forms of sexual violence. The first trial before the ECCC began in March 2009, and a joint trial of four senior leaders of the Khmer Rouge regime is expected in 2011. No gender crimes have been specifically included in charges before the ECCC as of 1 March 2009.

While the advances over the past 16 years since the establishment of the ICTY are extraordinary, they are still insufficient. Only a miniscule number of sex crime cases are actually prosecuted. In general, many investigators, prosecutors and judges remain largely uncomfortable with, and uninformed about, gender-related crimes. Others still do not view them as serious crimes. Prosecuting gender crimes is typically fraught with inherent difficulties and gratuitous obstacles. The crimes are notoriously under-reported, under-investigated and under-indicted. Nonetheless, the cases of sexual violence which have come before international courts – often only after sustained outside pressure and internal reluctance – have shattered traditional notions that sex crimes are mere by-products or side-effects of war.

---

[138]   See *Prosecutor* v. *Lubanga*, Case No. ICC-01/04, Warrant of Arrest, ICC-01/04-01/06 (-2-tEN 03-04-2006 1/5 UM PT), 10 February 2006.

6 The crime of aggression: is it amenable to judicial determination?

Faiza Patel King

In the decades since the Nuremberg Tribunal found the German leadership guilty of the crime of waging aggressive war, much ink has been spilled on the 'supreme' international crime. This river of ink has become a torrent since the Rome Conference adopted the Statute of the International Criminal Court[1] (ICC) and included a provision that brought aggression within the jurisdiction of the Court, but deferred until the First Review Conference of the Assembly of States Parties[2] the decision on the definition of the crime and the conditions under which it could be prosecuted. This provision was a compromise between those who believed that the ICC Statute would not be complete unless it included the crime of aggression and those who argued that the determination of aggression was too political an issue to put before a court.

This chapter of the *Handbook* will analyze the various lines of debate about the International Criminal Court and the crime of aggression using, as a functional lens, the issue of whether the crime of aggression is susceptible to judicial determination. In other words, is a court such as the ICC equipped to decide whether a particular use of force constitutes the crime of aggression?

To develop criteria regarding how to address this question, the first section of this chapter will look at situations where it has been asserted – in both domestic and international courts – that certain questions are by their nature too political to be judged by a court. As will be discussed later in the chapter, this is essentially the argument made by states that oppose the inclusion of aggression within the jurisdiction of the ICC or argue that the threshold determination of the state act should be made by the United Nations Security Council.[3] This section will conclude that while the political question doctrine has not gained much acceptance in the context of international cases, it nonetheless provides useful criteria in *a priori* deciding on institutional arrangements such as the exercise of jurisdiction over aggression by the ICC.

The second section of the chapter is a brief history of the negotiations leading up to the ICC Statute and those that followed. The chapter will then turn to an analysis of the nature of the crime of aggression: its elements and its unique twofold nature which requires a characterization of state action before a finding of individual criminal responsibility. This section will show that the elements of the crime of aggression, including the attribution issue, present

---

[1]   Rome Statute of the International Criminal Court, 17 July 1998, 2187 UNTS 90.

[2]   The Assembly of States Parties is composed of all states parties to the ICC Statute. The Statute provides that seven years after its entry into force, a Review Conference will be convened to review the Statute and consider amendments thereto. It is anticipated that this Review Conference, which is scheduled to take place in 2010, will consider the definition of aggression. ICC Statute, arts 112, 121, 123.

[3]   See text accompanying notes 98–105 *infra*.

questions of international criminal law of the type that are typically decided by courts so that there should be no qualms about entrusting them to the ICC. The fourth section of this chapter will examine the issue of how the ICC's jurisdiction would be triggered in aggression cases. This issue is still very much open to negotiation and the various options on the table will be analyzed using the criteria derived from the political question doctrine. The final section presents the conclusion that the crime of aggression is certainly amenable to judicial determination.

PRUDENTIAL CONSTRAINTS ON ADJUDICATION

One of the best-known doctrines constraining courts from exercising judicial power is the political question doctrine set out by the US Supreme Court in *Baker* v. *Carr*.[4] While there are many nuances of the doctrine as it is articulated in American case law, the basic principle is that a court may conclude that it is incompetent to decide a particular matter either because such matter has been confided to the superior authority of another branch, or because the court believes that judicial procedures and abilities are not adequate to the task of decision.[5] The basis of the doctrine is the separation of powers that underlies the constitutional order of the United States.[6] While a survey of national legislation is beyond the scope of this chapter, it is worth noting that similar doctrines exist in other domestic systems.[7]

Political question-type objections are frequently raised to resist the jurisdiction of the International Court of Justice (ICJ) in cases concerning allegations of the illegal use of force. In the jurisdiction phase of the *Case Concerning Military and Paramilitary Activities in and Against Nicaragua (Nicaragua* v. *United States)*[8] ('*Nicaragua* Jurisdiction Decision'), Nicaragua argued that the United States' backing of anti-Sandinista rebels (the Contras) and its mining of Nicaraguan harbors violated international law. The US raised a wide range of challenges to jurisdiction and admissibility, many of which were resonant of the political question doctrine. These included the following:

(a) the claim that the United States was engaged in an unlawful use of armed force, or breach of the peace, or act of aggression against Nicaragua was a matter which was committed

---

4   369 US 186 (1961).

5   *Ibid*. 217. Other aspects of the doctrine that were emphasized in *Baker* v. *Carr* are: the impossibility of deciding without an initial policy determination of a kind clearly for non-judicial discretion; the impossibility of a court's undertaking independent resolution without expressing lack of the respect due coordinate branches of government; an unusual need for unquestioning adherence to a political decision already made; and the potential of embarrassment from multifarious pronouncements by various departments on one question.

6   *Ibid*.

7   See Orna Ben-Naftali, *Justice-Ability: A Critique of the Alleged Non-Justiciability of Israel's Policy of Targeted Killings*, 1(2) J INT'L CRIM. JUSTICE 368 (August 2003); Micaela Frulli, *When are States Liable Towards Individuals for Serious Violations of Humanitarian Law? The Markovic Case*, 1(2) J INT'L CRIM. JUSTICE 408 (August 2003).

8   *Case Concerning Military and Paramilitary Activities In and Against Nicaragua (Nicaragua* v. *United States), 1986 ICJ Rep. 392, Jurisdiction Judgment, 26 November 1986 (hereinafter '*Nicaragua* Jurisdiction Decision').

by the Charter of the United Nations and the practice of the United Nations to the competence of other organs;[9]

(b) the ICJ should decline to hear the case because it would affect the United States' ongoing exercise of the right to individual or collective self-defense under article 51 of the UN
Charter;[10]

(c) the ICJ, as a judicial organ, was unable to deal with situations involving ongoing armed
conflict because it did not have available to it a fixed pattern of ascertainable facts.[11]

The ICJ firmly rejected all of these arguments. With respect to the first two arguments
(based essentially on the role of the UN Security Council in cases involving the use of force),
the Court found that there was no doctrine of separation of powers that prevented it from
hearing a case at the same time it was being considered by the Council.[12] Indeed, the ICJ
emphasized that it was not in the habit of shying away from cases because of political implications or because they involved the use of force.[13] With respect to the difficulty of establishing legally relevant facts, the ICJ held that this was not unusual with respect to the cases
that it heard and was, in any event, the responsibility of the litigants.[14]

The ICJ's opinion in the *Nicaragua* Jurisdiction Decision reflects its consistent jurisprudence up to that point.[15] Since then, the Court has seen a large increase in contentious cases
relating to the use of force;[16] to date, however, the ICJ has not declined jurisdiction in a case
on grounds such as those described above.

The International Criminal Tribunal for the Former Yugoslavia (ICTY) has gone even
further than the ICJ and explicitly held that the political question doctrine is no longer part of
'the horizon of contemporary international law'.[17] The ICTY specifically held that the polit-

---

9   *Ibid.* paras 89–90.
10 *Ibid.* paras 91–8.
11 *Ibid.* para. 99.
12 *Nicaragua* Jurisdiction Decision, note 8 *supra*, paras 94–5.
13 *Ibid.* para. 96
14 *Ibid.* para. 101.
15 See *Certain Expenses of the United Nations*, 1962 ICJ Rep. 151, 155, Advisory Opinion, 20
July 1962; *Interpretation of the Agreement of 25 March 1951 Between the WHO and Egypt,* 1980 ICJ
Rep. 87, Advisory Opinion 20 December 1980, para. 33.
16 See, for example, *Case Concerning the Application of the Convention on the Prevention and
Punishment of the Crime of Genocide (Bosnia and Herzegovina v. Serbia and Montenegro*, hereinafter
'Genocide case'), 1996 ICJ Rep. 595, Preliminary Objections Judgment, 11 July 1996; *Case
Concerning the Land and Maritime Boundary Between Cameroon and Nigeria (Cameroon v. Nigeria),*
1998 ICJ Rep. 275, Preliminary Objections Judgment , 11 June 1998; *Case Concerning the Legality of
the Use of Force (Yugoslavia v. United States)*, 1999 ICJ Rep. 916, Provisional Measures Order, 2 June
1999 (one of a series of cases filed by Yugoslavia against the NATO member states); *Case Concerning
Armed Activities on Territory of the Congo (DRC v. Uganda),* 2000 ICJ Rep. 111, Provisional Measures
Order, 1 July 2000; *Case Concerning Oil Platforms (Iran v. United States),* 2003 ICJ Rep. 161,
Judgment, 6 November 2003. The most recent example is the application filed by Georgia against the
Russian Federation in relation to the military intervention of the latter in Southern Ossetia and
Abkhazia. *Application of the International Convention on the Elimination of all Forms of Racial
Discrimination (Georgia v. Russian Federation),* Application Instituting Proceedings, 12 August 2008,
available at www.icj-cij.org/docket/files/140/14657.pdf (last visited on 22 September 2008).
17 *Prosecutor* v. *Tadic*, ICTY Appeals Chamber, 2 October 1995, Decision on the Defence
Motion for Interlocutory Appeal on Jurisdiction, paras 24–25 (hereinafter '*Tadic Jurisdiction*

ical question doctrine was no bar to its examination of the Security Council's Chapter VII establishment of the Tribunal as a measure to restore international peace and security.[18]

It has been argued that one of the key reasons for the diminished applicability of the political question doctrine in cases before international courts is the differences between the UN Charter and national constitutions. Specifically, the United Nations is a system of overlapping – rather than exclusive – spheres of responsibility so that the separation of powers rationale underlying the doctrine is not relevant in the international sphere.[19] It is also argued that the highly politicized nature of all decision-making in the international sphere means that if the ICJ were to avoid taking cases on the basis of the political question doctrine, it would soon have an empty docket.[20]

Even though the political question doctrine has basically been rejected by international tribunals as a basis of justiciability, it is nonetheless a useful lens for considering *a priori* whether a court should exercise jurisdiction over a particular type of crime. While the UN Charter may not provide for a strict separation of powers (unlike, say, the US Constitution), it does allocate responsibilities to the various organs of the United Nations. At the time of making international institutional arrangements, it is certainly relevant to ask whether a certain type of adjudication would appropriately be carried out by courts in light of the competencies of other UN organs. Indeed, this is precisely the type of argument that has been made by opponents of including aggression within the jurisdiction of the ICC.[21]

The part of the political question doctrine that relates to whether standards for deciding the case are either available to or discoverable by a court is also useful in considering whether the crime of aggression is susceptible to judicial determination. For example, even though the crime of aggression was prosecuted immediately after the Second World War, some states and commentators have argued that it is insufficiently defined to allow the exercise of jurisdiction by the ICC. This issue will presumably be settled once a definition is adopted by the Assembly of States Parties. Nonetheless, in deciding an aggression case, the ICC will undoubtedly face a number of novel issues of both criminal law and international law. Some of these issues can already be identified and this chapter will consider whether the ICC will be able to draw upon existing methods of inquiry to decide upon them.

A related issue is the Court's ability to make determinations of fact in cases involving the use of force. As is demonstrated in the discussion below, international courts have been increasingly faced with the task of fact-finding in cases involving armed conflict or other sensitive security matters and have demonstrated the capability to do so.[22]

Thus, in examining the question of whether the crime of aggression is *ab initio* susceptible to judicial determination, this chapter will consider whether any aspects of the adjudication of aggression would raise questions that are committed solely to another organ of the United Nations. It will also consider whether there are manageable standards for resolving the

---

Decision'), available at www.un.org/icty/tadic/appeal/decision-e/51002.htm (last visited 21 September 2008).

[18]   *Ibid.* para. 22.

[19]   Lara M. Pair, *Note and Comment: Judicial Activism in the ICJ Charter Interpretation*, 8 ILSA J Int'l & Comp. L 181, 198 (2001).

[20]   *Ibid.*

[21]   See text accompanying notes 98–102 *infra.*

[22]   See text accompanying notes 72–82 *infra.*

issue, both from a legal and a factual perspective. Before turning to this analysis, however, it will briefly review the history of the negotiations leading up to the ICC Statute.

FROM ROME TO THE REVIEW CONFERENCE

The ICC Statute defines the jurisdiction of the Court as being 'limited to the most serious crimes of concern to the international community as a whole'.[23] These are: (a) the crime of genocide; (b) crimes against humanity; (c) war crimes; and (d) the crime of aggression. While the first three of these are defined in articles 6 to 8 of the Statute, the crime of aggression is left for future delineation. Article 5(2) provides as follows:

> The Court shall exercise jurisdiction over the crime of aggression once a provision is adopted in accordance with articles 121 and 123 defining the crime and setting out the conditions under which the Court shall exercise jurisdiction with respect to this crime. Such a provision shall be consistent with the relevant provisions of the Charter of the United Nations.

The negotiations in Rome that led to the inclusion of article 5(2), essentially as a compromise, have been explained in a number of articles and books about the ICC. The basic divisions have, by and large, been characterized as follows: the first group consisted of some countries, like the United States and the United Kingdom, that were 'hesitant about accepting new legal restraints that would hamper their freedom of military or humanitarian intervention';[24] the second group comprised several Arab states that were keen to include aggression in the ICC Statute based on the General Assembly's 1974 definition of aggression; and the third and largest group was composed of 'many others, including the European Union and about thirty "non-aligned" countries, [that] argued that, without jurisdiction over aggression, the ICC would be unacceptable'.[25]

The position of each of these groups on the desirability of including aggression within the mandate of the ICC is directly linked to their view of the definition of the crime of aggression. The United States, for example, took the position that the crime of aggression was not sufficiently criminalized and therefore not susceptible to definition.[26] As noted above, the members of the Arab League were, by and large, pushing to include the crime of aggression within the ICC's Statute and to base the definition of aggression on General Assembly

---

[23]   ICC Statute, art. 5(1).

[24]   Benjamin B. Ferencz, *Enabling the International Criminal Court to Punish Aggression*, 6 WASH. UNIV. GLOBAL STUD. L REV. 551, 558 (2007). See also Niels Blokker, *The Crime of Aggression and the United Nations Security Council*, 20 LEIDEN J INT'L L 867, 860–70 (2007); Danilo Zolo, *Who is Afraid of Punishing Aggressors?*, 5 J INT'L CRIM. JUSTICE 799, 806 (2007); Noah Weisbord, *Prosecuting Aggression*, 49 HARVARD INT'L LJ 161, 170–1 (2008).

[25]   Ferencz, note 24 *supra*, at 558.

[26]   Ambassador Bill Richardson stated on 17 June 1998 that the Rome Conference should avoid defining 'crimes that are not yet clearly criminalized under international law', and for that reason 'it remains premature to attempt to define a crime of aggression for purposes of individual criminal responsibility'. Quoted in Pietro Gargiulo, *The Controversial Relationship Between the International Criminal Court and the Security Council*, in I ESSAYS ON THE ROME STATUTE OF THE INTERNATIONAL CRIMINAL COURT (F. Lattanzi and W.A. Schabas (eds), 1999).

Resolution 3314.[27] Finally, the objective of the European Union and remaining non-aligned countries was to include a definition of aggression that met the requirements of legality and practicality. The link between the definitional and policy positions of the three groups will be further explored later in this chapter.

Since no definition of aggression was agreed upon in Rome, the issue was referred to the Preparatory Commission for the ICC ('ICC PrepCom').[28] The mandate of the ICC PrepCom lasted until 2002, when the ICC Statute came into force and the Court itself was constituted. At that time, the coordinator for the ICC PrepCom Working Group on the Crime of Aggression issued a discussion paper that reflected the proposals that had garnered the most support amongst delegates, as well as the options that were on the table with regard to the main areas of disagreement.[29] The paper identified three main issues as requiring resolution: (1) the entity that would decide whether the threshold of state-level aggression had been met; (2) the contours of the crime of aggression; and (3) the requisite linkage between state-level aggression and individual responsibility for the crime of aggression.

The ICC PrepCom was followed by the Special Working Group on the Crime of Aggression (the 'Aggression Working Group'), which was established by the Assembly of States Parties of the ICC. This Group, which included interested UN member states, specialized agencies and accredited legal experts, was charged with submitting a proposal to the Assembly of States Parties for consideration by the first Review Conference for the Rome Statute.[30] The Aggression Working Group took the PrepCom's 2002 discussion paper as its starting point and the Group's chairman in turn produced three discussion papers. The first such paper, which was circulated in early 2007, showed several options for resolving each of the three issues outstanding from the ICC PrepCom.[31] This paper was followed by extensive negotiations, both informal ones that were held at Princeton University and formal sessions of the Aggression Working Group in New York.[32] The results of these discussions were reflected in the second paper issued by the chairman in the summer of 2008.[33] The last chairman's paper

---

[27]   For a discussion of General Assembly Res. 3314, see text accompanying notes 59–60 *infra*.

[28]   United Nations Diplomatic Conference of Plenipotentiaries on the Establishment of an International Criminal Court, Rome, Italy, 15 June 15 to 17 July 1998, Final Act, 17 July 1998, UN Doc. A/CONF.183/10, 9 (1998).

[29]   Preparatory Commission for the International Criminal Court, Working Group on the Crime of Aggression, 1–12 July 2002, *Discussion Paper Proposed by the Coordinator*, PCNICC/2002/WGCA/RT.1/Rev.2 (11 July 2002) (hereinafter 'PrepCom 2002 Discussion Paper').

[30]   ICC, Assembly of States Parties, 3rd plenary meeting, *Continuity of Work in Respect of the Crime of Aggression*, para. 2, ICC-ASP/1/Res.1, para. 2 (9 September 2002).

[31]   ICC, Assembly of States Parties, Special Working Group on the Crime of Aggression, Resumed 5th Sess., New York, 29 January to 1 February 2007, *Discussion Paper on the Crime of Aggression Proposed by the Chairman*, ICC-ASP/5/SWGCA/2 (16 January 2007) (hereinafter 'Chairman's 2007 Paper').

[32]   ICC, Assembly of States Parties, Special Working Group on the Crime of Aggression, 6th Sess., New York, 30 November to 14 December 2007, *Informal Inter-sessional Meeting of the Special Working Group on the Crime of Aggression, held at the Liechtenstein Institute on Self-Determination, Woodrow Wilson School, Princeton University, United States, from 11 to 14 June 2007*, ICC-ASP/6/SWGCA/INF.1 (25 July2007).

[33]   ICC, Assembly of States Parties, Special Working Group on the Crime of Aggression, Resumed 6th Sess., New York, 2–6 June 2008, *Discussion Paper on the Crime of Aggression Proposed by the Chairman* (Revision June 2008), ICC-ASP/6/SWGCA/2 (14 May 2008) (hereinafter 'Chairman's 2008 Paper').

that was part of the formal working group process was issued in 2009 ('Chairman's 2009 Paper').[34] This paper (which did not differ greatly from the 2008 version) reflected the progress made by the Aggression Working Group up until its final meeting in February 2009 and forms the primary basis for the following discussion.[35]

The Chairman's 2009 Paper and the most recent report of the Aggression Working Group indicate that there is a considerable degree of consensus on the definition of both the crime and the nexus between the state and the individual. But significant differences remain on which entity should make the initial determination of state aggression.

WHAT IS AGGRESSION?

The Chairman's 2009 Paper proposes a definition of aggression that would parallel the definitions of genocide, crimes against humanity and the crime of aggression contained in articles 6 to 8 of the ICC Statute. The text of the proposed definition is as follows.

> Article 8*bis*   Crime of aggression
> 1. For the purpose of this Statute, 'crime of aggression' means the planning, preparation, initiation or execution, by a person in a position effectively to exercise control over or to direct the political or military action of a State, of an act of aggression which, by its character, gravity and scale, constitutes a manifest violation of the Charter of the United Nations.

---

[34]   ICC, Assembly of States Parties, Special Working Group on the Crime of Aggression, Resumed 7th Sess., New York, 9–13 February 2009, *Discussion Paper on the Crime of Aggression Proposed by the Chairman* (Revision January 2009), ICC-ASP/7/SWGCA/INF.1, Annex (19 February 2009) (hereinafter 'Chairman's 2009 Paper').

[35]   The recent reports of the Aggression Working Group provide details regarding the negotiations and will also be relied upon. See ICC, Special Working Group on the Crime of Aggression, Resumed 7th Sess., New York, 9–13 February 2009, *Report of the Special Working Group on the Crime of Aggression*, ICC-ASP/7/20/Add.1, Annex II (February 2009) (hereinafter 'Aggression Working Group February 2009 Report'); ICC, Special Working Group on the Crime of Aggression, 7th Sess., The Hague, 14–22 November 2008, *Report of the Special Working Group on the Crime of Aggression*, ICC-ASP/7/20, Annex III (November 2008) (hereinafter 'Aggression Working Group November 2008 Report'). On the other hand, the informal meetings that have been held since the last session of the Aggression Working Group have focused primarily on the amendment procedure for the ICC Statute and the definition of the elements of the crime of aggression. The records of these meetings do not reflect significant changes with regard to the issues pertinent to this chapter. See ICC, Assembly of States Parties, 8th Sess., The Hague, 18–26 November 2009, *Informal Inter-Sessional Meeting on the Crime of Aggression, hosted by the Liechtenstein Institute on Self-Determination, Woodrow Wilson School, at the Princeton Club, New York, from 8–10 June 2009*, ICC-ASP/8/INF.2 (10 July 2009) (hereinafter 'Informal Meeeting June 2009 Report'). Finally, it should be noted that this chapter does not describe the historical evolution of the crime of aggression prior to the ICC Statute. This topic has been extensively covered in the documents prepared for the Rome Conference and in a number of scholarly articles. See, for example, Preparatory Commission for the International Criminal Court, Working Group on the Crime of Aggression, New York, 8–19 April 2002, *Historical Review of Developments Relating to Aggression*, PCNICC/2002/WGCA/L.1 (24 January 2002); Weisbord, note 24 *supra*, at 162–9; Alberto L. Zuppi, *Aggression as International Crime: Unattainable Crusade or Finally Conquering the Evil*, 26 PENN. STATE INT'L L. REV. 1, 5–22 (2007); Jennifer Trahan, *Defining 'Aggression': Why the Preparatory Commission for the International Criminal Court has Faced Such a Conundrum*, 24 LOY. LA INT'L & COMP. L REV. 439, 441–7 (2002).

2. For the purpose of paragraph 1, 'act of aggression' means the use of armed force by a State against the sovereignty, territorial integrity or political independence of another State, or in any other manner inconsistent with the Charter of the United Nations.

Any of the following acts, regardless of a declaration of war, shall, in accordance with United Nations General Assembly Resolution 3314 (XXIX) of 14 December 1974, qualify as an act of aggression:

(a)   the invasion or attack by the armed forces of a State of the territory of another State, or any military occupation, however temporary, resulting from such invasion or attack, or any annexation by the use of force of the territory of another State or part thereof;

(b)   bombardment by the armed forces of a State against the territory of another State or the use of any weapons by a State against the territory of another State;

(c)   the blockade of the ports or coasts of a State by the armed forces of another State;

(d)   an attack by the armed forces of a State on the land, sea or air forces, or marine and air fleets of another State;

(e)   the use of armed forces of one State which are within the territory of another State with the agreement of the receiving State, in contravention of the conditions provided for in the agreement or any extension of their presence in such territory beyond the termination of the agreement;

(f)   the action of a State in allowing its territory, which it has placed at the disposal of another State, to be used by that other State for perpetrating an act of aggression against a third State;

(g)   the sending by or on behalf of a State of armed bands, groups, irregulars or mercenaries, which carry out acts of armed force against another State of such gravity as to amount to the acts listed above, or its substantial involvement therein.[36]

This proposal incorporates many choices and compromises regarding the definition of the crime of aggression and deserves careful attention.

Individual Conduct

Paragraph 1 quoted above addresses the definition of the individual's conduct – in other words it describes the 'crime' of aggression of which an individual may be convicted. This is in contrast to paragraph 2 of the definition, which describes the state 'act' of aggression.

The first issue in regard to the individual crime of aggression is the form of participation in the crime that should be criminalized. The Chairman's 2009 Paper posits that the 'planning, preparation, initiation or execution' of an 'act of aggression'[37] would, under certain circumstances, be a crime. The conduct verbs selected for the definition, which seem to have garnered broad support from the beginning of negotiations, follow the Nuremberg precedent.[38] The wide definition of activity that is punishable as a crime is,

---

36   Chairman's 2009 Paper, note 34 *supra*, Annex at 2–3 .

37   Previously, some states had backed using the term 'armed attack' in place of 'act of aggression'. This discussion focused on the term to be used to describe the state conduct and will be examined in that context also in this chapter. See text accompanying notes 55–8 *infra*. In late 2007, these states agreed to the use of the term 'act of aggression'. ICC, Assembly of States Parties, Special Working Group on the Crime of Aggression, 6th Sess., New York, 2–6 June 2006, *Report of the Special Working Group on the Crime of Aggression*, ICC-ASP/6/SWGCA/1 (13 December 2007) (hereinafter 'Aggression Working Group December 2007 Report').

38   See ICC, Assembly of States Parties, Special Working Group on the Crime of Aggression, 6th Sess., New York, 30 November to 14 December 2007, *Informal Inter-sessional Meeting of the Special Working Group on the Crime of Aggression, held at the Liechtenstein Institute on Self-Determination,*

however, offset by the limited category of persons who can be prosecuted and the requirement of a level of gravity.

According to article 8*bis* proposed in the Chairman's 2009 Paper, the crime of aggression may only be committed by 'a person [who is] in a position effectively to exercise control over or to direct the political or military action of a State'. This text makes clear that the leadership position of the person being prosecuted is an element of the crime of aggression rather than a separate requirement. This was considered necessary by several states in order to ensure that the ICC would not have jurisdiction over secondary perpetrators.[39] It is also notable that the leadership element of the crime focuses on the position of the defendant. The defendant must be in a 'position' to control or direct the political or military action of a state. This could be read to suggest that the defendant must have some formal leadership position and that persons such as advisers could not be convicted of aggression regardless of the extent of their influence. This ambiguity was recognized in the inter-sessional discussions. It appears, however, that those who argued that broadening the wording of the leadership clause 'would cause more problems than it would solve'[40] won the day. Finally, the text makes clear that position alone is not sufficient to allow conviction for aggression; the defendant's position must give him or her 'effective control' or the authority to 'direct' the political or military apparatus of a state. This ensures that people in primarily ceremonial leadership positions (for example, a monarch in a constitutional monarchy or a president in some parliamentary systems) would not be subject to prosecution solely because of position.

In selecting the formulation discussed above, the Chairman's 2009 Paper maintains the integrity of the 'General Principles of Criminal Law' contained in Part 3 of the ICC Statute. In particular, article 25 of this section, the relevant portion of which is reproduced below, continues to apply:

Article 25   Individual criminal responsibility
In accordance with this Statute, a person shall be criminally responsible and liable for punishment for a crime within the jurisdiction of the Court if that person:
(a)   commits such a crime, whether as an individual, jointly with another or through another person, regardless of whether that other person is criminally responsible;
(b)   orders, solicits or induces the commission of such a crime which in fact occurs or is attempted;
(c)   for the purpose of facilitating the commission of such a crime, aids, abets or otherwise assists in its commission or its attempted commission, including providing the means for its commission;
(d)   in any other way contributes to the commission or attempted commission of such a crime by a group of persons acting with a common purpose. Such contribution shall be intentional and shall either:
   (i)   be made with the aim of furthering the criminal activity or criminal purpose of the group, where such activity or purpose involves the commission of a crime within the jurisdiction of the Court; or
   (ii)   be made in the knowledge of the intention of the group to commit the crime;
(e)   in respect of the crime of genocide, directly and publicly incites others to commit genocide;
(f)   attempts to commit such a crime by taking action that commences its execution by means of a substantial step, but the crime does not occur because of circumstances independent of the person's intentions. However, a person who abandons the effort to commit the crime or other-

---

Woodrow Wilson School, Princeton University, United States, from 11 to 14 June 2007, ICC-ASP/6/SWGCA/INF.1, 2 (25 July 2007) (hereinafter 'Princeton Meetings Report').
   [39]   *Ibid.* 3.
   [40]   Aggression Working Group December 2007 Report, note 37 *supra*, at. 2.

wise prevents the completion of the crime shall not be liable for punishment under this Statute for the attempt to commit the crime if that person completely and voluntarily gave up the criminal purpose.[41]

Articles 8*bis* and 25(3) must be read together in order to determine the individual conduct that leads to criminal responsibility for aggression.

The approach selected in the Chairman's 2009 Paper is the so-called 'differentiated' approach which details the type of actions that could be prosecuted under the ICC Statute by allowing article 25(3) to apply to the crime of aggression. This approach can be contrasted with the 'monistic' approach, which was included in the PrepCom 2002 Discussion Paper. Under the latter, all aspects of the conduct element of the crime of aggression would have been contained in article 8*bis*, and article 25(c) would not have been applicable. Article 8*bis* would therefore have read something like the following:

> For the purpose of the present Statute, a person commits a 'crime of aggression' when, being in a position effectively to exercise control over or to direct the political or military action of a State, that person orders or participates actively in the planning, preparation, initiation or execution of an act of aggression.[42]

The words 'orders or participates actively' contained in the monistic text would have replaced the forms of participation articulated in article 25(3) of the ICC Statute. This would certainly have been a clear and coherent definition but would have lacked the detail and specificity of the differentiated approach. The differentiated approach also has the advantage of treating aggression in the same way that the other crimes within the ICC's jurisdiction are treated.

A few points bear mention with respect to the selection of the differentiated approach as the currently preferred option. First, as one commentator has pointed out, the key political factor in defining the scope of the crime of aggression is that some states prefer a narrower definition while others would like to see a wider jurisdiction for the ICC. 'The problem in terms of choosing a monistic or differentiated approach based on scope is that it is far from clear which approach is more restricted.'[43] Aside from the political issue, it should be noted that article 25(3) covers a variety of conduct that is not necessarily compatible with a leadership crime like aggression. Article 25(3) criminalizes the following types of individual conduct: committing; ordering, soliciting or inducing; aiding, abetting or otherwise assisting, including by providing the means for commission; in any other way contributing to the commission of the crime by a group of persons acting with a common purpose; and attempt. In particular, the latter four categories of individual action (which correspond to article 25(3)(c) to (f)) seem unsuited to the crime of aggression.

---

[41]　ICC Statute, art. 25. The Chairman's 2009 Paper also suggests including a provision clarifying the 'leadership' element of the crime of aggression at the end of this provision. Chairman's 2009 Paper, note 34 *supra*, Annex, at 5. For a discussion of this proposal, see text accompanying notes 49–50 *infra*.

[42]　Chairman's 2007 Paper, note 31 *supra*, para. 1, variant (b). This approach is similar to the one advocated by the International Law Commission. See *Draft Code of Crimes against the Peace and Security of Mankind*, II YB INT'L COMM'N 15 (Pt 2) (1996), art. 16.

[43]　Weisboard, note 24 *supra*, at 193.

To understand this issue it is necessary to hearken back to the essential nature of the crime of aggression; it is, at its heart, the criminalization of conduct by a leader. In the other crimes under the jurisdiction of the ICC, the focus is generally on holding commanders and leaders liable for the conduct of those for whom they are responsible. Given the difficulty of proving this type of responsibility, particularly in the context of armed conflicts involving irregular forces (which have been most often seen in recent years) criminal statutes are designed to bring a wide range of associational conduct within their purview. Aggression, on the other hand, necessarily starts from the opposite premise: a conscious decision at the top echelons of government to follow a particular policy. Accordingly, it is difficult to fit individual conduct criminalized for other types of offenses to the crime of aggression. For example, one might ask how a top echelon political or military leader aids or abets in the decision to launch an aggressive war. If such a prosecution is brought, it is evident that it would not be against the key decision-makers but against a wider circle of persons who may or may not have been involved in the decision-making process. The circle of liability could be even larger in the case of a prosecution for conduct criminalized under article 25(3)(d), that is, contributing to the commission of the crime.

Another difficulty with maintaining the applicability of article 25(3) to the crime of aggression is that sub-paragraph (f) permits the prosecution of attempted crimes. In the case of aggression, a precondition of the individual crime is the existence of state-level aggression. It is therefore difficult to envisage a scenario where the individual conduct described in article 25(f) would be prosecuted in the context of aggression.

The Chairman's 2009 Paper attempts to ameliorate this problem by the insertion of a new article 25(3)*bis* which would provide that '[i]n respect of the crime of aggression, the provisions of this article shall apply only to persons in a position effectively to exercise control over or to direct the political or military action of a State'.[44] This provision does not add anything new to the Statute because the leadership requirement is itself part of the definition of the crime as set out in article 8*bis*. At most it serves as a reminder that, despite the broad range of actions criminalized by article 25(3), only the actions that are committed by the leaders of a country constitute the crime of aggression. Its insertion suggests that much of article 25(3) is not, in fact, applicable to the crime of aggression.[45]

Another element of the ICC Statute that does not apply to the crime of aggression and could explicitly be excluded is article 28, which is titled 'Responsibility of commanders and other superiors'. As discussed above, most crimes under the jurisdiction of the ICC require the establishment of command responsibility. Article 28 establishes specific standards for imposition of criminal liability based on a superior-subordinate relationship that are in addition to the conduct criminalized under article 25(3). Since this type of responsibility is clearly not relevant to the crime of aggression, the Statute could explicitly provide that this article does not apply to aggression.[46]

---

44   Chairman's 2009 Paper, note 34 *supra*, Annex, at 5.
45   The current form of the draft elements of the crime of aggression that are being developed may also be relevant to this issue. The current draft provides that an element of the crime of aggression is that '[t]he perpetrator planned, prepared, initiated or executed an act of aggression'. Informal Meeting June 2009 Report, note 35 *supra*, App. I, at 14.
46   Chairman's 2008 Paper, note 33 *supra*, at 2. Although this issue was raised in the Chairman's 2008 Paper, no discussion of the matter is reflected in subsequent records of discussions.

As is evident from the discussion above, the types of legal and factual issues that arise in determining whether individual conduct relating to a state act of aggression is sufficient to impose liability are typical of those that international criminal judges are called upon to decide. For example, determining the level of participation necessary to consider a defendant guilty of a particular crime is an issue that courts are faced with in any case involving a joint criminal enterprise or command responsibility. Indeed, the ICTY and the International Criminal Tribunal for Rwanda (ICTR) have had occasion to consider this very issue in a number of cases.[47] These types of issues have also been considered by the ICJ in determining state responsibility for armed actions.[48] Ensuring that the leadership requirement is met would require the ICC to consider issues relating to lines of responsibility within government and military institutions that are well within its competence. Indeed, such an analysis can be seen as a reverse engineering of the analysis that the ICC will be required to conduct with respect to command responsibility for other crimes under its jurisdiction. All-in-all, one can conclude that, with regard to this aspect of the crime of aggression, there is nothing to suggest that it is not amenable to judicial determination.

State Conduct

The Chairman's 2009 Paper proposes that only the most serious instances of aggression would result in individual criminal responsibility. It punishes the commission of 'an act of aggression which, by its character, gravity and scale, constitutes a manifest violation of the Charter of the United Nations'. The inclusion of a severity threshold in article 8*bis* as a filter for frivolous cases reflects an approach similar to that used with respect to the leadership element.[49] In terms of consistency with other parts of the Statute, the severity threshold for aggression is at variance with article 6 on genocide, which contains no qualifier.

The form of the qualifier is itself of great significance. By requiring that the act of aggression constitute a 'manifest violation' of the UN Charter, the provision would exclude acts that might appear to be aggression but are not obviously in violation of the Charter.[50] The qualifier seems aimed at providing a way to ensure that armed interventions of a humanitarian character (or otherwise in furtherance of Charter goals) could not be prosecuted as the crime of aggression. Two recent examples illustrate this point: the intervention of the North Atlantic Treaty Organization (NATO) in Kosovo and the US-led invasion of Iraq. In 1999, NATO,

---

[47] See, for example, *Prosecutor* v. *Aleksovski*, Case No. IT-95-14/1-A, Judgment, 24 March 2000; *Prosecutor* v. *Delalic*, Case No. IT-96-21-A, Judgment, 20 February 2001, paras 54–104; *Prosecutor* v. *Jokic*, Case No. IT-01-42/1-S, Judgment, 18 March 2004; *Prosecutor* v. *Krajisnik*, Case No. IT-01-42/1-S, Judgment, 27 September 2006; *Prosecutor* v. *Boskoski*, Case No. IT-04-82-T, Judgment, 10 July 2008. The ICTR's main case on responsibility (interestingly in the civilian context) is *Prosecutor* v. *Nahimana, Barayagwiza and Ngeze*, Case No. ICTR-99-52-T, Judgment, 3 December 2003.

[48] See, *Genocide case*, note 16 *supra*.

[49] See text accompanying note 43 *supra*.

[50] The current version of the draft elements of the crime of aggression makes clear that it is necessary only to establish that the 'perpetrator was aware of the factual circumstances establishing the inconsistency of the use of armed force by the State with the Charter of the United Nations'. It does not require knowledge of law or a legal analysis. *Informal Meeting June 2009 Report*, note 35 *supra*, App. I, at 14, 17.

without the authorization of the Security Council, commenced a 78-day bombing campaign against the Federal Republic of Yugoslavia on humanitarian grounds. Several commentators characterized the intervention as a breach of UN Charter provisions prohibiting the use of armed force, but did not identify it as an act of international aggression.[51] Prior to the invasion of Iraq in 2002, the United States and its allies advanced arguments before the Security Council as to the need to take military action to ensure that Iraq had in fact relinquished its weapons of mass destruction as had been required by Security Council Resolution 640. The question remains whether the justifications put forward in both cases – which were based on enforcement of elements of the Charter – would be considered sufficient to remove these actions from the ambit of the crime of aggression.[52]

The severity threshold serves as a counterbalance to the relatively wide definition of the state act of aggression included in paragraph 2 of article 8*bis*. The delineation of this definition has been a controversial and highly political process. As one commentator has noted, 'The finished crime would require a detailed description of the prohibited State/collective act – a contemporary answer to the historic debate over what constitutes an illegal or unjust war.'[53] Thus, while the Chairman's 2009 Paper contains a proposal that seems to steer a middle road between the various positions articulated by states, there is no certainty that it will be adopted by the Assembly of States Parties.

The basis for the definition of aggression has been UN General Assembly Resolution 3314. While Resolution 3314 has been criticized by the International Law Commission, powerful states and well-known scholars,[54] the ICJ found that at least part of the Resolution reflects customary international law,[55] and it is at the heart of the definition put forward in the Chairman's 2008 Paper. The Resolution begins as follows:

1974 Definition of Aggression: United Nations General Assembly Resolution 3314 (XXIX)

Article 1
Aggression is the use of armed force by a State against the sovereignty, territorial integrity or political independence of another State, or in any other manner inconsistent with the Charter of the United Nations, as set out in this definition.

Article 2
The first use of armed force by a State in contravention of the Charter shall constitute *prima facie* evidence of an act of aggression although the Security Council may, in conformity with the Charter, conclude that a determination that an act of aggression has been committed would not be justified in the light of other relevant circumstances including the fact that the acts concerned or their consequences are not of sufficient gravity.

---

[51]   See, for example, Richard A. Falk, *NATO's Kosovo Intervention: Kosovo, World Order, and the Future of International Law,* 93 Am. J Int'l L 847, 847–8 (1999); Ronald C. Santopadre, *Note: Deterioration of Limits on the Use of Force and Its Perils: A Rejection of the Kosovo Precedent,* 18 St. John's JL Comm. 369 (2003); Zolo, note 24 *supra*, at 804.

[52]   See Andreas L. Paulus, *Peace Through Justice? The Future of the Crime of Aggression in a Time of Crisis,* 50 Wayne L Rev. 1, 24 (2004).

[53]   Weisbord, note 24 *supra*, at 175.

[54]   See Theodor Meron, *Defining Aggression for the International Criminal Court,* 25 Suffolk Transnat'l L Rev. 1 (2001–2002).

[55]   *Case Concerning Military and Paramilitary Activities In and Against Nicaragua (Nicaragua v. United States),* 1986 ICJ Rep. 14, Merits Judgment, 27 June 1986, para. 195) (hereinafter '*Nicaragua Merits Judgment*').

Article 3
Any of the following acts, regardless of a declaration of war, shall, subject to and in accordance with the provisions of Article 2, qualify as an act of aggression:
(a) the invasion or attack by the armed forces of a State of the territory of another State, or any military occupation, however temporary, resulting from such invasion or attack, or any annexation by the use of force of the territory of another State or part thereof;
(b) bombardment by the armed forces of a State against the territory of another State or the use of any weapons by a State against the territory of another State;
(c) the blockade of the ports or coasts of a State by the armed forces of another State;
(d) an attack by the armed forces of a State on the land, sea or air forces, or marine and air fleets of another State;
(e) the use of armed forces of one State which are within the territory of another State with the agreement of the receiving State, in contravention of the conditions provided for in the agreement or any extension of their presence in such territory beyond the termination of the agreement;
(f) the action of a State in allowing its territory, which it has placed at the disposal of another State, to be used by that other State for perpetrating an act of aggression against a third State;
(g) the sending by or on behalf of a State of armed bands, groups, irregulars or mercenaries, which carry out acts of armed force against another State of such gravity as to amount to the acts listed above, or its substantial involvement therein.[56]

The remaining provisions of Resolution 3314 indicate that (1) the list contained in article 3 is not exhaustive and that the Security Council may decide that other acts constitute aggression; (2) there is no justification for aggression which is a crime giving rise to international responsibility; (3) no territorial or other advantages resulting from aggression are lawful; (4) the definition is without prejudice to the provisions of the Charter; (5) it is without prejudice to rights of people dominated by colonial, racist or alien regimes to struggle for self-determination; and (6) the provisions of the Resolution are interrelated and should be so construed.

The text proposed in the Chairman's 2009 Paper for inclusion in the ICC Statute includes only paragraphs 1 and 3 of General Asssembly Resolution 3314.[57] This formulation is an attempt at a compromise between those who wanted the full text of the Resolution incorporated into the Statute and those who wished to have only articles 1 and 3 incorporated. The rationale behind of each of these positions is aptly summarized in the Report of the Princeton Meetings:

- Resolution 3314 should be included in its entirety: because its provisions were interrelated, as evidenced by its article 8; this would underline that the list of acts in the definition is not exhaustive; and elements in addition to articles 1 and 3 were important aspects of the definition.
- The Statute should contain a reference to articles 1 and 3 of Resolution 3314 only: this would avoid the possibility of a person being convicted of aggression on the basis of state acts that the Security Council found to be aggression at a later date under article 4 of the Resolution.[58]

---

56 General Assembly Res. 3314 (XXIX), 14 December 19074, UN Doc. A/RES/3314 (1974).

57 The Chairman's 2008 Paper had also called for the inclusion of the full text of the Resolution as an annex to the ICC Statute. Chairman's 2008 Paper, note 33 *supra*, at 2. No similar exhortation is found in the 2009 version of paper. Since the ICC Statute does not currently include any Annexes or a provision on the status of Annexes to the Treaty, the effect of adding the entire resolution as an Annex to the Statute was, in any event, unclear.

58 Princeton Meetings Report, note 43 *supra*, at 8–9.

It is clear that articles 1 and 3 of Resolution 3314 form its core in terms of the legal definition of aggression and should be part of the ICC Statute.

Thus, if the chairman's proposal were adopted, the ICC Statute would not include the presumption that the first use of armed force by a state in contravention of the Charter constituted *prima facie* evidence of an act of aggression. It also would not include a provision allowing the Security Council to override this presumption. The removal of such an explicit presumption undoubtedly provides some comfort to the states that have expressed concern that the potential for charges of aggression would unduly hamper their ability to intervene militarily to advance Charter purposes.

Turning to the text of paragraph 2 of article 8*bis*, a few points bear emphasis. First, this provision states that, 'for the purpose of paragraph 1' (that is, for the purpose of defining a crime of aggression under the ICC Statute), the term 'act of aggression' means 'the use of armed force by a State against the sovereignty, territorial integrity or political independence of another State, or in any other manner inconsistent with the Charter of the United Nations'. Paragraph 2 is explicitly tied to the definition of the crime of aggression to clarify that it is not intended to be used for other purposes, such as determining state liability.

Second, as noted earlier, the Chairman's 2009 Paper describes the prohibited state act which would trigger individual criminal liability as an 'act of aggression'. In earlier discussions, there was considerable disagreement amongst delegations as to whether 'act of aggression' or 'armed attack' was the appropriate characterization of the state conduct.[59] Although both terms are drawn from the UN Charter, the term 'act of aggression' has the stronger connection to the Charter[60] and has a richer history of enforcement that provides it with texture and meaning. The debate about which term to use to describe the prohibited state act related primarily to the appropriate scope of the crime of aggression and the related issue of the acceptability of incorporating General Assembly Resolution 3314. 'Armed attack' is generally perceived as narrower than the term 'aggression'. It is one of the forms of aggression listed in Resolution 3314. Using the term 'armed attack' would also disengage the crime of aggression from the 1974 definition of the 'state act'.[61] However, as early as 2007, there was broad support for the use of the term 'act of aggression'[62] and this was incorporated in the Chairman's 2009 Paper.

Third, the Chairman's 2009 Paper does not fully settle the debate about whether the ICC Statute should include an exhaustive or illustrative list of acts that would qualify as acts of aggression.[63] The chapeau of the list of acts tracks the language of Resolution 3314 in that it provides that '[a]ny of the following acts, regardless of a declaration of war, shall, in accordance with United Nation's General Assembly Resolution 3314 (XXIX) of 14 December 1974, qualify as an act of aggression'. The use of this type of formulation was clarified in

---

[59]   *Ibid.* 8.

[60]   The term 'act of aggression' is used in art. 39 of the UN Charter and is the titular provision in Chapter VII ('Action with Respect to Threats to the Peace, Breaches of the Peace, and Acts of Aggression'). The term 'armed attack', in contrast, is used only in art. 51 in the context of self-defense ('Nothing in the present Charter shall impair the inherent right of individual or collective self-defense if an armed attack occurs against a Member of the United Nations, until the Security Council has taken measures necessary to maintain international peace and security.').

[61]   Weisbord, note 24 *supra*, at 184.

[62]   Aggression Working Group December 2007 Report, note 37 *supra*, at 3.

[63]   Princeton Meetings Report, note 38 *supra*, at 10.

Resolution 3314 by the inclusion of article 4, which states that 'the acts enumerated ... are not exhaustive'. However, since the latter is not included in the ICC Statute, the connection to that portion of Resolution 3314 is indirect (through the reference in the chapeau).

Fourth, the list of acts included in the Chairman's 2009 Paper exactly matches the list in Resolution 3314. This is an important step forward in that it suggests a consensus that all of these acts could potentially qualify as aggression and does away with the long-standing attempt of certain states to cherry-pick parts of the list for inclusion in the ICC Statute. Moreover, the expansiveness of the list offsets to a great degree the ambiguity regarding whether it is exhaustive.

There should be little concern that the list would allow a *de minimus* use of force to be considered as aggression within the purview of the ICC. The definition of the crime of aggression included in paragraph 1 of article 8*bis* clearly provides that it is only subject to prosecution when the 'act of aggression' on which it is premised 'by its character, gravity and scale, constitutes a manifest violation of the Charter of the United Nations'. Moreover, the jurisdictional trigger for prosecutions of the crime of aggression[64] serves an additional protective barrier to the bringing of cases where the underlying state act is of insufficient gravity.

The ICC Role in Deciding State-Level Aggression

The following section will consider issues relating to whether and how the Security Council, the General Assembly, the ICJ and the ICC should be involved in determining that state aggression exists at a level that allows the initiation of an individual criminal prosecution. Nonetheless, it is clear from the proposal contained in the Chairman's 2009 Paper that any such initial determination would be subject to challenge by the defendant at the trial stage.[65]

The ICC would therefore be called upon to decide whether a state used armed force against the sovereignty, territorial integrity or political independence of another state, or in any other manner inconsistent with the Charter of the United Nations. The list of acts currently listed in article 8*bis* will no doubt serve as its guide on this issue.

The aftermath of the Second World War was the last occasion where courts made findings of aggression. Both the Nuremberg Tribunal and the International Military Tribunal for the Far East convicted the German and Japanese leadership of the international crime of aggression.[66] Since then, there have been no international prosecutions of aggression. Nonetheless, in the 50-odd years since the Nuremberg and Far East Tribunals rendered their judgments, international courts have applied the rules regarding the use of force contained in the UN Charter, international treaties and customary law to make determinations relating to armed conflicts. These decisions suggest that a court such as the ICC , which includes judges with expertise in both criminal law and international law, would be in a position to identify standards of fact-finding and legal principles that would allow it to decide whether particular state actions constitute aggression for purposes of its Statute.

The ICJ has had occasion to consider whether actions by a state constituted a use of armed force and the character of such use on a number of occasions in recent years. The Court's

---

[64]   See text accompanying notes 94–105 *infra*.
[65]   See text accompanying note 92 *infra*.
[66]   International Military Tribunal (Nuremberg), *Judgments and Sentences*, 41 AM. J INT'L L 172, 186 (1947); *In re Hirota and others*, 15 ANN. DIG. 356, 362–3 (Int'l Mil. Trib. for the Far East, 1948).

decision in the *Case Concerning Military and Paramilitary Activities in and Against Nicaragua* is perhaps the seminal decision in this area. In that case, Nicaragua argued that US backing of anti-Sandinista rebels (the Contras) and the mining of Nicaraguan harbors violated international law. The United States countered that it was assisting third countries (Honduras, El Salvador and Costa Rica) in exercising their right to self-defense against attacks by the Sandinista government of Nicaragua.

The *Nicaragua* case demonstrates that the ICJ is not easily swayed by arguments relating to the difficulty of ascertaining facts in the context of an ongoing conflict. Although it was apparent in the *Nicaragua* case that disputed factual evidence would pose a challenge, the ICJ rejected this argument.[67] Indeed, in its decision on the merits, it explained and justified at length the system used to deal with factual issues.[68] Moreover, the ICJ made substantive decisions with regard to the characterization of aspects of the ongoing conflict. In the *Nicaragua* case, the ICJ was not asked to find that acts of aggression had been committed by the United states. It did, however, conclude that certain actions by the United states on the territory of Nicaragua and its laying of mines in Nicaraguan waters were a breach of its obligation not to use force against another state. In the context of the US claims of self-defense, the ICJ explained the meaning of the term 'armed attack', holding that in order to meet this definition (thereby triggering the right to self-defense), acts of force had to meet a certain threshold of gravity.[69]

These two themes, evident in the *Nicaragua* case, have marked the jurisprudence of the ICJ. The ICJ has the willingness to make factual findings relating to difficult situations involving ongoing armed conflict and security issues and the ability to find legal standards that allow for the analysis of such situations. For example, in the *Case Concerning the Legality of the Threat or Use of Nuclear Weapons*, the Court rejected the argument that it should decline jurisdiction because the case would require it to 'study various types of nuclear weapons and to evaluate highly complex and controversial technological, strategic and scientific information'.[70] In the *Case Concerning the Legal Consequences of the Construction of a Wall in the Occupied Palestinian Territory*, Israel argued that the ICJ should not take jurisdiction because it did not 'have at its disposal the requisite facts and evidence' and would have to make difficult and indeterminate enquiries, 'first, into the nature and scope of the security threat to which the wall is intended to respond and the effectiveness of that response, and, second, into the impact of the construction for the Palestinians'.[71] The Court nonetheless took jurisdiction and made the necessary factual determinations to render its opinion.

Two recent ICJ cases have evaluated facts of the sort that the ICC would be required to consider in an aggression case. The first such case arose in the context of disputes between the Democratic Republic of the Congo (DRC) and its neighbors, Burundi, Rwanda and Uganda. The DRC brought cases against these three states alleging that their unlawful invasion of its territory constituted aggression. At the request of the DRC, the cases against

67   *Nicaragua* Jurisdiction Decision, note 8 *supra*, paras 99–101.
68   *Nicaragua* Merits Decision, note 55 *supra*, paras 57–74.
69   *Ibid.* paras 103–4.
70   *Case Concerning the Legality of the Threat or Use of Nuclear Weapons*, 1996 ICJ Rep. 226, Advisory Opinion, 8 July 1996, para. 15.
71   *Case Concerning the Legal Consequences of the Construction of a Wall in the Occupied Palestinian Territory*, 2004 ICJ Rep. 136, Advisory Opinion, 9 July 2004, para. 55.

Burundi and Rwanda were discontinued. The case against Uganda, however, proceeded to a judgment on the merits.[72] The ICJ found that Uganda had conducted military operations inside the territory of the DRC, miles from their common border. The Court characterized Uganda's activities as an 'unlawful military intervention ... of such a magnitude and duration that the Court considers it to be a grave violation of the prohibition of the use of force expressed in Article 2, paragraph 4, of the Charter'.[73] Despite the scale of illegal armed intervention, the Court did not qualify Uganda's intervention as aggression.[74] While the ICJ did not find aggression in this particular case, there was no suggestion from the Court that it lacked the competence to make such a determination. Rather, the lack of an ICJ finding of aggression may most likely be attributed to the Court's desire to tread carefully in this sensitive area.[75]

In the *Case Concerning the Application of the Convention on the Prevention and Punishment of the Crime of Genocide (Bosnia and Herzegovina* v. *Serbia and Montenegro)* ('*Genocide* case'), the ICJ considered in great detail the factual record relating to alleged acts of genocide by the Republika Srpska against Bosnian civilians. It also examined the issue of whether the actions of the Republika Srpska could be attributed to the State of Serbia and Montenegro.[76]

Two points that have arisen in relation to the ICJ's fact-finding in armed conflict cases illuminate issues that may arise when the ICC is called upon to make a finding of state-level aggression. The first relates to the standard of proof required to show that the state-level aggression took place. In the *Genocide* case, the ICJ considered, in the context of state responsibility, the burden of proof, the standard of proof, and methods of proof with regard to genocide. The burden of proof was held to be on the applicant state, regardless of the fact that certain documentary evidence would be solely in the possession of the respondent state, which was not ready to provide it to the ICJ.[77] With regard to the standard of proof, the applicant had argued for the standard to be the normal 'balance of probabilities, inasmuch as what is alleged is breach of a treaty obligation'.[78] The respondent, not surprisingly, argued that a charge of such exceptional gravity against a state required proof 'such as to leave no room for reasonable doubt'.[79] The ICJ chose a path apparently in between the two contentions holding that any 'claims against a State involving charges of exceptional gravity must be proved by evidence that is fully conclusive'.[80] In cases before the ICC, the burden of proof is on the Prosecutor and, as an element of the crime, it would appear that the state act of aggression would be required to be proved beyond a reasonable doubt.[81]

---

72   *Case Concerning Armed Activities on the Territory of the Congo (Democratic Republic of the Congo* v. *Uganda)*, Judgment, 19 December 2005), available at www.icj-cij.org/docket/files/116/10455.pdf (last visited 20 October 2009).

73   *Ibid.* paras 153, 165.

74   Its failure to do so was roundly criticized in the Separate Opinions of Judges Elaraby and Simma. *Ibid.* Judge Simma, Separate Opinion, para. 2; Judge Elaraby, Separate Opinion, para. 20.

75   See Blokker, note 24 *supra*, at 886.

76   *Genocide* case, note 16 *supra*, paras 377–450.

77   *Ibid.* paras 204–8.

78   *Ibid.* para. 208.

79   *Ibid.*

80   *Genocide* case, note 16 *supra*, para. 209.

81   ICC Statute, art. 66.

With regard to the method of proof, in the *Genocide* case the ICJ catalogued the vast array of material provided to the Court by way of evidence. In addition to witness and expert testimony, the ICJ considered:

(a)   reports, resolutions and findings by various UN organs, such as the Secretary-General, the General Assembly, the Security Council and its Commission of Experts, the Commission on Human Rights, the Sub-Commission on the Prevention of Discrimination and Protection of Minorities and the Special Rapporteur on Human Rights in the former Yugoslavia;
(b)   documents from other intergovernmental organizations, such as the Conference for Security and Cooperation in Europe;
(c)   documents, evidence and decisions from the ICTY;
(d)   publications from governments;
(e)   documents from non-governmental organizations, media reports, articles and books.[82]

This listing gives an idea of the types of evidence that could be submitted by the ICC Prosecutor and any defendant in an aggression prosecution. It demonstrates that while factual issues relating to aggression may be challenging, there are means available for a court to decide these matters.

Like the ICJ, the ICTY has not shied away from factual and legal determinations relating to the use of force. The ICTY encountered challenges to its jurisdiction in its very first case on the grounds that there was no armed conflict and that the character of the conflict prevented prosecution of the defendant. With regard to the first challenge, the ICTY ruled that the fact that there were purportedly no armed activities in the particular areas where the alleged crimes had occurred did not mean that the crimes had not occurred in the context of a broader armed conflict. By reference to the Geneva Conventions and Protocols thereto, the Tribunal derived a means for determining the geographical and temporal scope of an armed conflict and applied this test to the factual record before it.[83] The ICTY addressed whether the conflict was international or internal and found a sufficient factual record (including Security Council resolutions relating to the conflict in the former Yugoslavia and various agreements entered into by the parties to the conflict with regard to the applicability of international humanitarian law) to find that the conflict was a mixed international-internal one.[84] It was also able to reach the legal conclusion that different provisions of its Statute were applicable with regard to different aspects of the conflict. For example, article 2 of the ICTY Statute referring to grave breaches of the Geneva Conventions was applicable only to crimes committed in the course of international hostilities,[85] while article 3 of the Statute covering violations of the laws and customs of war was held to be applicable in both internal and international conflicts.[86]

In sum, it is evident that international courts today are well able to decide upon both factual and legal questions relating to the use of force. With respect to an allegation of aggres-

---

[82]   *Genocide* case, note 16 *supra*, para. 211.
[83]   *Tadic Jurisdiction Decision*, note 117 *supra*, para. 70.
[84]   *Ibid.* paras 71–8.
[85]   *Ibid.* paras 80–2.
[86]   *Ibid.* para. 89

sion, the ICC would be called upon to determine whether the factual record established that activities of the sort listed in the definition of the state act of aggression had taken place. While developing the factual record would no doubt be a challenge for the Prosecutor, all courts addressing issues relating to conflict situations face these issues, and the record of the ICJ and the ICTY demonstrates that such factual evidence can and has been developed. Like the ICJ in the *Genocide* case, the ICC would have to consider what weight to give the findings of any other UN organ that is authorized (either as part of the jurisdictional trigger discussed below[87] or otherwise) to make findings with regard to the state act of aggression. To some extent, this will depend on the nature of the organ that is finally selected to make the decision and the actual form the decision takes. Here again, however, the practice of the ICJ and the ICTY in relying on UN documentation could serve as an example for the ICC.

With respect to the legal characterization, the ICC would have to decide whether a particular use of force meets the legal threshold of aggression and, if the proposal contained in the Chairman's 2009 Paper is accepted, whether the state act of aggression 'constitutes a manifest violation of the Charter of the United Nations'. In this context, the Court would no doubt be required to weigh any justifications put forward by the state accused of aggression and to decide whether they were justified or were pretexts for the use of force.

WHO MAKES THE THRESHOLD DETERMINATION OF THE STATE ACT OF AGGRESSION THAT TRIGGERS THE ICC'S JURISDICTION?

The most politically divisive issue relating to the crime of aggression is which UN organ should decide whether the prerequisite state act of aggression took place and how such a determination should trigger the ICC's jurisdiction? The proposal contained in the Chairman's 2009 Paper reflects some progress on this thorny issue, but still includes several alternatives with regard to which there is little consensus. This proposal is reproduced below:

Article 15bis   Exercise of jurisdiction over the crime of aggression
1. The Court may exercise jurisdiction over the crime of aggression in accordance with article 13, subject to the provisions of this article.
2. Where the Prosecutor concludes that there is a reasonable basis to proceed with an investigation in respect of a crime of aggression, he or she shall first ascertain whether the Security Council has made a determination of an act of aggression committed by the State concerned. The Prosecutor shall notify the Secretary-General of the United Nations of the situation before the Court, including any relevant information and documents.
3. Where the Security Council has made such a determination, the Prosecutor may proceed with the investigation in respect of a crime of aggression.
4. (*Alternative 1*) In the absence of such a determination, the Prosecutor may not proceed with the investigation in respect of a crime of aggression [*Option 1: end the paragraph here*] [*Option 2: add*: unless the Security Council has, in a resolution adopted under Chapter VII of the Charter of the United Nations, requested the Prosecutor to proceed with the investigation in respect of a crime of aggression.]
4. (*Alternative 2*) Where no such determination is made within [6] months after the date of notification, the Prosecutor may proceed with the investigation in respect of a crime of aggression [*Option 1: end the paragraph here*] [*Option 2: add*: provided that the Pre-Trial Chamber has authorized the

---

[87]   See text accompanying notes 94–105 *infra*.

commencement of the investigation in respect of a crime of aggression in accordance with the procedure contained in article 15.] [*Option 3: add*: provided that the General Assembly has determined that an act of aggression has been committed by the State referred to in article 8 *bis*.] [*Option 4: add*: provided that the International Court of Justice has determined that an act of aggression has been committed by the State referred to in article 8 *bis*.]

5. A determination of an act of aggression by an organ outside the Court shall be without prejudice to the Court's determination of an act of aggression under this Statute.

6. This article is without prejudice to the provisions relating to the exercise of jurisdiction with respect to other crimes referred to in article 5.[88]

This critical issue relates, of course, to the powers of various UN organs under the Charter with regard to the maintenance of peace and security in general, and determining the existence of state aggression in particular.

Alternative 1: The Security Council

The principal argument for allocating this function to the Security Council is that, under article 24 of the UN Charter, the Security Council has 'primary responsibility for the maintenance of international peace and security', and that under article 39 of the Charter:

> [t]he Security Council shall determine the existence of any threat to the peace, breach of the peace, or act of aggression and shall make recommendations, or decide what measures shall be taken in accordance with Articles 41 and 42, to maintain or restore international peace and security.

The primacy of the Council with respect to these matters was no doubt the impetus behind article 23(2) of the International Law Commission's draft Statute (which provided that a complaint relating to aggression 'may not be brought under this Statute unless the Security Council has first determined that the State has committed the act of aggression which is the subject of the complaint'),[89] and crucial for the proponents of alternative 1 set out in the Chairman's 2009 Paper.

Alternative 1 itself contains two options The first would completely prevent the Prosecutor from moving forward with an investigation in the absence of a finding of aggression by the Security Council; the second would allow an investigation to proceed if 'the Security Council has, in a resolution adopted under Chapter VII of the Charter of the United Nations, requested the Prosecutor to proceed with the investigation in respect of a crime of aggression'. As explained by the chairman, 'Alternative 1 makes the proceeding of an investigation into a crime of aggression conditional upon an active decision of the Security Council, namely either a substantive determination of aggression by the Council (option 1), or merely procedural authorization (option 2).'[90]

The first option under alternative 1, that is, requiring a specific determination of aggression, can be criticized on several grounds. The obvious difficulty is that it would prevent the ICC from proceeding unless there was the political will in the Security Council to make a

---

[88]   Chairman's 2009 Paper, note 34 *supra*, at 3–4.

[89]   *Draft Statute for an International Criminal Court*, II YB INT'L L COMM'N (Pt 2), (1994) at art. 23(2).

[90]   Chairman's 2008 Paper, note 33 *supra*, at 1.

finding of aggression.[91] Advocates of a strong role for the Security Council tend to favor such an arrangement, arguing that the Council's '[f]ailure to act in a particular case need not be proof of failure; it may be evidence of statesmanship'.[92] While this will certainly be the case in some situations, the possibility of an aggression prosecution by the ICC could also create reverse pressure on the Security Council to make a finding of aggression. Option 2 provides a way out of this by allowing the Security Council to authorize an aggression prosecution without necessarily making a finding that aggression occurred.

However, option 2 would not necessarily insulate the role of the Security Council from criticism based on the veto power of its five permanent members. The argument here, of course, is that no national of these states (or of states allied with them) would ever be prosecuted for aggression. Prosecutions for aggression would therefore continue to bear the taint of victor's justice that has followed them since Nuremberg. Some have proposed getting around the veto issue by positing that a decision under alternative 1, option 2 should be regarded as a procedural decision under article 27(2) of the Charter, which requires only 'an affirmative vote of nine members'.[93] The text currently proposed for this concept does not, however, make this clear.[94]

Alternative 2: The ICC, the General Assembly or the ICJ

Alternative 2 of the Chairman's 2009 Paper considers how an aggression prosecution could proceed even if the Security Council declines to take either of the routes made available to it under alternative 1. This alternative includes four options for what might happen if the Council does not act within six months of notification by the Prosecutor:

Option 1. the Prosecutor may proceed with the investigation.
Option 2. the Prosecutor may proceed with the investigation 'provided that the Pre-Trial Chamber has authorized the commencement of the investigation in respect of a crime of aggression in accordance with the procedure contained in article 15'.
Option 3. the Prosecutor may proceed with the investigation 'provided that the General Assembly has determined that an act of aggression has been committed by the State referred to in article 8 bis'.
Option 4. the Prosecutor may proceed with the investigation 'provided that the International Court of Justice has determined that an act of aggression has been committed by the State referred to in article 8 bis'.

---

[91]   Similar concerns were expressed with respect to the delaying mechanism contained in art. 16. See, for example, Gargiulo, note 26 *supra*, at 89, n. 57. This aspect of the relationship between the ICC and the Security Council is discussed at note 94 *infra*.

[92]   Meron, note 45 *supra*, at 13.

[93]   In contrast, art. 27(3) enshrines the veto power ('Decisions of the Security Council on all other matters shall be made by an affirmative vote of nine members including the concurring votes of the permanent members; provided that, in decisions under Chapter VI, and under paragraph 3 of Article 52, a party to a dispute shall abstain from voting.').

[94]   A third Security Council related option, which was presented and considered during 2008–2009 was the so-called 'red light' proposal. This would allow the Council to stop an ongoing investigation of aggression. Aggression Working Group February 2009 Report, note 35 *supra*, at 24. This proposal seems to duplicate the suspension power already found in art. 16 of the ICC Statute and did not garner much support. See, text accompanying note 100 *infra*.

The ICC

Options 1 and 2 – which would allow an aggression prosecution to commence without a determination by any other body as to the existence of sstate-level aggression – would leave this issue to the ICC itself to decide. The resistance to giving the ICC this mandate is based on the argument that this would violate the institutional peace and security structure of the UN Charter. This argument is resonant of the aspect of the political question doctrine that the judiciary should not make decisions relating to matters that are entrusted to another branch of government.

As has been convincingly argued by many commentators, the Security Council has primary, but not sole, responsibility for determining the existence of a threat to the peace, breach of the peace, or act of aggression.[95] As early as 1962, the ICJ held that the Security Council's responsibility in the area of peace and security was primary and not exclusive and that the UN Charter 'makes it abundantly clear ... that the General Assembly is also to be concerned with international peace and security'.[96] This position has been consistently reaffirmed by the Court.[97] As discussed above, the ICJ has frequently considered issues relating to peace and security, including in situations that were simultaneously under consideration by the Security Council.[98] Accordingly, there is nothing in the UN Charter structure that categorically prevents another organ from taking a role in determining the existence of a threat to the peace, breach of the peace, or act of aggression.

Moreover, under the ICC Statute, the Security Council can suspend criminal investigations and proceedings in the interests of international peace and security. Article 16 of the Statute provides:

> No investigation or prosecution may be commenced or proceeded with under this Statute for a period of 12 months after the Security Council, in a resolution adopted under Chapter VII of the Charter of the UN, has requested the Court to that effect; that request may be renewed by the Council under the same conditions.

Thus, the Security Council can act under Chapter VII (which allows it to take mandatory action in the interests of maintaining international peace and security) to stop ICC investigations and prosecutions. The availability of the suspension mechanism undermines the argument that the ICC's exercise of jurisdiction over the crime of aggression would hamper the Security Council in fulfilling its primary responsibility for the maintenance of international peace and security.

By allowing suspension, the ICC Statute also recognizes that prosecutions at the ICC (unlike those at the ICTY and the ICTR) are not necessarily measures to restore international peace and security. Rather, the role of the ICC is to provide a forum for holding individuals accountable for 'the most serious crimes of concern to the international community as a

---

[95]   See Blokker, note 24 *supra*, at 886.

[96]   *Certain Expenses of the United Nations (Article 17(2) of the Charter)*, Advisory Opinion, 20 July 1962, 1962 ICJ Rep. 151, 163.

[97]   See, for example, *Nicaragua Jurisdiction Decision*, note 8 *supra*, paras 94–5; *Case Concerning the Legal Consequences of the Construction of a Wall in the Occupied Palestinian Territory*, note 71 *supra*, para. 26.

[98]   See text accompanying notes 8–12 *supra*.

whole'. Since outlawing the illegitimate use of force by one sovereign state against another is surely the fundamental aim of the UN Charter, the purpose served by prosecuting aggression is to ensure that the norm against such uses of force is enforced at the individual level.

Another argument advanced against allowing the ICC to decide on the state act of aggression is that this type of inquiry would unduly politicize the Court. The latter argument has been articulated by Professor Meron:

> Moreover, to ask the ICC, in the absence of a determination by the Security Council, to decide that an act of aggression has taken place would force the ICC to become immersed in political controversies between states. Such an immersion would endanger the ICC's judicial role and image. Aggression is an act of state. Imagine the immense difficulties the ICC, as a court of individual criminal responsibility, would face in dealing even with relatively simple matters of aggression. Is it equipped to consider such matters as historical claims to territory, maritime boundaries, legitimate self-defense under Article 51, or legitimate reprisals? Do we want to expose the ICC to the inevitable accusations of politicization? And is the competence of the ICC, in any event, not limited to jurisdiction over natural persons? We must not turn the ICC into a political forum for discussing the legality of use of force by states.[99]

Taking these arguments in reverse order, it is clear that any threshold determination by the ICC relating to the state act of aggression relates only to its jurisdiction over individuals and not to state responsibility. Moreover, as is evident from the preceding section, regardless of whether the jurisdictional trigger for an aggression prosecution is pulled by the Security Council, the ICC would be required – as part of the trial of any individual for the crime of aggression – to decide on the issue of state aggression. Thus, the ICC, in any event, would affect the political landscape of aggression. Indeed, setting up a structure in which there is an inherent risk of inconsistent outcomes is perhaps more dangerous than removing aggression from the political sphere of the Security Council to the judicial sphere of the ICC. With regard to the ability of the ICC to rule on questions relating to the use of force, it is noted that the judges on the Court have expertise in both criminal law and international law so that it should be considered no less able to decide on these issues than the other international courts that have been called upon to do so.

Apart from the high politics surrounding the two broad alternatives discusssed above, it is worth exploring certain technical differences between them. These stem from the mechanism for triggering a case under the ICC Statute. Article 13 of the ICC Statute identifies three situations in which the Court may exercise its jurisdiction: (1) referral to the Prosecutor by a state party; (2) referral to the Prosecutor by the Security Council; and (3) investigations initiated by the Prosecutor.

In cases where the Prosecutor has initiated the investigation, he is required to follow the procedure set out in article 15 of the ICC Statute. Several elements of this process are important to our analysis and the corresponding provisions are reproduced below:

Article 15 Prosecutor
1. The Prosecutor may initiate investigations *proprio motu* on the basis of information on crimes within the jurisdiction of the Court.
2. The Prosecutor shall analyze the seriousness of the information received. For this purpose, he or she may seek additional information from States, organs of the United Nations, intergovernmental

---

[99] Meron, note 59 *supra*, at 13.

or non-governmental organizations, or other reliable sources that he or she deems appropriate, and may receive written or oral testimony at the seat of the Court.

3. If the Prosecutor concludes that there is a reasonable basis to proceed with an investigation, he or shall submit to the Pre-Trial Chamber a request for authorization of an investigation, together with any supporting material collected. Victims may make representations to the Pre-Trial Chamber, in accordance with the Rules of Procedure and Evidence.

The ICC Statute envisages a two-step process. First, the Prosecutor would initiate an investigation. This stage involves the analysis of information available to the Prosecutor and the seeking out of additional information. If, on the basis of his own investigation, the Prosecutor concludes that there is a reasonable basis to proceed, he may trigger the second stage and request authorization from a Pre-Trial Chamber.

Alternative 1 would not change this process for the crime of aggression. If the Security Council did not act within a specified period of time after notification by the Prosecutor, the normal process for investigations initiated by the Prosecutor would be followed.

Alternative 2 would change this process for the crime of aggression; the investigation could only proceed if 'the Pre-Trial Chamber has authorized the commencement of the investigation in respect of a crime of aggression in accordance with the procedure contained in article 15'.[100] It is not fully clear whether the two-step structure of article 15, paragraphs 1 to 3, is retained. Is the Prosecutor authorized to conduct any investigation before bringing it to the Pre-Trial Chamber for authorization or is that authorization required before the Prosecutor can proceed with the activities set out in article 15, paragraph 2?

If a Pre-Trial Chamber is involved, one must consider what the Chamber will have to decide in an aggression investigation. Article 15(4) provides:

> If the Pre-Trial Chamber, upon examination of the request and the supporting material, considers that there is a reasonable basis to proceed with an investigation, and that the case appears to fall within the jurisdiction of the Court, it shall authorize the commencement of the investigation, without prejudice to subsequent determinations by the Court with regard to the jurisdiction and admissibility of a case.

Since the state act of aggression is the *sine qua non* of the individual crime of aggression, the Pre-Trial Chamber will be required to find that there is a reasonable basis to proceed with respect to the state-level act and the individual act. This would likely be a *prima facie* type of determination and could be based on documentary evidence developed by other parts of the United Nations, including Security Council records.

The UN General Assembly or the ICJ

A number of non-aligned states have pushed for allowing the General Assembly or the ICJ to decide on the issue of state-level aggression. Proponents of the General Asssembly 'invoke the Uniting for Peace Resolution of 1950, whereby the General Assembly, faced with recur-

---

[100]   The Aggression Working Group also discussed the possibility of whether a Special Chamber should be constituted to consider the threshold question of state-level aggression. However, this proposal does not seem to have garnered much support. Aggression Working Group November 2008 Report, note 35 *supra*, at 51–2.

rent Security Council deadlocks, exerted authority over determinations relating to the use of force and subsequently condemned armed attacks in a number of violent crises'.[101] Not only has the ICJ recognized the role of the General Asssembly in the field of international peace and security, the practice of the United Nations shows that the Assembly has firmly asserted its role in the determination of state-level aggression. The Assembly adopted Resolution 3314, which is likely to be the basis of the definition of aggression in the ICC. Moreover, in six situations the Assembly has qualified state use of force as acts of aggression.[102] Opponents of General Asssembly involvement argue that the procedural and evidentiary standards of the Assembly are insufficiently rigorous.

The procedural and evidentiary standards of the General Assembly are not substantially different from those of the Security Council and, in any event, any determination by the General Assembly (like any determination by the Council or the ICJ) would have to be fully re-examined by the ICC at the trial stage.[103] While there is no technical bar to the General Assembly's making the determination of State level aggression, given the power structure within the United Nations, it seems highly unlikely that this will come to pass. From the point of view of the ICC, using the General Assembly rather than the Security Council as the jurisdictional trigger would not appear to make much difference in terms of the Court's ability to decide a particular case.

The ICJ seems a slightly more likely choice than the Assembly. Its proponents note the Court's experience in 'making legal determinations related to acts of aggression and point to the recent Armed Activities on the Territory of the Congo, the 1996 Nuclear Weapons Advisory Opinion, the 1986 Nicaragua Case, and the 1962 Certain Expenses of the United Nations in support of this view'.[104] Although, as with the General Assembly, critics have pointed out that the ICJ does not use the same high evidentiary standards that the ICC as a criminal court must follow, any determination would be re-examined at the trial stage. Moreover, many of the states that object to allowing the General Assembly to decide on aggression would likely also object to giving this role to the ICJ.

CONCLUSION

The discussion above reveals the complexities of the debate surrounding the crime of aggression and, in particular, the circumstances under which the ICC should exercise jurisdiction over it. There remains a great divide amongst commentators as to the political feasibility of reaching an agreement on the definition and jurisdictional trigger for the crime of aggression. The lens of this chapter is somewhat different in that it focuses instead on the ability of the ICC to decide on the crime of aggression. However, it is apparent that this aspect of the issue will itself be affected by the decision on the jurisdictional trigger.

---

[101]   Weisbord, note 24 *supra*, at 201, n. 159.
[102]   See Blokker, note 24 *supra*, at 881.
[103]   See text accompanying note 92 *supra*.
[104]   Yassin A. M'Boge, *The Council and the Court: Shared Objectives or Opposing Views on the Crime of Aggression*, JCD Research Paper No. 31/2010, 26, available at http://ssrn.com/abstract= 1641142.

To determine whether the crime of aggression is amenable to judicial determination by the ICC, this chapter examined the contours of the crime and, at every step, asked three questions.

1. Was the decision that the ICC would have to make committed to another organ of the United Nations?
2. Were there available or discoverable legal standards that the ICC could use in making its decision?
3. Would the ICC be able to make the necessary factual findings?

The first issue considered was individual criminal liability, with respect to which there is no question of a role for other UN organs; this is clearly a judicial task. It was demonstrated that the jurisprudence of the ICTY and ICTR showed that sufficient legal standards exist to allow the ICC to make the necessary determinations. Moreover, establishing a factual record on individual conduct is typical of criminal trials and has previously been undertaken in the international sphere.

Turning to the state act of aggression, it is noted that since the state action is an element of the crime of aggression, the ICC would have to examine the matter at the trial stage. As with the issue of individual liability, there is no question that during the trial, this is the responsibility of the Court and not any other UN organ. This section examined the jurisprudence of the ICJ in cases involving allegations of the use of force or aggression or other sensitive security issues, as well as the case law of the ICTY relating to the conflict in the Former Yugoslavia. It concluded that international courts have available to them standards for deciding questions relating to armed conflict, including whether certain state conduct can be categorized as aggression. This section also demonstrated the type of factual record that could be built with regard to an aggression case before the ICC.

The last section of this chapter considered the most controversial issue with respect to aggression prosecutions before the ICC: How should they be triggered? This section focused primarily on whether the decision on state-level aggression was the sole prerogative of the Security Council. Could the ICC decide on it without Council authorization? Analysis of the UN Charter and of the ICJ case law relating to the division of responsibilities among UN organs in the field of international peace and security demonstrated that the Security Council has primary, but not exclusive, competence in this field. Furthermore, this section considered arguments that allowing the ICC to make a determination of state-level aggression without Security Council authorization would hinder the Council's ability to carry out its mandate to maintain international peace and security and unduly politicize the Court. This section argued that because the Security Council can suspend ICC investigations and proceedings with a decision under Chapter VII of the UN Charter, its authority and ability to restore international peace and security would not be hampered by allowing the Court to decide on state-level aggression. Finally, with respect to the issue of possible politicization, this section pointed out that, given that the ICC will be required to decide on state-level aggression at the trial stage, perhaps a greater risk would be that of inconsistent outcomes.

In sum, this chapter concludes that judicial determination of the crime of aggression is indeed possible. There are, no doubt, difficult issues of law and fact that will require careful reflection and analysis by the ICC, but the crime itself is certainly amenable to judicial determination.

PART III

INTERNATIONAL CRIMINAL
COURTS AND TRIBUNALS

7 The contribution of non-governmental organizations to the creation of international criminal tribunals
Mark S. Ellis

INTRODUCTION

The establishment of international criminal tribunals marked a revolutionary change in the pursuit of international criminal justice. The success of these tribunals, however, would not have occurred without the support of non-governmental organizations (NGOs). NGOs have long played a multidimensional and indispensable role in advocating that the individuals responsible for gross violations of international law be brought to justice. These organizations have documented, lobbied, advised, coordinated, criticised, monitored and influenced public opinion in support of war crimes tribunals. They have provided resources and expertise to less developed states, and political support for developed states pursuing these accountability mechanisms. In so doing, NGOs have contributed to the overall legitimacy of the tribunals by ensuring that transparency and fair standards are employed in trials and by making certain that affected communities feel a sense of partnership with international justice. As one legal expert has stated:

> Over the past fifteen years, every tribunal has needed the support of NGOs to push governments to cooperate on the apprehension and transfer of indicted persons, provide intelligence and other information necessary to criminal investigations and trials, and help secure financial resources. Without the involvement of supportive governments and NGOs, many of these tribunals would have languished without defendants to try or key evidence to present.[1]

Non-governmental organizations have also ensured that tribunals remain responsible not only to the principle of international justice but to the international community at large. They have helped educate the public on the role of tribunals and establish best practices for future tribunals. NGOs have worked tirelessly, often without recognition and with meagre financial resources, to ensure that international justice is never compromised or forgotten. Their role has become crucial in the success of domestic and international criminal tribunals established to prosecute the worst offenders of international criminal law.

This chapter will explore the importance of NGOs in establishing newly formed international criminal tribunals and will address their roles at the various stages of the tribunals' formation. The chapter will detail NGO involvement in the creation of these tribunals, specifically the International Criminal Tribunal for the Former Yugoslavia (ICTY), the International Criminal Tribunal for Rwanda (ICTR) and the International Criminal Court (ICC). The chapter will also discuss the many functions NGOs assume after tribunals have

---

[1] Telephone Interview with Nina Bang-Jensen, Former Director of the Coalition for International Justice, 12 April 2007.

been established, including monitoring trials, arranging technical and legal assistance to the tribunals, and providing support for victims and witnesses.

ROLE OF NGOs IN THE CREATION OF TRIBUNALS

International Criminal Tribunal for the Former Yugoslavia

Outraged by reports of massive killings, ethnic cleansing and systematic rape in the Former Yugoslavia, the international community prompted the UN Security Council to establish the first international war crimes tribunal since Nuremberg. History will record, however, that NGOs were the crucial key in persuading the Security Council to act. The detailed documentation and evidence of war crimes that NGOs provided played an indispensable role in the establishment of the ICTY. Pressure that NGOs continually applied on the Security Council and UN Member States ensured that the Tribunal would become a reality. The work of Human Rights Watch (HRW) is a prime example of the important advocacy work undertaken by NGOs in support of the ICTY.

In response to the widespread atrocities in the former Yugoslavia, HRW was one of the first international NGOs to call for the creation of an international war crimes tribunal for the region.[2] HRW placed a permanent representative in the Former Yugoslavia during the conflict, and sent several missions to the region to conduct investigations and interview witnesses in support of creating a tribunal.[3] Its work led to the invaluable documentation of widespread and systematic religious and ethnically motivated violence and killings. Armed with this information, HRW issued a detailed report which outlined indisputable evidence that genocide was taking place in the Former Yugoslavia.[4] The report was a key factor in urging the UN Security Council to establish an international tribunal; in fact, HRW's report was published prior to Security Council Resolution 771, which called upon states and international organizations to submit information to the Council regarding the ongoing violations occurring in the Former Yugoslavia.[5] Moreover, the report contributed to the UN Commission of Experts finding violations of international humanitarian law in the region.[6]

Human Rights Watch continued to document detailed, first-hand accounts of crimes which were subsequently used by the ICTY.[7] This included the publication of an HRW report entitled, *Prosecute Now!* that meticulously outlined eight cases that were immediately ready for

---

[2]   Human Rights Watch, www.hrw.org/about/whoweare.html. See also WILLIAM KOREY, NGO'S AND THE UNIVERSAL DECLARATION OF HUMAN RIGHTS: 'A CURIOUS GRAPEVINE' 320 (Palgrave Macmillan, 2001).

[3]   *Ibid.* 321.

[4]   *Ibid.* See also HUMAN RIGHTS WATCH, I WAR CRIMES IN BOSNIA-HERZEGOVINA (1992), see www.hrw.org/doc/?t=europe_pub&c=bosher&document_limit=20,20,

[5]   HRW report was published on 1 August 1992 while Security Council Res. 771 was adopted on 13 August 1992.

[6]   M. Cherif Bassiouni, *The Commission of Experts Established Pursuant to Security Council Resolution 780: Investigating Violations of International Humanitarian Law in the Former Yugoslavia*, 5 CRIM. LF 279, 306 (1994).

[7]   HUMAN RIGHTS WATCH, II WAR CRIMES IN BOSNIA-HERCEGOVINA (1993), see www.hrw.org/doc/?t=justice_balkans&document_limit=160,20. See also Korey, note 2 *supra*, at 322.

prosecution.[8] The report provided the legal basis and potential evidence necessary to prosecute those first cases before the Tribunal. Other reports followed.[9]

It is important to note that NGOs like HRW were not solely concerned with the creation of the ICTY in and of itself; they also saw the Tribunal as a powerful instrument to end impunity for gross violations of international humanitarian law. Even though the ICTY was established in 1993, genocide was still occurring in the Former Yugoslavia as late as 1995. The perceived legitimacy and survival of the ICTY was at stake. Consequently, in 1995, a coalition of 27 NGOs took the unusual step of calling upon the United States and Western allies for 'multilateral military action' to end the genocide.[10] In addition to advocating military action, the joint statement called for the Serb leaders to be tried before the ICTY, and for sanctions to be imposed on Serbia unless it cooperated with the Tribunal. Among the signatories were the American Jewish Committee, the American Nurses Association, Human Rights Watch, the Anti-Defamation League, the American-Arab Anti-Discrimination Committee, Refugees International, World Vision, and Physicians for Human Rights. It is interesting to note that international sanctions are today imposed on Serbia for its failure to cooperate with the ICTY.

The NGO community also saw the ICTY as an important counter to Serbia's failed domestic legal system. The domestic attempt to undertake war crimes trials in the Former Yugoslavia was not working. The inadequacy and limitations of those domestic trials, including the lack of fairness and due process for those trials that did occur, was a major concern for the NGO community.[11] The reluctance of Serbia, Croatia and Bosnia-Herzegovina to prosecute their war criminals underscored the importance of establishing a non-political and unbiased international forum such as the ICTY. Their continuing failure to apprehend those who were indicted by the ICTY was also weakening the legitimacy of the newly created Tribunal.

The President of the ICTY, Antonio Cassese, echoed those concerns when he expressed disappointment that states were not complying with their obligations to adopt domestic legislation to apprehend war criminals pursuant to Security Council Resolution 827.[12] Without the ability to bring indicted war criminals before the ICTY, Cassese feared that the Tribunal would be rendered moot.[13] This led Amnesty International to issue a detailed policy paper describing how states could fulfil their obligations to cooperate with the ICTY.[14]

---

[8]   See Human Rights Watch, *Prosecute Now! Helsinki Watch Releases Eight Cases for War Crimes Tribunal on Former Yugoslavia* (1993), available at www.hrw.org/reports/1993/yugoslavia/. See also Korey, note 2 *supra*, at 324.

[9]   See Human Rights Watch, *War Crimes in Bosnia-Herzegovina: Bosanski Samac, Six War Criminals Named by Victims of 'Ethnic Cleansing'* (1993), available at www.hrw.org/reports/1994/bosnia/. See also Korey, note 2 *supra*, at 325.

[10]   Korey, note 2 *supra*, at 327. See also Dana Priest, *Coalition Calls for Action in Bosnia; Groups Want More Allied Military Force Used 'to Stop Genocide'*, WASHINGTON POST, 1 August 1995.

[11]   Human Rights Watch, *War Crimes Trials in the Former Yugoslavia* (1995), available at www.hrw.org/reports/1995/yugoslavia/.

[12]   Security Council Res. 827, 25 May 1993, UN Doc. S/RES/827 ('all States shall take any measures necessary under their domestic law to implement the provisions of the present resolution and the Statute').

[13]   Korey, note 12 *supra*, at 331.

[14]   See AMNESTY INTERNATIONAL, INTERNATIONAL CRIMINAL TRIBUNALS: HANDBOOK FOR GOVERNMENT COOPERATION (1996), available at http://web.amnesty.org/library/index/engior 400071996; see also Korey, note 12 *supra*, at 330, 331.

The ICTY did not turn a blind eye to the important role NGOs could play in advocating state compliance. The Tribunal actively sought direct assistance from NGOs to apply pressure on states to cooperate with the Tribunal. For example, HRW issued reports that urged NATO and Western leaders to arrest indicted war criminals in their respective jurisdictions.[15] Kenneth Roth, Executive Director of Human Rights Watch, stated that '[u]nless these men are apprehended, they will continue to undermine the peace process, prevent national reconciliation, and sabotage this rare opportunity to build an international system of justice'.[16] A coalition of NGOs, including HRW, Amnesty International, the Fédération Internationale des Ligues de Droits de l'Homme (FIDH), the International Helsinki Federation (IHF) and the Coalition for International Justice (CIJ), campaigned for the apprehension of war criminals at scheduled press conferences in Paris, Sarajevo, London and Washington.[17]

International Criminal Court

The establishment of the International Criminal Court serves as an indisputable example of NGO influence on the creation of war crimes tribunals in the history of international relations, and of its significant and lasting influence in forming a permanent international criminal court. The 1998 Rome Diplomatic Conference that created the ICC Statute illustrated this new, unique and cooperative form of multilateral diplomacy. Indeed, during the negotiations in Rome the media equated the influence of NGOs to that of an independent government.[18] The influence of NGOs on the ICC Statute is the clearest example of their role in establishing an international criminal tribunal.[19]

The unique role of NGOs in relation to the ICC first emerged during early efforts to establish an international criminal court.[20] It was not until 1994, however, that the International Law Commission (ILC) completed its work on a draft statute to officially establish an international criminal court. The UN General Assembly decided to establish an ad hoc committee to debate the draft statute, instead of going straight to a treaty conference, which dismayed many NGOs. This disappointment then led to the formation of the Coalition for an

---

[15]   See Human Rights Watch, *Bosnia-Herzegovina: A Failure in the Making* (1996), available at www.hrw.org/summaries/s.bosnia966.html; Human Rights Watch, *Human Rights Watch Calls on NATO to Apprehend the War Criminals in the Former Yugoslavia* (1997), available at http://hrw.org/english/docs/1997/07/08/yugosl8840.htm; Human Rights Watch, *'Arrest Now!' Campaign Calls for Apprehension of War Criminals in the Former Yugoslavia* (1997), available at http://hrw.org/english/docs/1997/07/10/yugosl8843.htm.

[16]   *Ibid.*

[17]   *Ibid.*

[18]   See Human Rights Watch, *World Report: International Criminal Court, the Role of NGOs* (1999), available at www.hrw.org/worldreport99/special/icc.html.

[19]   Jenia Iontcheva Turner, *Transnational Networks and International Criminal Justice,* 105 MICHIGAN L REV. 985, 1001 (2007).

[20]   See Marlie Glasius, *Expertise in the Cause of Justice: Global Civil Society Influence on the Statute for an International Criminal Court,* 146 GLOBAL CIVIL SOCIETY YB 138–9 (2002). (In 1872, a founder of the International Committee of the Red Cross, Gustav Moynier, proposed a permanent international criminal court.) See also Chronology of the International Criminal Court, available at www.icc-cpi.int/about/ataglance/chronology.html (last visited 9 August 2007). In 1949 the International Law Commission drafted a statute for an international criminal court.

International Criminal Court (CICC).[21] The CICC, with over 2,500 NGO members including Amnesty International, FIDH, HRW, the International Commission of Jurists, the International Bar Association, Human Rights First, Parliamentarians for Global Action, the World Federalist Movement and No Peace Without Justice (NPWJ), were involved at the earliest stages of the ICC's creation. The CICC was, without doubt, the most important and effective NGO in dealing with the ICC.

The Coalition's aim was to 'advocate for the establishment of an effective and just international criminal court'.[22] To this end, the CICC participated in every major phase of the ICC's establishment. For instance, it played an active role in those UN Preparatory Committee sessions responsible for preparing a widely accepted consolidated draft of the ICC Statute.[23] The CICC attended six sessions in which it lobbied state and UN negotiators, provided specialized documentation to advocate for key positions, and raised awareness of the proposed Court within the international community.[24] The CICC incorporated a variety of methods to educate the public on efforts to create an effective court. This effort included extensively documenting government papers, as well as organizing a number of highly regarded regional and international conferences.[25] Moreover, the CICC formed an alliance with a group of 'like-minded' states to collaborate on matters of substance and strategy.[26] These states conferred with one another on contentious issues through informal meetings and partnered to resolve them by organizing formal working groups.[27]

The real force of the CICC was demonstrated during the final days of the negotiations for the new Court. When the ICC Statute was negotiated at the Rome Diplomatic Conference between 15 June and 17 July 1998, the CICC network had over 800 individual organizations present; the CICC was larger than any state delegation.[28] The impact was immediate and immense. The Coalition's presence established undeniable proof of the legitimacy and importance of NGOs in promoting international justice.

The CICC's size allowed it to monitor a large number of simultaneous meetings. The CICC made its reports available to smaller government delegations that did not have significant resources, and provided coverage to the press, civil society groups and other interested parties by publishing the Conference's only regular news report[29] and by producing media packets for journalists.[30] Additionally, the Transnational Radical Party, an Italian NGO

---

21   See Glasius, note 20 *supra*.

22   WILLIAM PACE and MARK THIEROFF, PARTICIPATION OF NON GOVERNMENTAL ORGANIZATIONS IN THE INTERNATIONAL CRIMINAL COURT: THE MAKING OF THE ROME STATUTE 391 (Roy S. Lee ed., 1999).

23   Chronology of the International Criminal Court, available at www.icc-cpi.int/about/ataglance/chronology.html (last visited 9 August 2007).

24   Pace and Thieroff, note 22 *supra*, at 392. See also Glasius, note 25 *supra* , at 147–51.

25   For exhaustive list of documents prepared and archived by session see *History of ICC Preparatory Committee* available at CICC website www.iccnow.org/?mod=prepcommittee.

26   Zoe Pearson, *Non-Governmental Organizations and the International Criminal Court: Changing Landscapes of International Law*, 39 CORNELL INT'L LJ 243, 266 (2006).

27   See Human Rights Watch, *World Report: International Criminal Court, the Months Before the Rome Conference* (1999), available at www.hrw.org/worldreport99/special/icc.html.

28   Glasius, note 20 *supra*, at 147.

29   Print and electronic news coverage provided by Terra Viva, On-the-Record and CICC Monitor.

30   Pace and Thieroff, note 22 *supra*, at 394.

member of the CICC, provided each delegation with a radio, in order to follow the Conference live.[31]

Other organizations, such as Amnesty International, also circulated information about the negotiations to its members and the public at large.[32] No Peace Without Justice even raised public awareness through demonstrations.[33] Other NGO activities included publishing a petition signed by Heads of States, and a coalition of Nobel Prize winners calling for the ratification of the ICC Statute.

These activities not only raised awareness of the ICC Conference negotiations but also provided transparency to international negotiations that were often conducted in secret.[34] The CICC was able to keep track and publish countries' votes on key issues. This 'virtual vote' tally method assisted in securing votes on crucial issues.[35] Furthermore, this method provided smaller, less developed countries with information they would otherwise not have been able to obtain.

The NGO community helped to bring legitimacy to the participation of less developed countries during the Conference by providing crucial legal expertise to governments. The specialized documentation created by members of the CICC was often cited by state delegations and used by them as advocacy tools. For example, NPWJ provided valuable judicial assistance to the developing countries of Bosnia-Herzegovina and Sierra Leone during the ICC negotiations.[36]

The CICC's efforts contributed to the swift adoption of the ICC Statute and its success can be attributed to the sheer size of its membership and its unyielding perseverance.[37] However, equally as important was the CICC's strategic approach to its work. The Coalition employed techniques adopted by previous ad hoc tribunals to effectively organize and target key issues in the debate to establish the ICC. While the Coalition used both legal and moral arguments to persuade state delegates, they also effectively utilized their legal expertise and political savvy. The subsequent recognition of the CICC's efforts was unprecedented. The United Nations turned to the CICC to organize the accreditation of NGOs to the Rome Conference, a unique form of self-regulation not previously attempted.[38]

---

[31]   LEILA SADAT, THE INTERNATIONAL CRIMINAL COURT AND THE TRANSFORMATIONS OF INTERNATIONAL LAW: JUSTICE FOR THE NEW MILLENNIUM 3 (Transnational Publishers Inc., 2001).

[32]   Glasius, note 20 *supra*, at 150–1.

[33]   See Pearson, note 26 *supra*, at n. 145.

[34]   Marlie Glasius, *How Activists Shaped the Court: Crimes of War Project* (2003), available at www.crimesofwar.org/icc_magazine/icc-glasius.html.

[35]   *Ibid.* see Pace and Thieroff, note 22 *supra*, at 395.

[36]   No Peace Without Justice, *History Participation in the Negotiations and Technical Cooperation*, available at www.npwj.org/?q=node/2270#IMPLEMENTING. See also Pace and Thieroff, note 22 *supra*, at 394; Glasius, note 20 *supra*.

[37]   See Sadat, note 31 *supra*, at 5 (in part crediting the ultimate adoption of the ICC Statute to the Coalition's informational and lobbying campaign). See also Glasius, note 20 *supra*, at 159–60 (noting some reasons why the Peace Caucus in comparison to the Women's Caucus and independent Prosecutor was not successful).

[38]   Glasius, note 21 *supra*, at 147.

THE NGO ROLE IN INFLUENCING THE STATUTES OF INTERNATIONAL TRIBUNALS

In general, the Statute of any tribunal provides the backbone to its operation. In this arena as well, NGOs have made significant contributions to tribunal Statutes and their rules of procedure and evidence.

International Criminal Tribunal for the Former Yugoslavia

When the UN Security Council requested the Secretary-General to submit a report on the ICTY's proposed Statute and Rules of Procedure and Evidence, the NGO community also responded in force. The International Committee of the Red Cross (ICRC), the National Alliance of Women's Organizations (NAWO), Amnesty International, the American Bar Association (ABA) and Human Rights First (HRF) (formerly Lawyers Committee for Human Rights) all presented proposals for the Statute, each highlighting the particular NGO's dedicated interest.[39]

The NAWO focused on the important area of gender justice, submitting a proposal to ensure that gender-specific crimes such as rape, forced pregnancy and forced prostitution would be effectively prosecuted and that women would be involved throughout every phase of the prosecutorial process. To this end, the NAWO called for the ICTY's Statute to include gender crimes as both a war crime by itself and, when accompanied by specific intent, as a crime of genocide. By likening rape, forced prostitution and forced pregnancy to acts of torture and inhuman treatment, the NAWO argued that these crimes, in and by themselves, constituted grave breaches of the laws of war and should be explicitly listed as such in order to ensure effective prosecution.

The incorporation of rape as a sub-set of a crime against humanity and a crime of genocide in the Statutes of the ICTY and the ICTR was an unmitigated success. These Tribunal's Statutes provided the vital and much needed recognition that rape is a serious international crime. The Tribunals' decisions in cases such as *Prosecutor* v. *Kunarac, Kovac and Vukovic* (*'Foca* case'),[40] *Prosecutor* v. *Furundžija*[41] and *Prosecutor* v. *Akayesu*,[42] made significant advancements toward developing an international definition of rape and defining the specific elements of the crime. These developments were crucial in encouraging the ICC to adopt an agreed definition of rape in its Statute. In this way, the NGO community played an important role in helping to break the silence historically surrounding the crime of rape.[43]

The NAWO also called for equal representation of women at every level of the ICTY's formation. In addition to calling for the assurance of victims' rights and compensation, the

---

[39]   See Virginia Morris and Michael P. Scharf, *An Insider's Guide to the International Criminal Tribunal for the Former Yugoslavia*, AFRICAN YB INTERNATIONAL L 441–6 (1995).

[40]   Case No. IT-96-23/1-T, Judgment, 22 February 2001, available at www.un.org/icty/kunarac/trialc2/judgement/kun-tj010222e.pdf.

[41]   Case No. IT-95-17/1, Judgment, 10 December 1998.

[42]   Case no. IT-96-4-T, Judgment, 2 September 1998.

[43]   Mark Ellis, *Breaking the Silence: Rape as an International Crime*, 229 CASE WESTERN RESERVE J INTERNATIONAL L 38 (2007). See also 1949 Geneva Convention Relative to the Protection of Civilian Persons in Time of War, 12 August 1949, art. 27, 6 UST 3316, 75 UNTS 287.

NAWO underscored the importance of gender-sensitivity training for employees conducting investigations, in order to avoid retraumatizing victims. The International Women's Human Rights Law Clinic (IWHRLC) also stressed that the procedures adopted by the Tribunal should be gender neutral.

While the NAWO focused primarily on gender-specific crimes, other NGOs focused on ensuring that the ICTY met international standards of justice and fairness. Rampant politicalization of other tribunals prompted NGOs to advocate that all aspects of the ICTY, including its formation, selection of judges, personal and subject matter jurisdiction should occur through strict assurances of impartiality and independence.

HRF and other NGOs, including Amnesty International, the ABA and the IWHRLC, submitted proposals to ensure that the ICTY's Rules of Procedure and Evidence were just and fair.[44] The ABA, for example, created a special task force charged with analysing the draft rules. Their advocacy was an important step, because the United States was proposing a comprehensive set of rules on procedure and evidence, many of which were seen as contentious within the international community. For example, the United States' proposed that the Tribunal adopt a rule whereby national security information could not be disclosed to the public without the prior approval and consent of that state. It also argued to exempt disclosure of certain 'sensitive' intelligence. While the ABA took the US concerns of national security into consideration, it argued that all protected information supporting an indictment or trial should be disclosed to the accused. Otherwise, the US position could 'seriously impair the credibility and apparent integrity of the International Tribunal'.[45] The proposals set forth by the NGOs were well received by the ICTY and in its First Annual Report, the Tribunal's President, Antonio Cassese, acknowledged the important work of these NGOs in drafting the Rules of Procedure and Evidence.[46]

NGOs have also had considerable influence over other international tribunals as well. The Statutes and Rules of Procedure and Evidence for the Special Court for Sierra Leone (SCSL), the Extraordinary Chambers in the Courts of Cambodia (ECCC) and the ICC have all been improved through the input of NGOs.

Special Court for Sierra Leone

The Statute for the SCSL was greatly enhanced by NGOs. Because of the perverse role played by children in the Sierra Leone conflict, NGOs played a critical role in advocating for the rights of juveniles and for child-care rehabilitation.[47] NGOs were fearful that prosecuting juveniles could potentially harm their rehabilitation and reintegration back into the commu-

---

[44]   See Morris and Scharf, note 39 *supra*.

[45]   US Proposal for Rules of Evidence, rule 8.1.B (18 November 1993), reprinted in ABA section of International Law and Practice, *Report on the Proposed Rules of Procedure and Evidence of the International Tribunal to Adjudicate War Crimes in the Former Yugoslavia* 72 (1995). See also Laura Moranchek, *Protecting National Security Evidence While Prosecuting War Crimes: Problems and Lessons for International Justice from the ICTY*, 31 YALE JIL 477, 481–2 (2006).

[46]   ICTY First Annual Report, para. 55, available at www.un.org/icty/rappannu-e/1994/index.htm.

[47]   See Daphna Shraga, *The Second Generation UN-Based Tribunals: A Diversity of Mixed Jurisdictions*, in INTERNATIONALIZED CRIMINAL COURTS: SIERRA LEONE, EAST TIMOR, KOSOVO, AND CAMBODIA 15 (Cesare P.R. Romano, André Nollkaemper and Jann K. Kleffner eds, OUP, 2004).

nity. NGOs argued that mechanisms such as a truth and reconciliation commission were more appropriate when dealing with crimes committed by children. NGOs were adamant that prosecuting juveniles under international law alongside those who engineered mass genocide and other violent crimes was an abhorrent idea. Human Rights Watch was particularly focused on this issue and argued that children under the age of 18 at the time of the alleged crimes should not be included within the jurisdiction of the SCSL.[48]

The International Center for Transitional Justice (ICTJ) also played a prominent role in contributing to the Statute of the SCSL. In a joint project with the United Nations Development Programme (UNDP), the ICTJ funded two initiatives to provide technical assistance to the Court. The first was creating the Law Reform Initiative to assist in redrafting criminal law provisions. The second was supporting a local group of female activists who drafted a new law addressing gender equality.[49]

Extraordinary Chambers in the Courts of Cambodia

The ICTJ played an important role in commenting on the Draft Internal Rules for the ECCC and focused on several areas, including trials in absentia, protection and support for victims and witnesses, ECCC's power to award reparations, and public accessibility to the proceedings. The NGO raised important concerns about procedural rules within the ECCC and the unrealistic expectations of what the Court could achieve. The ICTJ also argued that the ECCC needed to ensure that the minimum obligations for fair trials were observed and the interests of victims would be protected.[50] Amnesty International and HRW joined in criticizing the Court for not meeting international standards of fairness.[51]

International Criminal Court

The CICC contributed to the creation of many of the progressive provisions of the ICC Statute and the Court's Rules of Procedure and Evidence. For example, the CICC insisted that the Prosecutor be able to initiate his own investigation. It also called for victims and witnesses to be afforded protection, and advocated for the inclusion of specific crimes in the Statute.[52]

The draft statute for the ICC included only two ways to open an investigation: either by state parties or by the UN Security Council.[53] Given the historical precedent of both states and the Security Council falling prey to politics over human rights abuses, the CICC feared that many crimes would go unpunished.[54] Consequently, the CICC vigorously advocated that the Statute allow the Prosecutor to initiate investigations independently.[55] The CICC also

---

[48]　Human Rights Watch, *Sierra Leone: Pressing Human Rights Concerns: Human Rights Watch Letter / Briefing for Ambassador Greenstock New York* (4 October 2000), available at www.hrw.org/press/2000/10/sl-brief-ltr.htm.

[49]　ICTJ, *Sierra Leone: ICTJ Activity*, available at www.ictj.org/en/where/region1/141.html.

[50]　See ICTJ website at www.ictj.org/images/content/6/0/601.pdf.

[51]　See Craig Etcheson, *The Politics of Genocide Justice in Cambodia*, in INTERNATIONALIZED CRIMINAL COURTS, note 47 *supra*.

[52]　See also Glasius, note 20 *supra*, at 153.

[53]　Draft Statute International Law Commission 1994, art. 25, UN Doc. A/49/10 (1994).

[54]　Glasius, note 20 *supra*, at 154.

[55]　*Ibid.*

advocated for a more radical proposal – to allow NGOs and victims themselves to initiate investigations. Although they considered it unlikely that states would agree to this more extreme measure, the CICC hoped that those states would seek a compromise and support the idea of an independent prosecutor. The CICC produced impressive position papers providing persuasive arguments for, and dispelling misinformation about, the benefits of an independent prosecutor.[56] The NGO also created rapid response teams to counter any false statements that opponents might circulate.[57]

The NGO community also focused on gender issues similar to those raised previously in relation to the ICTY and the ICTR. The CICC, led by the Women's Caucus, (representing over 300 women's organizations), vigorously demanded that violence against women be properly addressed in the ICC Statute.

It was in the area of gender justice that the NGO community achieved some of its most impressive gains. Ultimately, the ICC Statute incorporated many provisions ensuring gender justice, despite the strong opposition from the Vatican, Arab countries and religious groups who were extremely reluctant to incorporate the crime of 'forced pregnancy', who feared that inclusion would lead to acceptance of abortion.[58]

In the end, the ICC Statute codified the ad hoc tribunals' treatment of gender crimes as both crimes against humanity and war crimes, and included them as components of other crimes. However, the ICC Statute goes even further by specifically including sexual slavery, forced pregnancy, enforced prostitution and enforced sterilization within the Statute. The decision by the drafters of the Statute to include a specific reference to gender crimes was a defining moment in history. It demonstrated the significant progress by the international community to incorporate gender justice in the Statute and to align rape with the most heinous crimes under customary international law.[59]

Having successfully focused on issues of gender crimes, the NGO community turned its attention and expertise to the issue of victims' and witnesses' rights and protection. The CICC formed a Victims' Rights Working Group (VRWG), coordinated by the NGO Redress.[60]

Redress works to ensure victims' rights are protected within international legal systems and to ensure that victims understand their rights before international tribunals.[61] Redress was a strong advocate for the creation of the ICC, recognizing the opportunity to establish a 'victim friendly approach' to justice. Redress and other NGOs understood that the lack of reparation provisions for victims resulted in a negative impact on the ad hoc tribunals. Consequently, they pressed for strong victim rights in the ICC Statute.[62]

---

[56]   *Ibid.* See also, for example, Human Rights First (Lawyers Committee on Human Rights), *Automatic Jurisdiction, Independent Prosecutor Emerge as Most Contentious Issues in Rome*, MEDIA ALERT, 10 July 1998, available at www.humanrightsfirst.org/media/2001_1996/rome710.htm. See also UN Doc. A/CONF.183/C.1/L.59 (1998).

[57]   Glasius, note 20 *supra*, at 155.

[58]   Valerie Oosterve, *Integrating Gender into the International Criminal Court: Putting Theory into Practice*, Status of Women Canada (SWC), 24 October 2003, available at www.swc-cfc.gc.ca/cgi-bin/printview.pl?file=/resources/gba/gba-010601-dfait_e.html.

[59]   See Ellis, note 43 *supra*.

[60]   See Victims' Rights Working Group, www.vrwg.org/Who_We_Are.html.

[61]   See Redress, www.redress.org/victims_rights.html.

[62]   C. Ferstman (Director of Redress), *NGOs and the Role of Victims in International Criminal Justice, The Forum for International Criminal Justice and Conflict* (Oslo, 2 October 2006) available at http://new.prio.no/FICJC/Activities/Seminar-on-role-of-NGOs/.

As support for their position, these NGOs pointed out the absurd inequities resulting from the lack of reparation provisions in the ICTY and ICTR. Women infected by the AIDS virus through rape would be hard-pressed to receive medical treatment, while those convicted of rape would be entitled to therapy for the full duration of their prison terms.[63] The NGO community wanted to ensure that victims would have access to reparations, and would also have an active role in judicial proceedings.[64] Because the statutes for the ad hoc and hybrid tribunals (Sierra Leone, East Timor and Kosovo) failed to include these provisions, the VRWG actively campaigned for the protection and inclusion of victim and witness participation in the ICC Statute.[65]

Under the ICTY Rules of Procedure and Evidence, victims' relief is available only from the national courts.[66] Under the ICC Statute, however, victim reparations are included within the Court's jurisdiction, allowing it to 'determine the scope and extent of any damage, loss and injury to, or in respect of, victims'.[67] This provision entitles the Court to order those convicted to pay reparations to the victim, including restitution, compensation and rehabilitation.[68]

Another important area of focus by the NGO community was to ensure that the ICC Statute included a fair representation of male and female judges.[69] One of the most glaring deficiencies in the ICTR was its dearth of female judges. In fact, the Tribunal initially had only one female judge, who was largely responsible for the acknowledgment that widespread rape and sexual violence had occurred in Rwanda. The realization of that gender inequality resulted in the inclusion of an article in the ICC Statute that provided for 'a fair representation of female and male judges'.[70]

To the NGO community's credit, it did not ignore issues of defence which are too often an afterthought for international criminal tribunals. The International Criminal Defence Attorneys Association (ICDAA) pressed for guarantees of the accused's right to a fair trial before the ICC. The ICDAA developed and submitted position papers to the UN Preparatory Conference on the ICC Rules of Procedure and Evidence on such topics as the accused's right to freely choose counsel, disclosure of an informer's identity in cases where it is critical to the accused's defence, and balancing victims' rights to ensure they do not prejudice or trump the rights of the accused.[71] The ICDAA also vigorously campaigned to ensure that the ICC Rules of Procedure and Evidence included provisions recognizing the importance of an independent defence counsel and separate defence unit.[72] While they did not achieve all their

---

63   Reporters Without Borders, www.rsf.org/IMG/pdf/doc-2255.pdf.

64   See Glasius, note 20 *supra*, at 4 ('They worked to afford victims better protection, the right to have their own say, instead of just being an instrument of the Prosecution, and the right to reparation.').

65   ICC Statute, art. 68, 17 July 1998, 2187 UNTS 90.

66   Rules of Procedure and Evidence for the International Criminal Tribunal for the Former Yugoslavia, rule 106, UN Doc. IT/32/REV.38 (11 February 1994).

67   ICC Statute, art. 75(1).

68   *Ibid*. art. 75(2).

69   See Global Policy Forum, *NGOs Win Fight for Equal Representation of ICC Judges*, available at www.globalpolicy.org/ngos/role/globalact/int-inst/2002/0907icc.htm.

70   ICC Statute, art. 36(8)(a)(iii).

71   International Criminal Defence Attorneys Association, document presented during the UN Preparatory Conference on ICC Rules of Procedure and Evidence, Protection of Witnesses, 15 July 1999, available at www.hri.ca/partners/aiad-icdaa/icc/witnesses.htm.

72   International Criminal Defence Attorneys Association, *Achievements*, available at www.aiad-icdaa.org/about_us/achievements.php.

goals, rules 20 to 22 do recognize the important rights for the defence and created obligations upon the ICC Registry to ensure adequate support.[73] Most importantly, the NGO community was instrumental in creating the first International Criminal Bar to focus on defence-related issues and concerns.[74]

NGO ROLE IN ENSURING STATUTE RATIFICATION AND NATIONAL IMPLEMENTATION

The successful adoption of the ICC Statute did not lessen NGO involvement. Many NGOs continued working to ensure that the Statute was ratified by states parties. Key international NGOs involved in this effort were the CICC, Parliamentarians for Global Action (PGA), the NPWJ, the International Bar Association (IBA), the American NGO Coalition for the ICC (AMICC), Rights and Democracy, Redress and Women's Initiatives for Gender Justice (WIGJ).

The PGA, an NGO comprised of international legislators, was uniquely qualified to promote and support the ratification and national implementation of the ICC Statute. The PGA hosted events to encourage ICC ratification, and provided technical assistance to parliamentarians on implementing enabling legislation. It also established an annual parliamentary forum (the Consultative Assembly of Parliamentarians for the ICC and the Rule of Law) to discuss how states could adhere to and implement the ICC Statute.[75] In collaboration with the government of the Kingdom of Lesotho, the NPWJ also organized a conference to discuss the provisions of the ICC Statute and the challenges to implementing its provisions. It even seconded a legal expert to Lesotho to assist with drafting implementing legislation. Later, the NPWJ provided similar technical assistance to the government of Sierra Leone and the Mission of Timor-Leste.[76]

The IBA supported the ratification and national implementation process by hosting a series of conferences on the ICC. These sessions explored the role of national bars associations in promoting the Statute's ratification and implementation. The Association also worked to provide expert analysis of existing domestic laws and their compatibility with the ICC Statute. The IBA focused on ensuring broad participation and contribution to domestic drafting processes through information-sharing and coordination with other bar associations involved in similar initiatives.[77] For example, the IBA, in alliance with the Uganda Law Society, established a working group of Ugandan lawyers to push for implementing legislation in Uganda. Furthermore, in October 2007, the IBA's Governing Council unanimously approved a resolution calling for broad support of the ICC. It also specifically called on bar associations to support the process of adopting national implementing legislation.

---

[73]   International Criminal Court Rules of Procedure and Evidence, rules 20–22, UN Doc. PCNICC/2000/1/Add.1 (2000).

[74]   The International Criminal Bar is still a work in progress. International Criminal Defence Attorneys Association, *Achievements*, available at www.aiad-icdaa.org/about_us/achievements.php.

[75]   See Parliamentarians for Global Action, www.pgaction.org/prog.asp.

[76]   No Peace Without Justice, *Implementing Legislation for the Rome Statute of the International Criminal Court*, available at www.npwj.org/?q=node/2270#IMPLEMENTING.

[77]   IBA, *ICC Monitoring and Outreach Project*, available at www.ibanet.org/humanrights/ICC_Outreach.cfm.

Other NGOs, such as the AMICC and Rights and Democracy, assisted selected countries in understanding and supporting the ICC. The AMICC concentrated on advocating for US support and ratification of the ICC, while Rights and Democracy assisted African countries in the ratification and implementation process. The FIDH held a three-day regional seminar with the Human Rights Association of Turkey and the Human Rights Foundation of Turkey in Ankara, urging states to accede to the ICC Statute.

Additional NGOs have assisted states in ensuring that certain provisions of the ICC Statute, such as those relating to victim rights and gender rights, are effectively implemented. Redress created a detailed publication on how states can support the rights of victims before the ICC.[78] The publication includes an analysis of states' obligations to provide victim protection and cooperation in asset tracing, seizure and transfer, and also provides recommendations on how states can ensure these obligations through their own implementing legislation.

The WIGJ, on the other hand, has been actively involved in ensuring that gender rights are implemented through their Complementarity Project and Gender Report Card initiatives.[79] Through the Complementarity Project, the WIGJ monitors, reviews and conducts regional and legal assessments on domestic implementing legislation from a gender-based perspective. It does so by assessing whether domestic or implementing legislation includes gender-based crimes and whether those crimes are defined in accordance with the ICC Statute.[80] In addition to examining state implementation, the WIGJ assesses the work of the ICC in executing the gender provisions of the ICC Statute and issues an annual Gender Report Card covering such issues as equal representation, gender jurisprudence, and protection and support for victims of sexual violence.

ROLE OF NGOs AFTER TRIBUNALS ARE ESTABLISHED

Once international tribunals are established, NGOs continue their efforts in support. The tribunals have recognized the importance of NGOs and have actively welcomed their continued assistance, even when acting as constructive critics of the tribunals. This particular role has ensured that the tribunals retain legitimacy and adhere to international standards of fairness. These standards have emerged as key areas of focus for the NGO community and include providing evidentiary support and technical legal assistance, supporting outreach progress, monitoring the tribunals' work, assisting the prosecutor and supporting victim and witness units.

---

78   Redress, *State Cooperation and the Rights of Victims before the ICC* (2006), available at www.redress.org/publications/StateCooperation&RightsofVictims.pdf.

79   Women's Initiative for Gender Justice, *Gender Report Card*, available at www.iccwomen.org/publications/index.php.

80   For example, while Serbia and Montenegro's draft Criminal Code includes rape and enforced prostitution as a war crime it does not include other sexual violence. Women's Initiative for Gender Justice, Complementarity Project, *Overview Implementing Legislation* 32, available at www.iccwomen.org/whatwedo/projects/docs/Overview_Implementing_Legislation.pdf.

Providing Evidentiary Support

As noted, NGOs have played a crucial role in providing the tribunals with actual evidence of war crimes. They have provided the prosecutors' offices with background information on areas being investigated, information about those alleged to have committed the crimes, and on the willingness of states to investigate or prosecute alleged crimes.

Systematic collection and documentation of evidence by NGOs have greatly contributed to establishing crucial evidence of extensive violations and atrocities.[81] With the establishment of the Special Court for Sierra Leone, the NPWJ initiated a Conflict Mapping Program to reconstruct the ten-year Sierra Leonean conflict, and establish patterns of war crimes.[82] The NPWJ used testimonial data gathered from the field, along with existing combat information, to assemble the sequence of events of the conflict. Establishing essential facts created a 'big picture' of the conflict and assisted in ascertaining individual accountability. Ultimately, the NPWJ's detailed findings were published and made available to both the Office of the Prosecutor and Defence of the Special Court.[83]

Physicians for Human Rights (PHR) has uniquely assisted the ad hoc tribunals in gathering and analyzing the war crime evidence necessary to establish the scale and timeframe of human rights violations. PHR established teams of forensic scientists to locate mass gravesites, exhume bodies, conduct autopsies and report the evidence and findings to the tribunals. In particular, PHR was involved in exhuming and analyzing over 500 bodies from mass graves in the Srebrenica region of the Former Yugoslavia. That physical evidence was subsequently used during trials at the ICTY to prove that Bosnian Serb forces systematically massacred thousands of Muslim men and boys.[84]

In Kosovo, too, evidence was gathered by NGOs about the forced expulsion, arbitrary killings, torture and sexual assault of the Albanians. Physicians for Human Rights conducted the first epidemiological human rights-oriented study, randomly sampling over 1,200 refugees and assessing over 11,000 household members to establish widespread patterns of human rights violations by Serb forces against Kosovar refugees.[85] The Independent Law Commission asked the American Bar Association's Central European and Eurasia Initiative (ABA/CEELI) to establish a team of experts to review this information and compile data from other NGOs concerning the human rights violations in Kosovo. ABA/CEELI conducted comprehensive statistical studies to add clarity and precision to the potential evidence.

---

[81]   ICG, *Report of the International Crisis Group, Kosovo Spring* (March 1998); Amnesty International, *Orahovac, July–August 1998, Deaths, Displacement, Detentions: Many Unanswered Questions*, in Kosovo: A Decade of Unheeded Warnings (May1999). See Independent International Commission, *Kosovo Report*, Annex 1, 303 (OUP, 2000).

[82]   NPWJ, *Conflict Mapping in Sierra Leone: Violations of International Humanitarian Law from 1991 to 2002*, 7 (A. Smith *et al.*, 2004), available at www.specialcourt.org/outreach/ ConflictMapping/NPWJCMReport10MAR04.pdf.

[83]   See www.specialcourt.org/SLMission/NPWJStatusReport2002-2003.html#5. For the findings see www.specialcourt.org/SLMission/CMFullReport.html.

[84]   Physicians for Human Rights, http://physiciansforhumanrights.org/library/news-2001-08-02.html.

[85]   Physicians for Human Rights, *War Crimes in Kosovo: A Population-Based Assessment of Human Rights Violations Against Kosovar Albanians* (1999), available at http://physiciansforhuman rights.org/library/documents/reports/war-crimes-in-kosovo.pdf.

The NGO reports on the atrocities committed in Kosovo were particularly significant because official government field monitoring in the region was ending.[86] Thus, to ensure that the ICTY would continue to receive evidence to assist in prosecutions, ABA/CEELI established the Kosovo War Crimes Documentation Project to interview refugees and provide victim statements to the ICTY.[87] ABA/CEELI collaborated with a coalition of Albanian NGOs called the Center for Peace Through Justice (CPTJ) to gather critical refugee interviews. Other NGOs, including HRW, PHR and the American Association for the Advancement of Science (AAAS) were engaged in similar efforts.

Employing the statistical expertise of AAAS, NGOs were able to demonstrate evidence of ethnic cleansing against Kosovar Albanians. ABA/CEELI published a report entitled Political Killings in *Kosova/Kosovo* which reviewed and presented the data analysis.[88] In a particularly extraordinary event, this analysis was used by the ICTY Office of the Prosecutor in the trial of Slobodan Milosevic to refute the argument that the killings were simply a consequence of battles between the Kosovo Liberation Army and Serbian forces. Instead, the analysis proved that the Kosovo civilians were targets of an orchestrated campaign of ethnic cleansing. The report also encouraged organizations to work together in providing comprehensive analysis of data during future conflicts. The AAAS and the Chicago Kent College of Law collaborated to create an electronic database that would allow NGOs to gather future information on mass crimes in a structured and accurate manner.

ABA/CEELI's success in Kosovo led directly to the creation of the Sierra Leone War Crimes Documentation Project, which collected war crimes data and supported domestic organizations in data collection.[89] In partnership with the Coalition for International Justice, the ABA also collected data from refugees fleeing Darfur into Chad.[90]

The documentation of atrocities continues to expand. Entities like the International Crisis Group (ICG), in partnership with NPWJ[91] and the Documentation Centre of Cambodia (DC-Cam), have created similar successful documentation projects for the new war crimes tribunal in Cambodia. Indeed, as stated in a UN memorandum, '[i]t is expected that the [Extraordinary] Chambers will rely heavily on documentary evidence … [t]he bulk [of which] is held by the Documentation Centre of Cambodia'.[92]

---

[86]   American Bar Association, www.abanet.org/rol/focal_areas/war-crimes-kosovo-timeline. shtml.

[87]   *Ibid.*

[88]   See ABA, *From Publication to Testimony,* available at www.abanet.org/rol/focal_areas/war-crimes-publication-testimony.shtml. See also ABA, *Political Killings in Kosova/Kosovo* (March–June 1999), available at www.abanet.org/ceeli/publications/politicalkillings.PDF (finding a strong correlation between patterns of killings and refugee flow); see also ABA, *Killings and Refugee Flow in Kosovo*, available at www.abanet.org/ceeli/publications/polkilkos_020104.pdf (concluding that a coordinated campaign of expulsions and killings was conducted against Kosovar Albanians).

[89]   ABA, *The Rule of Law Initiative Sierra Leone War Crimes Documentation Project*, available at www.abanet.org/rol/focal_areas/war-crimes-sierra-leone-project-scope.shtml.

[90]   See www.abanet.org/rol/focal_areas/humanrights.shtml.

[91]   See *Reality Demands: Documenting Violations of International Humanitarian Law in Kosovo* (1999), available at www.crisisgroup.org/home/index.cfm?l=1&id=1865.

[92]   UN Memorandum, *Report of the Secretary-General on Khmer Rouge Trials*, para. 19, 12 October 2004, UN Doc. A/59/432.

Technical Legal Assistance

The international community has gradually moved its perception of NGOs away from that of human rights 'advocates' concerned with protest, to that of a legitimate resource of knowledge. In part, this shift can be attributed to the indispensable technical legal assistance that NGOs provided to the tribunals and to selected national judicial entities who have worked with these international legal institutions. The competencies of certain NGOs have also been extended to providing budgetary and administrative assistance.

Assisting the prosecutor

NGOs have played a crucial role in assisting the prosecution in various international tribunals by providing vital evidence, gathering information and analyzing data. While their role is limited by the jurisdiction of the Office of Prosecution, the prosecutor often seeks information from NGOs to assist in his/her investigations. NGO assistance has been particularly important when states have refused to cooperate with the tribunals, which makes investigative efforts difficult for prosecutorial teams.[93]

However, tribunals often impose limits upon investigatory NGOs. For example, the ICTY's Office of the Prosecutor has cautioned NGOs not to conduct in-depth interviews with potential witnesses and have established strict guidelines for collecting evidence.[94]

Beyond providing the prosecutor's office with evidence, NGOs have assisted with investigative efforts in non-compliant states, by applying needed political pressure. The Coalition for International Justice lobbied for the use of conditionality in pushing for the arrest and transfer of defendants to the tribunals. Their requests included trade sanctions, visa bans, financial reward programs for information leading to arrests, and denial of over-flight rights for uncooperative governments.

Advocate for investigations and prosecutions

As Human Rights Watch Helsinki pressed the ICTY to investigate and prosecute war criminals, other NGOs also urged international tribunals to initiate investigations and prosecute war crimes. The Coalition for Women's Human Rights in Conflict Situations (CWHRCS) compiled evidence of rape and sexual violence from NGOs including Amnesty International, HRW, FIDH, Initiative Congolaise pour la Justice et la Paix, and PlusNews, in order to demonstrate the prevalence of crimes of rape and sexual violence in the Democratic Republic of Congo (DRC).[95]

The first DRC crimes to be prosecuted by the ICC were triggered by detailed reports received from NGOs. The Prosecutor, Louis Moreno Ocampo, received two detailed reports regarding the situation in Ituri which lead him to identify that situation as 'the most signifi-

---

93   See Allison Marston Danner, *Enhancing the Legitimacy and Accountability of Prosecutorial Discretion at the International Criminal Court*, 97 AM. J INT'L L 510, 532 (2003).

94   *Ibid.*

95   Coalition for Women's Human Rights in Conflict Situations, Public records on sexual violence perpetrated in Ituri, Kivus, oriental Province and in Maniema (DRC) since 1 July 2002, available at www.womensrightscoalition.org/site/advocacyDossiers/congo/index_en.php.

cant to be followed'.[96] Amnesty International, FIDH and HRW called for measures to stop the atrocities, and appealed to the ICC and the international community to act.[97]

Many other women-focused NGOs have acted to ensure that gender-based crimes do not go unpunished and have vigorously campaigned for international tribunals to break the cycle of impunity for these types of crimes. The Women's Initiatives for Gender Justice, for one, has pushed the ICC to focus on crimes of sexual violence.[98]

In Kosovo, PHR called on the ICTY to amend the indictment of President Milosevic to focus on those military personnel who interfered with the provision of health services and who attacked health-care professionals treating the injured.[99] The indictment was, in fact, amended according to those requests. The indictment was further amended when over 30 international women's groups and individuals sent a letter to Prosecutor Carla Del Ponte calling for the inclusion of charges of sexual violence in the indictment against Slobodan Milosevic.[100]

Expert advisers
NGOs have provided tribunals with expert personnel to fill necessary positions, and have acted as expert advisers to the tribunals. The International Commission of Jurists supplied the ICTY with 22 legal assistants.[101] The ICTY also benefited from personnel provided by the European Action Council for Peace in the Balkans and Open Society Institute, and specifically from the IBA, who provided the ICTY with four law clerks to assist the judges of the Appeals Chamber in researching and drafting adjudications of pending cases. These law clerks have provided the Chamber with invaluable help as the tribunal nears its completion strategy.

The Special Court for Sierra Leone has also received assistance from the ICTJ. The ICTJ experts have advised the SCSL on issues regarding its relationship with the Truth and Reconciliation Commission, rules of procedure and evidence, legacy and outreach, victims, and other legal matters.[102]

In addition to helping tribunals with staff and advice, NGOs have greatly assisted states in working more effectively with the tribunals. For example, the NPWJ assisted the government of Sierra Leone with legal requests made by the SCSL.[103] That NGO often acted with dual

---

96   Human Rights Watch, *The International Criminal Court: How Nongovernmental Organizations Can Contribute to the Prosecution of War Criminals* (September 2004), available at http://hrw.org/backgrounder/africa/icc0904/icc0904.pdf.

97   AMNESTY INTERNATIONAL, ITURI: A NEED FOR PROTECTION, A THIRST FOR JUSTICE (AFR 62/032/2003, 2003), available at http://web.amnesty.org/library/pdf/AFR620322003ENGLISH/$File/AFR6203203.pdf.

98   Women's Initiatives for Gender Justice, *Mission and Objectives*, available at www.iccwomen.org/aboutus/mission.php.

99   Physicians for Human Rights, note 85 above.

100   For a list of the NGOs, see a Letter to Carla Del Ponte, Prosecutor, regarding the urgent need to include charges of sexual violence in the indictment against Milosevic (14 August 2001), available at www.womensrightscoalition.org/site/advocacyDossiers/formerYugoslavia/index_en.php.

101   ICTY, *Fourth Annual Report*, para. 107, available at www.un.org/icty/rappannu-e/1997/index.htm.

102   International Center for Transitional Justice, *Sierra Leone*, available at www.ictj.org/en/where/region1/141.html.

103   No Peace Without Justice, Criminal Justice Program, available at www.npwj.org/2007/05/30/internationalcriminaljuesticeprogram; No Peace Without Justice, Conflict Mapping in Sierra Leone; Violations of International Humanitarian Law from 1991 to 2002.

responsibility. The NPWJ legal advisers were asked to give expert opinions on initial appearances and pre-trial hearings before the SCSL; at the same time, it provided training to the Sierra Leonean State Counsel on procedural and substantive features of international trials.[104]

Training

NGOs have also provided technical legal assistance to tribunals by helping to train tribunal judges, prosecutors and defence attorneys in international humanitarian, human rights and criminal law. For example, the ICTJ organized training seminars for judges of the SCSL[105] and the IBA trained judges and lawyers in the Former Yugoslavia and Iraq on international human rights and humanitarian law.[106]

NGOs have provided training to domestic lawyers on international criminal law and on methods of advocating before an international tribunal. For example, the NPWJ established a Legal Profession Program in Sierra Leone to promote and train domestic lawyers in international human rights standards and humanitarian law.[107] It also conducted training seminars for the SCSL defense counsel and provided international experts to discuss their own roles and responsibilities in bringing cases before international tribunals.[108] Finally, the NPWJ established the International Human Rights and Humanitarian Law Library in Sierra Leone to provide legal materials for research on human rights and humanitarian law for lawyers, students and activists.[109]

The ABA provided training to Sudanese lawyers on how to defend cases brought before the ICC regarding the atrocities in Darfur. The program provided participants with the advocacy, interviewing and cross-examination skills specific to international war crimes. Sudanese lawyers were also provided with an overview of the relationship between Sudanese courts and the government, as well as a general review of international, criminal, civil and common law.[110]

Similarly, Redress and the Sudan Organisation Against Torture (SOAT) partnered to produce a handbook for Sudanese lawyers on national and international remedies for torture. This handbook provided Sudanese lawyers step-by-step guidance on how to gain justice for torture survivors, using both national and international legal institutions, including the ICC.[111]

NGOs have also played a major part in conducting gender-specific training. For example, both Rights and Democracy, and the CWHRCS provided training for the judges of the SCSL, focusing on international justice, women's rights and witness protection. Women's Initiatives for Gender Justice provided gender training seminars and training handbooks to ICC staff including the Registrar, Prosecutor and judges.[112]

---

[104]   NPWJ, *Sierra Leone Mission Final Narrative Status Report July 2002–October 2003*, available at www.specialcourt.org/SLMission/NPWJStatusReport2002-2003.html#2.
[105]   ICTJ, *Sierra Leone*, available at www.ictj.org/en/where/region1/141.html.
[106]   IBA Human Rights Institute, *Iraq*, available at www.ibanet.org/humanrights/Iraq.cfm.
[107]   See NPWJ, Mapping, note 103 *supra*.
[108]   NPWJ, *Sierra Leone*, note 104 *supra*.
[109]   See NPWJ, Mapping, note 103 *supra*.
[110]   See ABA Section of Litigation to Provide Advocacy Training to Sudanese Lawyers, www.abanet.org/litigation/pubserv/release_darfur.html.
[111]   Redress, *National and International Remedies for Lawyers: A Handbook for Sudanese Lawyers* (March 2005), available at www.redress.org/publications/Sudan05.pdf.
[112]   See ICC, *Gender in Practice, Guidelines and Methods to Address Gender Based Crime*

Budgetary/administrative assistance

NGOs have provided vital budgetary and administrative assistance to the tribunals to ensure that they have the adequate resources to function effectively and efficiently. For instance, the NGO Team on Budget and Finance of the CICC monitors the ICC's draft budget process before the Committee of Budget and Finance and the Assembly of State Parties. A strong NGO voice on budgetary issues strengthens the ICC's ability to conduct investigations, outreach, victim and witness protection, and legal representation.

The NGO voice has also been important in making recommendations on how the budget should adequately fund victims programs.[113] NGOs have been concerned over the inadequate investment in the ICC's Victim and Witness Unit, particularly in the lack of staff support. Furthermore, NGOs have pressed the ICC to urgently review its investment into outreach programs. Insufficient funding for field staff has reduced outreach programs and prevented the Court from effectively communicating with victims.[114]

The SCSL is funded by voluntary contributions from UN member states. Consequently, Human Rights Watch has consistently pressed governments to provide adequate funding for that Court's operation and to supplement the Court's outreach costs.[115]

In Cambodia, the Open Society Justice Initiative (OSJI) has been active in promoting greater funding for the ECCC by international donors and has voiced concerns that the budget's inadequacies could close down the ECCC entirely. OSJI has gone further than other NGOs by urging donors to review the ECCC's hiring process and for the Friends of the ECCC Group to monitor the budget and to ensure that the ECCC's budget is made public.[116]

Amicus Curiae Briefs

Despite the well-documented evidence sent to the tribunals' prosecutorial teams, NGOs are not always successful in their efforts to ensure prosecution. Therefore, NGOs often exercise a powerful and, at times, influential tool – the *amicus curiae* brief. All international criminal tribunals contain provisions within their respective rules of procedure and evidence that allow for *amicus* briefs to be filed by NGOs.[117]

---

in Armed Conflict, available at www.iccwomen.org/whatwedo/training/docs/Gender_Training_Handbook.pdf.

[113]   See www.iccnow.org/buildingthecourtnew/issues_campaigns/budget_finance/Budget200613 June05en.pdf.

[114]   Jonathan O'Donohue, *The Proposed 2006 Budget for the ICC: What Impact for Victims?*, 4 VRWG BULLETIN 2 (October 2005), available at www.redress.org/ICCBull/ENG04.pdf.

[115]   See http://hrw.org/english/docs/2007/05/31/sierra16027.htm.

[116]   See www.justiceinitiative.org/db/resource2?res_id=103452.

[117]   See ICTY Rules, rule 74 on *Amicus Curiae*, adopted 11 February 1994 ('A Chamber may, if it considers it desirable for the proper determination of the case, invite or grant leave to a State, organization or person to appear before it and make submissions on any issue specified by the Chamber.'); International Criminal Tribunal for Rwanda Rules of Procedure and Evidence, 29 June 1995, UN Doc. ITR/3/REV.1, rule 74 on *Amicus Curiae* ('A Chamber may, if it considers it desirable for the proper determination of the case, invite or grant leave to a State, organization or person to appear before it and make submissions on any issue specified by the Chamber.'). See also SCSL Rules, rule 74 on *Amicus Curiae*, amended 7 March 2003 ('A Chamber may, if it considers it desirable for the proper determination of the case, invite or grant leave to any State, organization or person to make submissions on any issue specified by the Chamber.'); ECCC Rules, rule 33 on *Amicus Curiae* Briefs, 12 June 2007 ('At

While NGOs provide a comprehensive legal analysis of a case through *amicus* briefs, they do not take an impartial 'friend of the court' stance.[118] On the contrary, NGOs strongly advocate for certain positions and have filed *amicus* briefs to assist in developing international law and to support individual rights. One of the main reasons tribunals invite NGOs to file briefs is because of their legal expertise on relevant subjects.[119] For instance, Redress, HRF and the ICJ have submitted *amicus* briefs to the SCSL, arguing that pre-trial amnesty given to perpetrators of crimes against humanity is a violation of international law.[120] The ICDAA has submitted *amicus* briefs to both the ICTR and ICTY on matters regarding an independent defence, including freedom of choice of defence counsel.[121]

An example that clearly underscores the importance of the use of *amicus* briefs by NGOs was the ICTR case of *Prosecutor* v. *Akayesu*.[122] Jean-Paul Akayesu, a bourgemastre of the Taba commune in Rwanda during the period in which thousands of Tutsis were killed, raped and terrorized by Hutus, was indicted by the ICTR for genocide and crimes against humanity. However, despite widespread accounts of rape and sexual violence that occurred in that region, Akayesu's indictment did not include charges of rape or sexual violence. Even after prosecution witnesses disclosed acts of rape during the trial, the prosecutor was reluctant to amend the indictment.[123]

---

any stage of the proceedings, the Co-Investigating Judges or the Chambers may, if they consider it desirable for the proper adjudication of the case, invite or grant leave to an organization or person to submit a written *amicus curiae* brief concerning any issue. The Co-Investigating Judges and the Chambers concerned shall determine what time limits, if any, shall apply to the filing of such briefs.'); see ICC Rules, rule 103 on *Amicus Curiae* and Other Forms of Submission ('At any stage of the proceedings, a Chamber may, if it considers it desirable for the proper determination of the case, invite or grant leave to a State, organization or person to submit, in writing or orally, any observation on any issue that the Chamber deems appropriate.').

[118]   See WILLIAM A. SCHABAS, THE UN INTERNATIONAL CRIMINAL TRIBUNALS: THE FORMER YUGOSLAVIA, RWANDA AND SIERRA LEONE, 619 (2006) ('Many *amicus curiae* have tended to be advocates for one side or another rather than neutral and independent "friends of the court" .').

[119]   See ICTY, *First Annual Report*, para. 96 ('In view of the highly specialized nature of the legal issues to be determined by it, the Tribunal has also made provision in its rules for the appearance before it by leave of *amici curiae* (rule 74). Not only will this enable the Tribunal to have access to independent expert advice on any matter it may wish but it will also permit other interested parties, such as States and NGOs, to present their views.'), see www.un.org/icty/rappannu-e/1994/index.htm; see also Special Court for Sierra Leone, Decision on the Application for Leave to file *Amicus Curiae* Brief and to present Oral Submissions, 1 November 2003, para. 3 ('Counsel invited under Rule 74 by the Court or its presiding judge, usually because of his or her expertise in the legal subject under question, will be expected to present all relevant material and if appropriate to express a view on the law'), see www.redress.org/casework/AmicusCuriaeBrief1-11-2003.pdf.

[120]   *Amicus Curiae* Brief, Special Court for Sierra Leone, available at www.redress.org/casework/AmicusCuriaeBrief-SCSL1.pdf.

[121]   For the theoretical version of the *amicus curiae* brief submitted to the ICTR, see International Criminal Defence Attorneys Association, Documents presented during the United Nations Preparatory Conference on ICC Rules of Procedure and Evidence, 26 July to 13 August 1999, available at www.hri.ca/partners/aiad-icdaa/icc/counsel.htm; see also International Criminal Defence Attorneys Association, *Documentations, Petitions and Appeals Briefs*, available at www.aiad-icdaa.org/documentation/petitions_appeals_briefs.php.

[122]   ICTR TC, Case No. ICTR-96-4-T, Judgment, 2 September 1998.

[123]   It should be noted that it was not until Judge Navanethem Pillay asked the witnesses whether they knew of instances of rape or sexual violence that the witnesses disclosed this to be so.

Consequently, the Coalition for Women's Rights in Armed Conflict Situations (CWRACS) filed an *amicus* brief signed by over 40 human rights organizations which called on the prosecutor to amend the indictment to include charges of rape and sexual violence as crimes against humanity.[124] There is little doubt that this brief affected the subsequent decision to amend Akayesu's indictment; it is an example of how NGO briefs can greatly contribute to shaping international criminal law. NGO concerns often represent public concerns and, therefore, NGOs can use *amicus* briefs as a way to bring to the tribunal's attention significant issues and interests of the community.[125] Moreover, by documenting such grave matters, NGOs ensure that history will always take account of the atrocities.

Supporting Outreach

Outreach efforts to affected countries and regions are an important tool for delivering justice and ending impunity. These efforts can assist in supporting international justice and building confidence in establishing the rule of law, particularly in post-conflict situations. More importantly, outreach efforts counter critics of international justice who try to manipulate and politicize the public's perception of tribunals.

Outreach efforts by international NGOs have generally consisted of disseminating information on the mandate and jurisdiction of the tribunals, the role of witnesses and victims, and the subsequent judicial proceedings in a manner that is clear and easily understandable to the affected community. The most successful outreach efforts have engaged the community in better understanding the judicial process so as to instil a sense of ownership and to build local capacity in national judicial systems. The various tribunals have recognized the important role that NGOs play in affected communities and have eagerly sought their assistance and involvement in this critical effort.[126]

Ad hoc tribunals

The importance of outreach became apparent in the early days of the ICTY and ICTR, when the delay in implementing outreach programs was detrimental to both tribunals. Because it relied solely on politically biased local media to disseminate information, the ICTY was particularly susceptible to misinformation campaigns.[127] Similarly, the ICTR's lack of an

---

[124] Coalition for Women's Rights in Armed Conflict Situations, *Amicus Brief* Respecting Amendment of the Indictment and Supplementation of the Evidence to Ensure the Prosecution of Rape and Other Sexual Violence within the Competence of the Tribunal, available at www.womens rightscoalition.org/site/advocacyDossiers/rwanda/Akayesu/amicusbrief_en.php.

[125] See *Akayesu* Judgment, note 122 supra, para. 417 (Chamber stating that while its determination was not based on public pressure it does take note of the public concern of the historical exclusion of sexual violence as represented by NGOs). See also *Amicus Denied by Trial Chamber of Furundzija* (Trial Chamber did not grant leave to *amicus* brief filed by Coalition for Women's Rights in Armed Conflict requesting the rescission of the witness disclosure order on her rape counseling and other confidential information), available at www.womensrightscoalition.org/site/advocacyDossiers/formerYugoslavia/Furundzija/amicusbrief.php.

[126] See, for example, ICTY, *Sixth Annual Report* (recognizing the need for an outreach program to rectify the negative image of the ICTY and also recognizing the important role of the NGOs in this endeavor), available at www.un.org/icty/rappannu-e/1999/AR99e.pdf.

[127] See NPWJ, *Outreach and the International Criminal Court* 2–3, available at www.iccnow.org/documents/NPWJOutreachPolicyICCSep04.pdf.

effective outreach program led to creating mistrust among a majority of Rwanda's population. A UN Expert Group reported that there was an overall lack of knowledge regarding both tribunals by their respective communities.[128] Recognizing the dangers of not implementing early outreach efforts, the ad hoc tribunals eventually established outreach programs.[129] Both tribunals, however, depended heavily on the support from international NGOs in reaching out to affected communities.

The ICTY and the Helsinki Committee for Human Rights in Republika Srpska initiated workshops to discuss proceedings of the ICTY in Brcko, Prijedor, Konjic, Srebrenica and Foca, regions where some of the most egregious atrocities occurred in the Former Yugoslavia.[130] The workshops, attended by both community leaders and victims, were structured to explain how cases are brought before the Tribunal.[131]

Under the remit of the War Crimes Documentation Project, ABA/CEELI and CIJ played a significant role in the ICTY's outreach. ABA/CEELI established programs throughout the Former Yugoslavia to speak directly to victims, human rights groups and legal organizations about the work of the ICTY.[132] The two NGOs used public outreach and educational campaigns to provide extensive information to local and international communities about war crimes and the events in Kosovo. Furthermore, the CIJ's Internet site was a key source of information that provided documents and publicity materials on the work of the ICTY and international justice. The CIJ also conducted advocacy and public education campaigns targeting decision-makers in Washington DC and other capitals, to the media and the public.

The ABA is currently assisting the Belgrade-based Humanitarian Law Center (HLC) as it transforms itself from a legal aid society into a war crimes documentation center. The HLC provides victims and witnesses of war crimes with legal support, serves as a repository for data and evidence related to war crimes committed during the Yugoslav conflict, and is linked to other documentation centers in Sarajevo and Zagreb.[133] In Kosovo, the ABA has engaged in outreach efforts to provide information to the general public about the ICTY and has partnered with the Center for Peace Through Justice to create an international humanitarian law guide in local languages.[134]

---

[128]   See Report of the Expert Group to Conduct a Review of the Effective Operation and Functioning of the ICTY and ICTR, para. 97, 22 November 1999, UN Doc. A/54/634.

[129]   An Outreach Program was established six years after the creation of the ICTY and five years after the establishment of the ICTR. See NPWJ, Outreach and the International Criminal Court, INTERNATIONAL CRIMINAL JUSTICE, POLICY SERIES No. 2, 4 (September 2004). See also Tracy Gurd, *Outreach in Cambodia: An Opportunity Too Good to Miss*, in THE EXTRAORDINARY CHAMBERS 118–20 (Open Society Justice Initiative, Spring 2006), available at http://www.justiceinitiative.org/db/resource2/fs/?file_id=16988 (questioning whether the ad hoc tribunals' late outreach efforts have been effective).

[130]   See Alexandra George, *OSCE BiH, Justice Requires Outreach: A Vital Communication Tool in Rendering Justice* (2007), available at www.oscebih.org/public/print_news.asp?id=2036.

[131]   See Balkan, *View From the Hague, SDS Badge Affixed to the Forehead of the One Beaten to Death* (24 November 2004), available at www.un.org/icty/bhs/outreach/articles/eng/article-041124e.htm.

[132]   GABRIELLE KIRK MACDONALD and RICHARD MAY, ESSAYS ON ICTY PROCEDURE AND EVIDENCE IN HONOUR OF GABRIELLE KIRK MCDONALD (BRILL, 2000).

[133]   See www.abanet.org/rol/focal_areas/humanrights.shtml#publicoutreach.

[134]   See www.abanet.org/rol/focal_areas/war-crimes-kosovo-project-scope.shtm.

Since 1996, Hirondelle News Agency based in Arusha, Tanzania has provided daily coverage of the ICTR in English, French, Swahili and Kinyarwanda.[135] Its objective is to provide independent information about the Tribunal so as to support reconciliation and justice. Internews has used radio and television to transmit information about the ICTR to remote villages. It also uses newsreels to report on ICTR judicial proceedings and provides a forum for citizens to interact with the Tribunal's personnel.[136]

Special Court for Sierra Leone
Prior to the SCSL's establishment of its own outreach program, the NPWJ formed an Outreach Program in Freetown, Sierra Leone to educate and disseminate information on the directives of the SCSL and combat any misinformation about the Court. The Program conducted seminars covering international humanitarian and criminal law for local NGOs throughout the provinces of Sierra Leone. It was through these seminars that the NPWJ were able to disseminate standardized information, leading to the establishment of a Special Court Working Group (SCWG).[137]

The NPWJ's outreach program, with the assistance of the SCWG, used various media outlets to educate the public about the Court. The programs included hosting radio shows and broadcasting publicly organized lectures about the SCSL on national television. The NPWJ also produced its own newspaper, the *Special Court Times*, with an accompanying 'pocket edition' which provided answers to frequently asked questions about the SCSL. The NPWJ even formed 'The Right Players', a group of Sierra Leonean dramatists who wrote and performed short plays, skits and songs about the SCSL across the Freetown area.[138]

The Court has since developed its own outreach program, crucial now with the start of the Charles Taylor trial. The SCSL has teamed up with the BBC World Service Trust and Search for Common Ground to provide the citizens of Sierra Leone with the media outlets necessary to follow the trial. To its credit, the Court has made extensive efforts to provide training programs, town hall meetings, school meetings, seminars, radio programs and video screenings of trials to the general public. It has also focused other programs on specific groups such as the military, police, student groups, members of the judiciary, prison officers, religious leaders and national and international NGOs.

And the outreach does work. A recent survey by the University of Sierra Leone of 10,000 people showed that 91 percent of respondents indicated that they strongly agreed that the Court's outreach program contributed to building peace in the region; 85 percent of respondents indicated that the program contributed to their knowledge of the Court, and 88 percent affirmed that the program was doing a good job.[139]

---

[135]   See www.hirondellenews.com/content/view/12/74/lang,en/.
[136]   See Internews, www.internews.org/regions/africa/default.shtm#rwanda.
[137]   NPWJ, *Mapping Report* (10 March 2004).
[138]   *Ibid.*
[139]   See United States Institute of Peace, www.usip.org/pubs/usipeace_briefings/2007/0821_special_court.html. See also Chatham House International Law, *The Special Court for Sierra Leone and How It Will End: A Summary of the Chatham House*, International Law Discussion Group Meeting, 9 July 2007, available at www.chathamhouse.org.uk/publications/papers/download/-/id/520/file/10261_il090707.pdf.

The International Center for Transitional Justice has also encouraged civil society involvement and local interest in the SCSL by conducting workshops and producing a *Citizen's Handbook for the Special Court*. Moreover, the ICTJ developed a unique forum under their National Vision for Sierra Leone project, in which citizens of Sierra Leone were able to voice their concerns regarding the Court.[140] Many believe that the SCSL has created 'one of the most successful outreach programs of any international or hybrid court to date'.[141]

International Criminal Court
The early failure to establish an outreach program in the ICTY and the ICTR was not repeated by the ICC. The new Court realized it required an outreach plan from the outset.[142] Valuable lessons were learned from the success of the SCSL; indeed, the ICC Registry paid particular attention to the input received from the NGOs.[143] Recognizing the important role that local NGOs play in affected communities, the Registry recruited them to help explain the ICC's role, mandate and judicial activities to the wider public. The Registry acknowledged that the potential support that NGOs could provide in communicating this information to networks was well beyond the reach of the Court.[144] Consequently, many NGOs have since been actively involved in the ICC's outreach activities.

The NPWJ published an early policy paper directed to the ICC on the most effective forms of outreach. One of the most important proposals was a recommendation to create a Public Education Program focused on partnerships with local NGO groups and organizations.[145] The NPWJ also played a significant role in support by organizing educational programs in various countries. For example, in Sierra Leone, the NPWJ organized workshops with a NGO coalition, involving the National Forum for Human Rights, the Lawyers Committee for Human Rights and the ICTJ, on the ICC and on how to implement the Court's provisions into Sierra Leonean law. That workshop led to the creation of a Sierra Leonean NGO Coalition specifically focused on the ICC.[146]

The IBA has developed an outreach program aimed at promoting better understanding of the ICC and its international and local impact on justice. The program aims to provide feedback to the Court, affected communities and the IBA's membership base through various outreach projects. To this end, the outreach program targets 'key countries' and works with local organizations to create a greater dialogue between them and the Court.

For example, in Uganda, the IBA worked with the Ugandan Law Society to bring together local traditional leaders, lawyers and civil society to discuss the importance of the ICC and

---

140   ICTJ, *Sierra Leone*, available at www.ictj.org/en/where/region1/141.html.
141   Human Rights Watch, *Justice in the Motion: The Trial Phase of the Special Court for Sierra Leone* 28 (October 2005), available at http://hrw.org/reports/2005sierraleone1105/sierraleone1105.pdf.
142   See IBA, *ICC Monitoring and Outreach Programme, First Outreach Report* 4 (June 2006), available at www.ibanet.org/images/downloads/ICC/06_2006_June_ICC_First_Outreach_Report_Final.pdf.
143   ICC Assembly of States Parties, *Strategic Plan for Outreach for the International Criminal Court*, para. 6, 29 September 2006, ICC-ASP/5/12, available at www.icc-cpi.int/library/asp/ICC-ASP-5-12_English.pdf.
144   *Ibid.* 18.
145   NPWJ, note 129 *supra*.
146   NPWJ, *Sierra Leone Mission: Narrative Status Report January–March 2003,* available at www.specialcourt.org/SLMission/NPWJStatusReportJan-Mar03.html.

its relevance to Uganda. Similar workshops have already been conducted in India, and the IBA is exploring ways of providing that same support in the Sudan.

Additionally, the IBA has advised the ICC to deepen its outreach in the Sudan and Uganda, and has identified key areas where the Court's outreach program must be strengthened. These areas include significantly increasing the level of outreach, particularly in Sudan; enhancing its visibility and accessibility to the local communities; beginning outreach well before investigations begin; ensuring outreach activities relate to the society in which the Court is placed; and making outreach a two-way participatory process.[147]

The Faith Based Caucus, supported by the CICC and AMICC, is a coalition of interfaith NGOs that has promoted the work of the ICC throughout the world by advocating for the ratification of the ICC Statute by all countries. The Caucus has primarily concentrated on religious and ecumenical communities examining the moral, ethical and religious issues surrounding the Court.[148]

Extraordinary Chambers in the Courts of Cambodia
The ECCC has benefited from a number of outreach efforts by various governmental and civil society groups. The Documentation Centre of Cambodia was initially established to collect documents relating to the Khmer Rouge atrocities, but in recent years has expanded its role. Through its outreach program, the DC-Cam has sent hundreds of students into the countryside to provide citizens with information about the upcoming trials. The Khmer Institute for Democracy has also made important contributions to outreach by creating films featuring well-known Cambodian folk singers who perform songs about the structure and aims of the ECCC. The Center for Social Development (CSD), a Cambodian NGO, has held several public forums focused on national justice and reconciliation. The forums have highlighted the need for the ECCC to increase its efforts to provide accessible information to the public regarding the ECCC.[149]

The IBA, in partnership with the Defence Office of the ECCC, provided training in international law for the Cambodian legal profession. Despite initial opposition from the Cambodian Bar Association, the workshops focused on issues including international standards of fairness, legal remedies and the role of international law in national jurisdictions. The workshops were vital in identifying key areas of outreach, including the need to increase the public's confidence in the ECCC and their knowledge about the workings of the ECCC. Furthermore, the workshops highlighted the need for better education, training and resources for Cambodian lawyers in international law.[150]

---

[147]   IBA Human Rights Institute Report, *ICC Monitoring and Outreach Programme Second Outreach Proposal May 2007*, available at www.ibanet.org/images/downloads/ICC/ICC%20 Outreach%20report_%20May%202007.pdf.

[148]   AMICC, *Foundation Statement of the Faith-Based Caucus for an International Criminal Court*, available at www.amicc.org/docs/Faith_caucus_stmt.pdf.

[149]   *Recent Developments at the Extraordinary Chambers in the Courts of Cambodia* (August 2007), available at www.soros.org/resources/articles_publications/publications/eccc_20070803/ eccc_20070803.pdf.

[150]   See IBA Press Release, *Threats by Cambodian Bar Force Cancellation of IBA Training in Support of the Khmer Rouge Tribunal* (24 November 2006), available at www.ibanet.org/iba/ article.cfm?article=100.

The Open Society Justice Initiative, in partnership with Bridges Across Borders (BAB), has also seconded an expert to the Khmer Institute for Democracy (KID) for 12 months to focus on outreach. Their outreach program includes providing information on the ECCC to citizens in the provinces, and then conveying their reactions and needs back to the ECCC.[151] While a considerable amount of work must still be done in support of the ECCC, the work of NGOs such as the OSJI is making a demonstrably positive impact.[152]

Monitoring the Tribunals' Work

The international NGO community has taken an active role in monitoring the work and proceedings of the tribunals. Strong NGO monitoring programs will be one of the most important contributions to lasting international justice.

International Criminal Tribunal for the Former Yugoslavia

The ICTY Office of the Prosecutor has on many occasions requested that NGOs evaluate and report on fairness standards of prosecutions undertaken by national courts under the concept of complementarity.[153] The Coalition for International Justice was one the most active NGOs to provide assistance to the ICTY in the form of monitoring and technical legal assistance. As new tribunals were created, CIJ's remit expanded to include the SCSL and the ECCC. When the CIJ ceased operations in 2006, it donated its Trial Reports Archive to the Institute for War and Peace Reporting (IWPR). During its tenure, CIJ produced some of the most comprehensive, in-depth legal reporting on the ICTY, especially regarding the trial of Slobodan Milosevic.

Since 1995, the IWPR has specialized in monitoring international tribunals, providing in-depth reports on the ICTY, and conducting comprehensive analyses of the Tribunal through a weekly regional report covering an expanse of issues. In a unique format, the IWPR documents the proceedings of trials in *Tribunal Update* which carries features and commentary on the wider issues surrounding war crimes. The IWPR is at the leading edge in this field, as it is the only specialist agency to have reported in-depth since the Tribunal's formation.

In response to the failure of the tribunals to adequately incorporate and address gender violence, a group of NGOs, including Pro-femmes in Rwanda, HRW, the Center for Constitutional Rights, the International Women's Human Rights Law Clinic, the University of Toronto's Working Group on Engendering the Rwandan Tribunal, and Rights and Democracy, formed the Coalition for Women's Human Rights in Conflict Situations (CWHRCS).[154] The Coalition has played a significant role in monitoring tribunals, particularly in seeing that crimes against women are investigated and effectively prosecuted. It

---

[151]   OPEN JUSTICE INITIATIVE, THE EXTRAORDINARY CHAMBERS, available at www.justice initiative.org/activities/ij/krt.

[152]   Gurd, note 129 *supra*.

[153]   Morten Bergsmo and Michael J. Keegan, *An Introduction for Human Rights Field Officers, Case Preparation for the International Criminal Tribunal for the Former Yugoslavia*, ch. 10, Annex 2, in MANUAL ON HUMAN RIGHTS MONITORING.

[154]   See CWHRCS, *About the Coalition: Background*, available at www.womensrightscoalition. org/site/about/mandate_en.php.

published Advocacy Dossiers for the ICTR, ICTY and the SCSL,[155] and strongly advocated that Slobodan Milosevic's indictment include charges of sexual violence.[156] The CWHRCS's most significant work, however, has been with the ICTR.

International Criminal Tribunal for Rwanda

Since 1996, Rights and Democracy, on behalf of the CWHRCS, has monitored gender crime prosecutions at the ICTR. In one unique and important study, the Coalition analyzed quantitative and qualitative data on sexual violence prosecutions and concluded that there was a declining trend in indictments at the ICTR. As a result of these conclusions, the Coalition decided to take action.

The CWHRCS expressed its grave concern to the ICTR Prosecutor about the alarming decline in the number of charges of sexual violence and exclusion of such charges in key prosecutions. The Coalition also questioned the overall lack of prosecutorial will and commitment to investigate and prosecute gender crimes.[157] Moreover, the Coalition explained its fear that without immediate action, many victims of rape and sexual violence would be without judicial recourse which would only serve to increase the cycle of impunity for crimes of sexual violence. In addition to issuing a press release on the Prosecutor's neglect in prosecuting and investigating these crimes,[158] the CWHRCS called upon UN Secretary-General, Kofi Annan, to reconsider the reappointment of the Prosecutor.[159] The Prosecutor was, in fact, replaced. The Coalition did not relent in its monitoring and advocacy for sexual violence prosecutions to be brought before the ICTR. Indeed, the Coalition was outraged in 2005 when the new Prosecutor, Hassan Jallow, decided to drop rape charges against the former commander Tharcisse Muvunyi. In response, it challenged the Prosecutor's decision directly and through the media.[160]

---

[155]   See CWHRCS, *Coalition Advocacy Dossiers*, available at www.womensrightscoalition. org/site/advocacyDossiers/index_en.php.

[156]   See generally CWHRCS, *International Criminal Tribunal for the Former Yugoslavia, Charging Sexual Violence Against Milosevic*, available at www.womensrightscoalition.org/site/ main_en.php.

[157]   See CWHRCS, Letter to Prosecutor Carla Del Ponte, 12 March 2003, available at www.womensrightscoalition.org/site/advocacyDossiers/rwanda/index_en.phpp.

[158]   See CWHRCS News Release, *Press Conference, Rwandan Rape Victims Denied Justice* (3 March 2003), available at www.womensrightscoalition.org/site/advocacyDossiers/rwanda/index_ en.php.

[159]   See CWHRCS, Letter to Kofi Annan, Secretary-General of the United Nations, concerning the reappointment of Carla Del Ponte as Prosecutor to the International Criminal Tribunal for Rwanda (24 July 2003), available at www.womensrightscoalition.org/site/advocacyDossiers/rwanda/index_en.php.

[160]   See CWHRCS, Coalition Letter to Prosecutor Jallow regarding the need to step-up sexual violence investigations in the case of former Commander Muvunyi, not drop rape charges (8 February 2005), available at www.womensrightscoalition.org/site/advocacyDossiers/rwanda/index_en.php; Hirondelle News Agency, *Women's Organisation Up in Arms Over Dropped Rape Charges Against Former Army Officer* (10 February 2005), available at www.womensrightscoalition.org/index_en.htm; Hirondelle News Agency, *Rwanda-ICTR Honeymoon Threatens To End Over Rape Charges* (11 February 2005), available at www.womensrightscoalition.org/site/advocacyDossiers/rwanda/ index_en.php.

Special Court for Sierra Leone
NGOs have created similar monitoring programs for the Special Court for Sierra Leone. Along with analyzing ongoing trials at the SCSL, the ICTJ is carefully monitoring the Charles Taylor trial in The Hague. Furthermore, in order to encourage civil society engagement with the Court, the ICTJ has established a local monitoring program in Sierra Leone.[161]

The Sierra Leone Court Monitoring Program (SLCMP) is an independent program comprised of Sierra Leonean lawyers and civil society members. Collaborating with the Sierra Leonean Coalition for Justice and Accountability, the SLCMP monitors proceedings at the SCSL in order to provide a fair, independent and critical assessment of the Court for local and international communities, as well as for the Court itself. In addition to hosting a radio program, the SLCMP issues reports, articles, newsletters and commentaries on both the procedural and substantive work of the Court. Moreover, it aims to increase local capacity for monitoring efforts.[162]

International Criminal Court
Recognizing the effectiveness of the monitoring system covering the SCSL, the ICC Registry decided to establish an alliance with NGOs when it created its own monitoring system.[163] The IWPR extended its ICTY monitoring program to cover the ICC, providing regular features and analysis of the ICC. The Belgium NGO Avocats sans frontières (ASF) also created an alliance with the ICC to monitor the proceedings of the ICC in the Thomas Lubanga trial and produce daily reports on the hearings.

The NGO Trial, a Swiss association working against impunity, reports on various proceedings in international criminal law and offers abstracts of the legal proceedings with links to relevant documents. One of the most important monitoring initiatives established by the CICC is the *ICC Monitor*. This newspaper has proved especially vital in reaching a world-wide audience and helps ensure that the ICC is fair, effective and independent.

The IBA also launched its own ICC monitoring program. The program monitors the proceedings of the Court and focuses on issues affecting fair trials, the rights of the accused, and the implementation of the Statute and Rules of Procedure and Evidence. To achieve these objectives, the IBA employs a full-time representative in The Hague to regularly monitor court proceedings and to liaise with other interested parties. The program also includes evaluations of legal, administrative and institutional issues which could potentially affect the impartiality of proceedings and the development of international justice.

Extraordinary Chambers in the Courts of Cambodia
In Cambodia, the Open Society Justice Initiative has actively monitored the ECCC and produces a monthly report on the ECCC's development. One of the most important international NGOs following the ECCC, OSJI has been at the forefront of pressing donor countries to contribute to the ECCC and ensuring that the ECCC's work is transparent. For example, it raised concerns that the ECCC's Cambodian staff were being hired on the basis of political

---

[161]   See International Center for Transitional Justice, *Sierra Leone*, available at www.ictj.org/en/where/region1/141.html.
[162]   Sierra Leone Court Monitoring Programme, *About SLCMP*, available at www.slcmp.org/drwebsite/aboutus/index.shtml.
[163]   29 September 2006, ICC–ASP/5/12, para. 98.

affiliations.[164] In June 2007, OSJI intensified its monitoring of the ECCC. In its report entitled *Progress and Challenges of the Extraordinary Chambers of the Courts of Cambodia*,[165] the NGO highlighted issues about pre-trial hearings, protection and support for potential witnesses, ensuring that the ECCC's operations are now more accessible to the Cambodian public through enhanced outreach, and instituting more transparent reporting on the ECCC's financial and administrative operations.

Supporting Victim and Witness Units

Witnesses put their lives, psychological wellbeing and families at risk when they testify in criminal trials. They are often the only direct evidence of the commission of the crimes. Successful prosecution of war crimes depends on credible witnesses who feel secure in testifying truthfully without fear of retribution. The NGOs who document evidence of atrocities gain direct contact with witnesses and victims, placing NGOs in a unique position to support and protect this vulnerable group.

NGOs have worked diligently to ensure that the Statutes of international tribunals include victim rights and protections. As a result, all but two of the international and hybrid tribunals have established a Victims and Witnesses Unit (VWU), providing psychological and legal counselling.[166] NGOs have made strident efforts to ensure that victims' rights are respected and that tribunals fulfill their obligations to protect those victimized by sexual violence. Special attention has been given to this group (mainly women and girls) because of the unique cultural circumstances and misunderstood manifestations that these crimes inflict on victims. Furthermore, NGOs have understood that special attention must be provided to victims of sexual violence because of the cultural stigma and the potential for retraumatization if victims are not assisted.

International Criminal Tribunal for Rwanda

In Rwanda, an African NGO, African Rights, published a report documenting how women who were victims of sexual violence were in grave danger of being threatened, attacked and even murdered because of the crime's cultural stigmatization.[167] Human Rights Watch and FIDH issued the groundbreaking report, *Shattered Lives, Sexual Violence During the Rwandan Genocide and Its Aftermath*. The report detailed the pervasive sexual violence that occurred in Rwanda and the overwhelming physical and psychological impact on women. The report also described the ICTR's investigatory defects and the general disregard for the sensitive nature required to work with victims.[168]

---

[164] Erik Wasson, *Open Society Justice Initiative NGO: Khmer Rouge Tribunal Budget Inadequate*, CAMBODIA DAILY, 10 October 2006, available at www.justiceinitiative.org/dlb/resource2?res_id=103452.

[165] *Recent Developments at the Extraordinary Chambers in the Courts of Cambodia* (August 2007), available at www.soros.org/resources/articles_publications/publications/eccc_20070803/eccc_20070803.pdf.

[166] The two tribunals that did not create such a body are the Khmer Rouge Tribunal and the East Timor Court.

[167] African Rights, *Rwanda – Killing the Evidence: Murder, Attacks, Arrests and Intimidation of Survivors and Witnesses* (April 1996).

[168] Human Rights Watch and FIDH, *Shattered Lives, Sexual Violence During the Rwandan Genocide and its Aftermath* (September 1996), available at www.hrw.org/reprts/1996/Rwanda.html.

Building on these reports, the Centre for Constitutional Rights (CCR), Rights and Democracy, International Women's Human Rights Law Clinic and MADRE (an international women's human rights organization), issued their own report underscoring the threat of intimidation to and killings of victims cooperating with the ICTR.[169] The Coalition for Women's Rights in Armed Conflict Situations subsequently used this report to recommend that the Prosecutor adopt effective witness protection measures at every stage of the proceedings. It also advised the use of gender specific factors during the investigatory process to develop trust with victims and to minimize feelings of shame and stigma associated with sexual violence.[170] The CWRACS suggested ways to assist the ICTR in this important undertaking, such as facilitating the relationship between the ICTR and Rwandan women's community, appointing a victim's advocate to assist witnesses who testify before the ICTR, assisting the Tribunal with staffing and potential secondments, and providing legal research and training on gender integration and justice. In response to these important suggestions, the Registrar established a separate Unit for Gender Issues and Assistance to Victims in order to improve ICTR's gender sensitivity in protecting and supporting witnesses.[171] The Registrar also reached out to the NGO community. The ICTR's Victims and Gender Support Unit selected Rwandan NGOs, including HAGURUKA (a Rwandan organization working to protect the rights of women and children), AVEGA (a Rwandan association for the widows of genocide), the Rwanda Women's Network and Pro-femmes Twese Hamwe, to assist in victim and witness legal, psychological, medical and resettlement services.[172]

The CWRACS also created a guide for Rwandan victims and grassroots organizations on how to access the ICTR. This included practical information on how to contact and participate in the Tribunal.[173] It also included a detailed explanation on the use of *amicus* briefs along with legal resources, such as text and jurisprudence to assist with any legal proceedings. Furthermore, the CWRACS created a comprehensive guide for ensuring that women victims were protected and their rights respected before the ICTR.[174] This guide includes established practices and guidelines in documenting gender human rights abuses and a general framework. It also includes detailed checklists and examples of how to ensure the protection of women's physical and psychological integrity.

Despite these attempts to create gender sensitive approaches towards the protection of victims and witnesses, allegations of victim and witness mistreatment within the ICTR

---

[169]   Connie Walsh, *Witness Protection, Gender and the ICTR* (1997), available at www.womens rightscoalition.org/site/advocacyDossiers/rwanda/index_en.php.

[170]   CWHRCS, Letter to Justice Louise Arbour, Chief Prosecutor of the ICTY and ICTR (17 October 1997), available at www.womensrightscoalition.org/site/advocacyDossiers/rwanda/index_ en.php.

[171]   See ICTR, *Fourth Annual Report*, A/54/315, para. 82, available at http://69.94.11.53/ ENGLISH/annualreports/a54/9925571e.htm.

[172]   See CWHRCS, *Analysis of Trends in Sexual Violence Prosecutions in Indictments by the International Criminal Tribunal for Rwanda (ICTR) from November 1995 to November 2002*, available at www.womensrightscoalition.org/site/advocacyDossiers/rwanda/index_en.php. See ICTR, *Fifth Annual Report*, para. 102, available at http://69.94.11.53/ENGLISH/annualreports/a55/0066997e.htm.

[173]   Gaelle Breton Le-Goff and Anne Saris, *Accessing the International Criminal Tribunal for Rwanda (ICTR)*, available at www.womensrightscoalition.org/site/advocacyDossiers/rwanda/index_ en.php.

[174]   Eva Gazurek and Anne Saris, *The Protection of Women as Witnesses and the ICTR* (2002), availabel at www.womensrightscoalition.org/site/advocacyDossiers/rwanda/index_en.php.

remained prevalent.[175] Consequently, victims and victim groups refused to work with the ICTR, which resulted in the Prosecutor's inability to gather evidence regarding sexual violence.[176] In response, FIDH sent a fact-finding mission in 2002 to Tanzania (Arusha) and Rwanda to critically examine this problem.[177] Reporting on the allegations, the FIDH took a neutral stance and recommended solutions to all parties – ICTR, the Rwandan government, NGOs and the international community.[178] Acting in a non-biased and constructive manner, the FIDH illustrated how an NGO can, at times, assume the role of mediator.

The ICTR was also assisted by the Irish NGO, Trocaire, in establishing the only trauma program designed especially for Rwandese women. In order to equip the ICTR with a better understanding of the effects of violence suffered by Rwandese women, the ICTR requested one of Trocaire's experienced counsellors to testify as an expert witness in Arusha.[179] Amnesty International supplemented this assistance with workshops focused on international witness protection in sexual violence cases. Their assistance provided the Tribunal with insight on the challenges of providing effective witness protection.[180]

International Criminal Tribunal for the Former Yugoslavia
The structure of witness protection and support in the ICTR is based on the experiences of the ICTY; both courts have similar victim and witness programs reflected in their Statutes. Despite an extensive Victims and Witness Section (VWS), in which qualified staff provide witnesses with counselling and assistance, the NGO community still strives to improve the ICTY witness protection programs. The CWHRCS has called upon the ICTY and other tribunals to guarantee witness safety before, during and after trials. In particular, one NGO member of the Coalition, Medica Mondiale, has pushed for extensive protection of witnesses, especially victims of sexual violence, in order to reduce the risk of retraumatization.

In the *Furundžija* case, the CWHRCS submitted an *amicus curiae* brief asking the ICTY to rescind its decision to allow witnesses' counselling and medical records to be disclosed to the defence.[181] A Kosovar NGO, the Association of Women Lawyers (NORMA), recommended that witnesses appearing before the ICTY retain legal counsel to represent them on issues of witness protection. Furthermore, NORMA called for donor governments to provide

---

[175]   See FIDH, *Victims in the Balance: Challenges Ahead for the International Criminal Tribunal for Rwanda* (No. 392/2, November 2002), available at www.iccnow.org/documents/ FIDHrwVictimsBalanceNov2003.pdf.

[176]   See note 168 *supra* (explaining that the difficulties encountered by the Prosecutor in gathering sexual violence evidence resulted from doubt by women victims and NGOs as to the Tribunal's ability to effectively prosecute crimes of sexual violence).

[177]   See www.iccnow.org/documents/FIDHrwvictimsBalanceNov2003.pdf.

[178]   See *Ibid.* (FIDH reported that allegations including lack of victim/witness confidentiality and lack of respect for victims during cross-examination were well-founded while other allegations were not founded or exaggerations).

[179]   See www.dd-rd.ca/site/publications/index.php?id=1279&page=7&subsection=catalogue.

[180]   Amnesty International, *International Criminal Tribunal for Rwanda: Trials and Tribulations*, AI Index: IOR 40/003/1998 (1 April 1998), available at http://web.amnesty.org/library/index/ engior400031998?open&of=eng-385.

[181]   CWHRCS, Application to file an Amicus Curiae Brief in the case of *Prosecutor* v. *Anto Furundzija*, Case No. IT-95-17/1-T.

funds for training local Kosovar Albanian lawyers on the rules and procedures of the ICTY.[182]

International Criminal Court

One of the most important features of the ICC Statute is the ability for victims to participate in the proceedings. This is a practice unique to the ICC, and marks the first time that victims can directly participate in an international criminal court's proceeding. According to the ICC Statute, in situations where 'the personal interests of the victims are affected', the Court may, at its discretion, allow the victims to present their views, so long as such participation does not prejudice the rights of the accused.[183] The practice not only allows victims to voice their opinions, but promotes closure and emotional healing.

The protection of victims and witnesses appearing before the ICC is the responsibility of the Victims and Witnesses Unit established under the authority of the ICC Registry. The VWU is required by the ICC Statute to work with the Office of the Prosecutor to provide protection and security arrangements to those who may be compromised by witness testimony. This increased collaboration allows the ICC's VWU to participate more in the investigative phase. Clearly, the work of NGOs has significantly contributed to the witness provisions in the ICC Statute.

One of the most influential NGOs working with the ICC to assist victims is the Fédération Internationale des Ligues des Droits de l'Homme. The FIDH has extended its Legal Action Group's mandate to help facilitate victim's participation and legal representation before the ICC. Their work has included a guide for victims on their rights before the ICC. The FIDH has also worked closely with the ICC; its efforts contributed directly to the ICC's decision to allow the first applications of victim participation under the ICC Statute in January 2006.

Redress, another important NGO, is the informal coordinator of the CICC's Victims' Rights Working Group. This group of NGOs and experts is committed to promoting and supporting victims appearing before the ICC.[184] They work to ensure that 'victims have a positive relationship with the Court, and that the processes will neither re-traumatise them or undermine their dignity'.[185] The ICC must continue to develop methods of implementing victim participation in a sympathetic way. The VRWG is instrumental in this process and works directly with the ICC Registrar to implement the victim participation provisions found in the ICC Statute and Rules of Procedure and Evidence. Their influence includes ensuring that national and international experts in victim trauma care are employed by the Court. A special feature, which has arisen from the participation of victims, is the creation of an Office of Public Counsel for Victims (OPCV) that provides support and assistance to victims.

To ensure that victims are aware of their rights under international law, Redress has produced a detailed and straightforward handbook, available in both Arabic and English, for victims in Darfur. The handbook provides victims with critical information about their roles

---

[182]   Human Rights Watch, *Federal Republic of Yugoslavia, Kosovo: Rape as a Weapon of 'Ethnic Cleansing'*, available at http://hrw.org/reports/2000/fry/Kosov003-03.htm#TopOfPage.

[183]   ICC Statute, art. 68(3).

[184]   Redress, www.redress.org/victims_rights.html.

[185]   VRWG, *Victim Participation at the International Criminal Court: Summary of Issues and Recommendations* (November 2003) available at www.redress.org/publications/VRWG_nov2003.pdf.

and rights before the ICC.[186] The guide outlines basic information about the Court, victims' expectations at different stages of the Court's procedures, and any precautionary measures that should be taken. Contrary to the experiences victims had before the ICTR, Redress attempts to set realistic expectations for victims by providing impartial and balanced information which will allow them to make informed decisions on appearing before the ICC.

Similar to the work of the Coalition for Women's Rights in Armed Conflict Situations at the ICTR, the Women's Initiatives for Gender Justice monitors the ICC to ensure gender justice is promoted.[187] One of its aims is to promote the rights of women victims and survivors through the Victim Trust Fund (VTF). The WIGJ provides training and develops handbooks for the ICC staff on the sensitivities of gender violence and the subsequent effect on its victims. It has also created information cards in English, French, Arabic, Spanish and Swahili on protection for victims and witnesses appearing before the ICC.[188] These multilingual cards succinctly summarize the basic and essential information for victims and witnesses.

ICC Victim Trust Fund

One of the most significant developments arising from the creation of the ICC was the establishment of a Victim Trust Fund.[189] The Fund was created for the sole benefit of victims and their families and is sourced from a variety methods, including member states reparation and assets collected through fines and forfeiture imposed by the ICC.[190] The creation of the VTF acknowledges that judicial remedies alone cannot provide solace for the victims; they need financial reparation as well.

While the decision to establish the VTF fell to the Assembly of States, NGOs were instrumental in advocating for the adoption of the Fund. The VRWG took the lead, vigorously lobbying against restrictive mandates. The Victim Trust Fund Team of the CICC developed lobbying materials to promote the implementation of the VTF. The CICC also lobbied the fourth session of the Assembly of States for the adoption of the draft regulations for the VTF, and worked with delegations on the text of the regulations.

Prior to the adoption of the regulations, Redress produced a detailed background report to assist the Assembly of States in developing criteria for managing the VTF. In the report, Redress suggested that the management criteria take detailed account of the types of crimes committed and the need for reparations, especially in light of the VTF's limited funds.

Special Court for Sierra Leone

The experiences of the ICTY and the ICTR in the protection of victims and witnesses proved to be valuable in the establishment of the SCSL. Once again, the NGO community recognized that lessons had to be learned in order to provide victims and witnesses with effective support. In a letter to the UN Security Council, Human Rights Watch detailed those matters it felt were

---

186   Redress, *Your Rights and the International Criminal Court, A Guide for Victims of International Crimes in Darfur*, available at www.redress.org/reports/SudanICCShortGuideEnglish. pdf.

187   Women's Initiatives for Gender Justice, *About Us*, available at www.iccwomen.org/aboutus/ history.php.

188   See www.iccwomen.org/publications/resources/index.php.

189   ICC Statute, art. 79.

190   ICC Rules, rules 94–9.

crucial to the effectiveness of the Court's ability to deliver justice. They included (1) handling defense and prosecution witness protection separately; (2) commencing programs at the investigative stage and continuing post-trial; (3) utilizing NGOs as intermediaries to facilitate investigative meetings with witnesses in safe locations, without compromising the identity of the witness; and (4) extensively training court personnel in dealing with sexual violence.[191]

The Victims and Witness Support Unit (VWSU) of the SCSL was established under the Court's Registry and adopted the advanced provisions of the ICTR's Rules of Evidence and Procedure concerning victim and witness protection.[192] Despite these efforts, concerns arose at both the investigative and trial level over the treatment of witnesses. In several instances, judges denigrated the witnesses' intelligence, another asked an amputee who had no arms to raise his hands and, on one occasion, still another revealed the identity of a child witness.[193] Consequently, the International Center for Transitional Justice partnered with the University of California, Berkeley, to organize training workshops for the SCSL judges at the ICTY and establish an exchange program with ICTY and ICC judges. Trial observers immediately noted a marked improvement in the treatment of witnesses by the Court; judges also remarked on the helpfulness of the training.[194]

Extraordinary Chambers in the Courts of Cambodia
The ECCC does have a small Witness Support Unit (WSU) under the Court Management Unit which has the responsibility of providing witness protection. However, the WSU is still in its infancy and lacks appropriate funding. In fact, the ECCC currently relies on assistance from an NGO to provide counselling, although the NGO itself has limited resources.[195] FIDH, together with the Cambodian League for the Promotion and Defence of Human Rights (LICADHO), recommended that the ECCC consult more with civil society about reparations for victims. A new coalition of NGOs, the Collective for the Victims of the Khmer Rouge (CVIC-KR), has been established to assist and represent victims at trials.[196]

CONCLUSION

NGOs have already proven indispensable to the creation and sustainability of international criminal tribunals. Their work has encompassed monitoring trials, arranging technical and

---

[191]   Recommendations for the Sierra Leone Special Court, Letter to Legal Advisors of UN Security Council Member States and Interested States (7 March 2002), available at http://hrw.org/press/2002/03/sleone0307-ltr.htm.

[192]   Rules of Procedure and Evidence of the Special Court of Sierra Leone, rule 34; ICTR Rules, rules 69 and 75.

[193]   Human Rights Watch, *Bringing Justice: The Special Court for Sierra Leone Accomplishments, Shortcomings, and Needed Support* (vol. 16, No. 8(A), September 2004), available at http://hrw.org/reports/2004/sierraleone0904/3.htm#_ftn71.

[194]   See www.ictj.org/en/where/region1/141.html.

[195]   Open Society Justice Initiative, *Progress and Challenges at the Extraordinary Chambers in the Courts of Cambodia* (June 2007), available at www.justiceinitiative.org/db/resource2/fs/?file_id=18559.

[196]   Laura McGrew, *Transitional Justice Approaches in Cambodia*, in THE EXTRAORDINARY CHAMBERS 144 (Open Society Justice Initiative, Spring 2006), available at www.justiceinitiative.org/db/resource2/fs/?file id= 16988.

legal assistance to the tribunals, and providing support for victims and witnesses. As the international tribunals continue to mature, NGOs will face new challenges as they identify ways to continue providing support. That said, if history is any judge, the NGO community will succeed in this endeavor.

As the international tribunals' completion strategies come to an end, a new phase in accountability will follow as domestic trials begin. The ICC's complementarity principle will enhance this new phase and should add to the growth of domestic war crimes courts. Consequently, the legacy of international tribunals will be dependent on the success of domestic judicial systems that will take over responsibility for the transferred cases. It is this stage of the process that is most compelling; these domestic courts often operate in post-conflict environments and are therefore debilitated by selective prosecutions, political interference, insufficient witness protection programs, and a general failure to meet international standards of justice.

As a result, NGOs will need to shift their focus to assisting domestic war crimes courts. Some efforts in this area have already begun. For example, the Sarajevo-based Research and Documentation Center now monitors domestic war crimes trials in Bosnia-Herzegovina, identifying impediments to the quality of justice delivered. It is also working with a number of national organizations to raise public awareness of the important role played by domestic war crimes courts.

In Serbia, the international community pressured the country to create a domestic process for bringing war criminals to justice. Serbia responded by establishing a Special War Crimes Chamber. Today, however, there is a continuing struggle between nationalists and reformists to control the country's government and the judiciary, which has debilitated the process of justice. In response, the Humanitarian Law Center, an influential Serbian NGO, has created an active outreach program to provide the public with accurate information on the work of the War Crimes Chamber. It has also successfully pressed the Chamber to provide more support for witnesses who testify at trials.

Bosnia and Serbia are only two examples of the myriad countries that face domestic war crimes prosecutions. Macedonia, Mexico, Poland, Argentina, Bolivia, Suriname, Iraq, Rwanda, Kenya, Liberia, Guatemala, Burundi, Lebanon, Congo, Ecuador, Somalia, Uganda, Chile and Senegal are either considering or in the process of establishing domestic war crimes courts. They all will face the daunting task of prosecuting the violators of international humanitarian law. The international community, and particularly NGOs, must commit to providing assistance to these new courts and ensuring that their operations remain consistent with international legal standards. This will be the new challenge for the NGO community and no doubt, it will be an arduous task. But it is a task absolutely essential in order to ensure that international justice and accountability are indelibly etched in national justice systems. Ultimately, this achievement will be the finest legacy of NGO involvement in international criminal law.

8 The ICC investigation into the conflict in Northern Uganda: beyond the dichotomy of peace versus justice

Katharina Peschke

INTRODUCTION

One cynical joke runs: 'If you murder one person, you are sent to prison. If you murder ten people, you are sent to a mental institution. If you murder ten thousand people, you are sent to a conference room for peace talks.' Does the message behind this quip still hold true today, in a time when more than 100 states are party to the Statute of the International Criminal Court? When will those responsible for the killing of thousands of people go to prison instead of participating in peace negotiations where, for the sake of peace, no one will insist that they be punished?

The last 15 years have seen the dramatically fast-paced coming-of-age of international criminal justice. The creation of two ad hoc tribunals, the International Criminal Tribunal for Yugoslavia (ICTY) and the International Criminal Tribunal for Rwanda (ICTR), was followed by the establishment of the International Criminal Court (ICC), which aspires to global reach. And as exemplified by the trials of Slobodan Milosevic, Charles Taylor and Jean Kambanda, individual criminal accountability has become a real possibility, even for the mighty.

Insistence on criminal accountability, however, remains controversial where it is seen to interfere with attempts to end a conflict. Three main positions can be sketched concerning the impact of international criminal justice on the prospects for peace.

The first argues that the threat of international criminal justice acts as a deterrent to those involved in the conflict. According to this optimistic theory, military leaders will be deterred from committing and allowing their troops to commit war crimes, crimes against humanity and genocide, if they can reasonably expect that they will face future criminal prosecution for those crimes.

A second, pessimistic, outlook takes the opposite view. Political or military leaders responsible for crimes punishable under the ICC Statute know that they risk being held criminally accountable at the end of the conflict. Instead of deterring them from future crimes, this knowledge provides a perverse incentive to prolong the conflict: political and military leaders may hope that as victors in the conflict, they will not be held criminally accountable because international criminal justice is frequently interpreted as the justice of the winners or 'victor's justice'. Victory is perceived to give political legitimacy. Furthermore, whilst conflict and chaos reign, perpetrators cannot easily be apprehended. The prospect of criminal accountability might thus actually entrench the conflict.

A third point of view argues that the threat of eventual criminal accountability neither increases nor decreases meaningfully the likelihood that war crimes, crimes against humanity and genocide are committed. Instead, such crimes follow their own perverse logic. If one understands crimes against humanity to emerge from what Immanuel Kant called the 'radical evil', the threat of future punishment does not enter the calculation of a potential perpetrator.

This chapter of the *Handbook* will attempt to make a contribution to the debate by examining the situation in Northern Uganda. It is an unusual situation in that peace negotiations between the government and the rebel Lord's Resistance Army (LRA) have been ongoing for several years, during which time the ICC has simultaneously been investigating the LRA leadership. This case study challenges the view that ICC investigations into ongoing conflicts will always constitute a significant obstacle to peace. Instead, it argues that the impact of ICC investigations depends on the dynamics of the specific conflict and is likely to have both negative and positive effects on a peace process. The study concludes that, in the Ugandan case, the impact of the ICC on peace prospects might in reality be quite limited. It contends, further, that undue emphasis on the role of the ICC should be avoided because otherwise the ICC might be unfairly made a scapegoat should peace efforts fail. As a more general matter, a narrow focus on the ICC's impact distracts attention from the question of how to address the wider need for transitional justice and reconciliation.

After this brief introduction, this chapter will examine the background of the conflict in Northern Uganda, including the ICC proceedings that led to arrest warrants against five senior leaders of the LRA. The article will continue with an analysis of the chronology of events, with a particular focus on any impact the ICC proceedings may have had on the development of the conflict. The chapter then examines the ways in which the drafters of the ICC Statute took into account the need to balance the (whether actually or only purportedly) competing demands of peace and justice. In particular, it will discuss the mechanisms built into the ICC Statute to allow the suspension of investigations for the sake of peace negotiations, or to allow a domestic solution to supersede the ICC proceedings under the principle of complementarity. Based on this more general discussion of legal tools, the article will consider the impact each possible option for ending the ICC proceedings could have on the peace process. Finally, based on the analysis of the Northern Uganda case study, the chapter will draw general conclusions applicable to ICC investigations into ongoing conflicts. And it will criticize calls to use procedural mechanisms not intended for this purpose to bring proceedings to a halt to favor peace negotiations. While the quest for justice and accountability cannot remain blind and deaf to the need to seize opportunities to end long-lasting armed conflicts, political decisions must be taken by political organs. The fledgling ICC must keep its aura as an impartial organ of justice and should not be burdened with political decisions which would compromise it.

THE CASE OF NORTHERN UGANDA

The debate about how the ICC's involvement in a situation of ongoing armed conflict affects the prospects for peace has been and still is very vivid with regard to the conflict in Northern Uganda.* International NGOs, such as Human Rights Watch (HRW) and International Crisis Group (ICG),[1] discuss the problem, as do local community leaders, such as clan chiefs and

---

*   This chapter was updated in 2009, and therefore does not take into account any subsequent developments on the peace and justice debate, including academic contributions and policy discussions.

[1]   N. Grono, *What Comes First, Peace or Justice?*, INTERNATIONAL HERALD TRIBUNE, 26 October 2006.

religious leaders in Northern Uganda.[2] The Office of the ICC Prosecutor has acknowledged and participates in the debate.[3]

The parties to the conflict drive the debate with their actions and take part in it. It was Uganda's President Museveni who asked the ICC Prosecutor to investigate the LRA leadership, and he has been making and revoking offers of amnesty for peace. On the other side when, in November 2006, then UN Envoy for Humanitarian Affairs, Jan Egeland, met LRA leader Joseph Kony, Kony asked him to intervene to cancel the ICC arrest warrants issued against him and his closest companions. He threatened that otherwise he would not sign any peace agreement.[4] Demands to end the ICC investigations did not only come from the indicted war crimes suspects themselves. In November 2004, the Acholi Paramount Chief Elect, head of the Northern Ugandan Acholi tribe that suffered much harm from the LRA, demanded: 'The ICC should write to both the LRA and the government of Uganda stating clearly its intention to halt any further investigation and prosecution and express its commitment to support the ongoing peace process. This will be a step in building confidence and trust on both sides.'[5] A woman in an internally displaced person (IDP) camp in Northern Uganda is reported to have asked: 'Kony will not come out because of the ICC, so to whom should we attribute our suffering?'[6]

Of course, it can also be argued that serious human rights abuses are the root cause of the conflict and must be addressed. The ICC's investigation therefore plays a vital role in bringing about a sustainable peace 'by ensuring that accountability and justice are present in the peace and reconciliation process in Northern Uganda'.[7]

To properly evaluate the merits of these differing claims, it is necessary to outline briefly the origins and history of the violent conflict in Northern Uganda and to take a close look at the chronological order in which advances and setbacks of both peace efforts and criminal proceedings have followed each other and interacted.

SOME GENERAL BACKGROUND ON THE CONFLICT IN NORTHERN UGANDA

The conflict in Northern Uganda began in 1986, soon after Yoweri Museveni took power and became President of Uganda, a position that he continues to hold more than 20 years later.

---

2   T. ALLEN, TRIAL JUSTICE, THE INTERNATIONAL CRIMINAL COURT AND THE LORD'S RESISTANCE ARMY 86 (London/New York, Zed Books in association with the International African Institute, 2006), citing a statement of Acholi Paramount Chief to the ICC Prosecutor of November 2004.

3   Office of the Prosecutor of the ICC, *Report on the Activities Performed During the First Three Years (June 2003–June 2006)* 3, 14–17 (2006).

4   BBC News, *UN Envoy Sees Uganda Rebel Chief,* 12 November 2006, available at http://news.bbc.co.uk/2/hi/africa/6139554.stm.

5   *Suggestions by the Acholi Religious and Cultural Leaders in Response to the Request by the International Criminal Court,* Gulu (12 November 2004), as cited in Allen, note 2 *supra,* at 86.

6   Quoted in T. McCornell, *Uganda: Peace vs. Justice,* OPEN DEMOCRACY.NET, 14 September 2006, available at www.opendemocracy.net/democracy-africa_democracy/uganda_peace_3903.jsp.

7   Human Rights Watch, *Uprooted and Forgotten: Impunity and Human Rights Abuses in Northern Uganda* 59 (September 2005), available at www.hrw.org/en/reports/2005/09/19/uprooted-and-forgotten.

The Lord's Resistance Army, a rebel group under the leadership of Joseph Kony, began fighting the Museveni government and the Ugandan People's Defense Forces (UPDF), the country's new army loyal to Museveni. The conflict is rooted in deep interethnic competition between populations in the North and in the South of Uganda over military and economic power, going back as far as colonial rule. The LRA leadership is made up of Acholi (a people in Northern Uganda). The LRA fights against the government of Museveni, which has its powerbase in Southern Uganda, causing many Northerners to feel disempowered. The issue, however, is not purely tribal; most victims of LRA atrocities are from the same Northern Acholi people as the LRA leadership. The LRA is not motivated by any clearly identifiable political agenda, making peace negotiations more difficult. While the LRA claims to represent the grievances of the Acholi people, the LRA's actions victimizing that same population directly contradict such a claim. In addition, the LRA has increasingly shifted its activities to Southern Sudan, the Northeastern Democratic Republic of Congo (DRC) and the Central African Republic, where civilians of other ethnicities in the region are also victimized.

One noteworthy element of the conflict is the fact that the LRA leader, Joseph Kony, portrays himself as a medium with direct contact to various spirits who guide his actions. These spirits that allegedly inhabit Kony include, among others, a female spirit called 'Silly Sindy' and a spirit referred to as 'Who are You?' who advises Kony on battle tactics.[8] The attribution of spiritual powers to Kony helps him to maintain control over his fighters and supports a belief in the Acholi population that he is invincible.

The conflict is characterized by serious human rights abuses against civilians in the region, including summary executions, recruitment of child soldiers, torture, sexual abuse and rape, forcible displacement and looting. This has resulted in many thousands of people killed and some 1.5 million IDPs in Northern Uganda,[9] many of whom have fled to camps where they live in deplorable conditions and remain dependent on outside help. Thousands of children have become 'night dwellers', walking at dusk kilometers from their villages to sleep in NGO-run centers or public spaces, such as on church grounds, where they feel safer from abduction.

The LRA base of combatants is drawn largely from abducted villagers, including young children. According to an October 2005 UNICEF situation report, an estimated 25,000 children have been abducted since the conflict began.[10] As part of initiation into the rebel movement, abductees are forced to commit inhuman acts, including killing, cannibalism and mutilations, such as cutting off hands, ears, noses or lips. Female abductees are forced to become the 'wives' of senior soldiers or are given as a sexual reward to male soldiers, resulting in rapes and forced pregnancies. People trying to flee the LRA are punished with death if caught. Even when abductees manage to return to their villages, they are often stigmatized and excluded from participating in community life.

---

[8]   Allen, note 2 *supra,* at 39; International Crisis Group, *Northern Uganda: Understanding and Solving the Conflict,* Africa Report No. 77, 4, 5 (Nairobi/Brussels, 14 April 2004).

[9]   This is a number often cited; see, for example, Allen, note 2 *supra,* overview. However, the figures available vary: according to UNICEF, in August 2005 the number of IDPs has risen to over 1.4 million; HRW estimated the number at 1.9 million in September 2005; for references see International Crisis Group, *A Strategy for Ending Northern Uganda's Crises,* Africa Briefing Paper No. 35, 7, n. 47 (Kampala/Brussels, 11 January 2006).

[10]   UNICEF Humanitarian Situation Report, *Northern Uganda*, 3 (October 2005).

The conflict is not confined to Northern Uganda; it also has an international dimension. For many years the LRA enjoyed the support of the Sudanese government. The central government in Khartoum saw the LRA as a force that could help in its own fight against the insurgency in Southern Sudan, which in turn was supported by the Ugandan government. More recently, the Sudanese support for the LRA has dwindled due to changed circumstances in Sudan, particularly since the conclusion of the Comprehensive Peace Agreement between the Sudanese government and the Sudanese People's Liberation Movement/Army (SPLM/A) in January 2005. In late 2001, the United States put the LRA on its list of terrorist organizations. This may have provided an additional incentive for the Sudanese government, which had been trying to improve its relations with the United States, to cut its ties with the LRA.[11]

In the course of the LRA conflict, violence spread to neighboring regions, in particular to Southern Sudan where, in the second half of the 1990s, the LRA established bases with the approval of the government in Khartoum. Since late 2005, the conflict has also affected the eastern region of the DRC where important figures of the LRA leadership have found a new safe-haven in the vicinity of the Garamba National Park. This has led to tensions between Uganda and the DRC because Museveni threatened at one stage to invade the DRC if Congolese authorities did not expel the LRA.[12] It is also believed that, in the Spring of 2007, LRA troops crossed into the Central African Republic.[13]

The conflict has seriously blemished the record of Museveni's government which was otherwise internationally credited with bringing relative stability to Uganda after the abusive regimes of Presidents Milton Obote and Idi Amin. At the same time, it appears that Museveni may have (had) some interest in a continuation of the conflict in the North because it helped him maintain the status quo in Ugandan politics.[14] In particular, the conflict has been an argument used to uphold the Southern Ugandan monopoly on power and wealth in the country, to delay reforms of the national army, and to suppress freedom of expression and political opposition in the name of his 'war against terrorism'.

For many years, Museveni has unsuccessfully pursued a military solution.[15] In March 2002, the Ugandan army launched a massive military offensive, named 'Operation Iron Fist', against the LRA bases in Southern Sudan. In response, LRA forces began crossing back into Uganda and carrying out brutal attacks, resulting in widespread displacement and suffering, including in Northern Ugandan regions previously not affected. In the second half of 2004, intense military pressure resulted in a significant drop of LRA activity in Northern Uganda. At the same time, the Ugandan government was also increasingly criticized internationally and doubts were raised about its commitment to a peaceful solution.

Earlier attempts to end the conflict through peace negotiations did not yield any results. The most promising initiative was that of Betty Bigombe, then a Minister with the Museveni government responsible for solving the conflict in Northern Uganda and an Acholi herself. In

---

[11]   ICG, note 9 *supra*, at 7.

[12]   *Ibid.* 6, n. 35.

[13]   *Uganda: Kony Heads to Central African Republic,* NEW VISION (KAMPALA), 19 February 2007.

[14]   See, for example, ICG, *Northern Uganda: Seizing the Opportunity for Peace*, Africa Report No. 124, p. 8 (Kampala/Nairobi/Brusssels, 26 April 2007).

[15]   ICG,. note 8 *supra*, Executive Summary.

February 1994, talks she initiated broke down after Museveni issued an ultimatum that the talks be concluded in seven days.[16]

In 2000, the Ugandan legislature passed the Amnesty Act, offering amnesty for all Ugandans involved in acts of a war-like nature who voluntarily came forward and abandoned their activities. Unfortunately, the Amnesty Act failed to end the conflict in Northern Uganda even though a considerable number of LRA fighters eventually abandoned the conflict. According to a study published in July 2005, by then about 14,000 former combatants had applied for amnesty, including approximately 6,000 LRA members.[17]

ICC PROCEEDINGS THAT LED TO THE ARREST WARRANTS AGAINST THE LRA LEADERSHIP

On 16 December 2003, after signing and ratifying the ICC Statute, the government of Uganda referred the situation in Northern Uganda to the Prosecutor of the ICC. In July 2004, after a thorough analysis of the available information, the ICC Prosecutor opened his investigation into the situation in Northern Uganda, the first in the young history of the ICC.

On 6 May 2005, the ICC Prosecutor filed an application for warrants of arrest against the LRA leader Joseph Kony, his deputy Vincent Otti, and against Raska Lukwiya, Okot Odhiambo and Dominic Ongwen, all three senior LRA commanders. These warrants accused them of crimes against humanity, including enslavement, sexual slavery, rape and murder, and war crimes, including intentionally directing attacks against the civilian population, enlisting children, and inducing rape and pillaging. On 8 July 2005, a Pre-Trial Chamber of the ICC issued arrest warrants under seal[18] so that the names of the indictees would not be made public in order not to alert them to the fact that they were now wanted for arrest. The Pre-Trial Chamber subsequently transmitted the warrants with requests for arrest and surrender to the governments of Uganda, the DRC and Sudan. On 13 October 2005, it unsealed the arrest warrants in accordance with an application by the ICC Prosecutor to that effect, a motion possibly prompted by leaks about the existence of the ICC arrest warrants.

RESPONSES TO THE UNSEALING OF THE ARREST WARRANTS

On 14 October 2005, in response to the unsealing of the arrest warrants, then UN Secretary-General, Kofi Annan, stated that they 'would send a powerful signal that those responsible for those crimes will be held accountable for their action'.[19] However, many directly

---

16   Allen, note 2 *supra*, at 48.

17   ICTJ and Human Rights Center, FORGOTTEN VOICES: *A Population-Based Survey on Attitudes about Peace and Justice in Northern Uganda* 17 (2005).

18   Office of the Prosecutor of the ICC, Decision on the Prosecutor's Application for Warrants of Arrest under Article 58, 8 July 2005, No. ICC-02/04-01/05-1-US-Exp 12-07-2005 2/11 UM, unsealed pursuant to Decision No. ICC-02/04-01/05-52, 13 October 2005, available at www.icc-cpi.int/iccdocs/doc/doc97108.PDF.

19   As cited in H. Moy, *Recent Developments: The International Criminal Courts Arrest Warrants and Uganda's Lords Resistance Army, Renewing the Debate over Amnesty and Complementarity*, 19 HARVARD HUMAN RIGHTS J 267, 269 (2006).

concerned with the conflict reacted less positively. In particular, Ugandan civil society organizations expressed their frustration with the ICC. Humanitarian organizations voiced fears that the LRA would retaliate against them and warned of a direct rise in violence in the region.[20] Betty Bigombe argued that the ICC indictments made reaching a peaceful solution in Uganda more difficult. She stated: '[y]ou can no longer talk to the LRA as before, the dynamics have changed'.[21] According to ICG interviews in November 2005, most members of the local population in Northern Uganda found the publication of the indictments premature and stated that more time should have been given to diplomatic efforts.[22]

In the aftermath of the unsealing of the arrest warrants, the crisis in Northern Uganda received increased international public attention. On 22 October 2005, tens of thousands marched in a 'GuluWalk Day' in over 35 cities worldwide, calling attention to the child victims in Northern Uganda. Media attention given to the crisis increased after staff of international relief groups and other foreigners were ambushed in October and November 2005, killing at least six people and leaving others injured. These attacks, which have been interpreted as a direct response by the LRA to the ICC arrest warrants, resulted in a temporary suspension and disruption of aid activities in Northern Uganda and in Southern Sudan, including a directive to temporarily abort all UN field missions in Northern Uganda.[23] However, with the looming prospect of serious peace negotiations, a process described in more detail below, a new era of relative calm began and humanitarian efforts could resume.

EFFORTS AT PEACE NEGOTIATIONS SINCE THE UNSEALING OF THE ARREST WARRANTS

On 29 November 2005, the LRA deputy leader Otti contacted the BBC World Service to call for renewed peace negotiations,[24] and in early 2006, the government of South Sudan ('the GoSS'), supported by NGOs and the Swiss government, expressed their willingness to assist in a possible peace process and established contacts with the Ugandan government and the LRA.[25] The newly established GoSS had an immediate interest in the conflict's resolution due to LRA attacks on its territory and against its inhabitants.

On 23 January 2006, in Garamba National Park, DRC, eight UN peace-keepers were killed in a fight between forces of the UN Mission to the DRC (MONUC) and the LRA. In March 2006, in Yambio, Southern Sudan, the LRA allegedly raided a UNICEF compound and

---

[20]   ICG, note 9 *supra*, at 3.

[21]   United Nations Office for the Coordination of Humanitarian Affairs, Integrated Regional Information Networks (IRIN), *Uganda: ICC Indictments to Affect Northern Peace Efforts, Says Mediator*, 10 October 2005, available at www.reliefweb.int/rw/RWB.NSF/db900SID/NKUA-6H2L5H?OpenDocument.

[22]   ICG, note 9 *supra*, at 9.

[23]   ICG, note 9 *supra*, at 3.

[24]   BBC News, Will Ross *Ugandan Rebel Urges Peace Talks*, 29 November 2005, available at http://news.bbc.co.uk/2/hi/africa/4483320.stm.

[25]   International Crisis Group, *Peace in Northern Uganda*, Africa Briefing Paper No. 41, 2 (Nairobi/Brussels, 13 September 2006).

engaged a group of UN peace-keepers in a fire-fight.[26] Both incidents were followed by UN Security Council Resolutions strongly condemning the LRA.[27]

In April 2006, over 50,000 people around the United States participated in the 'Global Night Commutes' solidarity marches in support of peace in Northern Uganda.[28]

Slowly, the conditions in Northern Uganda began to improve. In April 2006, resettlement of IDPs in the Lango and Teso subregions of northern Uganda began despite concerns of continued LRA activity.[29]

On 18 April 2006, the Ugandan Parliament passed an Amnesty Amendment Act to the Amnesty Act of 2003. It empowered the Minister of Internal Affairs to draw up a list of persons not eligible for the amnesty granted under the original Act, to be approved by Parliament.[30]

In the Spring of 2006, officials of the GoSS reaffirmed the offer to mediate, and a preliminary exchange of ideas with the government of Uganda and the LRA leadership began. In June, the GoSS issued official invitations to the LRA and the government of Uganda. Sporadic outbreaks of violence in and around Juba, the capital of Southern Sudan and the designated venue of the peace talks, accompanied these developments. UN and SPLM/A security officials have voiced suspicion that these acts of violence may have been staged by the government of the Sudan in Khartoum to implicate the LRA and undermine the negotiations.[31]

In early July 2006, Museveni announced that Kony and other LRA leaders indicted by the ICC were to be granted amnesty by the Ugandan government if they responded positively to the GoSS mediated talks and abandoned terrorism. In reply the ICC insisted on the prosecution of the indicted rebel leaders.[32]

On 14 July 2006, Uganda's government and the LRA formally opened talks in Juba to end the conflict. The talks were mediated by the GoSS and led by Riek Marchiar, Vice-President of the GoSS. In August 2006, the United Nations Mission to Sudan (UNMIS) publicly reiterated that it would not arrest any LRA leader travelling to the peace talks in Juba.[33] Nevertheless, the top LRA leaders refused to travel to Juba to participate directly in peace talks for fear of being arrested. Instead, they sent a delegation, which was criticized as being of too low a level to represent the LRA effectively.[34] Of the 15 LRA delegates in Juba, only two had been active LRA commanders.[35]

In August 2006, a Ugandan government delegation and members of the Juba mediation team visited Kony at his hide-out in the DRC. Chief GoSS mediator, Riek Marchiar, asked LRA deputy leader Vincent Otti to travel with him to Juba. Otti refused, allegedly out of fear

---

26   ICC, Pre-Trial Chamber II, 10 (October 2006), with further references.
27   UN Doc. SC1653 (2006), 3, para. 6; UN Doc. SC8672 (2006).
28   See www.invisiblechildren.com/theMovement/globalNightCommute.
29   United Nations Office for the Coordination of Humanitarian Affairs (OCHA), *Northern Uganda Briefing Paper* (May 2006), available at www.reliefweb.int/rw/rwb.nsf/db900SID/EVOD-6QLC36?OpenDocument.
30   ICG, note 25 *supra*, at 10.
31   *Ibid.* 6, n. 30.
32   BBC News, Mark Danner, *Africa's Mixed Amnesty Precedents*, 4 July 2006, available at <http://news.bbc.co.uk/2/hi/africa/5148226.stm>.
33   ICG, note 25 *supra*, at 4.
34   *Ibid.* 8.
35   *Ibid.* 8.

of the ICC indictments.[36] Later that month, UPDF soldiers killed the LRA's third-senior-most commander, Raska Lukwiya, one of the five ICC indictees.[37] At least 15 further LRA rebels were killed during the following two weeks. As a result, talks were temporarily delayed but resumed after a few days of respite to allow the LRA to mourn the death of Lukwiya.

On 26 August 2006, the Ugandan government and LRA leaders signed a truce calling for the cessation of hostilities. The LRA agreed to move its forces from Garamba in the DRC towards assembly points in Southern Sudan.[38]

After a pause in the negotiations, on 11 October 2006, the LRA proposed that Uganda adopt a federalist structure, which the Ugandan government spokesperson rejected.[39] On 20 October 2006, Museveni travelled to Juba to meet the LRA negotiators face-to-face for the first time in an attempt to revive the talks. A Ugandan government source reported that Museveni angrily rebuked the LRA team and referred to the LRA as 'unserious' in a subsequent address to GoSS officials.[40] The murder of several dozen civilians, including women and children, near Juba two days prior to Museveni's visit overshadowed the talks even though it remains unclear to date whether these crimes can be attributed to the LRA.[41]

On 1 November 2006, the LRA and the Ugandan government signed a second truce. The agreement mandated the LRA to assemble at two locations in Southern Sudan, Owiny Ki-Bul and Ri-Kwangba. Both Kony and Otti refused to go to either assembly point, citing their fear of arrest in accordance with the ICC warrants.[42]

On 16 November 2006, the UN Security Council issued a Presidential Statement, asking the LRA to release all women, children and other non-combatants, and to conclude the peace process expeditiously. The statement further invited 'United Nations Member States to support efforts to bring an end to this conflict … and to ensure that those responsible for serious violations of human rights and international humanitarian law are brought to justice'.[43]

At the end of November 2006, the LRA declared its withdrawal from the talks, claiming a violation of the truce by the UPDF based on the allegation that the UPDF had killed three of its fighters. Uganda denied the charge. To save the peace talks, in early December 2006,

---

[36] ICG, note 9, *supra*, at 4.

[37] See ICC Pre-Trial Chamber II, Prosecution's Request that the Warrant of Arrest for Raska LUKWIYA Be Withdrawn and Rendered Without Effect Because of his Death with (redacted) reference to a communication from the Ugandan government in n. 14, ICC Doc. No. ICC-02/04-01/05 (22 March 2007), available at www.icc-cpi.int/iccdocs/doc/doc297257.PDF.

[38] Steve Bloomfield, *Power of Forgiveness Offers Hope for Peace in War-torn Uganda*, THE INDEPENDENT (LONDON), 25 September 2006.

[39] IRIN, *UGANDA: Rebels Propose Federalist Solution at Juba Talks,* 11 October 2006, available at http://irinnews.org/report.aspx?reportid=61303.

[40] BBC News, *Museveni Meets Ugandan LRA Rebels,* 21 October 2006, available at http://news.bbc.co.uk/2/hi/africa/6072994.stm.

[41] ICG, note 8 *supra*; ICG, *Northern Uganda: Seizing the Opportunity for Peace*, Africa Report No. 124, 4, n. 27 (Kampala/Nairobi/Brussels, 26 April 2007) with further details.

[42] IRIN, *UGANDA: Revised Government-LRA Ceasefire Deal Signed,* 1 November 2006, available at http://irinnews.org/report.aspx?reportid=61460.

[43] UN Press Release, *Security Council Presidential Statement Demands release of Women, Children by Lord's Resistance Army, Expeditious Conclusion of the Peace Process*, 16 November 2006, UN Department of Public Information Doc. SC 8869, available at www.un.org/News/Press/docs/2006/sc8869.doc.htm.

UN Secretary-General, Kofi Annan, appointed Joaquim Chissano, former President of Mozambique, as UN Special Envoy to the conflict.[44]

On 18 December 2006, the ceasefire was extended for two more months.[45] At the same time, the LRA negotiators stated that they no longer felt safe and welcome in Southern Sudan. The Sudanese government had stated that the LRA were unwelcome in Sudan after it appeared that hungry LRA rebels had attacked and looted villages in the Southern Sudanese region of Eastern Equatoria.[46] As a result, the negotiations were suspended.

In December 2006 and January 2007, a total of 17 civilians were killed in a series of ambushes on the road that connects Juba with Uganda. On 26 January 2007, one UNMIS peace-keeper was killed and two were wounded in an ambush. It remains unclear who was responsible for these attacks.

On 26 April 2007, the Juba peace talks resumed due to efforts of UN Special Envoy Chissano and his team. Additional observers from Kenya, Tanzania, Mozambique, Congo and South Africa acted as informal facilitators. Security in Southern Sudan improved as LRA combatants, who had been destabilizing Eastern Equatoria, crossed the Nile and assembled with the bulk of the rebels west of Garamba National Park in Congo, near the Sudan border.

On 2 May 2007, an Agreement on Comprehensive Solutions to the Conflict was reached between the parties as part of the Juba peace talks. It provided general guidelines for addressing the long-term economic, political and social issues that afflict Northern Uganda but the agreement still lacked more detailed provisions.

From 3 to 20 June 2007, the Director of the Secretariat of the ICC Trust Fund for Victims visited Uganda and met with a wide range of people, including representatives of victims' communities, community leaders and government officials, to raise awareness about the Trust Fund's mandate and activities and lay concrete foundations for the first projects of the ICC Trust Fund for Victims in Northern Uganda.

On 29 June 2007, an Agreement on Basic Principles of Reconciliation and Accountability was concluded during the Juba peace talks. It lays a foundation for finding a compromise based on victims' needs and international standards. The parties agreed that reconciliation and accountability should be pursued locally, through both formal and informal measures.[47] The government agreed to establish a domestic legal framework to substitute the prosecutions by the ICC. This was to be complemented by alternative mechanisms, including traditional justice processes, and alternative sentences and reparations, which would be legally adopted and recognized. The parties further agreed that, after a preparatory period, they would negotiate an annex to 'set out elaborated principles and mechanisms for implementation'.[48] Basic details were left open to be defined in those negotiations, including the relationship between formal and alternative justice mechanisms.

---

44   UN News Service, *Annan Names Special Envoy to Help Resolve Northern Ugandan Conflict,* 4 December 2006, available at www.un.org/apps/news/story.asp?NewsID=20835&Cr=LRA&Cr1=#.

45   BBC News, Sarah Grainger, *Ugandan LRA Rebel Truce Extended*, 18 December 2006, available at http://news.bbc.co.uk/2/hi/africa/6190283.stm.

46   ICG, note 8 *supra*, at 4, n. 29.

47   Agreement on Basic Principles of Reconciliation and Accountability Between the Government of the Republic of Uganda and the Lord's Resistance Army/Movement ('Juba Agreement'), 29 June 2007, clause 4.1, available at www.beyondjuba.org/peace_agreements/Agreement_on_Accountability_And_Reconcilition.pdf.

48   *Ibid.* cl. 15.1.

In October 2007, LRA deputy and ICC indictee Vincent Otti died. According to news reports, he was killed during a high command meeting that Kony convened at his base camp in Garamba.

In November 2007, members of the LRA delegation to the Juba peace negotiations met with Museveni in Kampala, who stated that he would not ask the ICC to withdraw the arrest warrants before the signing of a peace deal. The LRA delegation then travelled to Northern Uganda for several weeks of consultation with victims on the question of accountability and reconciliation. The leader of the delegation, Martin Ojul, asked for forgiveness, stating to a local radio station that 'the LRA made plenty of mistakes' and asking for 'forgiveness for what happened to our people'.[49]

On 23 January 2008, Riek Machar finally confirmed the death of the LRA deputy leader, Vincent Otti, to the participants in the Juba peace talks. Subsequently, the LRA sacked the head of the LRA Juba negotiating team, Martin Ojul, and replaced him with Dr David Matsanga, who it was hoped would be able to break the deadlock with Kony concerning the ICC indictments.[50] The Juba peace talks resumed.

On 19 February 2008, the Ugandan government and the LRA signed an annex to the 2007 Agreement on Reconciliation and Accountability, adding further detail on how the Agreement should be implemented. This annex envisioned creating a special division of the Uganda High Court to try those accused of planning or carrying out war crimes and other widespread attacks on civilians during the LRA conflict.

On 23 February 2008, the Ugandan government and the LRA signed a permanent cease-fire agreement, coming into effect 24 hours after the signing by both sides of a comprehensive peace deal. One week later, the Pre-Trial Chamber of the ICC requested Uganda to provide detailed information on the steps it had taken to implement the Agreement on Reconciliation and Accountability and its annex. Soon thereafter, on 10 March 2008, an LRA delegation met with officials of the ICC Registry in The Hague to discuss legal and procedural issues relating to the LRA members facing the Court's arrest warrants.[51] The ICC Prosecutor, Luis Moreno-Ocampo, refused to meet LRA representatives and said the indictments would remain in place.[52]

On 12 March 2008, during a visit to London, President Museveni seemed hopeful that a comprehensive peace agreement was about to be concluded, and stated that the LRA leaders should be tried before local Ugandan courts rather than by the ICC.

For some weeks, LRA leader Kony delayed his signing of the peace agreement due to alleged health problems. Finally, on 10 April 2008, he failed to show up at a ceremony for the signing of the permanent truce, insisting first on the lifting of ICC arrest warrants against the LRA leadership and requesting further details on how *mato-oput*, an Acholi traditional justice process, would be applied and how exactly the special division of the High Court would work.[53]

---

[49]   BBC News, *Uganda Rebels Ask for Forgiveness*, 6 November 2007, available at http://news.bbc.co.uk/2/hi/africa/7080735.stm.

[50]   International Crisis Group, *Uganda: The Road to Peace, With or Without Kony*, Africa Report No. 146, 2 (Nairobi/Kampala/Juba/Brussels, 10 December 2008).

[51]   ICC Press Release, No. ICC-CPI-20080310-PR295, 10 March 2008.

[52]   BBC News, *ICC Rejects Uganda Rebel Overture*, 5 March 2008, http://news.bbc.co.uk/2/hi/africa/7277577.stm.

[53]   *Uganda: Rebel Chief Refuses to Sign Peace Deal*, New Vision, 10 April 2008, available at http://allafrica.com/stories/200804110001.html.

Kony then suspended the peace talks and appointed a new negotiating team. In response, the government of Uganda indefinitely suspended its participation in the Juba peace talks. In an ominous turn of events, the LRA began to rearm and to abduct new recruits not only in Southern Sudan, but also in the DRC and the Central African Republic.

In May 2008, the Ugandan government took the first steps in setting up a special division of the Uganda High Court to try those accused of planning or carrying out war crimes and other attacks on civilians during the conflict.[54] While still professing a commitment to peace, Kony failed to attend further meetings scheduled to discuss the Juba peace agreement in July, August and September 2008. After a deadline of 30 November 2008 was set, Kony did meet with Northern Ugandan elders but did not agree to sign the accords unconditionally.

The LRA continued to carry out attacks, in particular in Southern Sudan and in the DRC, resulting in the destruction of property and the killing of civilians. In response to ongoing LRA atrocities in the region, the UPDF, the Armed Forces of the Democratic Republic of Congo (FARDC) and the GoSS mapped out a military campaign against the LRA.

On 21 October 2008, the Pre-Trial Chamber II of the ICC decided to initiate proceedings against the LRA leaders. It then appointed a counsel for the defense and invited all parties to the case to submit observations on admissibility to the Court.

LRA atrocities continued and came to a new climax during the Christmas holiday of 2008, when the LRA reportedly attacked villages in the DRC, killing around 200 people in Faradje, Doruma and Gurga, including about 45 civilians who were hacked to death in a Catholic church near Doruma. Children were abducted, houses set on fire, and numerous buildings, including the hospital and the police barracks, looted. The United Nations Office for the Coordination of Humanitarian Affairs (OCHA) reported the entire population of Faradje, some 30,000 people, fled because of the LRA violence.[55]

The LRA violence continued in the DRC and in the region, displacing thousands of people in the Northeastern DRC.[56] Meanwhile, a military offensive by the coalition of Ugandan, Southern Sudanese and Congolese forces against the LRA continued. At the beginning of January 2009, groups of LRA fighters allegedly tried to enter the Central African Republic, while other groups of LRA fighters committed atrocities in Southern Sudan, allegedly killing more than 50 people in Western Equatoria State.

On 29 January 2009, Okot Odhiambo, one of the LRA members indicted by the ICC and the new deputy leader of the LRA, reportedly negotiated with the International Organisation for Migration (IOM) seeking safe passage to Uganda after having been wounded in fights with Ugandan forces in Northeastern Congo. Odhiambo also asked the Ugandan government for amnesty and assurance that he would not be handed over to the ICC.[57] However it appears that he did not return to Uganda, and the LRA denies the reports as defamation and an attempt to split the LRA.

---

54   BBC News, *Uganda Sets up War Crimes Court*), 26 May 2006, available at http://news.bbc.co.uk/2/hi/africa/7420461.stm.

55   IRIN, *DRC-Uganda: Deadly LRA Attacks Prompt Exodus in Northeastern DRC*, 30 December 2008, available at www.unhcr.org/refworld/docid/496321d4c.html.

56   IRIN, *DRC: Thousands Displaced by Latest LRA Attack*, 9 January 2009, available at www.unhcr.org/refworld/docid/496c5c448.html.

57   *Ugandan Rebel Deputy Leader Defects*, THE GUARDIAN, 29 January 2009, available at www.guardian.co.uk/world/2009/jan/29/uganda-rebels-odhiambo-defects.

In March 2009, Ugandan troops who had been fighting the LRA on Congolese territory with consent of the DRC government began withdrawing from the DRC. The UN Special Envoy for LRA-affected areas, Joaquim Chissano, called for a resumption of peace talks.

On 10 March 2009, the Pre-Trial Chamber II of the ICC rendered a decision concerning the admissibility of the case against Joseph Kony, Vincent Otti, Okot Odhiambo and Dominic Ongwen under article 19(1) of the ICC Statute. The Chamber declared the case admissible pending the adoption of relevant national legislation in Uganda and further practical steps to prosecute the indicted persons before Ugandan courts.

In a letter to the UN Security Council dated 26 May 2009,[58] UN Secretary-General, Ban Ki-Moon, suspended the mandate of UN Special Envoy for LRA-affected areas, Joaquim Chissano, as of 30 June 2009. The letter explained that Chissano had achieved negotiation of a peace agreement and that the onus now lay firmly with Kony to take the last step for peace and sign the final peace agreement. Accordingly, on 16 July 2009, Chissano gave a final briefing to the UN Security Council advocating that a peaceful resolution of the Northern Uganda conflict should be equally pursued alongside the military action.

At this time, it remains unclear whether and when LRA leader Kony will commit to a peace deal.

AN ANALYSIS OF THE CHRONOLOGY OF EVENTS

Even though the complexity of the conflict makes it difficult to establish clear causal links between events, the chronology of the developments in the LRA conflict allows for important conclusions concerning the impact of the ICC investigation. The chronology makes clear that many players with different agendas shaped events. In particular, the Juba peace negotiations appear to have depended on a complex interplay of various factors, including developments in the region, that is Uganda, the DRC, the Central African Republic and the Sudan.

The Juba negotiations were also affected by interventions and declarations by international players such as the UN peace-keeping Missions to the Sudan and the DRC (UNMIS and MONUC), the UN Security Council and the ICC. The LRA increasingly became a regional problem, affecting not only Northern Uganda but also the DRC, the Central African Republic and Southern Sudan. Furthermore, as the LRA began to operate outside of Northern Uganda, it appears that LRA fighters were increasingly of Southern Sudanese origin. This became a problem since the concerns of these non-Ugandan LRA members were not adequately addressed by the Juba peace talks.[59]

Given the fears of increased violence expressed by community leaders in Northern Uganda at the beginning of the ICC investigation, it is at first glance surprising that the Juba peace negotiations started eight months *after* the unsealing of the ICC arrest warrants. Initially, the peace talks seemed to offer good prospects for a successful end to the Northern Ugandan conflict: they were referred to as 'the best hope for a negotiated resolution of the conflict'.[60]

---

[58]   Security Council Doc. No. S/2009/281 (1 June 2009), available at www.securitycouncil report.org/atf/cf/%7B65BFCF9B-6D27-4E9C-8CD3-CF6E4FF96FF9%7D/Uganda%20S2009282.pdf.
[59]   ICG, note 50 *supra*.
[60]   ICG, note 8 *supra*, at 2.

However, since Kony's failure to sign the Juba accords in early 2008, LRA violence re-erupted, particularly in Southern Sudan and the DRC. On the other hand, LRA attacks decreased significantly in Northern Uganda itself and a growing number of IDPs have been able to return to their homes after years of living in dreadful conditions in IDP camps.

In more detail, an examination of the chronology allows for the following conclusions.

(1)   The ICC investigation brought growing attention to the long-standing Northern Ugandan conflict and thereby potentially increased the prospects for peace.

The Ugandan government's self-referral of the situation to the nascent ICC and the fact that it subsequently became the first investigation by that institution brought international attention to the long-neglected conflict in Northern Uganda. It has been argued that 'for Uganda the referral was an attempt to engage an otherwise aloof international community'.[61] The impact of the increased attention was not limited to the mobilization of the ICC itself. That attention also created broader public interest in the Northern Uganda conflict, increased media coverage, and contributed to worldwide solidarity actions such as the 'Guluwalks'. It was ultimately a factor contributing to a more visible UN involvement in the form of UN Security Council Resolutions and the appointment of a UN Special Envoy.

The attention also gave the LRA leadership an incentive to seek publicity. The importance of this development lies in the fact that during more than two decades of conflict, the LRA leadership had remained elusive, and it had consequently been difficult to decipher its inner dynamics. With increased international attention, the LRA leadership was given a forum that it used to discuss its ideas, including options for ending the fighting as exemplified by Kony's offer of a unilateral ceasefire.[62] A member of the Juba mediation team[63] has referred to this development as the 'coming out of the LRA' and observed that Vincent Otti had particularly 'discovered a taste for radio interviews'. So far, however, the public appearances of the LRA leadership have failed to shed light on the LRA's political agenda.[64]

In addition to influencing the LRA leadership, the increased media attention may also have been a factor in bringing the Ugandan government to participate in the Juba peace negotiations in an effort to restore its good international reputation, which has been increasingly tainted by the conflict.

(2)   The ICC arrest warrants provided motivation for the LRA's continued participation in the peace talks and brought accountability onto the agenda of the peace negotiations.

The ICC investigation and the unsealing of its arrest warrants have been credited with bringing about the Juba peace negotiations. The LRA leadership may have believed that in negotiations they could exchange an end to the hostilities for amnesty, or at least for a mitigation of penalties. The Ugandan diplomat, Ambassador Miriam Blaak, stated: 'I would like to emphasize that if it was not for the warrants of arrest hanging over the heads of the indictees, the LRA may not have agreed to the peace process.'[65] On the negative side, the

---

61   P. Akhavan, *The Lord's Resistance Army Case: Uganda's Submission of the First State Referral to the International Criminal Court*, 99 AMERICAN J INTERNATIONAL L 403, 404 (2005).

62   ICG, note 25 *supra*, at 4.

63   Interview with the author, 8 March 2007. The interview was conducted in writing and answers were received in an attachment to an email of 8 March 2007; copy retained by the author.

64   ICG, note 25 *supra*, at 7.

65   M. Blaak, *International Criminal Court (23 November 2006) Fifth Session of the Assembly of the State Parties in The Hague, 23 November 2006, Annex A: Statement Made on Behalf of Uganda* (The Hague, 23 November 2006), available at www.icc-cpi.int/library/cases/ICC-02-04-01-05-132-

arrest warrants were apparently a big factor in Kony's decision not to sign the accords negotiated thus far.

The Juba agreement and its annex show that the negotiating parties agreed upon the need to incorporate a reconciliation and accountability mechanism as part of any peace deal. Although criticized as insufficient to address serious weaknesses in the Ugandan justice system, these agreements can offer a real alternative to the ICC proceedings,[66] and are a first step in establishing a meaningful domestic framework capable of holding the perpetrators of the LRA conflict accountable within Uganda.

The arrest warrants also affect the indicted LRA leadership's physical and political isolation. This has both positive and negative effects upon the prospects for peace. While the isolation limits the ability of the LRA leadership to move and to act, it also makes them even more reclusive. Although, in August 2006, the negotiators did have direct contacts with the LRA leadership at their hide-out in the DRC, the indictees have repeatedly cited the ICC arrest warrants as a reason not to be physically present at the peace talks in Juba.[67] There is a discrepancy between the agenda of the LRA leadership and that of the predominantly diaspora LRA delegation negotiating in Juba. That delegation apparently has very limited authority within the LRA, which is obviously of concern for the outcome of the peace negotiations.[68] Furthermore, it seems that some of the accords reached in Juba were not communicated to or accepted by the LRA leader Joseph Kony[69] before the negotiations were completed. This may help to explain his continued reluctance to sign them.

(3)   The scale of LRA atrocities does not appear to be directly linked to the ICC arrest proceedings but instead seems to depend on other political factors.

After the ICC arrest warrants were issued there was, at least initially, a significant reduction in the number of crimes committed by the LRA. IDPs in Northern Uganda began to return to their homes. Acts of violence in Southern Sudan that took place just before the beginning of the peace talks, and before Museveni visited Juba in October 2006, cannot clearly be attributed to the LRA. Many suspect that violence was initiated by Khartoum to implicate the LRA and thereby undermine the negotiations.[70] Since the breakdown of the peace negotiations in early 2008, however, there have been significant new atrocities by the LRA, particularly in Southern Sudan and the DRC.

There are various possible reasons for the earlier decline in LRA atrocities. One plausible explanation would attribute the decline to the deterrent effect of arrest warrants. This explanation assumes that LRA leaders, afraid of their eventual apprehension, did not want to make things any worse for themselves by multiplying the number of atrocities committed.[71]

AnxA_English.pdf; similarly, the ICG noted, the arrest warrants 'have been important in bringing the LRA to the negotiating table'. ICG, note 24 *supra*.

[66]   Amnesty International, *Uganda: Agreement and Annex on Accountability and Reconciliation Falls Short of a Comprehensive Plan to End Impunity*, AI Index: AFR 59/001/2008 (21 March 2008).

[67]   ICG, note 25 *supra*, at 8.

[68]   ICG, note 25 *supra*, at 3.

[69]   ICG, note 50 *supra*.

[70]   ICG, note 25 *supra*, at 6, n. 30.

[71]   G. Evans, *Justice, Peace and the International Criminal Court*, presentation in response to the Second Public Hearing of the Office of the Prosecutor, the Prosecutorial Strategy for 2007–09, The Hague, 25 September 2006.

Although many remain skeptical of the deterrence argument, it is reasonable to conclude that the peace negotiations were advanced by the unsealing of the arrest warrants, and that the latter reinforced the willingness of all parties to enter into and obey the ceasefire. However, once the peace process stalled and regional governments pursued a military option, the level of LRA atrocities increased dramatically.

(4) The ICC depends upon states to carry out its arrest warrants, and it loses credibility when they lack the political will to do so.

The arrest warrants in the Uganda cases were issued in July 2005 and unsealed in October 2005. In the time that has passed since, no serious attempt has been made to carry them out. The trials against the LRA leadership cannot begin, however, without an arrest of the indictees.

The ICC's institutional weakness and dependency on the political will of states to carry out its arrest warrants seems to undermine the ICC's standing in the eyes of the local population in Northern Uganda. In the last few years, the United Nations Office of the High Commissioner for Human Rights (OHCHR) has organized group discussions with Northern Ugandans at massacre sites in Northern Uganda. While it became clear from those discussions that the local population had no uniform view of the ICC, it also became apparent that, in the eyes of many, the ICC was ineffective because it lacked a police force and could not secure the arrest of the indictees.[72]

(5) Problems related to the ICC's outreach efforts undermined the standing of the ICC in Northern Uganda.

Due to practical considerations, such as the need for witness protection,[73] and an effort to demonstrate respect for the ongoing peace talks, the ICC attempted to maintain a low public profile during the investigation in Northern Uganda. Initially, the ICC spoke mainly to community leaders. Subsequently, it adopted a more proactive information outreach policy, conducting workshops with traditional leaders, NGOs, local government representatives and religious leaders from across Northern and Eastern Uganda. The effectiveness of these efforts is far from clear, although a recent study based on interviews with 2,875 people in Northern Uganda claims there has been a significant increase in the number who know about the ICC.[74] However, their knowledge of the ICC's mandate and powers seems sketchy. The statement of one Acholi former abductee summarizes the ICC's outreach problem: 'We have heard of the ICC but we do not understand it properly.'[75]

The victims' assistance and reparation mechanism created by the ICC Statute provides a powerful tool enabling the ICC to engage communities affected by war crimes, genocide and crimes against humanity. Due to concerns about security, the ICC's Uganda office is based in Kampala, far from Northern Uganda, and this distance complicates victims' reparation claims. There have been positive developments, such as the June 2007 visit to Uganda of the Executive Director of the ICC Trust Fund for Victims and the fact that the Trust fund began

---

72   OHCHR staff member, interview with the author, 18 January 2007, Geneva.

73   ICG, note 9 *supra,* at 9.

74   ICTJ and the Berkeley-Tulane Initiative on Vulnerable Populations, *When the War Ends* 5 (8 December 2007). The study claims that about 60 percent of respondents knew about the ICC as opposed to only 27 percent in a similar study conducted in 2005.

75   OHCHR, *Making Peace Our Own* 50 (2007), available at http://transitionaljustice.ulster.ac.uk/pdfs/unohchr_tj_study_final_report.pdf.

assisting victims in Northern Uganda through projects aimed at providing material support and physical and psychological rehabilitation.

In addition, the appearance of a possible ICC bias towards the Ugandan government may have damaged the credibility of the ICC in Northern Uganda. A 2007 study of the OHCHR based on interviews with more than 1,700 conflict victims from all across Northern Uganda noted that:

> respondents expressed deep misgivings about the current capacity of domestic and international institutions of justice to effectively deliver on accountability in a fair and transparent manner. In particular, many focus groups underscored the failure of the ICC to follow through on the arrests of the LRA senior leadership, as well their perception that the ICC is one-sided for not having indicted any UPDF personnel.[76]

At the beginning of the Northern Uganda investigation, the ICC Prosecutor made the diplomatic mistake of hosting a press conference together with President Museveni, thereby creating the impression that the ICC Prosecutor did not contemplate looking into possible crimes committed by the government side.[77] More generally, it has been argued that President Museveni is using the ICC as the 'stick' in his 'carrot and stick' tactics against the LRA[78] and to appease international critics of his government. To correct the impression that he is acting upon instructions of President Museveni, ICC Prosecutor, Moreno-Ocampo, wrote a formal letter to the President of the ICC on 17 June 2004 stating: 'My Office has informed the Ugandan authorities that we must interpret the scope of the referral consistently with the principles of the Rome Statute, and hence we are analyzing the crimes within the situation in Northern Uganda by whomever committed.'[79]

In a later public document, Moreno-Ocampo explained:

> [T]he Office then analysed the gravity of crimes allegedly committed by different groups in Northern Uganda and found that the crimes allegedly committed by the LRA were of higher gravity than alleged crimes committed by any other group. The Office therefore started with an investigation of the LRA and is currently analyzing crimes committed by other groups, taking into consideration the gravity threshold and complementarity.[80]

But four years after the ICC had issued its arrest warrants against the LRA leadership and over five years after it began its investigation, there were no visible signs in Northern Uganda that an ICC investigation into UPDF crimes was under way. Until this changes, the ICC Prosecutor's assurances of impartiality will likely have little effect on public opinion in Northern Uganda.

(6)   The ICC is one of several factors in a complex process and is not the main obstacle to peace in Northern Uganda.

---

[76]   *Ibid.* 75.

[77]   P. Seils and M. Wierda, *The International Criminal Court and Conflict Mediation,* Occasional Paper of the International Center for Transitional Justice 10 (June 2005), available at www.ictj.org/images/content/1/1/119.pdf.

[78]   André-Michel Essoungou, *Chantage à la pax en Ouganda,* 54 Le Monde Diplomatique 13 (No. 637, April 2007).

[79]   Office of the Prosecutor of the ICC, Letter to President Kirsch, 17 June 2004.

[80]   International Criminal Court, *Background Documents for the Media* (March 2007), on file with the author.

It appears that the ICC's involvement has not been a decisive factor in the failure of the peace negotiations. On the contrary, it may have contributed to the bringing about of the Juba peace talks and the recorded decrease in atrocities.[81] Instead, it has been only one element in a complex process. Other factors, such as the changed political situation in Sudan, which for a long time had provided the LRA with support and a safe-haven from the UPDF, and the possible current military weakness of the LRA,[82] were also important. Another obstacle to reviving the peace talks may be the LRA leadership's fear of being attacked or arrested if they come to Southern Sudan. Conversely, the LRA may have been using the peace talks to gain tactical breathing space in which to rearm and regroup.[83]

(7)   Focus on the 'peace versus justice' question has diverted attention and resources from the question of how to initiate a wider reconciliation process.

The 2007 'Making Peace our Own' study by the OHCHR aimed at exploring perceptions among Northern Ugandans on themes of accountability, reconciliation and transitional justice. Based on its analysis of extensive consultations and interviews with a large number of conflict victims, the study concluded:

> Recent debates about the northern Ugandan conflict have been dominated by analyses based on artificial dichotomies, including peace versus justice, local versus international responses to harm, and the population's desire for forgiveness and reconciliation versus punishment. The effect of this polarization has been to cloud debates about the most appropriate ways to address conflict and its aftermath, implying either/or choices when combinations of these elements often better reflect popular perceptions and lead to more effective practical strategies.[84]

The ICC can offer formal justice for those leaders responsible for the worst atrocities, nothing more and nothing less. Uganda needs a wider and more comprehensive process of transitional justice, to which the ICC investigation can make a significant but only limited contribution. The present ICC Prosecutor is conscious of the limitations on the ICC's role. He has noted that 'the mandate of the Office is to ensure accountability for those who bear the greatest responsibility alongside national proceedings and other community initiatives'.[85]

In conclusion, one must not overstate the impact of the ICC investigation on the recent developments in the Northern Ugandan conflict.

ALTERNATIVES FOR ENDING THE ICC INVESTIGATION IN NORTHERN UGANDA

It appears that the issue of accountability has been an important factor in the reluctance of LRA leaders to commit to a peace agreement. Otti has warned there will be no peace deal

---

[81]   ICC official with the ICC Uganda investigation, interview with the author, The Hague, 30 March 2007, source requested to remain anonymous.

[82]   ICG, note 25 *supra*, at 8; also ICC official with the ICC Uganda investigation, interview with the author, The Hague, 30 March 2007.

[83]   ICG, note 25 *supra*, at 8; ICC official, interview with the author, The Hague, 30 March 2007.

[84]   *Making Peace Our Own,* note 74 *supra* at 1.

[85]   ICC *Background Documents for the Media,* note 80 *supra.*

unless international indictments for the top rebels are dropped.[86] Kony asked Egeland to intervene and to cancel the ICC arrest warrants. He threatened that otherwise he would not sign any peace agreement.[87] In fact, when Kony failed to sign the Juba accords in early 2008, his fear of being held criminally accountable before the ICC was reportedly the main factor he cited for not agreeing to sign the deal.[88] It is therefore highly unlikely that the LRA leadership will sign a peace agreement that will make them subject to criminal prosecution by the ICC.

As mentioned in the introduction, in drafting the ICC Statute, states parties were not oblivious to these competing demands. They included in the Statute a mechanism for temporarily suspending ICC proceedings and other mechanisms to end ICC proceedings for the purpose of yielding to domestic justice. Nonetheless, there is a continuing debate as to how these mechanisms should be understood and applied. This chapter argues that some of the approaches offered to prevent the ICC from interfering with the peace process are not compatible with a correct reading of the Statute and would undermine the ICC for years to come.

Government Revocation of the Referral to the ICC?

When President Museveni announced that Kony and other LRA leaders would be left unpunished if they abandoned terrorism, this statement was interpreted to mean that President Museveni intended to withdraw the Ugandan referral of the situation to the ICC. However, the government of Uganda cannot do so unilaterally. The ICC Statute does not explicitly address the issue, but its silence on the question of whether a state may withdraw its referral must be interpreted as excluding the 'self-withdrawal' of a state party referral. The *travaux preparatoires* of the ICC Statute do not suggest that a state party can 'withdraw' a referral once the jurisdiction of the ICC is triggered.[89] Moreover, it would contradict the ICC's mandate to end impunity if a state could simply decide to stop an ICC investigation once it has begun by withdrawing its referral.

UN Security Council Deferral of the Situation under Article 16 of the ICC Statute

Article 16 of the ICC Statute has been referred to as 'the vehicle for resolving conflict between the requirements of peace and justice where the Council assesses that the peace efforts need to be given priority over criminal justice'.[90] It reads:

---

    [86]   BBC News, 6 September 2006, as cited in ICG, note 24 *supra*, at 15, n. 111. Otti, who was thought to be supportive of peace talks, died in October 2007, as noted above.

    [87]   BBC News, *UN Envoy Sees Uganda Rebel Chief*, 12 November 2006, available at http://news.bbc.co.uk/2/hi/africa/6139554.stm.

    [88]   In an interview of 19 June 2008 (*US Demands Uganda Rebels Sign Final Peace Deal*) with Voice of America reporter Peter Clottey, then chief LRA negotiator David Matsanga stated that Kony would refuse to sign a final peace deal until the ICC arrest warrants against him and other rebel leaders were removed: 'General Joseph Kony cannot sign a peace agreement when he has warrants hanging on his head. He wants an explanation.' Available at www.voanews.com/english/archive/2008-06/2008-06-19-voa3.cfm?CFID=266012347&CFTOKEN=20591266&jsessionid=de305e8e31a0d7ba31397292 a6d51d641c53.

    [89]   Amnesty International Press Release, *Uganda: Government Cannot Prevent the International Criminal Court from Investigating Crimes*, 16 November 2004.

    [90]   M. Bergsmo and J. Pejic, *Article 16, Deferral of Investigation or Prosecution*, in COMMENTARY

No investigation or prosecution may be commenced or proceeded with under this Statute for a period of 12 months after the Security Council, in a resolution under Chapter VII of the Charter of the United Nations, has requested the Court to that effect; that request may be renewed by the Council under the same conditions.

Although potentially useful, this article also raises problems of selectivity and political control over 'prosecutorial discretion' and might have a negative impact on the credibility of the ICC.[91] It gives the UN Security Council unique new powers with regard to the ICC because the Security Council cannot defer cases pending before national courts or the International Court of Justice. And any deferral by the Security Council under article 16 will be public knowledge, as will the crimes that the ICC is being asked to desist from addressing. In a media age, where the public is exposed to the atrocities and violence through daily news images, Security Council deferral of a prosecution could be more difficult to justify politically than a simple failure to approve an investigation. The International Crisis Group[92] has described article 16 in the context of Northern Uganda as 'a flawed option' because 'the image of the Security Council intervening to reprieve a group as stigmatized as the LRA may appear to some an unacceptable affront to justice and victims, especially if a peace agreement does not include any substantial accountability mechanisms'.

Human Rights Watch rejects outright the idea of a Security Council intervention under article 16 in the situation of Northern Uganda. An HRW memorandum addressed to ICC states parties of November 2006 states:

> States parties should also make clear that a UN Security Council deferral under article 16 of the Rome Statute would be inappropriate in this instance, and states parties on the Security Council have a particular role to play in opposing an article 16 deferral. In the absence of credible alternatives at the national level, such a deferral would shield the LRA leadership from prosecution, perhaps indefinitely if renewed. It might also open the door to dangerous and inappropriate interference by the Security Council in the ICC.[93]

Some commentators, such as ICG's Vice President, Nick Grono, do not completely exclude the possibility of an article 16 deferral. Having argued that the ICC Prosecutor should continue with its investigation for now, he stated that, should the need arise to resolve the 'peace versus justice' dilemma, the UN Security Council is the right authority to do so. He concluded: 'The talks have a long way to go, but if they reach the stage that peace is likely, the ICC prosecutions should be put on hold to give the millions in northern Uganda a chance to enjoy the peace they have thirsted after for 20 years.'[94]

Despite such comments, a Security Council deferral in accordance with article 16 of the ICC Statute remains a very unlikely option in the case of Northern Uganda, particularly in

---

ON THE ROME STATUTE OF THE INTERNATIONAL CRIMINAL COURT: OBSERVERS NOTES, ARTICLE BY ARTICLE, 374 (O. Triffterer (ed.), Baden-Baden, Nomos Verlag, 1999.

[91] L. Condorelli and S. Villalpando, *Referral and Deferral by the Security Council*, in THE ROME STATUTE OF THE INTERNATIONAL CRIMINAL COURT, A COMMENTARY 644, 651–4, (A. Cassese, P. Gaeta and J.R.W.D. Jones eds, Oxford/New York, Oxford University Press, 2002).

[92] ICG, note 25 *supra.*

[93] Human Rights, in ROME STATUTE COMMENTARY, note 91 *supra*, at 644, 651–4. International Crisis Group, Memorandum for the Fifth Session of the Assembly of States Parties to the ICC, 29, *September Watch*, (November 2006).

[94] Grono, note 1 *supra.*

light of the shocking nature and scale of the atrocities committed in the course of the conflict. A Security Council deferral of the ICC investigation would be an affront to the victims without a wider, robust accountability mechanism in place. In any case, it is unlikely that the indicted LRA leaders would be satisfied with such a deferral given that it would apply only for a limited (even though renewable) period of 12 months. That restricts its potential utility as a bargaining chip.

One situation in which article 16 could play a role would be if the Ugandan government asked the Security Council for a referral until more adequate domestic mechanisms of criminal justice could be set up, but so far there is no indication that Uganda has any such plans.

Prosecutorial Discretion

Another option can be found in article 53 of the ICC Statute. On its face, article 53 may appear to give the ICC Prosecutor a role in balancing both 'peace and justice' concerns when conducting an investigation. Human Rights Watch has argued that the ICC Prosecutor, in response to pressure to abandon the ongoing investigation into the situation in Uganda, could have suggested during the early phase of the investigation that he could suspend investigations 'in the interests of justice'.[95]

Article 53, entitled 'Initiation of an Investigation', sets out the responsibilities of the Prosecutor with regard to investigations. In the relevant part, article 53(2) states:

> If, upon investigation, the Prosecutor concludes that there is not a sufficient basis for a prosecution because: ... (c) A prosecution is not in the interests of justice, taking into account all the circumstances, including the gravity of the crime, the interests of victims and the age or infirmity of the alleged perpetrator, and his or her role in the alleged crime;
> the Prosecutor shall inform the Pre-Trial Chamber and the State making a referral under article 14 or the Security Council in a case under article 13, paragraph (b), of his or her conclusion and the reasons for the conclusion.

The advantage of article 53 is that it does not require any involvement of the Security Council but is addressed solely to the ICC Prosecutor. Article 53 states that the ICC Prosecutor has the important responsibility of deciding 'whether to initiate an investigation' and, upon investigation, to decide whether there is 'sufficient basis for a prosecution'. In making this decision, the Prosecutor must consider various factors, and in doing so, he must act 'in the interest of justice'. The Prosecutor's decision is subject to review by the Pre-Trial Chamber.

The conceptual meaning of 'in the interests of justice' in article 53 of the ICC Statute was deliberately left open at the Rome Conference. The Prosecutor's efforts to interpret the phrase are illustrated by the fact that, at a biannual consultation with NGOs at the end of 2004, the Office of the Prosecutor circulated a 'Consultation Proposal on the Interests of Justice' to solicit comments by NGOs regarding the meaning of the phrase.[96]

According to the general rules of treaty interpretation as set out in article 31 of the Vienna Convention on the Law of Treaties, a treaty shall be interpreted according to 'the ordinary

---

    95   Human Rights Watch, *The Meaning of 'The Interest of Justice' in Article 53 of the Rome Statute,* Policy Paper, 1 (June 2005), available at www.hrw.org.
    96   *Ibid.* 1.

meaning' of the terms of the treaty 'in light of its object and purpose' and 'any relevant rules under international law'. Applying these rules, any recourse to article 53 for the purpose of stopping an ICC investigation on the basis that it interferes with peace negotiations should be excluded.

First, abandoning an otherwise appropriate investigation will hardly be 'in the interest of justice'. Nor will it be consistent with the ICC Statute, as the object and purpose of that treaty is to end impunity for crimes under its jurisdiction.

Second, the 'ordinary meaning' of the term 'in the interests of justice' must also be assessed in relation to how the term is otherwise used in the ICC Statute. This analysis indicates that it should be interpreted narrowly. For example, article 67 describes the right of the accused 'to have legal assistance assigned by the Court in any case where the interests of justice so require'. Here the term appears to mean nothing more than 'the good administration of justice'.

Third, from a systematic point of view, the way to resolve the dilemma between peace and justice clearly seems to be under article 16 of the ICC Statute, as discussed above. This is reaffirmed by the fact that article 42 of the ICC Statute explicitly states that the Prosecutor of the ICC shall act independently, and no member of his office shall 'seek or act on instructions from external sources'. In other words, the Prosecutor is meant to be a judicial, non-political organ. Accordingly, the Prosecutor should be guided by the interests of criminal justice and not by the broader interests of peace and security. Requiring the ICC Prosecutor to make prosecutorial decisions based on political factors, taking into account such far-reaching political imperatives as peace and security, would undermine both the perception and the reality of the Prosecutor as an independent organ beyond political influence.

Accordingly, the fact that peace negotiations are underway which might be disrupted by ICC proceedings is not in itself sufficient grounds for the Prosecutor to halt a prosecution under article 53 of the ICC Statute.[97]

It is quite possible that if and when a final peace agreement is reached it will contain an amnesty for the LRA leadership subject to certain conditions. In this case, the ICC Prosecutor might decide under certain circumstances to use his discretion under article 53 of the ICC Statute to abandon the investigation. The establishment of a robust accountability mechanism falling short of formal criminal trials could be one circumstance favoring such a decision. The issue was not settled in Rome. The Chairman of the Rome Conference and current President of the ICC, Phillipe Kirsch, stated in an interview after the adoption of the Statute that the use of the expression 'in the interests of justice' in article 53 reflected 'creative ambiguity' with regard to the controversial question of whether the Prosecutor should enjoy discretion to recognize an amnesty as an exception to the jurisdiction of the ICC.[98]

The threshold for such prosecutorial action must necessarily be very high and should include full disclosure of the crimes committed. It is difficult to imagine what kind of mechanism could fulfill the requirements of the ICC Statute. Something as simple as a blanket amnesty would not fulfill the ICC Statute requirements. Presently, no alternative accountability mechanism that could meet the ICC Statute standard exists in Uganda.

---

[97]   *Ibid.* 6.
[98]   Michael Scharf, *The Amnesty Exception to the Jurisdiction of the International Criminal Court*, 32 CORNELL INTERNATIONAL LJ, 507–27, 521–2 (No. 507, 1999).

Given the fact that the ICC Prosecutor repeatedly publicly insisted that the indicted LRA leaders must be arrested and brought to justice, it is unlikely that he will use his prosecutorial discretion to end the ICC proceedings against them unless there is reason to believe they will be held criminally accountable in a meaningful way.[99] His view on this issue was revealed on 5 March 2008 when there was still hope that Kony might sign the Juba peace accords if he was reassured that he would not be put on trial in The Hague. At that time, the Prosecutor refused to meet with a LRA delegation visiting the ICC, and insisted instead that the indictments would remain in place.[100]

Complementarity

The Juba peace accords themselves suggest that the most likely resolution of the tension between the ICC investigations and the conclusion of a peace agreement would be credible and fair domestic prosecutions before domestic Ugandan courts of all parties to the conflict responsible for serious crimes, with a possible role for traditional justice mechanisms.

Complementarity is one of the fundamental principles of ICC jurisdiction. The idea is that the ICC is subsidiary to national courts which have a sort of priority over it.[101] Accordingly, if a state wants to avoid or to end ICC proceedings, it can initiate domestic criminal proceedings. But under the ICC Statute, national proceedings can only bar the ICC's jurisdiction if they genuinely aim at bringing the perpetrators to justice in a fair trial. Article 17 of the ICC Statute entitled 'Issues of Admissibility' contains the core provisions outlining complementarity. Article 17, paragraph 1 states that cases are inadmissible before the ICC if they are already investigated or prosecuted by a state which has jurisdiction over it, 'unless the state is unwilling or unable genuinely to carry out the investigation or prosecution'. From the wording of the ICC Statute ('investigated,' 'prosecuted' and 'tried before court') it seems clear that its drafters did not intend that alternative justice mechanisms, not comparable to a criminal trial or closely similar, should be grounds for excluding ICC jurisdiction on the basis of complementarity.

The June 2007 Juba peace accords provide few details of what a Ugandan justice mechanism which brings both sustainable peace and meaningful justice to Northern Uganda could look like.

The agreement does explicitly call for 'the widest possible consultations' to take place 'at all stages of development and implementation of the principles and mechanisms of this Agreement'. And in fact, the consultations of the LRA leadership with the affected communities in Northern Uganda at the end of 2007 and the public apology of the leader of the LRA delegation towards the victims were first steps towards reconciliation.

The Juba accords also clarify that LRA and army leaders responsible for grave human rights abuses and other serious crimes must be held accountable under a formal legal process in Uganda, ideally by a special domestic tribunal for the LRA commanders and by courts martial for culpable army officers. Parliament may also provide for alternative sanctions.

---

[99]   See, for example, *Uganda's Kony 'Will Never Make Peace': ICC,* Reuters Africa, 14 July 2009, available at http://af.reuters.com/article/topNews/idAFJOE56D0FH20090714?pageNumber= 1&virtualBrandChannel=0.
[100]   See the chronology *supra*.
[101]   For a detailed and up-to-date discussion of complementarity, see Sarah Nouwen, Chapter 9.

Options discussed informally include, for example, prohibiting LRA leaders from holding political office for ten years, banishment from Acholiland for five years, confinement to a small area for a period of time, a ban from working with children and compulsory cooperation with a truth and reconciliation commission.[102] However, a special tribunal and the sanctions it may impose must have, as the ICG puts it, 'teeth to persuade the international judges'. The criminal charges and penalties must be comparable to those applicable before the ICC[103] for ICC judges to rule under article 19 of the ICC Statute that further ICC proceedings are inadmissible under the principle of complementary jurisdiction. Traditional justice is, as a result of the prolonged weakness of the formal justice sector, very important in Northern Uganda. Nonetheless, traditional justice approaches are not well adapted to deal with crimes of the scale for which the ICC indicted the LRA leaders, nor would they in themselves be enough to trigger complementarity under the ICC Statute. Traditional mechanisms such as the Acholi tradition of *mato-oput* can and should, nevertheless, play an important role in the wider reconciliation process in Northern Uganda.

Within the Juba accords themselves, the Annex of 19 February 2008 adds more specific details to the 29 June 2007 Agreement on Basic Principles of Reconciliation and Accountability. In clause 7 it provides that a 'special division of the High Court of Uganda shall be established to try individuals who are alleged to have committed serious crimes during the conflict'. However, neither the Agreement nor the Annex contain an explanation of how the special division will be constituted or what substantive law or rules of procedure and evidence will be applied. It is not clear how they will differ from other national criminal courts. Principle 9 of the Annex indicates that supplementary documents and legislation will address these issues. Amnesty International has expressed concern that:

> the proposal in the Agreement and the Annex to establish a special division of the High Court will do little to address the systemic problems with the justice system in northern Uganda which have contributed to impunity and the failure of the rule of law in the region.[104]

In response to these developments in Uganda aimed at setting up a domestic framework to bring the perpetrators of the LRA conflict to justice, the ICC Pre-trial Chamber II initiated proceedings under article 19(1) of the ICC Statute *proprio motu* in October 2008 to decide whether the case against the LRA leaders was admissible. It examined in particular how the Agreement and its Annex might affect the admissibility of the case in light of the principle of complementarity.

In its decision of 10 March 2009 on admissibility under article 19(1), the Pre-trial Chamber II noted that according to the submission of Uganda 'the implementation of the Agreement and its Annexure is still "in the initial stages"'[105] and took the view 'that it would

---

102   International Crisis Group, *Northern Uganda Peace Process: The Need to Maintain Momentum*, Africa Briefing No. 46, 7, n. 34 (14 September 2007).

103   *Ibid.* 8.

104   Amnesty International, *Uganda: Agreement and Annex on Accountability and Reconciliation Falls Short of a Comprehensive Plan to End Impunity*, 15, AI Index: AFR 59/001/2008 (21 March 2008).

105   International Criminal Court, Pre-Trial Chamber II, Decision No. ICC-02/04-01/05 on Admissibility of the Case under Article 19(I) of the Statute, Situation in Uganda in the Case of *Prosecutor* v. *Joseph Kony, Vincent Otti, Okot Odhiambo and Dominic Ongwen*, 10 March 2009, at 26.

be premature and therefore inappropriate to assess the features envisaged for the Special Division and its legal framework'[106] at this stage.

The Pre-Trial Chamber also clarified the question as to who has the ultimate authority to determine the admissibility of the case. It found that 'it is for the Court and not for Uganda to make such determination'.[107] In other words, when a domestic system is eventually set up to bring the indicted LRA leaders to justice in Uganda, it will still be the prerogative of the ICC and not that of Uganda to determine whether that system satisfies the requirements of the ICC Statute.

From the perspective of the 'peace versus justice' debate, if the ICC has no jurisdiction over a specific case due to the concept of complementarity, then justice has in the end prevailed. Only a robust action by a national justice mechanism would bring complementarity into play, and if it has, then the aim behind the creation of the ICC, namely to end impunity, has presumably been achieved:

> Under this system of complementarity, much of the work done toward achieving the goals of the Statute may take place in national systems around the world. Thus, the number of cases that reach the Court or its judicial proceedings should not be the sole or even decisive measure of its effectiveness. On the contrary, increasing numbers of genuine investigations and trials at the national level may well illustrate the successful functioning of the Rome system as a whole.[108]

THE WAY FORWARD

At the time of writing it is impossible to predict how the conflict in Northern Uganda will end and what the fate of the indicted LRA leaders will be.

The Juba accords appear to endorse a justice mechanism to hold accountable both the LRA leadership and army members that have committed crimes. But until a peace agreement is signed and implemented and credible domestic prosecutions are underway, there are still significant obstacles ahead. The deep mistrust of the LRA leadership towards Museveni raises the question of whether they would believe that they can get a fair trial before a special tribunal in Uganda. In addition, the fact that past leaders of former Ugandan rebel movements have been offered luxurious lives after signing peace deals, makes it unlikely that Kony and the other ICC indictees will want to settle for less and agree to stand trial.[109]

What, however, if the LRA leaders really are arrested and brought to the Hague for trial by the ICC before peace negotiations are concluded? Several factors indicate that such arrests would have a positive effect on the prospect of peace for Northern Uganda. The current Northern Ugandan delegation to the Juba talks remains dominated by the LRA. This is problematic, not least because of the crimes that the LRA committed against the population of Northern Uganda.[110] An arrest of the LRA leadership could enable the people of Northern

---

[106]   *Ibid.* 27.

[107]   *Ibid.* 27.

[108]   Office of the Prosecutor of the ICC, *Report on the Activities Performed During the First Three Years (June 2003–June 2006)*, at 22, 23.

[109]   ICG, note 102 *supra*, at 8.

[110]   See *Making Peace Our Own*, note 74 *supra* with reports that the local population is unhappy about the lack of legitimacy of the negotiators and fears that this may render the Juba peace talks ineffective.

Uganda to send a more representative delegation to future peace talks. Given the hierarchical structure of the organization[111] and the personality cult surrounding Kony, his arrest would also decisively weaken the LRA and possibly bring about its end.

Finally, if the ICC indictees can be neither arrested nor convinced to sign a peace agreement that would subject them to criminal trials, another possible option of last resort has at least been considered. This would involve offering to the indicted LRA leadership exile in a safe-haven and suspending proceedings under article 16 of the ICC Statute. The ICG report of 14 September 2007, for example, states, 'if safe-haven is at the end of the day genuinely the only way to achieve agreement that ends the long war, allows IDPs to return home for good and removes the regional LRA security threat the government may understandably want to pursue this option'.

However, it is vital for the international community to send a clear message so as not to undermine the credibility of the ICC and not to set an unwanted precedent of impunity that might apply to atrocities elsewhere (for example in Darfur.) Therefore, even commentators, such as the ICG, who seriously consider this option regard it 'as an absolute last resort to be contemplated as an alternative to the ICC or credible local prosecutions'. In this context one must also bear in mind the symbolic significance of the Northern Uganda investigation for the ICC as a fledgling institution. If the ICC's credibility were to be undermined by granting the indicted LRA leaders impunity of some sort, this would decisively weaken its future capability to contribute to the prevention of atrocities and thereby to promote peace globally. Richard Goldstone noted in this respect that:

> if you have a system of international justice you've got to follow through. If in some cases that's going to make peace negotiations difficult, that may be the price that has to be paid. The international community must keep a firm line and say are we going to have a better world because of an international court or not.[112]

CONCLUSION: WHAT LESSONS CAN BE LEARNED FROM THE EXAMPLE OF NORTHERN UGANDA?

The question of whether and how to include criminal accountability in peace negotiations is complex and thus it is not surprising that the examination of North Uganda as a case study has produced mixed conclusions. Pessimists, who predicted that a criminal investigation by an international tribunal would necessarily spoil the prospect for peace and even increase violence, were proved wrong by the fact that serious peace negotiations, a ceasefire, and a significant decrease of atrocities came about *after* the issuance of the ICC arrest warrants. The most important conclusion in the case of the Northern Ugandan conflict seems to be that the ICC is neither the *deus ex machina* for ending impunity and preventing future crimes, nor is it the main obstacle in the way of peace.

Another important observation is that the ICC has only limited options under its legal framework to end an ongoing investigation for the sake of peace. A key measure, the Security Council deferral under article 16 of the ICC Statute, is not in the ICC's hands.

---

[111] ICG, note 8 *supra,* at 5.

[112] Chris McGreal, *African Search for Peace Throws Court into Crisis,* THE GUARDIAN, 9 January 2007, accessible at www.guardian.co.uk/world/2007/jan/09/uganda.topstories3.

Finally, the impact of ICC involvement on ongoing conflicts must be assessed on a case-by-case basis. This is reflected in the fact that the ICC itself utilizes different strategies in different investigations. What is true for Northern Uganda may not be true elsewhere. In circumstances where an ICC investigation takes place against the will of a government in power and the primary focus of ICC investigations may directly implicate members of this government, the dynamics of the investigation will be very different from that of the dynamics in Uganda. In the case of Darfur, the ICC investigation likely contributed to making the Sudanese government more aggressively opposed to what it views as illegitimate intervention by outside actors. This Sudanese reaction may have prolonged and exacerbated the crisis in Darfur and contributed to the delay in the deployment of UN peace-keeping troops to the region. There are, however, some factors from the Northern Ugandan case study that appear to have general applicability to ICC investigations of ongoing conflict.

The ICC's dependence on the political will of governments and UN forces to carry out arrests and to allow it access to evidence clearly places limits on its actions. In situations of ongoing conflict, the dependence of the ICC on assistance by the states harboring (willingly or against their will) perpetrators and evidence is further exacerbated because conflict implies by its very nature a difficult security environment within which the ICC must work.

Insecure environments have negative 'knock-on' effects on the ability of the ICC to conduct outreach activities in the region. This in turn can have a negative effect upon the acceptance of the ICC's work by the local population.

An ICC investigation attracts international media attention. This will likely provoke a reaction from the parties to the conflict. On the positive side, moving a conflict into the eyes of the global public may create systemic pressure leading to the isolation of those targeted by ICC investigations, and may motivate governments to cut their support to these groups. It might furthermore provide an incentive for the parties to the conflict to engage in peace negotiations in order to attain or restore a positive international reputation. Reputation is a valuable asset for maintaining positive relations with partners in a world of interdependence.[113] On the other hand, ICC investigations might also make governments less cooperative and more aggressive, as seems to be the case in the present Sudanese response to the Darfur investigation.

Finally, as in the case of Uganda, ICC investigations will likely affect the public debate on how to solve the conflict. It is to be expected that some stakeholders in the conflict will welcome ICC intervention, while others will accuse it of constituting an obstacle to peace and seek to make it a scapegoat if peace efforts fail. A narrow focus on the ICC's role, however, will likely divert attention away from important issues, including the need for wider reconciliation. In the worst case, the parties to the conflict and also the international community may use the debate about the ICC's involvement to distract from the need to take decisive action to end the conflict through diplomacy or military intervention.

Time will tell whether the ICC will be successful in fulfilling its mandate to hold accountable those most responsible for genocide, war crimes, and crimes against humanity. Time will also reveal whether the UN Security Council will ever agree to act under article 16 to defer an ICC investigation into an ongoing conflict in the name of peace.

---

[113] Christopher Rudolph, *Constructing an Atrocity Regime: The Politics of War Crimes Tribunals*, 55 (3) INTERNATIONAL ORGANISATION 655, 681, (Summer 2001); also R. Keohane, *International Relations and International Law: Two Optics*, 38(2) HARVARD INTERNATIONAL LJ, 487, 501 (1997).

If the ICC does succeed with its initial cases in spite of the myriad difficulties it faces, it will hopefully attract an increasing number of states parties. The longer term hope must be for a new universal consciousness of accountability to develop which will affect all leaders and communities worldwide, including those who deem themselves untouchable today. Only then will the cynical joke cited at the beginning of this chapter no longer ring true.

9 Fine-tuning complementarity

Sarah M.H. Nouwen*

INTRODUCTION

Even before the ink of the ICC Statute had dried, the principle of complementarity was identified as the 'cornerstone'[1] of the world's first permanent International Criminal Court ('the Court' or 'ICC'). This principle provides that the Court can exercise its jurisdiction over a case only if the case is not being and has not been genuinely investigated or prosecuted by any state.[2] The principle has been considered a 'cornerstone' because it is seen to balance two fundamental values of international law: international justice and state sovereignty.[3] The rule embodying the complementarity principle determines when the ICC can exercise its jurisdiction in cases over which states could also claim a sovereign right to exercise jurisdiction.

Yet 'cornerstone' principles often suffer unhappy fates. When they become generally known by popular shortcut definitions, the precise provisions establishing the actual principles are ignored. Complementarity is often described, for instance, as the opposite of primacy, which is the jurisdictional arrangement in the Statutes of the Tribunals for the Former Yugoslavia (ICTY) and Rwanda (ICTR), according to which those international tribunals have priority over national proceedings.[4] However, closer examination reveals that both principles have the same starting point, namely the concurrent jurisdiction of both national and international courts over international crimes.[5] Similarly, as this chapter of the *Handbook* will

---

*   Gratitude is extended to Roger M. O'Keefe and Hannah Richardson for their ever useful comments. The usual disclaimers apply. This Chapter was last revised in September 2009.
¹   See, for example, Report of the Ad Hoc Committee on the Establishment of an International Criminal Court, UN Doc. A/50/22 (1995), 6, para. 29 and J.T. Holmes, *The Principle of Complementarity*, in R.S.K. LEE (ed.), THE INTERNATIONAL CRIMINAL COURT: THE MAKING OF THE ROME STATUTE: ISSUES, NEGOTIATIONS, RESULTS 41, 73 (The Hague London, Kluwer Law International, 1999).
²   Rome Statute of the International Criminal Court, Rome, 17 July 1998, 2187 UNTS 90, art. 17(1)(a), (b), (c), (2) and (3). Unless the text provides otherwise, references to articles in the body of this chapter are to articles of the ICC Statute. Unless otherwise indicated, all ICC documents are available at www.icc-cpi.int.
³   See, for example, I. Tallgren, *Completing the 'International Criminal Order': The Rhetoric of International Repression and the Notion of Complementarity in the Draft Statute for an International Criminal Court*, 67 NORDIC JIL 107 (1998). This chapter follows most of the literature by defining 'international justice' narrowly as the application and enforcement of international criminal law.
⁴   Apart from where it indicates otherwise, this dissertation uses the term 'proceedings' in the meaning of 'criminal process', including both investigations and prosecutions. This is in line with ICC Statute, art. 17, defining unwillingness (art. 17(2)) and inability (art. 17(3)) with reference to 'proceedings'. These definitions apply to the phases of both investigation and prosecution (art. 17(1)(a) and (1)(b)).
⁵   Contrast ICC, Trial Chamber II, Motifs de la décision orale relative à l'exception d'irrecevabilité de l'affaire (article 19 du Statut), ICC-01/04-01/07-1213, 16 June 2009, para. 45 ('Les

argue, the shorthand description of complementarity as meaning that a case is admissible where 'a state is unwilling or unable to investigate and prosecute', neglects fundamental aspects of complementarity as set forth in the ICC Statute. Critically assessing popular generalizations, this chapter discusses complementarity on the basis of the relevant provisions in the ICC Statute, rather than as a notion thought to exist separately from the Statute.

Analysing the Statute's substantive and procedural provisions, this chapter addresses several popular misunderstandings about complementarity. As regards substantive provisions, the chapter first addresses the misconception that complementarity always necessitates an assessment of 'unwillingness or inability'. In this context, the chapter discusses the Court's emerging case law on what constitutes a 'case', including the potential of the decisions so far to erode complementarity. Secondly, the chapter argues that complementarity does not require conduct to be domestically prosecuted as an international crime in order to render ICC proceedings inadmissible. Accordingly, the chapter puts into perspective the common claim that ICC states parties are required to incorporate the crimes of the ICC Statute into their domestic legislation. Fourthly, it argues that proceedings in states not parties to the Statute may render ICC cases inadmissible. Fifthly, the chapter discusses the importance of the requirement of 'genuine' national proceedings.

Turning to the procedural aspects of complementarity, the chapter argues that the admissibility assessment applies irrespective of the mechanisms triggering the Court's jurisdiction. It then argues that because the assessment is case-specific and not situation-specific, the ICC may pursue cases emerging from a situation, even if a state is pursuing one or more other cases emerging from that situation. Subsequently, the chapter explains why it is difficult for a state to end ICC involvement once the Office of the Prosecutor (OTP) has decided to open an investigation. Having highlighted that states are not prohibited from commencing proceedings after the ICC has done so, the chapter discusses several possible stages at which admissibility must or may be assessed. The chapter ends by noting that the admissibility assessment is dynamic in the sense that earlier findings of (in)admissibility can be reviewed. The conclusion evaluates these findings in light of considerations about the appropriate relationship between international and domestic courts.

THE ICC STATUTE'S SUBSTANTIVE PROVISIONS ON COMPLEMENTARITY

According to the Preamble's tenth recital and the Statute's opening article, the International Criminal Court 'shall be complementary to national criminal jurisdictions'. Without referring to 'complementarity,' article 17, the Statute's article on admissibility of cases, embodies the content of the principle:

Article 17   Issues of admissibility
1. Having regard to paragraph 10 of the Preamble and article 1, the Court shall determine that a case is inadmissible where:

---

auteurs du Statut entendaient bien faire de la Cour une juridiction complémentaire et non pas concurrente des juridictions nationales.'). ('The drafters of the Statute clearly intended the Court to complement national courts, not to compete with them.') (official court translation of the original French text).

(a)   the case is being investigated or prosecuted by a State which has jurisdiction over it, unless the State is unwilling or unable genuinely to carry out the investigation or prosecution;

(b)   the case has been investigated by a State which has jurisdiction over it and the State has decided not to prosecute the person concerned, unless the decision resulted from the unwillingness or inability of the State genuinely to prosecute;

(c)   the person concerned has already been tried for conduct which is the subject of the complaint, and a trial by the Court is not permitted under article 20, paragraph 3.[6] ...

2. In order to determine unwillingness in a particular case, the Court shall consider, having regard to the principles of due process recognized by international law, whether one or more of the following exist, as applicable:

(a)   the proceedings were or are being undertaken or the national decision was made for the purpose of shielding the person concerned from criminal responsibility for crimes within the jurisdiction of the Court referred to in article 5;

(b)   there has been an unjustified delay in the proceedings which in the circumstances is inconsistent with an intent to bring the person concerned to justice;

(c)   the proceedings were not or are not being conducted independently or impartially, and they were or are being conducted in a manner which, in the circumstances, is inconsistent with an intent to bring the person concerned to justice.

3. In order to determine inability in a particular case, the Court shall consider whether, due to a total or substantial collapse or unavailability of its national judicial system, the State is unable to obtain the accused or the necessary evidence and testimony or otherwise unable to carry out its proceedings.

The article thus provides three grounds for the inadmissibility of cases before the ICC that together reflect the complementarity principle:

1.   genuine ongoing domestic proceedings (either investigations or prosecutions);
2.   domestic investigations that have been concluded by a decision not to prosecute for reasons other than a lack of willingness or ability genuinely to prosecute;
3.   a concluded domestic prosecution in which the Statute's exceptions to the prohibition of double jeopardy do not apply.[7]

The article does not define when investigations should be considered to have started. However, since article 17(1)(b) concerns investigations that have been concluded by a decision 'not to prosecute', one can argue that, in order to qualify as an investigation under article 17, there must be a possibility of subsequently referring the case to a prosecuting body. Investigations by commissions of inquiry or truth commissions lacking such a mandate are unlikely to qualify as 'investigations' within the meaning of article 17.

---

[6]   ICC Statute, art. 17(1)(d) provides as a fourth ground of inadmissibility that '[t]he case is not of sufficient gravity to justify further action by the Court'. Not an element of complementarity, it is not reproduced above. The observations on the admissibility criteria in this chapter only concern the criteria embodying complementarity.

[7]   *Prosecutor* v. *Thomas Lubanga Dyilo,* Judgment on the Appeal of Mr. Thomas Lubanga Dyilo Against the Decision on the Defence Challenge to the Jurisdiction of the Court pursuant to Article 19(2)(a) of the Statute of 3 October 2006, ICC Appeals Chamber, ICC-01/04-01/06-772, 14 December 2006, para. 23 seems to consider *ne bis in idem* as an issue separate from complementarity. However, as the Pre-Trial Chamber acknowledged in *Prosecutor* v. *Thomas Lubanga Dyilo,* Decision on the Prosecutor's Application for a Warrant of Arrest, Article 58 (hereinafter '*Lubanga* Arrest Warrant Decision') ICC Pre-Trial Chamber I, ICC-01/04-01/06-8, 10 February 2006, para. 29, one limb of the Statute's rule of *ne bis in idem,* namely art. 20(3) (referred to in art. 17(1)(c)) regulates another instance in which the Court's claim to jurisdiction competes with a national court's.

As the next section will set out, close examination of article 17 reveals why shorthand definitions of complementarity according to which 'the Court may assume jurisdiction only when national jurisdictions are unwilling or unable to exercise it'[8] are misleading.

Unwillingness or Inability is Only a Secondary Question

Article 17 provides that the Court shall determine that a case is inadmissible where a case 'is being investigated or prosecuted', 'has been investigated' and 'has already been tried'. The references to ongoing or concluded proceedings reveal that, if there is no state investigating or prosecuting the case, none of the criteria of inadmissibility applies. In the absence of national investigations or prosecutions, cases are thus admissible without requiring, as a matter of law, a determination of unwillingness or inability.[9] Only when domestic proceedings in the case exist is it necessary to determine whether the state concerned is willing and able genuinely to carry out those proceedings. Accordingly, most ICC Chambers have not discussed unwillingness or inability when assessing admissibility, simply because there were no domestic proceedings, at least not in the same 'case' as defined by the Chambers.[10]

Since an assessment of willingness or ability is required only if there are domestic proceedings in the same case as the one before the ICC, the seemingly quotidian term 'case', the first component of article 17(1)(a), (b) and (d), has become all the more decisive. The definition of 'case' was not elaborated upon during the negotiations nor in the first commentaries on the Statute. Yet it became an issue in the very first case before the Court.

Thomas Lubanga Dyilo was in domestic detention on charges of crimes against humanity, genocide, murder, illegal detention and torture when Pre-Trial Chamber I issued an arrest warrant for him. In its decision, the Pre-Trial Chamber briefly reflected on the statement in the Democratic Republic of Congo (DRC) referral letter of 2004 that it was unable to investigate and prosecute. The Pre-Trial Chamber pointed out that recent developments indicated otherwise. After disagreeing in this respect with the OTP's argument for admissibility, the Pre-Trial Chamber concluded that an ability assessment was not even necessary since the Congolese case against Lubanga was not the same as the OTP's case. According to the Chamber, it is 'a *conditio sine qua non* for a case arising from the investigation of a situation to be inadmissible that the national proceedings encompass both the *person* and the *conduct* which is the subject of the case before the Court'.[11] Since the domestic charges against

---

8   M.H. Arsanjani and W.M. Reisman, *Developments at the International Criminal Court: The Law-in-Action of the International Criminal Court*, 99 AMERICAN JIL 385, 396 (2005).

9   See also, *inter alia*, ICC OTP, *Paper on Some Policy Issues before the Office of the Prosecutor* 5 (September 2003); ICC OTP, *Statement of the Prosecutor Luis Moreno Ocampo to Diplomatic Corps* 2 (12 February 2004); ICC OTP, *Report on Prosecutorial Strategy* 5 (14 September 2006) and ICC OTP, *Informal Expert Paper for the Office of the Prosecutor of the International Criminal Court: The Principle of Complementarity in Practice* 7–8, 11 (December 2003).

10   Motifs de la décision orale relative à l'exception d'irrecevabilité de l'affaire (Article 19 du Statut), note 5 *supra*, is an exception. The Chamber argued that since the DRC had referred the situation and had transferred the accused to the ICC it must be considered 'unwilling'. While acknowledging that the Statute does not explicitly provide for this form of 'unwillingness', the Chamber argued (at para. 77) that a state also lacks willingness if it prefers a person to be prosecuted by the ICC.

11   *Lubanga* Arrest Warrant Decision, note 7 *supra*, at 20, para. 31 (emphasis added).

Lubanga did not involve the conduct with which the Prosecutor[12] had charged him, namely enlisting, conscripting and using child soldiers, the Chamber held that 'the DRC cannot be considered to be acting in relation to the specific case before the Court'.[13] The Chamber thus reached the conclusion that neither the DRC nor any other state with jurisdiction 'is acting or has acted, in relation to such case'.[14] Consequently, the case was admissible, since none of the grounds for inadmissibility applied.[15]

The Pre-Trial Chamber reached the same conclusion when issuing an arrest warrant for the second person in the DRC situation, Germain Katanga. Even though he had been detained domestically on the basis of an arrest warrant with charges of crimes against humanity and the ICC Prosecutor also charged these crimes, the Pre-Trial Chamber found that 'the proceedings against Germain Katanga in the DRC do not encompass the same conduct which is the subject of the Prosecution Application'.[16] The Chamber applied the same logic to the arrest warrant for Mathieu Ngudjolo Chui, who had also been charged with crimes domestically.

In the Darfur situation, too, the issue of the same 'case' emerged. Like Lubanga, Katanga and Ngudjolo, Ali Kushayb was in domestic detention when the Chamber decided upon the Prosecutor's request for a summons to appear. Domestic investigations were ongoing into five separate incidents in five communities involving attacks accompanied by looting, burning houses, killing and forced disappearance. The ICC Prosecutor, in turn, accused Kushayb of having committed war crimes and crimes against humanity, charging him with killing, rape, torture, persecution, forcibly displacing civilians, depriving civilians of their liberty, pillaging and destroying property. One of the incidents involved the same locality as one of the incidents under domestic investigations. But the Prosecutor pointed out that the domestic investigations into that incident made 'no mention of rape or other inhumane treatment'.[17] The Prosecutor concluded that the case was admissible before the ICC because the domestic investigations did 'not relate to the same conduct which [wa]s the subject of the case before the Court: the national proceedings [we]re not in respect of the same *incidents* and address[ed] a significantly narrower range of *conduct*'.[18] The Prosecution thus added to the requirements of the same person and the same conduct another criterion for an investigation to amount to an investigation into the same 'case', namely the same incident.[19] In its decision

---

[12]   In the light of the gender of the current Prosecutor, this chapter refers to the Prosecutor as 'he'.

[13]   *Lubanga* Arrest Warrant Decision, note 7 *supra*, at 23, para. 39.

[14]   *Ibid*. 24, para. 40.

[15]   As became known when that part of the same decision was made public in July 2008, the Chamber used the same reasoning to determine the admissibility of the case against Bosco Ntaganda. He had been charged with 'joint criminal enterprise, arbitrary arrest, torture and complicity of assassination' in Congolese proceedings, but had not yet been arrested. See Decision on the Prosecutor's Application for Warrants of Arrest, Article 58 (hereinafter *Ntaganda* Arrest Warrant decision), ICC Pre-Trial Chamber I, Annex II, ICC-01/04-02/06-20-Anx2, 21 July 2008, paras 34–41.

[16]   Decision on the Evidence and Information Provided by the Prosecution for the Issuance of a Warrant of Arrest for Germain Katanga, ICC-01/04-01/07-55, 5 November 2007 (but taken on 6 July 2007), 8–9, para. 20.

[17]   Prosecutor's Application under Article 58(7), ICC-02/05-56, 27 February 2007, 90, para. 265.

[18]   *Ibid*. 91, para. 267 (emphasis added).

[19]   Decision on the Applications for Participation in the Proceedings of VPRS 1, VPRS 2, VPRS 3, VPRS 4, VPRS 5 and VPRS 6, ICC Pre-Trial Chamber I, ICC-01/04-101, 17 January 2006, para. 65 had also used the term incident when defining a 'case' in the context of victim participation.

to issue arrest warrants against Harun and Kushayb, Pre-Trial Chamber I did not engage with this extra requirement, but only repeated the criterion it had used in *Lubanga*, this time defining it negatively: 'for a case to be admissible, it is a condition *sine qua non* that national proceedings do not encompass both the person and the conduct which are the subject of the case before the Court'.[20] It concluded that the case appeared to be admissible.

Finally, when issuing the first arrest warrant in the Central African Republic situation, Pre-Trial Chamber III also found that there was no evidence indicating that the accused Jean-Pierre Bemba had been investigated or prosecuted at the national level for the crimes charged by the ICC Prosecutor. The Chamber added that the Central African Republic authorities seemed to have refrained from prosecuting Bemba because they believed he was immune from prosecution due to his status as Vice-President.[21] So while the Chamber concluded that the case appeared admissible, it did not specify whether that was because of a lack of domestic proceedings regarding the same conduct, or because domestic proceedings had been terminated due to immunities. If the latter, this would indicate unwillingness or inability genuinely to investigate and prosecute.

In all these instances the Pre-Trial Chambers have, or seem to have, chosen to argue that the domestic proceedings did not concern the same 'case' as the OTP's, rather than admitting that there were domestic proceedings and then going into the question whether the relevant domestic authorities were able and willing genuinely to conduct these proceedings. This evasion of politically sensitive questions has resulted in a strict definition of a 'case' that could entirely undermine complementarity. This is even more apparent if the definition includes the requirement cited by the Prosecutor in *Kushayb* that the domestic case must concern not only the same 'conduct' and 'person', but also the same 'incident' for it to be the same case. As a consequence, national prosecutors wishing to avoid ICC intervention are bound to select the person, conduct and incident that the ICC would prosecute. By contrast, the ICC Prosecutor has in practice total discretion as to which person, conduct and incident he decides to prosecute.[22] He could and did decide to charge Lubanga instead of the more notorious Nkunda, and to charge Lubanga with only war crimes, instead of also with crimes against humanity as had been done domestically. While the ICC Prosecutor has total discretion as to which person, conduct and incident he decides to prosecute, national prosecutors who wish to avoid ICC intervention are bound to select the person, conduct and incident that the ICC would prosecute. Even if national prosecutions encompassed persons with greater responsibility, different and arguably more serious crimes and different incidents, the OTP's case would still be admissible.

---

20   *Prosecutor* v. *Ahmad Muhammad Harun ('Ahmad Harun') and Ali Muhammad Al Abd-Al-Rahman ('Ali Kushayb')*, Decision on the Prosecution Application under Article 58(7) of the Statute (hereinafter *Harun and Kushayb*, Arrest Warrant decision), ICC Pre-Trial Chamber I, ICC-02/05-01/07-1, 27 April 2007, 9, para. 24.

21   Décision relative à la requête du Procureur aux fins de délivrance d'un mandat d'arrêt à l'encontre de Jean-Pierre Bemba Gombo (hereinafter *Bemba* Arrest Warrant decision), ICC Pre-Trial Chamber III, ICC-01/05-01/08-14, 11 June 2008, 11, para. 21. Footnotes omitted.

22   Article 53 suggests that the Prosecutor *must* investigate and prosecute after a referral if the criteria in art. 53 are fulfilled, but in practice the Prosecutor has much discretion, since it is difficult for the judges to force him to take a decision to investigate or prosecute or to overturn a decision not to.

If complementarity is to mean that states have the first right to investigate and prosecute, other Chambers might well consider deviating from this early case law.[23] This could require adjusting the complementarity test depending on the stage in which it is used – at the point of deciding to open an investigation into a situation, on the one hand, or at the point of deciding to open a case, on the other.[24] At the opening of an investigation, the criterion would be whether the state concerned is conducting or has conducted genuine proceedings with regard to crimes committed in the overall situation. At the moment when the Prosecutor requests the issuance of arrest warrants or summonses to appear, however, the complementarity assessment would be case-specific. States would be able to prevent or end ICC investigations by genuinely investigating and prosecuting crimes within the over-all situation. Only if they failed to do so and the ICC opened an investigation and selected cases would the state be compelled to investigate and prosecute exactly the same cases as identified by the OTP in order to end ICC proceedings. The next section will explain that such domestic proceedings would have to cover the same conduct but not necessarily the same crimes.

Domestic Case Must Concern the Same Conduct, Not Necessarily the Same Crime

In their definition of 'case', the Chambers have appropriately required the domestic case to cover the same 'conduct', not necessarily the same 'crime'. Requiring the legal qualification of the conduct in the domestic proceedings to be identical to the Court's would fly in the face of article 20(3), which prohibits the Court from trying a person who has already been tried for the same *conduct* by another court. It reads:

> Article 20   *Ne bis in idem*
> 3. No person who has been tried by another court for conduct also proscribed under article 6, 7 or 8 shall be tried by the Court with respect to the same conduct unless the proceedings in the other court:
> (a)   were for the purpose of shielding the person concerned from criminal responsibility for crimes within the jurisdiction of the Court; or
> (b)   otherwise were not conducted independently or impartially in accordance with the norms of due process recognized by international law and were conducted in a manner which, in the circumstances, was inconsistent with an intent to bring the person concerned to justice.

---

[23]   Motion Challenging the Admissibility of the Case by the Defence of Germain Katanga, pursuant to Article 19(2)(a), ICC-01/04-01/07-949, 11 March 2009 argued against this definition of the same 'case'. However, in Motifs de la décision orale relative à l'exception d'irrecevabilité de l'affaire (article 19 du Statut), note 5 *supra*, the Trial Chamber did not address the meaning of the same 'case' but argued that the DRC must be considered 'unwilling' as it had referred the situation and the accused to the Court.

[24]   Admittedly, art. 53, on the opening of an investigation and prosecution, does not make this distinction. However, it would be consistent with other parts of the Statute where a distinction between 'situation' and 'case' was inserted at the last moment of the ICC Statute negotiations in order to exclude the possibility of states' referring concrete cases rather than more general situations. See H. OLÁSOLO, THE TRIGGERING PROCEDURE OF THE INTERNATIONAL CRIMINAL COURT 147 (Martinus Nijhoff Publishers, 2005).

Hence, if a person has been tried by another court, the case is inadmissible before the ICC regardless of the legal qualification of the conduct in the other court. The only requirement for inadmissibility on this ground is that the person was tried for 'conduct which is the subject of the complaint',[25] or, more specifically, 'conduct also proscribed under article 6, 7 or 8'.[26]

The reference to 'conduct' rather than 'crime' indicates that states are free to determine the legal characterization of the conduct. The fact that the ICC Prosecutor disagrees with the legal qualification and considers, for instance, the conduct to constitute a crime against humanity rather than genocide, is no ground for admissibility. Nonetheless, the Pre-Trial Chambers' early case law on what constitutes a 'case', set out above, provides a reason for states to qualify conduct in the same way as the OTP did, if the OTP was the first to bring charges. Doing so would strengthen the argument that the domestic 'case', in the sense of person, conduct and perhaps even incident, is the same as that of the OTP.

The use of the term 'conduct' in article 20(3) contrasts clearly with the use of 'crime' in article 20(2) for the opposite situation, in which a domestic court wishes to try a case after the ICC.[27] This implies that domestic qualification of conduct as an ordinary crime instead of an international crime does not render a case admissible before the ICC.[28] It would be inconsistent with this clear choice of the word 'conduct' in article 20(3) to require prosecution for international crimes per se, by arguing that a lack of domestic criminalization of the crimes as defined in the ICC Statute is an indicator of 'unavailability' of the domestic system, amounting to inability. Similarly inconsistent with the clear choice of the term 'conduct' is the argument that prosecution for ordinary crimes amounts to 'shielding the person concerned from criminal responsibility *for crimes within the jurisdiction of the Court referred to in article 5*', as defined in articles 17(2)(a) and 20(3)(a).

The ICC Statute deviates in this respect from the Statutes of the ICTY and ICTR, which explicitly allow the tribunals to retry a case if the conduct has been prosecuted domestically as an ordinary crime.[29] The Appeals Chamber of those ad hoc tribunals even justified the Court's primacy with a reference to the risk that domestic courts might prosecute conduct constituting international crimes as ordinary crimes.[30] However, due to the widespread

---

25   ICC Statute, art. 17(1)(c).

26   *Ibid.* art. 20(3).

27   'No person shall be tried before another court for a crime referred to in article 5 for which that person has already been convicted or acquitted by the Court.' *Ibid.* art. 20(2).

28   *Report of the International Law Commission on the Work of its Forty-Sixth Session: Draft Statute for an International Criminal Court with Commentaries*, UN Doc. A/49/10 (1994), 58 describes trial of an 'ordinary crime' as one in which the act is tried as a common crime under domestic law instead of an international crime with the special characteristics of the international crimes as defined in the Statute.

29   Statute of the International Criminal Tribunal for the Former Yugoslavia, UN Doc. S/25704 (1993), Annex, as amended, art. 10(2)(a) and Statute of the International Criminal Tribunal for Rwanda, UN Doc. S/RES/955 (1994), Annex, as amended, art. 9(2)(a). For the ICTY, domestic characterization of conduct within its jurisdiction as an ordinary crime is a ground for claiming jurisdiction not only after but also during the domestic proceedings. See ICTY Rules of Procedure and Evidence, adopted on 11 February 1994, version of 22 September 2006 (IT/32/Rev. 39), rule 9(i). See also *Draft Code of Crimes Against the Peace and Security of Mankind*, II YB INTERNATIONAL LAW COMMISSION 15 (1996), art. 12(2)(a)(i).

30   *Prosecutor* v. *Duško Tadić*, Decision on the Defence Motion for Interlocutory Appeal, ICTY Appeals Chamber, IT-94-1-AR72, 2 October 1995, para. 58.

practice of domestic trials charging ordinary crimes instead of international crimes,[31] the distinction was deliberately deleted from the draft Statute of the ICC.[32]

The fact that proceedings for ordinary crimes can meet the complementarity threshold also puts into perspective the common misconception that states parties are required to incorporate the crimes of the ICC Statute into their domestic legislation.

No State Obligation to Criminalize in Domestic Law the Crimes in the ICC Statute

The argument that states parties must criminalize the ICC Statute crimes[33] under their domestic law is misplaced, first, because the Statute does not establish such an obligation. Indeed, contrary to the popular argument, the Statute does not even oblige states to make use of their primary right to investigate and prosecute war crimes, crimes against humanity or genocide.[34] The Statute's only provision explicitly referring to such a duty is the sixth preambular paragraph 'recalling that it is the duty of every State to exercise its criminal jurisdiction over those responsible for international crimes.' However, the general wording of the text of this provision militates against its creating an obligation for states parties domestically to investigate and prosecute the crimes within the Court's jurisdiction. It speaks of a duty of 'every State', whereas a treaty can impose obligations only on states parties.[35] It refers to a duty to prosecute 'international crimes' instead of only the international crimes within the Court's jurisdiction.[36] It equally fails to specify which titles of jurisdiction (for example, territorial, national or universal) states would be obliged to use. It refers to a state's duty to 'exercise its criminal jurisdiction', which does not necessarily require a state to conduct domestic investi-

---

    31   See also W.N. Ferdinandusse, Direct Application of International Criminal Law in National Courts 18–21 (The Hague, T.M.C. Asser Press, 2006).

    32   See for the draft Statute in which it was still included Report of the International Law Commission on the Work of its Forty-Sixth Session: Draft Statute for an International Criminal Court with Commentaries, UN Doc. A/49/10 (1994), 57 and for the suggestion to delete it *Ad Hoc Committee Report*, 9 para. 43 and 35, para. 179 (1995). In *Report of the Preparatory Committee on the Establishment of an International Criminal Court, vol. I, Proceedings of the Preparatory Committee During March–April and August 1996*, UN Doc. A/51/22 (1996), 39–40, para. 171 the issue returned. But, contrast C. Van den Wyngaert and T. Ongena, *Ne Bis in Idem Principle, Including the Issue of Amnesty*, in A. Cassese, P. Gaeta and J.R.W.D. Jones (eds), The Rome Statute of the International Criminal Court: A Commentary 705, 725–7 (Oxford University Press, 2002).

    33   See, *inter alia*, Z. Deen-Racsmány, *Lessons of the European Arrest Warrant for Domestic Implementation of the Obligation to Surrender Nationals to the International Criminal Court*, 20 Leiden JIL 167, 184–185 (2007) and C.K. Hall, *Expert Consultation Process on General Issues Relevant to the ICC Office of the Prosecutor: Suggestions Concerning International Criminal Court Prosecutorial Policy and External Relations*, 16, ICC-OTP 2003 (28 March 2003).

    34   See also, for example, *Report of the Commonwealth Expert Group on Implementing Legislation for the Rome Statute of the International Criminal Court* 1 (7–9 July 2004). Contrast J.K. Kleffner, *Complementarity in the Rome Statute and National Criminal Jurisdictions* 263–84 (thesis, Amsterdam, 2007) and W.W. Burke-White, *Proactive Complementarity: The International Criminal Court and National Courts in the Rome System of Justice*, 49(1) Harvard ILJ 53, 79 (2008).

    35   Vienna Convention on the Law of Treaties, Vienna, 23 May 1969, 1155 UNTS 331, art. 34.

    36   See also M. Bergsmo and O. Triffterer, *Rome Statute of the International Criminal Court: Preamble*, in O. Triffterer (ed.), Commentary on the Rome Statute of the International Criminal Court: Observers' Notes, Article by Article 1, 12 (Baden-Baden, Nomos Verlges, 1999).

gations and prosecutions. Arresting and transferring an accused to the ICC is an exercise of criminal jurisdiction, too.[37] Finally, the text does not establish but 'recalls' a suggested preexisting duty. However, there is no general duty on states to investigate and prosecute all types of international crimes. Only for some of the crimes within the Court's jurisdiction do certain treaties or even customary international law contain an obligation to criminalize and prosecute.[38] In sum, the preambular provision cited above does not establish a duty for states

---

[37]   The more specific obligation domestically to investigate and prosecute would be irreconcilable with the referrals of situations to the ICC by states which have jurisdiction over cases within the situation. See also *Lubanga* Arrest Warrant Decision, note 7 *supra*, para. 35.

[38]   For instance, with regard to genocide, the 1948 Convention on the Prevention and Punishment of the Crime of Genocide, 9 December 1948, 78 UNTS 277 (Genocide Convention), art. V, requires states parties 'to enact ... the necessary legislation to give effect to the provisions of the present Convention, and, in particular, to provide effective penalties for persons guilty of genocide'. Article VI determines that '[p]ersons charged with genocide ... shall be tried by a competent tribunal of the State in the territory of which the act was committed'. With regard to war crimes, the four Geneva Conventions of 1949 and the 1977 First Additional Protocol oblige contracting parties 'to enact any legislation necessary to provide effective penal sanctions for persons committing ... any of the grave breaches' defined in the Conventions and 'to search for persons alleged to have committed ... such grave breaches', and to 'bring such persons, regardless of their nationality, before its own courts' or to hand them over to another High Contracting Party. See Geneva Convention (I) for the Amelioration of the Condition of the Wounded and Sick in Armed Forces in the Field, Geneva, 12 August 1949, 75 UNTS 31, art. 49; Geneva Convention (II) for the Amelioration of the Condition of Wounded, Sick and Shipwrecked Members of Armed Forces at Sea, Geneva, 12 August 1949, 75 UNTS 85, art. 50; Geneva Convention (III) Relative to the Treatment of Prisoners of War, Geneva, 12 August 1949, 75 UNTS 135, art. 129; Geneva Convention (IV) Relative to the Protection of Civilian Persons in Time of War, Geneva, 12 August 1949, 75 UNTS 287, art. 146. The same rule applies for Protocol Additional to the Geneva Conventions of 12 August 1949, and Relating to the Protection of Victims of International Armed Conflicts (Protocol I), 8 June 1977, as a result of art. 85(1). Similar provisions can be found in the Convention for the Protection of Cultural Property in the Event of Armed Conflict with Regulations for the Execution of the Convention 1954, The Hague, 14 May 1954, art. 28 and Second Protocol to the Hague Convention of 1954 for the Protection of Cultural Property in the Event of Armed Conflict 1999, ch. 4; the Convention on the Safety of United Nations and Associated Personnel, New York, 9 December 1994, arts 9–16; the Convention on the Prohibition of the Development, Production, Stockpiling and Use of Chemical Weapons and on Their Destruction, art. 7(1); the Convention on the Prohibition of the Use, Stockpiling, Production and Transfer of Anti-Personnel Mines and on Their Destruction, Ottawa, 1997, art. 9; and Protocol on Prohibitions or Restrictions on the Use of Mines, Booby-Traps and Other Devices as amended on 3 May 1996 (Amended Protocol II), art. 14. State practice and *opinio juris* do not bear out the existence of such obligations in customary law with respect to these treaty crimes, crimes against humanity or war crimes pursuant to customary international law only. With respect to the treaty crime of genocide, ICJ, *Reservations to the Convention on Genocide*, 1951 ICJ Rep. 15, Advisory Opinion, 23 determines that 'the principles underlying the Convention are principles which are recognized by civilised nations as binding on States, even without any conventional obligation'. It is, however, ambiguous whether the 'principles underlying the Convention' include not only the prohibition to commit genocide, but also the obligation to criminalize and prosecute. State practice supporting such a finding is meagre. For some of the crimes that constitute crimes against humanity, specific treaties contain an obligation to criminalize and prosecute. See Convention Against Torture and Other Cruel, Inhuman or Degrading Treatment or Punishment, 1984, arts 4, 5, 7 and International Convention on the Suppression and Punishment of the Crime of Apartheid, 1973, arts IV and V, but the definition of the crimes in the Statute and in the specific treaties diverge. Kleffner, note 34 *supra*, at 28–9 argues that an independent obligation to prosecute these crimes flows from the obligation in human rights treaties to 'ensure' or 'secure' the human rights contained in these treaties in

to investigate or prosecute crimes within the Court's jurisdiction or to pass legislation to make that possible.

Of course, while not obliged to do so, states are free to incorporate the Statute's crimes into domestic law.[39] States may do so particularly if they wish to avoid ICC intervention by using the complementarity principle. Since it suffices to charge the conduct as an ordinary crime (see previous section), incorporation of the ICC Statute crimes into domestic legislation is then necessary only to the extent that the existing domestic law does not cover the conduct criminalized in the Statute. Recruitment of child soldiers, treatment of prisoners of war and modes of commission such as command responsibility could well be absent in ordinary penal legislation.

Proceedings in States Not Parties to the Statute Can Also Render a Case Inadmissible

A case is inadmissible where it is being genuinely investigated or prosecuted or has been genuinely investigated 'by a State which has jurisdiction over it'.[40] The references in article 17(1) to 'a State', in contradistinction to 'State Party', make it clear that genuine investigation or prosecution by any state, and not just by parties to the Statute, renders a case inadmissible. Accordingly, if Sudan, not a state party, conducts genuine domestic proceedings in the cases that the OTP has selected in the Darfur situation, the cases would be inadmissible. The fact that ICC jurisdiction was triggered by a UN Security Council referral has no impact on the admissibility assessment.[41]

Genuineness is the Key Qualification of Ability or Willingness to Conduct Proceedings

It has been established above that only if there are or have been domestic proceedings in the same 'case' does the question arise whether 'the State is unwilling or unable genuinely to carry out the [ongoing] investigation or prosecution' or whether 'the decision [not to prosecute] resulted from the unwillingness or inability of the State genuinely to prosecute'.[42] On the surface, there is perhaps some ambiguity about whether the qualifying term 'genuinely' in article 17(1)(a) applies to the unwillingness/inability[43] of a state or to the manner in which

---

conjunction with the right to an effective remedy, at least as long the rights have been violated within the state's jurisdiction. However, practice is too equivocal to substantiate such a rule. Although some decisions of human rights courts indeed refer to such an obligation in case of certain human rights violations (most notably the right to life and freedom from torture), there is insufficient evidence for the assertion that it always includes a non-derogable obligation for the state to prosecute and punish all the crimes within the Court's jurisdiction.

39   Indeed, many have done so upon ratification of the ICC Statute. For an overview, see, for example, Amnesty International, *The International Criminal Court Summary of Draft and Enacted Implementing Legislation*, AI Index: 2 IOR 40/041/2006 (November 2006).

40   ICC Statute, art. 17(1)(a) and (b).

41   See also the discussion of the procedural provisions on complementarity, *infra*.

42   ICC Statute, respectively art. 17(1)(a) and (b).

43   In this vein, see, for example, M.M. el Zeidy, *The Principle of Complementarity: A New Machinery to Implement International Criminal Law*, 23(2) Michigan JIL 869, 900 (2002) and M.A.

it acts 'to carry out' the investigation or prosecution. Any such ambiguity is dispelled by the rules of English grammar, the context of the unequivocal article 17(1)(b) and the French text of article 17.[44] It clearly means 'to carry out genuinely'.

Since the issue arises only in the case of ongoing or finalized investigations or ongoing prosecutions, the emphasis of the test is not on the empirical element of being 'able and willing' – the state seems to be so since proceedings are actually taking place – but on the more normative requirement to conduct these proceedings 'genuinely'.[45] Unwillingness and inability cannot be a ground for admissibility independent from the factor of a lack of genuineness. Thus, the attenuated reference in article 17(2) and (3), respectively, to 'unwillingness' and 'inability' must be taken to be shorthand for 'unwillingness genuinely to investigate or prosecute' and 'inability genuinely to investigate or prosecute'.

Like a chameleon, the word 'genuinely' adjusts its meaning according to its context. In the context of unwillingness, the meaning of 'genuinely' comes closest to 'in good faith' or 'not in a sham manner'. In combination with inability, the meaning of 'genuinely' is close to 'effectively', the drafters' attempts to avoid that word notwithstanding.[46]

A determination of unwillingness involves an assessment of a state's intentions, which are inherently subjective. States demanded 'objective' criteria for such an assessment.[47] Article 17(2) provides guidelines:

> In order to determine unwillingness in a particular case, the Court shall consider, having regard to the principles of due process recognized by international law, whether one or more of the following exist, as applicable:
> (a) the proceedings were or are being undertaken or the national decision was made for the purpose of shielding the person concerned from criminal responsibility for crimes within the jurisdiction of the Court referred to in article 5;
> (b) there has been an unjustified delay in the proceedings which in the circumstances is inconsistent with an intent to bring the person concerned to justice;
> (c) the proceedings were not or are not being conducted independently or impartially, and they were or are being conducted in a manner which, in the circumstances, is inconsistent with an intent to bring the person concerned to justice.

The three listed indicators of unwillingness reveal that the description of unwillingness is not concerned with a general unwillingness to conduct proceedings but with unwillingness to conduct genuine proceedings. In most instances in which a state is unwilling to carry out

---

Newton, *Comparative Complementarity: Domestic Jurisdiction Consistent with the Rome Statute of the International Criminal Court*, 167 MILITARY LR 20 (2001).

[44] Rome Statute of the International Criminal Court, Rome, 17 July 1998, 2187 UNTS 159 (French text), art. 17(1)(a) ('à moins que cet État n'ait pas la volonté ou soit dans l'incapacité de mener véritablement à bien l'enquête ou les poursuites') and 17(1)(b): ('à moins que cette décision ne soit l'effet du manque de volonté ou de l'incapacité de l'État de mener véritablement à bien des poursuites').

[45] See also D. Robinson, Comments on Chapter 4 of Claudia Cárdenas Aravena, in J.K. KLEFFNER and G. KOR (eds), COMPLEMENTARY VIEWS ON COMPLEMENTARITY: PROCEEDINGS OF THE INTERNATIONAL ROUNDTABLE ON THE COMPLEMENTARY NATURE OF THE INTERNATIONAL CRIMINAL COURT, AMSTERDAM, 25/26 JUNE 2004 141 (The Hague, TMC Asser, 2006).

[46] See *Preparatory Committee Report*, note 32 *supra*, at 38, describing the term 'ineffective' in the reference to complementarity in the Statute's Preamble as 'too subjective' and J.T. Holmes, Complementarity: National Court versus the ICC, in Cassese *et al.*, note 32 *supra*, at 667, 673–4.

[47] Holmes, note 1 *supra*, at 49.

proceedings, there will be no proceedings and the question of willingness does not arise. In all three circumstances it is the lack of an 'intent to bring the person concerned to justice' that undermines the genuineness. This is implicit in the first circumstance, namely proceedings 'made for the purpose of shielding the person concerned from criminal responsibility'. The second and third situations mention this lack of intent explicitly. Shielding from criminal responsibility is the most subjective ground, necessitating an inquiry into the intent of a state. It is sufficient to establish that the purpose is to shield the person from being held criminally responsible, irrespective of whether there are valid (political) reasons for that shielding (for instance, an official decision not to prosecute, as in article 17(1)(b), in exchange for the person's participation in peace negotiations).[48] On the other hand, the fact that a state has started proceedings merely to avoid the Court's doing so does not amount to shielding, as long as the state has the intent to bring the individual to justice.[49] The last two grounds are more objective. The absence of the intent to bring to justice need not be positively proven, but can be inferred from an unjustified delay or lack of impartiality and independence seemingly inconsistent with such an intent.[50]

Article 17(3) provides guidelines on the determination of inability:

> In order to determine inability in a particular case, the Court shall consider whether, due to a total or substantial collapse or unavailability of its national judicial system, the State is unable to obtain the accused or the necessary evidence and testimony or otherwise unable to carry out its proceedings.

Accordingly, the Court must consider both the causes and the consequences of inability to investigate or prosecute. As to causes, the provision mentions 'a total or substantial collapse or unavailability of its national system'. As regards the consequences thereof, the provision is more indeterminate. The expression 'otherwise unable to carry out its proceedings' allows the Court to determine that a state is unable in situations other than that of an inability to obtain the accused or the necessary evidence.[51]

The first two of the listed scenarios of inability, namely total or substantial collapse of the national judicial system, are the most obvious situations demonstrating a state's inability to conduct proceedings. In such situations, it is unlikely that any proceedings will take place, obviating the need for an ability assessment. However, if proceedings do take place, the state may not be able to conduct them genuinely, as evidenced by the state's being 'unable to obtain the accused or the necessary evidence and testimony or otherwise unable to carry out its proceedings'. Were these the only scenarios of inability, states could be found unable only in exceptional circumstances.[52]

However, the third scenario of inability, namely the unavailability of a national judicial system, expands the scope of the provision considerably. Both practical circumstances (for

---

[48]   Kleffner, note 34 *supra*, at 153.

[49]   See also L.N. Sadat and S.R. Carden, *The New International Criminal Court: An Uneasy Revolution*, 88 Georgetown LJ 381, 418 (2000).

[50]   See also S.A. Williams, *Article 17: Issues of Admissibility*, in Triffterer, note 36 *supra*, at 383, 393–4.

[51]   See, for example, Holmes, note 46 *supra*, at 678.

[52]   As is argued in M.C. Bassiouni, I The Legislative History of the International Criminal Court, International and Comparative Criminal Law Series, 138 (Ardsley, NY, Transnational Publishers, 2005) and Olásolo, note 24 *supra*, at 154 and 166.

example, a lack of judicial personnel, an insecure environment or a lack of essential cooperation by other states) and normative factors can render a system 'unavailable' genuinely to conduct proceedings. Examples are the applicability of amnesty or immunity laws,[53] the lack of the necessary extradition treaties or the absence of jurisdiction under domestic law. In many of these situations, it would be far-fetched to argue that the domestic justice system as such is 'unavailable'. But in the particular case the system would be unavailable to conduct proceedings genuinely. Consequently, it is not only states entangled in or emerging from armed conflict that can be found 'unable'. So too can states with fully-fledged functioning domestic justice systems provided that, in the particular case, the system is unavailable genuinely to conduct proceedings. In these circumstances of normative unavailability, the factors constituting the unavailability and flowing from the unavailability become hard to distinguish: the legislation or absence thereof renders the national justice system 'unavailable' and at the same time makes the state 'unable to obtain the accused or the necessary evidence and testimony or otherwise unable to carry out its proceedings'.

The requirement of genuineness is not explicitly stated in the third circumstance of inadmissibility, which is the situation that someone has been tried by another court (articles 17(1)(c) and 20(3)). However, the requirement is implicit in the two exceptions to this prohibition, namely where the proceedings were for the purpose of 'shielding the person concerned from criminal responsibility' or where the proceedings demonstrated 'a lack of independence and impartiality inconsistent with an intent to bring the person concerned to justice'. These are nearly identical to two of the three circumstances that evidence unwillingness to prosecute for purposes of complementarity. As has been argued, these circumstances do not reflect unwillingness as such, but unwillingness genuinely to conduct proceedings. Inability genuinely to conduct proceedings, a ground for admissibility during ongoing proceedings or after a decision not to prosecute, is not listed as one of the grounds rendering cases admissible after a concluded domestic trial. Consequently, if, for instance, 'due to a substantial collapse … of its national judicial system, the State [has been] unable to obtain … the necessary evidence', this form of 'inability' is no longer an exception to inadmissibility once a domestic trial has ended, even if the inability resulted in an acquittal. The case is admissible only if it is proved that the domestic proceedings were for the purpose of shielding the person from criminal responsibility or were not independent and impartial and were conducted in a manner inconsistent with the intent to bring the person to justice. A possible example is an acquittal in spite of an abundance of evidence pointing to the guilt of the accused. But when it cannot be proved that the evidence was intentionally ignored, the domestic justice system may have been simply 'unable' genuinely to prosecute, which, as such, does not render a concluded case admissible. The omission of inability from the grounds of admissibility after a finalized trial could be explained by the fact that, in many jurisdictions, grounds for a retrial, particularly if due to blunders of the prosecution, are very limited. It would be unacceptable for those states if the ICC had pervasive powers to retry. More generally, the states negotiating the ICC Statute wished to preclude the Court from acting as an appeals court by evaluating domestic justice systems' ability to conduct their proceedings.[54]

---

53   ICC OTP, *Expert Paper*, note 9 *supra*, at 15 and annex 4.
54   Holmes, note 46 *supra*, at 673.

The possible result, however, is an (undesirable) incentive for states to come to a rushed acquittal or conviction, as it is much harder for the Court to intervene in cases after finalized trials.

Considering the limited exceptions to the prohibition *ne bis in idem*, it is apparent that a case that has resulted in an acquittal, insignificant punishment or immediate pardon is not by definition admissible before the ICC. It must be proven that the proceedings were vitiated from the outset by a lack of genuineness, more precisely, by the absence of an intent to bring to justice, which can appear through shielding (article 20(3)(a)) or a lack of independence and impartiality (article 20(3)(b)). It is not easy to prove after the trial the absence of such an intent at the beginning of the proceedings.

ICC STATUTE'S PROCEDURAL PROVISIONS ON COMPLEMENTARITY

Complementarity Assessment Applies Irrespective of the Mechanism by which the Court's Jurisdiction is Triggered

Article 53(1) requires the Prosecutor to consider admissibility when deciding on whether to open an investigation, but applies only if the Security Council or a state party has referred a situation to the Court. Article 15(3) provides a special rule in respect of the Prosecutor's *proprio motu* investigations.[55] In practice, however, the test is the same, since rule 48 of the ICC Rules of Procedure and Evidence obliges the Prosecutor to consider the factors laid down in article 53(1) when making the determination whether there is a 'reasonable basis to proceed', as required by article 15(3).

As regards the referral of a situation by a state party, the Statute does not provide for a different procedure in the event that a state refers a situation in its own territory (a so-called 'self-referral'), as opposed to a situation in another state. Even in the case of a self-referral, the Prosecutor must decide whether or not to open an investigation, considering, among other things, whether the referring state or any other is conducting genuine domestic proceedings. A state cannot waive the admissibility assessment.[56]

Equally, in the case of a Security Council referral, the Prosecutor must decide whether or not to open an investigation[57] and must consider the admissibility criteria,[58] even if the

---

55   The distinction is confirmed by ICC Statute, art. 18(1), distinguishing between the reasonable basis referred to in art. 53(1) and *proprio motu* investigations on the basis of arts 13(c) and 15.

56   According to note 5 *supra*, para. 91, however, a self-referral, in combination with the state's cooperation with the Court and absence of an admissibility challenge by a state do indicate a lack of willingness to conduct proceedings on the side of the referring state.

57   As is confirmed by the Prosecutor's response to the Security Council referral of the situation in Darfur, see ICC OTP, *Report of the Prosecutor of the International Criminal Court, Mr. Luis Moreno Ocampo, to the Security Council Pursuant to UNSC 1593 (2005)* (29 June 2005) (hereinafter 'First Darfur Report'). But contrast L. Condorelli and S. Villalpando, *Referral and Deferral by the Security Council*, in *Cassese et al.*, note 32 *supra*, at 627, 643 and D.D. Ntanda Nsereko, *Article 18: Preliminary Rulings regarding Admissibility*, in Triffterer, note 36 *supra*, at 395, 398.

58   But contrast O. Triffterer, *Article 1*, in Triffterer, note 36 *supra*, at 38, 51, 59–60; K.L. Doherty and T.L.H. McCormack, '*Complementarity' as a Catalyst for Comprehensive Domestic Penal*

Council makes a determination on admissibility in its resolution referring the situation.[59] A situation referred by the Security Council is subject to different procedures only where the Statute so provides,[60] which it does with respect to neither the Prosecutor's duty to determine whether to open an investigation nor the applicability of the admissibility rules. The Security Council has no power to alter the Statute, and the Court can act only as provided for in the Statute. The Court, being neither a member[61] nor a subsidiary organ of the United Nations, is not bound by decisions of the Security Council.[62] The Security Council could influence the Court's proceedings, for instance, by obliging UN member states (not) to conduct domestic proceedings, (not) to allow the ICC to investigate, or (not) to transfer a person to the Court.[63] It could also instruct the UN member states that are parties to the ICC Statute to take certain decisions in the Assembly of States Parties.[64] If a Security Council decision prohibiting states from initiating or continuing proceedings were to be obeyed, the case would be admissible owing to the absence of domestic proceedings[65] or, in the case of stayed proceedings, owing to the domestic justice system's being rendered 'unavailable'.[66] The Court, however, is not bound by the Council's resolutions, and it 'shall determine that a case is inadmissible'[67] if one of the criteria for inadmissibility is fulfilled, for instance if a state has initiated genuine domestic proceedings in spite of the Council's decision.[68]

Pursuant to article 53(1), the Prosecutor must open an investigation after a referral unless he determines that 'there is no reasonable basis to proceed'. One of the three factors he must consider when taking this decision is whether '[t]he case is or would be admissible under article 17'.[69] Even though at this stage the Prosecutor has yet to open an investigation, the admissibility assessment is already case-specific.

Legislation, 5 U.C. Davis JILP 147, 151–2 (1999); M.C. Bassiouni, *The ICC – Quo Vadis?* 4(3) JICJ 421 (2006); and S.R. Ratner, *The International Criminal Court and the Limits of Global Judicialization*, 38 Texas ILJ 445, 447 (2003).

[59] But, contrast L. Arbour and M. Bergsmo, *Conspicious Absence of Jurisdictional Overreach*, 1 ILF 13, 19 (1999).

[60] See, for example, ICC Statute, art. 18.

[61] Pursuant to Charter of the United Nations, San Francisco, 6 June 1945, arts 3 and 4, only states can become UN members.

[62] See also D. Sarooshi, *Aspects of the Relationship Between the International Criminal Court and the United Nations*, 32 Netherlands YIL 27, 40 (2001). But, contrast R.H. Lauwaars, *The Interrelationship Between United Nations Law and the Law of Other International Organizations*, 82 Michigan LR 1604, 1605, 1606 and 1610 (1984).

[63] Pursuant to UN Charter, art. 103, obligations flowing from the Charter override other treaty obligations, for example, obligations flowing from the ICC Statute. UN Security Council decisions constitute such obligations flowing from the Charter pursuant to art. 25 ('The Members of the United Nations agree to accept and carry out the decisions of the Security Council').

[64] See UN Charter, art. 48, pursuant to which UN member states carry out Security Council resolutions directly 'and through their action in the appropriate international agencies of which they are members'.

[65] ICC Statute, art. 17(1). See also ICC OTP, *Expert Paper*, note 9 *supra*, at 22, para. 69.

[66] ICC Statute, art. 17(1) and (3). See also Condorelli and Villalpando, note 57 *supra*, at 640.

[67] ICC Statute, art. 17(1).

[68] But contrast P. Akhavan, *Developments at the International Criminal Court: The Lord's Resistance Army Case: Uganda's Submission of the First State Referral to the International Criminal Court'*, 99 American JIL 403, 411 (2005).

[69] ICC Statute, art. 53(1)(b). The other two factors are belief that a crime within the Court's jurisdiction has been committed and investigation not being in the interests of justice.

Complementarity Assessment is Case- and Not Situation-Specific

Where a 'situation' is referred to the Prosecutor, articles 53(1)(b) and 17 require the Prosecutor to assess whether 'the case is or would be admissible under article 17' before opening an investigation.[70] However, in this phase of the proceedings, the Prosecutor may not yet have identified concrete cases. Indeed, the Prosecutor will use his investigatory powers[71] to identify concrete cases within the more general situation that the Security Council or state[72] has referred or that the Prosecutor is investigating *proprio motu*. As the Prosecutor has interpreted it, the admissibility question in this pre-investigation phase is therefore whether there is 'sufficient information to believe that there are cases that would be admissible'.[73] Even though this stage of the proceedings still concern a general situation, the admissibility assessment is thus already case-specific and does not entail an examination of the overall activity, ability and willingness of the justice systems in the states with jurisdiction.[74] Complementarity is therefore unlikely to prevent the Prosecutor from opening an investigation: in situations in which crimes within the Court's jurisdiction have been committed on a massive scale, there will always be 'cases' (in the specific meaning that the Court has given to the term 'case')[75] that have not been prosecuted domestically.

Once an Investigation is Opened, it is Difficult for a State to End ICC Involvement

In the event that the Prosecutor decides to open an investigation, either *proprio motu* or after a referral of a situation by a state, article 18 provides interested states with an opportunity to compel the Prosecutor to defer to their national investigations. However, since the complementarity assessment is case- and not situation-specific, it will be difficult for a state entirely to end ICC involvement.

The Statute provides that, before commencing an investigation, the Prosecutor shall notify 'all States Parties and those States which, taking into account the information available, would normally exercise jurisdiction over the crimes concerned'.[76] But this obligation does not apply to an investigation begun pursuant to a Security Council referral. Since the state's right to request that the Prosecutor defer to its investigation is available only '[w]ithin one

---

70   Compare *ibid.* art. 53(1)(b) and (2)(b).

71   See *ibid.* art. 86.

72   *Ibid.* art. 13(a) and (b).

73   ICC OTP, First Darfur Report, note 57 *supra*, at 4. See also Holmes, note 46 *supra*, at 680.

74   In ICC OTP, First Darfur Report, note 57 *supra*, at 4, the Prosecutor when opening the investigation into Darfur indeed stressed that his decision on admissibility did 'not represent a determination on the Sudanese legal system as such, but ... is essentially the result of the absence of criminal proceedings in relation to the cases on which the OTP is likely to focus'. Earlier OTP documents, for instance ICC OTP, Press Release, *Communications Received by the Office of the Prosecutor of the ICC*, 16 July 2003, sometimes raised the impression of an assessment of the ability of the overall justice sector.

75   See notes 11–23 *supra* and the accompanying text.

76   ICC Statute, art. 18(1). Neither the Statute nor the ICC Rules indicates which states 'normally' exercise jurisdiction and thus must be notified. It would make sense for the Prosecutor to adopt a situation-by-situation approach, considering factors such as where initiatives for investigation or prosecution have been or are most likely to be taken (in view of the whereabouts of possible perpetrators, witnesses and evidence) and whether these states have jurisdiction under domestic and international law. See also Kleffner, note 34 *supra*, at 189–90.

month of receipt of *that* notification',[77] the entire procedure of article 18 is thus not applicable to situations referred by the Security Council.

The core of the procedure, set out in article 18(2), is that a notified state has a month to 'inform the Court that it is investigating or has investigated its nationals or others within its jurisdiction with respect to criminal acts which may constitute crimes [within the Court's jurisdiction] and which relate to the information provided in the notification to States'.[78] If a state so requests, 'the Prosecutor shall defer to the State's investigation of those persons'.[79] If the Prosecutor nevertheless wishes to investigate, he must apply to the Pre-Trial Chamber for authorization.[80] While the title of article 18 ('Preliminary rulings regarding admissibility') suggests otherwise, the procedure results in a ruling only if the Prosecutor requests the Pre-Trial Chamber to authorize an investigation in the face of a state's request for his deferral.

Article 18(2) provides that the Prosecutor 'shall defer to the State's investigations of those *persons*' which the state claims to have investigated or to continue to investigate. This shows that the deferral does not concern the investigation into the situation as a whole. If, in the Prosecutor's view, there are other potentially admissible cases not subject to domestic proceedings, he may still investigate the situation with respect to those other cases. On the other hand, the state need not have identified the specific persons yet. The reference to 'those persons' may be taken to suggest this, but the state is obliged to inform the Prosecutor in its deferral request only that it is investigating or has investigated 'criminal acts which may constitute crimes [within the Court's jurisdiction] and which relate to the information provided in the notification to States'.[81] The periodic information a state may be required to provide to the Prosecutor relates to the progress of 'its *investigations* and any subsequent prosecutions'.[82] When the Prosecutor opens an investigation into the rest of the situation, it may in practice prove difficult to demarcate the boundaries between the ICC's investigations and those of a state.

---

[77]   ICC Statute, art. 18(2), emphasis added.

[78]   *Ibid*. art. 18(2) and ICC Rules, rule 53.

[79]   ICC Statute, art. 18(2). If several states request deferral, the Prosecutor must decide upon each request individually. It is not up to the Prosecutor to resolve competing claims to jurisdiction. He can decide to defer to more than one state. During the deferral, the Prosecutor may ask the state concerned to inform him periodically of the progress of its proceedings, a request only states parties are obliged to respond to (*ibid*. art. 18(5)), and he may seek authorization from the Pre-Trial Chamber, on an exceptional basis, 'to pursue necessary investigative steps for the purpose of preserving evidence where there is a unique opportunity to obtain important evidence or there is a significant risk that such evidence may not be subsequently available' (*ibid*. art. 18(6)). The Prosecutor may review the deferral after six months or 'at any time when there has been a significant change of circumstances based on the State's unwillingness or inability genuinely to carry out the investigation' (*ibid*. art. 18(3)). It can be assumed that 'unwillingness or inability genuinely to carry out the investigation' is also the ground for the review after six months. The Pre-Trial Chamber, however, when deciding whether to authorize the investigation after the review (ICC Rules, rule 56(1)) still considers all 'the factors in article 17' (ICC Rules, rule 55(2)).

[80]   ICC Statute, art. 18(2) and ICC Rules, rule 54. Both the Prosecutor and the state concerned can appeal the Pre-Trial Chamber's decision (ICC Statute, art. 18(4)).

[81]   *Ibid*. art. 18(2).

[82]   *Ibid*. art. 18(5). Emphasis added.

The notification that the Prosecutor is obliged to give under article 18 must contain information about the acts that may constitute crimes within the jurisdiction of the Court,[83] but it need not inform states of which cases the Prosecutor intends to prosecute.[84] Indeed, the aim of the investigation to follow is to identify such cases. The procedure of article 18 is thus of little help to a state that wishes to prevent the ICC from investigating the situation as a whole but which itself has not yet identified all the cases that the ICC may wish to prosecute.[85]

Once the ICC's investigation of a situation has been opened, only the Prosecutor can end it. Whereas the state and the accused can challenge the admissibility of specific cases that the Prosecutor has identified for prosecution pursuant to article 19 (see below), the Statute does not provide them with an avenue for ending investigations. The Prosecutor may decide not to prosecute, which could be considered a decision to close the investigations. Yet the Statute does not provide a deadline for the Prosecutor to take such a decision. Nor does it bestow on the Pre-Trial Chamber, which has the power to review such a decision, powers to compel the Prosecutor to take a decision.[86] Without such a decision, an ICC investigation could be open-ended. However, as the next section argues, this does not prevent an interested state from starting domestic proceedings in an attempt to render a case inadmissible before the ICC.

States are Not Prohibited from Starting Proceedings After the ICC has Done So

Unlike in the Statutes for the ICTY and ICTR, there is no provision in the ICC Statute allowing the Court to request national courts to 'defer to its competence'.[87] The Statute obliges states parties merely to cooperate with the Court,[88] and it prohibits them from prosecuting the same crimes only after the Court has convicted or acquitted the person.[89] Until an acquittal or conviction by the ICC, states could, in theory, conduct national proceedings simultane-

---

[83]   ICC Rules, rule 52(1). Pursuant to rule 52(2) states may ask for more information. However, ICC Statute, art. 18(1) allows the Prosecutor to provide notification on a confidential basis or to limit the scope of the information provided if this is necessary to protect persons, to avoid destruction of evidence or to prevent persons from absconding.

[84]   See, in this light, the notifications of the investigations into the DRC (ICC OTP, Fax from the Prosecutor to all States Parties to the Rome Statute of the International Criminal Court, 21 June 2004, on file with author, OTP/20040621-Article 18 Notification (21 June 2004); Uganda (ICC OTP, Fax from the Prosecutor to all States Parties to the Rome Statute of the International Criminal Court, 28 July 2004, on file with author, OTP/20040728-Article18 Notification.Uganda (28 July 2004)); and Central African Republic (ICC OTP, Letter from the Prosecutor to all State Parties to the Rome Statute of the International Criminal Court, 21 May 2007, on file with author, CAR/Notif/21052007/LMO (21 May 2007)). None of these were very specific about the OTP's focus.

[85]   Indeed, as is evidenced by the many potential addressees of the notification (art. 18(1)) and the term 'investigations of its nationals or others within its jurisdiction' (art. 18(2)), art. 18 was inserted into the Statute primarily to give states other than that where the crime was committed a chance to investigate and prosecute, for instance on the basis of the active or passive personality principles.

[86]   See ICC Pre-Trial Chamber II, Situation in Uganda, Decision to Convene a Status Conference on the Investigation in Uganda in Relation to the Application of Article 53, ICC-02/04-01/05-68, Pre-Trial Chamber II, 2 December 2005 and ICC OTP, OTP Submission Providing Information on Status of the Investigation in Anticipation of the Status Conference to be Held on 13 January 2006, ICC-02/04-01/05-76, 11 January 2006.

[87]   See ICTR Statute, art. 8(2). See also ICTY Statute, art. 9(2).

[88]   ICC Statute, Part 9.

[89]   *Ibid.* art. 20(2).

ously with those of the Court. A state may even initiate national proceedings after the ICC has become involved. The fact that the state has initiated its investigations only after the Prosecutor's notification pursuant to article 18 provides no grounds for the OTP to refuse a deferral when requested in accordance with that provision.

In the absence of any article in the Statute to the contrary, states could initiate domestic proceedings even after the Court has issued arrest warrants in a specific case. If the state launching its domestic investigations were also requested by the Court to arrest and surrender the same person(s) to the ICC, the obligation to comply with the request[90] would be lifted pending the determination of any admissibility challenge.[91] It is still a matter of speculation what exactly is required for a successful admissibility challenge in the scenario where a state is trying to 'catch up' with ongoing proceedings before the ICC. The state must at least open an investigation, demonstrate that this encompasses the same case as the ICC's and, if contested by the Prosecutor, that it is willing and able to conduct proceedings genuinely.[92]

Admissibility is Assessed at Several Possible Stages of the ICC Proceedings

The judges are called upon to determine admissibility at several possible stages of the proceedings. The Prosecutor needs the Pre-Trial Chamber's authorization to launch an investigation *proprio motu*.[93] The test for the Pre-Trial Chamber is whether there is a 'reasonable basis to proceed'.[94] It is the same as the test the Prosecutor applies, and must therefore include an assessment of admissibility.[95] The judges must also consider admissibility when the Prosecutor requests the Pre-Trial Chamber to authorize an investigation despite a state's request for deferral,[96] and they are equally required to assess admissibility where it is challenged in a specific case.

Article 19 entitles a range of actors to raise admissibility before the Court. First, article 19(2)(a) grants the right to challenge admissibility to an accused and any person against whom the ICC has issued a warrant of arrest or a summons to appear.[97] Such a challenge may be based on any of the grounds of inadmissibility set out in article 17. This right is independent

---

[90] *Ibid.* arts 89 and 86.

[91] *Ibid.* art. 95.

[92] Decision on the Admissibility of the Case under Article 19(1) of the Statute, ICC Pre-Trial Chamber II, ICC-02/04-01/05-377, 10 March 2009, para. 49 suggests that the Chamber considers as relevant factors 'the substantive and procedural laws to be applied by the [national court], as well as the criteria presiding over the appointment of its members'. These factors as such, however, cannot determine the outcome of the admissibility assessment since the question must be whether the proceedings in the specific case are genuine (rather than whether the legislation applicable to the general situation is appropriate).

[93] ICC Statute, art. 15(3).

[94] *Ibid.* art. 15(4).

[95] ICC Rules, rule 48 and ICC Statute, art. 53(1)(b). This interpretation is supported by the fact that, pursuant to ICC Statute, art. 15(4), the Pre-Trial Chamber's determination is 'without prejudice to subsequent determinations by the Court with regard to the jurisdiction and admissibility of a case'.

[96] ICC Statute, art. 18(2).

[97] The Statute does not define when a person becomes 'the accused' (the ICC does not have an indictment procedure like the ICTY and ICTR) but a comparison of ICC Statute, arts 61 and 63 bears out that 'the person' becomes 'the accused' after the confirmation of charges. But contrast, C.K. Hall, *Article 19: Challenges to the Jurisdiction of the Court or the Admissibility of a Case*, in Triffterer, note 36 *supra*, at 409.

of any state's right to challenge admissibility. Secondly, article 19(2)(b) grants a right of challenge to 'a State which has jurisdiction over a case'. The only ground of inadmissibility this state may invoke is that 'it is investigating or prosecuting the case or has investigated or prosecuted'.[98] Unlike an accused, a state cannot invoke insufficient gravity as a ground for inadmissibility. Thirdly, article 19(2)(c) provides 'a State from which acceptance of jurisdiction is required under article 12' may challenge admissibility.[99] Finally, pursuant to article 19(3), the Prosecutor may seek a ruling from the Court regarding a question of jurisdiction or admissibility. This provision also grants victims and the referring entity the right to submit observations on issues of jurisdiction and admissibility.

The Pre-Trial Chamber has discretion to review admissibility when the Prosecutor decides not to open an investigation or not to prosecute and the referring entity (whether a state party or the Security Council) contests the decision. It stands to reason that the grounds for review are the same as the criteria by which the Prosecutor decides whether to investigate or prosecute, admissibility included. Though it cannot compel him to do so, the Pre-Trial Chamber can request that the Prosecutor review his decision.[100]

The Statute also provides that the Court 'may, on its own motion, determine the admissibility of a case in accordance with article 17'.[101] The same article provides that the Court 'shall satisfy itself that it has jurisdiction in any case brought before it'. The difference between 'shall' with respect to jurisdiction, and 'may' with respect to the Court's *proprio motu* power to determine admissibility could suggest that the Court is not obliged to consider admissibility in the event that neither the accused nor any state challenges it.[102] However, article 19(1) directs the Court to article 17, which provides, in paragraph 1, that the Court 'shall determine that a case is inadmissible' in the enumerated circumstances. This may oblige the Court to determine admissibility, even if it is not raised. Indeed, in Pre-Trial Chamber I's initial view, it was obliged to assess admissibility when deciding on issuing an arrest warrant: 'the term "shall" in the *chapeau* of article 17(1) of the Statute leaves the Chamber no discretion as to the declaration of the inadmissibility of a case once it is satisfied that the case "is not of sufficient gravity to justify further action by the Court"'.[103] Yet, in the appeal of the decision to deny an arrest warrant for Ntaganda on the ground of insufficient gravity, the Appeals Chamber stressed that the Court's *proprio motu* assessment of admissibility is discretionary.[104] On the issuance of an arrest warrant, a Chamber should 'exercise

---

[98]   ICC Statute, art. 19(2)(b).

[99]   *Ibid.* art. 12(2) requires acceptance of jurisdiction from either the state where the crimes were committed or the state of which the accused is a national, but not if the Security Council has referred the situation. In the scenario of a referral by the Security Council, the state where, or by whose nationals, the crimes were allegedly committed can challenge admissibility only under art. 19(2)(b). For the state, the difference is that art. 19(2)(c), unlike article 19(2)(b), allows challenges on all of the grounds of inadmissibility set out in art. 17, including insufficient gravity.

[100]   *Ibid.* art. 53(3)(a).

[101]   'The Court' in art. 19 must be interpreted to refer only to the Court's adjudicatory organs (the Pre-Trial, Trial and Appeals Chamber) and not to 'the Court' in the broad sense as defined in art. 34. This interpretation is supported by *ibid.* art. 19(6), which refers to the adjudicatory organs. See also Kleffner, note 34 *supra*, at 203.

[102]   In this vein, Hall, note 97 *supra*, at 203.

[103]   See *Lubanga* Arrest Warrant Decision, note 7 *supra*, para. 43.

[104]   Judgment on the Prosecutor's Appeal against the Decision of Pre-Trial Chamber I Entitled

such discretion only when it is appropriate in the circumstances of the case, bearing in mind the interests of the suspect'.[105] Such circumstances might include 'instances where a case is based on the established jurisprudence of the Court, uncontested facts that render a case clearly inadmissible or an ostensible case impelling the exercise of *proprio motu* review'.[106] In other circumstances a decision on admissibility in *ex parte* Prosecutor only proceedings is, according to the Appeals Chamber, detrimental to the suspect's interests.[107] Rather than as a rule that must be applied once the substantive criteria are met, the Appeals Chamber has thus interpreted article 17 as a rule that is applied only if a suspect/accused, state or a Chamber exercising its discretionary powers, uses the procedural avenues of article 19 to raise issues of admissibility. From the perspective of judicial economy there are good reasons for this. Otherwise, the Court would constantly have to assess admissibility and, in effect, make its own proceedings dependent on developments in national proceedings. However, the Appeal Chamber's decision does suggest that complementarity, as an admissibility criterion, is more the subjective right of a suspect/accused or state, than a grand principle that must be enforced in the public interest, whether to avoid the duplication of national and international proceedings or to encourage states to fulfil their role in the prosecution of international crimes. In this interpretation of the principle as a subjective right, complementarity is not assessed if it is not challenged or *proprio motu* raised by judges. As the Lubanga case illustrates, the case in which neither the state (having itself referred the situation) nor the accused (preferring a trial by the ICC to a national one) challenges admissibility despite the existence of national proceedings is not a mere hypothetical. The situation in Northern Uganda shows, however, that a state may also change its preference, first referring a situation to the Court and later deciding that it nonetheless wishes to challenge admissibility. The Statute allows this, since an initial assessment is not necessarily the final word on admissibility: the assessment is dynamic.

Assessment of Admissibility is Dynamic

The Court's finding on admissibility when it issues an arrest warrant or decides on an admissibility ruling requested by the Prosecutor is only preliminary, insofar as the actors with a right to challenge admissibility are not yet involved in the proceedings.[108] It could be argued that

---

'Decision on the Prosecutor's Application for Warrants of Arrest, Article 58', ICC Appeals Chamber, 13 July 2006, made public as ICC-01/04-169, 23 September 2008, para. 48.

[105] *Ibid*. para. 2. This decision was later applied in *Harun and Kushayb*, Arrest Warrant Decision, note 20 *supra*, at para. 18: 'article 19(1) of the Statute gives the Chamber discretion to make an initial determination of the admissibility of the case before the issuance of a warrant of arrest or a summons to appear. Such discretion should be exercised only if warranted by the circumstances of the case, bearing in mind the interest of the person concerned.'

[106] *Ibid*. para. 52.

[107] *Ibid*. para. 50. Note, however, that the Court's decision concerned the gravity component of article 17, rather than complementarity

[108] See also *Prosecutor* v. *Joseph Kony*, Arrest Warrant issued on 8 July 2005 as amended on 27 September 2005, ICC-02/04-01/05-53, 11, para. 38 (illustrative for the LRA cases); *Lubanga* Arrest Warrant Decision, note 7 *supra*, para. 20; *Ntaganda* Arrest Warrant Decision, note 15 *supra*, para. 20; *Prosecutor* v. *Ahmad Muhammad Harun ('Ahmad Harun') and Ali Muhammed Abd-Al-Rahman ('Ali Kushayb')*, ICC Pre-Trial Chamber I, Warrant of Arrest for Ahmad Harun, ICC-02/05-01/07-2, 27 April 2007, 2 and Warrant of Arrest for Ali Kushayb, ICC-02/05-01/07-3, 27 April 2007, 2, para. 2.5;

once these other actors have actually participated in proceedings which result in a finding of admissibility, they are thereafter estopped from challenging it unless they can show additional significant facts or a significant change of circumstances.[109] A significant additional fact or change of circumstances, which need not be unforeseen, could be that a state has started proceedings. Consequently, the preliminary ruling cannot guarantee admissibility.[110]

An actor wishing to challenge admissibility[111] – whether it be a person against whom a warrant or summons has been issued, the accused or a state – must do so in the period between the presentation of the case to the Court[112] and the commencement of the trial.[113] After the commencement of the trial, admissibility findings by the Court, whether *proprio motu* or as a response to a challenge or a request for a ruling, must be considered *res judicata*, unless a later challenge is allowed in exceptional circumstances. Such allowance can be made only in the event that the person concerned has already been tried.[114]

If the Prosecutor decides to defer an investigation based on the considerations set out in article 17 (the criminal proceedings of a state) he may, pursuant to article 19(11), request the state concerned to make available information on its domestic proceedings. Article 19(11) provides not only for the Prosecutor's right to request such information but also the authority to defer the investigation[115] at his own initiative and discretion. He can do so beyond the narrower circumstances in which article 18 applies.[116]

Katanga Arrest Warrant Decision, note 16 *supra*, para. 21; Decision on the Evidence and Information Provided by the Prosecution for the Issuance of a Warrant of Arrest for Mathieu Ngudjolo Chui, ICC-01/04-02/07-3 / ICC-01/04-01/07-262, Pre-trial Chamber I, 6 July 2007, para. 22; and *Bemba Gombo* Arrest Warrant Decision, note 21 *supra*, para. 22.

[109]   This is an analogical application of art. 18(7), which applies when a state wishes to challenge admissibility under art. 19 having already used the procedure provided for by art. 18.

[110]   As has been confirmed by Decision on the Admissibility of the Case under Article 19(1) of the Statute, note 92 *supra*, para. 28 ('the determination of admissibility is meant to be an ongoing process throughout the pre-trial phase, the outcome of which is subject to review depending on the evolution of the relevant factual scenario. Otherwise stated, the Statute as a whole enshrines the idea that a change in circumstances allows (or even, in some scenarios, compels) the Court to determine admissibility anew.').

[111]   Pursuant to art. 19(4), a person or state may challenge admissibility or jurisdiction only once.

[112]   Décision relative aux conclusions aux fins d'exception d'incompétence et d'irrecevabilité, ICC Pre-Trial Chamber I, ICC-02/05-34, 22 November 2006, confirms that art. 19(2) cannot be invoked by the ad hoc defence lawyer in the period before concrete cases have been identified.

[113]   According to Motifs de la décision orale relative à l'exception d'irrecevabilité de l'affaire (article 19 du Statut), note 5 *supra*, para. 49, the commencement of the trial is not the moment that the hearings begin, but the moment that the Trial Chamber is constituted. In other words, admissibility challenges other than those based on arts 17(1)(c) and 20(3) must be brought before the charges are confirmed. However, until the charges are confirmed it is difficult for parties to know whether the domestic case concerns the same persons, conduct and incidents as that of the ICC, which, as has been set out above, the Pre-Trial Chamber has considered the standard for rendering ICC cases inadmissible.

[114]   ICC Statute, arts 19(4) and 17(1)(c).

[115]   See also Olásolo, note 24 *supra*, at 159.

[116]   When a state successfully invokes art. 18(2), the Prosecutor must 'defer to' (in the sense of 'yield to') the domestic proceedings, whereas under art. 19(11) he only 'defers' (in the sense of 'post-pones') an investigation (the difference is confirmed by ICC Statute (French text), art. 18(2) ('le Procureur lui défère') and art. 19(11) ('le Procureur sursoit à enquêter'). While the Prosecutor cannot *proprio motu* end a 'deferral' undertaken pursuant to art. 18(2), he can decide to proceed with an investigation even after having earlier decided to 'defer' proceedings under art. 19(11).

Earlier Findings of Admissibility or Inadmissibility Can be Reviewed

The dynamic configuration[117] of the admissibility assessment discussed in the previous section gives states a chance to assert their primary right to exercise jurisdiction by conducting genuine domestic proceedings, even when these have been initiated after the ICC has become involved. This raises the question of the last point in ICC proceedings at which domestic proceedings can trigger a review of the admissibility of a case.

The first period during which states can influence the outcome of the admissibility test is during the preliminary examinations, which take place before the Prosecutor's decision on opening an investigation. The Statute obliges the Prosecutor to open an investigation in the case of a referral, unless the criteria of article 53(1) indicate that there is no reasonable basis to proceed. The Statute does not set a timeframe within which the Prosecutor must make this determination.[118] A state's domestic proceedings, even when initiated only after the referral, can persuade him to decide not to initiate an investigation. He may reconsider that decision 'at any time ... based on new facts or information',[119] without needing to seek the Pre-Trial Chamber's authorization.[120]

After the Prosecutor has decided to open an investigation, states still have several opportunities to end the ICC's involvement in a given case by conducting genuine domestic proceedings. In the circumstances described above, a state can use the procedure in article 18 to pre-empt the Prosecutor's investigation in any given case. If the state does not avail itself of this procedure or is not successful under it, its domestic proceedings could still end the ICC's involvement in a case given that the Prosecutor must continue to assess admissibility during the investigation.[121] The Prosecutor may defer his investigation (article 19(11)) or may decide not to open a prosecution (article 53(2)) in light of the domestic proceedings.[122] He may reconsider this decision 'at any time ... based on new facts or information'.[123]

---

[117]   Olásolo, note 24 *supra*, at 157.

[118]   The Prosecutor took over two years to decide whether to open an investigation after the referral of the situation in the Central African Republic. In Decision Requesting Information on the Status of the Preliminary Examination of the Situation in the Central African Republic, ICC Pre-Trial Chamber III, ICC-01/05-6, 30 November 2006, the Pre-Trial Chamber attempted to monitor the Prosecutor's consideration. In Prosecution's Report pursuant to Pre-Trial Chamber III's 30 November 2006 Decision Requesting Information on the Status of the Preliminary Examination of the Situation in the Central African Republic, ICC-01/05-7 (15 December 2006), para. 8, the Prosecutor argued that under art. 53(3) there is 'no exercise of prosecutorial discretion susceptible to judicial review by the [Pre-Trial] Chamber' until the Prosecutor decides not to proceed with an investigation or prosecution.

[119]   ICC Statute, art. 53(4).

[120]   The Statute does not provide for an expiry date for the right to reconsider, but, since future crimes cannot be referred, there must be a connection between the facts the Prosecutor wishes to prosecute and the time-period when the referral was made. In most instances, it will not be difficult to make a connection.

[121]   As is underscored in ICC OTP, First Darfur Report, note 57 *supra*, at 4.

[122]   M. Bergsmo and P. Kruger, *Article 53: Initiation of an Investigation*, in Triffterer, note 36 *supra*, at 701, 714, suggest that the word 'whether' in art. 53(4) means that the Prosecutor could also reconsider a decision to open an investigation (and prosecution). However, the word 'initiate' indicates that he can only reconsider a decision not to investigate (or prosecute). He cannot undo an initiation; he can only decide not to continue an investigation, which should be equated with the decision not to prosecute in art. 53(2).

[123]   ICC Statute, art. 53(4).

The Prosecutor's decision to prosecute materializes when he requests an arrest warrant or a summons to appear.[124] The Court has thus far examined admissibility *proprio motu* at this stage of the proceedings, but, as has been set out, its finding regarding admissibility at this stage is only preliminary. Thereafter a state can contest admissibility under article 19(2)(b) or (c) on the ground that it is conducting genuine domestic proceedings, even if it has started these only after the issuance of the arrest warrant. The fact that a state carries out domestic proceedings despite being obliged to transfer the person concerned to the ICC would not defeat the effect of those proceedings on the admissibility of a case before the ICC. This would not as such qualify as inability or unwillingness as defined in article 17(2) and (3) or as a ground allowing trial by the ICC despite a previous domestic trial under articles 17(1)(c) and 20(3). Hence, despite any such failure to comply, the case must be found inadmissible.

If, in light of domestic proceedings, the Prosecutor wishes to close a case, he can ask for a ruling on admissibility under article 19(3). If the Court decides that a case is inadmissible, whether *proprio motu* or pursuant to a request for a ruling from the Prosecutor or a challenge by a state or the accused, the Prosecutor can continue his investigation into the situation and identify other cases, unless he decides not to prosecute. If new facts regarding the admissibility of the case have arisen, he may request the Court to review the decision regarding admissibility.[125]

As already noted, states wishing to challenge admissibility must do so at the earliest opportunity and in any case will want to do so prior to or at the commencement of the trial.[126] At or after the commencement of trial, challenges to the admissibility can be based only on the ground that the person has already been tried.[127] A difficult situation could arise if a domestic court were to acquit or convict the accused *in absentia*. Pursuant to article 19(4), *ne bis in idem* may be raised as a ground for inadmissibility after the commencement of the trial only in exceptional circumstances and with leave of the Court. A concluded domestic trial could constitute such an exceptional circumstance. The fact that the verdict was rendered *in absentia* would not necessarily constitute one of the two exceptions to inadmissibility.

In comparison with the ICTY and ICTR, the ICC has fewer procedures for deferring cases to domestic jurisdictions while exercising supervisory powers. In due course the ICTY and ICTR have created a mechanism according to which the tribunals, at either the prosecutor's or a referral bench's initiative, can refer cases to domestic jurisdictions when they are satisfied that the accused will receive a fair trial and that the death penalty will not be imposed or carried out. The tribunals' prosecutors may send observers to monitor the domestic proceedings and can request the relevant tribunal to revoke an order referring the case to the domestic courts.[128]

The ICC cannot conditionally defer to domestic jurisdictions in this manner. When the Prosecutor 'defers to' (in the sense of 'yields to') domestic proceedings pursuant to article 18, he is able to acquire periodic information, to preserve evidence, to review such a decision and

---

[124]   See also VPRS 1-6 Decision, note 19 *supra*, distinguishing between situations and cases on the basis of the different kind of proceedings they entail. The Court distinguished between 'investigations' in the phase of a 'situation' and 'proceedings after the issuance of an arrest warrant' in the phase of 'a case'. The latter proceedings can be considered 'prosecution'.

[125]   ICC Statute, art. 19(10).
[126]   *Ibid.* art. 19(5).
[127]   *Ibid.* art. 19(4).
[128]   ICTY and ICTR Rules of Procedure and Evidence, rule 11*bis*.

ultimately to request the Pre-Trial Chamber to end the deferral.[129] When the Prosecutor 'defers' (in the sense of 'postpones') under the discretionary power granted in article 19(11), he can only ask for information, which he can later use to reconsider his decision. As they are not grounds for admissibility, domestic fair trial standards and the application of the death penalty cannot be criteria for considering or ending a deferral.

CONCLUSION

Complementarity, as the 'cornerstone' of the ICC Statute, has often been misunderstood. This chapter has attempted to flesh out the principle by reviewing both the substantive and procedural provisions of the ICC Statute that encapsulate it and the relevant evolving ICC jurisprudence. It has shown that in several respects the Statute does leave states the freedom to conduct domestic investigations and prosecutions of crimes within the ICC's jurisdiction, even after the ICC itself has already become involved. On the other hand, once the ICC Prosecutor has opened an investigation, it is quite difficult in practice for a state to bring the ICC's involvement to an end.

Ultimately, the true scope of the prerogative that complementarity reserves to states depends on the interpretation of relevant provisions of the Statute by the Prosecutor and the Judges' Chambers. It is the Court, and not states, which assesses the admissibility of cases before the ICC. The Court's first decisions on what constitutes a 'case' and until what moment admissibility may be challenged have severely limited the options for any state that wishes to avoid ICC intervention. Other decisions have emphasized judges' discretion whether or not *proprio motu* to review admissibility and have interpreted the concept of 'unwillingness' rather broadly. It is to be hoped that these first decisions are not indicative of a general trend to interpret and apply provisions in the Statute in such a way as to undermine complementarity and establish a *de facto* primacy for the ICC.

After all, complementarity is not, as it is often presented,[130] simply international justice's sacrifice to state sovereignty. International justice has much to gain from genuine domestic proceedings, particularly if they take place in the state where the crimes were committed. Apart from making justice more visible and comprehensible for perpetrators, victims and the society within which the crimes were committed, domestic proceedings can contribute to a stronger national justice sector. The ICC has an important role to play, but strong national justice systems will remain essential not only for investigating and prosecuting international crimes but also for preventing them.

---

[129]   ICC Statute, art. 18(5), (6), (3) and (2).

[130]   See, *inter alia*, B.S. Brown, *Primacy or Complementarity: Reconciling the Jurisdiction of National Courts and International Criminal Tribunals*, 23 YALE JIL 383, 389 (1998); J.I. Turner, *Nationalizing International Criminal Law*, 41(1) STANFORD JIL 1, 6 (2005); P. Sands, *After Pinochet: The Role of National Courts*, in P. SANDS (ed.), FROM NUREMBERG TO THE HAGUE: THE FUTURE OF INTERNATIONAL CRIMINAL JUSTICE 68, 75 (Cambridge University Press, 2003). See for an eloquent discussion of the complicated relationship between sovereignty and international criminal justice, R. Cryer, *International Criminal Law vs State Sovereignty: Another Round?* 16(5) EUROPEAN JIL 979 (2005) and M. Benzing, *The Complementarity Regime of the International Criminal Court: International Criminal Justice Between State Sovereignty and the Fight Against Impunity*, 7 MAX PLANCK YB UNITED NATIONS L 591, 597 (2003).

10 The hybrid experience of the Special Court for Sierra Leone

Clare da Silva

INTRODUCTION

The Special Court for Sierra Leone (SCSL) is one of a discrete number of 'hybrid' tribunals that have been established in recent years. As the name suggests, it was envisioned as a Court *for* Sierra Leone, established in response to the government's request, taking into account the special needs and requirements of Sierra Leone and located in the country where the crimes occurred. It is referred to as a 'hybrid' or 'mixed' tribunal because it was established through joint action of the United Nations and the government of Sierra Leone. The SCSL was conceived as an alternative model to the ad hoc tribunals that were created by decision of the United Nations Security Council.[1] This chapter will provide an overview of the conflict, the establishment of the SCSL, its structure, the trials and an analysis of the jurisprudence and legacy of the Court. It also addresses the relationship between the Court and the Sierra Leone Truth and Reconciliation Commission (TRC), which operated simultaneously for a brief period.

While it is too early to reach definitive conclusions on this 'hybrid' model, or the overall contribution of the SCSL, it is clear that it provides a number of important lessons for future mechanisms of international justice. Many of these lessons stem not from the model of the hybrid tribunal itself but from the practical application of this model in Sierra Leone. This chapter draws the conclusion that, in principle, the hybrid structure created a unique opportunity for the Court to address the local context and strengthen the domestic criminal justice system: both necessary elements to ensuring lasting peace. In practice, however, the Court has not developed coherent strategies for integrating domestic elements into its primarily international legal structure and for interfacing with the domestic criminal justice system. It is thus unclear whether this hybrid tribunal will have a lasting impact on the judicial institutions and legal culture of Sierra Leone.

THE COURT IN CONTEXT: A BRIEF HISTORY OF THE CONFLICT

Sierra Leone is a small West African nation located on the coast between Liberia and Guinea. On 23 March 1991, armed conflict broke out when approximately 100 fighters led by Foday Sankoh, and calling themselves the Revolutionary United Front (RUF), crossed the border from Liberia into Sierra Leone. Over the next 11 years, Sierra Leone was devastated by a

---

[1] These include the International Criminal Tribunals for the Former Yugoslavia and Rwanda (the ICTY and ICTR).

complex civil war, characterized by brutality against the civilian population and serious violations of human rights and international humanitarian law.

The conflict initially started as an attempt by the RUF to overthrow the dictatorial regime of Joseph Saidu Momoh and the All Peoples' Congress (APC), which had been the ruling party in Sierra Leone since 1968.[2] The RUF failed to generate broad popular support, however, as it quickly launched into a brutal campaign characterized by systematic violence against civilians and the forced recruitment of combatants to increase its numerical strength. In April 1992, its stated objective of popular revolution was rendered moot following a bloodless coup led by a group of young military officers, who displaced the APC government and installed the National Provisional Ruling Council (NPRC).

The NPRC expanded the size of the Sierra Leone Army (SLA) in an attempt to overrun the RUF, and it initially had successes. In 1993, the RUF was reduced to a confined area of forest territory on the Liberian border, though this did not bring an end to the conflict. In response, the RUF launched a 'guerrilla warfare' strategy, and it expanded its combat operations into every district of Sierra Leone. Community-based militias, drawing from traditional hunting societies, were gradually established to resist the RUF.[3]

Democratic elections were held in 1996 yet they were disrupted by extreme violence, which included forced amputation of limbs to deter citizens from voting. The elections ushered in a new Sierra Leone People's Party (SLPP) government headed by Ahmad Tejan Kabbah. Later that year, the new President signed a peace accord with the RUF in Abidjan, Côte d'Ivoire.[4] Despite the new peace accord, violence escalated almost immediately. In an attempt to increase the state security apparatus, President Kabbah formalized the community-based militias into the Civilian Defence Forces (CDF).

In May 1997, breakaway army officers overthrew President Kabbah in a coup and Corporal Johnny Paul Koroma was made head of the newly formed Armed Forces Revolutionary Council (AFRC). The AFRC forged a military and political alliance with the RUF, creating what was known as the 'People's Army' or 'junta.'

Immediately following the coup, President Kabbah went into exile in Guinea. The Deputy Minister of Defence, Chief Samuel Hinga Norman, remained in Sierra Leone and mobilized vast forces from the traditional hunting societies. These forces were deployed as CDF forces to oppose the AFRC military junta. In February 1998, a combination of Nigerian-led ECOMOG[5] troops and CDF forces restored Kabbah's government to power in the Western

---

2   2 *Witness to Truth: Final Report of the Sierra Leone Truth and Reconciliation Commission* ch. 1, *Executive Summary*, para. 19 (2004). The TRC notes that Momoh and his predecessor, Dr Siaka Stevens, had entrenched a system of central government which sustained itself through years of one-party rule, characterized by a small ruling elite's exploitation of the country, widespread corruption, nepotism, the plundering of state assets and economic decay. The TRC concluded that all the administrations of the post-independence period contributed to the structural and proximate contexts that led to the conflict in 1991.

3   The community-based militias were composed of a number of hunting societies, including Kamajors, Gbethis, Kampra, Tamaboros and Donsos. Kamajors were the dominant group in the CDF. For further detail on the CDF, see Danny Hoffman, *The Meaning of a Militia: Understanding the Civil Defence Forces of Sierra Leone*, 106 AFRICAN AFFAIRS 639 (2007).

4   Peace Agreement between the Government of Sierra Leone and the Revolutionary United Front of Sierra Leone, Abidjan, Côte d'Ivoire, 30 November 1996.

5   ECOMOG (Economic Community Cease-Fire Monitoring Group) is a non-standing military

Area of the country, though much of the country remained in rebel hands and the fighting continued.

In January 1999, rebels and ex-soldiers led by the AFRC entered the capital, Freetown, leaving 5,000 dead and much of the city destroyed in a week. The invasion was turned back by ECOMOG troops. After six more months of fighting throughout the country, all factions agreed to the Lomé Peace Agreement in July 1999.[6] The agreement was a combination of a military resolution, through the disarmament of combatants, and a political settlement that implemented a power-sharing arrangement between the RUF and the government. The Lomé Peace Agreement made broad concessions to the RUF, including a blanket amnesty granting unconditional and free pardon to all participants in the conflict.[7] The Agreement also mandated the creation of a Truth and Reconciliation Commission. At the signing of the Agreement, however, the United Nations representative appended a disclaimer to the document, stating that the United Nations did not recognize the amnesty and that, as a matter of international law, the amnesty provision would not apply to the international crimes of genocide, crimes against humanity, war crimes and other serious violations of international law.[8]

The United Nations Mission in Sierra Leone (UNAMSIL)[9] was installed in Spring 2000 with a mandate that included disarmament, demobilization and reintegration. In January 2002, the war was officially declared over. Elections were held in July 2002, and President Kabbah's SLPP was re-elected into power.[10]

NATURE OF THE ATROCITIES

The conflict in Sierra Leone has been described as one 'waged almost entirely against the civilian population'.[11] Combatant factions did not target conventional military targets, and there were few instances of pitched battles with combatant factions in direct confrontation. Rather the conflict consisted mainly of factions trading control of villages and towns, resulting in massive human rights violations against the civilian population.

The three main factions, comprised of the RUF, the AFRC and the CDF, engaged in atrocities against enemy combatants, suspected collaborators and civilians.[12] However, civilians

---

force that was set up by member states of the ECOWAS (Economic Community of West African States) to deal with the security problem that followed the collapse of the formal state structure in the Republic of Liberia in 1990.

[6] Peace Agreement between the Government of Sierra Leone and the RUF, Lomé, Togo, 7 July 1999 (Lomé Peace Agreement).

[7] Lomé Peace Agreement, art. IX.

[8] *Seventh Report of the Secretary-General on the United Nations Mission in Sierra Leone*, UN Doc. S/1999/836 (30 July 1999), para. 7. The United Nations was a signatory to the agreement as a moral guarantor.

[9] UNAMSIL was established by UN Security Council Resolution 1270/2000.

[10] For a fuller account of the conflict, see Paul Richards, *War and Peace in Sierra Leone*, 25 Fletcher Forum of World Affairs 41 (Summer 2001).

[11] TRC Final Report, note 2 *supra*, vol. 3a, ch. 4: *Nature of the Conflict*, para. 3.

[12] TRC Final Report, note 2 *supra*, vol. 2, ch. 2, *Findings*, para. 106: 'The RUF was the primary violator of human rights in the conflict. The AFRC was responsible for the second largest number of violations. The Sierra Leone Army (SLA) was the third biggest violator, followed by the Civil Defence Forces (CDF).'

bore the brunt of the conflict's brutality.[13] The conflict was characterized by mass displacement, sexual and gender-based violence, mass killing, abduction and forced recruitment into armed groups, and the use of forced labour to exploit Sierra Leone's diamond reserves to finance the war effort.

Another notorious feature of the conflict was the intentional amputation of hands and feet or arms and legs. The RUF and the AFRC committed most of these crimes. Other forms of mutilation, including cutting off noses, ears and lips, were widespread. Acts of cannibalism, particularly by the Kamajor members of the CDF, were also documented.

The conflict also involved the widespread use of child soldiers by the RUF, the AFRC and the CDF. UNICEF estimated that approximately 7,000 child soldiers fought in the war.[14] Many of these children were forcibly conscripted, and patterns of abduction and forcible drugging and abuse were well-documented. The impact of the conflict on children more broadly was also significant, with an estimated 15,000 children separated from their parents or families.[15]

While there are no confirmed figures, it is estimated that approximately 100,000 people were killed, and over two million were displaced during the course of the conflict.

CREATION OF THE SPECIAL COURT FOR SIERRA LEONE

One of the unique features of the Special Court for Sierra Leone is that a principal motivation for its creation was specifically to assist a failing peace process and to address security concerns in the country. As is evident from the *travaux préparatoires* of the negotiations between the United Nations and the Sierra Leone government, the SCSL was initially seen as a necessary measure to *prevent* the conflict from escalating, as well as a means of addressing the criminal responsibility of those who had perpetrated crimes.

Shortly after the Lomé Peace Accords were signed in July 1999, fighting had re-erupted and the peace process had broken down. In May 2000, Foday Sankoh, the leader of the RUF was taken into custody. There were concerns that his arrest and a national trial would further aggravate the conflict and fuel RUF desires to move towards Freetown. These concerns precipitated a request to the United Nations by President Kabbah for assistance in establishing a mixed national and international court in Sierra Leone to try a select group of perpetrators: 'members of the RUF and their accomplices'.[16] It was the government's view that international assistance through the form of an international tribunal would be a powerful tool in neutralizing the RUF and stabilizing the country.[17]

---

[13]   Throughout the 1990s a number of organizations documented the violations in Sierra Leone, including Human Rights Watch, the Campaign for Good Governance and the International Committee of the Red Cross. See, for example, Human Rights Watch, *Getting Away with Murder, Mutilation and Rape, New Testimony from Sierra Leone* (vol. 11, No. 3(A), July 1999).

[14]   Roisin DeBurca, *UNICEF Case Study on Children from the Fighting Forces in Sierra Leone*, Document Prepared for the International Conference on War-Affected Children (September 2000).

[15]   TRC Final Report, note 2 *supra*, vol. 3b, ch. 4, *Children and the Armed Conflict*, para. 143.

[16]   Letter from Ahmad Tejan Kabbah to the Secretary-General of the United Nations, UN Doc. S/2000/786 (12 June 2000).

[17]   Abdul Tejan Cole, *The Special Court for Sierra Leone: Conceptual Concerns and Alternatives*, 1 AFRICAN HUMAN RIGHTS J, 107 (2001).

In August 2000, the UN Security Council adopted Resolution 1315 authorizing the UN Secretary-General to enter into negotiations to establish such a court.[18] The resolution sets out the priorities of the international community, which included the need for 'a credible system of justice and accountability for the very serious crimes committed there [to] contribute to the process of national reconciliation and to the restoration and maintenance of peace …[19] and [to] expedite the process of bringing justice and reconciliation to Sierra Leone and the region'.[20]

While the Resolution 'reiterate[s] that the situation in Sierra Leone continues to constitute a threat to international peace and security in the region', the SCSL was not established according to the UN Security Council's Chapter VII authority, as was the case with the International Tribunals for the Former Yugoslavia and Rwanda (ICTY and ICTR), but rather by an international agreement whose negotiation was requested by the Security Council. This absence of Chapter VII authority impacts on the functioning of the Court in two significant ways. First, it means that the Court functions solely on voluntary contributions from UN member states, and second, the Court is deprived of the authority to compel other states to assist in carrying out its orders.[21]

On 16 January 2002, after 17 months of negotiations, the United Nations and the Sierra Leone government signed a bilateral agreement which created the legal framework for the Court, including as an annex the Statute of the Special Court for Sierra Leone.[22] Two days after the signing, President Kabbah declared the official end of the war.

STRUCTURE OF THE COURT

The creation of a new criminal court by a bilateral agreement between a state and the United Nations laid the groundwork for the Special Court's characterization as a 'hybrid legal institution'.[23] The hybrid tribunal model was conceived as a new model amidst growing international skepticism toward the ad hoc tribunals. The ICTY and ICTR had been criticized for the length of trials, the associated high costs, and the lack of a broader impact, particularly amongst victims of these conflicts.[24] The hybrid model was to focus on reducing the Court's

---

[18]   UN Security Council Resolution 1315 (2000), UN Doc. S/Res/1315 (2000).

[19]   *Ibid.* preambular para. 6. See also preambular para. 8: 'a strong and credible court that will meet the objectives of bringing justice and ensuring lasting peace'.

[20]   *Ibid.* preambular para. 11. See also *Report of the Security Council Mission to West Africa, 20–29 June 2004*, UN Doc. S/2004/525 (2 July, 2004), para. 39, which reiterated 'the importance of the Court for Sierra Leone's long-term reconciliation'.

[21]   For example, the lack of Chapter VII powers deprived the Court of the ability to compel Nigeria to carry out the arrest order for Charles Taylor when he was in exile in Nigeria.

[22]   Agreement between the United Nations and the Government of Sierra Leone on the Establishment of a Special Court for Sierra Leone, Annex to the *Report of the Secretary-General on the Establishment of a Special Court for Sierra Leone* (Statute of the Special Court), UN Doc. S/2000/915 (4 October 2000).

[23]   For example, President Kabbah referred to the Court as a 'hybrid institution' at the formal opening of the courthouse; see Statement of His Excellency Alhaji Dr Ahmad Tejan Kabbah, President of Sierra Leone at the Formal Opening of the Courthouse for the Special Court for Sierra Leone, 10 March 2004.

[24]   A number of the criticisms of the ad hoc tribunals are noted in the *Report of the Expert Group to Conduct a Review of the Effective Operations and Functioning of the International Tribunals for the Former Yugoslavia and Rwanda*, UN Doc. A/54/634 (22 November 1999).

budget, minimizing its scope, and streamlining its operations, while operating in the country where the conflict took place.

Beyond the administrative advantages deemed to be associated with the hybrid model, the Special Court for Sierra Leone has been much lauded as an innovative form of post-conflict justice. Much of this perceived innovation stems from President Kabbah's initial request to the United Nations and his vision to create a Special Court 'that will take into account the special needs and requirements of the Sierra Leone situation ... a court that is flexible in law and venue'.[25] The need to contextualize the court in the domestic setting within which it operates and to be responsive to the particular circumstances of Sierra Leone was the basis upon which the court was conceived.

One way that the Court attempts to ground itself within the national context is by incorporating both international and national crimes within its Statute. As the next section shows, this *de jure* relationship has little or no effect in practice, as the Court itself has ruled that it operates solely in the international legal sphere.

JURISDICTION OF THE COURT

Ratione materiae

This hybrid blend of law gives the court jurisdiction *ratione materiae* over two distinct bodies of law which are to be applied. The first is international criminal law including crimes against humanity,[26] serious violations of common article 3 of the Geneva Conventions and of Additional Protocol II,[27] intentional direction of attacks against humanitarian or peace-keeping personnel,[28] and conscription of children into armed forces or groups.[29]

The second body of law formally available to be applied is the law of Sierra Leone. Article 5 of the SCSL Statute draws from two pieces of domestic statutory law: the Prevention of Cruelty to Children Act of 1926 and the Malicious Damage Act of 1861. Some commentary on the SCSL merely notes in passing the presence of these Sierra Leone laws in the Statute.[30] Others have suggested that their inclusion can be seen as an attempt to legitimize and revitalize the existing domestic legal system, whose ineffectiveness as a democratic institution has been identified as a root cause of the conflict.[31] It has also been suggested that the inclusion of

---

25   Letter from Ahmad Tejan Kabbah to the Secretary-General of the United Nations, note 16 *supra*.

26   SCSL Statute, art. 2.

27   *Ibid*. art. 3.

28   *Ibid*. art 4(b): 'Intentionally directing attacks against personnel, installations, material, units or vehicles involved in a humanitarian assistance or peacekeeping mission in accordance with the Charter of the United Nations, as long as they are entitled to the protection given to civilians or civilian objects under the international law of armed conflict.'

29   *Ibid*. art. 4(c): 'Conscripting or enlisting children under the age of 15 years into armed forces or groups or using them to participate actively in hostilities.'

30   See, for example, WILLIAM SCHABAS, THE UN INTERNATIONAL CRIMINAL TRIBUNALS: THE FORMER YUGOSLAVIA, RWANDA AND SIERRA LEONE, (Cambridge University Press, 2006).

31   Daniel J. Macaluso, *Absolute and Free Pardon: The Effect of the Amnesty Provision in the Lomé Peace Agreement on the Jurisdiction of the Special Court for Sierra Leone*, 27 BROOK. J INT'L L 347, 362 (2002).

these laws was an attempt to ground the Court in the specific circumstances of the conflict, particularly with respect to crimes perpetrated against girls.[32]

Ironically, each of the domestic statutes mentioned predates Sierra Leone's independence from Britain, thus neither truly originates from Sierra Leone.[33] The 1926 Ordinance is described in the SCSL Statute as 'offences relating to the abuse of girls'[34] and is based largely on a British Imperial Statute.[35] The Malicious Damage Act was an English law adopted with other legislation into the jurisdiction of Sierra Leone in the late nineteenth century. Despite having been largely repealed in Britain in the second half of the twentieth century, this law is still in force in Sierra Leone.[36] The inclusion of laws that are largely a reflection of British legal norms of the nineteenth and early twentieth century is not an effective acknowledgement of the particular circumstances of present day Sierra Leone.

Further, while the Court is often described as a legal hybrid because of the inclusion of these two bodies of law, it is a *de jure* rather than a *de facto* hybrid. The prosecutor chose not to include crimes charged under article 5 of the Statute in the indictments; therefore, none of the indicted individuals have been accused of crimes under Sierra Leonean law. While there may be pragmatic reasons not to include violations of domestic law in the indictments (for example, potential complications that might arise out of the amnesty provisions of the Lomé Peace Agreement), it begs the question as to the inclusion of domestic offences in the first place. As some academics have noted, the legal hybrid nature of the Court is therefore largely rhetorical, 'an attempt to create a sense of innovation in the dispensation of international justice' though in practice the Court legally functions purely within the confines of public international law.[37]

A hybrid tribunal might potentially have generated wider and positive impacts on law reform and strengthened the domestic legal system. But through the complete dismissal of domestic law in the work of the Special Court, these opportunities have been lost. Bringing charges under the domestic laws and the subsequent investigations and evidence gathering that would have been required might have provided useful experience for local investigators and prosecutors that could have been applied to their future work within the domestic legal system. More attention given to the actual content of this domestic legislation might have also precipitated domestic legal reform processes, particularly with respect to legislation affecting the rights of women.[38]

---

[32]   *Ibid.* 363–6.

[33]   See Sara Kendall, *Beyond Justice: Figuring Jurisdiction at the Special Court for Sierra Leone*: *'Hybrid Law' and the Place of Jurisdiction* 16 (University of California at Berkeley, Department of Rhetoric, 2008) (forthcoming PhD, manuscript on file with author).

[34]   SCSL Statute, art. 5(a). The Act contains offences with antiquated language such as 'Abduction of a girl for immoral purposes, contrary to section 12', language which presupposes that abduction of a girl for 'moral purposes' would not be a crime. See SCSL Statute, art. 5(a)(iii).

[35]   Kendall, note 33 *supra*, citing Colonial Reports, Annual No. 1359, Sierra Leone, Report for 1926, 13.

[36]   *Ibid.* citing BANKOLE THOMPSON, THE CRIMINAL LAW OF SIERRA LEONE 149 (Lanham, University Press of America, 1999).

[37]   *Ibid.*

[38]   Despite the lack of impact from the SCSL, on 14 June 2007, the Sierra Leone Parliament passed three landmark 'gender bills' into law covering domestic violence, registration of customary marriage and the devolution of estates. See the Domestic Violence Act, No. 20 of 2007, being an Act to suppress domestic violence, to provide protection for the victims of domestic violence and to provide

Thirdly, a successful challenge by the Special Court to the validity of the Lomé Agreement amnesty provision relating to domestic crimes could have had a significant impact on the potential prosecution, within the legal law system, of perpetrators of crimes committed during the conflict. This could have played an important role complementary to the work of the Special Court: allowing for more prosecutions and reduced criticism directed towards the SC as to the small number of individuals indicted. Additionally, some application and interpretation of these domestic laws in the judgments of the Special Court would have provided legal precedent applicable within the domestic legal system; particularly important in a country where the last reported case was from 1972.

Temporal Jurisdiction

Even though the conflict began in 1991, the temporal jurisdiction of the SCSL runs from 30 November 1996, the date of the Abidjan Accord.[39] This truncated timeframe leaves out the formational years of the RUF and the NPRC regime. This timeframe is covered by the amnesty of the Lomé Agreement, namely crimes committed prior to July 1999. However, article 10 of the SCSL Statute states: 'An amnesty granted to any persons falling within the jurisdiction of the Special Court in respect of the crimes referred to in articles 2 to 4 of the present Statute shall not be a bar to prosecution.'[40]

Amnesties in International Law

Not surprisingly, the conflict between the granting of amnesty in the Lomé Agreement and the negation of that amnesty in the SCSL Statute formed the basis of a pre-trial motion by the accused challenging the assertion of jurisdiction by the Court over crimes committed prior to July 1999. In discussing the limits of amnesties in international law,[41] the Appeals Chamber first considered whether the SCSL had jurisdiction and the inherent power to review treaty provisions of the Statute or the Agreement on the grounds that they were unlawful.[42] The Appeals Chamber held that it was not vested with powers to declare statutory provisions of its own constitution unlawful.[43] This conclusion effectively dismissed the motion. However,

---

for other related matters; and the Devolution of Estates Act, No. 21 of 2007, being an Act to provide for surviving spouses, children, parents, relatives and other dependants of testate and intestate persons and to provide for other related matters, amending the Christian Marriage Act, the Muslim Marriage Act and the Administration of Estates Act. These are available at www.sierra-leone.org/laws.html.

[39] *Report of the Secretary-General on the Establishment of a Special Court for Sierra Leone*, note 22 *supra*, para. 27, states that this date was chosen because 'the choice of 30 November 1996 would have the benefit of putting the Sierra Leone conflict in perspective without unnecessarily extending the temporal jurisdiction of the Special Court'.

[40] SCSL Statute, art. 10.

[41] *Prosecutor* v. *Morris Kallon and Brima Bazzy Kamara,* Case Nos SCSL-2004-15-PT and SCSL-2004-16-PT, Decision on Challenge to Jurisdiction: Lomé Accord Amnesty, Appeals Chamber, 13 March 2004 (hereinafter 'Lomé Decision').

[42] *Ibid.* paras 61–5.

[43] *Ibid.* para. 61. This is in contradiction to the approach taken by the ICTY. As stated by Meisenburg: 'This finding departs from the *Tadić* jurisdiction decision of the ICTY Appeals Chamber. The Appeals judges of the SCSL argued that the ICTY and the SCSL were of a different nature, as the former was directly established by a Security Council resolution. Although the *Tadić* Decision was

the Appeals Chamber went on to state further that the crimes enumerated in articles 2 to 4 of the SCSL Statute were international crimes which could be prosecuted under the principle of universality.[44] Amnesties granted by Sierra Leone therefore could not cover crimes under international law, as such crimes were subject to universal jurisdiction,[45] and could therefore be prosecuted by other national and international authorities who would not be bound by that amnesty.

This decision is generally regarded as important for the development of international criminal law as it was the first decision by an international court to state that amnesty provisions are no bar to prosecuting international crimes.[46] However, the decision is also disappointing, as the Appeals Chamber chose not to examine the validity of amnesties in the domestic legal system of the state that granted that amnesty. Such a determination would have potentially had a significant impact on the national legal system, where the prosecution of crimes under domestic law covered by the Lomé Agreement is generally considered impossible.[47] Coupled with the Prosecutor's decision not to exercise his power to prosecute crimes under domestic law, the Special Court missed two key opportunities to have a broader impact on the national legal system.

Personal Jurisdiction

The personal jurisdiction of the SCSL is limited to persons 'who bear the greatest responsibility for serious violations of international humanitarian law and Sierra Leonean law committed in the territory of Sierra Leone since 30 November 1996'.[48] The 2000 *Report of the Secretary-General on the Establishment of a Special Court for Sierra Leone* had initially suggested the more general language of 'persons most responsible'.[49] According to the Secretary-General, this broader language would permit the prosecution of 'others in command authority down the chain of command' who could be regarded as 'most responsible' judging by the severity of the crime or its massive scale.[50] In the end, the Statute employs the most specific language of 'greatest responsibility'.[51]

---

highly controversial at the time, most authors acknowledged the fact that the ICTY was honestly willing to examine its own legality and the legality of provisions of its Statute.' See Simon M. Meisenberg, *Legality of Amnesties in International Humanitarian Law: The Lomé Decision of the Special Court for Sierra Leone*, 86 IRRC 837, 843 (2004).

[44]   *Lomé Decision*, note 41 *supra*, paras 68 and 70.

[45]   *Ibid.* para. 71.

[46]   Meisenberg, note 43 *supra*, at 843, noting that the ICTY in its *Furundžija* judgment limited its discussion on the validity of amnesties under international law in relationship to the crime of torture.

[47]   See, for example, Micaela Frulli, *The Special Court for Sierra Leone: Some Preliminary Comments*, 11 EJIL 857, 859 (2000).

[48]   SCSL Statute, art. 1. This is unlike the two UN tribunals for the Former Yugoslavia and Rwanda whose broad mandates require them to try 'persons responsible' for crimes under international law.

[49]   *Report of the Secretary-General on the Establishment of a Special Court for Sierra Leone*, note 22 *supra*, para. 29.

[50]   *Ibid.* para. 30.

[51]   For an interesting discussion see Carla del Ponte, *Prosecuting the Individuals Bearing the Highest Level of Responsibility*, 2(2) J INT'L CRIM. L 516 (June 2004).

ORGANS OF THE COURT

There are four main organs of the SCSL: Chambers, the Office of the Prosecutor, the Registry, and the Defence Office. It is through the composition of each of these organs that the hybrid nature of the Court can be more accurately characterized as an 'institutional' hybrid manifested through its personnel, rather than as a 'legal' hybrid criminal tribunal through an application of law.

Chambers

The SCSL is comprised of two Trial Chambers with three judges each and one Appeals Chamber with five judges. Article 12(1) of the SCSL Statute provides for a system of dual appointment of the judges. Each Trial Chamber is comprised of two international judges appointed by the UN Secretary-General and one appointed by the government of Sierra Leone. The Appeals Chamber is comprised of three judges appointed by the Secretary-General and two chosen by the Sierra Leone government. This structure attempts to preserve the input of the Sierra Leone government in judicial appointments, with the possibility of a blend of international and Sierra Leonean personnel. In practice, however, the government has not always appointed Sierra Leonean judges to these positions.

Office of the Prosecutor

The SCSL Statute provides for an Office of the Prosecutor (OTP) which 'acts independently as a special organ of the Special Court'.[52] The OTP functions autonomously with the assistance of its own evidence unit, criminal intelligence unit, legal operations section, witness management unit and an investigations section made up of international and national investigators. The Prosecutor is appointed by the Secretary-General and the Deputy-Prosecutor is appointed by the government of Sierra Leone, though this position is explicitly designated for a Sierra Leonean.[53] Efforts to ensure that Sierra Leoneans are well represented in professional positions in the OTP have been successful, with more than one-third of those posts filled by national staff.[54]

Historical narrative presented by the prosecution

Ultimately, an impartial historical record of the factual basis for each case should be established by the judgment of the Trial Chamber. In practice, however, the prosecution presents its case first and thus sets out the factual and contextual framework within which the evidence unfolds. Creating a narrative that Sierra Leoneans can identify with can give the SCSL greater

---

52 SCSL Statute, art. 15.
53 Special Court Agreement 2002 (Ratification) Act, 2002, art. (2). This Act implements the Special Court within the domestic jurisdiction of Sierra Leone. When the government of Sierra Leone chose a UK national for the Deputy Prosecutor position, it had to amend this Act in order to allow for their selection. This caused significant resentment from the Sierra Leone Bar Association and had a negative effect on the perceptions of the institutional hybrid nature of the Court.
54 International Centre for Transitional Justice (ICTJ), *The Special Court for Sierra Leone Under Scrutiny* 21 (March 2006).

domestic legitimacy. It also helps avoid the perception that the court is an international initiative imposing 'Western' perspectives, particularly of a conflict generally reduced to African barbarism.[55] Thus, while the prosecution has a dual responsibility to ensure that the narrative unfolds within the parameters of its mandate to meet its evidentiary burden, it also has the possibility of contributing to the creation of an impartial record for Sierra Leoneans.

A number of commentators expressed concerns over the Court's first Prosecutor's interpretation of the conflict, described by some as 'un-nuanced' and 'politically skewed'.[56] The International Crisis Group noted that a number of concerns had arisen about the way 'the prosecutor has interpreted Sierra Leone's conflict in various statements, the procedures surrounding some indictments, and in particular, the perceived Americanisation of the Court'.[57] In the Prosecutor's view, he had 'never seen a more black and white situation in my life, of good versus evil'.[58] Over-simplification of the conflict and disregard for other factors such as poverty, corruption and endemic mismanagement of state institutions risked alienating the Court from many Sierra Leoneans.

As the SCSL will produce a very limited number of judgments, creating an impartial record of events will be an important contribution of the Court to the population of Sierra Leone. The bench can only produce an authoritative record on the basis of the evidence presented in Court, and the prosecution's over-simplification of the conflict cannot assist in this task. While the subsequent Prosecutors have not employed such language or expressed similar views on the conflict, much of the contextual evidence for the trials had been presented prior to their appointments. The trial of Charles Taylor, which was the last trial to begin before the Special Court, presented a fresh opportunity for the prosecution to present a less rhetorical, emotive approach and a more fact-driven analysis of the conflict, which could ultimately create a more meaningful historical record of key events and players in the conflict.

The Registry

The Registry is responsible for those functions which support the SCSL process as a whole, including Finance, Personnel and Facilities Management. The Registry is also responsible for the Court Management section (which includes Court Records, the Library and the Language and Stenography Unit), Witness and Victims Support Unit (WVS), and the Detention Facility.

---

[55]   See, for example, Robert Kaplan, *The Coming Anarchy in Africa*, ATLANTIC MONTHLY, February 1994: 'A pre-modern formlessness governs the battlefield, evoking the wars in medieval Europe prior to the 1648 Peace of Westphalia, which ushered in the era of organized nation-states.'

[56]   James Cockayne, *The Fraying Shoestring: Rethinking Hybrid War Crimes Tribunals*, 28 FORDHAM INT'L LJ, 616, 654 (2005).

[57]   International Crisis Group, *The Special Court for Sierra Leone: Promises and Pitfalls of a New Model*, Africa Briefing No. 16 (August 4, 2003) stating 'in the eyes of many in Sierra Leone, it [the Court] suffers from a crisis of legitimacy'.

[58]   David Crane, Special Court for Sierra Leone Prosecutor Press Conference, Freetown (18 March 2003).

Defence Office and the Role of Local Counsel

The establishment of a Defence Office at the SCSL has been described as 'one of the most significant innovations in international justice … and one that can provide a major contribution to ensuring the rights of the accused are upheld'.[59] Although it technically falls under the authority of the Registry, the Defence Office is described by the Court as a 'fourth pillar' to the structure of international courts. It is meant to function as a counterbalance to the Office of the Prosecutor and a means of addressing an identified failing in the functioning of the ad hoc tribunals, where the rights of the accused were not adequately protected through the tribunals' institutional structures.

The Defence Office is comprised of the Principal Defender, a Deputy Principal Defender, and 'duty counsels' for each of the CDF, AFRC and RUF cases. In theory, this 'fourth pillar' is mean to provide legal and administrative support to the individual defence teams, as well as advocacy for general issues affecting the defence more broadly. In practice, however, the interests of the Defence Office and individual defence teams are not always harmonized, and the nature of this relationship needs to be more clearly determined in order to better serve the needs of the accused and of their counsel. Unlike the Office of the Prosecutor, the Defence Office is not animated by a unified objective, such as securing convictions against the accused parties. Instead, it must contend with competing interests, including its mandate to advocate broadly on behalf of the defence while overseeing the performance and budgets of individual defence teams. This dual role of advocacy and oversight sometimes places the 'fourth pillar' in an unclear relationship vis-à-vis individual defence teams, and it should be addressed explicitly in future efforts to set up an independent Defence Office.

As the hybrid nature of the SCSL manifests itself predominately through the composition of its personnel, one of the potential advantages of this model is the extent to which local lawyers can be involved in every aspect of the judicial process, including work for the prosecution, the defence and the bench. The prevalence of 'local' Sierra Leonean lawyers, particularly on the defence side, provides the most direct interface between the Special Court and the national legal system. Local lawyers offer local knowledge as well as a more nuanced understanding of the conflict and of Sierra Leonean culture, and their participation lends a greater sense of legitimacy to the process. It can also potentially serve as a way of increasing the skill-base of the local legal profession and opportunities for professional enhancement.

If it is carefully implemented and prioritized, the hybrid model can provide a valuable opportunity for exchanging skills between international and local lawyers and has the potential to strengthen the domestic legal system. This can occur through training programmes, through mutual educational seminars on relevant areas of law, and through informal mentoring on individual defence teams, which must be comprised of both Sierra Leonean and international counsel according to the SCSL Statute. However, this skills exchange has received minimal attention from the Court. While the model of the hybrid criminal tribunal provides for the possibility of leaving a meaningful legacy in terms of strengthening the national legal structures, there does not appear to be tangible change in the domestic legal system as a direct result of the Special Court's presence in Freetown.

---

[59] Human Rights Watch, Bringing Justice: the Special Court for Sierra Leone 22 (vol. 16, No. 8(A), September 2004).

The participation of local counsel was one way of connecting the SCSL more closely into the national context, though in practice the Special Court was more often used as a forum for advancing local political interests. In the CDF trial, several defence attorneys, and indeed the accused themselves, had long-standing political connections with the former SLPP President, Ahmed Tejan Kabbah. It may be that the domestic legacy of the court is less a matter of skills transfer and more a continuation of domestic politics in a new forum.

However, perhaps one of the important impacts that the Special Court has had in the domestic legal and political sphere was the decision of some Sierra Leonean lawyers, including Special Court defence counsel affiliated to the SLPP, to bring a case before the Sierra Leone Supreme Court alleging that Kabbah's establishment of the SCSL violated the Sierra Leone Constitution. The basis for this argument was that the Special Court altered the structure of judicial power within the country without the constitutional requirement of a referendum.[60] In a country where political allegiances run deep, the case represented an 'important phase in the shifting network of personal and political alliances that make up Sierra Leone national politics'.[61] The impact of the trials on the domestic political and legal realm was thus not entirely according to the design of the Special Court's architects, but rather a function of processes operating beyond the work of the Court itself.

TRIALS

The Prosecutor adopted a narrow interpretation of the mandate to prosecute only 'those who bear the greatest responsibility'. The Prosecutor's application of this phrase has been controversial, both because of the limited number of indictments that were issued and for its focus upon formal titles rather than upon an analysis of a particular individual's actual actions. In exercising his prosecutorial discretion, the Prosecutor indicted only 13 individuals associated with three factions of the conflict: the RUF, the AFRC and the CDF. In doing so he went beyond the Sierra Leonean President's original request to hold trials only for the RUF. Charles Taylor, the former President of Liberia, was also indicted. Of these 13 individuals, two of the highest-level RUF commanders have died[62] and the location of AFRC leader Johnny Paul Koroma remains unknown.

The indictment of these 13 individuals underscores the Prosecutor's interpretation of his mandate, which associates 'greatest responsibility' with those individuals who appeared at the top of a hierarchal command structure. An alternative approach would be to pursue those who bear the greatest responsibility for some of the conflict's most brutal atrocities even if they are formally below the top-level commanders. Such an approach would have accorded more with the Secretary-General's recommendation that those 'most responsible' be judged by the severity of the crime or its massive scale.[63] The Prosecutor chose to focus instead on

---

    60   Section 108(3) of the Sierra Leone Constitution (1991) requires that amendments to specified sections of the Constitution, including the judicial powers of the Republic, occur through referendum.
    61   Cockayne, note 56 *supra*, at 649.
    62   Fonday Sankoh, the alleged leader of the RUF, died in the custody of the Special Court. Sam 'Mosquito' Bockarie, another alleged high level RUF perpetrator, was killed allegedly under orders from Charles Taylor.
    63   *Report of the Secretary-General on the Establishment of a Special Court for Sierra Leone*, note 22 *supra*, para. 29.

an individual's position within the hierarchal command structure, and this approach is reflected in the indictments, which charge all indictees on the basis of superior criminal responsibility (perhaps better known as command responsibility) for the crimes charged pursuant to article 6(3) of the SCSL Statute.

While such an approach may have the virtue of simplicity, it fails to take into account some of the fundamental characteristics of the conflict, namely the involvement of a number of fighting factions which were fluid in composition, with complex and nuanced command relationships within them. The conflict also involved three factions with internal structures that did not necessarily reflect traditional military structures. For example, two of the accused in the CDF trial held the positions of 'Director of War' and 'High Priest', neither of which exists in traditional military structures.

This prosecutorial approach also creates an 'impunity gap', leaving a number of individuals who are arguably responsible for a significant number of the atrocities committed in the conflict either at large or working for the prosecution as so-called 'insider witnesses'. Insider witnesses are critical mainly in establishing command responsibility. With their intimate knowledge of operations, their leadership roles and high-level involvement in perpetuating crimes, they are often in the best position to testify as to the actual structure and control of an armed group. From a legal perspective, proving individual responsibility pursuant to command responsibility is a considerable challenge in light of the existing jurisprudence of the ICTR and the ICTY.[64] This jurisprudence requires the prosecution to establish three elements as the basis of command responsibility: the existence of a superior-subordinate relationship in which the superior has effective control over the subordinates directly committing the crime; that the superior knew or had reason to know that the criminal act was about to be or had been committed; and that the superior failed to take the necessary and reasonable measures to prevent the criminal act or punish the perpetrator thereof.[65] There have been relatively few convictions of individuals on the basis of command responsibility, largely because demonstrating the legal requirement of 'effective control' by a commander over his subordinates is very difficult.[66]

In light of the limited timeframe for its operation, limited budgets and limited mandate, the prosecution began its work with an uphill battle in having to demonstrate that these three factions operated within some formalized command structure. This also heightened the need to rely on numerous insider witnesses. The use of such witnesses, which the court's first Prosecutor referred to as 'dancing with the devil',[67] raises questions as to the extent to which

---

[64]   Beatrice I. Bonafé, *Finding a Proper Role for Command Responsibility*, 5 J International Criminal Justice 599, 602 (2007), noting that (as of April 2007) of the 99 accused persons who had faced trial before the ICTY and the ICTR, 54 were prosecuted on a theory of command responsibility and only 10 had been convicted.

[65]   *Ibid.*

[66]   *Ibid.* at 609 making the point that there have been many cases at the ad hoc tribunals where military commanders have been found not guilty under command responsibility because, despite their authority in an established chain of command, their 'effective control' over their subordinates could not be established beyond a reasonable doubt.

[67]   David Crane, *Dancing with the Devil: Prosecuting West Africa's Warlords: Building Initial Prosecutorial Strategy for an International Tribunal After Third World Armed Conflicts,* 37 Case W Res. J Int'l L 1 (2005): 'The devils we dance with everyday are not only the criminal actors being prosecuted, but the peripheral players who have been involved in this decade long tragedy.' See also, David M. Crane, Chapter 17 in this *Handbook*.

the Court is perceived as actually addressing impunity in Sierra Leone. It also raises questions as to whether there should have been more prosecutorial restraint on the extent of its reliance of such insiders to prove its case, given the fine line between indictees and insider witnesses, particularly in light of the overarching objective of promoting accountability through international criminal tribunals.[68]

Charles Taylor

The indictment against Charles Taylor was the first to be issued by the Prosecutor, and it was issued while he was still the President of Liberia. Taylor faces an 11-count indictment for crimes against humanity, violations of common article 3 of the Geneva Conventions and of Additional Protocol II, and other serious violations of international humanitarian law. Taylor is charged on the basis of his alleged role as a major backer of the RUF, his links with senior leaders in the RUF and the AFRC, and responsibility for Liberian forces fighting in support of the Sierra Leonean rebels.[69]

Taylor evaded trial in Nigeria in the years following his indictment. After his transfer to the SCSL, security issues surrounding Taylor's high profile case caused proceedings against him to be relocated to the premises of the ICC in The Hague,[70] redirecting significant attention and resources from the court's base in Freetown. The verdict of history regarding the legitimacy of the Special Court for Sierra Leone will be largely based on the outcome of the proceedings against Charles Taylor and much of the other work of the Court could potentially be overshadowed by this trial.

Sovereign immunity

While Taylor was still in exile in Nigeria, and therefore not yet in the protective custody of the Court, he filed a pre-trial motion challenging the Court's jurisdiction. This motion argued that Taylor was immune from its jurisdiction, as he was a Head of State at the time the indictment and the warrant for his arrest were issued.

In dismissing the motion, the Appeals Chamber noted that the motion turned largely on the legal status of the Court. A review of the constitutive instruments of the Court led the Appeals Chambers to conclude the Special Court is not a national court of Sierra Leone and is not part of the judicial system of Sierra Leone exercising the state's judicial powers. Rather the Appeals Chamber gave the decisive characterization of the Court as a 'truly international tribunal'.[71]

---

68   For example, Issa Sesay, the first accused in the RUF case, was first considered as an insider witness before he was indicted.

69   Charles Taylor's trial began on 7 January 2008, more than four and a half years after he was indicted.

70   Security Council Resolution 1688, 16 June 2006, authorized Taylor to be tried by the SCSL on the premises of the International Criminal Court in The Hague.

71   *Prosecutor* v. *Charles Ghankay Taylor*, Case No. SCSL-2003-01, Decision on Immunity from Jurisdiction, Appeals Chamber, 31 May 2004, para. 38. The characterization of the Court does not depend on whether the Prosecutor draws strictly from international law in the indictments. In her amicus curiae submission to the proceedings, Prof. Diane Orentlicher stated that 'although a court of mixed composition applying an amalgam of international and national law, the Special Court has the hallmarks of an international tribunal'. Submissions of the *Amicus Curiae* on Head of State Immunity in

The Appeals Chamber then reviewed article 6(2) of the SCSL Statute which states that 'the official position of any accused persons, whether as Head of State or Government or as a responsible government official, shall not relieve such person of criminal responsibility nor mitigate punishment'. After considering international jurisprudence, the Appeals Chamber held that it is now well established that the sovereign equality of states does not prevent a Head of State from being prosecuted before an international criminal tribunal or court.[72] Therefore, the fact that Taylor was a Head of State when the criminal proceedings were initiated against him is not a bar to his prosecution by the Court.

CDF, RUF and AFRC Trials

In addition to the trial of Charles Taylor, the remaining nine indictees were tried in three joint trials for each of the main factions in the conflict. Samuel Hinga Norman, the former Deputy Minister of Defence who coordinated the actions of the CDF while President Kabbah was in exile in Guinea, Moinina Fofana, who held the position of Director of War, and Allieu Kondewa, the 'High Priest' of the CDF, were indicted and tried in a joint CDF trial. Issa Sesay, Augustine Gbao and Morris Kallon, all allegedly senior commanders within the RUF, were tried in the RUF trial. Alex Tamba Brima, Ibrahim Bazzy Kamara and Santigie Borbor Kanu, all members of the AFRC Supreme Council[73] were tried in the AFRC joint trial.

The CDF indictees were charged with eight counts. The RUF and AFRC indictees faced an 18- and a 14-count indictment respectively. All indictments charge the accused with crimes against humanity, violations of common article 3 of the Geneva Conventions and of Additional Protocol II, and other serious violations of international humanitarian law.[74] The additional four counts in the RUF indictment pertain to the abduction of 300 UNAMSIL peace-keepers in 2000. Reflecting the close relationship between the two factions, particularly after the coup in 1997, both the RUF and AFRC indictments refer to nearly identical periods of time and geographical locations.

Joint Criminal Enterprise

While the SCSL Statute does not explicitly set it out as a mode of criminal liability,[75] the

---

Prosecutor v. *Charles Ghankay Taylor,* Case No. SCSL-2003-01, Appeals Chamber, 31 May 2004, 19. The Chamber held in another decision that the Court was 'an international tribunal exercising its jurisdiction in an entirely international sphere and not within the system of the national courts of Sierra Leone'. *Prosecutor* v. *Kallon, Norman, Kamara,* Case No. SCSL-04-14-PT-034, Decision on Constitutionality and Lack of Jurisdiction, 13 March 2004, para. 80.

[72]   *Prosecutor* v. *Charles Ghankay Taylor,* Decision on Immunity from Jurisdiction, note 71 *supra,* para. 53.

[73]   The Supreme Council was the highest political authority of the AFRC.

[74]   The final amendment indictment was a 14-count indictment. See *Prosecutor* v. *Brima et al.,* Case No. SCSL-04-16-PT, Further Amended Consolidated Indictment, 18 February 2005 (hereinafter 'AFRC Indictment'), and *Prosecutor* v. *Sesay et al.,* Case No. SCSL-2004-15-PT, Corrected Amended Consolidated Indicted, 2 August 2006 (hereinafter 'RUF Indictment').

[75]   It is only through a very liberal interpretation of art. 6(1) of the SCSL Statute that joint criminal enterprise as a form of criminal liability can be found. Article 6(1) states: 'A person who planned, instigated, ordered, committed or otherwise aided and abetted in the planning, preparation or execution of a crime referred to in articles 2 to 4 of the present Statute shall be individually responsible for the crime.'

prosecution's case in all the trials alleges a joint criminal enterprise (JCE), 'a common plan, purpose or design' to 'gain and exercise political power and control over the territory of Sierra Leone', particularly the diamond mining areas, that were allegedly shared by the RUF and the AFRC.[76] In a clear link to its case against Charles Taylor, which also alleges a JCE, the indictments in the RUF and AFRC cases state that 'the natural resources of Sierra Leone, in particular the diamonds, were to be provided to persons outside Sierra Leone in return for assistance in carrying out the joint criminal enterprise'.[77]

The prosecution over-simplified the nature of the conflict by relying upon JCE as a mode of liability, and this approach was rejected in the first judgment rendered by Special Court Trial Chamber II. Three categories of joint criminal enterprise have been identified in the jurisprudence of the international tribunals.[78] Regardless of the category, that jurisprudence clarifies that one of the basic elements is that the alleged 'common purpose' must itself be a crime under the relevant Statute.[79] In the initial judgment issued by the SCSL in the AFRC case, Trial Chamber II rejected aspects of the prosecution's case that relied on the JCE theory. Its judgment concluded that the common purpose of the enterprise in the form pled by the prosecution was not a crime within the Special Court's jurisdiction.[80] In addition to noting that gaining and exercising political power was not an inherently criminal activity, the Trial Chamber further stated that it was not possible to charge the *forseeability* of international crimes in a common purpose that is not inherently criminal.[81] According to the Chamber, the fundamental question was 'whether the *agreement* involved international crimes *at the inception* of the JCE'. The Chamber held that in this instance it did not.[82] This finding was over-turned by the Appeals Chamber, which stretched the JCE theory of liability even further, stating that 'although the objective of gaining and exercising political power and control over the territory of Sierra Leone may not be a crime under the Statute, the actions contemplated as a means to achieve that objective are crimes within the Statute'.[83]

CDF Trial and Balancing Court Mandates

The CDF indictment includes eight counts primarily consisting of war crimes and crimes against humanity. Charging members of the CDF with a joint criminal enterprise, and indeed indicting the CDF members in the first place, was controversial within Sierra Leone, as the CDF was widely regarded by the Sierra Leonean public as a resistance force against the

---

[76]   AFRC Indictment, note 74 *supra*, para. 33.

[77]   *Ibid.*

[78]   The three categories are described as basic, systemic and extended: *Prosecutor* v. *Tadić*, Case No. IT-94-I-A, Judgment, 15 July 1999, paras 196, 202, 204 (hereinafter 'Tadić Appeals Judgment').

[79]   *Ibid.* para. 227; *Prosecutor* v. *Fofana and Kondewa*, Case No. SCSL-04-14-T-785A, Judgment, 2 August 2007, para. 214.

[80]   *Prosecutor* v. *Brima et al.*, Case No. SCSL-04-16-T, Judgment, 20 June 2007, paras 61–8 (hereinafter 'AFRC Judgment').

[81]   *Ibid.* para. 70.

[82]   This question still seems not to have been settled as a matter of international criminal law. See, for example, *Prosecutor* v. *Brdjanin*, Case No. IT-99-36-A, Judgment, Appeals Chamber, 3 April 2007, para. 390.

[83]   *Prosecutor* v. *Brima et al.*, Case No. SCSL-2004-16-A, Appeals Chamber Judgment, 22 February 2008, para. 70 (hereinafter 'AFRC Appeal Judgment').

rebels.[84] Further, the original request by President Kabbah to the United Nations specifically requested assistance to set up a court to try members of the RUF. Though it is generally accepted that the vast majority of the atrocities committed during the war were committed by the RUF and the AFRC,[85] it is also clear that members of the CDF perpetrated a number of crimes. The first accused, Samuel Hinga Norman, was regarded by many Sierra Leoneans as a hero for having played a decisive role in restoring the Kabbah government to power through his work in mobilizing and coordinating the traditional Kamajor hunting societies to resist rebel forces. Norman was the Interior Minister in the Kabbah government and was viewed as a strong potential political opponent of the Vice-President at the time of his indictment and arrest in 2003. His political status only heightened the controversy surrounding his indictment. He remained a popular figure throughout the trial proceedings and remained so up to his death in 2007 following complications from surgery while awaiting judgment.

The indictment of the CDF leaders politicized the SCSL in the eyes of many Sierra Leoneans. For other Sierra Leoneans, however, it validated the Court's work. For example, following the arrest of Chief Norman, the National Chairman of the War-affected Amputees Association said:

> We are very pleased with actions taken by the Special Court ... We are the symbol of why this Court was created. We are the exhibits. Nothing will replace what we have lost. We know that the Special Court is on the victims' side and will make sure that this country is never again under attack.[86]

Despite its purely international legal status, as affirmed by the Court's own appellate chamber, the Special Court for Sierra Leone reflects and reproduces relationships within the domestic political sphere. Whether considering the role of local counsel, relationships between the indicted parties and the current power elite, or the exercise of prosecutorial discretion in indicting pro-government forces, political factors play a substantial role in the practices of the Special Court. The issue of whether the President of Sierra Leone could be compelled to testify before the Special Court was one such instance that revealed deeper political stakes.

Subpoena motion of President Kabbah

During the defence phase of the CDF trial, defense counsel requested President Kabbah to give testimony for the accused. In doing so, the role of the President during the war and the extent of his knowledge and control of the activities of the CDF was brought into the foreground. In their submissions, defense counsel argued that Kabbah had unique knowledge of the command structure of the CDF and would be able to assist in determining whether their clients in fact bore the 'greatest responsibility' for the alleged crimes.

As the Rules of Evidence and Procedure give only limited guidance regarding compulsory testimony, the Trial Chamber effectively devised its own test setting out the standard for the

---

[84]   ICTJ Report, note 54 *supra*, at 38.

[85]   TRC Final Report, note 2 *supra*, vol. 2, ch. 2, *Findings*, para. 106: 'The RUF was the primary violator of human rights in the conflict. The AFRC was responsible for the second largest number of violations. The Sierra Leone Army (SLA) was the third biggest violator, followed by the Civil Defence Forces (CDF).'

[86]   Quoted in Cockayne, note 56 *supra*, at 642.

issuance of a subpoena, and then found that the defense had failed to fulfill the requirements of the test. In dismissing the motion, the Trial Chamber stated that the standard to be met for the issuance of a subpoena was that the testimony was necessary for purposes of investigation or preparation or conduct of trial. The Trial Chamber determined that the defense failed to identify with sufficient specificity how the testimony would materially assist the case of the accused.[87] This was affirmed on appeal.[88] The decision received much public attention in Sierra Leone, as it could be interpreted as signaling that the President was effectively above the law.

One Trial Chamber judge actually advanced this claim in a separate concurring opinion. Justice Itoe argued that the President enjoyed sovereign immunity, and on that basis he was not required to appear as a witness. Because this view cannot be reconciled with the jurisprudence of the Court that a Head of State (Taylor) could be indicted by the SCSL, it left many in Sierra Leone with the perception that the decision was based on fundamentally political considerations rather than legal ones.

The CDF indictment, the trial, and the attempted subpoena of the President all threatened to undermine the way the SCSL is perceived by the Sierra Leonean public. The CDF trial and the indictment of CDF members also highlights fundamental tensions as to the primary purpose of the Court: is it to help to restore peace and to address security concerns domestically or is it to pursue accountability according to its international mandate, regardless of the domestic political consequences? While these objectives are not necessarily incompatible, the indictment of CDF members generated substantial criticism of the court within Sierra Leone, which was compounded by the Court's refusal to issue a subpoena to President Kabbah.[89]

ADVANCES AND RETREATS IN INTERNATIONAL CRIMINAL LAW

The jurisprudence of the Special Court has addressed a number of unique legal issues. Given the nature of the conflict, it is understandable that the Trial and Appeals Chambers would consider novel points of international law. Yet it remains to be seen whether other international or 'internationalized' courts will draw upon these decisions in advancing their own jurisprudence.

Child Soldiers

The pervasive use of child soldiers throughout the conflict by all factions led to the inclusion of article 4(c) of the SCSL Statute, which gives the Court power to prosecute individuals for

---

[87]   *Prosecutor v. Norman et al.,* Case No. SCSL-04-14-T, Decision on Motions by Moinina Fofana and Sam Hinga Norman for the Issuance of a *Subpoena ad Testificandum* to H.E. Alhaji Dr Ahmad Tejan Kabbah, President of the Republic of Sierra Leone, 13 June 2006.

[88]   *Prosecutor v. Norman et al.,* Case No. SCSL-04-14-T, Decision on Interlocutory Appeals Against Trial Chamber Decision Refusing to Subpoena the President of Sierra Leone, 11 September 2006.

[89]   The same Trial Chamber subsequently issued a subpoena to then former President Kabbah to appear as a witness in the RUF trial on behalf of the first accused. See *Prosecutor v. Sesay et al.,* Case No. SCSL-04-15-T, Written Reasoned Decision on Motion for Issuance of a Subpoena to H.E. Dr Ahmad Tejan Kabbah, Former President of the Republic of Sierra Leone, 30 June 2008.

'conscripting or enlisting children under the age of 15 years into armed forces or groups using them to participate actively in hostilities'. As this is the first time that an international criminal court has attempted to prosecute individuals for the recruitment and use of child soldiers, the defence contested it as a violation of the fundamental principle of *nullum crimen sine lege*, the principle of non-retroactivity. The burden was thus upon the prosecution to establish that child recruitment was recognized as a crime entailing individual criminal responsibility under customary international law at the time of the acts alleged in the indictments against the accused, which in this case date back to November 1996.

The defense argued that while Additional Protocol II to the Geneva Convention of 1977 and the Convention of the Rights of the Child may have created an obligation on the part of states to refrain from recruiting child soldiers, these instruments did not criminalize such activity. The defense further argued that although the 1998 Rome Statute of the International Criminal Court criminalizes child recruitment, it does not codify customary international law in doing so. However, the majority of the Appeals Chamber agreed with the prosecution's argument that based on the number of states that made the practice of child recruitment illegal under their domestic law, and subsequent international conventions addressing child recruitment, it was clear that child recruitment had crystallized as a crime under customary international law prior to November 1996.[90] On that basis, the Prosecutor proceeded on these charges in the three cases of the CDF, RUF and AFRC.

The decision was lauded by many as a significant advancement towards ending the use of child soldiers and bringing to account those who recruit or use children in conflict. A strong dissenting opinion opined that the reasoning of the majority of the Appeals Chamber failed to distinguish between the 'question of whether and when particular conduct becomes criminal … from the question of whether it should be'. The dissent noted that the UN Secretary-General originally proposed that the SCSL have jurisdiction over the more precise crime of 'abduction and forced recruitment of children under the age of 15 years for the purpose of using them to participate actively in hostilities'[91] as this was clearly a war crime by November 1996. Notwithstanding this proposal, the offence in article 4(c) of the SCSL Statute was changed to the much broader crime of 'conscripting, enlisting or using children in hostilities'. Rather than following the principle of strict legality, the majority of the Appeals Chamber appears to have concluded that under customary international law, the criminality of forced recruitment and abduction of children could reasonably be extended, by 1996, to the conscripting or enlisting of children.

Convictions on child soldiers

The AFRC judgment of the SCSL marks the first time that an international tribunal has considered and issued a verdict on the charge of conscription, enlistment and use of child soldiers as a crime under international law. The judgment confirmed that children were actively recruited into the AFRC through the primary method of abduction,[92] described by

---

90   *Prosecutor* v. *Norman*, Case No. SCSL-2004-14-AR72(E), Decision on Preliminary Motion based on Lack of Jurisdiction (Child Recruitment), 31 May 2004, para. 54.

91   *Ibid.* Dissenting Opinion of Justice Robertson, 31 May 2004, para. 4.

92   This finding was based on testimony both of former child soldiers and 'insider' witnesses who gave evidence either of their own abduction or of children who were abducted and then recruited as 'small boy units' or 'SBUs'.

the Court as a 'particularly egregious form of conscription', though a legal linkage between abduction and the recruitment of child soldiers is absent. Trial Chamber II also took a very broad approach to the term 'use', including all forms of labor utilized to assist the war effort. This included using children to guard diamond mines, to carry rice and other foodstuffs, and to participate in military training,

However, in the RUF judgment Trial Chamber I did distinguish between those activities that should be characterized as active participation in hostilities from those that should not. The accused were convicted of using children under 15 to participate in combat operations, to guard military objectives, to perpetrate crimes against civilians, and to be spies and body-guards.[93]

In the CDF judgment, one of the accused, Allieu Kondewa, was also convicted of enlist-ing child soldiers. Kondewa had the position of 'High Priest' for the CDF and was seen as having mystic powers, including the ability to 'immunize' Kamajors from bullets and to administer potions protecting them as they went into battle. He also carried out 'initiation' ceremonies whereby individuals joined the CDF. In holding Kondewa guilty of enlisting child soldiers, the Trial Chamber found that by initiating a child, albeit one who was already a part of the CDF, he had performed an act analogous to enlisting. Such reasoning effectively makes enlistment a crime that can happen repeatedly and in stages through various actions and by various individuals regardless of the fact that the initial crime of recruiting a child into a fighting faction has already occurred.[94]

The Special Court had a golden opportunity to make a significant contribution to the jurisprudence on the criminality of enlisting, conscripting or using child soldiers. In practice, however, the Court's interpretation and application of the law on this crime has been very broad and inconsistent, making it difficult to identify with any clarity the specific content of the crime.

Forced Marriage and Sexual Violence

Sexual violence crimes were widespread throughout the conflict. Women and girls were targeted by all factions and suffered abductions, were raped, were forced into sexual slavery and endured acts of great sexual violence.[95] The UN Secretary-General reported that sexual violence against women and girls was one of the most egregious practices committed during the decade-long conflict.[96]

As a result, the SCSL Statute has a gender-specific mandate. The Statute requires the Court to prosecute 'those bearing the greatest responsibility' for crimes within its jurisdiction, including acts of sexual violence. Article 2(g) of the SCSL Statute requires it to prosecute 'rape, sexual slavery, enforced prostitution, forced pregnancy and any other form of sexual

---

[93]   *Prosecutor* v. *Sesay et al.*, Case No. SCSL-04-15-T, Judgment, 2 March 2009, paras 1710–48.

[94]   The Appeals Chamber reversed this finding, noting that the child had already been enlisted before being intiatied, *Prosecutor* v. *Fofana and Kondewa*, Case No. SCSL-04-14-A, Appeal Judgment, 28 May 2008 (hereinafter 'CDF Appeal Judgment'), para. 145.

[95]   See, for example, Human Rights Watch, *We'll Kill You if You Cry': Sexual Violence In the Sierra Leone Conflict* (vol. 15, No 1(A), January 2003).

[96]   *Report of the Secretary-General on the Establishment of a Special Court for Sierra Leone*, note 22 *supra*, para. 12.

violence' as a crime against humanity; article 3(e) requires the Court to prosecute 'outrages upon personal dignity, in particular humiliating and degrading treatment, rape, enforced pregnancy, and any form of indecent assault' as a violation of common article 3 of the Geneva Conventions of 1949 and Additional Protocol II.

The SCSL Statute also directs the Prosecutor to pay special attention to gender-based violence in its investigations and staff hires. Article 15(4) of the Statute states:

> Given the nature of the crimes committed, and the particular sensitivities of girls, young women and children victims of rape, sexual assault, abduction and slavery of all kinds, due consideration should be given in the appointment of staff to the employment of prosecutors and investigators experienced in gender-related crimes and juvenile justice.

The emphasis placed on sexual violence offences in the Court's Statute has not always had the desired impact on its implementation and application by the Office of the Prosecutor and the Trial Chambers.

The indictments in the AFRC and RUF trials include numerous counts for alleged sexual violence, noting that '[w]idespread sexual violence committed against civilian women and girls included brutal rapes, often by multiple rapists, and forced marriages'.[97] The indictments set out a number of acts of alleged sexual violence, including abductions, using women as sex slaves, and forced marriage.[98]

The inclusion of forced marriage, charged as a crime against humanity in the indictment, reflects an innovation on the part of the prosecution extending beyond existing international jurisprudence. This charge reflected the common practice of soldiers and rebels of taking young women as their 'wives' and keeping them as domestic and sexual slaves. The prosecution stated that the factual evidence demonstrated that what women were subjected to exceeded sexual slavery. In many instances these crimes could be characterized as forced marriage, otherwise referred to in Sierra Leone as the 'bush wife' phenomenon. This factual distinction resulted in the prosecution requesting an amendment to the RUF and AFRC indictments to include forced marriage as a crime against humanity.[99]

In the AFRC trial, the three accused were convicted for gender-based crimes against humanity – rape, sexual slavery and inhumane acts (forced marriage) – as well as for the war crime of outrages upon personal dignity. The Appeals Chamber ruled that forced marriage could be a crime against humanity under the rubric of 'other inhumane acts', noting that the crime of forced marriage is not exclusively, or even predominantly, sexual and as such is not encompassed in the crime of sexual slavery.[100]

The decision to include forced marriage in the indictment as a crime against humanity was a positive and progressive step[101] representing a further recognition that gender crimes are

---

[97] AFRC Indictment, note 74 *supra*, para. 51.

[98] *Ibid.* paras 52–7.

[99] *Prosecutor* v. *Brima et al.*, Case No. SCSL-04-16-PT, Decision on Prosecution Request for Leave to Amend the Indictment, 6 May 2004. On 17 May 2004, six indictees were arraigned on new charges of 'other inhumane acts' relating to forced marriage.

[100] This reversed the findings of the Trial Chamber which over-simplified the crimes and viewed forced marriage primarily as a sexual crime alongside rape, sexual slavery and other forms of sexual violence, AFRC Judgment, note 80 *supra*, paras 711–13.

[101] This builds on the jurisprudence of the ICTY. See, for example, *Kunarac*, Case No. IT-96-23-

not limited to rape and sexual violence. It is an encouraging development for international criminal law that the factual distinction between sexual slavery and forced marriage was recognized by the Appeals Chamber.

Absence of Sexual Violence Evidence in CDF Trial

The main perpetrators of sexual violence, including sexual slavery, were the rebel forces of the RUF, the AFRC and the West Side Boys, a splinter group of the AFRC.[102] Sexual violence was committed less frequently by the CDF, perhaps due to the CDF's internal rule forbidding sexual intercourse before going to battle. This rule was apparently based on their belief that sexual abstinence preserves the power and potency of Kamajors. Some of this internal discipline was lost, however, as the CDF was formalized and gained more responsibility for national security. It remains true, however, that cases of sexual violence perpetrated by the CDF were less frequently documented.

As a result, the prosecution did not have sufficient evidence of sexual violence at the time of issuing its indictments for the CDF accused. This underlines some of the specific challenges involved in investigating such sensitive crimes in a post-conflict context. Despite the fact that the Court's own Statute recognizes the importance of addressing crimes of sexual violence, a pre-trial request to add charges of sexual violence was denied by the Trial Chamber. This request was denied primarily on the basis that it would prejudice the rights of the accused because the additions had not been brought in a timely fashion. The judges thought that granting leave to add sexual violence charges at that point, even though the trial had not yet begun, would amount to 'creating exceptions' for gender offences.[103] Despite precedents from the ad hoc tribunals permitting amendments to the indictment even after the trial had started,[104] the Chamber seemed to prioritize the responsibility of the prosecution to respect the fair trial rights of the accused over both the importance that gender crimes occupy in international criminal justice and the specific mandate of the Special Court to address those crimes.

This decision was further compounded by the subsequent refusal of the Trial Chamber to hear any testimony of sexual violence or gender crimes as evidence of 'physical violence and mental suffering'. Again this conclusion is inconsistent with the jurisprudence of other international tribunals, which have held that sexual violence can fall within the definition of 'other inhumane acts' or 'outrages upon personal dignity'.[105] According to the reasoning of the majority of the Trial Chamber, sexual violence crimes 'constitute part of a single, integrated, continuous transaction or *res gestae*'.[106] On this basis, most evidence by female witnesses of

---

PT, where a conviction was entered for enslavement as a crime against humanity involving rape, treatment of girls as private property and forced performance of household chores.

[102]   See generally, TRC Final Report, note 2 *supra*, vol. 3b, ch. 3, *Women and the Armed Conflict.*

[103]   *Prosecutor* v. *Norman et al.,* Case No. SCSL-04-14, Decision on Prosecution Request for Leave to Amend the Indictment, 20 May 2004.

[104]   *Prosecutor* v. *Akayesu,* Case No. ICTR-946-4-T, Judgment, 2 September 1998, permitting the amendment of the indictment to include charges of sexual violence five months into trial, as noted in Sara Kendall and Michelle Staggs, *Silencing Sexual Violence: Recent Developments in the CDF Case at the Special Court for Sierra Leone,* UC Berkeley War Crimes Studies Center, 5 (July 2005).

[105]   *Ibid.*

[106]   Oral ruling of testimony of Special Court Witness TF2-187, 1 June 2005, Majority Decision (Boutet J dissenting) delivered by Judge Thompson.

anything remotely deemed sexual was prohibited. For example, evidence of a miscarriage was excluded on the basis that it was inseparable from the rape that caused it. Evidence by a witness about making a complaint of rape to one of the accused was excluded. Evidence of women who were taken as Kamajor wives was excluded on the basis that it *might* lead to evidence of forced marriage.[107] In what has been described as 'a disturbing setback to international criminal law', evidence of amputations, beatings and imprisonments was accepted as evidence of physical violence and mental suffering, whereas rape and sexual violence was not.[108]

EXPEDITIOUS TRIALS?

The hybrid model of the SCSL was intended to expedite the trial process, addressing one of the main criticisms of the ad hoc tribunals. The Court began functioning in 2002 and was originally expected to function for approximately three years. More recent projections anticipate that trials and appeals for all cases will be completed in 2011, more than triple the time initially predicted. While initial delays in the trial proceedings were to be expected, the early pace of trials was remarkably slow and continued throughout the trial phase. The trial phase of the AFRC case took two years and five months and the CDF trial phase was completed in three years and two months. The RUF trial began on 5 July 2004, and judgment was released some four years and eight months later. These timelines do not include the appeal process.

The failure to expedite trials can be attributed to a number of factors, none of which point to deficiencies in the hybrid model of justice itself. The SCSL judges play a central role in managing the pace of the trial proceedings to ensure they are completed in a reasonable period of time and without compromising the rights of the accused. In practice, substantial delays have resulted from a lack of judicial management of the trial proceedings combined with inefficient judicial practices.[109] The length of the indictments, both in terms of the number of counts charged (from eight to 18) and the number of geographic areas covered, has also meant longer investigations and more witnesses. Also slowing things down was the Prosecutor's decision to charge each count broadly under both article 6(1), which provides for individual criminal responsibility through committing, ordering, instigating or aiding and abetting; and article 6(3), which provides for individual criminal responsibility on the basis of superior (or command) responsibility. Attempts to allege joint criminal enterprise as a further mode of criminal liability caused yet more delays. The combined effect of all the above factors made it impossible for the Court to complete trials within the initially anticipated timeframes.

---

107   November 2004 Transcript of Proceedings, 54 line 15.
108   *Prosecutor* v. *Norman et al.,* Case No. SCSL-04-14, Reasoned Majority Decision on Prosecution Motion for a Ruling on the Admissibility of Evidence, 24 May 2005 (released 23 June 2005), para. 19(iii)(b), in which the majority of the bench reasoned that 'other inhumane acts' could only be interpreted to cover acts of 'a non-sexual nature' and that sexual violence must be charged specifically and separately under the indictment. For a full report on the absence of sexual violence in the CDF case see Kendall and Staggs, note 104 *supra.* The Appeal Chamber did find that the 'Trial Chamber erred in denying a hearing of evidence for acts of sexual violence' but this does not change the fact that the trial record contains no evidence of sexual violence, CDF Appeal Judgment, note 94 *supra*, para.150.
109   See, for example, ICTJ Report, note 54 *supra*, at 20.

This experience highlights the need for criminal tribunals, hybrid or otherwise, to issue focused and specific indictments and not to fixate upon what some argue is their broader implicit mandate to create a full historical narrative of the conflict. This is particularly true in situations where another body, such as a Truth Commission, has been established for that purpose, as was the case in Sierra Leone. It also highlights the need to appoint professional judges with experience in criminal law who are committed to ensuring that proceedings recognize the rights of the accused, including the right to a fair and expeditious trial.

TRUTH AND RECONCILIATION COMMISSION

Sierra Leone is in the enviable position of having both a domestic Truth and Reconciliation Commission (TRC) and a special internationalized criminal court to assist the transitional justice process. The former does so by establishing an impartial record of the conflict and its historical roots. The latter institution is intended to end the impunity of those alleged to bear the 'greatest responsibility' for the crimes that were perpetrated. While these two institutions were established separately, it was suggested by the initial UN Planning Mission on the Establishment of the Special Court that the two institutions should remain independent, but should cooperate to set priorities.[110] Their strained interactions highlight the challenges each faced to achieving its stated mandate.

Initially, there were fears that the establishment of the SCSL would discourage both the disarmament process and the willingness of potential witnesses to testify before the TRC.[111] These concerns were reduced when the Special Court's Prosecutor announced that he would not use TRC testimony. Rather, the Special Court and the TRC would work together to 'fight impunity'.[112]

The relationship turned sour when the TRC requested access to Special Court detainees in order to conduct its public hearings. The request was denied by the Court on the grounds that the TRC's proposed hearings were an 'uncontrolled environment' which might create 'unpredictable trouble'.[113] While some of the Court's detainees ultimately gained limited access to the TRC process, the decision of the Court effectively ended any possible spirit of cooperation or mutual respect between the two institutions.

---

[110]   *Report of the Planning Mission on the Establishment of the Special Court for Sierra Leone*, annexed to Letter dated 6 March 2002 from the Secretary-General addressed to the President of the Security Council, UN Doc. S/2002/246 (8 March 2002), paras. 48–56.

[111]   See generally, Abdul Tejan-Cole, The Complementary and Conflicting Relationship Between the Special Court for Sierra Leone and the Truth and Reconciliation Commission, 6 YALE HUM. RTS AND DEV. LJ 139 (2003) and specifically, *Report of the Security Council Mission to Sierra Leone*, UN Doc. S/2000/992 (16 October 2000), para. 49, referring to 'the negative impact of the establishment and jurisdiction of the Court on the minds of ex-combatants who could be more reluctant to come forward to disarm for fear of prosecution'.

[112]   Special Court for Sierra Leone, Office of the Prosecutor, Press Release, *TRC Chairman and Special Court Prosecutor Join Hands to Fight Impunity*, 10 December 2002.

[113]   *Prosecutor* v. *Norman*, Case No. SCSL-2003-08-PT, Decision on Appeal by the TRC and Chief Samuel Hinga Norman JP against the Decision of his Lordship, Mr Justice Bankole Thompson Delivered on 30 October 2003 to Deny the TRC's Request to Hold a Public Hearing with Samuel Hinga Norman JP, 28 November 2003, paras 26, 30.

When the TRC issued its Final Report in October 2004 it was highly critical of the Special Court, stating:

> Sierra Leone, with its two institutions of transitional justice in operation at the same time … had the opportunity to offer the world a unique framework in moving from conflict to peace. Sadly, this opportunity was not seized. The two bodies had little contact and when they intersected at the operational level, the relationship was a troubled one … The Commission's ability to create a forum of exchange between victims and perpetrators was retarded by the presence of the Special Court … The Commission finds that the 'Practice Direction' formulated by the Registry of the Special Court to regulate contact between the Commission and the detainees did not adequately consider the spirit and purpose behind the Commission's mandate … The decision to deny Chief Hinga Norman and the other detainees their right to appear before the Commission represents an impairment, not only to the detainees but also to the people of Sierra Leone.[114]

The TRC Report further suggested that by establishing a Special Court which had partially overturned the validity of the amnesty granted by the Lomé Agreement, the United Nations 'may have sent an unfortunate message to combatants in future wars that they cannot trust peace agreements that contain amnesty clauses'.[115]

While the existence of these two institutions provided an opportunity for them to work together in synergy, in the end the SCSL and the TRC mutually undermined each other. Each institution has promoted divergent views on the best way forward to solidify peace in Sierra Leone. Their conflict also jeopardized efforts to generate one unified, accurate and impartial historical record of exactly what happened in that country.

APPLICATION OF THE HYBRID MODEL IN SIERRA LEONE: AN ASSESSMENT

As the SCSL moves closer to finishing its operations and with more thought being given to its legacy, the success of the Special Court as a transitional justice mechanism will be assessed in increasingly greater detail.

The Special Court is often perceived as nothing more than a scaled-down version of the ad hoc tribunals. In reality, the potential special value of this hybrid model stems from its ability to contextualize the application of transitional justice to the particular needs and circumstances of the population directly affected by the conflict. As a hybrid tribunal, the SCSL should balance adherence to international legal norms and precedents with a localized sensitivity and awareness. This can be done, in part, by recognizing the need for such a tribunal to have a broader impact within the domestic system in which it sits. The location of the Court in the country where the conflict occurred, and the resulting interaction with local political, legal and professional structures, together presented numerous opportunities and challenges for this model of criminal tribunal. This is the context in which to examine the success of this model as applied in Sierra Leone.

The model is sensible for its streamlined approach to exacting justice and for its recognition of the need for international courts to do more than just issue judgments. Rather,

---

114   TRC Final Report, note 2 *supra*, vol. 2, ch. 2, *Findings*, paras 558–73.
115   *Ibid.* para. 562.

international criminal tribunals should actively develop ways in which to interact with and have a positive impact on the broader domestic situation they are dealing with, especially the domestic legal sector. Without this interaction the Special Court, and similar hybrid tribunals, would be merely a limited mechanism for addressing criminal responsibility for a very small number of individuals. In addition to trying cases, these tribunals should address what has been consistently identified as one of the root causes of the conflict, that is, an ineffective and corrupt justice system. The Special Court should not isolate itself from the context in which it operates. Instead, it should improve that context. This is the novel contribution of the hybrid model.

The lessons that have been learned thus far from the SCSL can be divided into two themes: the effectiveness of the Court itself in bringing to justice 'those who bear the greatest responsibility' for the crimes perpetrated during the conflict; and the broader impact of the Court in strengthening the rule of law and the domestic legal system in Sierra Leone.

The mandate of the Special Court is to try 'those who bear the greatest responsibility'. It is in the interpretation and realization of this mandate that the Court has made its most questionable decisions. The Prosecutor indicted 13 individuals in total, of which ten will face trial. In choosing who to indict the Prosecutor must somehow have reasoned that they were the 13 most responsible, but the choice seems fundamentally flawed. The result is that those indictments are spread over a wide geographic area and over a long timeframe. The indictments also rely heavily upon the use of command responsibility and joint criminal enterprise as modes of criminal responsibility, and these can be notably difficult to prove.

The prosecution's approach has created considerable time and resource pressures but all focused on relatively few trials. When those trials have been completed and the Special Court has been dissolved, many of those responsible for serious crimes will be left untried, possibly perpetuating an 'impunity gap' in Sierra Leone. This leaves open the question of whether smaller-scale trials over a wider web of individuals might have better served the objectives of the court.

The broader impact of the court has yet to be determined, but its work thus far has already indicated some of the limits of its effect on the local context. Despite the efforts of an SCSL office dedicated solely to court outreach, the proceedings are not widely attended by Sierra Leoneans. From the symbolic reference to Sierra Leonean law in the SCSL Statute, to the possibility of using some domestic procedures under the Court's Rules, it is clear that elements of the domestic legal system are celebrated in theory but largely excluded in practice. Local counsel appear to move between domestic legal practice and their work at the Special Court with little overlap between the two legal worlds, and it appears unlikely that the decisions issuing from the Court will be used in domestic criminal cases.

Despite these ongoing challenges and limitations, the animating principles behind this model of hybrid justice offer valuable insights for future international tribunals. It is important for any international court to settle the specific case and thereby advance the development of international jurisprudence. But more can be done in terms of using those courts to address local conditions and institutional deficiencies as well. It remains to be seen how well the growing body of international law, and the increasingly professionalized body of international legal practitioners, will be able and willing to accommodate local laws, practices and conditions. Hybrid tribunals, such as the Special Court for Sierra Leone, are pioneering the process.

PART IV

DEFENCES AND THE DEVELOPMENT OF INTERNATIONAL FAIR TRIAL STANDARDS AND PROCEDURES

11 Protecting the fair trial rights of the accused in international criminal law: comparison of the International Criminal Court and the military commissions in Guantánamo

David Weissbrodt and Kristin K. Zinsmaster

INTRODUCTION

The United States government has been reluctant to ratify the Rome Statute of the International Criminal Court[1] (ICC) for a number of reasons,[2] including concerns about the absence of fair procedures. Instead of using the ICC for trying individuals who have arguably committed war crimes and other criminal offenses during the War on Terror, the US government has established military commissions to try 'unlawful enemy combatants'.[3] This chapter compares the fairness of the procedures afforded by the ICC and the US military commissions in an effort to examine the larger issue of the fundamental right to a fair trial.[4]

The concept of a fair trial is 'rather amorphous', but included within it are 'several more concrete, clear-cut guarantees', without any of which, fair proceedings are impossible.[5] Specific international fair trial standards have been established in such treaties and instruments as the Universal Declaration of Human Rights,[6] common article 3 of the Geneva

---

[1] Rome Statute of the International Criminal Court, 2187 UNTS 90, entered into force 1 July 2002.

[2] See John B. Bellinger, Legal Advisor, 'The United States and the International Criminal Court: Where We've Been and Where We're Going', Remarks to the DePaul University College of Law, 25 April 2008, available at www.state.gov/s/l/rls/104053.htm (pointing out Congress' early concerns that accused persons would be denied fair trial rights by an international tribunal); Supplemental Appropriations Act for Further Recovery From and Response to Terrorist Attacks on the United States, Pub. L No. 107–206, 116 Stat. 820, 900 (2002) (asserting that the ICC denies 'procedural protections … such as the right to trial by jury').

[3] This phrase is defined by and used in the Military Commissions Act of 2006, 10 USC s. 948a (2007). An 'unlawful enemy combatant' is one 'who has engaged in hostilities or who has purposefully and materially supported hostilities against the United States' or 'a person who before, on or after the date of the enactment of the Military Commissions Act of 2006, has been determined to be an unlawful enemy combatant by a Combatant Status Review Tribunal'.

[4] The US Supreme Court has reaffirmed the availability of *habeas corpus* to raise concerns about the fairness of military commissions. *Boumediene* v. *Bush*, 128 S Ct 2229 (2008).

[5] See generally STEFAN TRESCHEL, HUMAN RIGHTS IN CRIMINAL PROCEEDINGS 86 (2005) (providing an excellent survey of the right to a fair criminal trial).

[6] Universal Declaration of Human Rights, General Assembly Res. 217A (III), UN Doc A/810 (1948), 71 (UDHR).

Conventions,[7] Additional Protocol I of 1977,[8] the Civil and Political Covenant,[9] and the European Convention on Human Rights.[10] The right to a fair trial begins at the moment a government entity initiates the criminal investigation of an individual, 'continues through charge, arrest, preliminary hearings, trial, appeal, other post-conviction review, and punishment'[11] and encompasses such legal safeguards as the right to a speedy trial, including prompt notification of charges; the presumption of innocence; the right to counsel of one's choice; the right to equality of arms; the privilege against self-incrimination; the right to exclusion of evidence adduced by coercion; the right to confront witnesses and evidence, including the right to be present at trial; and the right to appellate review.[12]

The chapter begins with an overview of the ICC and the military commissions, and continues with a comparison of the fair trial rights afforded by each system.

INTERNATIONAL CRIMINAL COURT

Context: Promulgation and Relation to International Law

The foundation for an international criminal court to try those accused of war crimes and similar offenses was laid in the immediate aftermath of the Second World War. The Nuremberg and Tokyo tribunals were established to try alleged Nazi and Pacific war criminals, and international human rights law began to develop a focus on criminal responsibility. This focus, however, was not long-lived; after Nuremberg and related trials under Control Council Law No. 10,[13] proposals for a permanent international criminal court remained dormant in the United Nations for nearly half a century.[14]

---

[7]   See Geneva Convention Relative to the Protection of Civilian Persons in Time of War, 75 UNTS 287, art. 3, entered into force 21 October 1950.

[8]   Protocol Additional to the Geneva Conventions of 12 August 1949 Relating to the Protection of Victims of International Armed Conflicts (Protocol I), 1125 UNTS 3, entered into force 7 December 1978 [hereinafter 'Additional Protocol I'].

[9]   International Covenant on Civil and Political Rights, General Assembly Res. 2200A (XXI), 21 UN GAOR Suat (No. 16) 52, UN Doc. A/6316 (1966), 999 UNTS 171, entered into force 23 March 1976 (ICCPR).

[10]   Convention for the Protection of Human Rights and Fundamental Freedoms, 213 UNTS 222, entered into force 3 September 1953, as amended by Protocols Nos. 3, 5, 8 and 11 which entered into force on 21 September 1970, 20 December 1971, 1 January 1990 and 1 November 1998 respectively (ECHR).

[11]   DAVID WEISSBRODT, THE RIGHT TO A FAIR TRIAL 153 (2001).

[12]   See David Weissbrodt and Andrea W. Templeton, *Fair Trials? The Manual for Military Commissions in Light of Common Article 3 and Other International Law*, 26 MINN. JL INEQUALITY 353, 366–7 (2008).

[13]   The Control Council for Germany, comprised of Britain, France, the Soviet Union and the United States, authorized and carried out the trial of several thousands of cases not pursued by the tribunal at Nuremberg. See Control Council Law No. 10, Punishment of Persons Guilty of War Crimes, Crimes Against Peace and Against Humanity, 20 December 1945, 3 Official Gazette Control Council for Germany 50 (1946).

[14]   For a succinct history of key developments and periods of inactivity in the establishment of the Court, see International Criminal Court, *Chronology of the International Criminal Court*, available at www.icc-cpi.int/about/ataglance/chronology.html.

In 1990, the UN General Assembly requested that the International Law Commission (ILC) reopen its consideration of an international criminal court. Momentum behind the initiative for a permanent forum was strong, with supporters perhaps galvanized by the brutal nature of the conflicts in Yugoslavia and Rwanda,[15] as well as the establishment of ad hoc criminal tribunals for those two situations. In 1994, the ILC submitted a draft statute, and after three and a half years of review, diplomats from 150 nations convened in Rome to finalize the treaty that would formally create the ICC. The ICC Statute was adopted on 17 July 1998,[16] and came into force when it was ratified by the requisite 60 nations in 2002. There are now 106 states parties to the ICC Statute.[17]

The ICC is a permanent tribunal with its headquarters in The Hague. It has jurisdiction over genocide, crimes against humanity and war crimes – the 'most serious crimes of international concern'.[18] The court was established to prosecute these offenses to ensure that victims obtain public recognition and perhaps compensation, and also to deter future human rights abuses.[19] While the court is not a body of the United Nations, the two are formally related in that the Security Council may initiate or defer ICC investigations.[20] Investigations may also be initiated by states parties or by the Prosecutor. The ICC is governed by the principle of complementarity; it does not replace functioning judicial systems, but is an alternative where a functioning judiciary is unavailable or where a government refuses to prosecute crimes within its jurisdiction.[21]

Genocide is defined by the ICC Statute as killing or causing serious bodily or mental harm to a member of a national, ethnical, racial or religious group with the intent of destroying that group in whole or in part.[22] Crimes against humanity are characterized by a 'widespread or systematic attack directed against any civilian population', including many discrete offenses, such as murder, rape and enforced disappearance. Crimes against humanity must be committed pursuant to a state or organizational policy.[23] War crimes are defined as grave breaches of the Geneva Conventions: serious violations of the customary international law of war, and/or violations of common article 3 in conflicts not of an international nature.[24] The ICC Statute lists several acts which constitute the above breaches, including willful killing, torture and intentionally directing attacks at civilian targets.[25]

---

[15]   See, for example, Milena Sterio, *The Evolution of International Law*, 31 BC INT'L AND COM at L REV. 213, 234 (2008); Coalition for the International Criminal Court, *History of the ICC*, available at www.iccnow.org/?mod=icchistory.

[16]   See ICC Statute.

[17]   For the most current listing of parties to the Statute, see International Criminal Court, *States Parties to the Rome Statute*, available at www.icc-cpi.int/statesparties.html.

[18]   Jerry Fowler, *The Rome Treaty for an International Criminal Court: A Framework for International Justice for Future Generations*, 6 HUM. RTS BRIEF 1 (1998), available at www.wcl.american.edu/hrbrief/06/1fowler.cfm.

[19]   See Martti Koskenniemi, *Between Impunity and Show Trials*, in 6 MAX PLANCK YB UN L 1 (Jochen A. Frowein and Rüdiger Wolfrum eds, 2002).

[20]   See Fowler, note 18 *supra*. When the Security Council initiates an investigation, it is not necessary that the state involved be a party to the Statute.

[21]   See *ibid.*

[22]   ICC Statute, art. 6.

[23]   *Ibid.* art. 7.

[24]   *Ibid.* art. 8.

[25]   *Ibid.* The ICC will also exercise jurisdiction over the crime of aggression once a provision has been set out defining that crime and the Court's jurisdiction over it, pursuant to ICC Statute, art. 5.

The ICC Statute incorporates the fundamental guarantees of the right to fair trial recognized in international law. The Statute thus reflects earlier instruments that establish this right, including the Universal Declaration of Human Rights, the International Covenant on Civil and Political Rights (ICCPR), common article 3 of the Geneva Conventions, Additional Protocol I of 1977, and the European Convention on Human Rights.

The Universal Declaration of Human Rights (UDHR), adopted in 1948, states, in article 10 that: 'Everyone is entitled in full equality to a fair and public hearing by an independent tribunal, in the determination of his rights and obligations and of any criminal charge against him.'[26] Article 11 provides for the presumption of innocence, public trial and the 'guarantees necessary for [one's] defense'. Other safeguards found in the UDHR include, for example, the right to be free from arbitrary arrest and detention (article 9) and the right to be free from torture and other inhuman treatment (article 5).

The ICCPR, adopted in 1966 and entered into force in 1976, further elaborates on and codifies (particularly in articles 14 and 15, but also in articles 9, 6 and 7) the right to a fair trial identified in the UDHR. Article 14 recognizes the right to 'a fair trial and public hearing by a competent, independent and impartial tribunal'.[27] Certain 'minimum guarantees' are also recognized, including the right to be informed of charges in a language one understands; the right to have adequate time and facilities available to prepare a defense; the right to be tried without undue delay in one's presence and with the assistance of counsel of one's choosing; the right to examine all witnesses and to call witnesses of one's own; the right to have the free assistance of an interpreter; and the privilege against self-incrimination.[28] The right to appeal one's conviction is established by article 14.[29] Other fair trial protections scattered throughout the ICCPR include the right to be promptly informed of the reason for one's arrest (article 9), the right not to be deprived of one's life arbitrarily (article 6), and the right to be free from torture (article 7). Human Rights Committee jurisprudence has interpreted the above fair trial provisions to be non-derogable.[30]

Common article 3 of the four Geneva Conventions contains fair trial guarantees in times of non-international armed conflict for both prisoners of war[31] and civilians.[32] It prohibits, in pertinent part, '[t]he passing of sentences and the carrying out of executions without previous judgment pronounced by a regularly constituted court, affording all of the judicial guarantees which are recognized as indispensable by civilized peoples'.[33] The first Additional Protocol to the Geneva Conventions, in its article 75, extends fair trial guarantees in an international armed conflict to all persons, including those arrested for actions relating to the conflict.[34] The guarantees provided include the right to be informed of charges in a language one under-

---

26   UDHR, note 6 *supra*, art. 10.
27   ICCPR, note 9 *supra*, art. 14.
28   *Ibid.* art. 14(3).
29   *Ibid.* art. 14(5).
30   See Human Rights Committee, General Comment 29, States of Emergency (art. 4), UN Doc. CCPR/C/21/Rev.1/Add.11 (2001).
31   See Geneva Convention Relative to the Treatment of Prisoners of War, 75 UNTS 135, art. 3, entered into force 21 October 1950.
32   See Geneva Convention relative to the Protection of Civilian Persons in Time of War, 75 UNTS 287, art. 3, entered into force 21 October 1950.
33   Common article 3, note 7 *supra*, art. 3(1)(d).
34   Additional Protocol I, note 8 *supra*, art. 75.

stands; the right to be presumed innocent; the right to be present at trial; the privilege against self-incrimination; the right to examine and call witnesses; and the right to be advised of judicial remedies upon conviction.[35]

The European Convention on Human Rights (ECHR), adopted in 1950 and entered into force in 1953, protects fair trial procedures principally in article 6. Article 6(1) provides that a person is entitled to a public hearing within a reasonable time by an independent and impartial tribunal.[36] Article 6(2) stipulates that a person charged with a criminal offense shall be presumed innocent until proved guilty,[37] and article 6(3) addresses many of the procedural fair trial rights detailed above, in the context of the other instruments and treaties. In particular, article 6(3) provides that the accused must be promptly informed of charges in a language he understands; must have adequate time and facilities to prepare his defense; be allowed to defend himself or receive legal assistance (free of charge, if the accused cannot afford such services); to examine witnesses against him; and to have free assistance of an interpreter if necessary.[38] The European Court of Human Rights (ECtHR) has developed a considerable jurisprudence interpreting article 6, especially regarding the principles of undue delay and equality of arms.[39]

This review of the international treaties and instruments reveals a well-established pattern of fundamental guarantees. The procedural safeguards deemed necessary to provide a fair trial for the accused appear in all of the above documents, although in slightly different forms, and are substantially reproduced in the ICC Statute.

Fair Trial Guarantees of the ICC Statute

The ICC Statute incorporates fundamental guarantees of the right to fair trial recognized at international law to ensure that in the determination of any charge, a person accused of genocide, crimes against humanity or war crimes receives an impartial, public and fair hearing.

The fair trial rights explicitly protected by the ICC Statute (followed by the article in which each safeguard is found) are the right to prompt information of the reasons for arrest or detention (art. 67); the right to be tried without undue delay (art. 67); the right to be presumed innocent until proved guilty beyond a reasonable doubt (art. 66); the right to counsel of one's choice (arts 55, 67); the privilege against self-incrimination (art. 55); the right to have deemed inadmissible evidence obtained in violation of the Statute (art. 69); the right to have witnesses examined (art. 67); and the right to appeal a conviction (art. 81).

The guarantees found in the ICC Statute provide a great deal of protection for the rights of the accused, similar to other international tribunals, including the bodies that interpret the instruments and treaties discussed above, as well as the ad hoc tribunals for the Former Yugoslavia and Rwanda.

---

[35]   *Ibid.*
[36]   ECHR, note 10 *supra*, art. 6(1).
[37]   *Ibid.* art. 6(2).
[38]   *Ibid.* art. 6(3).
[39]   See, for example, *Moreira de Azevedo* v. *Portugal,* 189 Eur. Ct HR (ser. A) (1990); *Neumeister* v. *Austria,* 1 EHRR 91 (1968); *Schouten and Meldrum* v. *The Netherlands,* 19 EHRR 390 (1994); *Hentrich* v. *France,* 18 EHRR 440 (1994); *Kudla* v. *Poland,* Eur. Ct HR Appl. No. 30210/96 (2000); *LeCompte* v. *Belgium,* 58 Eur. Ct HR (ser. A) (1983).

Current Jurisprudence

The ICC is currently investigating four situations: Darfur, the Democratic Republic of Congo, Uganda and the Central African Republic.[40] In connection with these investigations, eight arrest warrants have been issued, and four arrests made since 2002.[41] The ICC has issued only procedural decisions, but this jurisprudence has interpreted the right to a fair trial to some extent. For example, the Court imposed a stay on the proceedings in *Prosecutor* v. *Thomas Lubanga Dyilo*, finding that non-disclosure of possibly exculpatory evidence on the part of the prosecution constituted a denial of the fair trial protections required by the ICC Statute.[42] The Court has also recognized the importance of having adequate time to prepare one's defense[43] and the importance of maintaining transparency and the public nature of hearings[44] by issuing decisions postponing certain proceedings and unsealing evidentiary documents. Additional case law interpreting fair trial principles comes from the other treaty bodies, including the Human Rights Committee and the European Court of Human Rights.

The Human Rights Committee has considered numerous cases on issues relating to the right to a fair trial, most recently involving allegations of torture. In *Chikunova* v. *Uzbekistan*, the Committee found violations of articles 14 and 7 of the ICCPR. The government, by not responding in a timely manner to allegations of torture on the part of police, failed to ensure that the petitioner's son would be free from torture and not forced to confess guilt.[45] The Committee also held that being provided with a single visit by counsel after two days of detention in a capital case, did not afford 'adequate time … for the preparation of [the accused's] defense',[46] a violation of article 14(3)(b). In *Agabekova* v. *Uzbekistan*, the Committee similarly held that, in the light of the detailed descriptions of inhuman treatment, the state party had failed in its duty to investigate under article 7.[47]

The Committee has interpreted the 'prompt trial' requirement by asserting that trials must proceed 'without undue delay', both in the first instance and on appeal.[48] In *Tcholatch* v. *Canada*, the Committee found that a delay of three years between placing a child in protec-

---

[40]   See International Criminal Court, *Situations and Cases* available at www.icc-cpi.int/cases.html.

[41]   See *ibid.*

[42]   See International Criminal Court, Press Release, *Trial Chamber Imposes a Stay on the Proceedings of the Case Against Thomas Lubanga Dyilo*, 16 June 2008, available at www.icc-cpi.int/press/pressreleases/381.html.

[43]   See, for example, International Criminal Court, Press Release, *Confirmation of Charges Hearing Postponed in the Case Against Germain Katanga and Mathieu Ngudjolo Chui*, 28 April 2008, available at www.icc-cpi.int/press/pressreleases/361.html.

[44]   See, for example, International Criminal Court, Press Release, *Unsealing and Reclassification of Certain Documents in the Case of Prosecutor* v. *Germain Katanga*, 7 November 2007, available at www.icc-cpi.int/press/pressreleases/299.html.

[45]   See *Chikunova* v. *Uzbekistan*, Communication No. 1043/2002, UN Doc. CCPR/C/89/D/1043/2002 (2007).

[46]   ICCPR, note 9 *supra*, art. 14(3)(b).

[47]   See *Agabekova* v. *Uzbekistan*, Communication No. 1071/2002, UN Doc. CCPR/C/89/D/1071/2002 (2007).

[48]   Human Rights Committee, General Comment 13, Article 14 (Twenty-first session, 1984), Compilation of General Comments and General Recommendations Adopted by Human Rights Treaty Bodies, UN Doc. HR\GEN\1\Rev. 1 (1994), 14.

tive custody and trial on the child protection issue was undue.[49] In *Henry and Douglas* v. *Jamaica*, the Committee found that a lapse of 30 months between the petitioner's arrest and trial constituted undue delay in the absence of any justification. It also found excessive the delay of three years and four and a half months between the trial's conclusion from the dismissal of the appeal.[50]

The Human Rights Committee has also interpreted ICCPR, article 4, which identifies certain rights as non-derogable (those rights which cannot be the subject of suspension during periods of emergency). Article 4 does not specify article 14 (the right to a fair trial), but the Committee issued a General Comment in 2001, which stated, 'any trial leading to the imposition of the death penalty during a state of emergency must conform to the provisions of the Covenant, including all the requirements of articles 14 and 15'.[51]

Article 6(1) of the ECHR guarantees the right to trial within a reasonable time in criminal proceedings.[52] Article 5(3) provides that 'everyone arrested or detained … shall be brought promptly before a judge … and shall be entitled to trial within a reasonable time'.[53] The ECtHR has frequently heard cases regarding these speedy trial provisions, and declared in *Moreira de Azevedo* v. *Portugal* that the ECHR 'stresses the importance of administering justice without delays which might jeopardize its effectiveness and credibility'.[54] Scrutiny of the reasonable time requirement begins when 'the situation of the person concerned has been substantially affected as a result of suspicion against him'[55] and lasts until acquittal, dismissal or conviction.[56] The ECtHR said that the reasonableness of the length of proceedings must be assessed in the light of the circumstances of the case, with regard to its complexity, the conduct of the parties, and the authorities dealing with the case.[57] The ECtHR has also found that delay due to a backlog in the legal system constitutes a violation of article 6(1).[58]

The principle of equality of arms between the accused and the prosecutor has also been interpreted by the ECtHR. Under this principle, the ECtHR has examined a number of cases dealing with expert witnesses, finding a lack of equal treatment when an expert appearing for the prosecution had a stronger procedural position than another expert appearing for the defense.[59]

---

[49]   See *Tcholatch* v. *Canada*, Communication No. 1052/2002, UN Doc. CCPR/C/89/D/1052/2002 (2007).

[50]   See *Henry and Douglas* v. *Jamaica*, Communication No. 571/1994, UN Doc. CCPR/C/57/D/571/1994 (1996).

[51]   Human Rights Committee, General Comment 29, States of Emergency (Article 4), UN Doc. CCPR/C/21/Rev. 1/Add.11 (2001).

[52]   ECHR, note 10 *supra*, art. 6(1).

[53]   *Ibid.* art. 5(3).

[54]   *Moreira de Azevedo* v. *Portugal*, 189 Eur. Ct HR (ser. A) (1990).

[55]   *Neumeister* v. *Austria*, 1 EHRR 91 (1968).

[56]   See *Eckle* case, 51 Eur. Ct HR (ser. A)(1982), at 33.

[57]   See *Bucholz* case, 42 Eur. Ct HR (ser. A) (1981).

[58]   See *Hentrich* v. *France*, 18 EHRR 440 (1994).

[59]   See *Bonsich* case, 92 Eur. Ct HR (ser. A) (1985).

MILITARY COMMISSIONS

Context : The War on Terror and the Military Commissions Act of 2006

The US Department of Defense initiated military commissions as authorized by the Military Commissions Act of 2006 (MCA) to try 'unlawful enemy combatants' detained in the course of the War on Terror.[60] The War on Terror encompasses a number of international and non-international conflicts, with the primary conflicts being in Afghanistan and Iraq.[61] Beginning on 7 October 2001, the United States bombed and sent troops to Afghanistan in response to the 11 September 2001 attacks by al Qaeda on the United States.[62] The scope of the War on Terror increased dramatically with the inception of the conflict in Iraq on 20 March 2003, when an international coalition led by the United States invaded Iraq in an effort 'to disarm Iraq of weapons of mass destruction, to end Saddam Hussein's support for terrorism, and to free the Iraqi people'.[63] In both Afghanistan and Iraq, the United States captured and detained enemy combatants; the United States now faces the dilemma of what to do with these detainees.[64] The detention facility at Guantánamo was constructed in a vain effort to deprive detainees of their rights.[65] Top US policy-makers have expressed the view that the facility should be closed, but it is not clear how this can be accomplished. In essence the United States is said to be 'stuck'.[66]

Putting aside for now the argument that 'this war is different' – in other words, the enemy more elusive, the tactics more extreme[67] – the trial procedures to which the detainees should be entitled ultimately should depend upon their status at international law.[68] Taliban prisoners

---

[60]   Military Commissions Act of 2006, 10 USC s. 948a (2007). The MCA is not the government's first attempt at creating military commission jurisdiction. The general power of the President to establish military commissions in appropriate circumstances was recognized in *Hamdi* v. *Rumsfeld*, 542 US 507, 518 (2004). The Supreme Court later found, however, that the first military commissions established in the context of the War on Terror lacked jurisdiction because their 'structure and procedures violated both the Uniform Code of Military Justice (UCMJ) and the Geneva Conventions', *Hamdan* v. *Rumsfeld*, 126 S Ct 2749, 2759 (2006), and because Congress had not expressly authorized the commissions, *Hamdan*, 126 S Ct at 2775. It was after the decision in *Hamdan* that Congress passed the MCA, which provided the requisite congressional authorization and supposedly met the concerns of the court in *Hamdan*. That portion of the MCA which strips the federal courts *habeas corpus* jurisdiction over Guantánamo detainees, however, has since been deemed unconstitutional. *Boumediene* v. *Bush*, 128 S Ct at 2274.

[61]   JOSEPH MARGULIES, GUANTANAMO AND THE ABUSE OF PRESIDENTIAL POWER 3 (2006).

[62]   See *ibid.*

[63]   Radio address, 'President Discusses Beginning of Operation Iraqi Freedom', 22 March 2003, available at www.whitehouse.gov/news/releases/2003/03/20030322/html (transcript of radio address and audio file available on website).

[64]   See JUDGES, TRANSITION, AND HUMAN RIGHTS (John Morison, Kieran McEvoy and Gordon Anthony eds, 2007).

[65]   The Supreme Court held that detainees at Guantánamo Bay *do* possess at least some constitutional rights, thereby removing this so-called rationale for the facility's existence. *Boumediene*, 128 S Ct at 2274.

[66]   William Glaberson, *Detention Camp Remains, but Not Its Rationale*, New York TIMES, 13 June 2008, available at www.nytimes.com/2008/06/13/washington/13gitmo.html?scp=9&sq=Robert %20Gates%20Guantanamo&st=cse.

[67]   See for example, 152 CONG. REC. S10, 243–74, at 10,243 (2006) (statement of Senator Frist).

[68]   See Weissbrodt and Templeton, note 12 *supra*, at 357.

detained during the international armed conflict with Afghanistan qualify as prisoners of war (POWs), and thus should be covered by the Third Geneva Convention,[69] while individuals detained following the close of this conflict were taken in the context of a non-international armed conflict and should be covered under common article 3 of all four Geneva Conventions.[70] Individuals taken during the initial stages of the war in Iraq ought either to be covered under the Third Geneva Convention, if they are POWs,[71] or under the Fourth Geneva Convention, if they are civilians.[72] The United Nations declared the international armed conflict in Iraq to be officially over in 2005,[73] thus those persons detained in the context of the Iraq war after 2005 are covered under common article 3.[74] Those individuals who were initially detained outside of these conflicts, for example, in Bosnia,[75] are now under US control and covered under the ICCPR.[76] Ultimately, however, the precise status assigned to each detainee is irrelevant: the same fair trial guarantees apply to each of the categories above.[77] The treaties and instruments under which any of the detainees fall contain the inter-related fair trial standards which were described in the previous section.

The US government, however, has made the determination that some of the detainees are neither POWs, entitled to a court martial under the Third Geneva Convention, nor are they civilians entitled to a regularly constituted court. Instead, pursuant to a hearing process known as the Combatant Status Review Tribunal (CSRT), almost all detainees have been designated as 'unlawful enemy combatants', and thus subject to prosecution by military commission under the MCA.[78] This new category does not exist under international humanitarian law,[79] and is only justified, in the eyes of its supporters, because the War on Terror is 'different'.[80]

---

[69]   Geneva Convention on POWs, note 31 *supra*, art. 4. Note, however, that this definition assumes the prisoner is part of the Taliban or regular army. The Geneva Convention would not apply to Al Qaeda, or non-combatants, though art. 5 of the Geneva Convention on POWs gives them the same protections. *Ibid*. 140–2.

[70]   Common article 3, note 7 *supra*.

[71]   Geneva Convention on POWs, note 31 *supra*, at 288–90.

[72]   Geneva Convention on Civilians, note 32 *supra*.

[73]   Security Council Res. 1637, 11 November 2005, UN Doc. S/RES/1637 (2005).

[74]   Common article 3, note 7 *supra*, art. 3.

[75]   Extraordinary rendition is one source of detention outside of these conflicts. See, for example, *Boudellaa* v. *Bosnia and Herzegovina*, Case No. CH/02/8679, Decision on Admissibility and Merits, Human Rights Chamber for Bosnia and Herzegovina, 11 October 2002, at 69.

[76]   ICCPR, note 9 *supra*.

[77]   See Weissbrodt and Templeton, note 12 *supra*, at 358–9.

[78]   See US Department of Defence, *Manual for Military Communications,* Part II: Rules for Military Commission, 103(a)(24) (2007), available at http://www.defenselink.mil/pubs/pdfs/The%20Manual%20for%20Military%20Commissions.pdf (hereinafter, 'Manual Rules'). The Manual contains four parts; in this chapter, 'RMC' refers to Part II, Rules for Military Commissions, and 'MCRE' refers to U.S Dept. of Def., Manual for Military Comm'ns, Part III, The Military Commission Rules of Evidence, available at www.defenselink.mil.pubs/pdfs/The%20Manual%20for%20Military%20Commissions.pdf.

[79]   See Weissbrodt and Templeton, note 12 *supra*, at 362–3.

[80]   See 152 Cong. Rec., note 67 *supra*, at 10,243. The term 'enemy combatant' was coined by the US Supreme Court in *Ex parte Quirin*, in the context of the Second World War, 317 US 1, 31 (1942). By labeling the so-called Nazi saboteurs 'enemy combatants', the Court was able to find that the men were not entitled to civilian trials, but would be subject to military commissions. *Quirin*, 317 US at 44. The category does not, however, exist at international law.

Enacted on 17 October 2006, the MCA's specific purpose is 'to try [those] alien unlawful enemy combatants engaged in hostilities against the United States for violations of the law of war and other offenses triable by military commission'.[81] Congress passed the Act as a renewed attempt at convening military commissions – a response to the US Supreme Court's ruling in *Hamdan* v. *Rumsfeld*,[82] where the Court held that the President's initial attempt at trying detainees before military commissions was not authorized either by congressional legislation or the President's war powers.[83] The Secretary of Defense published the *Manual for Military Commissions* of 18 January 2007 ('the Manual'), in accordance with the MCA, to govern the commissions' proceedings. The Manual sets forth guidelines[84] for trials of 'unlawful enemy combatants' at Guantánamo Bay and other US detention sites. Pursuant to these guidelines, prosecutors renewed their effort to charge some detainees and bring them to trial.[85] The prosecutors now face bringing the detainees to justice amidst already prolonged detention, considerable indications that many of the detainees have been severely ill-treated,[86] criticism of the military commissions by the Supreme Court,[87] and international pressure to comply with human rights and international humanitarian law obligations.[88]

Trying the detainees in the War on Terror requires protection of the right to a fair trial for both reputational and legal reasons. The United States considers itself a leader in promoting human rights; to cease protecting fair trial rights would damage this reputation.[89] Furthermore, human rights treaties obligate the United States to guarantee the right to a fair trial. If the United States fails to provide fair trial protections to the detainees, US soldiers captured in future conflicts may be unfairly treated.[90] Practical concerns also weigh in favor of providing fair trial protections at the outset; unfair procedures are unlikely to survive in the long run. Adhering to unfair practices will demand continuous appeals and ultimately waste the time and resources of those persons detained, as well as the courts.

---

[81]   Military Commissions Act of 2006, 10 USC s. 948b (2007).

[82]   126 US 2749 (2006).

[83]   *Ibid.* 2774–5.

[84]   See RMC, note 78 *supra*.

[85]   See for example, William Glaberson, *Court Advances Military Tribunals for Detainees*, NEW YORK TIMES, 25 September 2007, A1 (describing the trial court and appellate decisions in the case of Canadian detainee Omar Ahmed Khadr).

[86]   See generally STEVEN H. MILES, MD, OATH BETRAYED: TORTURE, MEDICAL COMPLICITY AND THE WAR ON TERROR 8–9 (2006) (summarizing and analyzing the information available regarding US interrogation tactics, including ill-treatment, at Guantánamo Bay and elsewhere). See also Jenny S. Martinez, *Process and Substance in the War on Terror* 108 COLUM. L REV 1013, 1073–4 (2008) (providing further documentation and support for the perpetration of ill-treatment on the part of the US government).

[87]   See *Boumediene* v. *Bush*, 128 S Ct 2229 (2008).

[88]   See Theodor Meron, *The Humanization of Humanitarian Law*, 94 AM. J INT'L L 239, 266 (2000) (stating that human rights law should be a part of the interpretation and application of international humanitarian law specifically in the case of 'regularly constituted courts' under common article 3); see also *Testimony of Elisa Massimino: Hearing Before the H. Comm. on Armed Services in the Military Commission Act and the Future of Detention at Guantanamo Bay*, 110th Cong. (2007) (statement of Elisa Massimino, Washington Director, Human Rights First) (discussing the negative effects of the manner and prolonged nature of the Guantánamo Bay detentions).

[89]   See Weissbrodt aand Templeton, note 12 *supra*, at 103.

[90]   *Ibid.*

Fortunately, the MCA mandates that the Manual be interpreted in such a way as to protect fair trial rights.[91] Secretary of Defense Robert Gates demonstrably intended the Manual to comply with common article 3[92] in several places, including the Executive Summary, which states, '[this Manual] is intended to ensure that alien unlawful enemy combatants who are suspected of war crimes and certain other offenses are prosecuted before regularly constituted courts affording all the judicial guarantees which are recognized as indispensable by civilized people'.[93] Of course, simply tracking the language of common article 3 is not sufficient to make the military commissions compliant with that provision or any other standard. Interpreting the Manual in light of the relevant international standards, it does protect certain fair trial rights, but it also contains several provisions which may not afford the procedural safeguards necessary to make the commissions legal under international standards.

Fair Trial Guarantees and Shortfalls of the Military Commissions

The *Manual for Military Commissions* does guarantee several of the fair trial rights necessary to conform to internationally accepted norms, but fails to protect other necessary safeguards. With regard to what the Manual *does* protect, Rules for Military Commissions (RMC), rule 290(e)(5)(A) establishes the proper standard for findings, noting that '[t]he accused must be presumed to be innocent until the accused's guilt is established by legal and competent evidence beyond reasonable doubt'.[94] However, no definition of competent evidence is given in the Manual, which raises concerns, particularly if the evidence is adduced by torture or ill-treatment. RMC rule 910(c) provides substantial protections regarding counsel for the defendant, including the right to be represented by counsel,[95] though that right only applies after the detainee is accused and is not applicable during pre-trial questioning and investigation. Also, the right to counsel may be hindered by restrictions invoked under the national security privilege. Additionally, the Manual partially guarantees the defendant's right not to testify against himself through RMC, rule 910(a)(1), which allows the defendant to plead not guilty.[96]

The more problematic portions of the Manual, with regard to fair trial rights, come in the context of the right to notice, the right to counsel during interrogations, the right to confront witnesses, the right to be present at trial, the right to a public trial, the right to review by a higher court, and the privilege against self-incrimination. RMC, rule 308 addresses a defendant's right

---

[91] See Military Commissions Act of 2006, 10 USC s. 948b (2007) (providing that 'A military commission established under this chapter is a regularly constituted court, affording all the necessary "judicial guarantees which are recognized as indispensable by civilized peoples" for purposes of common Article 3 of the Geneva Conventions.'). The argument that this language is merely a statement of compliance with the Geneva Conventions, advanced by the Military Judge in *United States* v. *Khadr*, is unpersuasive in light of the principle of statutory construction which demands that every word of a statute be read so as not to render it insignificant or superfluous. See *United States* v. *Khadr*, Ruling on Defense Motion to Dismiss for Lack of Jurisdiction for Failure to Comply with Common Article 3 (Military Commission, 2 May 2008) (on file with author); *TRW Inc.* v. *Andrews*, 534 US 19, 31 (2001) (citing *Duncan* v. *Walker*, 533 US 167, 174 (2001)).

[92] RMC, *Executive Summary*, at 1.

[93] *Ibid.*; see common article 3, note 7 *supra*.

[94] See RMC, rule 920(e)(5)(A).

[95] *Ibid.* rule 910(c), Preamble, para. 19(f)(2).

[96] *Ibid.* rule 910(a)(1).

to notice and states that a detainee must be made aware of the charges against him or her 'as soon as practicable'.[97] This language provides a considerable amount of leeway, especially in light of the fact that many detainees in US custody have been held for months or years without charges and without counsel.[98] Furthermore, rule 909(b) presumes that the defendant is mentally capable of standing trial,[99] without taking into account the fact that prolonged detention may in fact diminish that capacity to a great extent.[100]

RMC, rule 701(f), concerning the treatment of classified information for purposes of national security,[101] also raises concerns for fair trial rights. Information becomes classified for the purposes of Military Commissions Rules of Evidence, rule 505(b)(3) through an *in camera* proceeding, which may exclude the request of the counsel for the defendant or may be made *ex parte*, in writing, 'outside the presence of the accused and defense counsel'.[102] National security may also be invoked under RMC, rule 806(b)(2)(a), which authorizes closure of a session to 'protect information the disclosure of which could reasonably be expected to damage national security'.[103] While generally a state possesses the right to exclude the press and public from portions of hearings under exceptional circumstances,[104]

---

[97]   *Ibid.* rule 308.

[98]   See, for example, Andrew Grey, *Guantanamo Trials on Track for Summer: Pentagon*, REUTERS, 28 February 2007, available at www.reuters.com/articlePrint?articleId=USN28169496200 70228; Stephen Labaton, *Court Endorses Curbs on Appeal by U.S. Detainees*, NEW YORK TIMES, 21 February 2007; William Glaberson, *A U.S. Trial by Its Looks, But Only So*, NEW YORK TIMES, 29 July 2008.

[99]   See RMC, rule 909(b).

[100]   See generally Joanna Dingwall, *Unlawful Confinement as a War Crime: The Jurisprudence of the Yugoslav Tribunal and the Common Core of International Humanitarian Law Applicable to Contemporary Armed Conflicts*, 9 J CONFLICT AND SECURITY L 133, 177 (2004) (stating that 'the recognition that isolation may amount to cruel treatment [is] evidence that inclusion of unlawful confinement as a war crime in internal armed conflict has a basis in customary international law').

[101]   See RMC, rule 701(f) ('Classified information shall be protected and is privileged from disclosure if disclosure would be detrimental to the national security. This rule applies to all stages of proceedings in military commissions, including the discovery phase.').

[102]   See MCRE, rule 505(b)(3). While the former chief prosecutor for the military commissions, Morris Davis, defended the Manual rules by arguing that 'the [Military Commissions Act] gives the accused the right to be present for all open sessions of the trial', he neglected to address the denial of an accused's rights at the point where trial procedures are closed. See Morris D. Davis, *In Defense of Guantanamo Bay*, POCKET PART: AN ONLINE COMPANION TO THE YALE LJ 30 (13 August 2007), available at yalelawjournal.org/2007/08/13/davis.html. Mr Davis later changed his mind about the overall fairness of the proceedings. *See* William Glaberson, *Claim of Pressure for Closed Guantanamo Trials*, NEW YORK TIMES, 20 October 2007, available at http://www.nytimes.com/2007/10/20/us/national special3/20gitmo.html.

[103]   See RMC, rule 806(b)(2)(A). This closure includes information regarding 'intelligence or law enforcement sources, methods, or activities'. *Ibid.* Compare William Schabas, *Fair Trials and National Security Evidence*, 4 INT'L COMMENT ON EVIDENCE (2006), available at www.bepress.com/ ice/vol4/iss1/art9 (pointing to the danger of drawing inferences in international criminal trials from state claims to withhold evidence on grounds of national security). The Obama administration supports revised legislation 'incorporating classified information procedures that are more similar to those applicable in federal court, but appropriately modified for the military commissions context, and to reflect lessons learned in terrorism prosecutions'. Brad Wiegmann aand Mark Martins, Memorandum for the Attorney General and the Secretary of Defense, Detention Policy Task Force 4 (20 July 2009).

[104]   See ICCPR, note 9 *supra*, art. 14 (allowing for the exclusion of the press and public for reasons of 'public order (*ordre public*) or national security in a democratic society'); see also *United States ex*

these provisions, if taken to the extreme, threaten a defendant's rights to confront the witnesses and evidence, to be present at trial, and to have a public trial.

The military commissions also lack adequate protections for the right to appeal, as well as adequate *habeas corpus* procedures.[105] The personal jurisdiction of a military commission extends to those deemed 'alien unlawful enemy combatants', which status is determined at the CSRT hearing[106] described above. The CSRT finding is thus deemed dispositive for purposes of jurisdiction. In theory, a defendant will already have had the opportunity to challenge his or her detention prior to coming before the military commission. In fact, however, the defendant's status is questionable, as the CSRT process inherently violates the right to a fair trial and *habeas corpus*.[107] With regard to appellate review, the MCA does seem to guarantee the right to review by the US Court of Appeals for the District of Colombia Circuit, and, if necessary, the Supreme Court.[108] Under RMC, rule 1201, however, the Court of Military Commission Review performs the initial review of decisions by the commissions.[109] Unfortunately, RMC, rule 1201 then provides that '[n]o relief may be granted unless an error of law prejudiced a substantial trial right of the accused'.[110] This limitation may restrict appeals to issues of law and would not permit challenges to convictions for insufficient evidence to support the conviction or review of sentences.

The treatment by military commissions of evidence procured through coercive methods also raises fair trial concerns. The definition of coercion may include methods that rise to the level of cruel, inhuman and degrading treatment, forbidden by all of the international treaties and instruments discussed above.[111] The Manual, while it rightly excludes statements

---

rel. Knauff v. *Shaughnessy*, 338 US 537, 551 (1950) (Jackson J, dissenting) ('In the name of security the police state justifies its arbitrary oppressions on evidence that is secret'). For more on accommodating national security via *in camera* inspection and the exclusion of the general public see Geneva Convention on POWs, note 31 *supra*, art. 105 ('[E]xceptionally ... held *in camera* in the interest of State security'); ICC Statute, art. 68(2) ('[T]o protect victims and witnesses or an accused, [the court may] conduct any part of the proceedings in camera.'), art. 72 (regarding protection of national security information).

105   See Joan Fitzpatrick, *Jurisdiction of Military Commissions and the Ambiguous War on Terrorism*, 96 AM. J INT'L L 345, n. 2 (2002) (outlining issues regarding the legality of the appeals process under the 13 November 2002 order negating the possibility of a review of the outcome of military commission proceedings); *Boumediene*, note 87 *supra*, 128 S Ct at 2240 (finding that the MCA operates as an unconstitutional suspension of the writ of *habeas corpus*).

106   RMC, rule 202(b), *Discussion*. At least one military commission, however, has questioned a defendant's classification. See *United States* v. *Khadr*, Order on Jurisdiction (US CM Comm'n, 4 June 2007), available at http://www.defenselink.mil/news/jun2007/khadrJudgesDismissalOrder (June%204).pdf.

107   In determining a detainee's status, the CSRT review asks whether the detainee is an 'alien unlawful enemy combatant' under 10 USC s. 948a(1)(ii). See RMC, rule 202(b), *Discussion*. This is not the correct question under the Geneva Convention on POWs. See Geneva Convention on POWs, note 31 *supra*, arts 4, 5. Further, the CSRT process has been found to 'fall well short of the procedures and adversarial mechanisms that would eliminate the need for *habeas corpus* review'. *Boumediene*, note 87 *supra*, 128 S Ct at 2260.

108   RMC, rule 1205, *Further Review*.

109   *Ibid.* rule 1201.

110   *Ibid.* rule 1201(d)(1). The Obama administration has announced its support for legislation 'reforming the appellate process to give reviewing courts more authority to correct both legal and factual errors at the trial level'. Wiegmann and Martins, note 103 *supra*, at 4.

111   See Rosemary Pattenden, *Admissibility in Criminal Proceedings of Third Party and Real*

adduced by torture, specifically allows for 'statements in which the degree of coercion is disputed ... if reliable, probative, and the admission would best serve the interests of justice'[112] and 'admission of an accused's allegedly coerced statements if they comport with s. 948r'.[113] In light of the fact that the Bush administration authorized 'coercive' interrogation conduct[114] 'so brutal that it essentially amounts to torture',[115] this provision arguably allows for evidence procured by torture to be admitted at trial. This process not only violates international norms regarding torture and ill-treatment,[116] but also the fair trial right against self-incrimination because a witness from whom such statements are obtained will say whatever he or she believes may stop the infliction of pain – rather than the truth.[117] Such techniques may easily lead to coerced confessions.

Evidence Obtained by Methods Prohibited by UNCAT, 10 INT'L J. EVID. AND PROOF 6 (2006) (examining international standards of what constitutes torture and noting that 'it is a grave crime to extract information from prisoners or civilians by torture or ill-treatment'); see also ICC Statute, art. 8(2)(a)(ii) (declaring that grave breaches of the Geneva Convention include torture or inhuman treatment); Geneva Convention on POWs, note 31 *supra*, arts 3, 17, 130. Human Rights Committee jurisprudence further elucidates the parameters of what constitutes cruel, inhuman and degrading treatment. In *Conteris* v. *Uruguay*, the Human Rights Committee found that a confession obtained only after ill-treatment violated the accused's right not to be compelled to confess guilt under ICCPR, art. 14(3)(g). UN Human Rights Committee, Communication No. 139/1983, UN Doc. A/40/40 (1985), para. 10. Arrested by security police for crimes associated with subverting the constitution, the victim spent three months in *incommunicado* detention. *Ibid.* para. 1.4. Subjected to various forms of torture, he eventually signed a confession. *Ibid.* The Human Rights Committee held that he did not voluntarily sign the confession. *Ibid.* para. 9.2. See also *El-Megreisi* v. *Libyan Arab Jamahiriya*, UN Human Rights Committee, Communication No. 440/1990, UN Doc. CCPR/C/50/D/440/1990 (1994), para 5.4 (holding that the detainee, 'by being subjected to prolonged *incommunicado* detention in an unknown location is the victim of torture and cruel and inhuman treatment, in violation of Articles 7 and 10').

112   RMC, Preamble, para. (1)(g), citing 10 USC s. 948r(b), (c) (2006).

113   RMC, Preamble, para. (1)(h)(3), citing 10 USC s. 949(b)(2)(B) (2006).

114   Memorandum from William J. Haynes II, General Counsel, Department of Defence, to Donald Rumsfeld, Secretary of Defence, Counter-Resistance Techniques (27 November 2002), available at www.slate.com/features/whatistorture/LegalMemos.html (memo signed as approved by Secretary of Defense Donald Rumsfeld).

115   See Press Release, *Statement of Senator John McCain on Detainee Amendments on (1) The Army Field Manual and (2) Cruel, Inhumane, Degrading Treatment*, 4 November 2005, available at http://mccain.senate.gov (arguing for the passage of the Detainee Treatment Act because without it the United States 'is the only country in the world that asserts a legal right to engage in cruel and inhumane treatment').

116   See UDHR, note 6 *supra*, art. 5; ICCPR, note 9 *supra*, art. 7; common article 3, note 7 *supra*, at 3(1)(a); ECHR, note 10 *supra*, art. 3; Additional Protocol I, note 8 *supra*, art. 75; ICC Statute, art. 55. Each of these instruments, in much the same language, prohibits 'any form of coercion, duress or threat, or torture or any other form of cruel, inhuman or degrading treatment or punishment'. On 15 May 2009, the Obama administration notified Congress of five rule changes in the military commissions, including a provision that 'statements that have been obtained from detainees using cruel, inhuman and degrading interrogation methods will no longer be admitted as evidence at trial'. Statement of President Barack Obama on Military Commissions, 15 May 2009, available at www.gpoaccess.gov/presdocs/2009/DCPD-200900364.pdf; Wiegmann and Martins, note 103 *supra*, at 4. The Obama administration also supports 'adopting a "voluntariness" standard for the admission of statements of the accused, while taking into account the challenges and realities of the battlefield ' *Ibid.* 4. Congress is considering legislation to implement those changes. *Ibid* 3–4.

117   See Center for Victims of Torture, *Eight Lessons of Torture*, available at www.cvt.org/main.php/Advocacy/TheCampaigntoStopTorture/WhatCVTknowsaboutTorture (explaining why torture does not yield reliable information).

Current Jurisprudence

The military commissions remain a largely untested system. As of August 2009, the commissions have referred charges against 24 defendants.[118] The commissions have made rulings on certain pre-trial motions in some of these cases, but have proceeded to the trial phase in only one. On 18 July 2008, a US District Court and the military commission in Guantánamo rejected all arguments for a stay in the case of Salim Hamdan,[119] and his military commission trial began on 21 July.[120]

The manner in which the military commissions will interpret the MCA and the Manual, and the extent to which fair trial rights will be protected or ignored, remains to be seen. The fact that many of those awaiting trial have been detained for years without a finding of undue delay and may remain detained even if found not guilty, does not bode well for a fair trial in this context.

RIGHT-BY-RIGHT COMPARISON: THE MILITARY COMMISSIONS AND THE ICC

Right to a Speedy Trial

The ICC Statute guarantees the right to a speedy trial in article 67(c), which provides '[in] the determination of any charge, the accused shall be entitled … [t]o be tried without undue delay'.[121] Article 67(a) provides that an accused person must be informed of the charges against him or her 'promptly and in detail'.[122] To provide one example of how the ICC has implemented these requirements, a first appearance hearing in the case of *Prosecutor* v.

---

[118]   See Military Commissions, *Commission Cases*, available at www.defenselink.mil/news/commissions.html.

[119]   See Scott Shane and William Glaberson, *Rulings Clear Military Trial of a Detainee*, New York Times, 18 July 2008.

[120]   See William Glaberson and Eric Lichtblau, *Military Trial Begins for Guantánamo Detainee*, New York Times, 22 July 2008. In March 2007, David Matthew Hicks, an Australian national who had been detained at Guantánamo, plead guilty to one charge of material support to terrorism in the Military Commission under the Military Commissions Act of 2006. As part of the pre-trial agreement, Hick's sentence was limited to nine months confinement. The Military Commission decided a sentence of seven years confinement, although six years and three months were suspended pursuant to the pre-trial agreement. Hicks served his sentence in Australia. US Department of Defense, News Release, *Detainee Convicted of Terrorism Charge at Guantanamo Trial*, 30 March 2007, available at www.defenselink.mil/releases/release.aspx?releaseid=10678. Charges against one other defendant, Ahmed Khalfan Ghailani, were dismissed without prejudice; he was transferred to federal court for trial. William Glaberson, *Detainee to be Transferred to U.S. for Trial*, New York Times, 22 May 2009, A16 ('Pledging trials of terrorism suspects in federal courts "whenever feasible", President Obama said Thursday that for the first time a Guantánamo detainee would be transferred into the United States to face charges.') See also an account of the status of the Guantánamo detainees, Chisun Lee, *An Examination of 33 Gitmo Detainee Lawsuits*, available at www.propublica.org/special/an-examination-of-31-gitmo-detainee-lawsuits-722.

[121]   ICC Statute, art. 67(c).

[122]   *Ibid.* art. 67(a).

Thomas Lubanga Dyilo was held three days after Mr Lubanga Dyilo's arrest by ICC officials.[123] At this hearing, the goal of the Court was to 'ensure that a number of [the accused's] rights have indeed been respected',[124] including the right to be promptly informed of his charges. Other pre-trial matters in this case were dealt with in a continuous manner beginning almost immediately upon Mr Lubanga Dyilo's arrest, and confirmation of his charges began in November 2006.[125] While Mr Lubanga Dyilo was ultimately released prior to trial because of the Trial Chamber's concerns that his rights to a fair trial had been irreconcilably violated,[126] it appears that absent these concerns, he would have been tried on schedule, in 2008.

With regard to the military commissions, the MCA indirectly affords the right to a speedy trial under section 948b(f), which provides 'judicial guarantees which are recognized as indispensable by civilized peoples'[127] under common article 3. The *Manual for Military Commissions*, however, does not protect the accused's right to a speedy trial in practice. For example, there is no timeframe – not even a vague requirement of 'promptness' – within which the accused must be charged.[128] Indeed, many of those detained pursuant to the MCA have been held in custody for upwards of five years and with no trial process initiated.[129] Without any time constraint for charging, the military commissions fail in practice to provide the accused the right to a speedy trial. The fact that a trial must commence 120 days after the accused person is charged[130] fails to address the issue of years-long detentions without counsel and without any outside contact prior to charging, and the 'speed' suggested by this requirement is too little, far too late.

Right to the Presumption of Innocence

The ICC Statute provides, in its article 66(a), that the accused 'shall be presumed innocent until proved guilty before the Court in accordance with applicable law'.[131] That article goes on to provide that proof of guilt is the responsibility of the Prosecutor and that guilt must be

---

[123]   Transcript of First Appearance Hearing in Open Session at 1, *Prosecutor* v. *Thomas Lubanga Dyilo*, Case No. ICC-01/04-01/06, available at www.icc-cpi.int/library/cases/ICC-01-04-01-06-T-3_English.pdf (hereinafter 'Initial Hearing Transcript'); International Criminal Court, Press Release, *First Arrest for the International Criminal Court*, 17 March 2006, available at www.icc-cpi.int/pressrelease_details&id=132.html.
[124]   Initial Hearing Transcript, note 123 *supra*, at 8.
[125]   See Summary of Press Releases in *Lubanga Dyilo*, available at www.icc-cpi.int/cases/RDC/c0106/c0106_pr.html (site provides a timeline of events in the pre-trial phase of this case).
[126]   See International Criminal Court, Press Release, *Trial Chamber Imposes a Stay on the Proceedings of the Case Against Thomas Lubanga Dyilo*, 16 June 2008, available at www.icc-cpi.int/press/pressreleases/381.html (hereinafter 'Imposing Stay Press Release'). See also Marlise Simons, *International Court Says It May Discard First Case*, NEW YORK TIMES, 17 June 2008, available at www.nytimes.com/2008/06/17/world/europe/17hague.html?_r=1&scp=1&sq=International+Court+says+it+may&st=nyt&oref=slogin. http://www.icc-cpi.int/press/pressreleases/381.html.
[127]   Military Commissions Act of 2006, 10 USC s. 948b(f).
[128]   See RMC, rule 707.
[129]   See, for example, *United States* v. *Khadr*, Defense Reply to Prosecution Response to Defense Motion to Dismiss All Charges (Equal Protection), (Military Commission, 24 January 2008), available at www.defenselink.mil/news/Feb2008/d20080201khadr.pdf.
[130]   See RMC, rule 707(a)(2).
[131]   ICC Statute, art. 66.

established beyond a reasonable doubt.[132] The ICC Statute contains no exceptions to the above provisions. Since the ICC has yet to complete a full trial, the commitment of that body specifically to the presumption of innocence is difficult to determine; however, the Trial Chamber has indicated its willingness to hold the Prosecutor to high standards in other instances, suggesting that this context would be no different.[133]

Under the MCA, the accused also supposedly has the right to be presumed innocent. '[T]he accused must be presumed to be innocent until his guilt is established by legal and competent evidence beyond a reasonable doubt.'[134] The national security privilege provided for by the Manual, however, abrogates the right to be presumed innocent by providing measures that assume an inability to trust the accused. For example, trial counsel can move to protect classified information *ex parte*.[135] This provision indicates a predetermination that the accused cannot be trusted or might retaliate against witnesses, which is ultimately incompatible with any presumption of innocence. Further, the general admissibility of hearsay evidence and the fact that the government may conceal the sources of its evidence effectively transfer the burden of proving innocence to the accused.[136] This ultimately results in the presumption of *guilt*. The accused person is in effect forced to prove his or her own innocence, in direct violation of this fair trial right.

Right to Counsel

The ICC Statute provides for the right to counsel in the context of an ongoing investigation in article 55, which reads in pertinent part, 'the person shall also have the [right] … [t]o have legal assistance of the person's choosing'[137] as well as the right to have that assistance provided free of charge, if the person cannot otherwise afford it.[138] This same right is provided in article 67, in the context of the trial.[139] This right to counsel is not limited by article 72, which speaks to national security information, as that article does not require the withholding of information from the accused on the part of the attorney.[140] Returning to the

---

132   *Ibid.*
133   See Imposing Stay Press Release, note 126 *supra*. The Trial Chamber, in later making the decision to release Mr Lubanga Dyilo, found that the manner in which the Prosecutor informed the defense of the available evidence did not meet fair trial standards. The Chamber's willingness to hold the Prosecutor responsible for this shortcoming, even when the decision may result in the release of a prisoner, is illustrative.
134   Military Commissions Act of 2006, 10 USC s. 949l(c)(1).
135   See MCA, 10 USC s. 949d(f)(2)(C); MCRC, rule 505(e)(5)(B).
136   See MCA, 10 USC s. 949a(b)(2)(E)(i) (allowing hearsay evidence to be presumptively admitted at trial); MCA, s. 949d(f)(2)(B) (allowing trial counsel to 'protect' the sources of the evidence sought to be introduced by refusing to disclose such sources to the defense). The Obama administration indicated its support for 'further regulating the use of hearsay, to bring the rule more in line with the rules in federal court or courts-martial while preserving an important exception pertaining to the unique circumstances of military and intelligence operations' See Wiegmann and Martins, note 103 *supra*, at 4. The 'use of hearsay will be limited, so that the burden will no longer be on the party who objects to hearsay to disprove its reliability'. Statement of President Barack Obama on Military Commissions, 15 May 2009, available at www.gpoaccess.gov/presdocs/2009/DCPD-200900364.pdf.
137   ICC Statute, art. 55.
138   *Ibid.*
139   See *ibid.* art. 67.
140   See *ibid.* art. 72.

example of the initial appearance of Mr Lubanga Dyilo, the Trial Chamber was careful to make clear to the accused that he had the right to counsel.[141] Further, the Chamber sought to ascertain at which points in the questioning that had already taken place Mr Lubanga Dyilo had been accompanied by counsel.[142] The Chamber was also careful to note that the accused could choose his own attorney pursuant to his trial strategy and need not employ the attorney assisting him in his initial appearance.[143]

The MCA affords the accused the right to counsel by providing, in section 948k(a)(1), that '[m]ilitary defense counsel shall be detailed for each military commission under this chapter'.[144] In addition to mandating a military attorney, rather than providing for the 'counsel of one's choice',[145] this general right to counsel is further limited in practice by rule 505 of the Military Commissions Rules of Evidence. This rule directs the military judge to 'enter an appropriate protective order to guard against the compromise of the information disclosed to the defense'.[146] The order may '[prohibit] the disclosure of the information except as authorized by the military judge'.[147] This provision may be used to prevent defense counsel from discussing important information with her client, leading the accused to suffer a lack of critical information which would allow him to make informed decisions relative to his defense. The accused is ultimately denied this information by his own counsel, the very person who is supposed to be his champion. This situation, in addition to the vast cultural and religious barriers already present between military commission detainees and their detailed defense attorneys, precludes any establishment of trust and candor, which necessarily characterize the attorney/client relationship. The right to counsel is impermissibly burdened.

Right to Equality of Arms

The ICC Statute provides for equality of arms between the prosecution and the defense in article 67. That article begins by asserting that the accused shall be 'entitled to the following minimum guarantees, *in full equality*' (emphasis added), and goes on to list many of the fair trial provisions discussed elsewhere in this chapter.[148] Article 67 also provides specifically that the accused shall have access to favorable witnesses 'under the same conditions' as those witnesses testifying for the prosecution and that the accused must have 'adequate time and facilities for the preparation of the defence'.[149] The ICC has recognized the importance of this equality, especially regarding preparation time, in the context of the first appearance of Mr Lubanga Dyilo,[150] as well as in a working document entitled *The Course of Action and*

---

141   Initial Hearing Transcript, note 123 *supra*, at 6.
142   *Ibid.* 3.
143   *Ibid.* 6.
144   MCA, 10 USC s. 948k(a)(1).
145   The ability to choose one's attorney freely is required by the ICC Statute, art. 67(1)(b), as well as by other international treaties and instruments, see, for example, ICCPR, note 9 *supra*, art. 14; ECHR, note 10 *supra*, art. 6.
146   MCRE, rule 505(e)(1).
147   *Ibid.* rule 505(e)(1)(A).
148   ICC Statute, art. 67.
149   *Ibid.*
150   In this hearing, the Trial Chamber was careful to point out to Mr Lubanga that he was at all times entitled to adequate time and facilities to prepare his defense. Initial Hearing Transcript, note 123 *supra*, at 4.

Procedure Following the Arrest and Surrender of a Suspect to the Court.[151] Further, the Trial Chamber reaffirmed its commitment to equality of arms when it made the decision to release Mr Lubanga Dyilo. This decision was made in light of the fact that the prosecution possessed certain, possibly exculpatory, evidence to which the defense did not have access.[152] This situation put the prosecution and defense on uneven playing fields, precluding the possibility of a fair trial.[153]

MCA, section 948b(f) guarantees procedural equality of arms only indirectly, stating that military commissions must offer all 'judicial guarantees which are recognized as indispensable by civilized peoples'[154] under common article 3. A number of inequalities between the prosecution and defense allowed by the Manual, however, violate this protection. First, the prosecution has an unlimited amount of time to prepare for trial, while the defense can be forced to trial with 120 days notice.[155] Second, trial counsel in a military commission has a more extensive right to object to cross-examination and may object to 'any question, line of inquiry, or motion to admit evidence that would require the disclosure of classified information'.[156] Third, trial counsel may move *ex parte* to withhold classified information from the accused.[157] Fourth, expedited interlocutory appeals are available to trial counsel, but not to the defense.[158] Fifth, the government may refuse to disclose its sources, methods and activities that produced the evidence it introduces at trial, leaving the defense unable to inquire into reliability and probative value of incriminating evidence.[159] Under these circumstances, the defense in a military commission is at a disadvantage; equality between the two sides exists only in theory.

Privilege Against Self-Incrimination

The ICC Statute affords the accused the privilege against self-incrimination by stating that no one may be 'compelled to testify or to confess guilt' and that everyone has the right 'to remain silent, without such silence being a consideration in the determination of guilt or innocence'.[160] The Statute also forbids the use of coercion and/or torture in the course of an investigation.[161] The privilege against self-incrimination is made known to accused persons when they are arrested by ICC officials, and again at the accused's initial appearance in the Trial Chamber.[162]

---

[151]   *The Course of Action and Procedure Following the Arrest and Surrender of a Suspect to the Court*, ICC Doc. ICC-PIDS-PRI-1/07_En, available at www.icc-cpi.int/library/cases/Course_of_action _en.pdf.

[152]   Imposing Stay Press Release, note 126 *supra*.

[153]   *Ibid.*

[154]   MCA, 10 USC s. 948b(f).

[155]   See RMC, rule 707(a)(2).

[156]   MCA, 10 USC s. 949d(f)(2)(C); MCRE, rule 505(f)(1).

[157]   See MCA, 10 USC s. 949d(f)(2)(C); MCRE, rule 505(f)(1).

[158]   See MCA, 10 USC s. 950d; RMC, rule 908.

[159]   See MCA, 10 USC s. 949d(f)(2)(B); RMC, rule 701(f). The Obama administration has announced its support for 'adopting clear rules requiring the government to disclose exculpatory evidence to the accused'. Wiegmann and Martins, note 103 *supra*, at 4.

[160]   ICC Statute, art. 55(2)(b).

[161]   *Ibid.* art. 55(1)(b).

[162]   See, for example, Initial Hearing Transcript, note 123 *supra*, at 5.

Under the MCA, the accused also enjoys the privilege against self-incrimination; section 948r states that '[n]o person shall be required to testify against himself at a proceeding of a military commission under this chapter'.[163] The Manual, however, threatens this right by allowing uncorroborated confessions to be admitted in evidence, requiring only that someone heard the accused confess.[164] The problem of uncorroborated confessions is aggravated by the fact that coerced testimony is also allowed in evidence if the totality of the circumstances make such a statement reliable and probative.[165] This is true regardless of the fact that, when subject to coercive interrogation techniques, a person will say what his or her interrogators want to hear, rather than a statement of the truth. Because the Manual thus allows for confessions that are uncorroborated and adduced without warning, the privilege against self-incrimination is insufficiently protected.

Right to Exclusion of Evidence Adduced by Coercive Methods

The ICC Statute provides, in article 55, that persons subject to investigation 'shall not be subjected to any form of coercion, duress or threat, to torture, or to any other form of cruel, inhuman, or degrading treatment or punishment'.[166] The Statute goes on to provide, in its article 69, that '[e]vidence obtained by means of a violation of this Statute or internationally recognized human rights shall not be admissible if: (a) [t]he violation casts substantial doubt on the reliability of the evidence; or (b) [t]he admission of the evidence would be antithetical to and would seriously damage the integrity of the proceedings'.[167] These provisions, read together, demand that evidence adduced by coercive means be excluded at trial.

'A statement obtained by use of torture shall not be admissible in a military commission under this chapter.'[168] according to MCA, section 948r(b). If a statement was made under a 'disputed degree of coercion', however, the military judge may admit it if the 'totality of the circumstances renders the statement reliable and possessing sufficient probative value' and 'the interests of justice would best be served by admission'.[169] This test for admission necessarily allows evidence adduced by torture or inhuman treatment to be admitted in evidence at military commissions, contrary to the fact that such evidence is unreliable for the reasons discussed above. What is more, since the government may withhold sources and the methods through which it obtained statements under MCA, section 949d(f)(2)(B), coerced evidence may be admitted without the defense's awareness.[170] Trial counsel can offer coerced evidence; claim the privilege against disclosure of sources; and use it at trial without the illegal provenance of the evidence ever being disclosed to the defense. Not only does this situation create an unacceptable incentive to engage in severe abuse and undermine the right to

---

[163]   MCA, 10 USC s. 948r.
[164]   See MCRE, rule 304(g)(1).
[165]   See MCA, 10 USC s. 948r; MCRE, rule 304(g)(1). The Obama administration supports 'adopting a "voluntariness" standard for the admission of statements of the accused, while taking into account the challenges and realities of the battlefield'. Wiegmann and Martins, note 103 *supra*, at 4; see also note 116 *supra*.
[166]   ICC Statute, art. 55.
[167]   *Ibid.* art. 69.
[168]   MCA, 10 USC s. 948r(b).
[169]   *Ibid.* s. 948r(d)(2).
[170]   See MCA, 10 USC s. 949d(f)(2)(B).

fair trial, it outrages the values of civilization and reflects perhaps the most poorly on the United States of any of the shortcomings of the military commission system.

Right to Confrontation of Witnesses and Evidence

The ICC Statute protects the right to confrontation in articles 63 and 67. An accused person has the right to 'examine or have examined, the witnesses against him or her and to obtain the attendance and examination of witnesses on his or her behalf under the same conditions as witnesses against him or her'[171] (article 67(e)). Every accused person also has the right, under article 63, to be present at his or her trial.[172] This right is subject to the exception for situations in which the accused impermissibly disrupts the trial, in which case that person is removed and able to watch and instruct counsel only via communications technology.[173] This is a very limited exception under the Statute and must be employed only after other means of control have failed, and then only for as long as absolutely necessary. It is reserved for 'exceptional circumstances'.[174] While these fair trial rights to confrontation have not yet been tested in the trial setting, the ICC Trial Chamber has made clear to accused persons their right to prepare their defense, including the calling and examination of all witnesses.[175] Accused persons have the right to call favorable witnesses and cross-examine the witnesses called by the Prosecutor not only at trial, but also at the confirmation of charges hearing.[176]

The MCA generally provides for the right to call witnesses, the right to cross-examine adverse witnesses, and the right to be present at one's trial, but the Manual again contains provisions that violate each of these component protections of the right to confrontation.

The right to call witnesses is protected by section 949j(a), which states that the '[d]efense counsel in a military commission ... shall have reasonable opportunity to obtain witnesses ... as provided in regulations prescribed by the Secretary of Defense'.[177] This right is undercut by provisions in the Manual which provide the prosecution with a superior right to call witnesses (by subjecting only the defense to having their witnesses contested on the basis of national security)[178] and which allow the trial to continue despite the absence of an essential witness.[179] A continuance in order to obtain a witness essential to a fair trial must be granted *only* 'if the reason for the witness' unavailability is within the control of the United States'.[180] These two problems make it impossible for the military commission to ensure the equal right to call witnesses required in a fair trial.

The MCA provides in section 949a(b)(1)(A) that '[t]he accused shall be permitted ... to cross-examine the witnesses who testify against him'.[181] A number of Manual provisions make this general grant of the right to cross-examine ineffective. First, the general admissibility of

---

[171]   ICC Statute, art. 67.
[172]   *Ibid.* art. 63.
[173]   *Ibid.*
[174]   *Ibid.*
[175]   See, for example, Initial Hearing Transcript, note 123, *supra*, at 4.
[176]   *Ibid.*
[177]   MCA, 10 USC s. 949j(a).
[178]   RMC, rule 703(c)(2)(D).
[179]   RMC, rule 703(b)(3)(B).
[180]   *Ibid.*
[181]   MCA, 10 USC s. 949a(b)(1)(A).

hearsay evidence[182] denies the accused his right to cross-examine, because the declarant need not be present. The accused is confronted with unreliable statements, but is unable to demonstrate their lack of probative value. Second, the military judge must limit cross-examination of government witnesses upon request of the government.[183] In light of these limitations, the full right to cross-examine witnesses is compromised in military commissions.

The MCA provides the right to be present at military commission proceedings. The accused 'shall be present at all sessions of the military commission (other than those for deliberation and voting), except when excluded under section 949d'.[184] The MCA also, however, allows the military judge to exclude the accused from *ex parte* reviews of trial counsel's claims of national security privilege in certain circumstances 'at trial'.[185] In practice, the accused may be excluded whenever the military judge considers claims of national security. This exception to the accused's right to be present at trial means that right is not observed in the military commissions to the extent required for a fair trial.

Right to Appeal One's Conviction

The ICC Statute allows any person convicted to appeal his or her conviction and/or the sentence imposed under article 81. This appeal may be made on any of the following grounds: procedural error, error of law or error of fact, in addition to '[a]ny other ground that affects the fairness or reliability of the proceedings or decision'.[186] The commitment of the Court to the right to appeal has not yet been tested. The provisions of article 81, however, are broad enough to comport with the fair trial standards recognized in other treaties and instruments at international law.[187]

The accused in a military commission has the right to review by a higher court, pursuant to section 950c.[188] The Court of Military Commission Review, however, can act only with respect to errors of law, rather than with respect to the facts of the case.[189] This standard of review fails to provide the comprehensive right to appeal required by international fair trial standards

CONCLUSION

Examining the fundamental right to fair trial by comparing these two very different institutional settings illustrates the nature and content of fair trials. Furthermore, examining the issue in the above manner allows for a thoughtful consideration of the importance of the right

---

[182]   As discussed above, the admission of hearsay evidence is presumptively allowed by the MCA, 10 USC s. 949a(b)(2)(E)(i).

[183]   See MCA, 10 USC s. 949d(f)(2)(C); MCRE, rule 505(e)(2).

[184]   MCA, 10 USC s. 949a(b)(1)(B).

[185]   MCA, 10 USC s. 949d(f)(3).

[186]   ICC Statute, art. 81.

[187]   This standard comports with, for example, *Report of the Secretary-General Pursuant to Paragraph 2 of Resolution 808 (1993)* S/25704 (3 May 1993) para. 117, available at www.un.org/icty/legaldoc-e/basic/statut/s25704.htm.

[188]   See MCA, 10 USC s. 950c

[189]   *Ibid.*

itself and the manner in which current policy is able, or should be able, to reflect that importance in all circumstances. Given the tremendous delay, uncertainty and judicial opposition generated by the military commissions, in addition to the notable fair trial shortfalls, it might have been wise for the United States to refer prosecutions of accused terrorists to the ICC rather than trying to use the military commissions. The ICC would provide a fairer trial and generate greater international acceptance. By creating a new set of procedures with many defects, the United States has undermined its own objectives of achieving prompt and effective justice.

12 Self-representation of the accused before international tribunals: an absolute right or a qualified privilege?

Michael P. Scharf

INTRODUCTION

Echoing the wording of article 14 of the International Covenant on Civil and Political Rights (ICCPR),[1] the Statutes of the International Criminal Tribunal for Rwanda (ICTR), and all of the other modern war crimes tribunals provide that the defendant has the right 'to defend himself in person or through legal assistance of his own choosing'.[2] Relying on this language, former leaders standing trial for war crimes often seek to act as their own lawyers in order to transform the proceedings into a political stage.[3] Is this a necessary evil attendant to the right to a fair trial under conventional and customary international law, as Judge Richard May, who presided over the trial of Slobodan Milosevic, concluded?[4] Or can the Covenant, customary international law and the Statutes of the international tribunals be read as permitting a war crimes tribunal to appoint counsel over the objections of the defendant, as the ICTR held in the *Barayagwiza* case?[5]

How war crimes tribunals answer this question in the future will have a significant effect on their ability to contribute to peace, reconciliation and the rule of law by establishing a historic record of atrocities committed by the former regime that is accepted by the target

---

[1] International Covenant on Civil and Political Rights, 19 December 1996, 999 UNTS 171 (ICCPR), art. 14(3)(d) ('In the determination of any criminal charge against him, everyone shall be entitled ... to be tried in his presence, and to defend himself in person or through legal assistance of his own choosing').

[2] This clause is contained in the Statutes of the ICTR, ICTY, SCSL, IST and ICC.

[3] Michael P. Scharf, *Making a Spectacle of Himself, Milosevic Wants a Stage, Not the Right to Provide His Own Defense*, THE WASHINGTON POST, 29 August 2004, B2 (Outlook Section).

[4] *Prosecutor* v. *Milošević*, Case No. IT-99-37-PT, Transcript, 30 August 2001, 18 (Status Conference): 'We have to act in accordance with the Statute and our Rules which, in any event, reflect the position under customary international law, which is that the [defendant] has a right to counsel, but he also has a right not to have counsel. He has a right to defend himself, and it is quite clear that he has chosen to defend himself. He has made that abundantly clear. The strategy that the Chamber has employed of appointing an *amicus curiae* will take care of the problems that you have outlined, but I stress that it would be wrong for the Chamber to impose counsel on the [defendant], because that would be in breach of the position under customary international law. Judge May later confirmed his ruling in a published decision: *Prosecutor* v. *Milošević*, Case No. IT-02-54, Reasons for Decision on the Prosecution Motion Concerning Assignment of Counsel), 4 April 2003, available at www.un.org/icty/milosevic/trialc/decision-e/040403.htm (hereinafter '*Milošević* Reasoned Decision').

[5] *Prosecutor* v. *Jean-Bosco Barayagwiza*, Case No. ICTR-97-19-T, Decision on Defence Counsel Motion to Withdraw, 2 November 2000). All documents from this case are available through the ICTR website, www.ictr.org.

population.[6] In the 2001–2005 trial of Slobodan Milosevic, for example, the tactic of self-representation enabled the former Serb leader to: (1) generate the illusion that he was a solitary individual pitted against an army of foreign lawyers and investigators, when in fact he had a squadron of legal counsel assisting him from behind the scenes; (2) make unfettered caustic speeches throughout the trial which were not restricted by the rules of relevance or subject to cross-examination by the prosecution; and (3) repeatedly challenge the legitimacy of the proceedings and treat the witnesses, prosecutors and judges in a manner that would earn ordinary defense counsel expulsion from the courtroom. These tactics were not helping Milošević's case in the courtroom, but opinion polls in Serbia indicated that they had the affect of convincing a majority of the Serb people that his trial was unfair and that he was not guilty of the charges.[7] Self-representation thus enabled Milosevic to cloud the historic record and to transform himself into a martyr, rather than a discredited war criminal. Suspicion surrounding the circumstances of Milosevic's death just before the conclusion of his trial has only reinforced these widely-held views.

Seeking to accomplish the same result, former Iraqi leader Saddam Hussein took advantage of Iraqi legal tradition which permits a defendant to act as his own co-counsel, to cross examine witnesses when his lawyer was through with them, and to address the court at will. During his trial in 2005–2006, Saddam[8] exploited these opportunities by making frequent political speeches and inciting his followers (who were watching the television broadcasts of the proceedings) to kill American occupiers and Iraqi government collaborators. In his interactions with the court, he told the judge to 'go to hell' and called the judge at various times a 'homosexual', a 'dog', and a 'whore-monger'.[9]

Given these examples of abuse, we must ask whether self-representation is indeed a fundamental right enshrined in international law? To that end, this chapter explores the negotiating record, scholarly commentary and international jurisprudence related to the self-representation provision of the ICCPR on which the self-representation language of the Statutes of the several war crimes tribunals is based. Next, it explores the two main reasons why a court in a major war crimes trial should be able to require the defendant to work through counsel: (1) the likelihood that a defendant will act in a disruptive manner; and (2) the unique need in a

---

6   For a detailed discussion of the roles of justice in the aftermath of conflict, see Paul R. Williams and Michael P. Scharf, Peace With Justice? 11–22 (2002). In the context of rebuilding Iraq, see Michael P. Scharf, Is It International Enough? A Critique of the Iraqi Special Tribunal in Light of the Goals of International Justice, 2 J Int'l Crim. Just. 330, 331 (2004).

7   Michael P. Scharf, *The Legacy of the Milošević Trial*, 37 New England L Rev. 915, 930 n. 85 (citing Andre Purvis, *Star Power in Serbia; Slobodan Milošević's Performance at his War Crimes Trial has Won Him Increased Popularity at Home*, Time (Europe), 30 September 2002, 46); *ibid.* 930 n. 83 (citing Joseph Lelyveld, *The Defendant; Slobodan Milošević's Trial, and the Debate Surrounding International Courts*, New Yorker, 27 May 2002, 82 (citing opinion polls in which less than 25 percent of the people in Serbia felt that Milošević was getting a fair trial, and only 33 percent thought that he was actually responsible for war crimes); Dosan Stojanovic, Milošević Wins Serb Parliament Seat, Plain Dealer (Cleveland), 30 December 2003, A9 (reporting that Milošević used his trial presentations to successfully campaign for a seat in the Serb Parliament).

8   Saddam was the former Iraqi leader's given name; Hussein was the name of his father; and al-Tikriti was the name of the village in which he was born. Thus, in Iraq he was commonly referred to just as 'Saddam'.

9   See Michael P. Scharf, *Chaos in the Courtroom: Controlling Disruptive Defendants and Contumacious Counsel in War Crimes Trials*, 39 Case Western Reserve J Int'l L 155, 163–5 (2007).

complex war crimes case for an orderly trial. Finally, it examines the conflicting positions taken by the ICTR, the Special Court for Sierra Leone (SCSL) and the International Criminal Tribunal for the Former Yugoslavia (ICTY), on this issue. The analysis contained herein suggests that the underlying purpose of the defendant's right 'to defend himself in person or through legal assistance of his own choosing' is to ensure a fair trial, an objective that can best be met in cases of former leaders accused of international crimes by assigning highly qualified stand-by counsel, ready and willing to step in whenever the self-represented defendant abuses the privilege of self-representation.

ICCPR, ARTICLE 14(3)(D): NEGOTIATING RECORD, SCHOLARLY COMMENTARY AND JURISPRUDENCE

It is helpful to examine the drafting history of article 14(3)(d) of the ICCPR in order to locate the origins of the self-representation provision and its true meaning. The United States provided the first substantive contributions to the First Session of the Drafting Committee of the Universal Declaration of Human Rights (UDHR), held from 9 to 25 June 1947. These provisions later became part of article 14 of the ICCPR, but were originally intended to be included in the proposed articles 6 and 27 of the UDHR. It is noteworthy that the initial proposal for the text that eventually became article 14 of the ICCPR included only the right to consult with and be represented by counsel; there was no mention of a right to self-representation.[10] At the Second Session of the Drafting Committee, the United States introduced a revised draft article, which provided that everyone is entitled to the aid of counsel.[11] It was not until the draft wording at the end of the Committee's Fifth Session that the eventual article 14 of the ICCPR added that, in the determination of any criminal charge, the accused is entitled '[t]o defend himself in person or through legal assistance which shall include the right to legal assistance of his own choosing, or, if he does not have such, to be informed of his right and, if unobtainable by him, to have legal assistance assigned'.[12]

---

[10]   See DAVID WEISSBRODT, THE RIGHT TO A FAIR TRIAL UNDER THE UNIVERSAL DECLARATION OF HUMAN RIGHTS AND THE INTERNATIONAL COVENANT ON CIVIL AND POLITICAL RIGHTS 43–5 (2001). Weissbrodt quotes *Comments on the Secretariat Outline*, 1, UN Doc. E/CN.4/AC.1/8 (1947), art. 6 as follows: 'No one shall be deprived of life or personal liberty, or be convicted or punished for crime in any manner, save by judgment of a competent and impartial tribunal, in conformity with law, after a fair and public trial at which he has had the opportunity for a full hearing, the right to be confronted with the witnesses against him, the right of compulsory process for obtaining witnesses in his favour, and the right to consult with and be represented by counsel.'

Further, according to *Comments on the Secretariat Outline*, 5, UN Doc. E/CN.4/AC.1/8 (1947), art. 27 'Every person has the right to have any civil claims or liabilities determined without undue delay by a competent and impartial tribunal before which he has the opportunity for a fair hearing, and has the right to consult with and be represented by counsel., Weissbrodt, *supra*, 45.

[11]   See *ibid.* at 45 (quoting *Comments on the Secretariat Outline*, 7, UN Doc. E/CN.4/AC.3/SR.9 (1947), where it says 'In the determination of his rights and obligations, everyone is entitled to a fair hearing before an independent and impartial tribunal and the aid of counsel. No one shall be convicted and punished for crime except after public trial pursuant to law in effect at the time of the commission of the act charged.').

[12]   Weissbrodt, note 10 *supra*, at 54 (quoting *Summary Record of the 110th Meeting*, 8, UN Doc. E/CN.4/SR.110 (1979)).

At the Sixth Session, the United States stressed that, in its legal system, the defendant has the right to refuse the assigned counsel and ask for another if the assigned counsel does not perform properly. According to the official records, no discussion ensued concerning an absolute right to represent oneself; rather the delegates were solely concerned about the right to access counsel, the choice of counsel, and who pays for counsel if the defendant is indigent.[13] This evinces the limited weight the drafters placed on the wording which the *Milošević* Trial Chamber has interpreted as creating an absolute right to self-representation.

It is noteworthy that distinguished scholars in the field have not read this clause as requiring an unfettered right of self-representation. According to Professor Cherif Bassiouni, 'the right to self-representation complements the right to counsel and is not meant as a substitute thereof'.[14] The purpose of the right to self-representation is to assure 'the accused of the right to participate in his or her defense, including directing the defense, rejecting appointed counsel, and conducting his or her own defense *under certain circumstances*'.[15] But this right is not unqualified as, Bassiouni continues, 'representation of counsel is not only a matter of interest to the accused, but is also paramount to due process of the law and to the integrity of the judicial process'.[16] Accordingly, this can be accomplished only by ensuring that such self-representation is adequate and effective.[17] It logically follows that a court 'should appoint professional counsel to supplement self-representation; conversely, whenever it is in the best interest of justice and in the interest of adequate and effective representation of the accused, *the court should disallow self-representation and appoint professional counsel*'.[18]

It is also important to recognize that while most common law countries (including the United States) recognize a right of self-representation, civil law countries including France, Germany and Belgium, among others, do not feel compelled to permit a defendant to represent him or herself.[19] In civil law countries, defense counsel can be imposed on the defendant in serious cases, which happen to be most criminal cases with the potential for long sentences. In France, during a trial, the presence of a lawyer is required before the *Court daisies*, which has jurisdiction to try felonies (offenses punished by imprisonment with

---

[13]   Weissbrodt, note 10 *supra*, at 57.

[14]   M. Cherif Bassiouni, *Human Rights in the Context of Criminal Justice: Ibidentifying International Procedural Protections and Equivalent Protections in National Constitutions*, 3 Duke J Comat and Int'l L 235, 283 (1993).

[15]   *Ibid.* (emphasis added). Bassiouni studied 139 constitutions to determine the level of international protections given to a defendant with respect to various types of rights. He found that the right to self-representation is guaranteed in only 33 of the national constitutions that he surveyed.

[16]   *Ibid.*

[17]   *Ibid.*

[18]   *Ibid.* 283–4 (emphasis added).

[19]   *Prosecutor* v. *Vojislav Šešelj*, Case No. IT-03-67-PT, Decision on Prosecution's Motion for Order Appointing Counsel to Assist Vojislav Šešelj 9 May 2003, paras 16–17). This decision also referred to s. 731 of the Danish Administration of Justice Act as requiring mandatory defense counsel in 'specific circumstances'. Moreover, art. 71 of the Criminal Procedure Act of the Federal Republic of Yugoslavia provided that the defendant would be assigned defense counsel if the criminal offense had a penalty of more than ten years in prison. The decision also noted that defense counsel was mandatory even if the defendant had the 'requisite legal qualifications'. Article 66 of the Criminal Procedure Code for the Federation of Bosnia and Herzegovina of 20 November 1998 similarly provided.

hard labor, for life, or for a fixed period of time).[20] Germany similarly requires mandatory defense counsel in certain situations, including where the defendant is charged with a serious offense, where the presiding judge finds that the assistance of defense counsel appears necessary because of the difficult factual or legal situation, or where it is evident that the defendant cannot defend himself.[21] In Belgium, the President of the court must verify whether the defendant has selected counsel of his choice to represent him in front of the *Court daisies*; if the defendant has not so selected, the President must designate counsel for the defendant.[22]

Given the contrary widespread practice of the civil law countries, it would be difficult to properly conclude that the right to self-representation has in fact attained the level of customary international law, as Judge May concluded in the *Milošević* case. Moreover, the jurisprudence of the European Court of Human Rights (ECtHR) provides further evidence that Judge May was mistaken. Interpreting a clause in the European Convention on Human Rights with the same language as article 14(d)(3) of the ICCPR, the ECHR has 'taken a relatively restrictive stance and affirmed the right of States to assign a defense counsel against the will of the accused in the administration of justice'.[23] Judge May dismissed the importance of this precedent because of the fact that the nature of the proceedings at the ICTY is adversarial, and the imposition of defense counsel is a feature of the inquisitorial system, which is most prevalent among the European states.[24] However, international and hybrid courts such as the ICTY, ICTR, International Criminal Court (ICC), SCSL and Iraqi Special Tribunal (IST) are *sui generis*, representing a blending of the common law and civil law approaches.[25] Thus, the practice of the civil law countries should not be discounted.

---

[20]   Valerie Dervieux, *The French System*, in EUROPEAN CRIMINAL PROCEDURES 218, 231 (Mireille Delmas-Marty and J.R. Spencer eds, 2002); THE FRENCH CODE OF CRIMINAL PROCEDURE, American Series of Foreign Penal Codes (Gerald L. Kock and Richard S. Frase trans., March 1988).

[21]   See Strafprozeßordnung (Code of Criminal Procedure), art. 140, available at www.iuscoma-torg/gla/statutes/StPO.htm; Rudolphe Juy-Birmann, *The German System*, in EUROPEAN CRIMINAL PROCEDURES 304–5 (Mireille Delmas-Marty and J.R. Spencer eds, 2002).

[22]   See Belgian Coded Instruction Criminelle, art. 293, available at www.juridat.be/cgi_loi/legislation.at

[23]   MANFRED NOWAK, UN COVENANT ON CIVIL AND POLITICAL RIGHTS: CCPR COMMENTARY 259 (1993).

[24]   *Prosecutor* v. *Milošević*, Case No. IT-02-54, Reasons for Decision on the Prosecution Motion Concerning Assignment of Counsel, 4 April 2003, available at www.un.org/icty/milosevic/trialc/decision-e/040403.htm (hereinafter '*Milošević* Reasoned Decision'), paras 24–5.

[25]   See Sean D. Murphy, *Progress and Jurisprudence of the International Criminal Tribunal for the Former Yugoslavia*, 93 AM. J INT'L L 57, 80 (1999) (quoting an ICTY Trial Chamber: '[N]either the rules issuing from the common law tradition in respect of the admissibility of hearsay evidence nor the general principle prevailing in the civil law systems, according to which, barring exceptions, all relevant evidence is admissible, including hearsay evidence, because it is the judge who finally takes a decision on the weight to ascribe to it, are directly applicable before this Tribunal. The International Tribunal is, in fact, a *sui generis* institution with its own rules of procedure which do not merely constitute a transposition of national legal systems. The same holds for the conduct of the trial which, contrary to the Defence arguments, is not similar to an adversarial trial, but is moving towards a more hybrid system.').

RATIONALE FOR REQUIRING A FORMER LEADER TO ACT THROUGH COUNSEL

Likelihood that the Defendant Will Act in a Disruptive Manner

The likelihood that a defendant will act in a disruptive manner may be inherent with certain types of defendants, especially former leaders who publicly challenge the court's authority to try them. It is particularly useful, then, to examine US jurisprudence on limiting the right of self-representation in the case of disruptive defendants.

In *Faretta* v. *California*, the US Supreme Court held that a defendant has a Sixth Amendment right to conduct his or her own defense in a criminal case.[26] However, it is important to recognize that the Supreme Court qualified this pronouncement by stating that such a 'right of self-representation is not a license to abuse the dignity of the courtroom'.[27] As discussed below, since *Faretta*, several courts have found that self-representation may be terminated if the defendant acts in a disruptive manner.

Under American jurisprudence, the right to counsel is the paramount right in relation to the right to self-representation.[28] As the US Court of Appeals for the First Circuit has reasoned, 'if [the right to counsel is] wrongly denied, the defendant is likely to be more seriously injured than if denied his right to proceed *pro se*'.[29] In *Tuitt* v. *Fair*, the appellant, convicted of armed robbery and carrying a firearm without lawful authority, alleged that his right to counsel was infringed when he was denied his requests for a continuance and for a substitution of counsel, or for permission to proceed unrepresented.[30] On appeal, the First Circuit held that '[t]he right to counsel is subject to practical constraints',[31] such that 'the right of an accused to choose his own counsel cannot be insisted upon in a manner that will obstruct reasonable and orderly court procedure'.[32] Similarly, in *United States* v. *Mack*, the US Court of Appeals for the Ninth Circuit stated that a defendant's right to self-representation does not overcome the court's right to maintain order in the courtroom.[33] The court further reasoned that '[a] defendant does not forfeit his right to representation at trial when he acts out. He merely forfeits his right to represent himself in the proceeding'.[34] The US Court of Appeals for the Second Circuit in *United States* v. *Cauley* refused to allow a disruptive defendant to dismiss his legal aid lawyer and proceed unrepresented.[35] The court found that

---

[26]   *Faretta* v. *California*, 422 U.S. 806, 835 (1975).

[27]   *Ibid.* 834 n. 46.

[28]   *Tuitt* v. *Fair*, 822 F.2d 166, 177 (1st Cir. 1987); *United States* v. *Mack*, 362 F.3d 597, 601 (9th Cir. 2004); *United States* v. *Cauley*, 697 F.2d 486, 491 (2d Cir. 1983); *United States* v. *West*, 877 F.2d 281, 286–7 (4th Cir. 1989); *United States* v. *Harris*, 317 F.Suat2d 542, 544–5 (DNJ 2004).

[29]   *Tuitt*, 822 F.2d at 177.

[30]   *Ibid.*

[31]   *Ibid.*

[32]   *United States* v. *Poulack*, 556 F.2d 83, 86 (1st Cir. 1977).

[33]   *Mack*, 362 F.3d at 601 (referring to when the appeals court reversed the trial court's conviction because the district court removed the defendant from the courtroom, leaving nobody to represent him. The court found this was a structural error which violated the defendant's rights under the Sixth Amendment).

[34]   *Ibid.*

[35]   *United States* v. *Cauley*, 697 F.2d 486, 491 (2d Cir. 1983).

his 'behavior in court was that of an easily angered man',[36] and noted that the defendant 'interrupted the cross-examination … with shouted obscenities'.[37] He also refused to answer questions posed to him. In *United States* v. *West*, the US Court of Appeals for the Fourth Circuit held similarly.[38] The appellant in that case attacked the court's 'integrity and dignity by characterizing it as the "home team" on the side of the government'.[39] The court held that the lower court was correct in finding that the appellant forfeited his right to self-representation by 'flouting the responsibility' given to him.[40] Most recently, in *United States* v. *Harris*, the federal district court in New Jersey turned down a defendant's request to self-representation.[41] As justification for this, the court found that the defendant refused to acknowledge the authority of the court, showed disrespect for the court, and that his attempts to proceed unrepresented were meant to disrupt the court.[42]

The above forms of disruption have accompanied the cases of former leaders before war crimes tribunals. As the descriptions of Milošević's and Saddam Hussein's antics in the introduction illustrate, such individuals openly question the legitimacy of the court, act disrespectfully to the judges, make speeches during cross-examination, and browbeat witnesses. In the ordinary case, the judges would threaten to expel from the courtroom, impose fines or prison time, or to suspend the license of an attorney who acted in such a manner, but these modes of discipline are not available to the judges with respect to a defendant who is serving as his own attorney. This type of inherently disruptive behavior, then, can justify appointment of stand-by defense counsel over the objection of the accused in war crimes trials.

Complexity of the Case and the Need for an Orderly Trial

War crimes tribunals are initiated in response to some of the gravest of atrocities committed in the history of mankind. Cases involving former leaders accused of war crimes are particularly complex. Consequently, the right to self-representation may be inherently incompatible with war crimes trials involving such defendants in four respects. First, war crimes tribunals prosecute violations of international humanitarian law, and have the overwhelming obligation of bringing the perpetrators to justice. The gamut of legal skills used in ordinary domestic criminal cases is insufficient for the trial of an accused war criminal.[43] Defense counsel must be fluent in substantive and procedural legal aspects of international humanitarian law, comparative law, and trial and written advocacy skills.[44] Second, international courts such as the ICTR, ICTY, SCSL, ICC and IST are *sui generis*, representing a blending of the common law and civil law approaches.[45] The judges are from both systems, and the procedural and

---

[36]   *Ibid.* 490.
[37]   *Ibid.* 491.
[38]   *United States* v. *West*, 877 F.2d 281, 286 (4th Cir. 1989).
[39]   *Ibid.* at 287.
[40]   *Ibid.*
[41]   *United States* v. *Harris*, 317 F.Suat2d 542, 546 (DNJ 2004).
[42]   *Ibid.* 546.
[43]   Mark S. Ellis, *Achieving Justice Before the International War Crimes Tribunal: Challenges for the Defense Counsel*, 7 Duke J Comat and Int'l L 519, 523 (1997).
[44]   Mark S. Ellis, *The Evolution of Defense Counsel Appearing Before the International Criminal Tribunal for the Former Yugoslavia*, 37 New Eng. L Rev. 949, 970–1 (2003).
[45]   See generally Murphy, note 25 *supra*, at 80.

substantive outcomes will depend on a mixture of the two legal systems. Even though the procedure tends to be closer to an adversarial model, characteristic of common law countries, the international courts can be characterized as hybrid, creating unique challenges to even the most experienced and skilled international lawyer.[46] Third, mounting a defense to a war crimes charge has proven to be quite daunting. In the first ICTY case of *Prosecutor* v. *Tadić*, for example, defense counsel was already spending 12 to 14 hours a day, six days a week in preparation for cross-examinations and direct examinations of witnesses.[47] Finally, due to the nature of the crimes and the geographic location of the courts in relation to the actual 'crime scenes', access to the sites, evidence and witnesses is especially challenging.[48]

Although domestic courts in common law countries do not impose defense counsel on an unwilling defendant in the absence of disruptive conduct, some courts have propounded on the matter of competent self-representation in complex cases and offer useful commentary. The Supreme Court of India, for example, has found that the fairness of a trial may be implicated in circumstances where a self-represented defendant cannot understand all the legal implications of the trial and appellate proceedings, as intricate questions of law and fact are involved which require the skillful handling of a competent lawyer, especially when the best of the public prosecutors appear on the other side of the courtroom.[49] The Australian High Court has similarly opined that defendants do not have the right to represent themselves on appeal because 'the most important part of the oral discussion – the testing of the arguments by a Socratic dialogue – is rarely effective in the case of applicants who are without legal representation ... because they generally lack the experience and legal knowledge to respond effectively to the justices' questions'.[50]

The concept of 'equality of arms' further supports the position that a defendant in a trial for war crimes should not have the absolute right of self-representation. Article 19(1) of the ICTR Statute and article 20(1) of the ICTY Statute firmly embrace the right to 'equality of arms'.[51] The jurisprudence of both Tribunals has dealt extensively with the issue of 'equality of arms' between the prosecution and the defense. Thus, in *Prosecutor* v. *Tadić*, the Appeals Chamber took the view that 'equality of arms obligates a judicial body to ensure that neither party is put at a disadvantage when presenting its case'.[52] To that end, these international tribunals make provision for specific rules on the appointment, qualifications and assignment of defense counsel in the Rules of Procedure,[53] as well as codes of conduct and directives for

---

[46]   See STEVEN R. RATNER AND JASON S. ABRAMS, ACCOUNTABILITY FOR HUMAN RIGHTS ATROCITIES IN INTERNATIONAL LAW: BEYOND THE NUREMBERG LEGACY 194 (2001).

[47]   Ellis, *Achieving Justice*, note 43 *supra*, at 529.

[48]   See, for example, Ellis, *Achieving Justice*, note 43 *supra*, at 533.

[49]   *Hussainara Khatoon et al.* (IV) v. *Home Secretary*, AIR 1979 SC 1369, 1374–5 (State of Bihar, Patna) (referring to when the Supreme Court of India held that there is a constitutional right of every defendant who is unable to secure the legal services of a lawyer to have counsel assigned, provided that the defendant wants legal representation); R.V. KEKLAR, R.V. KELKAR'S CRIMINAL PROCEDURE 472 (1993).

[50]   *Milat* v. *R*, 205 ALR 338, 340 (2004).

[51]   ICTY Statute, art. 20(1), available at www.un.org/icty/legaldoc/index.htm; ICTR Statute, art. 19(1), available at www.un.org/icty/ENGLISH/basicdocs/statute.html.

[52]   *Prosecutor* v. *Dusko Tadić*, Case No. IT-94-1-A, Judgment, 15 July 1999, para. 48, available at www.un.org/icty/tadic/appeal/judgement/tad-aj990715e.pdf.

[53]   See ICTY Rules of Procedure, rules 44–6; see ICTR Rules of Procedure and Evidence, rules 44–6, available at www.ictr.org/ENGLISH/rules/260503/270503e&fnew.pdf.

the assignment of defense counsel.[54] It seems at odds with a system that makes such an effort to promote 'equality of arms' and extensive qualifications upon defense counsel to accept that potentially unqualified defendants would be allowed to act alone as their own lawyer. After all, the most legally gifted of defendants, such as Tadić and Saddam Hussein,[55] would, notwithstanding their own training, have difficulty following the rules of procedure of an international court, as well as standard international criminal law practices.

CASE LAW OF THE ICTR, SCSL AND ICTY

International Criminal Tribunal for Rwanda

The ICTR was the first international tribunal to face the question of a defendant's right to self-representation, holding in the case of Jean-Bosco Barayagwiza that defense counsel could be assigned over the objection of the accused.[56] Barayagwiza, like Milosevic, was a lawyer by training and a former high level government official.[57] The ICTR Trial Chamber took the right to self-representation as articulated in the Statute as a starting point, but noted that according to international (and some national) jurisprudence, this right is not absolute.[58]

The Registrar declined Barayagwiza's request on 5 January 2000 for the withdrawal of his counsel, J.P.L. Nyaberi.[59] Barayagwiza sought the withdrawal citing reasons of 'lack of competence, honesty, loyalty, diligence, and interest'.[60] The Registrar's decision was confirmed by the President of the ICTR on 19 January 2000,[61] but on 31 January 2000, the Appeals Chamber ordered the withdrawal of Barayagwiza's defense counsel, J.P.L. Nyaberi, and ordered the assignment of new counsel and co-counsel for Barayagwiza.[62] Barayagwiza

---

[54]   In the ICTR, see the Directive on Assignment of Defence Counsel, available at www.ictr.org/ENGLISH/basicdocs/defence/index.htm; see also Code of Professional Conduct for Defence Council, available at www.ictr.org/ENGLISH/basicdocs/codeconduct.htm. In the ICTY, see the Directive on Assignment of Defence Counsel, and the Code of Professional Conduct for Defence Counsel Appearing Before the International Tribunal, available at www.un.org/icty/legaldoc/index.htm.

[55]   BBC News World Edition, *Profile: Vojislav Šešelj*, 29 December 2003, available at http://news.bbc.co.uk/2/hi/europe/2317765.stm (stating that Šešelj is highly educated, became the youngest Ph.D holder in Yugoslavia, and went on to teach first at the University of Michigan and then at Sarajevo universities); see *Key Milošević Ally Defects to the Opposition: Rightwing Maverick Offers His Support to Kostunica's Coalition*, THE GUARDIAN (London), 30 September 2000, 19 (stating that Šešelj graduated at the top of his class in law school in Belgrade); DUSKO DODER AND LOUISE BRANSON, MILOŠEVIĆ: PORTRAIT OF A TYRANT 24 (1999) (stating that Milošević is himself a lawyer who graduated near the top of his class from the University of Belgrade School of Law).

[56]   *Prosecutor* v. *Jean-Bosco Barayagwiza*, Case No. ICTR-97-19-T, Decision on Defence Counsel Motion to Withdraw, 2 November 2000). All documents from this case are available through the ICTR website, www.ictr.org.

[57]   *Prosecutor* v. *Jean-Bosco Barayagwiza*, Case No. ICTR-99-52-T, Judgment, 3 December 2003, para. 6.

[58]   See generally *Prosecutor* v. *Jean-Bosco Barayagwiza*, note 56 *supra*.

[59]   *Prosecutor* v. *Jean-Bosco Barayagwiza*, Case No. ICTR-99-52-T, Judgment, 3 December 2003, para. 82.

[60]   *Ibid*.

[61]   *Ibid*.

[62]   *Ibid*.

declined to accept the assigned counsel, and instructed him not to represent him at the trial.[63] The ICTR Trial Chamber ordered counsel to continue representing Barayagwiza. Counsel filed a motion to withdraw on 26 October 2000, given his client's instructions not to represent him at trial, which was denied on 2 November 2000, on the basis that the ICTR Trial Chamber had to ensure the rights of Barayagwiza.[64]

The ICTR Trial Chamber held Barayagwiza's behavior to be 'an attempt to obstruct proceedings. In such a situation, it cannot reasonably be argued that Counsel is under an obligation to follow them, and that [*sic*] not do so would constitute grounds for withdrawal.'[65] It referred to the 'well established principle in human rights law that the judiciary must ensure the rights of the accused, taking into account what is at stake for him'.[66] The ICTR Trial Chamber further noted that assigned counsel 'represents the interest of the Tribunal to ensure that the Accused receives a fair trial. The aim is to obtain efficient representation and adversarial proceedings'.[67] In a separate concurring opinion, Judge Gunawardana stressed the effect a decision to grant the withdrawal of counsel would have on the administration of justice of the trial.[68] He submitted that article 20(4)(d) of the ICTR Statute, the provision founded on ICCPR, article 14(3)(d), is an enabling provision for the appointment of a 'standby counsel', and in such circumstances the ICTR should make use of court-appointed standby counsel.[69]

Special Court for Sierra Leone

The Special Court for Sierra Leone Statute has a similar provision concerning the right to counsel.[70] In a recent decision, an SCSL Trial Chamber found that the defendant Samual Hinga Norman could not represent himself without the assistance of standby counsel.[71] Norman, who like Milosevic was a lawyer by training and a former high level government official, indicated in a letter of 3 June 2004, after the opening statement of the Prosecutor, that he wished to represent himself and that he was dispensing with his defense counsel who had been acting on his behalf since March 2003.[72]

In requiring the appointment of standby counsel, the SCSL Trial Chamber sought to distinguish Norman's situation from that in *Milošević* in two respects: First, the SCSL noted that Norman was being tried with two co-defendants.[73] Second, Norman did not signal his intention

---

63   *Ibid.* para. 83.
64   *Ibid.*
65   *Prosecutor v. Jean-Bosco Barayagwiza*, Case No. ICTR-97-19-T, Decision on Defence Counsel Motion to Withdraw, 2 November 20001, para. 24.
66   *Ibid.* para. 23.
67   *Ibid.* para. 21.
68   *Ibid.* Concurring and Separate Opinion of Judge Gunawardana).
69   *Ibid.*
70   See SCSL Statute, art. 17(4)(d), available at www.sc-sl.org/scsl-statute.html.
71   *Prosecutor v. Sam Hinga Norman*, Case No. SCSL-04-14-T, Decision on the Application of Samuel Hinga Norman for Self-Representation under art. 17(4)(d) of the Statute of the Special Court, 8 June 2004, para. 32.
72   *Ibid.* paras 3–5.
73   *Ibid.* para. 19.

to represent himself from the outset.[74] The SCSL Trial Chamber then turned to the characteristics of the trial that made it impossible for Norman to represent himself. According to the SCSL Trial Chamber, the right of counsel is an essential and necessary component of a fair trial.[75] Without counsel, the judges are forced to be a proactive participant in the proceedings instead of the arbiter, which is one of the greatest characteristics of an adversarial proceeding.[76] The SCSL Trial Chamber turned to the complexity of the case and the intricacies of international criminal law, as well as the national and international interest in the 'expeditious completion of the trial'.[77] The trial judges were also concerned with the impact on the court's timetable.[78]

International Criminal Tribunal for the Former Yugoslavia: Milošević revisited

On 22 September 2004, with the *Milošević* trial about to begin the defense phase, the Trial Chamber (now composed of Patrick Robinson, O-Gon Kwon and Iain Bonomy (replacing the deceased Richard May)) decided to revisit Judge May's ruling that Slobodan Milosevic had an absolute right to represent himself in the courtroom. As discussed above, there were two independent grounds upon which Judge May's ruling could potentially have been reversed. First, the Trial Chamber might have held that the language of the ICTY Statute does not in fact give the defendant the right to self-representation. The language from the Yugoslavia Tribunal Statute originally came from an identically worded clause contained in the European Convention on Human Rights and in the ICCPR. The negotiating record of these treaties indicates that the drafters' concern was with effective representation, not self-representation. In other words, the drafters felt that a defendant should have a right to either be represented by a lawyer or to represent himself; they did not state that each defendant must be asked to choose between the two. Unlike Britain and the United States, most countries of the world do not allow criminal defendants to represent themselves under any circumstances, and this has been deemed consistent with international law by the ECtHR.[79]

Second, even if Judge May was correct in his reading of the law, as providing a right to self-representation, the Trial Chamber could find that he was wrong to treat that right as absolute. As authority for his position, Judge May cited the US Supreme Court's 1975 ruling in *Faretta* v. *California*,[80] which held that there was a fundamental right to self-representation in US courts. But the US high court also added a caveat, which Judge May overlooked, stating that 'the right of self-representation is not a license to abuse the dignity of the courtroom'.[81] US appellate courts have subsequently held that the right of self-representation is

---

[74]   *Ibid.*

[75]   *Ibid.* para. 26.

[76]   *Ibid* .

[77]   *Ibid.* Norman objected to the idea of standby counsel and threatened to boycott attendance, before eventually agreeing to the decision to have his former legal team serve as standby counsel, in conformity with the definition outlined by the Šešelj Trial Chamber. Statement by the Trial Chamber on the State of the Proceedings in the Trial of the CDF Group of Indictees, 15 June 2004.

[78]   *Ibid.*

[79]   Nowak, note 23 *supra*, at 259; *Croissant* v. *Germany*, 16 Eur. Ct HR 135, 151 (1992), para 29, available at http://hudoc.echr.coe.int/Hudoc1doc/HEJUD/sift/321.txt.

[80]   *Faretta* v. *California*, 422 US 806, 841 (1975).

[81]   *Ibid.* 834 n. 46.

subject to exceptions – such as when the defendant acts in a disruptive manner or when self-representation interferes with the dignity or integrity of the proceedings.[82]

In its ruling on 22 September 2004 the Trial Chamber focused on this second ground, ruling that Milošević's poor health, which repeatedly disrupted the trial, justified appointment of counsel to represent him in court for the remainder of the proceedings. In its view:

> If at any stage of a trial there is a real prospect that it will be disrupted and the integrity of the trial undermined with the risk that it will not be conducted fairly, then the Trial Chamber has a duty to put in place a regime which will avoid that. Should self-representation have that impact, we conclude that it is open to the Trial Chamber to assign counsel to conduct the defense case, if the Accused will not appoint his own counsel.

Following the Trial Chamber's decision of 22 September 2004 Milošević refused to cooperate in any way with assigned counsel. Believing that they could not adequately represent the defendant without such cooperation, assigned counsel brought an interlocutory appeal to the ICTY Appeals Chamber (consisting of Theodor Meron, Fausto Pocar, Florence Mumba, Mehmet Guney and Innes Monica Weinberg de Roca). The Appeals Chamber decision, which was authored by Judge Meron, represented an obvious attempt at compromise. Based on the language of the ICTY Statute (without any analysis of the negotiating record of the international instruments from which the language originated), the Appeals Chamber agreed that defendants have 'a presumptive right to represent themselves before the Tribunal'.[83] The Appeals Chamber also agreed with the Trial Chamber that the right was subject to limitations. According to the Appeals Chamber, the test to be applied is that 'the right may be curtailed on the grounds that a defendant's self-representation is substantially and persistently obstructing the proper and expeditious conduct of his trial'.[84] Applying this test, the Appeals Chamber concluded that the Trial Chamber had not abused its discretion in deciding to restrict Milošević's right to self-representation.

However, the Appeals Chamber felt that the Trial Chamber's order requiring Milošević to act through appointed counsel went too far, and that the proportionality principle required that a more 'carefully calibrated set of restrictions' be imposed on Milošević's trial participation. Specifically, the Appeals Chamber ruled that when he is physically able to do so, Milošević must be permitted to take the lead in presenting his case – choosing which witnesses to present, questioning those witnesses, giving the closing statement, and making the basic strategic decisions about the presentation of his defense. 'If Milošević's health problems resurface with sufficient gravity, however, the presence of Assigned Counsel will enable the trial to continue even if Milošević is temporarily unable to participate.'[85] This ruling assumed, of course, that Milošević would be alive for the remainder of the trial, and the whole issue was rendered moot a few months later when he was found dead in his cell due to 'natural causes'.

---

82   *United States* v. *Mack*, 362 F.3d 597, 601 (9th Cir. 2004); *United States* v. *West*, 877 F.2d 281, 287 (4th Cir. 1989); *Tuitt* v. *Fair*, 822 F.2d 166, 177 (1st Cir. 1987); *United States* v. *Cauley*, 697 F.2d 486, 491 (2d Cir. 1983); *United States* v. *Harris*, 317 F.Suat2d 542, 544–5 (DNJ 2004).
83   *Prosecutor* v. *Milošević*, Case No. IT-02-54-AR73.7, Decision on Interlocutory Appeal of the Trial Chamber's Decision on the Assignment of Defense Counsel, 1 November 2004, para. 9.
84   *Ibid.* para. 13.
85   *Ibid.*

Six months after Milošević's death, another Serb leader, Vojislav Šešelj, decided that he, too, would utilize the right of self-representation as a means of disrupting his trial before the ICTY. Šešelj made his unruly intentions clear on the eve of trial when he published three books in Serbia entitled *Genocidal Israeli Diplomat Theodor Meron* (about the President of the ICTY), *In the Jaws of the Whore Del Ponte* (about the Chief Prosecutor of the Tribunal), and *The Lying Hague Homosexual, Geoffrey Nice* (about the lead trial prosecutor).[86] Šešelj tried repeatedly to provoke the judges at pre-trial hearings and made numerous obscene and improper statements in his pre-trial motions, including one submission which stated, 'You, all you members of The Hague Tribunal Registry, can only accept to suck my cock.'[87]

On the eve of trial in August 2006, the Trial Chamber revoked Šešelj's right to self-representation, stating:

> While it is clear that the conduct of the Accused brings into question his willingness to follow the 'ground rules' of the proceedings and to respect the decorum of the Court, more fundamentally, in the Chamber's view, this behaviour compromises the dignity of the tribunal and jeopardizes the very foundations upon which its proper functioning is based.[88]

The Appeals Chamber agreed that the Trial Chamber could revoke the right to self-representation where the Trial Chamber found 'that appropriate circumstances, rising to the level of substantial and persistent obstruction to the proper and expeditious conduct of the trial exist'.[89] The Appeals Chamber, however, held that the Trial Chamber had to first give the defendant an explicit warning. The Trial Chamber subsequently did so, and in light of Šešelj's continuing disruptive behavior, appointed counsel over his objection to represent him for the trial.

CONCLUSION

As Robert Jackson, the Chief Prosecutor at the Nuremberg trial, observed 60 years ago, war crimes trials, whether before international tribunals or domestic courts, seek to establish a credible historic record of abuses and elevate the rule of law over the force of might, thereby facilitating the restoration of peace and the transition to democracy.[90] While tolerating dissent is a healthy manifestation of a democratic government, 'a courtroom is not an arena in which dissension, particularly of a disruptive nature, may supplant, or even take precedence over, the task of administering justice'.[91] This is especially true in a war crimes trial.

---

[86]   *Prosecutor* v. *Šešelj*, Case No. IT-03-67-PT, Decision on Assignment of Counsel, 21 August 2006, para 30.

[87]   *Ibid*. para. 48.

[88]   *Ibid*. para. 77.

[89]   *Prosecutor* v. *Šešelj*, Case No. IT-03-67-AR73.3, Decision on Appeal Against the Trial Chamber's Decision on Assignment of Counsel, 20 October 2006, para. 21.

[90]   Robert H. Jackson, *Report to the President* (7 June 1945), quoted in MICHAEL P. SCHARF, BALKAN JUSTICE 37 (1997) ('We must establish incredible events by credible evidence'.); see also Robert H. Jackson, Opening Speech for the Prosecution at Nuremberg, 21 November 1945 quoted in II TRIAL OF THE MAJOR WAR CRIMINALS BEFORE THE INTERNATIONAL MILITARY TRIBUNAL NUREMBERG, 98–9 (1946).

[91]   *United States* v. *Dougherty*, 473 F.2d 1113 (DC Cir. 1972) (Aams J, concurring and dissenting).

Unlike other forms of acceptable political expression, a disruptive self-represented defendant who interferes with the 'grandeur of court procedure' (as Hannah Arendt once described the judicial process)[92] threatens the proper administration of criminal justice in several fundamental ways. First, disruptive conduct renders it more difficult for the defendant and any co-defendants to obtain a fair trial. Second, it hampers the court's ability to facilitate the testimony of victims and other witnesses. Third, it undermines the public's confidence in and respect for the legal process.

There are those who would argue that a defendant has a right, through his own disruptive and obstructionist conduct, to an unfair trial, but modern war crimes tribunals have wisely held that the defendant's right to employ disruptive tactics which seek to discredit the judicial process must give way to the tribunal's obligation to protect 'the integrity of the proceedings' and 'to ensure that the administration of justice is not brought into disrepute'.[93] The duty of a war crimes tribunal to ensure that a trial is fair has been interpreted as including concerns that go beyond just those of the accused.

This chapter has demonstrated the fallacy of Judge May's conclusion in the *Milošević* Case that a defendant in a war crimes trial has an absolute right to self-representation under conventional and customary international law. In contrast to Judge May's position in *Milošević*, the ICTR in *Barayagwiza* and the SCSL in *Norman* each recognized that assignment of counsel to an unwilling defendant is permissible under international law and is sometimes necessary to safeguard the legitimacy of the proceedings. After three years of Milošević's disruptions, the ICTY finally reversed Judge May's ruling and required the former Serb leader to be represented by counsel over his objection.

It is noteworthy that in doing so, the *Milošević* Appeals Chamber concluded that self-representation was a fundamental (though qualified) right. In issuing that determination, the Appeals Chamber impliedly overruled the reasoning of the ICTY Trial Chamber in the case of *Prosecutor* v. *Šešelj*, which had ordered that the defendant Vojislav Šešelj be represented by 'standby counsel'.[94] In order to rein in the defendant's disruptive behavior in the courtroom, the *Šešelj* Trial Chamber had taken the position that ICCPR, article 14(3)(d), and similar provisions in the ICTY Statute, do not declare that the right to work through legal counsel is derivative of the primary right to represent oneself. As the *Šešelj* Trial Chamber observed: 'It would be a misunderstanding of the word "or" in the phrase "to defend himself in person or through legal assistance of his own choosing" to conclude that self-representation excludes the appointment of counsel to assist the Accused or vice versa.'[95] In justifying its decision to appoint counsel over the defendant's objection, the *Šešelj* Trial Chamber concluded that '[t]he complex legal, evidential and procedural issues that arise in a case of this magnitude may fall outside the competence even of a legally qualified accused, especially where that accused is in detention without access to all the facilities he may need. Moreover, the Tribunal has a legitimate interest in ensuring that the trial proceeds in a timely manner without interruptions,

---

[92] Hannah Arendt, *Civil Disobedience*, in IS LAW DEAD? 212 (Eugene V. Rostow ed., 1971).

[93] See, for example, *Prosecutor* v. *Norman et al.*, Case No. SCSL-04-14-T, Decision on the Application of Samuel Hinga Norman for Self-Representation under art. 17(4)(d) of the Statute of the Special Court, 17 January 2005, para. 28.

[94] *Prosecutor* v. *Vojislav Šešelj*, Case No. IT-03-67-PT, Decision on Prosecution's Motion for Order Appointing Counsel to Assist Vojislav Šešelj), 9 May 2003.

[95] *Ibid.* para. 29.

adjournments or disruptions.'[96] In contrast to the *Šešelj* Trial Chamber's position that the ICCPR language does not require that a defendant be given a right to choose self-representation if appointed counsel is available, by interpreting the phrase as creating a presumptive right of self-representation, the ICTY Appeals Chamber decision may inadvertently fuel a spate of cases before the ECtHR, challenging the practice throughout Europe of requiring defendants to act through counsel.

In the final analysis, principles of justice and human rights require that former leaders like Milošević and Saddam Hussein be given fair trials. This chapter has made the case that self-representation is not in fact an absolute right, but a qualified privilege. In a major war crimes trial, a fair trial can best be guaranteed by appointing stand-by defense counsel, ready and willing to step in when a self-represented defendant attempts to disrupt or hijack the proceedings. Since most war crimes tribunal courtrooms are partitioned by sound-proof glass, a judge may effectively deal with minor disruptions by simply turning off the defendant's microphone. In the case of persistent disruptions, the judge should give a specific warning before revoking the right of self-representation and turning over the reins to the stand-by counsel. In addition, the defendant should be accorded at least a chance to reclaim the right if he manifests a willingness to conduct himself consistently with the decorum and respect inherent in the concept of courts and judicial proceedings.

---

[96]   *Ibid.* para. 21.

13 Defences in international criminal law

*Kai Ambos**

INTRODUCTION

With the establishment of the International Criminal Court (ICC),[1] the first comprehensive codification of international criminal law (ICL) was achieved. The strong support of the ICC by civil society, academic institutions and more than a hundred states has quickly turned the ICC Statute and its complementary norms into the fundamental reference points of modern ICL. As to 'defences', however, the Statute is silent; it does not even mention this term. The drafters consciously avoided certain 'catch words' too closely associated with either the common law or the civil law system. They wanted to make sure the Statute would be truly universal and would not be interpreted by way of recourse to a specific type of national systems.[2]

Article 31[3] of the ICC Statute contains explicit rules regarding 'grounds for excluding criminal responsibility' distinguishing between mental disease or defect, intoxication, self-defence and duress/necessity.[4] This list is not exhaustive. Pursuant to article 31(3), the Court may consider others grounds for excluding individual criminal responsibility. The Statute sets out some of these explicitly[5] such as mistake of fact and mistake of law (article 32) and superior orders (article 33). Additional grounds for excluding criminal responsibility may arise from any source of law as referred to in article 21 of the ICC Statute, especially from customary

*   I am grateful to my senior research assistant Dr. Stefanie Bock and student research assistant Moritz Eckhardt for invaluable assistance in preparing this chapter.
1   Rome Statute of the International Criminal Court, 17 July 1998, A/CONF.183/9, entry into force on 1 July 2002.
2   Kai Ambos (1999), *The General Principles of the Rome Statute*, 10 CRIMINAL LAW FORUM, 1, 2 (1999); Kai Ambos, *Other Grounds for Excluding Criminal Responsibility*, in ANTONIO CASSESE, PAOLA GAETA and JOHN R.W.D. JONES (eds), I THE ROME STATUTE OF THE INTERNATIONAL CRIMINAL COURT, A COMMENTARY 1028 (New York, Oxford University Press, 2002); Albin Eser, *Article 31. Grounds for Excluding Criminal Responsibility*, in OTTO TRIFFTERER (ed.), COMMENTARY ON THE ROME STATUTE OF THE INTERNATIONAL CRIMINAL COURT, para. 17 (2nd edn, München,: Beck *et al.*, 2008); William Schabas (2007), AN INTRODUCTION TO THE INTERNATIONAL CRIMINAL COURT 226 (3rd edn, Cambridge University Press, 2007).
3   Articles without further reference belong to the ICC Statute.
4   The 'general part' of art. 31 reads as follows: '1. In addition to other grounds for excluding criminal responsibility provided for in this Statute, a person shall not be criminally responsible if, at the time of that person's conduct: ...   2. The Court shall determine the applicability of the grounds for excluding criminal responsibility provided for in this Statute to the case before it.   3. At trial, the Court may consider a ground for excluding criminal responsibility other than those referred to in paragraph 1 where such a ground is derived from applicable law as set forth in article 21. The procedures relating to the consideration of such a ground shall be provided for in the Rules of Procedure and Evidence.'
5   Eser, note 2 *supra*, para. 7.

international law or general principles of law.[6] In this regard, the classical humanitarian law defences of military necessity and reprisal are of particular importance.[7] The case law, especially from the UN ad hoc Tribunals for the Former Yugoslavia[8] and Rwanda,[9] may serve as an important source for aiding in the interpretation and application of these defences.

Apart from these substantive defences relating to the conduct in question, the ICC Statute also provides for procedural defences[10] addressed to the jurisdiction and the right of a court to try an accused.[11] The latter include, for example, the exclusion of jurisdiction over persons under 18 years (article 26), immunities (article 27), as well as amnesties and the statute of limitations not regulated in the Statute. These procedural defences are beyond the scope of this chapter but are partly treated in other chapters of this *Handbook*.[12] The analysis in this chapter will follow the structure of articles 31 to 33 and complement these articles with some considerations on other defences.

PRELIMINARY CONCEPTUAL QUESTIONS

Justification and Excuse

Apart from distinguishing between substantive and procedural defences, civil law systems normally distinguish between justificatory and exculpatory substantive defences as well. A justification excludes criminal responsibility for an act which fulfils the elements of the offence definition (*actus reus*) but is regarded as lawful because the actor acted on the basis of a permissive norm which negates the effect of the *actus reus*, for example self-defence.[13] In contrast, an excuse exists when the act itself is wrongful, but the individual wrongdoer cannot be blamed for having carried it out because he was unable to recognize the unlawfulness of his conduct or because he could not be expected to act lawfully.[14] Although this differentiation is reasonable and sometimes even necessary for achieving a

---

[6]   Ambos, *General Principles*, note 2 *supra*, at 18; Massimo Scaliotti, '*Defences before the International Criminal Court: Substantive Grounds for Excluding Criminal Responsibility*, Part 1', 1 INTERNATIONAL CRIMINAL L REV, 111, 120 (2001); Gerhard Werle, *Principles of International Criminal Law*, para. 539 (2nd edn, The Hague, TMC Asser Press, 2009), see also Eser, note 2 *supra*, para. 15.

[7]   See the discussion of other defences, *infra*.

[8]   Security Council Res. 827, 25 May 1993, UN Doc. S/RES/827 (1993).

[9]   Security Council Res. 955, 8 November 1994, UN Doc. S/RES/955 (1994).

[10]   For an overview see Ambos, *General Principles*, note 2 *supra*, at 22 *et seq.*

[11]   For the distinction between substantive and procedural defences in this context, see ROBERT CRYER, HÅKAN FRIMAN, DARRYL ROBINSON and ELIZABETH WILMSHURST, AN INTRODUCTION TO INTERNATIONAL CRIMINAL LAW AND PROCEDURE, 402 (2nd edn, New York, Cambridge University Press, 2010).

[12]   As to amnesties, see William A. Schabas, Chapter 16 and Katharina Peschke, Chapter 8. As to immunities, see David Weissbrodt and Kristin K. Zinsmaster, Chapter 11.

[13]   Kai Ambos, *May a State Torture Suspects to Save the Life of Innocents?*, 6 J INTERNATIONAL CRIMINAL JUSTICE 261, 278 (2008); Antonio Cassese, INTERNATIONAL CRIMINAL LAW 255 (2nd edn, New York, Oxford University Press, 2008; Héctor Olásolo, UNLAWFUL ATTACKS IN COMBAT SITUATIONS, 235 (Leiden, Martinus Nijhoff Publishers, 2008). See also Cryer *et al.*, note 11 *supra*, at 403.

[14]   Cryer *et al.*, note 11 *supra*, at 403; Ambos, note 13 *supra*, at 285–6; Cassese, note 13 *supra*, at 256; Olásolo, note 13 *supra*, at 235.

just result,[15] the ICC Statute (essentially following the traditional common law approach) leaves open the question whether a specific defence qualifies as a justification or an excuse.[16] But even though the text of the ICC Statute does not distinguish justification from excuse, the rationale of this distinction should nevertheless be taken into account in interpreting the relevant provisions. This holds especially true for the duress/necessity defence in connection with the killing of innocent persons.[17]

Relevant Time

As to the decisive time at which a ground of exclusion must exist, the chapeau of article 31 refers to the 'time of that person's conduct'. Thus, the ICC Statute follows the 'act theory', instead of the so-called 'ubiquity principle', according to which the place and the result of the actual conduct are equally relevant.[18] The act theory is in line with the case law of the International Criminal Tribunal for Former Yugoslavia (ICTY).[19] This is the correct approach since both the prohibition and the substantive defences are linked to the conduct, while the result may be accidental or beyond the actor's control.[20]

MENTAL DISEASE OR DEFECT (ARTICLE 31(1)(a))[21]

ICC Statute, article 31(1)(a) excludes criminal responsibility if the actor, due to a mental disease or defect, is not able to recognize the unlawfulness of his conduct and/or control it according to the requirements of the law.[22] No one is to be held responsible if he cannot 'appreciate the unlawfulness or nature of his conduct' or he lacks capacity to control it because of a defect or disease which lies beyond his responsibility. This ground of exclusion exists in various legal systems;[23] its nature is that of an excuse because it addresses the actor's

---

15 Eser, note 2 *supra*, para. 17. See also the detailed analysis on the question whether a state may torture suspects to save the life of innocents in Ambos, note 13 *supra*, at 261 *et seq.*

16 See also Reinhard Merkel, *Gründe für den Ausschluss der Strafbarkeit im Völkerstrafrecht*, 114 Zeitschrift für die gesamte Strafrechtswissenschaft 437 (2002); Cherif M. Bassiouni, The Legislative History of the International Criminal Court: Introduction, Analysis, and Integrated Text, 158 (Ardsley, International Publishers, 2005); Eser, note 2 *supra*, paras 2, 17.

17 See the discussion of duress and necessity, *infra*.

18 Kai Ambos, *Other Grounds for Excluding Criminal Responsibility*, in Antonio Cassese, Paola Gaeta and John R.W.D. Jones (eds), I The Rome Statute of the International Criminal Court, A Commentary 1003, 1028 (New York, Oxford University Press, 2002); Eser, note 2 *supra*, para. 21.

19 See *Prosecutor* v. *Delalic et al.*, Case No. IT-96-21-T, TC II, Judgment, 16 November 1998, para. 1181.

20 Eser, note 2 *supra* 2, para. 21.

21 ICC statute, art. 31(1)(a) reads as follows: 'a person shall not be criminally responsible if ... (a) The person suffers from a mental disease or defect that destroys that person's capacity to appreciate the unlawfulness or nature of his or her conduct, or capacity to control his or her conduct to conform to the requirements of law'.

22 See also the definition of diminished responsibility in *Prosecutor* v. *Delalic et al.*, note 19 *supra*, para. 1169.

23 See the analysis in Ambos, note 118 *supra*, at 1019 *et seq.*

personal capacity of control based on his mental state. In cases of this defence, an accused's lack of capacity to control his conduct does not affect the lawfulness or unlawfulness of that conduct; the conduct remains unlawful. For example, consider the case of a mentally deranged combatant who shoots a civilian. The shooting is an unlawful act (war crime) but because of the combatant's mental defect, the soldier cannot be held legally responsible.

Despite several submissions by the defence,[24] mental diseases or defects as grounds for excluding criminal responsibility have not yet played an important role in international jurisprudence. Based on rule 67 of the ICTY Rules of Procedure and Evidence,[25] the ICTY distinguishes between insanity and diminished mental responsibility. Accordingly, *insanity* requires that the accused is, at the time of commission, unaware of what he is doing or incapable of forming a rational judgment as to whether his conduct is right or wrong. In contrast, *diminished responsibility* is based on the premise that, while recognizing the wrongful nature of his conduct, the accused, due to his mental abnormality, is unable to control (fully) his actions.[26] This abnormality must be supported by medical evidence. In addition, conduct exclusively motivated by emotions, such as jealousy, rage or hate, is excluded.[27] Thus, contrary to article 31(1)(a), diminished mental responsibility presupposes some residual responsibility, that is, it entails only a limitation, not the complete elimination of the actor's capacities.[28] It is not a defence *stricto sensu* excluding criminal responsibility, but only a partial defence resulting at best in a more lenient sentence.[29]

The exclusion of responsibility pursuant to article 31(1)(a) has two requirements. First, there must be a more than momentary defective mental (not psychological or emotional)[30] state.[31] A second requirement is the absence of the capacity to (cognitively) appreciate the

---

[24]   See, for example, *Prosecutor* v. *Banović*, Case No. IT-02-65/1-S, TC III, Sentencing Judgment, 28 October 2003, para. 79; *Prosecutor* v. *Sikirika et al.*, Case No. IT-95-8-S, TC III, Sentencing Judgment, 13 November 2001, para. 189; *Prosecutor* v. *Delalic et al.*, note 19 *supra*, para. 1156; *Prosecutor* v. *Vasiljevic*, Case No. IT-98-32-T, TC II, Judgment, 29. November 2002, para. 280; *Prosecutor* v. *Todorović*, Case No. IT-95-9/1-S, TC I, Sentencing Judgment, 31 July 2001, para. 94. See also the analysis by Massimo Scaliotti, *Defences Before the International Criminal Court: Substantive Grounds for Excluding Criminal Responsibility, Part 2'*, 2 INTERNATIONAL CRIMINAL L REV. 1, 20 (2002).

[25]   Rules of Procedure and Evidence adopted on 11 February 1994 as amended on 10 December 2009, IT/32/Rev. 42. The relevant part of ICTY Rules, rule 67 reads as follows '(B) Within the time-limit prescribed by the Trial Chamber or by the pre-trial judge ... (i) the defence shall notify the Prosecutor of its intent to offer: ... (b) any special defence, including that of diminished or lack of mental responsibility.'

[26]   *Prosecutor* v. *Delalic et al.*, note 19 *supra*, para. 1156. The word 'fully' was inserted by the author.

[27]   *Ibid.* para. 1166.

[28]   *Prosecutor* v. *Delalic et al.*, Case No. IT-96-21-A, Appeal Chamber Judgment, 20 February 2001, para. 587. See also Eser, note 2 *supra*, para. 29.

[29]   *Prosecutor* v. *Delalic et al.*, note 19 *supra*, para. 1162; *Prosecutor* v. *Delalic et al.*, note 28 *supra*, para. 582 *et seq.*; *Prosecutor* v. *Vasiljevic*, note 24 *supra*, para. 282; *Prosecutor* v. *Todorović*, note 24 *supra*, para. 93; Kriangsak Kittichaisaree, INTERNATIONAL CRIMINAL LAW, 262 (New York, Oxford University Press, 2001); Alexander Zahar and Göran Sluiter, INTERNATIONAL CRIMINAL LAW, 439 (Oxford, Oxford University Press, 2008).

[30]   See Werle, note 6 *supra*, para. 599; Cassese, note 13 *supra*, at 266; Eser, note 2 *supra*, para. 23.

[31]   See Eser, note 2 *supra*, para. 23, correctly stating that the wording is narrow (with regard to the *mental* state) and broad (with regard to the recognition of any 'defect') at the same time and that,

unlawfulness of the conduct or to control it (volitionally).[32] In essence, the actor does not know what he is doing and therefore cannot be blamed for his conduct. Responsibility may be excluded by a lack of intent if the mental defect is so serious as to exclude the actor's awareness or ability to act at all.

Notwithstanding the differences in the legal consequences, the defences of 'diminished mental responsibility' and 'mental disease or defect' have a considerable overlap. If one follows the line of the ICTY's jurisprudence, the main challenge for the defence in invoking article 31(1)(a) will be the *burden of proof*. The reasoning in *Delalic* is based on the presumption of sanity, that is, the defendant is deemed sane until the contrary is proven.[33] Similarly, with regard to diminished responsibility/insanity, the Chamber places the burden of proof on the defence.[34] The situation may be different if, as in the case of the ICC, the Prosecutor is not merely a party to the proceedings but is supposed to act as an impartial agent of justice.[35] Pursuant to ICC Statute, article 54(1)(a), the Prosecutor is under the legal obligation to establish the truth and, in doing so, investigate incriminating and exonerating circumstances equally. This means, at least in theory, that the Prosecutor must not concentrate solely on demonstrating the guilt of a suspect, but should pay equal attention to gathering any exculpatory evidence. If this obligation is to be taken seriously, then the Prosecutor must present exculpatory evidence which could contribute to the absolution of the accused.[36]

Despite the possibility of gaining useful help from the Prosecutor's investigations, the burden will be upon the defence to adduce the facts indicating a mental defect. The *Delalic* Trial Chamber pointed out that the standard of proof is 'not as heavy as the Prosecutor's burden in establishing the guilt of the accused', the defence must only be proved 'on the balance of probabilities'.[37] The Appeals Chamber confirmed this standard, stating that the defendant has to show that he was, 'more probably than not', suffering from a mental defect.[38] There is some controversy, however, as to whether the rule prohibiting any reversal

---

therefore, the word 'suffers' should be interpreted in requiring 'more than only a momentary disturbance'. In a similar vein, Werle, note 6 *supra*, para. 599.

[32]   See more detail in Eser, note 2 *supra*, para. 28–9.

[33]   *Prosecutor* v. *Delalic et al.*, note 19 *supra*, para. 1157. Cf. also Kittichaisaree, note 29 *supra*, at 262.

[34]   *Prosecutor* v. *Delalic et al.*, note 19 *supra*, para. 1172. See also *Prosecutor* v. *Delalic et al.*, note 28 *supra*, paras 582, 590; *Prosecutor* v. *Vasiljevic*, note 24 *supra*, para. 282.

[35]   *Situation in the Congo*, Case No. ICC-01/04-84, Prosecution's Reply on the Applications for Participation 01/04-1/dp to 01/04-6/dp of 15 August 2005, para. 32; *Prosecutor* v. *Thomas Lubanga Dyilo*, Case No. ICC-01/04–01/05-734, Defence Response to the Appeals Chamber Order of 24 November 2006 of 29 November 2006, para. 27; *Situation in Uganda*, Case No. ICC-02/04-85, Prosecution's Reply under Rule 89 (1) to the Applications for Participation of Applicants a/0010/06, a/0064/06 to a/a/0070/06, a/0081/06 to a/0104/06 and a/0111/06 to a/0127/06 in the Uganda Situation of 28 February 2007, para. 32; *Situation in the Congo*, Case No. ICC-01/04-419, Request for Leave to Appeal the Decision on the Request of the OPCD on the Production of Relevant Supporting Documentation Pursuant to Regulation 86(2)(e) of the Regulations of the Court and on the Disclosure of Exculpatory Materials by the Prosecutor of 13 December 2007, para. 32.

[36]   See, in a similar vein Roger S. Clark, *Drafting a General Part to a Penal Code: Some Thoughts Inspired by the Negotiations on the Rome Statute of the International Criminal Court and by the Court's First Substantive Law Discussion in the Lubanga Dyilo Confirmation Proceedings*, 19 Criminal Law Forum 519, 532 (2008).

[37]   *Prosecutor* v. *Delalic et al.*, note 19 *supra*, para. 1172.

[38]   *Prosecutor* v. *Delalic et al.*, note 28 *supra*, para. 582.

of the burden of proof to the detriment of the accused[39] reduces the standard of proof even more to the point where mere reasonable doubts might be sufficient to establish a defence based on the mental state.[40] This is an open question to be decided by the ICC; but in any case, demonstrating probability goes beyond indicating mere doubts.

These considerations regarding the burden and standard of proof apply *mutatis mutandis* to all defences.[41] The defence of insanity, however, poses specific evidentiary problems. For after a certain lapse of time, even the best experts will find it difficult to present a reliable statement about the defendant's mental health at an earlier time when the prohibited acts were committed. In most cases, courts have to rely exclusively on the information provided by the accused, without having an opportunity to cross-check his story with other sources. This significantly reduces the probative value of the expert evidence.[42] If the Tribunal concludes that the defendant was insane at the time he committed the crime, the defendant must not be convicted because he cannot be blamed for his conduct. If he poses a threat to himself or to others, preventive measures to protect society may be taken.[43]

INTOXICATION (ARTICLE 31(1)(b))[44]

In ICTY proceedings, several accused have claimed to have committed their crimes under the influence of drugs or alcohol.[45] Intoxication could give rise to a form of diminished mental responsibility.[46] The jurisprudence takes, however, a restrictive approach. The *Kvocka* Trial Chamber held that a state of intoxication could only constitute a mitigating circumstance if it was brought about by force or coercion, but not if the defendant produced this situation voluntarily or consciously. The Chamber further held, following the approach of some Arabic states and societies,[47] that 'particularly in contexts where violence is the norm and weapons are carried, intentionally consuming drugs or alcohol constitutes an aggravating rather than a mitigating factor'.[48]

---

39   See ICC Statute, art. 67(1)(i).
40   In this sense Schabas, note 2 *supra*, at 227. See also Scaliotti, note 24 *supra*, at 27 *et seq.*
41   See also the discussion by Scaliotti, note 6 *supra*, at 123 *et seq.*
42   See *Prosecutor* v. *Delalic et al.,* note 19 *supra*, paras 1181 *et seq.* Confirmed in *Prosecutor* v. *Delalic et al.,* note 28 *supra*, paras 593–4. See also *Prosecutor* v. *Vasiljevic,* note 24 *supra*, para. 286.
43   Scaliotti, note 24 *supra*, at 27.
44   ICC Statute, art. 31(1)(b) reads as follows: 'a person shall not be criminally responsible if … (b) The person is in a state of intoxication that destroys that person's capacity to appreciate the unlawfulness or nature of his or her conduct, or capacity to control his or her conduct to conform to the requirements of law, unless the person has become voluntarily intoxicated under such circumstances that the person knew, or disregarded the risk, that, as a result of the intoxication, he or she was likely to engage in conduct constituting a crime within the jurisdiction of the Court.'
45   See, for example, *Prosecutor* v. *Kvocka et al.,* Case No. IT-98-30/1-T, TC I Judgment, 2 November 2002, para. 706; *Prosecutor* v. *Todorović,* note 24 *supra*, para. 90; *Prosecutor* v. *Vasiljevic,* note 24 *supra*, para. 284.
46   Compare *Prosecutor* v. *Mrdja,* Case N o. IT-02-59-S, TC I, Decision on the Defence Motion for Medical Examination and Variation of Scheduling Order, 15 September 2003.
47   See Eser, note 2 *supra*, para. 35.
48   *Prosecutor* v. *Kvocka et al.,* note 45 *supra*, para. 706.

A comparative overview of several national legal systems[49] shows that intoxication – as opposed to mental disease – is not universally recognized as a defence. Rather, whether a national legal system recognizes an exemption from responsibility under the intoxication defence depends to a great extent on the socio-cultural context of the society concerned, in particular its attitude towards alcohol.[50] Therefore, ICC Statute, article 31(1)(b) tries to strike a balance between completely disregarding and unconditionally recognizing intoxication as a ground of exclusion.

With regard to its scope of application, the question arises whether intoxication is applicable to all core crimes. The question was answered by an explanatory footnote stating that 'voluntary intoxication as a ground for excluding criminal responsibility would generally not apply in cases of genocide or crimes against humanity, but might apply to isolated acts constituting war crimes'.[51] The reason for this limitation was the general feeling among delegations that it borders on the absurd to admit such a defence in the face of such serious crimes as genocide and crimes against humanity. As a matter of fact, article 31(1)(b) is not expressly limited to war crimes. Thus, one may argue that it should be at least applicable to low level perpetrators who have committed only a few underlying acts within the framework of a broader pattern of genocide and/or crimes against humanity.[52]

Article 31(1)(b) presupposes a certain degree of intoxication. Given that intoxication is to be understood as 'a diminished ability to act with full mental and physical capabilities because of alcohol or drug consumption',[53] it requires a sort of toxic impact, for example, the consumption of an exogenic substance. Thus, responsibility is not excluded if an abnormal mental state is produced by external circumstances.[54] In addition, as in the case of a mental disease defence, it is required that the intoxication destroys the defendant's ability to control and assess his conduct. Thus, the intoxication defence raises similar evidentiary problems as discussed above.[55]

Further, article 31(1)(b) adopts the *actio libera in causa* ('*alic*') principle excluding the defence if 'the person has become voluntary intoxicated under such circumstances that the person knew, or disregarded the risk, that, as a result of the intoxication, he was likely to engage in conduct constituting a crime within the jurisdiction of the Court'. The underlying rationale of this principle is to prevent a *mala fide* intoxication, or rather intentionally bringing about intoxication – as a 'free act' ('*actio libera*') – with the preconceived intent to commit a crime in the resulting state, all in order to then invoke this state as a ground for excluding responsibility.[56] In this case, the actor is punished for the crime committed as if he committed it with full responsibility; he was free and fully responsible when he set the cause ('*in causa*') and thus is blamed for the intentional and attributable '*actio libera*' which brought about the state of non-responsibility. The principle is generally recognized in both

---

49   Ambos, note 18 *supra*, at 1019 *et seq.*
50   *Ibid.* 1021; Eser, note 2 *supra*, para. 30. See also the comparative overview in Scaliotti, note 24 *supra*, at 29 *et seq.*
51   UN Doc. A/CONF.183/C.1/WGGP/L.4/Add.1/Rev.1 (1998), 4, n. 8.
52   In this sense see Eser, note 2 *supra*, para. 31.
53   Bryan A. Garner (ed.), BLACK'S LAW DICTIONARY (8th edn, St Paul, Thomson West, 2007).
54   Eser, note 2 *supra*, para. 33.
55   See note 32 *supra* 32 *et seq.* and main text.
56   Ambos, note18 *supra*, at 1030; Eser, note 2 *supra*, para. 35.

continental and common law and is codified in many national codes.[57] It is, however, hotly disputed whether a reckless or negligent alic also entails criminal responsibility; for example, it is not settled whether an actor is fully responsible if he does not possess the criminal intent when becoming intoxicated and negligently fails to recognize the risk that he could commit a crime in his later state of intoxication.[58] Pursuant to article 31(1)(b) the intoxication defence is already precluded if the person 'disregarded' the risk of committing a crime. This term clearly indicates that the relevant provision does not only recognize the intentional *alic* but something below this mental standard.[59] The exact meaning of 'disregarded' is, however, unclear.

The American Law Institute (ALI)'s Model Penal Code differentiates between negligence and recklessness. In the first variant, the agent 'should be aware of substantial and unjustifiable risk',[60] while in the latter case he 'consciously disregards a substantial and unjustifiable risk'.[61] The wording of article 31(1)(b) is very similar to this definition of recklessness. This would appear to indicate that at least in case of a reckless *alic,* the defendant is not spared from criminal responsibility.[62] Thus, the exclusion of the intoxication defence is based on two cumulative preconditions: (1) the person became intentionally drunk or otherwise intoxicated, and (2) the person knowingly or recklessly took the risk that, due to the intoxication, he would be likely to commit or otherwise get involved in a core crime of the ICC.[63] The second requirement, however, poses evidentiary problems. It is difficult enough to prove that a defendant voluntarily became drunk in order to commit an isolated crime, such as murder, but it is almost impossible to prove that he became drunk to commit 'a crime within the jurisdiction of the Court', that is, a particularly atrocious crime.[64]

In sum, the ICC Statute recognizes intoxication as a full defence not only if and as long as the person was involuntary intoxicated,[65] but also if the defendant voluntary became drunk, unaware of the risk that this could result in the committing of a core crime. In the latter case, the situation fundamentally differs from article 31(1)(a) because the existence of a mental defect or disease lies beyond the responsibility of the defendant, while the intoxication is the result of his free and autonomous decision (*'actio libera'*) to consume drugs or alcohol. Normally, the person concerned knows that this will affect his capacity of self-control and appreciation and, thus, he may still be blameworthy. In judicial practice, the *alic* should be of little importance since the ICC will, already for the evidentiary reasons indicated, focus on the prosecution of sober commanders and civilian superiors (usually responsible for the plan-

---

57   See George P. Fletcher, RETHINKING CRIMINAL LAW 846–7 (Boston, Little, Brown 1978; Kai Ambos, *Der Anfang vom Ende der Actio Libera in Causa?* 55 NEUE JURISTISCHE WOCHENSCHRIFT 2296, 2298 (1997); also Jean Pradel, DROIT PÉNAL COMPARÉ para. 113 (3rd edn, Paris, Dalloz 2008).

58   See the comparative overview in Pradel, note 57 *supra*, para. 113.

59   For a different interpretation, which is, however, apparently inspired by the official German translation of 'disregarding the risk', see Merkel, note 16 *supra*, at 444.

60   See Model penal Code s. 2.02(2)(d).

61   See *ibid.* s. 2.02(2)(c).

62   See also Werle, note 6 *supra*, para. 608; Eser, note 2 *supra*, para. 35.

63   Eser, note 2 *supra*, para. 35.

64   See also Scaliotti, note 24 *supra*, at 37–8; Ambos, note 18 *supra*, at 1030–1; Eser, note 2 *supra*, para. 36. As to different solutions offered by national law see also Ambos, note 18 *supra*, at 1031.

65   For example, soldiers may be unknowingly intoxicated with a drug and therefore commit crimes, as apparently occurred with US soldiers in Vietnam who were dosed with LSD.

ning and organization of atrocities) rather than focus on the pursuit of drunken soldiers directly committing war crimes.[66]

SELF-DEFENCE AND DEFENCE OF OTHERS (ARTICLE 31(1)(c))[67]

ICC Statute, article 31(1)(c) allows for *proportionate* self-defence and defence of others against an imminent and unlawful use of force which endangers a person or property of particular importance. Thus, the provision has two basic requirements: (1) the existence of a certain danger to a person or property brought about by the unlawful use of force, and (2) a proportionate reaction against it.[68] While no detailed codification of this criminal defence previously existed,[69] it constitutes a classical ground of justification and is recognized as such in comparative law.[70] Still, its requirements remain a subject of some controversy.

As to the defence situation – the 'imminent and unlawful use of force' producing a 'danger' to a person or property – the provision opts for an objective *ex ante* test,[71] that is, the situation must exist objectively (not only in the actor's mind) at the time of the counter-action. The 'subjectification' of legitimate defence, as particularly known in some common law countries,[72] is thereby rejected. Thus, if the actor reasonably believed that the force or danger existed, he does not act objectively in self-defence but may invoke the rules on mistake of fact or law.[73]

The other elements of the first requirement are less complicated. 'Force' must be understood broadly, encompassing physical coercion and psychological threats; the 'force' must be 'imminent', that is, immediately antecedent, presently exercised or still enduring. This means that both a pre-emptive strike against a feared attack and a retaliation against a successful attack are excluded.[74] The use of force is 'unlawful' if not legally permitted.[75] Given this broad definition, only the 'danger' brought about by the use of force can restrict the scope of

---

66   See also Scaliotti, note 24 *supra*, at 37.

67   ICC Statute, art. 31(1)(c) reads as follows: 'a person shall not be criminally responsible if, at the time of that person's conduct: … (c) The person acts reasonably to defend himself or herself or another person or, in the case of war crimes, property which is essential for the survival of the person or another person or property which is essential for accomplishing a military mission, against an imminent and unlawful use of force in a manner proportionate to the degree of danger to the person or the other person or property protected. The fact that the person was involved in a defensive operation conducted by forces shall not in itself constitute a ground for excluding criminal responsibility under this subparagraph.'

68   *Prosecutor v. Kordić and Čerkez,* Case No. IT-95-14/2-T, TC III, Judgment, 26 February 2001, para. 451.

69   See thereto Ambos, note 18 *supra*, at 1004 *et seq.*, 1015 *et seq.*

70   *Prosecutor v. Kordić and Čerkez,* note 68 *supra*, para. 451; GEORGE P. FLETCHER, BASIC CONCEPTS OF CRIMINAL LAW 130 (New York, Oxford University Press, 1998); Pradel, note 57 *supra*, at 102; see also Eser, note 2 *supra*, para. 37 all with further references.

71   Eser, note 2 *supra*, para. 45.

72   See the comparative overview by Ambos, note 18 *supra*, at 1021 *et seq.*

73   See the discussion of mistake of fact and mistake of law, *infra*

74   Fletcher, note 70 *supra*, at 133–4: 'Legitimate self-defense must be neither too soon nor too late'. See also with regard to terrorist attacks or threats ('ticking bomb scenario') Ambos, note 13 *supra*, at 273–4.

75   Cryer *et al.*, note 11 *supra*, at 409.

the application of self-defence.[76] Certainly, danger must imply a serious risk to the life or physical integrity of a person; as to property, a special qualifier indicates that danger to just *any* property is not sufficient to trigger the defence.[77] In fact, the protection of property is limited to war crimes situations in which the property is 'essential for the survival of the person or another person' or 'essential for accomplishing a military mission'.[78] The property defence was a point of major discussion during the Rome Conference.[79] This is understandable since the difference in value attached to life and physical integrity, on the one hand, and property, on the other, justifies a clear distinction in the protection afforded to these legal interests. Thus, a teleological and systematic interpretation taking into account the second sentence of sub-paragraph (c) may be necessary to avoid the use of the property clause 'as a readily available "panacea" in any sort of military confrontation'.[80]

The defence must be *reasonable,* for example, the defence must be necessary and appropriate to prevent or avert the danger.[81] Thus, a reasonable reaction must create only such harm to the aggressor as is absolutely necessary to repel the danger, and the means applied must not be inept or inefficient.[82] In other words, the counter-action must be a suitable and minimally severe, but equally effective means to avert the danger.[83] Apart from that, the defence must be *proportionate*, that is, it may not cause disproportionately greater harm than that sought to be avoided.[84] The proportionality element provides for a balancing of the conflicting interests between the defender and the aggressor[85] and, in this sense, brings self-defence close to the necessity defence. In concrete terms, this means that the killing of an aggressor is only admissible as *ultima ratio* to avoid one's own or another's death or serious bodily harm.[86]

Finally, self-defence has a *subjective element*. This requirement may be deduced from the wording of article 31(1)(c) (a defender has to act 'to defend himself')[87] or derived from general principles of comparative law according to article 31(3) in connection with article 21(1)(c).[88] It is generally recognized that the defender must at least know about the attack; it is controversial, though, whether he must also be motivated by this knowledge, that is, act with a kind of will to defend himself.[89] This additional volitional threshold should be rejected because it would require too much and is not demanded by the rationale of the subjective

---

[76]   Ambos, note 18 *supra*, at 1032–3.

[77]   Eser, note 2 *supra*, para. 43.

[78]   A/CONF.183/C.1/WGGP/L.4/Add. 3 (1998), 2.

[79]   See Scaliotti, note 6 *supra*, at 165 *et seq.*

[80]   See in more detail Eser, note 2 *supra*, para. 44.

[81]   Eser, note 2 *supra*, para. 47.

[82]   See also Fletcher, note 70 *supra*, at 135.

[83]   See also Ambos, note 13 *supra*, at 275.

[84]   See also Fletcher, note 70 *supra*, at 135; Thomas Weigend, Notwehr im Völkerstrafrecht, in Ulrich Sieber et al. (eds), Festschrift für Klaus Tiedemann 1439, 1449 (Köln, Carl Heymanns Verlag, 2008).

[85]   See also Fletcher, note 70 *supra*, at 136.

[86]   In this vein also Werle, note 6 *supra*, para. 549; Eser, note 2 *supra*, para. 47.

[87]   Eser, note 2 *supra*, para. 48.

[88]   Ambos, note 18 *supra*, at 1035.

[89]   This broader view is taken by Fletcher, note 70 *supra*, at 137; Werle, note 6 *supra*, para. 550; but see Claus Roxin, I Strafrecht Allgemeiner Teil (4th edn, München, Beck 2006) at s. 14 para. 97 *et seq.*; s. 15 paras 129–30.

element. This element constitutes an *additional* requirement which lends stronger legitimacy to the defender's claim that his conduct was justified and lawful. If it is not present, the defence act is only half-lawful. On the one hand, the wrongful result (*Erfolgsunwert*) of the offence (the prohibitive norm) is negated by the objective situation of self-defence (the permissive norm). At the same time, the wrongful act or conduct (*Handlungs-* or *Verhaltensunwert*) continues to exist because the actor did not act with knowledge that it was a matter of self-defence but only on the occasion of such a situation.[90] He therefore does not deserve the benefit of a full exclusion from criminal responsibility. Of course, his knowledge of this situation would be sufficient to award him the full effect of the defence. In sum, the use of force cannot be justified by the mere objective existence of the use of force; it also requires that the defender acted in good faith, knowing that he had been attacked and perhaps even believing that he was entitled to self-defence.

The second sentence of sub-paragraph (c) clarifies the difference between *collective* and *individual* self-defence. Participation in a collective defensive operation does not in itself exclude criminal responsibility; rather the actor's conduct must remain within the limits of legitimate individual self-defence as defined in the first sentence of subparagraph (c).[91] Still another question is whether the recourse to individual self-defence presupposes that the collective self-defence operation itself is lawful. The argument that it does is unconvincing if, as understood here,[92] collective and individual self-defence are not interrelated but independent from each other. Collective self-defence relates to inter-state conflicts and is therefore state-centric and sovereignty oriented in the sense of classical public international law: a right to self-defence by and against collective entities. In contrast, individual self-defence relates to conflicts between two or more individuals and tries to find an adequate solution to their conflict by giving the person attacked an individual right of self-defence against the aggressor. Thus, individual self-defence is governed by the emerging rules of ICL based on comparative criminal law. Consequently, the legality or illegality of a collective defence operation is independent of any determination, recognition or rejection of an individual right of self-defence related to acts within the framework of this operation.[93]

The recognition of self-defence is heavily criticised by Eric David. In his view, ICC Statute, article 31(1)(c) disturbs the balance between military necessity and the protection of fundamental human rights which is an integral part of the definition of war crimes.[94] Referring to the ICTY Judgment in *Kordić and Čerkez*[95] he points out that military operations

---

[90]   See Roxin, note 89 *supra*, s. 14 paras 96, 104 *et seq.*

[91]   *Prosecutor* v. *Kordić and Čerkez,* note *supra* 68, para. 452.

[92]   I do not use the term 'collective' and 'individual' in the sense of UN Charter art. 51, namely as defence of one state against another state or a group of states against one or many states or as defence of a third state, etc., but in a criminal law sense as explained in the text. As to the meaning of the different terms see also Eser, note 2 *supra*, para. 39.

[93]   Compare Werle, note 6 *supra*, para. 552; Eser, note 2 *supra* , para. 39; Weigend, note 84 *supra*, at 1441. For a different view apparently see John C. Dehn, Permissible Perfidy? Analysing the Colombian Hostage Rescue, the Capture of Rebel Leaders and the World's Reaction, 6 J INTERNATIONAL CRIMINAL JUSTICE 627, 646 *et seq.* (2008), who, however, seems to overlook ICC Statute, art. 31(1)(c) clause 2.

[94]   Eric David, PRINCIPES DE DROIT DES CONFLICTS ARMÉS, para. 4.352 (4th edn, Bruxelles, Brylant, 2008).

[95]   *Prosecutor* v. *Kordić and Čerkez,* note 68 *supra*, para. 452.

in self-defence do not provide a justification for serious violations of international humanitarian law (IHL).[96] In his view, ICL has to obey the absolute prohibitions of IHL.[97] Therefore, a justification of war crimes is said to violate *jus cogens*. Consequently, David regards article 31(1)(c) as null and void.[98] Apparently, Belgium (David's home state) adopted his view; it declared along with the ratification of the ICC Statute that article 31(1)(c) could only be applied and interpreted 'having regard to the rules of IHL which may not be derogated from'.[99]

This view is unconvincing, however. First of all, it rests on an (admittedly widespread)[100] conceptual misunderstanding as to the relationship between human rights and humanitarian law, on the one hand, and ICL on the other. These areas of law are concerned with structurally different subject matters directed at different addressees (collective state responsibility versus individual criminal responsibility).[101] A prohibition of humanitarian law, absolute as it may be, is only addressed to *states*; it does not automatically or necessarily entail the criminal responsibility of *individuals*.[102] While it is certainly true that human rights and humanitarian law strongly influence ICL, one must not ignore the fundamental structural differences between them. A tendency to conflate IHL and ICL contributes to the broadening of criminal liability under the latter based on an almost reflexive recourse to the rationale of the former.[103] Even if one accepts that IHL and ICL are interdependent, IHL still cannot repeal the inherent right of individual self-defence. Article 31(1)(c) expresses the exceptional way in which that right, as a rule of international *criminal* law, cannot be displaced by international *humanitarian* law; at best, the latter may call for a more restrictive approach to that right.[104]

DURESS AND NECESSITY (ARTICLE 31(1)(d))[105]

General

Necessity and duress are generally recognized as two separate defences in comparative

---

[96]   David, note 94 *supra*, para. 4.352.

[97]   *Ibid.* para. 4.353.

[98]   *Ibid.* para. 4.354.

[99]   See thereto Schabas, note 2 *supra*, at 229; Weigend, note 84 *supra*, at 1440 n. 7.

[100]   For a recent account see Darryl Robinson, *The Identity Crisis of International Criminal Law*, 21 LEIDEN J INTERNATIONAL L 925, 929 *et seq.* (2008) identifying and criticizing the substantive and structural conflation between these areas of law advocated by human rights activists, NGOs and certain academics.

[101]   Weigend, note 84 *supra*, at 1443.

[102]   Ambos, note 13 *supra*, at 269.

[103]   Compare Robinson, note 100 *supra*, at 946 *et seq.* criticizing the excessive broadening of liability.

[104]   In a similar vein Weigend, note 84 *supra*, at 1444 *et seq.*

[105]   ICC Statute, art. 31 (1)(d) reads as follows: 'a person shall not be criminally responsible if … (d) The conduct which is alleged to constitute a crime within the jurisdiction of the Court has been caused by duress resulting from a threat of imminent death or of continuing or imminent serious bodily harm against that person or another person, and the person acts necessarily and reasonably to avoid this threat, provided that the person does not intend to cause a greater harm than the one sought to be avoided. Such a threat may either be: (i) made by other persons; or (ii) constituted by other circumstances beyond that person's control.'

criminal law.[106] Despite this fact, one finds that in ICL neither the official codifications of the International Law Commission nor the Rome Statute of the ICC have so far considered it necessary to distinguish between them.[107] This is unfortunate. Well-established and reasonable distinctions should not be blurred. While duress refers to the lack of freedom of will or choice in the face of an immediate threat,[108] necessity is based on a choice of evils with the decision taken in favour of the lesser evil.[109] Thus, in the case of *necessity*, the unlawfulness of the incriminating act, said to be the lesser evil, is eliminated by the higher legal interest which the actor purports to serve. The principal remaining controversy concerns just how much higher or greater this protected interest must be.[110] When applied to the protection of a *higher* legal interest, necessity permits an act which is actually prohibited (fulfilling the elements of an offence) and thus renders this act lawful, that is, it is a *justification*.[111] In the case of *duress*, on the other hand, such a justification cannot be invoked; it can only be argued that the accused cannot fairly be expected to resist the threat. In other words, the underlying rationale of duress is not the balancing of competing legal interests but the criterion of *Zumutbarkeit* (that is, could it fairly be expected that the person concerned would resist the threat?).[112] The personal or actor-oriented nature of duress makes clear that it is merely an *excuse*.[113] The legal consequences of the distinction will be illustrated below when we consider the possibility of the duress defence against the killing of innocent civilians.[114]

Article 31(1)(d) of the ICC Statute, by its terms, apparently subsumes necessity under the rubric of duress as grounds for excluding criminal responsibility. It applies when the following elements are present:

(a)   a threat of imminent death or continuing or imminent serious bodily harm against the person concerned or a third person made by other persons or by circumstances beyond that person's control;
(b)   a necessary and reasonable reaction to avoid this threat;
(c)   on the subjective level, the corresponding intent (not intending to cause a greater harm than the one sought to be avoided).

The provision contains *objective* elements of both necessity and duress. The 'threat' element applies to necessity and duress, while the 'necessary and reasonable reaction'

---

106   See Fletcher, note 70 *supra*, at 138 *et seq.*, 164; Pradel, note 57 *supra*, para. 103, 114.
107   See Ambos, note 18 *supra*, at 1035–6.
108   See Pradel, note 57 *supra*, para. 114; CHERIF M. BASSIOUNI, CRIMES AGAINST HUMANITY IN INTERNATIONAL CRIMINAL LAW 484 (2nd edn, The Hague, Kluwer International, 1999); Ambos, note 18 *supra*, at 1036 with further references.
109   See also Eser, note 2 *supra*, para. 49.
110   See the comparative overview by Pradel, note 57 *supra*, para. 103.
111   See the overview in Christiane Nill-Theobald, DEFENCES' BEI KRIEGSVERBRECHEN AM BEISPIEL DEUTSCHLANDS UND DER USA 213–15 (Freiburg, Max Planck Institute for Foreign and International Criminal Law, 1998); Eser, note 2 *supra*, para. 49; see also Ambos, note 13 *supra*, at 280 stressing the importance of the balancing test.
112   See Fletcher, note 57 *supra*, at 833; Ambos, note 18 *supra*, at 1037.
113   See Nill-Theobald, note 111 *supra*, at 268–70, 274, 279; Eser, note 2 *supra*, para. 49.
114   See the section on special considerations applicable to the killing of innocent civilians, *infra*.

element applies only to necessity. It also introduces a new *subjective* requirement which relates to the 'choice of evils' criterion.[115]

Threat of Death or Serious Bodily Harm

Prima facie, it appears that a threat may exist even if there has been no use of force within the meaning of sub-paragraph (c); this would correspond to the general distinction between self-defence and necessity in comparative law,[116] the former requiring a quite focused attack ('use of force') and the latter a broader danger ('threat'). Yet, the qualifier referring to 'death' or 'harm against that person' makes clear that a threat in the sense of sub-paragraph (d) is to be understood more narrowly than the use of force in the case of self-defence. While the latter may encompass psychological threats, *lato sensu,* sub-paragraph (d) only recognizes such threats if they entail physical acts and/or consequences, that is, 'imminent' death or bodily harm.[117] As to the temporal requirement ('continuing' or 'imminent'), the already mentioned difference between attack (narrower) and danger (broader) implies that it should be understood more broadly in the case of duress/necessity.[118] Nevertheless, the threat must be present; the materialization of the danger cannot lie too far in the future.[119] Sub-paragraph (d) also encompasses continuing threats which may result in death or serious harm at any time.[120] An abstract danger or a mere increased general probability of harm is not sufficient.[121]

The pressure itself must be directed against the person concerned or against *any* third person. Thus, the provision does not require a special relationship between the person threatened and the actor.[122] But in case of altruistic necessity (solely for the benefit of others) the actor is only justified if the threat to the other person is serious enough to compel a reasonable person to commit an international crime.[123]

As to its origin, the threat must be 'made by other persons' or 'constituted by other circumstances'. Thus, not the source but the gravity of the danger is of particular importance.[124] But not even the existence of overwhelming pressure constitutes duress if the actor himself *caused* the danger. This requirement is implicitly contained in article 31(1)(d)(ii) in the reference to 'circumstances beyond that person's control' (clearer in the French version: 'circon-

---

[115] Ambos, note 18 *supra*, at 1037–8.

[116] Compare Ambos, note 13 *supra*, at 281.

[117] See also Cryer *et al.*, note 11 *supra*, at 412; Werle, note 6 *supra*, para, 560; Eser, note 2 *supra*, para. 53. In a similar vein *Prosecutor* v. *Erdemović*, Case No. IT-96-26, Appeals Chamber, Separate and Dissenting Opinion of Judge Cassese, 7 October 1997, para. 14 holding that necessity requires 'threats to life and limb'.

[118] Ambos, note 13 *supra*, at 281. Cryer *et al.*, note 11 *supra*, at 412 also argue for a different interpretation of the temporal requirements in sub-paras (c) and (d).

[119] See Kai Ambos, DER ALLGEMEINE TEIL DES VÖLKERSTRAFRECHTS 850 (Berlin, Duncker & Humblot, 2002); Ambos, note 13 *supra*, at 281 with a critical analysis of the ticking bomb cases and the relevant case law; see also Dehn, note 93 *supra*, at 645.

[120] Ambos, note 119 *supra*, at 850; Werle, note 6 *supra*, para. 560. Compare also Dehn, note 93 *supra*, at 645–6.

[121] Werle, note 6 *supra*, para. 560; Eser, note 2 *supra*, para. 53.

[122] Eser, note 2 *supra*, para. 55.

[123] See in more detail Eser, note 2 *supra*, para. 55 *et seq.*

[124] As to the different approach in traditional common law see Ambos, note 18 *supra*, at 1023 *et seq.*

stances indépendantes de sa volonté'). In other words, circumstances within the person's control or even caused by the person do not fulfil this requirement.[125] This issue is related to the question whether necessity and duress are excluded if the defendant has voluntary exposed himself to danger. The delegates in Rome could not agree on a definition of self-exposure that would preclude these defences and therefore it will be up to the Court to decide the issue.[126]

Another limitation to this ground for excluding responsibility can follow from the actor's status. If the actor belongs to a special profession, he may be expected to tolerate greater dangers and higher risks than ordinary people. Soldiers, for example, have a special duty to take on dangers inherent in their profession.[127] However, while soldiers must certainly face higher risks than ordinary persons with regard to tasks typically related to the exercise of their functions, they are not obliged passively to accept their certain death or serious bodily harm. Also, a soldier is not expected to comply with an illegal order to commit an international crime. The commission of such crimes does not belong to the tasks typically related to a soldier's functions.[128] Finally, as will be argued in detail below, their special status does not, as a general matter, preclude soldiers from invoking duress as a defence in the cases where innocent persons have been killed.[129]

The issue of status reinforces our earlier conclusion that the kind of threat required relates to the criterion of what can reasonably be expected from a person acting under duress (*Zumutbarkeit*). This question cannot be decided in abstract terms, but only in light of the specific circumstances and above all, the personal characteristics of the actor.[130]

Necessary and Reasonable Reaction

In order to fall within the defence of duress/necessity the reaction has to be 'necessary' and 'reasonable'. The difference from sub-paragraph (c) on self-defence is that a 'proportionate' reaction is not explicitly required. Yet, this difference may be only of a terminological nature because the term 'reasonable' can be an umbrella term encompassing 'necessary', 'proportionate', etc.[131] In this sense, it is clear that the means used have to be apt and efficient, that the harm should be limited to that absolutely necessary to avoid the threat, and that, most importantly, the reaction should not cause greater harm than that sought to be avoided.[132] It is unfortunate that, despite this substantive similarity, the terms used in sub-paragraphs (c) and (d) were not harmonized.

---

[125]   Werle, note 6 *supra*, para. 565; Cryer *et al.*, note 11 *supra*, at 412; Eser, note 2 *supra*, para. 54. See also Judge Cassese, note 117 *supra*, para. 16.

[126]   Scaliotti, note 6 *supra*, at 153; Werle, note 6 *supra*, para. 566.

[127]   With special reference to the German law see Werle, note 6 *supra*, para. 567; Ambos, note 18 *supra*, at 1039. The same applies to policemen, firemen and other professionals with a special duty, see Roxin, note 89 *supra*, s. 22 para. 39.

[128]   See Nill-Theobald, note 111 *supra*, at 260–1.

[129]   See the section on special considerations applicable to the killing of innocent civilians, *infra*.

[130]   Eser, note 2 *supra*, para. 56 *et seq.*

[131]   See also Cryer *et al.*, note 11 *supra*, at 412–3.

[132]   Ambos, note 2 *supra*, at 1040; Eser, note 2 *supra*, para. 59.

Subjective Requirements

The general subjective requirement, that is, the actor's knowledge that he is acting under duress, has a solid basis in comparative law.[133] This general requirement can be deduced from the wording of the second requirement of sub-paragraph (d) that 'the person acts necessarily and reasonably to avoid this threat.' Thus, the act is linked to and determined by the threat and the actor has to act with the knowledge of the threat. One could go even further and require the actor's reaction to be motivated by the will to avert the danger. This stricter requirement can be found in national law[134] and may be explained by the conceptual difference between self-defence and duress/necessity. Since the person acting in self-defence has a stronger right than the one acting under duress/necessity, the mental requirement for the former must be less demanding than for the latter. Therefore, while the requirement of a specific motivation in the case of self-defence is controversial,[135] it may be more acceptable in the case of duress/necessity.[136] The requirement that acts be motivated by the will to avert the danger should make the duress/necessity defence inapplicable in all cases where the actor voluntarily, ambitiously and with self-interest participates in a crime.[137]

In contrast, the specific subjective requirement of the 'provided that' clause in article 31(1)(d) is a compromise formula unprecedented in comparative law.[138] In fact, this formula introduces the common law 'subjectification'[139] of defences through the back door. It is not objectively required, at least not explicitly, that the actor avoids a greater harm; rather, he need only intend to do so.[140] In other words, duress is excluded – on the subjective level – if the actor intended to cause a greater harm, a fact that would have to be proved by the prosecution. According to Bassiouni, this formula 'excludes decision-makers, senior executors and even mid-level ones leaving it open only to low level executors'.[141] This idea is not entirely correct. While it is true that decision-makers and senior executors cannot invoke duress, this has little to do with the 'provided that' clause. Instead their inability to invoke duress is due to the general structure of the defence which implies, on a factual level, pressure or coercion from 'top to bottom'. In other words, the people at the top cannot invoke duress because they cannot be coerced. In contrast, 'mid-level' officials can potentially be coerced by their superiors to an extent that would, in principle, entitle them to invoke duress.

Special Considerations Applicable to the Killing of Innocent Civilians

In *Erdemović*,[142] the ICTY was called upon to decide whether the killing of innocent civil-

---

[133]   See the comparative overview by Ambos, note 2 *supra*, at 1023 *et seq.* and Nill-Theobald, note 111 *supra*, at 229, 230, 259, 277, 280.

[134]   See on the German law Nill-Theobald, note 111 *supra*, at 229, 277: '*Gefahrabwendungswille*'; see also the comparative (legislative) overview by Ambos, note 2 *supra*, at 1023 *et seq.*

[135]   See note 89 *supra* and main text.

[136]   See Werle, note 6 *supra* 6, para. 563.

[137]   See Nill-Theobald, note 111 *supra*, at 259.

[138]   Werle, note 6 *supra*, para. 564. See also the critical remarks by Scaliotti, note 6 *supra*, at 156.

[139]   See note 72 *supra* and main text.

[140]   See also Eser, note 2 *supra*, para. 60.

[141]   Bassiouni, note 108 *supra*, at 491.

[142]   *Prosecutor* v. *Erdemović*, Case No. IT-96-22-T, TC I, Sentencing Judgment, 29 November 1996.

ians may give rise to a ground excluding responsibility (be it a justification or excuse) if the killer acted under the threat of his own death and that of his family. Dražen Erdemović was an ethnic Croat, who served in the overwhelmingly ethnic Serb Army of Republika Srpska. When he and his unit were told to massacre Muslim men and boys at Srebrenica he initially refused. He was then told that his choice was either to shoot the Muslim men, or to hand his gun to another and join the line of those to be killed. Under the duress of this threat, he then killed a number of them. He felt great remorse and admitted participating in the killings. His case raised the issue of whether the duress he suffered could serve as a defence at least in part excusing his otherwise culpable actions.

After the ICTY Trial Chamber ruled that duress could under certain strict conditions act as a defence in such a situation,[143] the Appeals Chamber reversed that decision by a narrow three to two majority.[144] Erdemović was ultimately sentenced to five years imprisonment by Trial Chamber II, which did at least consider the duress situation as a mitigating factor.[145]

Given the threat faced by Erdemović his conviction is not satisfying. A situation of such extreme duress calls for a differentiated solution based on a balancing of legal interests. Even if the actor's resistance to an order to kill would save innocent lives, the defence of duress cannot be completely excluded. Rather, the application of duress in such cases would duly take into account the exceptional situation of the actor and comply with the principle of culpability (*nullum crimen sine culpa*) instead of ascribing liability on the basis of abstract, non-legal policy considerations. Recognition of the duress defence rests on the assumption that the ordinary person is too weak to refuse an order if there is a risk that he will be killed. There are no doubt heroic exceptions, but a few extraordinary individuals do not change human nature. The underlying philosophical rationale for recognizing (extreme) duress as a defence is that we cannot expect others to live up to a such a high standard if we cannot guarantee that we ourselves would uphold it under similar circumstances. A human and therefore honest and realistic concept of criminal law must take into account the human weakness of each individual[146] and therefore must reject an abstract call for heroism as the standard of criminal law.[147] The sentencing judgment in *Erdemović* has already pointed in the direction of a more tolerant view, conceding a considerable mitigation of punishment with a statement demonstrating the importance of a recognized defence of duress.[148] It does indeed appear 'illogical', as Judge Stephen correctly pointed out, 'to admit duress generally as a matter of mitigation

---

[143]   *Ibid.* paras 16–20.

[144]   *Prosecutor* v. *Erdemović*, Case No. IT-96-22-A, Appeals Chamber Judgment, 7 October 1997, para. 19. The majority view was expressed in the opinions of Judges McDonald and Vohrah, Judge Li concurring; the minority view in the opinions of Judges Cassese and Stephen. For a thorough analysis of the judgment and the separate opinions see Ambos, note 18 *supra*, at 1010 *et seq.*

[145]   *Prosecutor* v. *Erdemović*, Case No. IT-96-22-T*bis*, TC III, Sentencing Judgment, 5 March 1998, paras. 8, 23.

[146]   On the 'human claim' as the basis of this position see Nill-Theobald, note 111 *supra*, at 269 with further references. For a similar position as to ordinary crimes, see Alan Reed, *Duress and Provocation as Excuses to Murder: Salutary Lessons from Recent Anglo-American Jurisprudence*, 6 J TRANSNATIONAL LAW AND POLICY 51, 53 (1996).

[147]   Ambos, note 18 *supra*, at 1024. In a similar vein Reed, note 146 *supra*, at 55: 'the standard is that of the reasonable man, not the reasonable hero'.

[148]   *Prosecutor* v. *Erdemović*, note 145 *supra*, para. 17.

but wholly exclude it as a defence in the case of murder'.[149] The rejection of duress as a defence in war crimes cases has normally been due to the defence's failure to prove the corresponding factual circumstances, in particular a credible serious threat against the defendant, rather than to the non-recognition of this defence as a matter of law.[150] Comparative analysis shows that modern criminal law, in both civil law *and* common law countries, no longer absolutely excludes duress as a defence in cases where innocent persons have been killed.[151] This result also seems logical in view of the purposes of punishment. The punishment of a person acting under duress is not necessary in order to prevent future crimes because presumably the same person would, under normal circumstances, act in accordance with the law, and therefore his attitude need not be corrected.[152] Thus, the question should not be whether duress can be invoked as a defence to the killing of innocent persons, but what the requirements of such a defence are and how, from a theoretical point of view, it is to be classified.

The first part of this question, concerning the requirements, is answered by article 31(1)(d) as analysed and interpreted above.[153] The drafters of the ICC Statute consciously departed from the *Erdemović* precedent and did not explicitly exclude the killing of innocents from the scope of the exclusionary ground.[154] Clearly, even if the actor may, on a personal level, be exempted from culpability (by an excuse), the law has to express its disapproval of atrocious crimes. This can be achieved by qualifying the acts as unlawful and wrongful under any circumstance, independent of the actor's (individual) culpability which may be negated by the duress. From this it follows that duress in general, and sub-paragraph (d) in particular, must be classified as an *excuse*.[155] In other words, the commission of the 'serious crimes of concern to the international community as a whole' which are within the jurisdiction of the ICC[156] can never be *justified* on the basis of a balancing of interests but can, in appropriate cases, be *excused* on the basis of compassion for and understanding of the actor's human weakness.[157]

The view that extreme duress in such cases can only operate as an excuse is not incompatible with the general objection against allowing arguments based on necessity to justify

---

[149]   *Prosecutor* v. *Erdemović*, Case No. IT-96-26, Appeals Chamber, Separate and Dissenting Opinion of Judge Stephen, 7 October 1997, para. 46.

[150]   See the similar conclusion of Abbe L. Dienstag, *Comment: Fedorenko v. United States. War Crimes, the Defense of Duress, and American Nationality Law*, 82 COLUMBIA L REV. 120, 141–2, 146–7 (1982) with regard to the American and the Nuremberg case law.

[151]   Nill-Theobald, note 111 *supra*, at 212–13, 267–8 with further references. See also Reed, note 146 *supra*, at 61–3; Ambos, note 18 *supra*, at 1044 and the analysis of the (international) jurisprudence by Cassese, note 13 *supra*, at 285 *et seq.*

[152]   See in more detail Ambos, note 18 *supra*, at 1045 *et seq.*

[153]   See also Werle, note 6 *supra*, para. 562.

[154]   As to the drafting history see Scaliotti, note 6 *supra*, at 156–7; Schabas, note 2 *supra*, at 229.

[155]   See also Cassese, note 13 *supra*, at 289.

[156]   ICC Statute, art. 5.

[157]   See also the same view defended by Nill-Theobald, note 111 *supra*, especially at 222–3, 226, 228–30, 274, 279, with regard to war crimes. In a similar vein *Prosecutor* v. *Erdemović*, Case No. IT-96-26, Appeals Chamber, Separate Opinion of Judge McDonald and Judge Vohrah, 7 October 1997, para. 85; Jan C. Nemitz and S. Wirth, *Der aktuelle Fall: Legal Aspects of the Appeals decision in the Erdemovic Case: The Plea of Guilty and Duress in International Humanitarian Law* 11 HUMANITÄRES VÖLKERRECHT-INFORMATIONSSCHRIFTEN 43, 52–3 (1998).

war crimes, crimes against humanity and genocide.[158] While necessity as a justification implies a balancing of conflicting interests and presupposes a (hardly conceivable) prevalence of the protected interest over the interest violated by the commission of an international crime,[159] duress as an excuse does not imply such a balancing exercise. On the contrary, the excuse of duress recognizes that the act committed by the person concerned is unlawful and in this sense does not weaken the general validity of the law. It only exempts the specific actor from personal responsibility, excusing his behaviour on a purely personal level by presuming he cannot be blamed for the act because any ordinary person would have behaved in the same way. A categorical exclusion of duress in the case of international crimes would overlook this structural difference between necessity and duress and, in fact, mix up the two defences, inventing a rule for duress that should properly apply only to the case of necessity. Since duress understood both in this sense and in sub-paragraph (d) can offer only a *personal* excuse, and since the question can arise both in the case of ordinary domestic crimes and international crimes, there is no cogent reason why the defence of duress should be excluded in a general and absolute way from the latter.[160] From the individual's point of view, the situations regulated by ICL are not so different from the ones regulated by national criminal law as to justify denying him, categorically, the right to invoke the excuse of duress in ICL. While the risks to life and physical integrity are greater during armed conflict, the individual combatant similarly runs a higher risk of becoming entangled in life-threatening situations. Thus, the factual and legal circumstances of a concrete case always determine whether duress as an excuse is applicable and whether its requirements are fulfilled.

MISTAKE OF FACT AND MISTAKE OF LAW (ARTICLE 32)[161]

ICC Statute, article 32 is based on the traditional distinction, in principle still valid in common law systems, between a mistake of fact and a mistake of law.[162] While the former is

---

[158]   See the discussion reproduced in Nill-Theobald, note 111 *supra*, at 197–8; also Bassiouni, note 108 *supra*, at 484, 490.

[159]   Indeed, a balancing of life against life is not possible. See with references to the relevant case law Ambos, note 18 *supra*, at 1046.

[160]   In a similar vein Claus Kreß, *Zur Methode der Rechtsfindung im Allgemeinen Teil des Völkerstrafrechts. Die Bewertung von Tötungen im Nötigungsnotstand durch die Rechtsmittelkammer des Internationalen Straftribunals für das ehemalige Jugoslawien im Fall Erdemovic*, 111 ZEITSCHRIFT FÜR DIE GESAMTE STRAFRECHTSWISSENSCHAFT 597, 618 (1999); Nill-Theobald, note 111 *supra*, at 278–9; Sander Janssen, *Mental Condition Defences in Supranational Criminal Law*, 4 INTERNATIONAL CRIMINAL L REV. 83, 97 (2004). See also Cassese, note 13 *supra*, at 289 who wants to take into account whether the crime would have been carried out in any event by other persons than the accused. For a stricter view see Dienstag, note 150 *supra*, at 148 *et seq.*; Yoram Dinstein, *International Criminal Law*, 20 ISRAEL L. REV. 206, 235 (1985).

[161]   ICC Statute, art. 32 reads as follows: 'Article 32 Mistake of fact or mistake of law   1. A mistake of fact shall be a ground for excluding criminal responsibility only if it negates the mental element required by the crime. 2. A mistake of law as to whether a particular type of conduct is a crime within the jurisdiction of the Court shall not be a ground for excluding criminal responsibility. A mistake of law may, however, be a ground for excluding criminal responsibility if it negates the mental element required by such a crime, or as provided for in article 33.'

[162]   Scaliotti, note 24 *supra*, at 12; Ambos, note 2 *supra*, at 29; Cryer *et al.*, note 11 *supra*, at 414.

relevant as a rule, the latter is not, as expressed by the old Roman principle *error iuris nocet* or *ignorantia iuris neminem excusat* (ignorance of the law is no excuse).[163] Yet, this rule has exceptions, and article 32 itself states that a mistake of either type can be relevant only if it 'negates the mental element'. Thus, the crucial issue is not so much the nature of the mistake (as one of fact or law) but the conceptual meaning of 'mental element'. In ICL, this concept must, in accordance with article 30, be understood as referring to the intent of the actor to engage in conduct and his knowledge of the awareness of its consequences when committing the material elements of the offence (*actus reus*). Thus, in a narrow sense, it refers only to the psychological relation between the actor and the act.[164] Clearly, if one were to interpret this concept more broadly, to include consciousness of the legal wrong (in the sense of the traditional *mens rea* as 'guilty mind'),[165] then not only mistakes of fact, but also those of law would, as a rule, be relevant because either affects, by definition, the actor's capacity to appreciate the unlawfulness of his conduct.[166]

As noted above, a *mistake of fact* (article 32(1)) excludes responsibility, as a rule, if the defendant is lacking the mental element (*mens rea*). Paragraph 1 refers to the ignorance of the factual (descriptive) elements in the definition of the offence, while paragraph 2 (*mistake of law*) encompasses an erroneous evaluation of the (criminal) law or the normative (legal) elements of the definition of the offence. Thus, if a soldier confuses the civilian in front of him with a combatant and shoots him, he is mistaken about a factual element relating to the war crime of 'wilful killing' of civilians as defined in article 8(2)(a)(i) of the ICC Statute. Article 32(1) applies to this situation and the soldier's responsibility is excluded since his mistake 'negates the mental element required by the crime'. The soldier does not identify the person in front of him as a civilian and therefore is unaware of the 'civilian' element required by article 8(2)(a)(i) in its factual sense. In contrast, if the same soldier is fully aware of the factual situation, that is, identifies the person in front of him as a civilian, but wrongfully

---

For a third category of a 'mistake of mixed fact and law', 'mistake of legal fact' or 'mistake of legal element', that is, a mistake standing between a pure mistake of fact or law referring to the definition of a legal element in a crime, see Kevin Jon Heller, *Mistake of Legal Element, the Common Law, and Article 32 of the Rome Statute*, 6 J INTERNATIONAL CRIMINAL JUSTICE 419 (2008).

[163] For the historical development of this Roman Law principle see Mingxuan Gao, *Rechtfertigung und Entschuldigung im Fall des Irrtums*, in ALBIN ESER AND HARUO NISHIHARA (eds), RECHTFERTIGUNG UND ENTSCHULDIGUNG 379 (Freiburg, Germany: Max Planck Institute for Foreign and International Criminal Law, 1995).

[164] Ambos, note 119 *supra*, at 760; Eser, note 2 *supra*, at 937; Hans-Heinrich Jescheck, '*The General Principles of International Criminal Law Set Out in Nuremberg, as Mirrored in the ICC Statute*', 2 J INTERNATIONAL CRIMINAL JUSTICE 38, 47 (2004).

[165] See the old principle from canon law (twelfth to sixteenth centuries) '*actus non facit reum nisi mens sit rea*' ('the act does not make guilty unless the mind is guilty'), adopted in common law by Edward Coke (1552–1634) (cf. Gao, note 163 *supra*, at 383 with further references). Most modern common law writers understand *mens rea*, however, in a narrow sense, see, for example, Andrew Ashworth, PRINCIPLES OF CRIMINAL LAW 5–7, 75. 154 (6th edn, New York, Oxford University Press, 2009); DAVID ORMEROD, SMITH AND HOGAN: CRIMINAL LAW 96 (12th edn, New York, Oxford University Press, 2008) ('A person may ... have *mens rea* though neither he nor any reasonable person would regard his state of mind as blameworthy'); A.P. Simester, J.R. Spencer, G.R. Spencer and G.J. Virgo, CRIMINAL LAW THEORY AND DOCTRINE 125 (4th edn, Portland, Hart Publishing, 2010); Fletcher, note 57 *supra*, at 298 *et seq.*

[166] On the special situation with regard to a mistake on the unlawfulness of an order, see the discussion of superior orders, *infra*.

assumes that the law allows shooting even civilians during an armed conflict, he acts based upon an erroneous evaluation of (humanitarian and international criminal) law which does not affect his intent to shoot and eventually kill a civilian.[167]

The delimitation between descriptive and normative elements, and thus between factual and legal mistakes, is not always that clear-cut. The basic definition according to which descriptive elements may be perceived with the five senses, while normative elements cannot because they are defined by law and therefore value based,[168] offers little guidance when elements have both a descriptive and a normative content. Normative elements often have a factual basis.[169] Returning to the above example, the correct normative evaluation that civilians are protected persons and therefore must not be shot presupposes the correct factual perception that the person in front of the soldier is indeed a civilian. Or take, for example, the killing of a peace-keeper: Before concluding that a peace-keeper is a protected person he must be correctly identified as a peace-keeper in the first place. These cases of a (possible) mistake about the factual basis for a normative evaluation should correctly be treated as (relevant) mistakes of fact.[170]

The ICC had to deal with a possible mistake of law in its very first confirmation of charges decision in the *Lubgana* case.[171] Lubanga, charged with the war crime of enlisting and conscripting children (ICC Statutes, article 8(2)(b)(xxvi) and (e)(vii)), argued that he could not have known that the relevant acts were prohibited since neither Uganda nor the Congo 'brought to the knowledge of the inhabitants of Ituri the fact that the Rome Statute had been ratified'.[172] While this submission raises the possibility of a mistake of law because of ignorance of the relevant conduct's (criminal) prohibition,[173] it clearly follows from clause 1 of article 32(2) that a mistake about the criminalization of certain conduct under the ICC Statute is per se irrelevant.[174] In any case, the Chamber rejected Lubanga's submission on factual grounds[175] and thus omitted any substantive discussion of article 32(2).

---

[167]   Ambos, note 18 *supra*, at 807; Eser, note 2 *supra*, at 937 *et seq.*; Werle, note 6 *supra*, para. 573; for the same result Otto Triffterer, *Article 32. Mistake of Fact or Mistake of Law*, in OTTO TRIFFTERER (ed.), COMMENTARY ON THE ROME STATUTE OF THE INTERNATIONAL CRIMINAL COURT para. 24 (2nd edn, München, Beck *et al.*, 2008); Heller, note 162 *supra*, at 420–1. See also Thomas Weigend, *Zur Frage eines "internationalen" Allgemeinen Teils*, in BERND SCHÜNEMANN ET AL. (eds), FESTSCHRIFT FÜR CLAUS ROXIN 1375, 1391 (Berlin, Walter de Gruyter, 2001).

[168]   Ambos, note 119 *supra*, at 786; Roxin, note 89 *supra*, s. 10 para. 10 *et seq.*; Triffterer, note 167 *supra*, para. 21.

[169]   Triffterer, note 167 *supra*, para. 22.

[170]   Eser, note 2 *supra*, at 938 *et seq.*; Werle, note 6 *supra*, para. 573; Triffterer, note 167 *supra*, para. 24.

[171]   *Prosecutor* v. *Lubanga*, Case No. ICC-01/04-01/06-803, PTC I, Decision on the Confirmation of Charges, 29 January 2001.

[172]   *Ibid.* para. 296.

[173]   Originally, the defence had argued that a conviction of Lubanga would violate the principle of legality. This argument is, however, based on a profound misunderstanding of art. 22. See thereto Thomas Weigend, *Intent, Mistake of Law, and Co-Perpetration in the Lubanga Decision on Confirmation of Charges*, 6 J INTERNATIONAL CRIMINAL JUSTICE 471, 474 (2008); Kai Ambos, *Commentary*, in ANDRÉ KLIP and GÖRAN SLUITER (eds), ANNOTATED LEADING CASES OF INTERNATIONAL CRIMINAL TRIBUNALS, XXIII, *International Criminal Court* (Antwerp, Intersentia, 2009), at n. 46 and accompanying text.

Still, the *Lubanga* case shows that mistake issues are likely to come up regularly before the ICC in the future.[176] In fact, a slightly more sophisticated argument could have raised a somewhat more difficult issue for the Pre-trial Chamber. If Lubanga had, for example, argued that he was aware of the general prohibition of enlisting and conscripting children but was convinced that this provision was only applicable to the *forcible*[177] recruitment of children,[178] the Chamber would have been faced with the difficult question whether an erroneous evaluation of very specific normative elements of a crime (*in casu* 'conscripting or enlisting', article 8(2)(b)(xxvi) and (e)(vii)) can be a ground for excluding criminal responsibility. The issue was discussed in the post-Rome Preparatory Commission and it was considered 'sufficiently evident' that 'the Prosecutor is not obliged to prove that the accused personally completed the correct normative evaluation'.[179] The general introduction to the final version of the ICC's Elements of the Crimes confirms that 'with respect to mental elements associated with elements involving value judgement … it is not necessary that the perpetrator personally completed a particular value judgement'.[180] While it is therefore clear from the *travaux* that the delegations wanted to exclude the possibility of a relevant mistake of law as to normative elements of the definition of the offence, this is not necessarily a convincing solution.[181] One need only take a closer look at the wording of article 32(2) according to which even a mistake of law 'may' be a ground for excluding criminal responsibility 'if it negates the mental element'. While the interpretation of the term 'may' is disputed,[182] it is clear from this wording that a mistake (in fact, as said before, 'any' mistake) becomes relevant once it 'negates' the mental element. Thus, the crucial question always remains when this is actually the case. I have tried to explain elsewhere that this must normally be affirmed with regard to normative elements of the offence.[183]

---

[174]   See also Ambos, note 119 *supra*, at 817 *et seq.*; Eser, note 2 *supra*, at 940; Cryer *et al.*, note 11 *supra*, at 415; Triffterer, note 167 *supra* 167, para. 31.

[175]   Compare *Prosecutor* v. *Lubanga*, note 171 *supra*, para. 316 (presented evidence does not 'show that Thomas Lubanga Dyilo might have made any such mistake in the context in which the crimes were committed').

[176]   For the relevance of mistakes concerning IHL in particular, see Heller, note 162 *supra*, at 430–2.

[177]   On voluntary recruitment see *Prosecutor* v. *Lubanga*, note 171 *supra*, paras. 242–58 and thereto Ambos, note 173 *supra*, at n. 17 and accompanying text.

[178]   See Weigend, note 173 *supra*, at 475.

[179]   Preparatory Commission for the International Criminal Court, Working Group on Elements for Crimes (9 February 2000), Outcome of an intersessional meeting of the Preparatory Commission for the International Criminal Court held in Siracusa from 31 January to 6 February 2000, PCNICC/2000/WGEC/INF/1.

[180]   Elements of the Crimes, ICC-ASP/1/3, 9 September 2002, General Introduction, para. 4.

[181]   In a similar vein Clark, note 36 *supra*, at 536–7.

[182]   According to Triffterer, note 167 *supra*, para. 39, the word 'may' gives the Chamber discretion to decide whether or not a mistake of law which negates the mental element excludes criminal responsibility. Contrary to my former view (see Ambos, note 119 *supra*, at 811–12), it seems, however, more convincing to me that the negation of the mental element always excludes the actor's criminal responsibility. 'May' then only makes clear that not every mistake of law is relevant (Kai Ambos, Internationales Strafrecht (2nd edn, München, Beck, 2008), at s. 7 para. 102 n. 438 with further references; see also Weigend, note 167 *supra*, at 1391 n. 66; Cryer *et al.*, note 11 *supra*, at 415; Heller, note 162 *supra*, at 442).

[183]   Ambos, note 119 *supra*, at 811 *et seq.* For a broad interpretation also Heller, note 162 *supra*,

While mistakes referring to the (descriptive or normative) elements of the offence (*direct* mistakes) fall clearly under article 32, the situation is even more complex with regard to mistakes about the requirements of a defence (*indirect* mistakes). Such mistakes also have a factual and a normative side, that is, the mistake may refer to the factual existence or requirements of a defence or to its normative existence or requirements. In the case of self-defence, for example, the actor may wrongly perceive a gesture or bodily movement by another person as an attack (so-called putative self-defence) and thus react with a counter-attack, or he may in fact be attacked but misread the legal contours of his right to counter-attack, that is, overstep the scope of his right to defend himself. As in the case of direct mistakes, the rule regarding relevance of factual mistakes (article 32(1)) and the irrelevance of normative mistakes (article 32(2)) applies. For the latter group of cases this rule must be upheld since a 'normative defence-mistake' does not affect the actor's *mens rea* as to the objective elements of the offence; he acts with intent anyway.[184] A part of the doctrine adopts the same position with regard to 'factual defence-mistakes'.[185] While this view is correct insofar as such a mistake does not affect the actor's intent as to the elements of the definition of the offence,[186] it overlooks the salient fact that such an actor does not intentionally commit a wrong. In fact, he does not want to break the law or act unlawfully since he believes himself to be acting in accordance with the law. If this belief had been true, he would have been justified. Thus, conceiving the permissive norm ('defence') as the flipside of the prohibition ('offence'), such an actor participates in a similar (indirect) mistake as a person who is (directly) mistaken about the existence of an element of the offence definition. As a consequence, article 32(1) should apply by way of analogy to all (indirect) mistakes about the existence or factual requirements of a defence.[187]

The above considerations have shown that the traditional *error iuris* or *ignorantia iuris* doctrine as codified in article 32(2) is unduly strict and inconsistent with the principle of culpability. While in most cases the actor making a (direct or indirect) mistake of law will act with intent, and therefore his mistake will be irrelevant, another equally relevant question is whether his ignorance of the law can be blamed on him. The respective actor does not deserve conviction and punishment unless he can be blamed for his ignorance. Article 32 is concerned exclusively with the effect of the mistake on the mental element, and therefore does not sufficiently account for this second, more value-oriented, level of analysis. Linked to that is the problem that the *error iuris* doctrine rests on a *presumption of knowledge* of the law which is a fiction bordering on the absurd. In the midst of the complex and fragmented regimes of criminal law which exist in today's world, nobody can be expected to know all offences and defences, let alone their most highly normative elements. The *error iuris* doctrine dates back

---

at 419 *et seq.* arguing that his third category of a 'mistake of legal element' (note 162 *supra*) leads regularly to an acquittal since in such a situation the perpetrator cannot be said to have acted knowingly with regard to that element.

[184] Ambos, note 119 *supra*, at 819 *et seq.*; Weigend, note 167 *supra*, at 1391; Werle, Völkerstrafrecht, Völkerstrafrecht, 2nd ed. Tübingen, Mohr Siebeck, 2007, para. 534.

[185] See Cryer *et al.*, note 11 *supra*, at 415.

[186] Ambos, note 119 *supra*, at 809 *et seq.*; Werle, note 6 *supra*, para. 575; Triffterer, note 167 *supra*, para. 14.

[187] Ambos, note 119 *supra*, at 808 *et seq.* (810, 811). In a similar vein Triffterer, note 167 *supra*, para. 14; more reluctant Werle, note 6 *supra*, para. 575. For a different view see Scaliotti, note 24 *supra*, at 14 *et seq.*

to a time when, in principle, only the '*mala in se*' (acts wrong in themselves or inherently wrong) were considered crimes, while modern criminal law is full of '*mala prohibita*' (acts wrong only because they are prohibited by law). But the *mala in se/mala prohibita* distinction is only convincing as long as one does not get bogged down in the subtleties of the qualification of concrete crimes.[188] This is also true in ICL, particularly with regard to war crimes. As a consequence, article 32(2) should be interpreted in a more flexible or liberal way via recourse to a criterion of *avoidability* or *reasonableness*, which would enable the judges to find practical and just solutions on a case-by-case basis.[189] These criteria have a solid basis in comparative law and could therefore be introduced by way of article 21.[190]

SUPERIOR ORDERS (ARTICLE 33)[191]

While the Nuremberg precedent and the subsequent law rejected, without further ado, the notion of superior orders as a ground excluding responsibility,[192] ICC Statute, article 33 adopts a more sophisticated approach affirming, on the one hand, the traditional rejection of the defence but allowing, on the other, for its application under certain conditions. The negotiations were quite controversial. First, it was debated whether the provision deserved to be treated as a separate article at all or if it should rather be built into article 31 as the United States suggested. Further and more importantly, there was considerable disagreement as to the legal consequences of acting on superior orders. During informal deliberations the United States, supported by the academic authority of Theodor Meron (then a member of its delegation and a Law Professor at New York University), took the somewhat surprising position, reversing its own Nuremberg precedent, that superior orders constitutes a substantive defence. This was rejected by other delegations upholding the Nuremberg precedent and the subsequent law, according to which acting on orders can never constitute a defence. The

---

[188]   I have tried to explain this point earlier in Kai Ambos, *Nulla Poena Sine Lege in International Criminal Law*, in Roelof Haveman and Olaoluwa Olusanya (eds), Sentencing and Sanctioning in Supranational Criminal Law 17, 21–2 (Antwerp, Intersentia, 2006) referring to Carl Schmitt, *Das internationalrechtliche Verbrechen des Angriffskrieges und der Grundsatz 'Nullum crimen, nulla poena sine lege'*, Legal Brief of 1945, edited by H. Quaritsch, Berlin, Duncker & Humblot, 1994), at 21–2.

[189]   Ambos, note 119 *supra*, at 822 *et seq.*; Bassiouni, note 108 *supra*, at 414–5; Triffterer, note 167 *supra*, para. 38. Critically Clark, note 36 *supra*, at 534–5; Heller, note 162 *supra*, at 440–1 who, however, only deals with reasonableness as a possible limitation for 'mistakes of legal elements'.

[190]   Triffterer, note 167 *supra*, para. 38.

[191]   ICC Statute, art. 33 reads as follows: 'Article 33 Superior orders and prescription of law   1. The fact that a crime within the jurisdiction of the Court has been committed by a person pursuant to an order of a Government or of a superior, whether military or civilian, shall not relieve that person of criminal responsibility unless: (a) the person was under a legal obligation to obey orders of the Government or the superior in question; (b) the person did not know that the order was unlawful; and (c) the order was not manifestly unlawful.   2. For the purposes of this article, orders to commit genocide or crimes against humanity are manifestly unlawful.'

[192]   See IMT Statute (82 UNTS 280), art. 8; Tokyo Statute, art. 6 (reprinted in G.K. McDonald and O. Swaak-Goldman (eds.), II Substantive and Procedural Aspects of International Criminal Law Pt 1, 73 (2000), Nuremberg Principle IV, II YB International Law Commission 374 (1950); ICTY Statute, art. 7(4) and ICTR Statute, art. 6(4): ('The fact that an accused person acted pursuant to an order of a government or of a superior shall not relieve him or her of criminal responsibility, but may be considered in mitigation of punishment).').

compromise formulation incorporated into the ICC Statute takes things a step beyond Nuremberg insofar as the availability of the defence is excluded as a rule but can, under exceptional circumstances, be invoked if three limiting, cumulative conditions are met:

(a) the person was under a legal obligation to obey orders of the government or the superior in question;
(b) the person did not know that the order was unlawful; and
(c) the order was not manifestly unlawful.

As the second condition shows, superior order is an extended form of the mistake of law defence.[193] But as the third condition makes clear, the defendant may be relieved of criminal responsibility (more exactly excused, not justified)[194] only for ignorance of the simple, that is not *manifest*, unlawfulness of the order.[195] This 'manifest illegality test'[196] is complemented by article 33(2) which establishes that 'orders to commit genocide or crimes against humanity are manifestly unlawful'.[197] Thus, by legislative *fiat*, article 33 solely applies to war crimes.[198] War crimes are a serious matter, and thus one could certainly argue that most orders to commit them should also be qualified as manifestly unlawful.[199] But the seriousness of the ICC's core crimes cannot discharge the Chamber from establishing the subordinate's culpability in every particular case.[200] How, in this regard, is the reference to article 33 in clause 2 of article 32(2) to be interpreted? In its oblique reference to article 33, article 32 (2) recognizes an exception to its otherwise strict *error iuris* rule in the case of superior orders to commit war crimes. Take, for example, the highly practical case of a soldier who kills a civilian on the basis of an order he believes is lawful. He acts with intent and in this sense commits the war crime of killing civilians by fulfilling its objective and subjective elements. But does his error concerning the validity and exonerating effect of the order, that is an *error iuris*, affect the soldier's culpability? According to articles 32(2) and 33(1), that mistake of law may relieve the subordinate of criminal responsibility for war crimes if he cannot be blamed for not having recognized the unlawfulness of the orders he has followed.[201]

---

[193] Scaliotti, note 6 *supra*, at 140; Cryer *et al.*, note 11 *supra*, at 418.

[194] Olásolo, note 13 *supra*, at 244; Otto Triffterer, *Article 33. Superior Orders and Prescription of Law*, in OTTO TRIFFTERER (ed.), COMMENTARY ON THE ROME STATUTE OF THE INTERNATIONAL CRIMINAL COURT para. 29 (2nd edn, München, Beck *et al.*, 2008).

[195] Schabas, note 2 *supra*, at 231. See also Cryer *et al.*, note 11 *supra*, at 418.

[196] On this test or principle originally Morris Greenspan, THE MODERN LAW OF LAND WARFARE 440 (Berkeley, University of California Press, 1959); L.C. Green, *The Man in the Field and the Maxim Ignorantia Juris Rule*, 19 ARCHIV DES VÖLKERRECHTS 169, 237–8, 243 *et seq* (1980/81).

[197] This paragraph was drafted to accommodate customary law concerns as voiced, for example, by Paola Gaeta, *The Defence of Superior Orders: The Statute of the International Criminal Court versus Customary International Law*, 10 EUROPEAN J INTERNATIONAL L 172 (1999).

[198] Werle, note 6 *supra*, para. 594; Cassese, note 13 *supra*, at 279. Obviously, the crime of aggression, as now defined in the new art. 8*bis*, also falls under art. 33 (Triffterer, note 194 *supra*, para. 30).

[199] Charles Garraway, *Superior Orders and the International Criminal Court: Justice Delivered or Justice Denied*, INTERNATIONAL REVIEW OF THE RED CROSS 791 (1999); Cassese, note 13 *supra*, at 279. Gaeta, note 197 *supra*, at 190, even wants to extend the legal presumption of art. 33(2) to war crimes and thus render the defence of superior orders totally invalid.

[200] Ambos, note 119 *supra*, at 836. Dehn, note 93 *supra*, at 646 argues that the order of perfidious acts might under certain circumstances not be manifestly illegal.

[201] See also Ambos, note 182 *supra*, s. 7 para. 103. In the same vein George P. Fletcher, THE

In practice, article 33 is likely to have only a very limited scope of application. Historically, the superior orders defence has often been pled but has almost never been recognized as an *autonomous* ground of excluding responsibility.[202] More often, the fact that a crime was committed pursuant to an order was considered relevant only within the framework of the mistake or duress defences.[203] Dinstein sees superior orders merely as part of a defence based on a lack of *mens rea.*[204] In any case, the prosecutorial strategy of international criminal tribunals tends to focus on the responsibility of those at the highest decision-making level,[205] and this will reduce the importance of the superior orders defence in the future.

OTHER DEFENCES

As indicated above, the ICC Statute does not provide a complete list of all possible grounds for excluding criminal responsibility but article 31(3) allows the court to consider the derivation of other non-specified grounds from the sources of applicable law as set forth in article 21. The most important of these will be discussed here.

Military Necessity

Military necessity has traditionally been defined as 'an urgent need, admitting of no delay, for the taking by a commander of measures, which are indispensable for forcing as quickly as possible the complete surrender of the enemy'.[206] That such a notion is part of IHL is indicative of the compromise character of that law, a law always seeking to strike the right balance between military and humanitarian requirements.[207] The increasing 'humanization' of armed

---

GRAMMAR OF CRIMINAL LAW 109 (Oxford University Press, 2007); Olásolo, note 13 *supra*, at 244; Triffterer, note 194 *supra*, para. 31.

[202]   Compare Werle, note 6 *supra*, para. 588 and the historical overview by Cryer *et al.*, note 11 *supra*, at 415 *et seq.* As to drafting history see Ambos, note 2 *supra*, at 30–1.

[203]   Ambos, note 119 *supra*, at 836–7; Cryer *et al.*, note 11 *supra*, at 419–20; Zahar and Sluiter, note 29 *supra*, at 426. See also Judge Cassese, note 117 *supra*, para. 15.

[204]   Yoram Dinstein, WAR, AGGRESSION AND SELF DEFENCE 87 (4th edn, New York, Cambridge University Press, 2005): 'the fact of obedience to orders constitutes not a defence per se but only a factual element that may be taken into account in conjunction with the other circumstances of the given case within the compass of a defence based on a lack of *mens rea,* that is, mistake of law or fact or compulsion'.

[205]   ICC OTP, *Paper on Some Policy Issues before the Office of the Prosecutor* 3, 7 (September 2003); ICC OTP, *Report on Prosecutorial Strategy* (14 September 2006); Security Council Res. 1503 (2003) and 1534 (2003). See also SCSL Statute, art. 1, established through the Agreement between the United Nations and the Government of Sierra Leone on the Establishment of the Special Court for Sierra Leone, signed on 16 January 2002, available at www.sc-sl.org.

[206]   William G. Downey, *'The Law of War and Military Necessity'*, 47 AMERICAN J INTERNATIONAL L, 47, 251, 254 (1953). As to the historical development of military necessity see Kai Ambos, § 9 VStGB, in WOLFGANG JOECKS, KLAUS MIEBACH and OTTO LAGODNY (eds), MÜNCHENER KOMMENTAR ZUM STRAFGESETZBUCH, Band 6/2, *Nebenstrafrecht III, Völkerstrafgesetzbuch*, para. 17 (München, Beck, 2009).

[207]   Payam Akhavan, *'Reconciling Crimes Against Humanity with the Laws of War'*, 6 J INTERNATIONAL CRIMINAL JUSTICE 21, 28 (2008); Robert Kolb, *Droit international pénal*, in ROBERT KOLB (ed), DROIT PÉNAL INTERNATIONAL 214 (Bruxelles, Helbing Lichtenhan, 2008); Christopher Greenwood, *'Historical Development and Legal Basis'*, in DIETER FLECK (ed), THE HANDBOOK OF INTERNATIONAL HUMANITARIAN LAW para. 132 (2nd edn, New York, Oxford University Press, 2008).

conflict reflected in the steady expansion of IHL has led to the decreasing importance of military necessity. Indeed, today it is almost universally accepted that mere considerations of military necessity cannot justify breaches of humanitarian law per se; but insofar as these considerations have been taken into account in drafting IHL, they have become an integral part of it.[208]

As a consequence, military necessity cannot be considered a general defence applicable to all war crimes. The concept recognizes the value of military advantage but it can never justify an attack on civilians.[209] It may exclude criminal responsibility only where it is expressly included in an offence, that is, where it is itself an element of the offence.[210] In the ICC Statute, it is an element in the war crime of extensive destruction and appropriation of property (article 8(2)(a)(iv)) and that of destroying or seizing the enemy's property (article 8(2)(b)(xiii), (e)(xii)).[211] In addition, footnote 47 of the Elements of the Crimes provides that appropriations justified by military necessity cannot constitute the crime of pillaging.[212] In sum, military necessity can only, at most, exclude criminal responsibility for war crimes against property.

Reprisals

The law of reprisals is a classical instrument of IHL which is meant to contribute to its enforcement.[213] Coercive measures which would normally be contrary to international law may be considered legally permissible if they are taken as a last resort and as a proportionate response to a previous violation of international law. In essence, reprisal involves retaliation by one party to a conflict in order to stop the adversary from continuing to

---

[208] Downey, note 206 *supra*, at 262; Greenwood, note 207 *supra*, para. 133.

[209] *Prosecutor* v. *Galić*, Case No. IT-98-29-T, TC I, Judgment, 5 December 2003, para. 44 n. 76 ('destroying a particular military objective will provide some type of advantage in weakening the enemy military forces. Under no circumstance are civilians to be considered legitimate military targets. Consequently, attacking civilians or the civilian population as such cannot be justified by invoking military necessity.'). In *Prosecutor* v. *Blåskić*, Case No. TC I, IT-95-14-T, TC I, Judgment, 3 March 2000, para. 180, the Trial Chamber, however, held '[t]argeting civilians or civilian property is an offence when not justified by military necessity'. This view was explicitly rejected by *Prosecutor* v. *Galić*, *supra*, para. 44.

[210] Werle, note 6 *supra*, para. 614; Cryer *et al.*, note 11 *supra*, at 423; Kolb, note 207 *supra*, at 214; see also *Prosecutor* v. *Katanga and Ngudjolo*, Case No. ICC-01/04/07-717, TC I, Decision on the Confirmation of Charges, 30 September 2008, para. 318; Ambos, note 182 *supra*, s. 6 para. 23; Ambos, note 173 *supra*, para. 17. For a more extensive application of military necessity, however, Akhavan, note 207 *supra*, at 34 with further references.

[211] In addition, art. 8(2)(b)(xx) contains indirectly (*e contrario*) a reference to military necessity by criminalizing the use of weapons and methods of warfare which cause 'unnecessary suffering'.

[212] Elements of the Crimes, note 180 *supra*, Pt II-B. See also Andreas Zimmermann, *Article 8. War Crimes, para. 2(b)(xvi)*, in Otto Trifferer (ed.), Commentary on the Rome Statute of the International Criminal Court para. 170 (2nd edn, München, Beck *et al.*, 2008).

[213] Christopher Greenwood, *The Twilight of the Law of Belligerent Reprisals*, 20 Netherlands YB International L, 35, 36 (1989); Rüdiger Wolfrum and Dieter Fleck, *Enforcement of International Humanitarian Law*, in Dieter Fleck (ed.), The Handbook of International Humanitarian Law para. 1406 (2nd edn, New York, Oxford University Press, 2008). Compare also Dehn, note 93 *supra*, at 652.

violate international law.[214] A different question is, however, whether this instrument, rooted in *humanitarian* law may qualify as a defence in international *criminal* law. The first limitation is that reprisals presuppose a link to an armed conflict and therefore cannot exclude criminal responsibility for crimes committed in times of peace – especially not if they qualify as genocide or crimes against humanity.[215] Going one step further, however, the increasing 'humanization' of IHL has raised doubts about the applicability of reprisals to war crimes. In this sense, the *Kupreškic et al.* ICTY Trial Chamber held that 'reprisals against civilians are inherently a barbarous means' since they are not only 'arbitrary but are also not directed specifically at the individual authors of the initial violation'.[216] In the Chamber's view, 'the reprisal killing of innocent persons … can safely be characterized as a blatant infringement of the most fundamental principles of human rights'.[217] On the basis of such humanitarian or human rights considerations, the applicability of reprisals has been increasingly restricted, excluding certain groups of (protected) persons and objects completely.[218] The *Kupreškic* Trial Chamber, referring to Articles 51(6) and 52(1) of the First Additional Protocol to the Geneva Conventions (Additional Protocol I),[219] even concluded, without distinguishing between international and non-international armed conflicts, that customary international law not only prohibits reprisals against civilians who find themselves in the hands of the adversary but also against civilians in the combat zone.[220] This jurisprudence implies that reprisals should no longer qualify as an admissible defence.[221]

---

[214]   Greenwood, note 213 *supra*, at 37; C. Greenwood, *Belligerent Reprisals in the Jurisprudence of the International Criminal Law for the Former Yugoslavia*, in HORST FISCHER, CLAUS KREß and SASCHA ROLF LÜDER (eds), INTERNATIONAL AND NATIONAL PROSECUTION OF CRIMES UNDER INTERNATIONAL LAW 541 (Berlin, Berlin Verlag, 2001); Cryer, note 11 *supra*, at 422; Cassese, note 13 *supra*, at 258; Stefan Oeter, *Methods and Means of Combat*, in DIETER FLECK (ed.), THE HANDBOOK OF INTERNATIONAL HUMANITARIAN LAW para. 476 (2nd edn, New York, Oxford University Press, 2008).

[215]   Werle, note 6 *supra*, para. 613.

[216]   *Prosecutor* v. *Kupreškic et al.*, Case No. IT-95-16-T, TC II, Judgment, 14 January 2000, para. 528. Compare thereto the analysis by Greenwood, note 214 *supra*, at 549 *et seq.*

[217]   *Prosecutor* v. *Kupreškic et al.*, note 216 *supra*, para. 529.

[218]   It is, for example, expressly forbidden to take reprisals against the wounded, sick, personnel, buildings or protected equipment (art. 46 of Geneva Convention (I) for the Amelioration of the Condition of the Wounded and Sick in Armed Forces in the Field, 12 August 1949, 75 UNTS 31), shipwrecked (art. 47 of the Geneva Convention (II) for the Amelioration of the Condition of Wounded, Sick and Shipwrecked Members of Armed Forces at Sea, 12 August 1949, 75 UNTS 85), prisoners of war (art. 13(3) of Geneva Convention (III) Relative to the Treatment of Prisoners of War, 12 August 1949, 75 UNTS 135), and civilians and their property on occupied territory (art. 33(3) of Geneva Convention (IV) Relative to the Protection of Civilian Persons in Time of War, 12 August 1949, 75 UNTS 287). For an overview see Greenwood, note 213 *supra*, at 50; Ambos, note 182 *supra*, s. 6 para. 23; Oeter, note 214 *supra*, para. 479.

[219]   Protocol Additional to the Geneva Conventions of 12 August 1949, and Relating to the Protection of Victims of International Armed Conflicts (AP I), 8 June 1977, 1125 UNTS 3. AP I, art. 51(6) reads as follows: 'Attacks against the civilian population or civilians by way of reprisals are prohibited.' Article 52(1) states 'The civilian population and individual civilians shall enjoy general protection against dangers arising from military operations. To give effect to this protection, the following rules, which are additional to other applicable rules of international law, shall be observed in all circumstances.'

[220]   *Prosecutor* v. *Kupreškic et al.*, note 216 *supra*, paras 527, 531.

[221]   In this vein Jescheck, note 164 *supra*, at 52. See also Jean-François Quéguiner, *Dix ans après la création du Tribunal pénal international pour l'ex-Yougoslavie: évaluation de l'apport de sa jurisprudence au droit international humanitaire*, 850 INTERNATIONAL REVIEW OF THE RED CROSS 271, 293 *et seq.* (2003); Kolb, note 207 *supra*, at 213–14.

Notwithstanding the above, it is questionable whether the reprisal prohibition contained in Additional Protocol I is indeed part of customary international law.[222] As is well known, Additional Protocol I has not been ratified by major (military) powers such as the United States, India, Israel and Turkey. In addition, 'countermeasures' and 'armed reprisals' are still an accepted state practice.[223] Accordingly, the United Kingdom has expressly rejected the *Kupreškic* Judgment by declaring that the 'court's reasoning is unconvincing and the assertion that there is a prohibition in customary law flies in the face of most of the state practice that exists. The UK does not accept the position as stated in this judgment.'[224]

It is also far from clear that an absolute prohibition of reprisals would be desirable at all. Even if one takes into account that reprisals may produce an escalating spiral of atrocities,[225] they are nevertheless one of the few enforcement mechanisms available under IHL.[226] This issue was raised in *Kupreškic et al.* but was not satisfactorily resolved. The Trial Chamber took the view that the prosecution and punishment of war crimes and crimes against humanity by national or international courts is an efficient alternative means of producing compliance with international law.[227] But even today, eleven years after the *Kupreškic* Judgment and eight years after the entry into force of the ICC Statute, one has to concede that ICL is still in its initial stages and has yet to prove its efficiency in producing compliance. Thus, there may still be a need for reprisals as an additional enforcement mechanism.

In any case, even if one takes the view that customary international law does not provide for an *absolute* prohibition of reprisals, they are subject to a number of stringent requirements.[228] The *Kupreškic* Chamber specified them as follows:

(a) the principle whereby they must be a *last resort* in attempts *to impose compliance* by the adversary with legal standards (which entails, amongst other things, that they may be exercised only after a prior warning has been given which has failed to bring about the discontinuance of the adversary's crimes);

(b) the obligation to take *special precautions* before implementing them (they may be taken only after a decision to this effect has been made at the highest political or military level; in other words they may not be decided by local commanders);

(c) the principle of *proportionality* (which entails not only that the reprisals must not be excessive compared to the precedent unlawful act of warfare, but also that they must stop as soon as that unlawful act has been discontinued); and

(d) elementary *considerations of humanity*.[229]

---

[222] Greenwood, note 213 *supra*, at 63; Greenwood, note 214 *supra*, at 556; Ambos, note 119 *supra*, at 398. The absolute prohibition of reprisals against civilians was a controversial issue during the drafting process of AP I, see Quéguiner, note 221 *supra*, at 293. Compare also Greenwood, note 214 *supra*, at 543 *et seq.*

[223] Ambos, note 119 *supra*, at 398.

[224] UK Ministry of Defence (2004), THE MANUAL OF LAW OF ARMED CONFLICT 421, n. 62 (New York, Oxford University Press, 2004).

[225] Greenwood, note 213 *supra*, at 36; Oeter, note 214 *supra*, para. 476. Compare also Dehn, note 93 *supra*, at 652.

[226] See thereto the instructive discussion by Greenwood, note 213 *supra*, at 56 *et seq.* and the response by Frits Kalshoven, *Belligerent Reprisals Revisited*, 21 NETHERLANDS YB INTERNATIONAL LAW 43, 58 *et seq* (1990). Compare also Oeter, note 214 *supra*, para. 479.

[227] *Prosecutor* v. *Kupreškic et al.*, note 216 *supra*, para. 530.

[228] Cryer *et al.*, note 11 *supra*, at 422.

[229] *Prosecutor* v. *Kupreškic et al.*, note 216 *supra*, para. 535 (emphasis added). In a similar vein Greenwood, note 213 *supra*, at 40 *et seq.*; Oeter, note 214 *supra*, para. 476 *et seq.*

In sum, if reprisals are an admissible defence at all, they may exclude criminal responsibility only in limited, rather extraordinary circumstances.[230]

Consent of the Victim

It is a general norm in criminal law that consent can only exclude criminal responsibility if the consenting victim is entitled to dispose exclusively of the (individual) legal interest protected by the offence or offences concerned. If, in contrast, the offences also protect *collective* interests then the individual's consent cannot have an exonerating effect. Collective interests belong to a collective entity, which is normally the respective state or society, and thus cannot be disposed of by an individual's decision alone. As to crimes under ICL this means that, as a rule, it does not admit of the consent defence[231] since ICL purports to protect a collective interest *par excellence*, that is, the international peace, security and wellbeing of the world.[232] The defence of consent is problematical even in the exceptional case of offences that explicitly require the perpetrator to act against the victim's will, such as sexual offences or deprivation of liberty. The potentially exonerating effect of consent[233] will normally not operate here because of the coercive circumstances likely to prevail in cases of ICL. In other words, the general situation of coercion and pressure under which the perpetrators act strongly suggests that voluntary consent is not possible.[234]

Inapplicability of the *Tu-Quoque* Principle

The *tu-quoque* principle traditionally purports to exclude criminal responsibility for war crimes on the ground that the adversary in the armed conflict has committed similar

---

[230]   See also Cryer *et al.*, note 11 *supra*, at 422; Ambos, note 119 *supra*, at 402.

[231]   Fernando Mantovani, *The General Principles of International Criminal Law: The Viewpoint of a National Criminal Lawyer*, 1 J International Criminal Justice 26, 35 (2003); Wolfgang Schomburg and Ines Peterson, *'Genuine Consent to Sexual Violence Under International Criminal Law'*, 101 American J International L, 121, 125 (2007); Werle, note 6 *supra*, para. 615.

[232]   See Preamble to the ICC Statute.

[233]   Compare Werle, note 6 *supra*, para. 615; Schomburg and Peterson, note 231 *supra*, at 125; Cryer *et al.*, note 11 *supra*, at 420. See in particular with regard to sexual assaults *Prosecutor* v. *Kunarac*, Case No. IT-96-23&23/1, TC I, Judgment, 22 February 2001, para. 460; *Prosecutor* v. *Semanza*, Case No. ICTR-97-20-T, TC III, Judgment, 15 May 2003, para. 346; *Prosecutor* v. *Muhimana*, Case No. ICTR-95-1B-T, TC III, Judgment, 28 April 2005, para. 546. See also the case law analysis by Schomburg and Peterson, note 231 *supra*, at 132 *et seq*.

[234]   *Prosecutor* v. *Muhimana*, note 233 *supra*, para. 546; Schomburg and Peterson, note 231 *supra*, at 138; Mikaela Heikkilä, International Criminal Tribunals and Victims of Crime 130 (Saarijärvi, Gummerus Printing, 2004) therefore takes the view that 'victim consent should not at all be regarded as relevant'. See also the restrictive rule 70 of the ICC Rules of Procedure and Evidence, ICC-ASP/1/3, 9 September 2002, Pt II-A, which states: 'Principles of Evidence in Cases of Sexual Violence   In cases of sexual violence, the Court shall be guided by and, where appropriate, apply the following principles: (a) Consent cannot be inferred by reason of any words or conduct of a victim where force, threat of force, coercion or taking advantage of a coercive environment undermined the victim's ability to give voluntary and genuine consent; (b) Consent cannot be inferred by reason of any words or conduct of a victim where the victim is incapable of giving genuine consent; (c) Consent cannot be inferred by reason of the silence of, or lack of resistance by, a victim to the alleged sexual violence; (d) Credibility, character or predisposition to sexual availability of a victim or witness cannot be inferred by reason of the sexual nature of the prior or subsequent conduct of a victim or witness.'

offences.[235] The defence was raised many times at Nuremberg but was just as often rejected, most clearly in the *Ministries* case:

> But if we assume, *arguendo*, that Russia's action was wholly untenable and its guilt as deep as that of the Third Reich, nevertheless, this cannot in law avail the defendants or lessen the guilt of those of the Third Reich who were themselves responsible.[236]

In the same vein, the *Kupreškic* Chamber rightly held that this defence is incompatible with the 'absolute nature of most obligations imposed by rules of international humanitarian law'.[237] As the norms prohibiting war crimes, crimes against humanity and genocide are *ius cogens*, and therefore have a non-derogable and overriding character,[238] the recognition of the *tu-quoque* principle would not only affect the efficiency of ICL[239] but would render moot the binding character of the relevant norms. The obligations imposed by IHL ought to be fulfilled regardless of whether others comply with them or disregard them. Thus, the *tu-quoque* principle cannot constitute a valid defence at all.[240]

---

[235]   *Prosecutor* v. *Kupreškic et al.*, note 216 *supra*, para. 515; Jescheck, note 164 *supra*, at 52.

[236]   *United States* v. *von Weizsäcker et al.* (*Ministries* case, case 11), 12 December 1949, in US Government Printing Office (ed.), XIV Trials of War Criminals (TWC), 308, 322; see also *United States* v. *von Leeb et al.* (*High Command* case, case 12), 28 October 1948, XI TWC 462, 482; *United States* v. *Ohlendorf et al.* (*Einsatzgruppen* case, case 9), 10 April 1948, IV TWC 411, 457, 467. See also Ambos, note 119 *supra*, at 123 *et seq.*

[237]   *Prosecutor* v. *Kupreškic et al.*, note 216 *supra*, para. 518.

[238]   *Prosecutor* v. *Kupreškic et al.*, note 216 *supra*, para. 520.

[239]   Jescheck, note 164 *supra*, at. 52.

[240]   Compare only *Prosecutor* v. *Kupreškic et al.*, note 216 *supra*, para. 520; Bassiouni, note 108 *supra*, at 502 *et seq.*; Jescheck, note 164 *supra*, at 52; Schabas, note 2 *supra*, at 227; Werle, note 6 *supra*, para. 617; see also Ambos, note 119 *supra*, at 374–5.

PART V

PROSECUTIONS BY NATIONAL COURTS

14 Extradition and mutual legal assistance: recent trends in inter-state cooperation to combat international crimes

Ved P. Nanda

INTRODUCTION

In this era of globalization, worldwide concern with international terrorism and other cross-border crimes, such as narcotics trafficking, trafficking in persons, arms smuggling, financial crimes, massive tax cheating and major frauds, have led to several multilateral, regional and bilateral interstate efforts to combat such crimes. In the aftermath of the tragic events of 11 September 2001, the United Nations and several regional organizations, especially the European Union and the Organization of American States (OAS), undertook new initiatives to respond to the threats of terrorism. For example, the UN Security Council invoked Chapter VII of the UN Charter to authorize the use of force in self-defense to combat international terrorism. This indeed was a transformative decision, which was followed by the Security Council's sanctioning of stringent financial measures by states to address the menace of terrorism.

In recent years, the United States has fostered closer law enforcement cooperation with other countries and with the European Union. Compounding the 9/11 concerns for Europe (since key logistical and planning centers for terrorist attacks on the United States were found to be in Germany and Spain) were the 2004 terrorist bombings in Madrid and terrorist attacks on the London transport system in 2005. The EU responded by creating a counter-terrorism coordinator and by the adoption of a new EU counter-terrorism strategy. It is worth noting that the main hurdles in creating effective mechanisms to promote inter-state cooperation have been sovereignty-related issues, some of which still impede the needed progress.

The recent EU initiatives have included efforts to harmonize national laws and to enhance cooperation among member states' police, intelligence and judicial authorities; establishment of a European Arrest Warrant (EAW); and both strengthening the EU's joint criminal intelligence agency, Europol, and also establishing a new institution to improve prosecutorial cooperation in cross-border crimes known as Eurojust. The Organization of American States has initiated regular meetings of senior justice officials of member states to enhance legal and judicial cooperation in the Americas. Since their first meeting in 1997 they have strengthened law enforcement cooperation and information exchange.

The tools undertaken to combat terrorism and other international crimes have included new treaties on extradition and mutual legal assistance. The purpose is to simplify, streamline and modernize the extradition process and to enhance prosecutorial cooperation. This chapter will highlight a few selected developments in these related areas to illustrate contemporary efforts and the prevailing trend toward enhancing interstate cooperative efforts in criminal matters. The next section focuses on extradition, followed by a section on multilateral legal assistance and a concluding section.

EXTRADITION

Extradition will be discussed here in two parts: general considerations and extradition and human rights.

General Considerations

As it was succinctly stated in 1935 in a Harvard study, *Draft Convention on Extradition*, extradition 'is the formal surrender of a person by a State to another State for prosecution or punishment'.[1] While practices similar to extradition can be traced back to ancient history, 'extradition' in its modern incarnation is of recent origin, approximately the mid-eighteenth century.[2] The purpose is to ensure that the state most affected by a crime has the fugitive offender returned to it so that s/he can be held accountable for the crime.

In essence, extradition reflects international cooperative efforts aimed at accomplishing the twin objectives of punishing serious crimes and allowing custody of the offender to the most interested state. Citing Grotius, *Restatement (Third) of the Foreign Relations Law of the United States* notes that by 1776, a general principle of international law had evolved to the effect that 'every state was obliged to grant extradition freely and without qualification or restriction, or to punish a wrongdoer itself'.[3]

In modern practice, extradition generally occurs pursuant to bilateral treaties. However, multilateral and regional treaties on extradition include: 1990 UN Model Treaty on Extradition,[4] 1957 European Convention on Extradition,[5] 1995 EU Convention on Extradition,[6] 1994 Economic Community of West African States Convention on Extradition,[7] and 1933 Inter-American Convention on Extradition.[8] A related convention is the 1983 Council of Europe Convention on the Transfer of Sentenced Persons.[9] The EAW is a recent development, which will be discussed later. As the *Restatement* notes, under an extradition treaty a state party:

---

[1] Harvard Research in International Law, *Draft Convention on Extradition,* 29 Am. J Int'l L 21 (Supp. 1935).

[2] See, for example, Christopher L. Blakesley, Terrorism, Drugs, International Law, and the Protection of Human Liberty: A Comparative Study of International Law, its Nature, Role, and Impact in Matters of Terrorism, Drug Trafficking, War, and Extradition 171 (1992).

[3] I *Restatement (Third) of the Foreign Relations Law of the United States*, introductory note to 7B, 557 (1986), citing Grotius, II De Jure Belli ac Pacis, ch. 21, ss. 3–4 (Scott ed., 1925) (hereinafter *Restatement*).

[4] UN Model Treaty on Extradition, General Assembly Res. 45/116, Annex, 45 UN GAOR Supp. (No. 49A) 212, UN Doc. A/45/49 (1990).

[5] European Convention on Extradition, 13 December 1957, ETS No. 24, 359 UNTS 273. The Convention was amended by its 1975 Additional Protocol, 15 October 1975, ETS No. 86, and further amended by the 1978 Second Additional Protocol (17 March 1978, ETS No. 98).

[6] Convention drawn up on the basis of art. K.3 of the Treaty on European Union, on simplified extradition procedure between the Member States of the European Union OJ C78, 30 March 1995.

[7] ECOWAS Convention on Extradition (A/P1/8/94), signed on 6 August 1994 in Abuja, Nigeria.

[8] Inter-American Convention on Extradition, OAS Treaty Series No. 34, 26 December 1933, entered into force 26 December 1934.

[9] Council of Europe Convention on the Transfer of Sentenced Persons, Strasbourg, 21 March 1983, ETS No. 112, available at http://conventions.coe.int/Treaty/en/Treaties/Html/112.htm.

is obligated to comply with the request of another state party to that treaty to arrest and deliver a person duly shown to be sought by that state (a) for trial on a charge of having committed a crime covered by the treaty within the jurisdiction of the requesting state, or (b) for punishment after conviction of such a crime and flight from that state, provided that none of the grounds for refusal to extradite set forth in [the treaty] is applicable.[10]

The process of extraditing a fugitive from the United States to another country is governed by the extradition treaty between the United States and the country requesting extradition, and the federal extradition statute[11] which authorizes the extradition of fugitive aliens even in the absence of a treaty.[12] The statute also authorizes the application of extradition procedures to surrender persons to the international war crimes Tribunals for Yugoslavia and Rwanda.[13] The United States has entered into extradition treaties with most countries and is also a party to the Inter-American Convention on Extradition.[14] In 2003, the United States signed an agreement on extradition with the European Union.[15]

In the United States, extradition has been traditionally viewed as an executive function, a prerogative derived from the President's powers to conduct foreign affairs. Following a formal request for extradition, the judicial role in an extradition hearing has been limited to making a non-discretionary determination as to whether the defendant is subject to surrender to the requesting state.

The federal extradition statute requires a court to determine whether there is sufficient evidence 'to sustain the charge [against the accused] under the provisions of the proper treaty or convention'.[16] As the Third Circuit Court of Appeals said in *Sidali* v. *INS*,[17] 'the court determines whether there is probable cause to believe that the defendant is guilty of the crimes charged. If the evidence is sufficient, the court makes a finding of the extraditability and certifies the case to the Secretary of State.'[18] It is the Secretary of State who makes the final decision to extradite.

---

10   I *Restatement*, note 3 *supra*, s. 475, at 559.

11   18 U.S.C. s. 3181 *et seq.*

12   18 USC s. 3181(b) states: 'The provisions of this chapter shall be construed to permit, in the exercise of comity, the surrender of persons, other than citizens, nationals, or permanent residents of the United States, who have committed crimes of violence against nationals of the United States in foreign countries without regard to the existence of any treaty of extradition with such foreign government if the Attorney General certifies, in writing, that: (1) evidence has been presented by the foreign government that indicates that had the offenses been committed in the United States, they would constitute crimes of violence as defined under section 16 of this title; and (2) the offenses charged are not of a political nature.'

13   18 USC s. 3181, note, PL 104–132, s. 443, 110 Stat. 1280 (1996).

14   For a list, see 18 USC s. 3181.

15   Council of the European Union, Agreement on Extradition between the European Union and the United States, EU/USA/EXTR/en1-en21; EU/USA/EXTR/NOTE/en1-en2, 3 June 2003 (supplementing bilateral treaties between the United States and member states of the European Union with replacement of some bilateral treaty provisions by the Convention provisions, thus harmonizing and strengthening existing US bilateral treaties with individual EU member states).

16   18 USC s. 3184.

17   *Sidali* v. *INS*, 107 F.3d 191 (3d Cir. 1997).

18   *Ibid.* 195. For a thorough discussion of the standard of probable cause in extradition proceedings, which is established by federal law, see *In re Extradition of Ortiz,* 444 F.2d 876, 883–5 (ND Ill. 2006). The court stated: 'Probable cause will be found where there is evidence sufficient to cause a person of ordinary prudence and caution to conscientiously entertain a reasonable belief of the guilt of

After an adverse ruling, the accused's only remedy is to seek a writ of *habeas corpus*, which 'is available only to inquire whether the magistrate had jurisdiction, whether the offense charged is within the treaty and, by a somewhat liberal extension, whether there is any evidence warranting the finding that there was reasonable ground to believe the accused guilty'.[19]

Traditionally, specific crimes are listed in extradition treaties and extradition is limited to those listed crimes which are punished by each of the parties to the treaty. As the US Supreme Court explained the law in the 1922 case of *Collins* v. *Loisel*,[20] dual criminality:

> does not require that the name by which the crime is described in the two countries shall be the same; nor that the scope of the liability shall be coextensive, or, in other respects, the same in the two countries. It is enough if the particular act charged is criminal in both jurisdictions.[21]

However, some US treaty partners construe the dual criminality requirement more narrowly than does the United States. As the Congressional Research Service report for Congress states, 'In the past, some have been unable to find equivalents for attempt, conspiracy, RICO [the Racketeer-Influenced and Corrupt Organization Act, 18 USC ss. 1961–1966], CCE [the Continuing Criminal Enterprise Act, 21 USC s. 848], and crimes with prominent federal jurisdictional elements.'[22]

The recent landmark settlement that UBS, Switzerland's biggest bank, reached with the US government, admitting that the bank had enabled clients to evade US taxes, shows that Switzerland makes a rather fuzzy distinction between tax fraud, which is a crime under Swiss law, and tax evasion, which is not. The Swiss bank agreed to pay US$780 million in fines and turn over about 250 client names to the United States.[23] The United States, however, demanded that UBS also disclose as many as 50,000 American clients who violated US tax laws as UBS hid their accounts from US authorities.[24]

Modern practice, however, has been to insert a general 'dual criminality' clause in extradition treaties, stating that serious offenses punishable under the laws of both parties for a prison sentence of more than one year are extraditable offenses. To illustrate, the US extradition treaty with France, which entered into force in 2002, states in article 2, paragraph 1,

---

the accused. … There are crucial distinctions between the assessment to be made in an extradition hearing and one to be made in a preliminary hearing under Rule 5.1. These distinctions are ultimately grounded on the fundamental principle of comity that, among nations, 'no one can rightfully impose a rule on another'. At an extradition hearing, the defendant's right to challenge the evidence introduced against him is quite limited. He can offer evidence that explains the requesting country's proof, but he cannot submit evidence that contradicts it.' *Ibid.* 884.

[19]   *Eain* v. *Wilkes*, 641 F.2d 504, 509 (7th Cir. 1981), quoting *Fernandez* v. *Phillips*, 268 US 311, 312 (1925).

[20]   *Collins* v. *Loisel*, 259 US 309 (1922).

[21]   *Ibid.* 312.

[22]   Charles Doyle, *Extradition To and From the United States: Overview of the Law and Recent Treaties* 10 (Congressional Research Service (CRS) Report for Congress, 98-958A, 3 August 2007) (hereinafter CRS Report for Congress).

[23]   Joanna Chung et al., *UBS Agrees to Pay $780m over US Tax Evasions*, FINANCIAL TIMES (US), 19 February 2009, 1.

[24]   Adrian Cox et al., *US Lawsuit Says 52,000 Hid UBS Accounts*, FINANCIAL TIMES (US), 20 February 2009, 1.

'Acts shall be extraditable if they are punished under the laws in both States by deprivation of liberty for a maximum of at least one year or by a more severe penalty'.[25]

In the new US extradition treaty with the United Kingdom, which was signed in 2003,[26] the parties agreed to extradite for any 'extraditable offense' similarly defined as in the United States–France extradition treaty. The Secretary of State's letter of submittal to the President asserted that the use of such a 'dual criminality' clause to define extraditable offences 'obviates the need to renegotiate or supplement the Treaty as additional offenses become punishable under the laws in both States'.[27] The 2003 Extradition Agreement between the European Union and the United States similarly defines an extraditable offense.[28]

The *Restatement* notes that most international agreements today provide that a person who is sought for prosecution or for enforcement of a sentence will not be extradited 'if the offense with which he is charged or of which he has been convicted is not punishable as a serious crime in both the requesting and requested state'.[29]

An apt illustration of the application of dual criminality in the United States is a 2007 federal district court case, *In re Extradition of Exoo*.[30] The United States initiated the action for extradition to Ireland of the accused, who was charged with aiding, abetting and counseling a suicide, a violation of Irish law. The question was whether the dual criminality requirement was met. The United States asserted that the court must first look to federal law and in its absence to the law of the state where the accused was found. Further, in the absence of a corresponding law in that state, the court must look to the law of the preponderance or majority of states.[31]

The United States urged the court to look to the law of the preponderance of states. The court thus 'examined and compared the law of Ireland and the fifty states to determine the extent to which the States' laws are "substantially analogous", "relate to the same general offense" or involve conduct which is criminal in both countries'.[32] It concluded that dual criminality did not exist because of its finding that the conduct with which the accused was charged in Ireland was not made felonious under the law of the preponderance of states, which precluded extradition.[33]

---

[25]   Extradition Treaty Between France and the United States, entered into force 1 February 2002, art. 2, para. 1, 2179 UNTS 341 (2002).

[26]   Extradition Treaty Between the United Kingdom and the United States, 31 March 2003, arts 1, 2(1), S Treaty Doc. No. 108-23 (2003), entered into force 26 April 2007. See Cm 7146, (June 2007), available at www.statewatch.org/news/2007/jun/uk-usa-extradition-treaty.pdf. The US Senate gave its consent to the treaty in September 2006. See John R. Cook, *Contemporary Practice of the United States Relating to International Law,* 101 AM. J INT'L L 199 (2007).

[27]   United Kingdom–United States Extradition Treaty, note 26 *supra*, art. V (Secretary of State's letter of submittal to the President).

[28]   Agreement on Extradition between the European Union and the United States, 25 June 2003, OJ L181/27 (2003), art. 4. The Agreement is designed to supplement bilateral agreements on extradition between the United States and EU member states. Under art. 10, the Agreement provides a detailed list of criteria for a requested state to take into account when faced with competing extradition requests from several states. Under art. 4 it also broadens the range of extraditable offenses.

[29]   I *Restatement*, note 3 *supra*, s. 476c.

[30]   *In re Extradition of Exoo,* 522 F.Supp.2d 766 (SDWVa. 2007).

[31]   *Ibid.* 770.

[32]   *Ibid.* 779.

[33]   *Ibid.* 785.

The European Union's Council Framework Decision on the European Arrest Warrant[34] has revolutionized the traditional process of extradition between and among the member states of the EU by giving effect to the 'principle of mutual recognition in criminal matters', as it partially abolishes the dual criminality requirement and authorizes the extradition of nationals. This initiative, which followed the 9/11 attacks, was aimed at integrating criminal matters within the EU, and has removed some of the hurdles in seeking extradition of individuals accused or convicted of certain serious criminal acts. The Framework Decision uses the term 'surrender' instead of 'extradition'. It also refers to 'executing state' in place of the traditional reference in extradition treaties to 'requested state' and to 'issuing state' instead of 'requesting state'. The procedure for surrender is simplified because the transmission of arrest warrants is not done through diplomatic channels or ministries but directly between competent judicial authorities.[35]

The EAW overturns the traditional practice in many civil law states, including continental Europe, that nationals are not extradited.[36] This practice is so well entrenched in Europe that even the European Convention on Extradition[37] provides that contracting parties 'shall have the right to refuse extradition of their nationals'.[38] However, the EAW does give a nod to this practice as it states that:

> where a person who is the subject of a European arrest warrant for the purpose of prosecution is a national or resident of the executing Member State, surrender may be subject to the condition that the person, after being heard, is returned to the executing Member State in order to serve there the custodial sentence or detention order passed against him in the issuing Member State.[39]

The substitution of 'surrender' for 'extradition' is aimed at ensuring that the prohibition, constitutional or statutory, against extraditing a national does not apply. The International Criminal Court similarly uses the term 'surrender', as its Statute reads:

---

34   Council Framework Decision 2002/584/JHA of 13 June 2002 on the European Arrest Warrant and the Surrender Procedure between Member States, OJ L190/1–20 (2002). See also Presidency Conclusions European Council Tampere, art. 33 SN 200/99 (15–16 October 1999), available at www.europarl.europa.du/summits/tam_en.htm; Commission staff working document, Annex to the Report from the Commission on the Implementation of the Council Framework Decision, COM(2007)407 final, SEC/2007/0979 final (11 July 2007); European Commission, Freedom, Security and Justice, *European Arrest Warrant Replaces Extradition Between EU Member States,* available at http://ec.europa.eu/justice_home/fsj/criminal/extradition_en.htm. For a discussion of the EAW, see text at note 36 *infra.* See also Zsuzsanna Deen-Racsmány, *Lessons of the European Arrest Warrant for Domestic Implementation of the Obligation to Surrender Nationals to the International Criminal Court,* 20 LEIDEN J INT'L L 167 (2007) (the EU and the ICC provisions offer useful guidance to domestic legislatures involved with implementing obligations under the ICC Statute to ensure that ICC requests concerning the surrender of nationals can be honored).

35   See EAW, note 34 *supra,* preambular para. 9; arts 3, 4, 7, 9, 15 and 17.

36   *Ibid.* perambular para. 1.

37   1957 European Convention on Extradition, note 5 *supra.*

38   EAW, note 34 *supra,* art. 6(1). This provision was included to allow as many states as possible to become parties to the Convention, since the laws of several European states proscribe extradition of their nationals. See Explanatory Report to the European Convention on Extradition, ETS No. 24, art. 6. For the recent refusal of the Russian Federation to extradite one of their nationals to the United Kingdom for his alleged murder of a naturalized British citizen in London in November 2006, see Jacques Hartmann, *The Lugovoy Extradition Case,* 57 INT'L AND COMP. LQ 194 (2008).

39   EAW, note 34 *supra,* art 5.

(a)   'Surrender' means the delivering up of a person by a State to the Court, pursuant to this Statute.

(b)   'Extradition' means the delivering up of a person by one State to another as provided by treaty, convention or national legislation.[40]

It is equally noteworthy that the EAW partially abolishes the dual criminality requirement regarding 32 enumerated crimes. Thus, persons may be surrendered for the alleged commission of acts that do not constitute a crime in the surrendering state where the acts may have taken place. The issue came for determination before the European Court of Justice (ECJ) in *Advocaten vor de Wereld VZW* v. *Leden van de Ministerraad*,[41] as a Belgian non-profit organization brought an action before the Belgian Constitutional Court challenging the EAW and thus seeking annulment of the Belgian law incorporating the provisions of the Framework Decision.[42] The ECJ concluded that 'there was no breach of the principle of equality and non-discrimination and that the validity of the Framework Decision must be upheld'.[43] As an EU instrument which incorporated the principle of mutual recognition into criminal matters, the EAW is an apt example of the EU's efforts to enhance cooperation of prosecutors and judges among member states.

Among the offenses for which extradition may or must be denied, the one most common in many treaties has been the political offense. As a US federal appellate court stated in a 2006 case, *Vo* v. *Benov*:[44]

> The political offense doctrine covers two types of crimes … The first are 'relative' political offenses, which are "otherwise common crimes committed in connection with a political act', or 'common crimes … committed for political motives or in a political context' … For this type of crime, we use the two-prong 'incidence' test to decide whether a crime falls under the political offense exception … The second are 'pure' political offenses, such as treason, sedition, and espionage … Because these crimes are by definition political, courts generally do not apply the incidence test to them …
>
> For a crime to qualify for the political offense exception under the incidence test, there must be (1) the occurrence of an uprising or other violent political disturbance at the time of the charged offense, and (2) a charged offense that is incidental to, in the course of, or in furtherance of the uprising.[45]

As countries continue to face the threat of terrorism and violent crimes, many multinational agreements obligate states to cooperate in combating such crimes by extraditing or prosecuting the offender. States are also renegotiating and updating their extradition treaties by excluding such crimes from the definition of political crimes, and new extradition treaties follow this contemporary practice. The 2003 United Kingdom–United States Extradition

---

40   Rome Statute of the International Criminal Court, UN Doc. A/Conf.183/9 (1998), 37 ILM 999 (1998), art. 102. This provision was modeled on the Statute of the International Criminal Tribunal for the Former Yugoslavia, 32 ILM 1159 (1993), art. 29) and the Statute of the International Criminal Tribunal for Rwanda, 33 ILM 1598 (1994), art 28.

41   *Advocaten vor de Wereld VZW* v. *Leden van de Ministerraad,* Case No. C-303/05, available at http://curia.europa.eu/jurisp/cgi-bin/form.pl?lang=en.

42   For a comment, see Christine Janssens, *Case Law: Case C-303/05, Advocaten vor de Wereld VZW v. Leden van de Ministerraad,* 14 COLUM. J EUR. L 169 (Winter 2007/2008).

43   *Ibid.* 174.

44   *Vo* v. *Benov*, 447 F.3d 1235 (9th Cir. 2006) (citations omitted).

45   *Ibid.* 1241.

Treaty,[46] which modernized and streamlined the earlier bilateral agreements between the two countries, will be frequently referred to here as an apt illustration of contemporary bilateral agreements on extradition. Article 4 of the Treaty enumerates seven exceptions to the definition of political offense. It is reproduced here in full as it establishes a model of extradition treaties excluding a number of major crimes, including terrorism, from the political offense exception:

> Political and Military Offenses
> 1. Extradition shall not be granted if the offense for which extradition is requested is a political offense.
> 2. For the purposes of this Treaty, the following offenses shall not be considered political offenses:
> (a)   an offense for which both Parties have the obligation pursuant to a multilateral international agreement to extradite the person sought or to submit the case to their competent authorities for decision as to prosecution;
> (b)   a murder or other violent crime against the person of a Head of State of one of the Parties, or of a member of the Head of State's family;
> (c)   murder, manslaughter, malicious wounding, or inflicting grievous bodily harm;
> (d)   an offense involving kidnapping, abduction, or any form of unlawful detention, including the taking of a hostage;
> (e)   placing or using, or threatening the placement or use of, an explosive, incendiary, or destructive device or firearm capable of endangering life, of causing grievous bodily harm, or of causing substantial property damage;
> (f)   possession of an explosive, incendiary, or destructive device capable of endangering life, of causing grievous bodily harm, or of causing substantial property damage;
> (g)   an attempt or a conspiracy to commit, participation in the commission of, aiding or abetting, counseling or procuring the commission of, or being an accessory before or after the fact to any of the foregoing offenses.
> 3. Notwithstanding the terms of paragraph 2 of this Article, extradition shall not be granted if the competent authority of the Requested State determines that the request was politically motivated. In the United States, the executive branch is the competent authority for the purposes of this Article.
> 4. The competent authority of the Requested State may refuse extradition for offenses under military law that are not offenses under ordinary criminal law. In the United States, the executive branch is the competent authority for the purposes of this Article.

The place where the crime is committed may become an issue when a state seeks extradition of the offender. May a state, for example, claim extra-territorial jurisdiction, seeking extradition of a person for a crime committed outside its territory, based on the claim that its laws provide for punishment for such crimes? While acknowledging territoriality as the primary basis of a state's jurisdiction regarding the reach of its criminal laws, the United States and some other states as well are now claiming extra-territorial reach of their criminal laws, in light of the increasing threat of terrorism and drug trafficking. The following provision in the 2003 United Kingdom–United States Extradition Treaty illustrates how the parties are attempting to resolve the issue:

> If the offense has been committed outside the territory of the Requesting State, extradition shall be granted in accordance with the provisions of the Treaty if the laws in the Requested State provide for the punishment of such conduct committed outside its territory in similar circumstances. If the laws in the Requested State do not provide for the punishment of such conduct committed outside

---

[46]   See note 26 *supra*.

of its territory in similar circumstances, the executive authority of the Requested State, in its discretion, may grant extradition provided that all other requirements of this Treaty are met.[47]

There are a few more general considerations to be noted here, specifically the doctrine of *non bis in idem* (double jeopardy and/or double punishment), the doctrine of specialty, and the matter of limitation periods. Many extradition treaties include provisions denying extradition under the doctrine of *non bis in idem* when the person sought has been convicted or acquitted in the requested state for the same offense for which extradition is requested. Some clauses may bar extradition for a second prosecution of the 'same acts' or the 'same event' instead of the 'same offense'.[48]

The pertinent provision in the United Kingdom–United States Extradition Treaty also provides that 'when the person sought has been convicted or acquitted in a third state in respect of the conduct for which extradition is requested', the requested state may refuse extradition.[49] It also provides, however, that extradition shall not be denied if the competent authorities of the requested state:

(a) have decided not to prosecute the person sought for the acts for which extradition is requested;
(b) have decided to discontinue any criminal proceedings which have been instituted against the person sought for those acts; or
(c) are still investigating the person sought for the same acts for which extradition is sought.[50]

Explaining the doctrine of specialty, the US Supreme Court stated in the 1886 case of *United States* v. *Rauscher*:[51]

a person who has been brought within the jurisdiction of the court by virtue of proceedings under an extradition treaty, can only be tried for one of the offences described in that treaty, and for the offence with which he is charged in the proceedings for his extradition, until a reasonable time and opportunity have been given him, after his release or trial upon such charge, to return to the country from whose asylum he had been forcibly taken under those proceedings.

Many extradition treaties contain such a provision. The pertinent provision in the United Kingdom–United States treaty reads in part:

1. A person extradited under this Treaty may not be detained, tried, or punished in the Requesting State except for:
(a) any offense for which extradition was granted, or a differently denominated offense based on the same facts as the offense on which extradition was granted, provided such offense is extraditable, or is a lesser included offense;
(b) any offense committed after the extradition of the person; or
(c) any offense for which the executive authority of the Requested State waives the rule of specialty and thereby consents to the person's detention, trial, or punishment. ...

---

47 *Ibid.* art. 2(4).
48 See generally CRS Report for Congress, note 22 *supra*, at 14.
49 United Kingdom–United States Extradition Treaty, note 26 *supra*, art. 5(2).
50 *Ibid.* art. 5(3).
51 *United States* v. *Rauscher*, 119 US 407 (1886).

2. A person extradited under this Treaty may not be the subject of onward extradition or surrender for any offense committed prior to extradition to the Requesting State unless the Requested State consents.[52]

Extradition treaties may also preclude extradition if prosecution for the offense charged, or the penalty's enforcement, has lapsed under the applicable limitation period, which could be that of the requested state, the requesting state, or either. However, some contemporary treaties disregard the limitation period in either state.[53]

Human Rights and Extradition

General

Inter-state relations and comity are the prime drivers of the traditional practice of extradition. With the advent of international human rights law in the post-UN period, the rights of the individual, which were ignored under the traditional practice, are increasingly impacting extradition. To illustrate, while the non-inquiry rule, under which human rights considerations are not taken into account, still prevails in the United States, contemporary practice in several countries is to reject the rule and subject extradition to judicial scrutiny. This rule is rationalized on the bases of comity and foreign policy considerations.

US practice

A 2006 Third Circuit Court of Appeals case, *Hoxha* v. *Levi*, is a recent application of the non-inquiry rule in the United States. The court there stated that this 'principle serves interests of international comity by relegating to political actors the sensitive foreign policy judgments that are often involved in the question of whether to refuse an extradition request'.[54] And, as early as 1901, Justice Harlan stated in *Neely* v. *Henkel*:[55]

> When an American citizen commits a crime in a foreign country he cannot complain if required to submit to such modes of trial and to such punishment as the laws of that country may prescribe for its own people, unless a different mode be provided for by treaty stipulations between that country and the United States.[56]

In *Hoxha*, a naturalized US citizen petitioned for *habeas corpus*, seeking to block his extradition to Albania, his birth country, where he would stand trial for murder. The petition was rejected although he had asserted that if extradited he would 'be tortured and may be killed by the Albanian authorities'.[57] The Third Circuit affirmed the District Court's finding that Hoxha's humanitarian arguments were irrelevant.[58] The court stated: 'Under the traditional doctrine of "non-inquiry", such humanitarian considerations are within the purview of

---

52   United Kingdom–United States Extradition Treaty, note 226 *supra*, art. 18(1)–(2).
53   See *ibid.* art. 6, which reads: 'The decision by the Requested State whether to grant the request for extradition shall be made without regard to any state of limitations in either State.'
54   *Hoxha* v. *Levi*, 465 F.3d 554, 563 (3rd Cir. 2006).
55   *Neely* v. *Henkel*, 180 US 109 (1901).
56   *Ibid.* 123.
57   *Hoxha*, 465 F.3d at 563.
58   *Ibid.* 565.

the executive branch and generally should not be addressed by the courts in deciding whether a petitioner is extraditable.'[59]

It is noteworthy that the District Court was cognizant of State Department reports that Albanian police were accused of torturing suspects in their prisons. Also, while acknowledging the allegations that US authorities had collaborated with foreign agents to send terrorist suspects to nations that use 'deplorable and illegal interrogation practices', the court trusted:

> that the State Department will seriously examine the charges of torture that Hoxha has levied against Albanian authorities and faithfully uphold this Government's clear policy of refusing to extradite a person when there are substantial grounds for believing that person would be subjected to torture.[60]

Hoxha is one of numerous cases where the US courts have applied the rule of non-inquiry in the face of evidence that extraditees may face egregious violations of their human rights.[61] One case, however, especially stands out and I will briefly discuss it here. The case is a 2005 Ninth Circuit decision, *Prasopat* v. *Banov*,[62] where the court ruled on foreign policy grounds that the accused should be extradited to Thailand even if he, as a US citizen, may be executed as punishment for a non-violent drug offense for which the United States does not impose capital punishment.

The court did discuss the possibility of a humanitarian exception to extradition but accepted the government's argument that it was for the Secretary of State to deny extradition on humanitarian grounds, since the Secretary of State's decision may be based on foreign policy considerations and not merely on considerations relating to the individual facing extradition.[63] Thus, it applied the rule of non-inquiry, holding that 'an extradition magistrate lacks discretion to inquire into the conditions that might await a fugitive upon return to the requesting country'.[64]

Several recent international human rights norms, established as customary international law and embodied in international treaties, demand a revisiting of this state-centered focus. Thus, the non-inquiry rule, under which the court is considered not to be the proper place for evaluating humanitarian considerations, which belong exclusively to the purview of the executive, is rejected in the emerging practice of many countries.

---

[59] *Ibid.* 563. The court quoted *Sidali*, 107 F.3d at 195, n. 7: '[W]e note that it is the function of the Secretary of State – not the courts – to determine whether extradition should be denied on humanitarian grounds.' The court also quoted *United States* v. *Kin-Hong*, 110 F.3d 103, 110 (1st Cir. 1997): 'Under the rule of non-inquiry, courts refrain from investigating the fairness of a requesting nation's justice system, and from inquiring into the procedures or treatment which await a surrendered fugitive in the requesting country.'

[60] *Hoxha* v. *Levi*, 371 F.Supp.2d 651, 660 n.3 (ED Pa. 2005).

[61] See Andrew J. Parmenter, *Comment: Death by Non-Inquiry: The Ninth Circuit Permits the Extradition of a U.S. Citizen Facing the Death Penalty for a Non-Violent Drug Offense (Prasopat v. Banov F.3d 1009 (9th Cir. 2005))*, 45 WASHBURN LJ 657, 664 n. 76 (2006). See also Michael P. Shea, *Expanding Judicial Scrutiny of Human Rights in Extradition Cases After Soering*, 17 YALE J INT'L L 85 (1992).

[62] *Prasopat* v. *Banov*, 421 F.3d 1009 (9th Cir. 2005).

[63] *Ibid.* 421 F.3d at 1016.

[64] *Ibid.*

The pertinent human rights treaties include the International Covenant on Civil and Political Rights (ICCPR),[65] which guarantees the right to life and the right not to be tortured or subjected to cruel, inhuman or degrading punishment; the United Nations Convention Against Torture and Other Cruel, Inhuman or Degrading Treatment or Punishment (CAT);[66] and several regional conventions on human rights, especially the European Convention for the Protection of Human Rights and Fundamental Freedoms (ECHR).[67]

The US Congress incorporated the prohibition against torture by stating in the Foreign Affairs Reform and Restructuring Act: 'It shall be the policy of the United States not to … extradite … any person to a country in which there are substantial grounds for believing the person would be in danger of being subjected to torture, regardless of whether the person is physically present in the United States.'[68] The Secretary of State is bound to enforce the policy,[69] and as the Act does not create a private cause of action, there is no basis for judicial review. But the questions are: why should the Secretary of State's decision to extradite after the court has certified extraditability be not subject to judicial review when fundamental human rights are implicated? Why should not the Congress enact this much needed reform?

In the international setting, the abolition of the death penalty in many jurisdictions has caused special extradition problems. As a result, several abolitionist states provide in their extradition treaties that they have the right to deny extradition in capital cases or without sufficient assurances that the death penalty will not be imposed or carried out if imposed on the fugitive if s/he is surrendered.[70] Consequently, domestic courts in several such jurisdictions follow this rule and refuse extradition if not satisfied by the assurances given.[71]

---

[65]   International Covenant on Civil and Political Rights (ICCPR), 16 December 1966, entered into force 23 March 1976, 999 UNTS, reprinted in 6 ILM 368 (1976).

[66]   UN Convention Against Torture and Other Cruel, Inhuman or Degrading Treatment or Punishment, 10 December 1984, entered into force 26 June 1987, 1465 UNTS 85.

[67]   European Convention for the Protection of Human Rights and Fundamental Freedoms, 4 November 1950, ETS No. 5, 213 UNTS 222.

[68]   Foreign Affairs Reform and Restructuring Act of 1988 (FARRA), Pub.L No. 105-277 (a), div. G, Title XXII, s. 2242, 112 Stat. 2681–822 (21 October 1998) (codified as Note to 8 USC s. 1231) (providing that 'it shall be the policy of the United States not to expel, extradite, or otherwise effect the involuntary return of any person to a country in which there are substantial grounds for believing the person would be in danger of being subjected to torture').

[69]   *Ibid.* s. 2242(b); 22 CFR Pt 95.

[70]   The United Kingdom–United States Extradition Treaty, note 26 *supra*, states at art. 7: 'Article 7   When the offense for which extradition is sought is punishable by death under the laws in the Requesting State and is not punishable by death under the laws in the Requested State, the executive authority in the Requested State may refuse extradition unless the Requesting State provides an assurance that the death penalty will not be imposed or, if imposed, will not be carried out.'

[71]   See, for example, Andrea Bianchi, *International Decision: Venezia* v. *Ministero di Grazia e Giustizia*, 91 AM. J INT'L L 727 (1997) (discussing the Italian Constitutional Court's ruling). The author states, 'The ruling of the Italian Constitutional Court in the *Venezia* case attests to the increasing difficulty in obtaining extradition from European countries of fugitives charged with crimes punishable by death in the United States and elsewhere.' *Ibid.* at 733. See also *Short* v. *Netherlands*, (1990) 76 Rechtspraak van der Week 358 (Hoge Raod, the Netherlands), reprinted in 29 ILM 1388 (1991); and *Mohamed* v. *President of Republic of South Africa*, [2001] 3 S Afr. LR 893 (Const. Ct), reprinted in 127 ILR 468 (2006).

Complaints before the UN Human Rights Committee

The UN Human Rights Committee has received several complaints claiming violations of the ICCPR[72] in respect of extradition cases. In 2003 the Committee considered a 'disguised extradition' case, *Judge* v. *Canada*.[73] The accused, a wanted fugitive who had escaped after being convicted of murder and sentenced to death, was simply deported from Canada to the United States without any assurances concerning the death penalty and thus the fugitive invoked articles 6, 7, 10 and 14 of the ICCPR to complain that his rights were violated. Consequently, the Committee had to determine whether Canada, an abolitionist state, had violated Judge's right to life, to an effective remedy, and not to be subjected to serious ill- treatment.

The Human Rights Committee concluded that Canada had violated article 6 of the ICCPR by deporting Judge without ensuring that the death penalty would not be carried out. In the Committee's words:

> For countries that *have* abolished the death penalty, there is an obligation not to expose a person to the real risk of its application. Thus, they may not remove, either by deportation or extradition, individuals from their jurisdiction if it may be reasonably anticipated that they will be sentenced to death, without ensuring that the death sentence would not be carried out.[74]

In *Everett* v. *Spain*,[75] a 2004 Human Rights Committee decision, the Committee acknowledged that several ICCPR articles apply to the extradition process, and that extradition could be challenged alleging future ill-treatment. Professor Joanna Harrington has concluded, after a thorough study of extradition complaints brought before the Human Rights Committee invoking the ICCPR:

> The test for finding ... a violation [under ICCPR] is whether the anticipated consequences of the extradition to the individual concerned constitute a real and substantial risk that flows as a necessary and foreseeable consequence from the decision to extradite, with the grounds for such a violation being limited, at least internationally, to the right to life and the right to be free from serious forms of ill-treatment such as torture.[76]

Jurisprudence of the European Court of Human Rights

The European Court of Human Rights (ECtHR) has established impressive jurisprudence in the last decade mandating the observance of fundamental human rights in the extradition process. A few cases illustrating this practice will be discussed here.

In its 1999 landmark case, *Soering* v. *United Kingdom*,[77] the ECtHR interpreted the ECHR,[78] especially article 3 of the Convention, which prohibits torture and cruel, inhuman

---

72   ICCPR, note 65 *supra*.

73   *Judge* v. *Canada,* Communication No. 829/1998, UN Doc. CCPR/C/78/D/829/1998, Report of the Human Rights Committee, UN GAOR, 58th Sess., Supp. (No. 40), UN Doc. A/58/40, vol. 2, Annex VG (2003) (views adopted 5 August 2003), reprinted in 42 ILM 1214 (2004).

74   *Ibid.* para. 10.4 (emphasis in original).

75   Report of the Human Rights Committee, UN GAOR, 59th Sess., Supp. (No. 40), UN Doc. A/59/40, vol. 2 (2004) Annex XF (*Everett* v. *Spain*, Communication No. 961/2000, UN Doc. CCPR/C/81/D/961/2000) (decision adopted 9 July 2004).

76   Joanna Harrington, *The Absent Dialogue: Extradition and the International Covenant on Civil and Political Rights,* 32 QUEEN's LJ 82, 131 (2006).

77   *Soering* v. *United Kingdom*, Eur. Ct HR (Ser. A), No. 161, 11 Eur. HR Rep. 439 (7 July 1999).

78   See note 67 *supra*.

or degrading treatment or punishment, and held that the United Kingdom would violate its obligations under the Convention should it proceed with extradition. The issue was whether the 'death row' phenomenon likely to be experienced by the individual in that case, if convicted and condemned to death in Virginia, would constitute a violation of his rights under article 3 of the ECHR. In the ECtHR's view:

> having regard to the very long period of time spent on death row in such extreme conditions, with the ever-present and mounting anguish of awaiting execution of the death penalty, and to the personal circumstances of the applicant, especially his age and mental state at the time of the offense, the applicant's extradition to the United States would expose him to a real risk of treatment going beyond the threshold set by Article 3.[79]

The 2005 judgment of the ECtHR in *Shayamev* v. *Georgia*[80] confirms the recent trend of what has been called the 'judicialization of the extradition process'.[81] The case involved Chechen guerrillas detained in Georgia whose extradition was sought by the Russian Federation on charges of having attacked a Russian army patrol in Chechnya. The ECtHR was requested to order provisional measures to prohibit the extradition of any of them to Russia. The Court ordered the requested provisional measures; however, the order was not communicated to Georgia in time and five of the 13 guerrillas were handed over to Russia, pursuant to the requirements of the European Convention on Extradition.[82] Russia subsequently refused to honor the ECtHR's request for an on-site visit so that the Court could establish the facts of the case and acquire a better understanding of the situation.

After stating that the ECHR 'prohibits in absolute terms any treatment contrary to Article 3, whatever the actions of the victim', the Court added: 'Articles 2 and 3 of the Convention do not provide for any restriction and are not subject to any derogation according to Article 15 even in times of public danger threatening the life of the nation.'[83] The ECtHR held that the extradition procedure employed by the Georgian authorities amounted to a breach of article 3 of the ECHR, prohibiting inhuman and degrading treatment, because of the 'lack of procedural guarantees, the detainees' ignorance concerning their fate, and the needless anxiety and uncertainty that they experienced'.[84]

The Court found that 'it is imperative that an applicant's complaint that extradition may have consequences contrary to Articles 2 and 3 of the Convention be examined meticulously by a national authority', and that the state in question must give the complaint 'an independent and rigorous examination', and must also stay the extradition process pending the outcome of the investigation.[85]

Professor Gavouneli considers the case a landmark as it brings 'within its domain – and therefore subject to review – not only the technicalities of the extradition procedure, but also

---

[79] *Ibid.* para. 111.
[80] *Shayamev* v. *Georgia*, App. No. 36378/02, ECtHR, 12 April 2005. For a comment on the case, see Maria Gavouneli, *Shayamev & 12 Others* v. *Georgia & Russia, App. No. 36378 (02)*, available at www.echr.coe.int; 100 AM. J INT'L L 674 (2006).
[81] See Gavouneli, note 80 *supra*, at 679–83.
[82] European Convention on Extradition, note 5 *supra*.
[83] Gavouneli, note 80 *supra*, at 677, quoting from para. 335 of the Court's decision.
[84] Gavouneli, note 80 *supra*, at 678.
[85] *Ibid.* quoting from paras 448 and 446 of the Court's decision.

the ultimate decision on whether or not to carry out the extradition – a decision that has been political rather than legal, [thus] codifying the extradition procedure as an integral part of the ECHR's human rights protection system'.[86] Among several other such judgments of the ECtHR, it blocked Russia from extraditing a group of Uzbek refugees to Uzbekistan where they feared they would be tortured on their return.[87] This was one among many cases where the Court has rejected diplomatic assurances against torture as insufficient and unreliable.

In *Saadi* v. *Italy,* the ECtHR reiterated its prior jurisprudence interpreting article 3 of the ECHR as obligating states not to return or extradite individuals to states in which they face a real risk of torture, or inhuman or degrading treatment. Thus, it reasserted the states' *non-refoulement* obligation under article 3.[88] In this case, Italy arrested Naseem Saadi, a Tunisian national, on suspicion of involvement in international terrorism. He was subsequently released, but during his detention in Italy a military court in Tunisia had convicted him *in absentia* on charges of incitement to terrorism and membership in a terrorist organization operating abroad, sentencing him to 20 years' imprisonment.

Saadi had asserted that, if deported to Tunisia, he would be subjected to torture. He claimed 'that it was "a matter of common knowledge" that persons suspected of terrorist activities, in particular those connected with Islamist fundamentalism, were frequently tortured in Tunisia'[89] and thus he invoked article 3 of the ECHR.

Italy argued that it had received diplomatic assurances from Tunisia[90] and had therefore fulfilled its obligation under article 3 not to remove an individual to a state if there was a real risk that s/he would be subjected to torture or inhuman or degrading treatment. Along with this, Italy also challenged the ECtHR's jurisprudence on states' *non-refoulement* obligations in light of the prevalent environment of international terrorism.The Court acknowledged the need to take into account 'the scale of the terrorist threat in the world of today and of the objective difficulties of combating it effectively'.[91] But it was unequivocal in its uncompromising assertion about the nature of the article 3 prohibitions, as it stated that the danger of terrorism 'must not, however, call into question the absolute nature of article 3'.[92]

In the ECtHR's words:

> Since protection against the treatment prohibited by Article 3 is absolute, that provision imposes an obligation not to extradite or expel any person who, in the receiving country, would run the real risk of being subjected to such treatment. As the Court has repeatedly held, there can be no derogation from that rule.[93]

---

[86] Gavouneli, note 80 *supra*, at 680.

[87] *Ismoilov* v. *Russia,* App. No. 2947/06, ECtHR, 24 April 2008.

[88] *Saadi* v. *Italy,* App. No. 37201/06, ECtHR 28 February 2008. For a comment on this case, see Fiona de Londras, *Saadi* v. *Italy: European Court of Human Rights Reasserts the Absolute Prohibition of Refoulement in Terrorism Extradition Cases,* 12 ASIL INSIGHTS, No. 9 (13 May 2008). See also Aoifi Duffy, *Expulsion to Face Torture? Non-Refoulement in International Law,* 20 INT'L J REFUGEE L 373 (2008).

[89] *Saadi,* note 88 *supra*, para. 98.

[90] By *note verbale* dated 10 July 2007, the Tunisian Minister of Foreign Affairs 'confirm[ed] that the Tunisian laws in force guarantee and protect the rights of prisoners in Tunisia and secure to them the right to a fair trial', and pointed out that 'Tunisia has voluntarily acceded to the relevant international treaties and conventions'. *Ibid.* para. 55.

[91] *Ibid.*, para. 114.

[92] *Ibid.*, para. 137.

[93] *Ibid.*, para. 138.

The Court:

> reaffirm[ed] that for a planned forcible expulsion to be in breach of the Convention it is necessary – and sufficient – for substantial grounds to have been shown for believing that there is a real risk that the person concerned will be subjected in the receiving country to treatment prohibited by Article 3.[94]

In a later case, *Ben Khemais,*[95] with similar facts, Italy deported Ben Khemais, a Tunisian national, to Tunisia, where the Tunis military court had sentenced him *in absentia* to ten years' imprisonment for membership in a terrorist organization. Italy had ignored the ECtHR's interim order to stay his deportation.[96] A Chamber of the Court, holding that the deportation had violated article 3, awarded the applicant 10,000 euros under ECHR, article 41, the 'just satisfaction' provision of the Convention, as non-pecuniary damages, and 5,000 euros for costs and expenses. According to the court in Italy, he 'represented a threat to national security' because of his contacts with terrorists.

The ECtHR reiterated its earlier conclusion in the *Saadi* case that, based upon international reports and visits by the International Committee of the Red Cross to Tunisian prisons, it 'could not exclude the risk of subjection to treatment contrary to Article 3'. Consequently, it rejected the Italian government's argument that 'the assurances given by the Tunisian authorities secured effective protection against the serious risk of ill-treatment incurred by the applicant', reiterating 'the principle affirmed by the Parliamentary Assembly of the Council of Europe ... in its resolution no. 1433 (2005), according to which diplomatic assurances could not be relied on unless the absence of a risk of ill-treatment was firmly established'.[97]

Two instances of interim measures ordered by the ECtHR will be briefly noted here. On 1 August 2008, Mustafa Kamal Mustafa (Abu Hamza) sought interim measures to prevent his extradition to the United States from the United Kingdom. The United States was seeking his surrender on charges alleging that his activities supported terrorism and on conspiracy charges to take Western hostages in Yemen. He was serving a seven-year sentence in Britain and had exhausted his appeals against extradition.[98] On 4 August 2008, the acting President of the Chamber to which the case had been allocated decided that under rule 39 of the Rules of Court, Abu Hamza should not be extradited to the United States until the ECtHR had given due consideration of the matter.[99]

Similarly, on 19 February 2009, the acting President of the Chamber to which another case had been allocated decided that under rule 39 of the Rules of Court the government of the United Kingdom should not extradite the applicant, Omar Othman (Abu Qatada), to Jordan

---

[94]   *Ibid.,* para. 140.

[95]   *Ben Khemais* v. *Italy,* App. No. 246/07, ECtHR 24 February 2009. The judgment is available only in French. See Press Release Issued by the Registrar No. 142, *Chamber Judgment,* 24 February 2009, available at http://echr.coe.int/echr/en/hudoc.

[96]   Under rule 39 of the Rules of Court, the ECtHR may indicate to the parties any interim measure which it considers should be adopted in the interests of the parties or of the proper conduct of the proceedings.

[97]   *Ben Khemais,* note 97 *supra.*

[98]   Press Release Issued by the Registrar No. 569, 4 August 2008, available at http://cmiskp.echr.coe.int. For a brief account, see BBC News, *Abu Hamza Extradition is Delayed,* 5 August 2008, available at http://news.bbc.co.uk.

[99]   *Ibid.*

until the ECtHR had given due consideration of the matter. The applicant had complained that although the Jordanian government had given the United Kingdom assurances to the contrary, he was at real risk of being subjected to ill-treatment in breach of article 3, as well as of articles 5 (right to liberty and security) and 6 (right to a fair trial) of the ECHR.[100]

Convention Against Torture and Other Cruel, Inhuman or Degrading Treatment or Punishment[101]

Article 22 of the CAT provides that the Committee Against Torture 'shall consider communications received ... in the light of all information made available to it by or on behalf of the individual and by the State party concerned'.[102] The Committee adopted guidelines in its 1997 General Comment[103] for states parties and authors of communications on article 3 of the CAT, which prohibited states parties to 'expel, return (*refouler*) or extradite a person to another State where there are substantial grounds for believing that he would be in danger of being subjected to torture'. In the Committee's view, 'another state' in article 3 referred to 'the State to which the individual concerned is being expelled, returned or extradited, as well as to any State to which the author may subsequently be expelled, returned or extradited'.[104]

The Committee observed that the standard for meeting the threshold of the 'substantial grounds' requirement in article 3 was that 'the risk of torture must be assessed on grounds that go beyond mere theory or suspicion. However, the risk does not have to meet the test of being highly probable', although such danger has to be personal and present.[105] The burden is upon the author to present 'a factual basis for the author's position sufficient to require a response from the State party'.[106]

A 1993 decision of the Committee Against Torture, *Mutombo* v. *Switzerland*,[107] is a typical illustration of the Committee's interpretation of the Convention's mandate. Mutombo, a

---

[100]   Press Release Issued by the Registrar No. 131, 19 February 2009, available at http://cmiskp.echr.coe.int.

[101]   See note 66 *supra*.

[102]   CAT, art. 22(4).

[103]   Office of the High Commissioner for Human Rights, *General Comment No. 01: Implementation of Article 3 of the Convention in the Context of Article 22* , A/53/44, Annex 9, CAT *General Comment No. 01, November 21, 1997*, available at www.unhchr.ch.tbs.doc.

[104]   *Ibid.* para. 2.

[105]   *Ibid.* paras 6, 7.

[106]   *Ibid.* para. 5.

[107]   *Mutombo* v. *Switzerland*, Communication No. 13/1993, UN Doc. A/49/44, 45 (1994). The following are a few other illustrative decisions by the Committee Against Torture: *Agiza* v. *Sweden*, Communication No. 233/2003, Sweden 24 May 2005, UN Doc. CAT/C/34/d/233/2003, reprinted in 44 ILM 1103 (2005) (while acknowledging that measures taken to fight terrorism, including denial of safe haven, are legitimate as well as important, the Committee found Sweden in violation of art. 3 by returning him to Egypt and said that Sweden was under an obligation to prevent similar violations in the future); *AS* v. *Sweden,* Communication No. 149/1999, 24 November 2000, UN Doc. CAT/C/25/D/149/1999 (15 February 2001) (the Committee decided that Sweden was under an obligation not to return the author to Iran, where she was under a sentence of death by stoning for adultery); *Falcon* v. *Canada,* noted in 17 INT'L J REFUGEE L 416 (2005) (the Committee concluded that the complainant's removal to Mexico where he had been tortured would constitute a violation by Canada of art. 3 of the Convention); and *TPS* v. *Canada,* Communication No. 99/1997, 4 September 2000, UN Doc. CAT/C/24/D/99/1997 (the complainant's removal from Canada to India was found by the Committee not to constitute a violation of art. 3 of the Convention by Canada).

citizen of Zaire, was living in Switzerland and was seeking recognition as a refugee at the time of his communication to the Committee. He had illegally entered Italy prior to illegally entering into Switzerland. He claimed a violation of article 3 of the CAT by Switzerland as it had ordered his expulsion to Zaire. The Swiss Federal Refugee Office had rejected his application to be recognized as a refugee.

Mutombo claimed that he had deserted the Zairian army because of discrimination he suffered on account of his ethnic background. He said that he was subsequently arrested and detained, first in the military camp and then under a 15-year sentence from a military tribunal. He claimed that he was repeatedly tortured, not given any medical treatment, and consequently had suffered partial loss of his eyesight and a head injury.

The Swiss authorities based their rejection of his claim on what they asserted were several contradictions in his testimony and on general unreliability of his allegations. Switzerland further argued that Mutombo had not met the requirement that 'substantial grounds' existed that he would be in concrete danger of being tortured if he was sent back to Zaire. Switzerland also argued that Mutombo's allegation, invoking article 3, paragraph 2 of the CAT that there existed in Zaire 'a consistent pattern of gross, flagrant or mass violations of human rights', would not suffice as a valid invocation unless he could show that he faced a real risk of being subjected to torture.

The Committee considered Mutombo's ethnic background, his alleged political affiliation, his desertion from the army, his detention history, and his escape from Zaire, and concluded that 'his return to Zaire would have the foreseeable and necessary consequence of exposing him to a real risk of being detained and tortured'.[108] It added that 'the belief that "substantial grounds" exist within the meaning of article 3, paragraph 1, is strengthened by "the existence in the State concerned of a consistent pattern of gross, flagrant or mass violations of human rights", within the meaning of article 3, paragraph 2'.[109]

The Committee decided that Switzerland was obligated to refrain from expelling Mutombo to Zaire or to any other country where he might run a real risk of being subjected to torture or of being expelled or returned to Zaire.[110] Mutombo's expulsion or return to Zaire thus would constitute a violation by Switzerland of article 3 of the CAT.[111]

Appraisal

The contemporary trend is generally for states to consider human rights issues when responding to requests for extradition. However, this trend has yet to find acceptance in the United States, where extradition is treated as *sui generis,* with the resulting exclusion of the judiciary from reviewing the extradition process's compatibility with certain fundamental human rights, such as the right to be free from torture and the principle of specialty. This indeed is out of sync with the powerful prevailing world-wide human rights movement. The US

---

[108]   *Ibid.* at para. 9.4.

[109]   *Ibid.* art. 3, para. 2 reads: 'For the purpose of determining whether there are such grounds, the competent authorities shall take into account all relevant considerations including, where applicable, the existence in the State concerned of a consistent pattern of gross, flagrant or mass violations of human rights.'

[110]   Mutombo, note 107 *supra*, para. 10.

[111]   *Ibid.* para. 9.7.

Congress needs to update the statute on extradition, which is antiquated and in dire need of modernizing. A reform of the process in the United States is long overdue.[112]

MUTUAL LEGAL ASSISTANCE AGREEMENTS

General

Mutual legal assistance treaties (MLATs) generally provide for the exchange of information and evidence in criminal and ancillary matters in support of criminal investigations and prosecutions. Requests under MLATs do not require a court order and do not go through diplomatic channels but through an established direct channel of communication between central authorities who are designated by treaty partners and are responsible for the execution of requests. MLATs also confer a binding legal obligation to provide assistance once the treaty requirements are met. Thus, compared with other formal means of international legal assistance, such as letters rogatory, MLATs are more effective instruments.

States have entered into bilateral MLATs, as well as regional and multilateral mutual assistance agreements, for decades. However, an appreciation of the need to effectively respond to cross-border criminal threats, including terrorism, drug trafficking and organized transnational crime, has given rise to the creation of new institutions in many countries and the negotiation of strengthened extradition agreements and MLATs, primarily in Europe and the Western Hemisphere. Under many of the newer treaties, treaty partners can also obtain banking and other financial records which become useful tools in fighting money laundering.

During the 1990s states negotiated several multilateral agreements to combat terrorism and transnational crimes. Interstate cooperation lies at the core of these agreements, which include the United Nations Convention Against Transnational Organized Crime (UNCTOC),[113] the UN Convention Against Terrorist Financing,[114] the Council of Europe Cybercrime Convention,[115] the OECD Anti-Bribery Convention,[116] and the OAS Convention Against Illicit Firearms Trafficking.[117] Three Protocols, one each on trafficking

---

[112]   For several recommendations regarding the new approach the United States should follow, see M. Cherif Bassiouni, *Reforming International Extradition: Lessons of the Past for a Radical New Approach*, 25 LOY. LA INT'L AND COMP. L REV. 389, 402–7 (2003). Professor Bassiouni calls for extradition's integration 'into a single comprehensive code of international cooperation in penal matters that includes all of these modalities, which are dealt with discretely in many treaties as well as addressed in several parts of US legislation. The following modalities are addressed in a compartmentalized fashion: extradition (treaties and legislation), mutual legal assistance (treaties and no legislation except for 'Letters Rogatory'), transfer of sentenced persons (treaties and national legislation), freezing and seizing of assets (treaties and no international legislation, only domestic).' *Ibid.* 405.

[113]   United Nations Convention against Transnational Organized Crime, General Assembly Res. 55/25, UN GAOR, 55th Sess., Annex I, at XXX, UN Doc. A/55/25 (2001), art. 1.

[114]   International Convention for the Suppression of the Financing of Terrorism, New York, 9 December 1999, 2178 UNTS 197.

[115]   Council of Europe, Convention on Cybercrime, Budapest, 23 November 2001, available at http://conventions.coe.int/Treaty/EN/Treaties/Html/185.htm.

[116]   OECD Convention on Combating Bribery of Foreign Public Officials in International Business Transactions, entered into force 15 February 1999, available at www.oecd.org.

[117]   Organization of American States, Inter-American Convention Against the Illicit

in women and children, migrant smuggling and illicit firearms,[118] supplemented the UNCTOC Convention. Multilateral efforts also resulted in agreements such as that against money laundering.[119] The 2003 UN Convention against Corruption[120] followed the US initiative in convening the Global Forum against Corruption in 1999.[121]

As an illustration of these multilateral efforts, the UNCTOC is a recognition by member states of the seriousness of the problems posed by organized crime, as well as the need to enhance international cooperation in order to address those problems. Thus, the Convention is aimed at combating organized crime more effectively and is the main international instrument for that purpose. It enacts expansive frameworks for extradition, mutual legal assistance and law enforcement cooperation.

The then-UN Secretary-General, Kofi Annan, called the UNCTOC a 'watershed event' in the international community's 'fight against organized crime'.[122] States parties are required under the Convention to criminalize the offenses of participation in an organized criminal group, money laundering, corruption and obstruction of justice in their domestic legislation.[123] If there is no extradition treaty between the parties, the Convention provides a legal basis for extradition, as states are to make crimes under the UNCTOC extraditable offenses.[124]

Under article 18 of the UNCTOC, states parties are obligated to 'afford one another the widest measure of mutual legal assistance in investigations, prosecutions and judicial proceedings in relation to the offences covered by this Convention', and also are reciprocally obligated to provide similar assistance when the requesting state party has reasonable grounds to suspect that such offense is transnational in nature.[125] Mutual legal assistance under the Convention extends to taking evidence; service of judicial documents; executing searches and

---

Manufacturing of and Trafficking in Firearms, Ammunition, Explosives, and Other Related Materials, Washington, DC, 14 November 1997, entered into force July 1, 1998.

[118]   Protocol to Prevent, Suppress and Punish Trafficking in Persons, Especially Women and Children, Supplementing the United Nations Convention Against Transnational Organized Crime, New York, 15 November 2000, entered into force 25 December 2003, UN Doc. A/55/383; Protocol Against the Smuggling of Migrants by Land, Sea and Air, Supplementing the United Nations Convention Against Transnational Organized Crime, New York, 15 November 2000, entered into force 28 January 2004, UN Doc. A/55/383; Protocol Against the Illicit Manufacturing of and Trafficking in Firearms, Their Parts and Components and Ammunition, Supplementing the United Nations Convention Against Transnational Organized Crime, New York, 31 May 2001, entered into force 3 July 2005, UN Doc. A/55/383/Add.2.

[119]   For a description see OECD Financial Action Task Force, *Policy Brief: Money Laundering* (July 1999), available at http://www1.worldbank.org/finance/assets/images/PB9906_en.pdf.

[120]   United Nations Convention Against Corruption, General Assembly Res. 58/4, 31 October 2003, 2349 UNTS 41. See also *An Effective International Legal Instrument Against Corruption*, General Assembly Res. 55/61, UN GAOR, 55th Sess., Annex, UN Doc. A/RES/55/61 (2001) (indicative list of international legal instruments, documents and recommendations against corruption).

[121]   Global Forum on Fighting Corruption, launched by the US government and held in Washington, DC, in 1999. The Second Global Forum was held at The Hague, Netherlands, in 2001. See *Global Forum Against Corruption, Ongoing Challenges, Shared Responsibilities* (31 May 2003), available at www.abanet.org/intlaw.

[122]   UN Office on Drugs and Crime, *United Nations Convention Against Transnational Organized Crime and the Protocols Thereto* iv (2004).

[123]   *Ibid.* arts 5, 6, 8 and 23.

[124]   *Ibid.* arts 4 and 16.

[125]   *Ibid.* art. 18(1).

seizures and freezing assets; examining objects and sites; and providing information and copies of documents, including 'government, bank, financial, corporate or business records'.[126] The Convention also provides for joint investigation by the parties.[127]

The Protocol on trafficking in women and children, which supplements the UNCTOC, was the first binding international instrument with an agreed definition on trafficking in persons. The definition is designed to facilitate efficient international cooperation in investigating and prosecuting cases against those trafficking in persons.

The second Protocol, on migrant smuggling, was designed not only to prevent and combat the smuggling of migrants but also to promote cooperation among states parties and also to protect the smuggled migrants' rights.

The third Protocol, on illicit firearms, was the first legally binding international agreement on small arms aimed at promoting, facilitating and strengthening cooperation among states parties with the objective of preventing, combating and eradicating the illicit manufacture of and traffic in firearms.

Western Hemisphere

In the regional setting, in 1992 the Organization of American States adopted the Inter-American Convention on Mutual Assistance in Criminal Matters,[128] followed by an Optional Protocol.[129] In 1997, the OAS initiated the first Meeting of Ministers of Justice and Ministers and Attorneys General of the Americas (REMJA).[130] The meeting was aimed at considering 'issues contributing to enhanced legal and judicial cooperation in the Americas'.[131] Since then, most senior justice officials of the OAS member states have met several times, the most recent being REMJA VII in April 2008. In all these years they have worked to strengthen law enforcement cooperation and enhance information exchange, and have initiated the creation of a Hemispheric Plan of Action to combat transnational organized crime.[132]

In September 2007, at the third meeting of Central Authorities and Other Experts in Mutual Assistance in Criminal Matters and Extradition, held in Bogotá, Colombia, a Model Law on Mutual Assistance in Criminal Matters was made available to the member states.[133] The Model Law provides a set of non-binding guidelines for member states' legislation. The scope of mutual assistance under the Model Law is similar to that of the UNCTOC, as it

---

[126]   *Ibid.* art. 18(3).

[127]   *Ibid.* art. 19.

[128]   Inter-American Convention on Mutual Assistance in Criminal Matters, 23 May 1992, entered into force April 14, 1996, OASTS No. 75, available at www.oas.org/juridico/English/treaties/a-55.html. The United States signed the Convention on 10 January 1995, and ratified it on 25 May 2001.

[129]   Optional Protocol Related to the Inter-American Convention on Mutual Assistance in Criminal Matters, adopted 11 June 1993, OASTS No. 77, available at www.oas.org/juridico/english/Sigs/a-59.html. The United States signed the Protocol on 10 January 1995, and ratified it on 5 January 2001.

[130]   Reunion Extraordinaria de los Ministeros de Justicia de las Americas, Organization of American States (OAS), Resolution of Meeting of Ministers of Justice, AG/RES. 1482 (XXXVII-O/97) (5 June 1997), available atwww.oas.org/juridico/english/ga-res97/eres1482.

[131]   *Ibid.* P 2.

[132]   See generally David P. Warner, *Law Enforcement Cooperation in the Organization of American States: A Focus on REMJA,* 37 U MIAMI INTER-AM L REV. 387 (Spring/Summer, 2006).

[133]   Model Law of Mutual Assistance in Criminal Matters, OEA/Ser.K/XXXIV, PENAL/doc.20/07 rev. 1 (14 September 2007).

provides for requests to deliver documents and court records; to provide information and evidence and perform forensic tests; to seize, attach and confiscate property; and to 'identify, seize, attach and confiscate criminal proceeds'.[134]

Requests for assistance in criminal matters may be denied under the Model Law if the act is classified as a political crime; and war crimes, military crimes, crimes against humanity, genocide and other crimes against international law, and acts of terrorism are not to be considered political crimes. Also, the request is to be denied when 'the circumstances included in the request suggest that one or more persons are being persecuted on account of their race, religion, nationality, gender, or political views'. If the person under investigation has been convicted for the same act in the requested state, the request is to be denied.[135] The principle of reciprocity provides the foundation for assistance under the Model Law. Each state is to designate a single central authority responsible for processing requests for assistance and to act as a clearing-house for information.[136]

The meeting recommended that the Model Law be posted on the Hemispheric Information Exchange Network for Mutual Assistance in Criminal Matters and Extradition.[137] It also recommended that the member states support the proposals regarding guidelines to 'best practices with respect to the collection of statements, documents, and physical evidence', and 'best practices with respect to mutual legal assistance in connection with the investigation, freezing, seizure, and confiscation of assets that are either the proceeds of or instrument for crimes'.[138] The Model Law is not a treaty binding on states. Instead, as its name suggests, it provides a model for the legislation of states in the field of mutual legal assistance. It also informs the discussions of REMJA at various regional meetings.

The meetings have been fruitful and effective in enhancing law enforcement and judicial cooperation in criminal matters. Justice reform in member states has been supported through the establishment of the Justice Studies Center of the Americas.[139] Meetings, networks, training, technical cooperation and sharing of information among the pertinent national officials has led to increased mutual assistance in criminal matters, including extradition, and issues such as illicit drug trafficking and corruption, and other international crimes. Also, there have been increased cooperative efforts against cybercrime and trafficking in persons, and for penitentiary and prison policies and forensic investigation:[140]

> Participating States have been urged to ratify or accede to international agreements and to support the strengthening of the Hemispheric Information Exchange Network for Mutual Assistance in Criminal Matters and Extradition, including:
> (a)   the Inter-American Convention Against Corruption, and the Declaration on the Mechanism for Follow-up for its Implementation (MESICIC) ('Document of Buenos Aires');

---

134   *Ibid.* ch. I.
135   *Ibid.* ch. III.
136   *Ibid.* ch. II.
137   Meeting of Ministers of Justice and of Ministers aand Attorneys General of the Americas, Recommendations of the Third Meeting of Central Authorities and Other Experts on Mutual Assistance in Criminal Matters and Extradition, OEA/Ser.K/XXXIV, PENAL/doc.26/07 rev. 1 (14 September 2007), at II.2(b).
138   *Ibid.* II.3.
139   *Ibid.* IX.
140   *Ibid.* III, V, VI and VII.

(b) the Inter-American Convention on Mutual Assistance in Criminal Matters, and its Optional Protocol;
(c) the Inter-American Convention on Serving Criminal Sentences Abroad;
(d) the Inter-American Convention Against the Illicit Manufacturing of and Trafficking in Firearms, Ammunition, Explosives, and Other Related Materials (CIFTA);
(e) the United Nations Convention against Transnational Organized Crime, and its protocols; and
(f) the United Nations Convention Against Corruption.[141]

As noted above, the initiative on a Hemispheric Plan of Action Against Transnational Organized Crime is another special accomplishment of the REMJA process.[142]

Europe

In 1959, members of the Council of Europe agreed to the European Convention on Mutual Assistance in Criminal Matters.[143] This followed the 1957 European Convention on Extradition.[144] In 1975, an Additional Protocol supplemented the Convention by 'strengthening the protection of humanity and of individuals',[145] and a Second Additional Protocol in 1978 added fiscal offenses as an appropriate area for mutual assistance.[146] Under the EU's Convention on Cybercrime, which opened for signature in November 2001, the Council of Europe's Project on Cybercrime addresses issues such as networks, illegal access to information, attacks on computer systems, distribution of illegal content, cyberlaundering and cyberterrorism.[147] This was followed in 2003 by the Additional Protocol on the Criminalization of Acts of a Racist and Xenophobic Nature Committed through Computer Systems.[148] In 2003, the European Union entered into an Agreement on Mutual Legal Assistance with the United States.[149]

The European Union created two new organizations primarily aimed at enhancing cooperation between and among member states: the European Police Office (Europol), officially opened in 1998 as the law enforcement organization designed to improve the effectiveness and cooperation of the competent authorities in the member states in the prevention and

---

[141]   *Ibid.* I(1).
[142]   AG/RES. 2334 (XXXVIII O/08) (3 June 2008). See Permanent Council of the Organization of American States Committee on Hemispheric Security, available at www.oas.org/CSH/english/TOC.asp.
[143]   Council of Europe, European Convention on Mutual Assistance in Criminal Matters, 20 April 1959, ETS 30.
[144]   1957 European Convention on Extradition, note 5 *supra.*
[145]   Council of Europe, Additional Protocol to the European Convention on Extradition, ETS No. 86, Strasbourg, 15 October 1975, available at www.unicri.it/wwd/justice/docs/JudicialCoop/1975_Add_Protocol_coe_Extradition.pdf.
[146]   Council of Europe, Additional Protocol to the European Convention on Mutual Assistance in Criminal Matters, 17 March 1978, ETS 99, available at http://conventions.coe.int/en/Treaties/html/099.htm.
[147]   Council of Europe, Convention on Cybercrime, November 2001, ETS 185.
[148]   Council of Europe, Additional Protocol to the Convention on Cybercrime, January 2003, ETS 189.
[149]   Council of the European Union, Agreement on Mutual Legal Assistance Between the European Union and the United States, EU/USA/MLA/en1-en23; EU/USA/MLA/NOTE/en1-en4, 3 June 2003 (authorizing US access to European bank account information, speeding MLA request processing and permitting joint investigations).

combating of international crimes; and Eurojust, established in 2002 as the world's first permanent network of judicial authorities.

Since its inception, Europol has been actively involved in forming and strengthening the European strategy to prevent organized crime and working with the EU member states to curb terrorism, unlawful drug trafficking and other international organized crimes, ranging from human trafficking and child pornography to counterfeiting euros and smuggling of people.[150] Europol has also entered into a cooperation agreement with the United States to enhance cooperation between them in:

> preventing, detecting, suppressing, and investigating serious forms of international crime in specific areas – unlawful drug trafficking; trafficking in nuclear and radioactive substances; illegal immigrant smuggling; trade in human beings; motor vehicle crime; terrorist activities and crimes committed in the course of such activities; forgery of money and means of payment; and illegal money laundering activities and related criminal offenses.[151]

The European Union established Eurojust to enhance the effectiveness of its member states with the investigation and prosecution of serious cross-border and organized crime. It brings together investigators and prosecutors and as a permanent body in the European legal setting it enhances Europe-wide cooperation on criminal justice cases by facilitating the execution of international mutual legal assistance and the implementation of extradition requests. Twenty-seven national members, representing each member state, are senior experienced prosecutors and judges. An administrative team supports Eurojust's work. Eurojust has entered into agreements with many countries, including the United States and the European Union's anti-fraud organization, OLAF,[152] and works also with Europol.

United States

The United States entered into its first mutual legal assistance treaty in 1977 with Switzerland,[153] followed by several more similar bilateral treaties for mutual judicial assistance. After the 11 September 2001 terrorist attacks, the realization had grown in the United States that there were shortcomings in its intelligence operations and its law enforcement cooperation mechanisms, and that information sharing among different agencies was not effective.[154] The 9/11 Commission (the National Commission on Terrorist Attacks Upon the

---

[150]   For the scope of Europol's activities, see Press Releases from 1 October 1998 to March 2009, Europol, Press Releases, European Law Enforcement Cooperation, available at www.europol.europa.eu.

[151]   Agreement between the United States and the European Police Office to Enhance Cooperation in Preventing, Detecting, Suppressing, and Investigating Serious Forms of International Crime, with Annex, signed at Brussels, 6 December 2001, entered into force 7 December 2001, TIAS; Supplemental Agreement Between the Europol Police Office and the United States on the Exchange of Personal Data and Related Information, signed at Copenhagen, 20 December 2002, entered into force 21 December 2002, TIAS.

[152]   These agreements are available at Eurojust's website, www.eurojust.europa.eu. For Eurojust's range and scope of activities, see *ibid.* for Press Releases.

[153]   Treaty with the Swiss Confederation on Mutual Assistance in Criminal Matters, 27 UST 2019, TIAS 8302, entered into force 23 January 1977; S Exec. Rep. F, 94th Cong., 2d Sess. 35 (1976).

[154]   See generally US GPO, *The 9/11 Commission Report – Final Report of the National Commission on Terrorist Attacks upon the United States* (2004).

United States) recommended in its 2004 report that the United States should 'engage other nations in developing a comprehensive coalition strategy' against terrorism, and that such issues should be addressed through several multilateral institutions.[155] It also called for developing 'joint strategies for targeting terrorist travel, or for hammering out a common strategy for the places where terrorists may be finding sanctuary'.[156]

The United States revamped its national institutional structure by integrating several law enforcement agencies, such as Customs and the Immigration and the Naturalization Service, into a Department of Homeland Security, which also had responsibility over cyberterrorism and seaport, airport and airline security.

The United States currently has several mutual legal assistance treaties, including those with all the G-8 partners, the latest of these having been agreed in 2003 with Germany[157] and Japan.[158] Among others, the United States entered into an MLAT with India in 2005[159] and with Malaysia in January 2009.[160] The agreements with the countries in the European Union and the Western Hemisphere have already been noted above.

CONCLUSION

The menace of cross-border crimes has certainly spurred increased activity between and among states to enter into extradition treaties as well as mutual legal assistance treaties. As terrorists, drug traffickers and human traffickers do not heed the constraints of territorial boundaries, states have responded by entering into bilateral, regional and multilateral agreements to combat terrorism, organized crime and other international criminal activities. At the same time, human rights issues are often raised by these arrangements. What is needed is to strike an appropriate balance so that international criminal activities are effectively combated while fundamental human rights are fully protected.

Bilateral, regional and international agreements and institutions have led the way in devising new norms, modernizing extradition treaties and streamlining and strengthening mutual

---

155   *Ibid.* at 379.

156   *Ibid.*

157   Mutual Legal Assistance Treaty between the United States and the Federal Republic of Germany on Mutual Legal Assistance in Criminal Matters, signed at Washington, 14 October 2003, Treaty No. 108-27 (transmitted to the Senate, 16 November 2004). This is the first US MLAT to include special investigative techniques among permissible types of assistance, such as telecommunications surveillance, undercover investigations and controlled deliveries, in accordance with the parties' domestic law in execution of requests for assistance. *Ibid.* art. 12.

158   Mutual Legal Assistance Treaty with Japan, signed at Washington, 5 August 2003, S Treaty Doc. No. 108-12 (2003). In addition to assistance with the typical investigations, prosecutions and other proceedings in criminal matters, the Treaty also permits assistance in connection with an administrative investigation of suspected criminal conduct, such as the SEC's investigation of suspected securities fraud. *Ibid.* art. 1(3).

159   Treaty on Mutual Legal Assistance in Criminal Matters, signed at New Delhi, 17 October 2001, entered into force 3 October 2005, TIAS See US Embassy News Press Release, *US–India Treaty on Mutual Legal Assistance in Criminal Matters Ratified*, 3 October 2005, available at www.new delhiusembassy.gov/pr100305a.html.

160   See Foo Yee Ping, *Malaysia–US Treaty Takes Effect*, THE STAR ONLINE, 23 January 2009, available at www.thestar.com.my/news/story.

assistance mechanisms in criminal matters. Simultaneously, the burgeoning jurisprudence of human rights draws special attention to the importance of observing fundamental human rights even in times of upheaval and challenges to national security. Ultimately, it falls to national authorities to find and implement effective yet just solutions. Maintaining this delicate balance presents a challenge requiring not only principled and enlightened action by the judiciary, but also by the political branches of government.

15 Universal jurisdiction

Naomi Roht-Arriaza and Menaka Fernando

Universal jurisdiction is a jurisdictional principle of international criminal law that allows a state to prosecute certain crimes based on the nature of the crime, regardless of where the crimes occurred or whether the prosecuting state has any territorial or nationality-based connection to them. Crimes for which universal jurisdiction may apply include war crimes, crimes against humanity, genocide, torture and enforced disappearances.[1]

The doctrine of universality was traditionally associated with the crime of piracy, but gained wider application in the post-Second World War era with the prosecution of Nazi-era crimes. For example, Israel utilized the concept of universal jurisdiction in prosecuting Adolf Eichmann in Jerusalem in 1961 when the Israeli Attorney-General charged Eichmann with war crimes and crimes against humanity. He was abducted from Argentina and brought to stand trial in Israel, a state that did not exist at the time the crimes were committed. He was convicted and executed.[2]

Universal jurisdiction was not used extensively again until the 1990s, when – for the first time – the doctrine was utilized for crimes outside the post-Second World War context. In 1993, Belgium passed its expansive Act Concerning Grave Breaches of International Humanitarian Law in order to implement its obligations under the 1949 Geneva Conventions. The first prosecutions and convictions under the new law were four Rwandan defendants present in Belgium, who were prosecuted for war crimes against Tutsi and internally displaced persons during Rwanda's genocide in 1994.[3] A number of cases in Germany concerning genocide in Bosnia-Herzegovina soon followed.[4] In 1998, Spain's invocation of universal jurisdiction to file charges against the military leadership in Argentina and Chile for the death and disappearances of Spanish and Chilean citizens in the mid-1970s launched the principle onto the center stage of the international criminal legal and policy debate.

---

[1]   Amnesty International advocates the expansion of this list of crimes for which universal jurisdiction should be exercised to include extra-judicial executions, as these six crimes 'represent the gravest crimes under international law. In the last century, there were millions of victims of these crimes, but only a handful of those responsible for the crimes were brought to justice.' Amnesty International, *Universal Jurisdiction: Questions and Answers* (December 2001), available at www.amnesty.org/en/library/asset/IOR53/020/2001/en/dom-IOR530202001en.pdf.

[2]   Attorney-General of the Government of Israel v. Eichmann, Supreme Court of Israel, 36 ILR 277, 299 (1962).

[3]   *Prosecutor* v. *Higaniro et al.* (Cour d'Assises de l'Arrondissement Administratif de Bruxelles-Capital, President Maes, Judges Louveaux and Massart, 8 June 2001). This was known as the 'Butare Four' case, see L. Reydams, *Belgium's First Judicial Application of Universal Jurisdiction: The Butare Four Case*, 1 J INT'L CRIM. JUST. 428 (2003).

[4]   For example, *Public Prosecutor* v. *Jorgic*, Bundesgerichtshof, 11 December 1998; *Public Prosecutor* v. *Djajic*, Bayerisches Oberstes Landgericht, 23 May 1997; *Public Prosecutor* v. *Sokolovic*, Bundersgerichshof, 21 February 2001, all digested in L. REYDAMS, UNIVERSAL JURISDICTION: INTERNATIONAL AND MUNICIPAL LEGAL PERSPECTIVES (Oxford University Press, 2003).

UNIVERSAL JURISDICTION AND THE STATE OBLIGATION TO PROSECUTE OR EXTRADITE

The crimes for which a state may exercise universal jurisdiction may be found in multilateral treaties, customary international law and domestic statutes. Some treaties require the exercise of a form of universal jurisdiction. For example, the Geneva Conventions of 1949 define certain 'grave breaches' subject to a mandatory enforcement regime. States that have ratified the treaties are required either to prosecute perpetrators of 'grave breaches' of the Geneva Conventions or to extradite them to a state that will do so. The UN Convention Against Torture and Other Cruel, Inhuman and Degrading Treatment or Punishment (CAT) provides for the same with regard to the crime of torture, as does the Inter-American Torture Convention and the UN and Inter-American Conventions on Forced Disappearances with respect to those suspected of those crimes. This type of 'extradite or prosecute' provision also forms part of a number of treaties aimed at suppressing terrorist acts.[5] The International Criminal Tribunal for the Former Yugoslavia (ICTY) affirmed that torture is a crime that warrants universal jurisdiction. The Tribunal said:

> This legal basis for States' universal jurisdiction over torture bears out and strengthens the legal foundation for such jurisdiction found by other courts in the inherently universal character of the crime. It has been held that international crimes being universally condemned wherever they occur, every State has the right to prosecute and punish the authors of such crimes. [6]

In the absence of a treaty, states may exercise universal jurisdiction for certain crimes under customary international law. Genocide and crimes against humanity fall into this category. For example, the courts of Spain and Germany have held that even though the Convention on the Prevention and Punishment of the Crime of Genocide (1948) ('Genocide Convention') does not by its terms provide for universal jurisdiction, it does not foreclose other bases of jurisdiction (such as universal jurisdiction) because the Convention sets out only minimum requirements. The majority view is that universal jurisdiction exercised under customary international law is permissive, not mandatory; states may exercise it, but are not required to do so.

Often, states' domestic legislation and practices inform the exercise of universal jurisdiction as well. As far as is known, Austria was the first state to incorporate the principle of universality and its related doctrine of 'prosecute or extradite' into its penal code in 1803. Argentina did so in 1885. According to current Amnesty International estimates, more than 125 states have enacted some type of universal jurisdiction legislation.[7] Courts routinely cite

---

[5]   For example, Convention for the Suppression of Unlawful Seizure of Aircraft, 16 December 1970, art. 7, 22 UST 1641, TIAS No. 7192, 860 UNTS 105, 109; Convention for the Suppression of Unlawful Acts Against the Safety of Civil Aviation, 23 September 1971, art. 7, 24 UST 565, TIAS No. 7570; International Convention Against the Taking of Hostages, 17 December 1979, art. 8, UN General Asssemly Res. 34/146, UN Doc. A/C6/34/46 (1979).

[6]   *Prosecutor* v. *Furundzija*, Case No. IT-95-17/1, ICTY Trial Chamber Judgment, 10 December 1998, 156 (1998).

[7]   Amnesty International, *Universal Jurisdiction: Questions and Answers*, note 1 *supra*, at 8, AI Index: IOR 53/020/2001 (December 2001), available at www.amnesty.org/en/library/asset/IOR53/020/2001/en/009a145b-d8b9-11dd-ad8c-f3d4445c118e/ior530202001en.pdf.

to the decisions of other national courts in ruling on the applicability of universal jurisdiction norms.

Finally, the universality principle is supported by an abundance of 'soft law' in the form of United Nations General Assembly Resolutions and Special Rapporteur reports. For example, the 1973 United Nations Resolution on Principles of International Cooperation in the Detection, Arrest, Extradition, and Punishment of Persons Guilty of War Crimes and Crimes Against Humanity declares that '[w]ar crimes and crimes against humanity, wherever they are committed, shall be subject to investigation and the persons against whom there is evidence that they have committed such crimes shall be subject to tracing arrest, trial and, if found guilty, to punishment' and that '[s]tates shall assist each other in detecting, arresting and bringing to trial persons suspected of having committed such crimes and, if they are found guilty, in punishing them'.[8]

THE PINOCHET CASE[9]

In 1973, a military junta led by General Pinochet successfully conducted a coup d'etat and overthrew Chile's democratically-elected government under President Salvador Allende. The new military dictatorship suspended the Constitution, silenced political critics and engaged in a terror campaign that resulted in the abduction, torture, disappearance and execution of thousands of individuals. The Chilean government passed an amnesty law that immunized the government for atrocities committed between 1973 and 1978. Pinochet lost a plebiscite on his rule in 1988, and civilian government resumed in 1991. Despite losing the election, Pinochet remained head of the army and, later, 'Senator for Life', which, along with the amnesty law, afforded him the cloak of limited immunity against prosecution within Chilean borders.

This cloak offered less protection, however, in the international arena. In 1996, Spanish investigating magistrates began an investigation in the Spanish federal court (Audiencia Nacional) of Argentine and Chilean military officials. Jurisdiction was granted by article 23.4 of Spain's Organic Law of Judicial Power, which provided for universal jurisdiction over genocide, terrorism and other offenses in treaties to which Spain is a party.[10] The investigations were consolidated and assigned to Judge Baltazar Garzón, who in 1998 issued an arrest

---

[8] Principles of International Co-operation in the Detection, Arrest, Extradition and Punishment of Persons Guilty of War Crimes and Crimes Against Humanity, General Assembly Res. 3074, 28 UN GAOR Supp. (No. 30) at 78, UN Doc. A/9030 (1973). See also Basic Principles and Guidelines on the Right to a Remedy and Reparation for Victims of Gross Violations of International Human Rights Law and Serious Violations of International Humanitarian Law, General Assembly Res. 60/147, 16 December 2005, UN Doc. A/Res/60/147 (2005); International Law Commission, *Third Report on the Obligation to Extradite or Prosecute ('aut dedere aut judicare')*, UN Doc. A/CN.4/603 (10 June 2008); Updated Set of Principles for the Protection and Promotion of Human Rights Through Action to Combat Impunity, UN Doc. E/CN.4/2005/102/Add.1.

[9] For a more detailed discussion of these cases, and other matters covered in this chapter, see NAOMI ROHT-ARRIAZA, THE PINOCHET EFFECT: TRANSNATIONAL JUSTICE IN THE AGE OF HUMAN RIGHTS (Philadelphia, Penn Press, 2005), especially ch. 5, *The European Cases*, at 118–49.

[10] See Maria del Carmen Marquez Carrasco and Joaquin Alcaide Fernandez, *International Decision: In Re Pinochet: Spanish National Court, Criminal Division (Plenary Session). Case 19/97, November 4, 1998; Case 1/98, November 5, 1998*, 93 AJIL 690 (1999).

warrant and extradition request for Pinochet.[11] At the time, Pinochet was in the United Kingdom for business and medical treatment. The United Kingdom's lower Divisional Court quashed the warrants on grounds of the immunity afforded him by virtue of being a former Head of State. An initial House of Lords ruling, three to two, that no immunity applied, was set aside on conflict-of-interest grounds. In a landmark six to one decision, a second panel held that as a former Head of State, Pinochet was not entitled to immunity from prosecution for charges of torture, conspiracy to torture and conspiracy to murder.[12] The court held that immunity for former Heads of State, like former diplomats, only extended to their official acts. Torture, as a crime under international law, could not be an official act. Once the countries involved ratified the UN Convention Against Torture, they were bound to prosecute or extradite suspected torturers, and adherence to the Convention was logically incompatible with immunity. However, the one judge, in dissent, argued that if the Convention had meant to lift the customary law of immunity, the drafters would have done so explicitly.

Although the British courts approved his extradition, Pinochet was eventually returned to Chile on grounds of ill-health. In 2001, and again in 2004, the Chilean Supreme Court of Justice stripped Pinochet of his immunity and deemed him mentally competent to stand trial. Evidence came to light of his role in numerous crimes, and of his amassing huge wealth on a modest civil servant's salary. While awaiting trial in December 2006, General Pinochet suffered a heart attack and died at the age of 91.[13] Although the former Chilean Head of State was never brought to trial, most of his remaining lieutenants have been tried and convicted, and his reputation for brutality and thievery outlives him. Moreover, the *Pinochet* proceedings left a lasting legacy in the evolution of universal jurisdiction principles.

The *Pinochet* Legacy

In the aftermath of the *Pinochet* case, courts in Spain and Belgium – which exercise the most well-known universal jurisdiction laws – saw a flurry of extra-territorial cases that ultimately had the effect, at least temporarily, of scaling back the doctrine's application. For example, in 1999, Rigoberta Menchú, the Guatemalan indigenous rights advocate and winner of the Nobel Peace Prize, led the effort to file genocide, terrorism and torture charges in Spanish courts against Guatemalan officials for the atrocities committed during Guatemala's internal armed conflict from 1960 to 1996 that left over 200,000 people dead or missing. In 2000, a Spanish appellate court held that Spain had no jurisdiction to hear the complaint because a Spanish inquiry had to be subsidiary to the state in which the alleged incidents occurred. The Supreme Court partially affirmed the dismissal in 2003, holding that for universal jurisdiction to conform to international law, there needed to be a tie between the case and Spain, and thus the only charges that could proceed were those involving Spanish citizens.[14] It took two

---

[11]   The arrest warrant was affirmed in November 1998 by the full Audiencia Nacional. That decision is available in English in REED BRODY and MICHAEL RATNER (eds), THE PINOCHET PAPERS (Kluwer, 2000).

[12]   *R. v. Bow Street Metropolitan Stipendiary Magistrate and Others, ex parte Pinochet Ugarte*, House of Lords, [1999] 1 AC 147, reprinted in 38 ILM 68 (1999).

[13]   See Larry Rohter, *A Bitter Legacy of Division Survives Pinochet*, NEW YORK TIMES, 12 December 2006, sec. A, col. 4, Foreign Desk News Analysis, 8.

[14]   For cites and analysis see Naomi Roht-Arriaza, *Guatemala Genocide Case*, 100 AM. J INT'L L 207 (2006).

more years for the Spanish courts to adopt a version of universal jurisdiction which was less restrictive, in the sense that it would truly allow prosecution of serious international crimes even in the absence of a territorial or nationality-based connection to them.

A few years later, the International Court of Justice (ICJ) avoided the question of whether universal jurisdiction was valid, but ruled on the scope of immunities of high-ranking government officials in a way that, in effect, limited the exercise of universal jurisdiction. This occurred in the case concerning the *Yerodia* arrest warrant[15] described below.

In April 2000, under its universal jurisdiction statute, Belgium issued an arrest warrant and extradition request for Abdulaye Yerodia Ndombasi, the Foreign Minister of the Democratic Republic of Congo (DRC) at that time. The warrant charged that Yerodia Ndombasi incited racial hostilities by publicly calling for the massacre of Tutsis, resulting in hundreds of deaths – acts which Belgium alleged constituted war crimes and crimes against humanity under Belgian and international law. In response, the DRC filed a complaint with the ICJ, accusing Belgium of violating the foreign minister's immunity. The Court found in favor of the DRC. The Court ignored the nature of the crimes the former Foreign Minister had been charged with, finding that sitting Foreign Ministers and Heads of State have personal immunity. This immunity did not necessarily create impunity, according to the Court, because immunities under international law would not bar prosecution when the national state institutes proceedings against its own officials; when it waives their immunity before another state; when the case is before an international criminal court; or 'in respect to acts committed prior or subsequent to his or her period of office, as well as in respect of acts committed during that period of office in a private capacity'. The Court's language about private acts was problematic because it was unclear when acts by public officials could be considered 'private'. How would it apply in the case of a Pinochet or other high-ranking official? Could torture or summary execution ever be 'private' when their definition involves an official acting in an official capacity? If read to preclude prosecution in those cases, the Court's decision would set the law back decades. Militating against this result is a concurring opinion which held that international crimes could never constitute official acts.[16]

Although controversial, the *Yerodia* decision soon became obscured by more high profile universal jurisdiction cases in the Belgian courts. For example, on 18 June 2001, 23 Lebanese-Palestinian petitioners filed a complaint against former Israeli Prime Minister Ariel Sharon alleging war crimes, crimes against humanity and genocide during Israel's invasion of Lebanon in 1982. Next, in March 2003, cases were filed against former US President George H.W. Bush, Vice President Dick Cheney, former Secretary of State Colin Powell and Norman Schwarzkopf, commander of the Coalition Forces during the Gulf War of 1991, for the bombing of a Baghdad air raid shelter during the Gulf War of 1991. Soon after, the Belgian courts saw cases against General Tommy Franks and other US officials for acts committed during the US invasion of Iraq in 2003. The cases caused an outcry, and the Belgian Parliament ultimately succumbed to intense pressure from the United States and repealed its universal jurisdiction statute in July 2003. Belgium's new law only allows jurisdiction if one of the parties is Belgian or resides in Belgium or if Belgium is obligated to

---

15   *Democratic Republic of Congo* v. *Belgium*, ICJ, Arrest Warrant of 11 April 2000, ICJ Rep. 3 (2002). The decisions, pleadings, and basic documents of the International Court of Justice are available at www.icj-cij.org.

16   *Ibid.* separate opinion of Judges Higgins, Buergenthal and Koojimans.

exercise jurisdiction by treaty.[17] It also removes the ability of complainants to go directly to the courts in cases not involving a link to Belgium, putting the decision to proceed entirely into the hands of a prosecutor.

Despite the major setback that the Belgian repeal represents, a few cases were grandfathered in. One concerned Hissene Habré, the former dictator of Chad from 1982 to 1990, who currently resides in Senegal. In 2000, Chadian victims in Senegal attempted to open an investigation into Habré's crimes, but the higher courts of that country rejected the charges of torture on grounds that Senegal, although a party to the CAT, never incorporated the jurisdictional provisions of the Convention into local law. The complainants then turned to Belgium. Two Belgian arrest warrants were issued against Habré for crimes against humanity and torture, and a Belgian investigating magistrate visited Chad to take testimony. In 2005, Senegal denied a Belgian extradition request but, in 2006, agreed to an African Union request to prosecute the former dictator on behalf of Africa.

Senegal then instituted legal reforms to remove obstacles to the trial. In September 2008, 14 victims filed complaints with the Senegalese prosecutor alleging crimes against humanity and torture by Habré. The victims and a coalition of African and international human rights organizations expect the case to reach trial, although to date it has stalled over funding issues. Indeed, the constant delays led Belgium, in February 2009, to file a complaint in the ICJ against Senegal for non-compliance with its treaty obligation to extradite or prosecute. In May 2009, the ICJ denied the Belgian request for provisional measures.[18] This case has immense significance because it is the first high profile universal jurisdiction case inching toward trial in a Southern developing country's judicial system.

By mid-decade, the initial backlash against the use of universal jurisdiction had faded somewhat. Cases in the Netherlands, the United Kingdom and Denmark involving defendants who were living in those countries resulted in trials and some convictions on torture and related charges. In September 2005, the Spanish Constitutional Court held that jurisdiction based solely on the nature of the crime was proper in the case against Guatemalan officials. The court held that no tie of nationality or national interest was necessary as a jurisdictional prerequisite given the plain language of Spanish law and the imperative of combating impunity and international crimes. As a result, the *Guatemala Genocide* case was reopened and, since 2006, the Spanish judge, Santiago Pedraz, has been hearing witnesses and experts and requesting the extradition of named defendants to stand trial. (Extradition to Spain would be a necessary first step because Spain does not allow trial *in absentia*.) Other Spanish magistrates have opened investigations into allegations of international crimes in El Salvador, Tibet, Rwanda, Palestine and Western Sahara. However, in 2009, the Spanish Parliament agreed to cut back the law to exclude cases that have no tie to Spain or where Spanish interests are not involved,[19] a partial replay of the Belgian experience. The final shape of the

---

[17]   *Belgium Scales Back Its War Crimes Law Under US Pressure*, NEW YORK TIMES, 2 August 2003, sec. A, col. 1, Foreign Desk, 6.

[18]   Marlise Simons, *Belgium Sues to Compel Prosecution of a Chadian*, NEW YORK TIMES, 22 February 2009, sec. A, col. 0, Foreign Desk, 8.

[19]   See Victoria Burnett, *Vote on Changes to Inquiry Law*, NEW YORK TIMES, 26 June 2009, sec. A, col, 0, Foreign Desk, World Briefing Europe, 7; see also Victoria Burnett and Marlise Simons, *Push in Spain to Limit Reach of the Courts*, NEW YORK TIMES, 21 May 2009, sec. A, col. 0, Foreign Desk, 10.

legislative reform, and the effect it will have on the existing cases, is unclear as of the date of writing.

To date, efforts to prosecute high-ranking officials of the US government for torture and related crimes have not been successful. A coalition of US and German human rights lawyers petitioned a German investigating judge to look into the crimes at Abu Graib prison in Iraq and named Donald Rumsfeld and other high-ranking US current and former officials as defendants. Even though the German law on universal jurisdiction seems very broad, the prosecutor, under heavy US pressure, decided not to proceed on grounds that the case could be adequately investigated in the United States. A later attempt to investigate Rumsfeld in France was rejected on grounds of immunity.[20]

UNIVERSAL JURISDICTION IN THE UNITED STATES

In the United States, legislation is necessary to allow the criminal prosecution of crimes recognized under customary international law. Congress has enacted numerous statutes that allow a type of universal jurisdiction for various crimes such as the destruction of aircraft and aircraft facilities, violence at international airports, hostage-taking and torture. For example, the implementing legislation of the CAT provides federal jurisdiction over torture committed abroad.[21] Based on a violation of this statute, a federal grand jury in Miami indicted Charles Taylor, Jr for commanding and committing torture in Liberia as head of an anti-terrorist unit called the 'Demon Forces' from 1997 to 1998. He was convicted in October 2008 and sentenced to 97 years in prison. This marks the first conviction for a violation of the federal anti-torture statute in the United States. In December 2007, Congress finally passed a Bill allowing the prosecution of genocide by non-US citizens outside the United States when the offender is found within the United States.[22] Recruitment of child soldiers and trafficking are also now the subject of US legislation that allows prosecution if the offender is found within the United States, no matter where the crime took place or the nationality of those involved.[23]

Although limited in its application, the doctrine of universality has gained some traction in US courts. For example, a New York district court endorsed the principle in 2000 with the case brought against Osama Bin Laden and 14 other defendants charged with conspiracy to murder and use weapons of mass destruction against US nationals and to destroy US property. The court held that it had jurisdiction to hear most of the counts based on domestic and international law, partly because 'universal jurisdiction is increasingly accepted for certain acts of terrorism, such as … indiscriminate violent assaults on people at large'.[24] Nevertheless, the application of universal jurisdiction in US courts has been limited, as is apparent from the Second Circuit Court of Appeals holding in *United States* v. *Yousef*.[25] In

---

[20]   See Craig Whitlock, *European Nations May Investigate Bush Officials Over Prisoner Treatment*, WASHINGTON POST, 22 April 2009, sec. A, A04.

[21]   18 USC s. 2340.

[22]   18 USC s. 1091.

[23]   Child Soldiers Accountability Act of 2007, 18 USC s. 2442 (2008); Trafficking in Persons Accountability Act of 2008, S 1703 110th Cong.

[24]   *United States* v. *Bin Laden*, 92 F.Supp.2d 189, 222 (SDNY 2000) (citing *Restatement (Third) of Foreign Relations Law* s. 404) (internal quotations omitted).

[25]   327 F.3d 56 (2d Cir. 2003).

Yousef, the court held that the principle of universality was not applicable to defendants tried on terrorism charges relating to bombings of a theater in Manila and a Philippine Airlines commercial jet with no link to the United States. The court held that 'the universality principle permits jurisdiction over only a limited set of crimes that cannot be expanded judicially', and that jurisdiction is permitted over piracy, war crimes and crimes against humanity, but not terrorism.[26] The court explained that universal jurisdiction is appropriate 'only where crimes (1) are universally condemned by the community of nations, and (2) by their nature occur either outside of a State or where there is no State capable of punishing, or competent to punish, the crime (as in a time of war)'.[27]

Several commentators refer to the US Alien Tort Statute (ATS) as a kind of civil universal jurisdiction. The ATS, which dates back to 1789, allows suits by aliens for a tort in violation of the law of nations or a treaty of the United States.[28] The ATS has resulted in civil damages awards against over a dozen perpetrators, although far fewer have actually been collected. Additionally, in 1991, Congress passed the Torture Victims Protection Act, which allows civil suits by US citizens for torture or extra-judicial killing committed outside the United States, although in both cases the defendant must be served legal papers within the United States to establish jurisdiction.[29]

DILEMMAS AND DEBATES

The case for the exercise of universal jurisdiction is strengthened when the accused resides in a repressive regime where credible domestic proceedings are not an option. As Lord Browne-Wilkinson stated in his opinion in the *Pinochet* extradition proceedings:

> a totalitarian regime will not permit adjudication by its own courts on its own shortcomings. Hence the demand for some international machinery to repress state torture which is not dependent upon the local courts where the torture was committed.[30]

If the broad international consensus is that some crimes are heinous and important enough to be internationally condemned, yet prosecution at home is impossible, alternative forums are needed. One option would be to turn to the International Criminal Court (ICC), but the ICC can take few cases and has serious jurisdictional limitations.[31] Ad hoc tribunals, such as the ICTY and International Criminal Tribunal for Rwanda (ICTR), or hybrid courts, like those of Sierra Leone or Cambodia, are another option, but the political will (and cost) involved in setting up such a court make it unlikely that they will be used often. Thus, universal jurisdiction-based national prosecutions may often be the only option. Moreover, while all complex criminal investigations are costly, the use of domestic courts to investigate human rights violations can occur within institutions already in place and as a matter of routine, rather than requiring specific additional resources and executive decisions by states to proceed.

---

[26]   *Ibid.* 103.
[27]   *Ibid.* 106.
[28]   28 USC s. 1350.
[29]   *Ibid.*
[30]   See Ex Parte Pinochet, note 12 *supra.*
[31]   The ICC can only investigate cases referred to it by the UN Security Council, or where either

It has sometimes been suggested that the exercise of universal jurisdiction by the courts of one state implies a judgment that the judiciary of another is not competent to handle the case. This view reflects an assumption that the preferred forum would normally be the territorial state (where the crime was committed). This is sometimes referred to as the 'subsidiarity' issue. Spain's current law does not by its terms demand subsidiarity, only that the defendant has not been convicted, acquitted or pardoned elsewhere. At one point, the Spanish Supreme Court articulated a standard of 'effective' prosecution at home, which was presumably meant to exclude sham or desultory efforts. A German court, as noted above, dismissed the *Rumsfeld* complaint because it found he could be investigated in the United States.

There is nothing in treaty law requiring subsidiarity, or preferring one forum over another, although article VI of the Genocide Convention does state that those charged with genocide 'shall be tried by a competent tribunal of the State in the territory of which the act was committed, or by such international penal tribunal as may have jurisdiction'. Other jurisdictional bases are not mentioned in that 1948 treaty but this alone cannot exclude their application in the twenty-first century.

The question of the relationship between territory and forum raises the larger concern of the democratic legitimacy of a universal jurisdiction-based prosecution where the judges are not constrained by the politics or culture of the country where the crimes took place. On the one hand, this provides victims with some security and gives impartiality to the court's efforts, but it also means that prosecutors and judges 'are completely unaccountable to the citizens of the nation whose fate they are ruling upon'.[32] As a result, critics fear that such courts 'will invariably be less disciplined and prudent than would otherwise be the case'.[33] Henry Kissinger has called this the 'tyranny of the judges'.[34] Judges might, for example, set aside carefully-crafted post-armed conflict settlements that granted conditional or partial amnesty to some or all perpetrators. And they might be more willing to do so when the effects would be felt far from home. Similarly, states exercising universal jurisdiction are open to charges of post-colonial paternalism, particularly in cases in which the prosecuting state is the former colonizer and the extraditing state is the former colony (such is the case with Belgium and Rwanda). Additionally, other nations, such as Spain, have faced charges of hypocrisy. For example, it took Spain over 30 years to confront its own Francoist legacy, and it never prosecuted those responsible, even as Spanish judges considered prosecutions in a half-dozen other places. In response, proponents of an expanded universal jurisdiction argue that, as more states actually exercise their legal obligations and responsibilities, the paternalistic overtones will diminish, and fewer and fewer states will wait 30 years to begin confronting their own post-armed conflict legacies.

---

the state where the crimes were committed or the state of nationality of the suspect agrees to the investigation. Additionally, the ICC can only investigate crimes that occurred after 2002, or after the date the relevant states became parties to the treaty.

32   Jack Goldsmith and Stephen D. Krasner, *The Limits of Idealism*, DEDALUS 47, 51 (Winter 2003).

33   Diane F. Orentlicher, *Whose Justice? Reconciling Universal Jurisdiction with Democratic Principles*, 92 GEO. LJ 1057, 1063 (2004).

34   Kissinger has personal reasons for concern. Courts in France and Chile have asked to question him about his knowledge of crimes committed when he was in the US government. See Roht-Arriaza, note 9 *supra*, ch. 6.

Another set of concerns relates to the nature and extent of ties needed between the perpetrator and the forum state. As the Spanish Constitutional Court found, requiring a tie to nationality of either victims or perpetrators changes the idea of universality and replicates other grounds of jurisdiction already existing in international law. How then can chaos be avoided as competing jurisdictions try to exercise power over the same facts or same defendants? In part, this is merely a theoretical concern; as to date, the problem has been more that too few jurisdictions are pursuing universal jurisdiction prosecutions, rather than too many. Practical concerns about the ability to extradite, to obtain witnesses or information, or to otherwise try the case may require prosecutors and judges to exercise a prudential course of restraint where there are no ties to the forum, but that is very different from a bright-line jurisdictional rule.

The related questions of whether a defendant needs to be present in the jurisdiction of the court, and at what stage, go to the heart of what universal jurisdiction is about. Even if most states require the presence of the defendant for a final trial and conviction, can a court investigate, issue a warrant, request extradition of the defendant, and satisfy the presence requirement through extradition? At what point in that sequence does the defendant have to be there? Or is presence acting merely as a proxy for ties to the forum?

If the defendant has to be present for the judicial process to commence, it will be difficult ever to get to the arrest stage. This is because ex-dictators and torturers are unlikely to linger somewhere long enough for a conscientious prosecutor or investigating judge to put together the case file or dossier needed, especially once they get wind of an investigation. Universal jurisdiction, under that scenario, will still play a constructive role, but it will be more to ensure that dictators stay at home and that there is 'no safe haven' for such people, than it is to see that they are actually brought to justice. Courts will not often be able to put together the evidence and testimony that might jump-start a domestic prosecution if the 'investigate and extradite' route is closed; indeed, most prosecutions to date under a form of universality have involved refugees or immigrants to the prosecuting country. Under a 'presence of the defendant' rule, the *Pinochet* case would never have happened. British human rights groups tried four times to start a prosecution against him on various trips to the United Kingdom, but each time he left before the slow machinery of the justice system (and the requisite political will) could be brought to bear. Without the Spanish extradition request, it would have been much more difficult to kick-start that machinery into operation.

A final dilemma involves the role of victim initiatives in universal jurisdiction cases. From the perspective of states, the ability of victims to go directly to an investigating magistrate or state prosecutor without initial action or approval by a state official opens up the system in a way that could have major diplomatic repercussions. From the victims' perspective, however, the bottom-up approach that forces a state's domestic courts to take heed of complaints about foreign officials is more beneficial to victims' needs than the more top-down approach taken by international courts like the ad hoc tribunals set up for Rwanda and Yugoslavia. The capacity to take complaints and evidence directly to an investigating magistrate gives victims much more initiative and control over the case, which in itself can be a form of vindication.

Universal jurisdiction will continue to play a significant, if opportunistic, role in international criminal justice. Its utility does not come solely, or even mainly, from the ability to capture errant dictators and torturers. Nor does it come from the possible deterrence value, either on atrocities or, more modestly, on post-atrocity travel by perpetrators. These effects would be difficult to measure in any case. Rather, the primary value lies in the ability of a transnational investigation based on universal jurisdiction to prompt investigations and prosecutions at home, in the territorial state. Some cases did this – for example, the *Pinochet* litigation undoubtedly changed forever Chile's domestic political and legal panorama. The investigations into Argentine military atrocities prompted new investigations, judicial and legislative annulments of the amnesty law, and a new willingness to extradite human rights offenders if they are not tried domestically. The *Habré* case seems to have had some similar catalytic effects in Chad. Even in Guatemala, under much more adverse conditions, the Spanish investigation yielded a year's detention of a number of high-ranking former military leaders, new evidence, and renewed attention to the issue including, grudgingly, that of the public prosecutor. It is these internal catalytic effects that may prove, over time, to be the greatest argument in favor of universal jurisdiction.

PART VI

THE FUTURE OF INTERNATIONAL CRIMINAL LAW

16 National amnesties, truth commissions and international criminal tribunals

William A. Schabas

Amnesty is defined by the *Oxford English Dictionary* as 'an act of forgetfulness, an intentional overlooking, a general pardon, esp. for a political offence'. The word is used in many languages, apparently derived from the same word in both Greek and Latin, *amnestia*, which means 'forgetfulness'. The profound suspicion of criminal justice systems manifested at an early stage in the development of human rights law is reflected in the name chosen by one of the premier human rights non-governmental organizations, Amnesty International. But Amnesty International no longer looks very favourably on amnesties, as a general rule. Moreover, there is a growing body of authority indicating that amnesties are not only frowned upon by human rights law, they may even be prohibited.[1]

Often amnesties are explicitly set out in peace agreements. Such conventions make up a long list, going back to the mother of all international treaties, the 1848 Peace of Westphalia.[2] The Lomé Agreement that ended the civil war in Sierra Leone provides a recent example, although amnesty provisions in peace treaties are as old as international law itself. Another comes from the dawn of international criminal justice, at the end of the First World War. The Treaty of Lausanne of 1923, which ended the war and determined the consequences of its aftermath with respect to Turkey, contained a 'Declaration of Amnesty' for all offences committed between 1 August 1914 and 20 November 1922.[3] It replaced the Treaty of Sèvres of 1920, which was never accepted by Turkey. The Treaty of Sèvres authorized prosecution by the victorious allies not only of 'violations of the laws and customs of war', but also for the 'massacres committed during the continuance of the state of war on territory which

---

[1] See, for example, ANDREAS O'SHEA, AMNESTY FOR CRIME IN INTERNATIONAL LAW AND PRACTICE (The Hague, Kluwer Law International, 2002); NAOMI ROHT-ARRIAZA (ed.), IMPUNITY AND HUMAN RIGHTS IN INTERNATIONAL LAW AND POLITICS (New York, Oxford University Press, 1995); J. Gavron, *Amnesties in the Light of Developments in International Law and the Establishment of the International Criminal Court*, 51 INTERNATIONAL AND COMPARATIVE LQ 91 (2002); Douglas Cassel, *Accountability for International Crime and Serious Violations of Fundamental Human Rights: Lessons from the Americas: Guidelines for International Response to Amnesties for Atrocities* 59 LAW AND CONTEMPORARY PROBLEMS 197 (1996); John Dugard, *Dealing with Crimes of a Past Regime: Is Amnesty Still an Option?*, 12 LEIDEN J INTERNATIONAL L 1001 (1999); Yasmin Naqvi, *Amnesty for War Crimes: Defining the International Recognition*, 85 INTERNATIONAL REVIEW OF THE RED CROSS 583 (2003).

[2] For a list, see Fania Domb, *Treatment of War Crimes in Peace Settlements: Prosecution or Amnesty?*, in Y. DINSTEIN and M. TABORY (eds.), WAR CRIMES IN INTERNATIONAL LAW (The Hague, Martinus Nijhoff, 1996).

[3] Treaty of Lausanne between Principal Allied and Associated Powers and Turkey, (1923) 28 LNTS 11.

formed part of the Turkish Empire on August 1, 1914',[4] a reference to what today we would call the Armenian genocide.[5]

Sometimes *de facto* amnesty follows from a political decision not to prosecute crimes committed during a conflict rather than from a formal agreement or declaration. They may also be the result of an offer of asylum which has, as its consequence, the removal of a threat of criminal prosecution. The exile of Napoleon to Elba, and later St Helena, furnishes an historic example.[6] A modern one would be Nigeria's promise of refuge to Charles Taylor as part of the deal brokered by its President to end the civil war in Liberia.

Amnesties are often associated with truth and reconciliation commissions. Although in reality very few truth and reconciliation commissions have had any authority or power with respect to amnesty, the discussion has been largely defined by the South African Truth and Reconciliation Commission.[7] One of its subordinate bodies was authorized to provide witnesses with amnesty, to the extent that they had presented the Truth and Reconciliation Commission with full disclosure about crimes in which they had participated. The Sierra Leone Truth and Reconciliation Commission was born as a result of the amnesty in the Lomé Peace Agreement. Although it was agreed that there would be no criminal prosecution, the Agreement called for a Truth and Reconciliation Commission in order to provide some measure of accountability for atrocities committed during the conflict.

Both amnesties and truth commissions are creatures of national law, although their origins may lie in treaties, and their funding and infrastructure may depend upon international donors or international organizations. They result from enactments of sovereign legislatures. Theoretically, it would be open to the United Nations Security Council to establish a truth commission, just as it could also declare an amnesty, but there are no precedents. In a few cases, the Security Council has forbidden the prosecution of war crimes by both national and international criminal tribunals with the exception of the state of nationality (the 'sending state') of the offender.[8] It is also expressly empowered by the Rome Statute of the International Criminal Court to prevent prosecution by the Court in certain circumstances,[9] an authority it has exercised twice.[10]

EVOLVING ATTITUDES TO AMNESTY

The Statute of the Special Court for Sierra Leone declares that '[a]n amnesty granted to any person falling within the jurisdiction of the Special Court in respect of the crimes referred to

---

⁴   [1920] UKTS 11; DeMartens, *Recueil général des traités*, 99, 3e série, 12, 1924, 720 (French version), arts 227, 230.

⁵   PETER BALAKIAN, BURNING TIGRIS (New York, HarperCollins, 2003); TANER AKÇAM, A SHAMEFUL ACT: THE ARMENIAN GENOCIDE AND THE QUESTION OF TURKISH RESPONSIBILITY (New York, Holt, 2007).

⁶   See GARY BASS, STAY THE HAND OF VENGEANCE (Princeton University Press, 2001).

⁷   *Rule of Law Tools for Post-Conflict States: Truth Commissions* 11–12 (Geneva and New York, Office of the United Nations High Commissioner for Human Rights, 2006).

⁸   UN Doc. S/RES/1497 (2003), para. 7; UN Doc. S/RES/1593 (2005), para. 6.

⁹   Rome Statute of the International Criminal Court, 2187 UNTS 90 (2002), art. 16.

¹⁰   UN Doc. S/RES/1422 (2002), para. 1; UN Doc. S/RES/1487 (2003), para. 1.

in articles 2 to 4 of the present Statute shall not be a bar to prosecution'.[11] In his preliminary report on the draft Statute of the Court, the Secretary-General explained: 'With the denial of legal effect to the amnesty granted at Lomé, to the extent of its illegality under international law, the obstacle to the determination of a beginning date of the temporal jurisdiction of the Court within the pre-Lomé period has been removed.'[12] Echoing the Secretary-General's reference to the 'illegality under international law' of amnesty with respect to genocide, crimes against humanity and war crimes, the Appeals Chamber of the Special Court for Sierra Leone has stated that, in its view, the amnesty was 'not only incompatible with, but is in breach of an obligation of a State towards the international community as a whole'.[13]

There is no similar provision in the Statutes of any of the other international criminal tribunals, nor has amnesty ever been invoked by defendants before those institutions. It seems that in Japan, following the Second World War, an Imperial Rescript granting an amnesty by general pardon for war crimes committed by members of the Japanese Armed Forces during the Second World War was issued on 3 November 1946. It had no effect upon war crimes trials held by the victorious allies, including the International Military Tribunal for the Far East.[14] When the Rome Statute of the International Criminal Court was being negotiated, the question of how the new institution might deal with amnesty was considered from time to time, generally at the behest of South Africa, whose Truth and Reconciliation Commission was then in its heyday. There is barely a trace of this discussion in the official record, essentially because states understood that unanimity or consensus on such a difficult issue was unlikely and possibly because their own views were unclear or in ferment at the time.

Indeed, the position of international law on the issue of amnesty has probably evolved over recent decades. In terms of the principle of amnesties, there are only two references in major multilateral treaties, both of them favourable to the concept. Article 6(4) of the International Covenant on Civil and Political Rights (ICCPR) declares: 'Anyone sentenced to death shall have the right to seek pardon or commutation of the sentence. Amnesty, pardon or commutation of the sentence of death may be granted in all cases.' The context suggests that it applies to specific cases of imposition of capital punishment, rather than to situations of post-conflict justice. Much more relevant is article 6(5) of the Protocol Additional (II) to the 1949 Geneva Conventions and Relating to the Protection of Victims of Non-International Armed Conflicts, which states that '[a]t the end of hostilities, the authorities in power shall endeavour to grant the broadest possible amnesty to persons who have participated in the armed conflict, or those deprived of their liberty for reasons related to the armed conflict, whether they are interned or detained'.[15]

---

[11]   Statute of the Special Court for Sierra Leone, art. 10.

[12]   *Report of the Secretary-General on the Establishment of a Special Court for Sierra Leone*, UN Doc. S/2000/915, para. 24.

[13]   *Prosecutor* v. *Kallon*, Case No. SCSL-04-15AR72(E) and *Prosecutor* v. *Kamara*, Case No. SCSL-04-16-AR72(E), Decision on Challenge to Jurisdiction: Lomé Accord Amnesty, 13 March 2004, para. 73. See also *Prosecutor* v. *Kondewa*, Case No. SCSL-2004-14-AR72(E), Separate Opinion of Justice Robertson, 25 May 2004.

[14]   R. John Pritchard, *The Gift of Clemency following British War Crimes Trials in the Far East, 1946–1948*, 7 CRIMINAL LAW FORUM 15, 22–3 (1996).

[15]   Protocol Additional to the 1949 Geneva Conventions and Relating to the Protection of Victims of Non-International Armed Conflicts, 1125 UNTS 609 (1979).

Some argue that there has been no development in the law on this subject since Additional Protocol II was adopted in 1977 and that article 6(5) was never intended to authorize or encourage amnesty for serious violations of international humanitarian law, such as war crimes, crimes against humanity and genocide. In the customary law study published by the International Committee of the Red Cross in 2004, article 6(5) of Additional Protocol II is reformulated with the addition of a final phrase to the text, making an exception to the provision which is generally most favourable to amnesty in the case of 'persons suspected of, or accused of or sentenced for war crimes'.[16] The commentary explains that the intent of the drafters of the Protocol was to exclude war crimes from such an amnesty. Thus, the additional phrase is said to clarify the intent of those who drafted Additional Protocol II, rather than amplify or develop it. Citing the International Committee of the Red Cross, Diane Orentlicher, in her report to the United Nations Commission on Human Rights, also refers to the *travaux préparatoires* of Additional Protocol II as authority for the proposition that amnesty cannot be extended to war crimes, crimes against humanity and genocide.[17]

Evidence that the drafters of article 6(5) of Additional Protocol II meant to exclude serious violations of international humanitarian law is actually very slender. The record shows that when article 6(5) of the Protocol was adopted, the representative of the Soviet Union declared that, in his country's opinion, the provision could not be interpreted as applying to war criminals and those who had committed crimes against humanity. This is apparently the only mention of the issue in the record of the Diplomatic Conference of 1974–1977 at which the Protocol was adopted. More than three decades have passed, and it is now perhaps more difficult to recall the international context of the time. Suffice it to say that an isolated statement from the Soviet Union at a diplomatic conference is probably better interpreted as evidence of an absence of agreement than as proof of consensus or acquiescence. A single statement of this nature is scant authority for the interpretation of a treaty provision. Moreover, we know that the drafters of Additional Protocol II quite intentionally excluded the concept of war crimes in non-international armed conflict altogether. Why would they have excluded the concept of war crimes in non-international armed conflict, but at the same time intended to refer implicitly to this non-existent notion in the amnesty provision? The rejection of the very concept of war crimes during non-international armed conflict persisted until the mid-1990s[18] and has continued to be questioned by large states as recently as the 1998 Diplomatic Conference at which the ICC Statute was adopted.[19]

The evolving position of public international law on this subject is reflected in changing practice within the United Nations itself. In Sierra Leone, for example, the United Nations was one of the moral guarantors of the Abidjan Peace Agreement of 30 November 1996. That peace treaty included an amnesty clause to which the United Nations made no objection at the time.[20] Three years later, at Lomé, the attitude had changed, and the Secretary-General

---

16   JEAN-MARIE HENCKAERTS and LOUISE DOSWALD-BECK, CUSTOMARY INTERNATIONAL HUMANITARIAN LAW (Cambridge University Press, 2005), rule 159.

17   UN Doc. E/CN.4/2004/88, para. 27.

18   See *Prosecutor* v. *Tadić*, Case No. IT-94-1-AR72, Separate Opinion of Judge Li on the Defence Motion for Interlocutory Appeal on Jurisdiction, 2 October 1995, para. 9.

19   UN Doc. A/CONF.183/SR.9, para. 30; UN Doc. A/CONF. 183/C. 1/SR.25, para. 36.

20   Peace Agreement between the Government of the Republic of Sierra Leone and the Revolutionary United Front of Sierra Leone (RUF), 30 November 1996, art. 14. This was noted by

instructed his Special Representative to make the following declaration: 'The United Nations holds the understanding that the amnesty provisions of the Agreement shall not apply to international crimes of genocide, crimes against humanity, war crimes and other serious violations of international humanitarian law.'[21] In 2000, when the establishment of the Special Court for Sierra Leone was proposed, the Secretary-General wrote:

> While recognizing that amnesty is an accepted legal concept and a gesture of peace and reconciliation at the end of a civil war or an internal armed conflict, the United Nations has consistently maintained the position that amnesty cannot be granted in respect of international crimes, such as genocide, crimes against humanity or other serious violations of international humanitarian law.[22]

But this wasn't a very accurate statement because, in Sierra Leone itself, the United Nations had endorsed the idea of amnesty as recently as 1996. The famous statement in the Lomé Peace Agreement was probably the first manifestation of an anti-amnesty policy within the United Nations Secretariat with respect to peace agreements.[23] In 2005, a Report by the Secretary-General proposed that the Security Council '[r]eject any endorsement of amnesty for genocide, war crimes, or crimes against humanity, including those relating to ethnic, gender and sexually based international crimes, ensure that no such amnesty previously granted is a bar to prosecution before any United Nations-created or assisted court.'[24]

A fairly good assessment of law and practice appears in the reasoning of Lord Lloyd of the United Kingdom's House of Lords in the *Pinochet* case, in 1998.

> Further light is shed on state practice by the widespread adoption of amnesties for those who have committed crimes against humanity including torture. Chile was not the first in the field. There was an amnesty at the end of the Franco-Algerian War in 1962. In 1971 India and Bangladesh agreed not to pursue charges of genocide against Pakistan troops accused of killing about one million East Pakistanis. General amnesties have also become common in recent years, especially in South America, covering members of former regimes accused of torture and other atrocities. Some of these have had the blessing of the United Nations, as a means of restoring peace and democratic government ... It has not been argued that these amnesties are as such contrary to international law by reason of the failure to prosecute the individual perpetrators.[25]

---

defence counsel, in *Prosecutor* v. *Kallon*, Case No. SCSL -04-15AR72(E) and *Prosecutor* v. *Kamara*, Case No. SCSL -04-16-AR72(E), Decision on Challenge to Jurisdiction: Lomé Accord Amnesty, 13 March 2004, para. 58, as well as in the final report of the Sierra Leone Truth and Reconciliation Commission: 3B *Witness to Truth: Report of the Sierra Leone Truth and Reconciliation Commission* (Freetown, 2004), ch. 6, para. 8.

21   UN Doc. S/RES/1315 (2000), Preamble, para. 5.

22   *Report of the Secretary-General on the Establishment of a Special Court for Sierra Leone*, UN Doc. S/2000/915, para. 22. A footnote reference to art. 6(5) of Additional Protocol II appears after the first comma in the citation.

23   In 1999, the Secretary-General issued Guidelines for United Nations Representatives on Certain Aspects of Negotiations for Conflict Resolution.

24   *Report of the Secretary-General, The Rule of Law and Transitional Justice in Conflict and Post-conflict Societies*, UN Doc. S/2004/616, at 20. See also *Set of Principles for the Protection and Promotion of Human Rights through Action to Combat Impunity*, UN Doc. E/CN.4/2005/102/Add.1, Principle 24.

25   *R* v. *Bow Street Metropolitan Stipendiary Magistrate, ex parte Pinochet*, [1998] 4 All ER 897 (HL), at 929 h–i.

There can be no doubt that there is a trend towards condemning amnesties, but the claim that they are contrary to international law is unsupported by treaties and recent state practice. A likely explanation of why some international lawyers tend to exaggerate the reality is their concern that if the door to amnesty is left even slightly ajar, unprincipled politicians will pry it wide open. It is better to tell peace negotiators that amnesty is simply not an option, they reason, rather than let them retain it in their tool-box as a mechanism to end conflict in appropriate situations, however rare these may be.

Although there is no text in public international law instruments prohibiting amnesty, this may be an implied consequence of the norm by which states are required either to prosecute or extradite persons suspected of committing serious violations of international humanitarian law. Such an obligation is set out quite clearly in the so-called 'grave breach' provisions of the four Geneva Conventions and of Additional Protocol I.[26] The duty is also affirmed in two human rights treaties, dealing with torture[27] and enforced disappearance.[28] Debate persists about whether, in addition to the treaty sources, the obligation to extradite or prosecute is also imposed by customary international law with respect to international crimes in general, including genocide, crimes against humanity and war crimes other than grave breaches.[29]

VICTIMS AND THE RIGHT TO JUSTICE

In the absence of any clear treaty provision declaring amnesty to be contrary to international law, and indeed given an important suggestion to the contrary in Protocol Additional II, efforts to provide a legal basis for the anti-amnesty provision have focused upon the rights of victims, in particular the right to reparation and to a remedy. It is contended that victims have a right to see justice done, and that the rights of the victims are violated by amnesty. According to the Basic Principles and Guidelines on the Right to a Remedy and Reparation for Victims of Gross Violations of International Human Rights Law and Serious Violations of International Humanitarian Law, adopted by the Commission on Human Rights in 2005:

> [i]n cases of gross violations of international human rights law and serious violations of international humanitarian law constituting crimes under international law, States have the duty to investigate and, if there is sufficient evidence, the duty to submit to prosecution the person allegedly responsible for the violations and, if found guilty, the duty to punish her or him.[30]

---

[26]   Convention for the Amelioration of the Condition of the Wounded and Sick in Armed Forces in the Field, 75 UNTS 31 (1949), art. 50; Convention for the Amelioration of the Condition of Wounded, Sick and Shipwrecked Members of Armed Forces at Sea, 75 UNTS 85 (1950), art. 51; Convention Relative to the Treatment of Prisoners of War, 75 UNTS 135 (1950), art. 130; Convention Relative to the Protection of Civilian Persons in Time of War, 75 UNTS 287 (1950), art. 147; Protocol Additional to the 1949 Geneva Conventions and Relating to the Protection of Victims of International Armed Conflicts, 1125 UNTS 3 (1979), art. 85.
[27]   Convention Against Torture and Other Cruel, Inhuman or Degrading Treatment or Punishment, 1465 UNTS 85 (1987), art. 7.
[28]   International Convention for the Protection of All Persons from Enforced Disappearance, UN Doc. A/61/488, art. 11.
[29]   *Report of the International Law Commission, Fifty-ninth Session, 7 May–5 June and 9 July–10 August 2007*, UN Doc. A/62/10, para. 354.
[30]   UN Doc. E/CN.4/RES/2005/35, para. 4.

There is much authority, in the case law of the European Court of Human Rights (ECtHR),[31] the Human Rights Committee[32] and the Inter-American Court of Human Rights,[33] for the proposition that fundamental rights are breached where a state fails to investigate, prosecute and punish. In a recent case, the ECtHR held that Bulgaria had breached the European Convention on Human Rights because it did not adequately investigate a complaint of so-called 'date rape'.[34] Another recent case involves a violent attack on Jehovah's Witnesses during a religious meeting. A Chamber of the ECtHR wrote:

> Article 3 of the [European] Convention [on Human Rights] gives rise to a positive obligation to conduct an official investigation (see *Assenov and Others v. Bulgaria*, judgment of 28 October 1998, *Reports* 1998-VIII, p. 3290, para. 102). Such a positive obligation cannot be considered in principle to be limited solely to cases of ill-treatment by State agents (see *M.C. v. Bulgaria*, cited above, para. 151). Thus, the authorities have an obligation to take action as soon as an official complaint has been lodged. Even in the absence of an express complaint, an investigation should be undertaken if there are other sufficiently clear indications that torture or ill-treatment might have occurred. A requirement of promptness and reasonable expedition is implicit in this context. A prompt response by the authorities in investigating allegations of ill-treatment may generally be regarded as essential in maintaining public confidence in their maintenance of the rule of law and in preventing any appearance of collusion in or tolerance of unlawful acts. Tolerance by the authorities towards such acts cannot but undermine public confidence in the principle of lawfulness and the State's maintenance of the rule of law (see *Batı and Others v. Turkey*, nos. 33097/96 and 57834/00, para. 136, ECHR 2004-IV (extracts); *Abdülsamet Yaman v. Turkey*, no. 32446/96, para. 60, 2 November 2004; and, *mutatis mutandis, Paul and Audrey Edwards v. United Kingdom,* no. 46477/99, para. 72, ECHR 2002-II).[35]

These pronouncements from the human rights bodies apply to all crimes, or at least to crimes involving violence against the person, and not only to war crimes, crimes against humanity and genocide. Indeed, there seems to be no basis in international human rights law for making any distinction between the rights of the victim of a domestic-variety murder or rape and the rights of the victim of a murder *qua* crime against humanity. From the standpoint of the individual victim, how could the legal qualification of such a crime have any real significance? Should one victim be denied justice, as a matter of principle, because the perpetrator did not have the exalted *mens rea* necessary for a finding of crimes against humanity? To the extent that the duty to prosecute, which is based in the rights of victims to redress and justice, finds its roots in international human rights law, then amnesties ought to be prohibited altogether, and not only for serious violations of international humanitarian law, namely genocide, crimes against humanity and war crimes. But there is no serious suggestion in the case law or the academic commentary that amnesties be prohibited altogether. Such a proposition flies in the face of article 6(5) of Additional Protocol II, even if one accepts the restrictive gloss placed upon it by the International Committee of the Red Cross and certain

---

31   *Streletz, Kessler and Krenz* v. *Germany*, Applications Nos 34044/96, 35532/97 and 44801/98, 22 March 2001, para. 86.

32   *Bautista de Arellana* v. *Colombia*, Case No. 563/1993, UN Doc. CCPR/C/55/D/563/1993, paras 8.3. 10.

33   *Velasquez Rodriguez* v. *Honduras*, Judgment, 29 July 1988, Series C, No. 4.

34   *MC* v. *Bulgaria*, Application No. 39272/98, ECHR 2003-XII, para. 149.

35   *Case of 97 Members of the Glldani Congregation of Jehovah's Witnesses and 4 Others* v. *Georgia*, Application No. 71156/01, Judgment, 3 May 2007, para. 97.

academic commentators. The *reductio ad absurdum* demonstrates the fallacy of the initial proposition.

Once the issue is framed within the setting of international human rights law, the fact that the right to reparation and remedy cannot be absolute and may be limited becomes clearer. In international criminal law discussions, the prohibition of amnesty is often presented in an absolute fashion, as if it was not subject to limitations or exceptions. But with rare exceptions, human rights are generally framed as being subject to some form of reasonable limitation, even when the texts themselves do not appear to allow this. Thus, in the application of the fundamental rights of defendants to a fair trial, international criminal tribunals have held that the right to defend oneself in person,[36] and the right to be present at trial,[37] are not absolute. Both of these rights are set out in article 14(3) of the ICCPR in an apparently absolute manner.[38] If these rights are subject to reasonable limitations, why then are the rights to reparation and remedy not also subject to limitation?

Human rights law often distinguishes between negative and positive rights. A negative right only requires that the state abstain from intervening, whereas a positive right compels state action, including allocation of resources. This distinction was one of the arguments that prompted the division of fundamental rights, as set out in the Universal Declaration of Human Rights, into two broad categories, with the result that we have two human rights treaties of universal application: the International Covenant on Civil and Political Rights and the International Covenant on Economic, Social and Cultural Rights. In the case of civil and political rights, where the obligations are primarily 'negative' in nature, states are required to implement these rights immediately.[39] On the other hand, where economic, social and cultural rights are concerned, there is a more modest obligation 'to take steps, individually and through international assistance and co-operation, especially economic and technical, to the maximum of its available resources, with a view to achieving progressively the full realization of the rights recognized in the present Covenant by all appropriate means, including particularly the adoption of legislative measures'.[40]

The right to reparation and remedy involves allocation of resources, something that suggests that it cannot be an absolute and unqualified right. Justice systems are expensive undertakings, and their scope and coverage inevitably reflect policy decisions where other imperatives of government derived from fundamental rights, such as education and medical care, are involved. In other words, the right of victims of human rights violations to reparation and remedy is inevitably balanced against other fundamental rights. This proposition does not seem difficult to accept. Indeed, it has an obvious reflection at the international level, where the United Nations assigns portions of its own budget to international criminal justice. The Special Court for Sierra Leone (SCSL) was provided with a relatively small budget, at

---

[36]   *Prosecutor* v. *Milošević*, Case No. IT-02-54-AR73.7, Decision on Interlocutory Appeal of the Trial Chamber's Decision on the Assignment of Defence Counsel, 1 November 2004, paras 12–13; *Prosecutor* v. *Šešelj*, Case No. IT-03-67-AR73.3, Decision on Appeal Against the Trial Chamber's Decision on Assignment of Counsel, 20 October 2006, para. 8.

[37]   *Prosecutor* v. *Karamera et al.*, Case No. ICTR-98-44-AR73.10, Decision on Nzizorera's Interlocutory Appeal Concerning his Right to be Present at Trial, 5 October 2007, para. 15

[38]   *International Covenant on Civil and Political Rights*, 999 UNTS 171 (1976).

[39]   *Ibid.* art. 2.

[40]   *International Covenant on Economic, Social and Cultural Rights*, 993 UNTS 3 (1976), art. 2(1).

least compared with its elder siblings, the International Criminal Tribunal for the Former Yugoslavia and the International Criminal Tribunal for Rwanda. Thus, to the extent that reparation and remedy involve expenditure of resources, be they of the state or of intergovernmental organizations, we are dealing with a qualified rather than an absolute right.

Amnesty does not, of course, involve a balancing between the right to justice and the right to education. In some cases, egregious amnesties are offered to aging dictators, like Augusto Pinochet, more or less as a retirement gift. It would be difficult to imagine that such considerations could be equated with matters like the right to education and the right to medical care. But what about amnesties that are granted as part of a peace process in order to bring an end to armed conflict? Are they not driven by a legitimate social value, indeed a fundamental right, namely that of everyone to live in peace? If the right to justice can be balanced with the rights to education and health, can it not also be balanced with the right to peace?

This more nuanced approach to amnesty was adopted by the Sierra Leone Truth and Reconciliation Commission. In its final report, the Commission concluded:

> Accordingly, those who argue that peace cannot be bartered in exchange for justice, under any circumstances, must be prepared to justify the likely prolongation of an armed conflict. Amnesties may be undesirable in many cases. Indeed there are examples of abusive amnesties proclaimed by dictators in the dying days of tyrannical regimes. The Commission also recognizes the principle that it is generally desirable to prosecute perpetrators of serious human rights abuses, particularly when they rise to the level of gravity of crimes against humanity. However amnesties should not be excluded entirely from the mechanisms available to those attempting to negotiate a cessation of hostilities after periods of brutal armed conflict. Disallowing amnesty in all cases is to deny the reality of violent conflict and the urgent need to bring such strife and suffering to an end.
>
>   The Commission is unable to declare that it considers amnesty too high a price to pay for the delivery of peace to Sierra Leone, under the circumstances that prevailed in July 1999. It is true that the Lomé Agreement did not immediately return the country to peacetime. Yet it provided the framework for a process that pacified the combatants and, five years later, has returned Sierra Leoneans to a context in which they need not fear daily violence and atrocity.[41]

The Commission's view is certainly a minority voice in the current debate. But at the very least, it usefully recalls that there is no unanimity on these issues.

APPROACH OF THE INTERNATIONAL CRIMINAL COURT

The SCSL applied article 10 of its Statute and refused to consider the amnesty of the Lomé Agreement. Nothing in the SCSL Statute authorized the judges to do otherwise. It was clearly the will of those who established the SCSL, including the UN Security Council, that the amnesty in the Lomé Agreement be disregarded. The same cannot be said of the International Criminal Court, however. There is no provision in the ICC Statute that is comparable to article 10 of the SCSL Statute. As mentioned earlier in this chapter, during the drafting of the ICC Statute, the very issue of how the Court would deal with future amnesties was frequently considered, often at the behest of the South African delegates. Because of the impossibility of reaching consensus on this matter, any definitive conclusion on the matter was avoided.

---

[41]   3B *Witness to Truth: Report of the Sierra Leone Truth and Reconciliation Commission* (Freetown, 2004), ch. 6, paras 11–12.

Two provisions of the ICC Statute reflect the ambiguity of the drafters, articles 17 and 53.[42] Article 17 of the ICC Statute is the principal provision concerning the admissibility of cases. Article 17 entitles the judges of the Court to decline to hear a case:

> 1. Having regard to paragraph 10 of the Preamble and article 1, the Court shall determine that a case is inadmissible where:
>
> (a)   the case is being investigated or prosecuted by a State which has jurisdiction over it, unless the State is unwilling or unable genuinely to carry out the investigation or prosecution;
>
> (b)   the case has been investigated by a State which has jurisdiction over it and the State has decided not to prosecute the person concerned, unless the decision resulted from the unwillingness or inability of the State genuinely to prosecute;
>
> (c)   the person concerned has already been tried for conduct which is the subject of the complaint, and a trial by the Court is not permitted under article 20, paragraph 3;
>
> (d)   the case is not of sufficient gravity to justify further action by the Court.

Paragraph 10 of the Preamble states: 'Emphasizing that the International Criminal Court established under this Statute shall be complementary to national criminal jurisdictions.'

There has been much speculation that article 17 might be applied by judges of the Court with considerable deference towards alternative mechanisms of accountability and, more specifically, truth and reconciliation commissions. It can be argued that 'investigation' is a concept that is broad enough to encompass the work of a truth commission. But article 17 marries 'investigation' to 'prosecution', and therefore it seems difficult to square the work of a truth commission with the first three paragraphs of article 17(1). More potential to make room for a truth commission can be derived from article 17(1)(d), which authorizes the judges of the Court to declare inadmissible a case that is not of 'sufficient gravity to justify further action by the Court'. A truth commission process addresses impunity and provides a degree of accountability for atrocities, with the consequence that the objective gravity of the acts in question declines in overall importance, above all in relation to other possible crimes within the jurisdiction of the Court.

Article 53 is the other relevant provision of the ICC Statute. It authorizes the Prosecutor to decline to investigate or prosecute when this does not serve 'the interests of justice'. There have been suggestions that this 'interests of justice' criterion would enable the Prosecutor to decline to prosecute when a truth commission process with an acceptable level of legitimacy in civil society is underway. Given the malleability of the 'interests of justice' concept, much will depend upon the personal vision of the Prosecutor. In 2007, the first Prosecutor, Luis Moreno-Ocampo, issued a policy paper outlining his interpretation of the 'interests of justice' concept as set out in article 53. He described the issue as 'one of the most complex aspects' of the ICC Statute. 'It is the point where many of the philosophical and operational challenges in the pursuit of international criminal justice coincide (albeit implicitly), but there is no clear guidance on what the content of the idea is,' he explained. The Prosecutor noted that although

---

[42]   See, generally, Michael P. Scharf, *The Amnesty Exception to the Jurisdiction of the International Criminal Court*, 32 Cornell International LJ 507 (1999); D. Majzub, *Peace or Justice? Amnesties and the International Criminal Court*, 3 Melbourne J International Law 247 (2002); Darryl Robinson, *Serving the Interests of Justice: Amnesties, Truth Commissions and the International Criminal Court*, 14 European J International L 481 (2003); Charles Villa Vicencio, *Why Perpetrators Should not Always be Prosecuted: Where the International Criminal Court and Truth Commissions Meet*, 49 Emory LJ 205 (2000).

the phrase 'interests of justice' appears in several places in the ICC Statute and Rules of Procedure and Evidence, it is never defined, nor do the *travaux préparatoires* provide any assistance in construction of the provision.[43]

According to the Prosecutor, the exercise of discretion not to proceed with a case on the grounds that it would not be in the 'interests of justice' is 'exceptional in nature', and 'there is a presumption in favour of investigation or prosecution'.[44] The Prosecutor observed that '[m]any developments in the last ten or fifteen years point to a consistent trend imposing a duty on States to prosecute crimes of international concern committed within their jurisdiction'.[45] Here he cited, in a footnote, a Press Telease issued by the United Nations Security Council on 22 June 2006:

> Touching on another issue highlighted in today's debate, Nicolas Michel, Under-Secretary-General for Legal Affairs and United Nations Legal Counsel, said that ending impunity for perpetrators of crimes against humanity was one of the principal evolutions in the culture of the world community and international law over the past 15 years. 'Justice should never be sacrificed by granting amnesty in ending conflicts', he said, adding that justice and peace should be considered as complementary demands and that the international community should 'consider ways of dovetailing one with the other'. The trend was confirmed in the statement of the President of the Security Council where he stated that, 'The Council intends to continue forcefully to fight impunity with appropriate means and draws attention to the full range of justice and reconciliation mechanisms to be considered, including national, international and 'mixed" criminal courts and tribunals, and truth and reconciliation commissions.'[46]

Although the Prosecutor did not explore this, there are obvious distinctions in the Press Release between the views of the United Nations Legal Counsel and those of the President of the Security Council. The former essentially condemns the phenomenon of amnesty as a mechanism of conflict resolution, whereas the latter seems open to 'the full range of justice and reconciliation mechanisms', including 'truth and reconciliation commissions'. If anything, they ought to have implied uncertainty about the issue rather than confirm a 'consistent trend'.

Be that as it may, the Prosecutor proceeded to develop an interpretation of 'interests of justice' that suggests little or no sympathy with alternative accountability mechanisms, such as truth commissions, as a justification for a decision not to proceed in a particular case. The Prosecutor pointed to paragraph 6 of the Preamble to the ICC Statute, which recalls that 'it is the duty of every State to exercise its criminal jurisdiction over those responsible for international crimes'. He added that criteria for application of the 'interests of justice' concept set out in article 53 'will naturally be guided by the objects and purposes of the Statute – namely the prevention of serious crimes of concern to the international community through ending impunity'.[47] Finally, the Prosecutor insisted that 'there is a difference between the concepts of the interests of justice and the interests of peace and that the latter falls within the mandate of institutions other than the Office of the Prosecutor'.[48] The implied reference here is to the

---

[43] *Policy Paper on the Interests of Justice* 2 (September 2007).
[44] *Ibid.* 1.
[45] *Ibid.* 3.
[46] *Ibid.* n. 5.
[47] *Ibid.* 1.
[48] *Ibid.*

UN Security Council, which is authorized by article 16 of the ICC Statute to defer prosecutions before the Court. But while it may be true that the Security Council is mandated to attend to 'the interests of peace', it too has viewed this as comprising the 'interests of justice', as can be seen by its establishment of the ad hoc international criminal tribunals.[49] Perhaps it is wiser to take the view that the interests of justice and the interests of peace cannot be separated, or at least that there is a region where they overlap. Where they coincide, both institutions operating in the field, Security Council and International Criminal Court, have a duty to reconcile the two related interests.

From the standpoint of statutory construction, separating the 'interests of justice' from the 'interests of peace' may be reading too much into the text of article 53. As the Prosecutor's position paper concedes, there is really nothing in the drafting history of the ICC Statute to assist in the interpretation of the phrase. It is certainly not at all obvious that the drafters intended any such distinction. There is ample authority within the Statute itself that the drafters prized the achievement and maintenance of peace, as the Prosecutor noted in his policy paper. The Prosecutor referred to the Preamble (paragraph 3: 'Recognizing that such grave crimes threaten the peace, security and well-being of the world') but he might have added the inclusion of the crime of aggression among the crimes within the jurisdiction of the Court.[50] The term 'interests of justice' is commonly used in legal drafting where it has proven impossible to provide any precise language in a situation where discretion and common sense must be exercised. An equally valid interpretation of the 'interests of justice' in article 53 would be that the Prosecutor is to consider a range of factors, including the risk that proceeding with arrest and trial might complicate rather than assist initiatives at peace-making.

In the policy paper, the Prosecutor noted that the ICC Statute creates 'a new legal framework' that 'necessarily impacts on conflict management efforts'.[51] He said: 'The issue is no longer about whether we agree or disagree with the pursuit of justice in moral or practical terms: it is the law. Any political or security initiative must be compatible with the new legal framework insofar as it involves parties bound by the Rome Statute.'[52] The proposition that the law has changed because of the ICC Statute implies that previous experiments with transitional justice, such as the South African experience, might no longer be acceptable. Indeed, this is what certain commentators have proposed.[53]

This may well be a step too far. The South African apartheid system has been at the core of international human rights activity since the 1960s. No other single issue (the Chilean junta and the Occupied Territories are close competitors) galvanized the human rights machinery of the United Nations. The South African experiment presents an extremely attractive model of peaceful transition from an oppressive, racist regime to a pluralist modern democracy. At its helm was the moral conscience of the modern world, Nelson Mandela. South Africa's approach is sometimes misunderstood. Although the Truth and Reconciliation Commission had the authority to grant amnesty in specific cases, there was a more global amnesty granted

---

[49]   UN Doc. S/RES/827 (1993); UN Doc. S/RES/955 (1994).
[50]   Rome Statute of the International Criminal Court, 2187 UNTS 90 (2002), art. 5(1).
[51]   *Policy Paper on the Interests of Justice* 4 (September 2007).
[52]   *Ibid.*
[53]   Marieka Weirda, *Truth Commissions, Accountability and the International Criminal Court*, in Willem J.M. van Genugten, Michael Scharf and Sasha E. Radin (eds), Criminal Jurisdiction 100 Years After the 1907 Hague Peace Conference 120–5 (The Hague, TMC Asser Press, 2009).

at the political level by which the overarching international offence of the previous regime, namely the crime against humanity of apartheid,[54] went unpunished. According to the report of the South African Truth and Reconciliation Commission:

> The definition of apartheid as a crime against humanity has given rise to a concern that persons who are seen to have been responsible for apartheid policies and practices might become liable to international prosecutions. The Commission believes that international recognition should be given to the fact that the Promotion of Unity and Reconciliation Act, and the processes of this Commission itself, have sought to deal appropriately with the matter of responsibility for such policies.[55]

It would appear that the international community has responded favourably to this appeal from the Truth and Reconciliation Commission. It has almost certainly done so not out of a sense of legal obligation but rather because of its willingness to accept the South African model. Otherwise, we would expect to find resolutions of the United Nations General Assembly calling for the creation of an international tribunal to deal with impunity for apartheid, as in the case of Cambodia under the Khmer Rouge, for example, or initiatives on the exercise of universal jurisdiction, as in the case of the Argentine dictatorship or the Guatemalan civil war. Why are there no credible initiatives to unleash the Security Council, or indictments by hyperactive national prosecutors, or calls for prosecution from the major international non-governmental organizations, to deal with what has amounted to total impunity for the paradigmatic human rights violation of the past half-century? This is explained by near-universal respect, indeed admiration, for the approach taken in the South African transition. In other words, the Prosecutor may have overstated the case when he declared that 'developments in the last ten or fifteen years point to a consistent trend imposing a duty on States to prosecute crimes of international concern committed within their jurisdiction'. Of course, there is no shortage of uncompromising statements from special rapporteurs and similar experts about the predominance of justice over peace. But the discourse seems contradicted by the practice of states and by international civil society in the case of South Africa. Where there is a credible transition process without criminal prosecution and which is associated with *de facto* or *de jure* amnesty, as in South Africa, such a process is met not with disdain but with general acceptance. The South African experience stands as a valuable and effective model, and it may prove helpful to other societies confronted with similar problems. To dismiss it would be a great shame.

PARALLEL COURTS AND TRUTH COMMISSIONS

International prosecution and truth commissions are often presented as alternatives. But it is not at all inconceivable that the two institutions operate contemporaneously and in parallel, each making its own contribution to accountability for gross and systematic violations of human rights or serious violations of international humanitarian law. Given that the

---

[54]   Convention on the Nonapplicability of Statutory Limitations to War Crimes and Crimes Against Humanity, 754 UNTS 73 (1970), art. 1(b); International Convention on the Suppression and Punishment of the Crime of Apartheid, 1015 UNTS 243 (1976), art. 1; Rome Statute of the International Criminal Court, 2187 UNTS 90 (2002), art. 7(1)(j).

[55]   5 *Truth and Reconciliation Commission Report* 349 (1998).

International Criminal Court now applies to the territory of more than 100 states, for the majority of the world's countries there is now no choice between the two. Truth commissions, in these cases at least, must labour under the watchful eye of the Prosecutor of the International Criminal Court. The Prosecutor has indicated that he sees a useful and positive role for truth commissions:

> The pursuit of criminal justice provides one part of the necessary response to serious crimes of international concern which, by itself, may prove to be insufficient as the Office is conducting focused investigations and prosecutions. As such, it fully endorses the complementary role that can be played by domestic prosecutions, truth seeking, reparations programs, institutional reform and traditional justice mechanisms in the pursuit of a broader justice. The Office notes the valuable role such measures may play in dealing with large numbers of offenders and in addressing the impunity gap.[56]

For this reason, attention should be paid to the relationship of international courts and truth commissions when they operate at the same time. The most developed model of this is probably the post-conflict justice process in Sierra Leone, where the Special Court for Sierra Leone and the Sierra Leone Truth and Reconciliation Commission operated alongside one another from 2002 to 2004.

Sierra Leone's Truth and Reconciliation Commission was a product of the Lomé Peace Agreement of 7 July 1999, a negotiated truce between the government of Sierra Leone and the rebel Revolutionary United Front.[57] As originally conceived, there was never any thought of defining how the Sierra Leone Truth and Reconciliation Commission would relate to criminal prosecutions. Given the amnesty clause in the Lomé Agreement, the Commission was presented as an alternative to prosecutions, not a complement to them. This changed a year later, and well before the Truth and Reconciliation Commission was formally established in July 2002. A resurgence in the conflict prompted Sierra Leone's President to request that the United Nations establish an international criminal tribunal.[58] The concept was immediately endorsed by the Security Council, which instructed the Secretary-General to negotiate an agreement between the United Nations and the government of Sierra Leone for the establishment of a court. The Preamble to the Security Council Resolution acknowledged the Commission's position within the overall context of post-conflict justice, noting 'the steps taken by the Government of Sierra Leone in creating a national truth and reconciliation process, as required by Article XXVI of the Lomé Peace Agreement (S/1999/777) to contribute to the promotion of the rule of law'.[59] The Security Council subsequently referred to the complementary role of the Truth and Reconciliation Commission within the overall context of post-conflict justice in Sierra Leone in its correspondence with the Secretary-General concerning establishment of the Special Court.[60] The Secretary-General shared the view that the Commission was a complementary institution to the SCSL, writing in a 2001

---

[56]   *Policy Paper on the Interests of Justice* 7–8 (September 2007).

[57]   Peace Agreement between the Government of Sierra Leone and the Revolutionary United Front of Sierra Leone, Lomé, 7 July 1999, art. XXVI.

[58]   Letter dated 9 August 2000 from the Permanent Representative of Sierra Leone to the United Nations addressed to the President of the Security Council, UN Doc. S/2000/786, Annex.

[59]   UN Doc. S/RES/1315 (2000).

[60]   Letter dated 22 December 2000 from the President of the Security Council addressed to the Secretary-General, UN Doc. S/2000/1234, at 1; Letter dated 31 January 2001 from the President of the Security Council addressed to the Secretary-General, UN Doc. S/2001/95.

report that '[t]hese two institutions are mutually reinforcing instruments through which impunity will be brought to an end and long-term reconciliation may be achieved'.[61] In a letter to the UN Security Council, dated 12 January 2001, the Secretary-General said that 'care must be taken to ensure that the Special Court for Sierra Leone and the Truth and Reconciliation Commission will operate in a complementary and mutually supportive manner, fully respectful of their distinct but related functions'.[62]

For about 18 months (the lifespan of the Truth and Reconciliation Commission), the two institutions operated in parallel. By sheer coincidence, they were located in neighbouring premises on Freetown's Jomo Kenyatta Road. Operating from different perspectives, both institutions attempted to investigate and understand the complex conflict that brought Sierra Leone to its knees during the 1990s. Although prior to the establishment of the two bodies, their relationship had received much attention within the United Nations and in NGO circles, the terms of this relationship was never clarified in any formal sense. Rather, a *modus vivendi* was achieved by which the Commission and the SCSL worked without major incident and with a public profile of cordiality. Both repeatedly explained to the people of Sierra Leone that there was no formal cooperation between the two bodies, but that they respected the role of the other institution and appreciated its contribution to post-conflict justice. Indeed, the complementary relationship was unblemished until, in the final months of the Truth and Reconciliation Commission's activities, a dispute arose.

In late 2003, three prisoners who had been indicted by the SCSL asked to testify in a public hearing before the Truth and Reconciliation Commission. The Prosecutor opposed the request, and ultimately the issue was litigated before judges of the SCSL. On 28 November 2003, the President of the Appeals Chamber, Geoffrey Robertson, gave each side 'half a loaf', ruling that the accused could testify, but not publicly.[63] His judgment now represents the principal judicial examination of the relationship between truth commissions and criminal prosecution and will doubtless influence future efforts at transitional justice where truth commissions and courts operate simultaneously.

Judge Robertson described the issue as a 'novel and difficult question', but also 'one that is likely to recur for other indictees and in other post-war situations where the local and international community considers that the establishment of both a Special Court and a Truth Commission will assist in the restoration of peace and justice'.[64] Citing its submissions on the motion, which underscored the importance of hearing Hinga Norman, Judge Robertson said: 'I endorse this claim, so far as it goes. The TRC certainly can have the indictee's evidence, if (and only if) he is prepared to take the risk of volunteering it.'[65] But Judge Robertson was not enamoured with the idea of any public hearing: 'There shall be no public hearing of the kind requested or any other kind prior to the conclusion of the trial.' He explained:

---

61   *Eleventh Report of the Secretary-General on the United Nations Mission in Sierra Leone*, UN Doc. S/2001/857, para. 66.

62   Letter dated 12 January 2001 from the Secretary-General addressed to the President of the Security Council, UN Doc. S/2001/40, para. 9.

63   *Prosecutor* v. *Norman*, Case No. SCSL-2003-08-PT, Decision on Appeal by the Truth and Reconciliation Commission for Sierra Leone and Chief Samuel Hinga Norman JP against the Decision of His Lordship, Mr Justice Bankole Thompson delivered on 30 October 2003 to Deny the TRC's Request to Hold a Public Hearing with Chief Samuel Hinga Norman JP, 28 November 2003.

64   *Ibid.* para. 2.

65   *Ibid.* para 19.

Let me return to first principles. Truth Commissions and International Courts are both instruments for effectuating the promise made by states that victims of human rights violations shall have an effective remedy. Criminal courts offer the most effective remedy – a trial, followed by punishment of those found guilty, in this case of those who bear the greatest responsibility. TRC reports can assist society to move forward and beyond the hatreds that fuelled the war. Truth commissions offer two distinct prospects for victims – of truth, i.e. learning how and why they or their loved ones were murdered or mutilated, and of reconciliation, through understanding and forgiveness of those perpetrators who genuinely confess and regret. It seems to me that these are separate and severable objectives.[66]

Judge Robertson concluded that '[t]he work of the Special Court and the TRC is complementary and each must accommodate the existence of the other'.[67] The denial of the application for a public hearing was not easy for the Commission to digest, and some saw it as a repudiation. In reality, while reasonable people might disagree with Judge Robertson's ruling, he sought a way to reconcile conflicting concerns and to allow the operations of both bodies to proceed.

That the two bodies concluded the period of their parallel operation with tension and conflict gives a misleading impression of the nature of their relationship. The final report of the Commission probably does not assist in this regard either, as it is the product of compromises within the organization between those with different assessments of the significance of the two institutions to post-conflict justice and reconciliation. In fact, the quarrel over testimony by indicted prisoners was the only significant dispute between the Truth and Reconciliation Commission and the Special Court. And it showed that when issues did arise between the two institutions, an appropriate mechanism and procedure could be devised to resolve differences. The real lesson of the Sierra Leone experiment is that truth commissions and courts can work productively together, even if they only work in parallel. This complementary relationship may have a synergistic effect on the search for post-conflict justice as part of the struggle against impunity.[68]

---

66   *Ibid.* para. 33 (reference omitted).
67   *Ibid.* para. 44.
68   The author, who was one of the three members of the Sierra Leone Truth and Reconciliation Commission who were not nationals of Sierra Leone, has developed some of these ideas in earlier publications, to which the reader is referred for a more thorough examination of these issues: William Schabas, *The Relationship Between Truth Commissions and International Courts: The Case of Sierra Leone*, 25 HUMAN RIGHTS QUARTERLY 1035 (2003); William Schabas, *'Internationalised' Courts and their Relationship with Alternative Accountability Mechanisms: The Case of Sierra Leone*, in PROCEEDINGS OF THE 31ST ANNUAL CONFERENCE OF THE CANADIAN COUNCIL ON INTERNATIONAL LAW, 322–50 (The Hague/London/New York, Kluwer Law International, 2004); William Schabas, *Addressing Impunity in Developing Countries: Lessons from Rwanda and Sierra Leone*, in HÉLÈNE DUMONT and ANNE-MARIE BOISVERT (eds), LA VOIE VERS LA COUR PÉNALE INTERNATIONALE: TOUS LES CHEMINS MÈNENT À ROME 159–78 (Montréal, Les Éditions Thémis, 2004); William Schabas, *Truth Commissions and Courts Working in Parallel: The Sierra Leone Experience*, PROCEEDINGS OF THE 98TH ANNUAL MEETING, AMERICAN SOCIETY OF INTERNATIONAL LAW 189 (2004); William Schabas, *Internationalised Courts and their Relationship with Alternative Accountability Mechanisms: The Case of Sierra Leone*, in CESARE P.R. ROMANO, ANDRÉ NOLLKAEMPER and JANN K. KLEFFNER (eds), INTERNATIONALISED CRIMINAL COURTS AND TRIBUNALS, SIERRA LEONE, EAST TIMOR, KOSOVO AND CAMBODIA 157–80 (Oxford University Press, 2004); William Schabas, *Conjoined Twins of Transitional Justice? The Sierra Leone Truth and Reconciliation Commission and the Special Court*, 2 J INTERNATIONAL CRIMINAL JUSTICE 1082 (2004).

Although accountability mechanisms, be they criminal court or truth commission or something in between, focus to a large extent on the role of individuals in the perpetration of atrocity, they also play an important role in clarifying the historical narrative of the conflict. One of the consequences of the operation of more than one transitional justice system is that different views of the historical facts may emerge. This seems to be the case in Sierra Leone. There are two widespread and competing explanations for the conflict in Sierra Leone, one that largely blames external forces – Liberia's Taylor, Libya's Gaddafi, and the international diamond smuggling mafias – and the other that focuses on internal causes – corruption, bad governance and the lingering legacies of colonialism. The Truth and Reconciliation Commission unequivocally opted for the second of these two visions in explaining the civil war's origins and causes. Its report explains that rebellion, driven by the country's frustrated and disillusioned youth, was probably the inexorable result of the post-colonial dictatorships. Regrettably, the 'rebels' had little if any ideological underpinning, and they soon fell into the same corrupt, abusive ways as those whom they had condemned and pledged to overthrow. The report notes that essentially all sides in the conflict were responsible for serious violations of human rights and international humanitarian law.

It would be misleading to suggest that the report of the Truth and Reconciliation Commission shifts the blame for violations and abuses of human rights and international humanitarian law away from the Revolutionary United Front (RUF), which launched the war in 1991. The Commission acknowledged that the majority of atrocities could be laid at the feet of the RUF and its recently deceased leader, Foday Sankoh. But the Commission did not subscribe to the 'just war' theory so fashionable in Sierra Leone's ruling circles, by which any means were acceptable in order to suppress the rebellion. Nor did it denounce the rebellion as an inherently perverse or negative development, given the wretched state of governance in Sierra Leone in the early 1990s. Furthermore, the atrocities committed by the pro-government Civilian Defence Forces (CDF), and notably by one subgroup of them known as the *Kamajors*, were on a par with the worst the RUF had to offer.

A rather different perspective emerges from the judgments of the Special Court for Sierra Leone. The Prosecutor had taken some care to adopt a somewhat balanced approach, with three of the 13 indictments directed at leaders of the pro-government CDF.[69] However, the detailed description of the charges in the indictments tended to emphasize the role of external factors, including Libyan President Muammar al-Gaddafi, whose role had not been deemed to be of any real significance by the Truth and Reconciliation Commission. The first trial judgments of the Special Court reinforce the 'just war' approach, which had been dismissed by the Truth and Reconciliation Commission. Thus, although two of the leaders of the CDF were convicted (the third, Hinga Norman, died in custody before the end of the trial) of war crimes and crimes against humanity, they were sentenced to relatively insignificant terms of imprisonment of six and eight years.[70] By contrast, the three leaders of the Armed Forces Revolutionary Council were convicted and sentenced to terms of 45 and 50 years. The Trial Chamber considered the support of the CDF for the democratically elected regime to be

---

[69] *Prosecutor* v. *Norman*, Case No. SCSL-03-08-I, Indictment, 7 March 2003; *Prosecutor* v. *Fofana*, Case No. SCSL-03-11-I, Indictment, 7 March 2003; *Prosecutor* v. *Kondewa*, Case No. SCSL-03-12-I, Indictment, 24 June 2003; *Prosecutor* v. *Norman et al.*, Case No. SCSL-04-14-I, Consolidated Indictment, 4 February 2004.

[70] *Prosecutor* v. *Fofana et al.*, Case No. SCSL-04-14-T, Judgment, 2 August 2007.

an important mitigating factor.[71] One of the three judges on the Trial Chamber voted to acquit the defendants altogether.[72] He took the view that their defence of a democratic regime essentially excused their crimes, a position that may be politically popular among some elements in Sierra Leone but that is utterly untenable from the standpoint of international criminal law.

CONCLUSION

Some uncertainty shrouds issues relating to the relationship of international criminal tribunals, such as the International Criminal Court, and other accountability mechanisms such as truth and reconciliation commissions. As John Dugard has written, the law is, 'to put it mildly, unsettled'.[73] Where truth and reconciliation commissions are proposed as a substitute for prosecution, this may amount to *de facto* amnesty. There is a growing trend in international law and policy to condemn measures that stay the hand of criminal justice. Recognized sources of international law are equivocal on this point, and it is difficult to demonstrate that amnesty is prohibited as a question of international law. The provisions of the ICC Statute may be applied in either direction, depending upon the discretion of the Prosecutor and the assessment by judges of vague concepts such as 'gravity' and 'social unrest'.

---

[71]   *Prosecutor* v. *Fofana et al.*, Case No. SCSL-04-14-T, Judgment on the Sentencing of Moinina Fofana and Allieu Kondewa, 9 October 2007, paras 80, 86.

[72]   *Prosecutor* v. *Fofana et al.*, Case No. SCSL-04-14-T, Separate Concurring and Partially Dissenting Opinion of Hon. Justice Bankole Thompson filed pursuant to art. 18 of the Statute, 2 August 2007.

[73]   John Dugard, *Dealing with Crimes of a Past Regime: Is Amnesty Still an Option?*, 12 LEIDEN J INTERNATIONAL L 1001, 1015 (1999).

17 Dancing in the dark – politics, law and peace in Sierra Leone: a case study

David M. Crane

INTRODUCTION

It was a hot and humid day in Liberia. Tension electrified the humid and fetid air. At the base of the stairs of an Air Nigeria plane stood the recently defrocked President of Liberia, Charles Ghankay Taylor. He seemed stunned. Pale, trying to maintain his composure, he spoke with halting words, seemingly trying to say something significant at this historic moment in the life of West Africa. At the end of his brief remarks to the media gathered around him, he boldly stated, '… and God willing, I'll be back'. This indicted war criminal then turned and walked up the stairs for a flight to the seaside town of Calabar, Nigeria, escorted by various supporting Presidents from all over Africa. They almost seemed to be shielding him from something that even they could not understand. As the plane lifted off into the rain-laden clouds, the end of a ten-year reign of terror began to unravel. Had the rule of law finally proved to be more powerful than the rule of the gun? No one was sure, but the words Taylor spoke rang clearly in our minds and in the minds of the people of West Africa: 'I'll be back.'[1]

Fast forward almost three years later to a sleepy university town in Ontario. It was a bright clear day. I was the guest of the faculty of law at the University of Western Ontario to speak about my time as the Chief Prosecutor of the Special Court for Sierra Leone (SCSL), the world's first hybrid international war crimes tribunal. Throughout the day, I had been monitoring important events in West Africa as the indicted former President of Liberia was handed over by the President of Nigeria to the newly elected President of Liberia, who promptly handed him over to the United Nations peace-keepers for transfer to the Special Court.

It had been a long day as my cell phone had been ringing since 4 a.m. that morning from contacts in West Africa informing me that an allegedly 'missing' Taylor had been found and was finally being handed over for trial. As the world woke up, the press began to reach out for my reaction. It was, after all, my name on the indictment. I was the one who had taken down the most powerful warlord in Africa with the stroke of my pen on 3 March 2003.[2] Around noon, I received a call from my former Deputy Prosecutor, the current Chief Prosecutor, briefing me about his perspectives on the transfer. He assured me he would have someone contact me the moment Charles Taylor entered the compound of the SCSL in Freetown, Sierra Leone. Later that afternoon, I was giving my main speech to the students of the university when my cell phone vibrated on my hip. It was my former special assistant and

---

[1]   I sat at my headquarters watching this dramatic scene play out in front of the world on CNN in Freetown, Sierra Leone, the country next to Liberia.

[2]   *Prosecutor* v. *Taylor*, Case No. SCSL-03-01-I, Indictment, 7 March 2003, see Appendix A to this chapter.

political adviser, Harpinder Atwahl, telling me that the helicopter had landed, and Taylor was stepping out of it, heading for his cell. In the background, thousands of Sierra Leoneans cheered in the hills and rooftops surrounding the Court compound. I thanked her and hung up. I then announced to the audience that Charles Taylor was now in the custody of the Special Court for Sierra Leone. The audience cheered. It was a great day for the rule of law.[3]

At the end of the day, the basis for the handover of former President Charles Taylor was not a legal decision, but a political one. It was all about politics, the bright red thread that runs through any international legal process. International courts and tribunals are essentially creatures of political events, such as internal armed conflict, and of political compromise, usually at the United Nations Security Council, after much debate and consideration. This certainly was the case in West Africa, a region of the world in the grip of one of the world's most notorious joint criminal enterprises that literally spanned a vast majority of the world.[4] A ten-year civil war within Sierra Leone and its corollary conflict in Liberia was sucking the lifeblood out of the sad string of corrupt and tenuous governments, ranging from Senegal in the West to Nigeria in the East.[5] Two countries were destroyed with a third beginning to feel the political heat.[6] It had to stop. President Tejan Kabbah reached out to the UN Secretary-General seeking assistance with an immediate deployment of a peace enforcement package to bolster the faltering Lomé Peace Accords signed by the warring parties in 1999.[7]

After a year-long planning process, authorized by the Security Council, a new type of justice mechanism was created. Unlike the other ad hoc international criminal tribunals, this new 'hybrid' court would be a joint venture between the United Nations and the government of Sierra Leone. As such, its jurisdiction and its composition would involve both international and Sierra Leonean elements and individuals.[8] The frustrated and skeptical Security Council also wanted a more efficient and effective method to deal with the atrocities that took place in Sierra Leone and drafted a mandate that would be politically acceptable to the Council

---

[3]   I had told the audience of around 300 people that I might be getting that fateful phone call and that I intended to take it even in the middle of my speech.

[4]   Joint criminal enterprise holds an individual responsible for committing acts with others that follow a 'common plan, design or purpose which amounts to or involves the commission of a crime'. *Prosecutor v. Kupreskic et al.*, Case No. IT-95-16-T, ICTY Trial Chamber, Judgment, 14 January 2000, para. 772; *Prosecutor v. Vasiljevic*, Case No. IT-98-32-T, ICTY Trial Chamber, Judgment, 29 November 2002), cited in Allison Marston Danner and Jenny S. Martinez, *Guilty Associations: Joint Criminal Enterprise, Command Responsibility and the Development of International Criminal Law* 26 n. 103 (Vanderbilt Univ. Law School, Public. Law and Legal Theory Working Paper Series, Working Paper No. 04-09; Stanford Law School, Public Law and Legal Theory Working Paper Series, Research Paper No. 87, 2004).

[5]   For an overview of the conflict, see David Pratt, *Sierra Leone: The Forgotten Crisis*, available at www.globalsecurity.org/military/library/report/1999/crisis-e.htm. For a more detailed history of the 11-year civil war, see Babafemi Akinrinade, *International Humanitarian Law and the Conflict in Sierra Leone*, 15 NOTRE DAME JL ETHICS AND PUB. POL'Y 391 (2001).

[6]   The third country was Cote d'Ivoire.

[7]   Letter from Ahmad Tejan Kabbah, President of Sierra Leone, to Secretary-General Kofi Annan, UN Doc. S/2000/786 (12 June 2000) Annex; Lomé Peace Agreement between the Government of Sierra Leone and the Revolutionary United Front of Sierra Leone, 7 July 1999, available at www.usip.org/library/pa/sl/sierra_leone_07071999_toc.html.

[8]   Agreement between the United Nations and the Government of Sierra Leone on the Establishment of a Special Court for Sierra Leone, arts 1, 2 (16 January 2002).

itself, the region and the combatants.[9] The political compromise turned out to be a mandate of 'greatest responsibility' for what was now called the Special Court for Sierra Leone.[10] It would be the debut for this limited and more realistic *in personem* jurisdiction.[11] Absent these two key words in the mandate, this new justice mechanism would not have seen the light of day. Politics created the Court and its mandate, and it was the chaff that blew about during my time as Chief Prosecutor.

In this chapter, I will highlight the bright red thread of politics that bound the activities of the SCSL, both chronologically, and then by topic, and then end with some reflections.

THE BEGINNING

Greatest responsibility. There was concern that the creation of a West African justice mechanism would evolve into an endless and expensive proposition, reflective of the challenge faced by the various ad hoc tribunals. To address this concern, many states and permanent representatives on the Security Council ensured that there was only a very narrowly defined mandate. Greatest responsibility would evolve to be the standard, and in my mind, was correctly drafted. It is important to reflect at this point that politics plays an important role in the implementation of justice and can temper the passion surrounding these tragic events in a way that injects reality as to what can be accomplished. This reality was produced in the deliberations regarding this new West African model.

Temporal jurisdiction. Closely related to the mandate and the subject matter of the SCSL, drafters also wanted to narrow the time period in which the Prosecutor could consider various crimes. It reflected a political decision tailored to speed the process along and save money for donors. Hence, the temporal jurisdiction would begin on 30 November 1996, the day of the signing of the Abidjan Peace Accords.[12]

An American Chief Prosecutor. As the creation of the SCSL moved forward, the United States began to maneuver to ensure that the first Chief Prosecutor of the Court would be an American.[13] The Bush administration pushed hard for this, even using the personal intervention of then-Secretary of State Colin Powell.[14] The Americans did not want to lose control of the process.[15] However, the law requires that the Prosecutor can seek neither counsel nor

---

[9] Statute of the Special Court for Sierra Leone (16 January 2002).

[10] See *Report of the Secretary-General to the Security Council on the Establishment of a Special Court for Sierra Leone*, UN Doc. S/2000/915 (4 October 2000).

[11] SSCSL Statute, art. 15.

[12] *Ibid.* art. 15; Abidjan Peace Accords between the Government of the Republic of Sierra Leone and the Revolutionary United Front of Sierra Leone, 30 November 1996, available at www.usip.org/library/pa/sl/sierra_leone_11301996.html.

[13] Emails from US government officials to David Crane, Department of Defense (January 2002) (on file with author).

[14] *Ibid.*

[15] Ironically, they were not happy when their nominee was too successful in taking down the entire joint criminal enterprise in West Africa, indicting a Head of State, and threatening to indict two others. At one point, President Bush tried to remove me as the Chief Prosecutor, but was checked by a constitutionally equal branch of the government. The US Congress was a bipartisan supporter throughout the process and took action to block these efforts by the Administration. Emails from US government officials to David Crane, Department of Defense (January 2002) (on file with author).

advice from any person or entity related to the prosecutions. I took that standard very seriously, and no country, politician or diplomat ever approached me on how to charge any person in the process.

The Prosecution Plan. After my appointment in April 2002, I finalized a ten-phased prosecution plan that would carry out the prosecution of those who bore the greatest responsibility. I unveiled its general parameters to the world at the US Institute of Peace in Washington, DC the following month. I invited governmental and non-governmental agencies, civil society, and others to ensure that they felt included in our work. My intent was to work together towards a common goal, ensuring that all the stakeholders were comfortable with where the prosecution was headed.

THE MIDDLE

Fund-raising. A lack of funds was (and still is) the 'sword of Damocles' that hung over the SCSL's leadership. Monetary assistance was the mechanism with with interested states could exert their influence and shape, to the extent they legally could, the direction of the Court. This function consumed the majority of my time once the prosecution plan was in place.

Political hand-holding. Closely tied to fundraising is the time needed to talk to key players, domestically, regionally and internationally. I traveled a great deal, ensuring that the political stakeholders achieved a certain comfort level. They needed to be assured that matters were under control and that they had some type of input in the process. Though I never discussed the actual investigation or cases, I ensured that those politicians understood various perspectives and responded to their questions. At the end of the day, I would spend 70 percent of my time fund-raising and meeting political stakeholders from across the spectrum.

Charging. Both civil society and the international community had concerns as to who actually bore the greatest responsibility. My sense was that most of the constituents, particularly at the regional and international level, wanted a quick and narrowly focused investigation and trial of a few local boy generals and rebel leaders. Civil society, on the other hand, wanted a more expansive prosecution that would also target what I called regional monsters, just below those who at the national and regional level bore the greatest responsibility. Finally, we had the major players in the guise of the United States, the United Kingdom and the United Nations, that were not interested in seeing a Head of State indicted, even though they clearly put the legal capability to do so in the SCSL's mandate.[16] I considered and weighed the law, the facts, and the politics before I finally settled on the 13 who were eventually charged.[17] It is important to point out that there was reliable and sufficient evidence to

---

[16]   SCSL Statute, art. 1.

[17]   RUF leaders Foday Sankoh, Sam Bockarie, Issa Hassan Sesay, Morris Kallon and Augustine Gbao; CDF leaders Sam Hinga Norman, Moinina Fofana and Allieu Kondewa; AFRC leaders Johnny Paul Koroma, Alex Tamba Brima, Brima Bazzy Kamara, and Santigie Borbor Kanu; Liberian President Charles Taylor. The charges against Sankoh and Bockarie were dropped after their deaths were confirmed. The trial against Norman was terminated after his death in 2007. Koroma is the only indictee not detained, although reports indicate he was killed in 2003, and the SCSL is awaiting forensic data on remains discovered by investigators. Tanu Jalloh, *Sierra Leone: Johnny Paul's Dead Body Found in Liberia*, CONCORD TIMES, 11 September 2008.

charge three sitting Heads of State, but I only chose to indict the most directly culpable as I feared that the political 'blow back' would end the Court's work. Thus, the Presidents of Libya and Burkina Faso were not indicted.

The Truth and Reconciliation Commission. A body created domestically, pursuant to the Lomé Peace Accords in 1999, the Truth and Reconciliation Commission (TRC) was initially the only mechanism that would hold accountable those who destroyed Sierra Leone. About a year later, President Kabbah sought other forms of accountability in the shape of a court.[18] When I became Chief Prosecutor, I felt that this was a unique political opportunity for me. I had always believed that you had to have both truth and justice to create a sustainable and long-term peace in a society transitioning from war. I was determined that it could happen in Sierra Leone and worked hard to do just that for the entire life of the TRC. Despite the initial rocky start of the TRC and the political naivety of its first executive director, Bishop Joe Humper and I became both colleagues and friends, each of us doing our work in bringing Sierra Leone back from the brink. Bishop Humper was always fond of saying to me: 'David, we are two pilgrims traveling on different paths towards the same goal … Jerusalem.'

Charles Taylor. I recall handing to a very surprised Assistant Secretary of State and the American Ambassador to Sierra Leone the signed indictment of Charles Taylor at the Ambassador's house in April 2003. I would eventually discreetly show the document to other interested parties to ensure that the international community would realize that the first indictment of a Head of State in Africa for war crimes and crimes against humanity was completed. It was all part of a plan to focus the world's attention on the civil war in Africa and on President Charles Taylor's role in this ten-year tragedy that saw the destruction of two countries and the murder, rape, maiming and mutilation of approximately 1.2 million human beings.[19]

The unsealing of the indictment against Charles Taylor was purely political. It was my intent to shame and embarrass him before his peers, the several African Presidents in attendance at the Accra Peace Conference, and to show the people of Africa that, at the stroke of a pen, the most powerful warlord in Africa could be brought down. It was high stakes international politics and, in my mind, it worked.[20]

THE END?

Getting Taylor. Of course, the international community, particularly the African community, was not prepared for the unsealing of the indictment against President Charles Taylor. It reacted in shock and anger that a 'minor American bureaucrat' would have the audacity to indict one of their own for international crimes, as they hustled him off to Calabar.[21] I never

---

[18]   Letter from Ahmad Tejan Kabbah, President of Sierra Leone, to Secretary-General Kofi Annan, UNDoc. S/2000/786 (12 June 2000) Annex.

[19]   Interview by NPR with David Crane, *Charles Taylor's Lasting Impact on West Africa* (4 June 2007).

[20]   See Appendix A to this chapter for the original indictment against President Charles Taylor, signed on 3 March 2003.

[21]   See Elizabeth Blunt, *Taylor's New Nigerian Home*, BBC, 11 Sugust 2003, available at http://news.bbc.co.uk/2/hi/africa/3142101.stm.

expected to see an immediate handover, as I knew the decision to hand Taylor over would be purely a political decision, not a legal one.[22] Yet, I did not think it would take almost three years.[23]

The political build-up. Our next step was to continue to build the case against Charles Taylor internationally. I traveled extensively, giving interviews to the press, meeting with civil society, and discussing Taylor's handover with various political leaders. Privately, almost everyone wanted him turned over for a fair trial, but publicly they had to be politically careful as the combined influence of the United States, the United Kingdom and Nigeria was daunting and very problematic. I learned that patience is a virtue, something I did not know I possessed, at least not to this extent.

In the first year, we perfected the indictment, built interest through the media and public speeches, and sought an international arrest warrant via Interpol. We also began to quietly go through Taylor's possessions at the White Dove plantation and follow his various bank accounts, seizing monies where we could. In February 2005, I sent my Deputy Prosecutor to work with the European Union to seek a resolution calling for Taylor's handover. Our intent was to build up the political base in Europe before going to the United Nations and the United States.

In late February, the European Parliament passed a resolution 95 to 0 calling for an immediate handover of Taylor and for the United Nations Security Council to seize themselves of the matter to effect the handover.[24] In April, I sent my Chief of Investigations to begin working with the US Congress and its relevant committees to draft a joint resolution calling for Nigeria to hand over Taylor. While he was there in Washington, I traveled to the United Nations and spent a month working with the members of the Security Council and other interested states, such as Canada and the Netherlands, to have the Taylor issue put on the Agenda for review and consideration in May. We had chosen the month of May because Denmark would be in the role of President of the Security Council. We had worked for six months previously to get the Danes to agree to champion our cause, which they did.

At the end of May, the Security Council issued a declaration that Taylor needed to face justice for what he had done in West Africa and seized themselves of the matter to ensure that this happened.[25] The vote was 15 to 0.[26] Each permanent representative spoke on the matter,

---

[22]   See Appendix B to this chaper regarding Senator Patrick Leahy's address to the President of the Senate in support of the author's action.

[23]   See Craig Timberg, *A Warlord's Exile Divides His Hosts*, WASHINGTON POST, 9 October 2005, available at www.washingtonpost.com/wp-dyn/content/article/2005/10/08/AR2005100801243.html; *Liberia to Nigeria: Hand Over Charles Taylor*, CNN, 17 March 2006, available at www.cnn.com/2006/WORLD/africa/03/17/liberia.taylor/index.html; *Nigeria Agrees to Hand Taylor Over to Liberia*, CNN, 25 March 2006, available at http://www.cnn.com/2006/WORLD/africa/03/25/taylor.liberia/index.html.

[24]   Resolution on the Special Court for Sierra Leone: Case of Charles Taylor, paras. 1, 6, Eur. Parl. Doc. B6-0136/05 (21 February 2005), available at www.europarl.europa.eu/sides/getDoc.do?type=MOTION&reference=B6-2005-0136&language=EN.

[25]   UN Security Council President, Press statement, Special Court for Sierra Leone, UN Doc. SC/8392, AFR/1167 (24 May 2005); see also Security Council Res. 1638, UN Doc. S/Res/1638 (11 November 2005).

[26]   The author was present when this vote was taken on 23 May 2005.

many calling for an immediate handover for trial.[27] Shortly thereafter, the US Congress called on the Bush administration to work to have Taylor turned over immediately for trial as well.[28] In the House of Representatives, the vote was 421 to 1 in favor; in the Senate it was unanimous consent.[29] The platform of political will to get Nigeria to hand over Taylor was in place. It would take another several months and a key regional election to make it happen, but it did, barely.[30]

The handover. In the end, it was my understanding that it took a message from President Bush via his national security adviser to the visiting President of Nigeria requiring that the latter find and turn Taylor over immediately or President Bush would not see him the next day at the White House.[31] Two hours later, the 'missing' Taylor was found, seized in Nigeria heading for Cameroon (and back to Lofa County in Liberia).[32] Later, Taylor was turned over to the Liberians and then was handed over to security personnel from the SCSL.[33]

CONCLUDING THOUGHTS

It is a naive prosecutor that does not understand the role that politics and diplomacy play in a successful prosecution. A prosecutor is not only a lawyer, but a manager, leader, visionary, in some ways an evangelist, as well as a politician and diplomat. When all is said and done, it is politics that threatens the very existence of the tribunal and determines its place in history, as well as how the victims and public perceive whether justice has been done.

---

[27]   See generally Laolu Akande, *UN Mandates Taylor's Arrest in Liberia*, THE GUARDIAN, 13 November 2005, reprinted in Open Society Justice Initiative, available at www.justiceinitiative.org/db/resource2?res_id=103016.

[28]   H.R. Con. Res. 127, 109th Cong. (2005). Specifically, Representatives Frank R. Wolf from Virginia, Tom Lantos from California, Ed Royce from California, Henry J. Hyde from Illinois, Chris Smith from New Jersey, Sue Kelly from New York, Betty McCollum from Minnesota, Vic Snyder from Arkansas and Dianne Watson from California, and Senators Patrick J. Leahy from Vermont, Lincoln Chafee from Rhode Island, Barack Obama from Illinois, Jack Reed from Rhode Island and Russ Feingold from Wisconsin were instrumental in compelling the Administration to put pressure on Nigeria. See U.S. Lawmakers Call for Action on Liberia's Charles Taylor, Washington File (Bureau of International Information Programs, 16 December 2005), available at http://news.findlaw./com/wash/s/20051215/200512151801341.html..

[29]   See clerk.house.gov/evs/2005/roll155.xml; http://www.govtrack.us/congress/bill.xpd?bill=hc109-127.

[30]   Liberia held elections on 11 October 2005, electing Africa's first female head of state, Ellen Johnson-Sirleaf. See generally David S. Belt, *Liberia's Uneasy Peace*, PBS Online NewsHour, 15 November 2005; *Dispute in Liberia Over Taylor Handover*, Voice of America, 24 March 2006, available at www.voanews.com/english/archive/2006-03/2006-03-24-voa48.cfm.

[31]   Personal discussion between author and Sir Desmond DeSilva, London (June 2008); *President Bush Welcomes President OBasanjo of Nigeria to the White House*, White House Press release, 29 March 2006; see generally *Nigeria Agrees to Hand Taylor Over to Liberia*, CNN, 25 March 2006, available at www.cnn.com/2006/WORLD/africa/03/25/taylor.liberia.index.html.

[32]   Lydia Polgreen, *Liberian Warlord Charles Taylor Caught in Nigeria*, INTERNATIONAL HERALD TRIBUNE, 29 March 2006, available at www.iht.com/articles/2006/03/29/africa/web.0329taylor.php.

[33]   *Liberia's Ex-Leader Handed Over for War Crimes Trial*, THE GUARDIAN, 30 March 2006.

We do very little in factoring in all this in selecting the leadership of a tribunal. In most instances, the UN Secretary-General has gotten it right; in some, he has not. The reality is that we have been lucky. It is clear that, in the future, the afore-mentioned traits must be considered in selecting a Chief Prosecutor who dutifully does the will of the various constituents, while considering and utilizing politics to the advantage of justice.

APPENDIX A

Prosecutor v. Charles Ghankay Taylor, Case No. SCSL-03-1, Special Court for Sierra Leone, Charles Ghankay Macarthur Dapkpana Taylor Indictment, 3 March 2003, David M. Crane, Prosecutor

The Prosecutor, Special Court for Sierra Leone, under article 15 of the Statute of the Special Court for Sierra Leone (the Statute) charges Charles Ghankay Taylor also known as (aka) Charles Ghankay Macarthur Dapkpana Taylor with crimes against humanity, violations of Article 3 common to the Geneva Conventions and of Additional Protocol II and other serious violations of international humanitarian law, in violation of Articles 2, 3 and 4 of the Statute as set forth below:

The Accused

1. Charles Ghankay Taylor also known as (aka) Charles Ghankay Macarthur Dapkpana Taylor (the Accused) was born on or about 28 January 1948 at Arthington in the Republic of Liberia.

General allegations

2. At all times relevant to this Indictment, a state of armed conflict existed within Sierra Leone. For the purposes of this Indictment, organized armed factions involved in this conflict included the Revolutionary United Front (RUF), the Civil Defence Forces (CDF) and the Armed Forces Revolutionary Council (AFRC).

3. A nexus existed between the armed conflict and all acts or omissions charged herein as Violations of Article 3 common to the Geneva Conventions and of Additional Protocol II and as Other Serious Violations of International Humanitarian Law.

4. The organized armed group that became known as the RUF, led by Foday Saybana Sankoh aka Popay aka Papa aka Pa, was founded about 1988 or 1989 in Libya. The RUF, under the leadership of Foday Saybana Sankoh, began organized armed operations in Sierra Leone in March 1991. During the ensuing armed conflict, the RUF forces were also referred to as 'RUF', 'rebels' and 'People's Army'.

5. The CDF was comprised of Sierra Leonean traditional hunters, including the Kamajors, Gbethis, Kapras, Tamaboros and Donsos. The CDF fought against the RUF and AFRC.

6. On 30 November 1996, in Abidjan, Ivory Coast, Foday Saybana Sankoh and Ahmed Tejan Kabbah, President of the Republic of Sierra Leone, signed a peace agreement which brought a temporary cessation to active hostilities. Thereafter, the active hostilities recommenced.

7. The AFRC was founded by members of the Armed Forces of Sierra Leone who seized power from the elected government of the Republic of Sierra Leone via a coup d'état on 25

May 1997. Soldiers of the Sierra Leone Army (SLA) comprised the majority of the AFRC membership. On that date Johnny Paul Koroma aka JPK became the leader and Chairman of the AFRC. The AFRC forces were also referred to as 'Junta', 'soldiers', 'SLA', and 'ex-SLA'.

8. Shortly after the AFRC seized power, at the invitation of Johnny Paul Koroma, and upon the order of Foday Saybana Sankoh, leader of the RUF, the RUF joined with the AFRC. The AFRC and RUF acted jointly thereafter. The AFRC/RUF Junta forces (Junta) were also referred to as 'Junta', 'rebels', 'soldiers', 'SLA', 'ex-SLA' and 'People's Army'.

9. After the 25 May 1997 coup d'état, a governing body, the Supreme Council, was created within the Junta. The governing body included leaders of both the AFRC and RUF.

10. The Junta was forced from power by forces acting on behalf of the ousted government of President Kabbah about 14 February 1998. President Kabbah's government returned in March 1998. After the Junta was removed from power the AFRC/RUF alliance continued.

11. On 7 July 1999, in Lomé, Togo, Foday Saybana Sankoh and Ahmed Tejan Kabbah, President of the Republic of Sierra Leone, signed a peace agreement. However, active hostilities continued.

12. The Accused and all members of the organized armed factions engaged in fighting within Sierra Leone were required to abide by International Humanitarian Law and the laws and customs governing the conduct of armed conflicts, including the Geneva Conventions of 12 August 1949, and Additional Protocol II to the Geneva Conventions, to which the Republic of Sierra Leone acceded on 21 October 1986.

13. All offences alleged herein were committed within the territory of Sierra Leone after 30 November 1996.

14. All acts and omissions charged herein as Crimes Against Humanity were committed as part of a widespread or systematic attack directed against the civilian population of Sierra Leone.

15. The words civilian or civilian population used in this Indictment refer to persons who took no active part in the hostilities, or who were no longer taking an active part in the hostilities.

Individual criminal responsibility

16. Paragraphs 1 through 15 are incorporated by reference.

17. In the late 1980's Charles Ghankay Taylor received military training in Libya from representatives of the Government of Mu'ammar Al-Qadhafi. While in Libya the Accused met and made common cause with Foday Saybana Sankoh.

18. While in Libya, the Accused formed or joined the National Patriotic Front of Liberia (NPFL). At all times relevant to this Indictment the Accused was the leader of the NPFL and/or the President of the Republic of Liberia.

19. In December 1989 the NPFL, led by the Accused, began conducting organized armed attacks in Liberia. The Accused and the NPFL were assisted in these attacks by Foday Saybana Sankoh and his followers.

20. To obtain access to the mineral wealth of the Republic of Sierra Leone, in particular the diamond wealth of Sierra Leone, and to destabilize the State, the Accused provided financial support, military training, personnel, arms, ammunition and other support and encouragement to the RUF, led by Foday Saybana Sankoh, in preparation for RUF armed action in the Republic of Sierra Leone, and during the subsequent armed conflict in Sierra Leone.

21. Throughout the course of the armed conflict in Sierra Leone, the RUF and the AFRC/RUF alliance, under the authority, command and control of Foday Saybana Sankoh, Johnny Paul Koroma and other leaders of the RUF, AFRC and AFRC/RUF alliance, engaged in notorious, widespread or systematic attacks against the civilian population of Sierra Leone.

22. At all times relevant to this Indictment, Charles Ghankay Taylor supported and encouraged all actions of the RUF and AFRC/RUF alliance, and acted in concert with Foday Saybana Sankoh and other leaders of the RUF and AFRC/RUF alliance. Foday Saybana Sankoh was incarcerated in Nigeria and Sierra Leone and subjected to restricted movement in Sierra Leone from about March 1997 until about April 1999. During this time the Accused, in concert with Foday Saybana Sankoh, provided guidance and direction to the RUF, including Sam Bockarie aka Mosquito aka Maskita.

23. The RUF and the AFRC shared a common plan, purpose or design (joint criminal enterprise) which was to take any actions necessary to gain and exercise political power and control over the territory of Sierra Leone, in particular the diamond mining areas. The natural resources of Sierra Leone, in particular the diamonds, were to be provided to persons outside Sierra Leone in return for assistance in carrying out the joint criminal enterprise.

24. The joint criminal enterprise included gaining and exercising control over the population of Sierra Leone in order to prevent or minimize resistance to their geographic control, and to use members of the population to provide support to the members of the joint criminal enterprise. The crimes alleged in this Indictment, including unlawful killings, abductions, forced labour, physical and sexual violence, use of child soldiers, looting and burning of civilian structures, were either actions within the joint criminal enterprise or were a reasonably foreseeable consequence of the joint criminal enterprise.

25. The Accused participated in this joint criminal enterprise as part of his continuing efforts to gain access to the mineral wealth of Sierra Leone and to destabilize the Government of Sierra Leone.

26. Charles Ghankay Taylor, by his acts or omissions, is individually criminally responsible pursuant to Article 6.1. of the Statute for the crimes referred to in Articles 2, 3 and 4 of the Statute as alleged in this Indictment, which crimes the Accused planned, instigated, ordered, committed or in whose planning, preparation or execution the Accused otherwise aided and abetted, or which crimes were within a joint criminal enterprise in which the Accused participated or were a reasonably foreseeable consequence of the joint criminal enterprise in which the Accused participated.

27. In addition, or alternatively, pursuant to Article 6.3. of the Statute, Charles Ghankay Taylor, while holding positions of superior responsibility and exercising command and control over his subordinates, is individually criminally responsible for the crimes referred to in Articles 2, 3 and 4 of the Statute. The Accused is responsible for the criminal acts of his subordinates in that he knew or had reason to know that the subordinate was about to commit such acts or had done so and the Accused failed to take the necessary and reasonable measures to prevent such acts or to punish the perpetrators thereof.

Charges

28. Paragraphs 16 through 27 are incorporated by reference.

29. At all times relevant to this Indictment, members of the RUF, AFRC, Junta and/or AFRC/RUF forces (AFRC/RUF), supported and encouraged by, acting in concert with and/or subordinate to Charles Ghankay Taylor, conducted armed attacks throughout the territory of

the Republic of Sierra Leone, including, but not limited, to Bo, Kono, Kenema, Bombali and Kailahun Districts and Freetown. Targets of the armed attacks included civilians and humanitarian assistance personnel and peacekeepers assigned to the United Nations Mission in Sierra Leone (UNAMSIL), which had been created by United Nations Security Council Resolution 1270 (1999).

30. These attacks were carried out primarily to terrorize the civilian population, but also were used to punish the population for failing to provide sufficient support to the AFRC/RUF, or for allegedly providing support to the Kabbah government or to pro-government forces. The attacks included unlawful killings, physical and sexual violence against civilian men, women and children, abductions and looting and destruction of civilian property. Many civilians saw these crimes committed; others returned to their homes or places of refuge to find the results of these crimes – dead bodies, mutilated victims and looted and burnt property.

31. As part of the campaign of terror and punishment the AFRC/RUF routinely captured and abducted members of the civilian population. Captured women and girls were raped; many of them were abducted and used as sex slaves and as forced labour. Some of these women and girls were held captive for years. Men and boys who were abducted were also used as forced labour; some of them were also held captive for years. Many abducted boys and girls were given combat training and used in active fighting. AFRC/RUF also physically mutilated men, women and children, including amputating their hands or feet and carving 'AFRC' and 'RUF' on their bodies.

Counts 1–2: Terrorizing the civilian population and collective punishments

32. Members of the AFRC/RUF supported and encouraged by, acting in concert with and/or subordinate to Charles Ghankay Taylor committed the crimes set forth below in paragraphs 33 through 58 and charged in Counts 3 through 13, as part of a campaign to terrorize the civilian population of the Republic of Sierra Leone, and did terrorize that population. The AFRC/RUF also committed the crimes to punish the civilian population for allegedly supporting the elected government of President Ahmed Tejan Kabbah and factions aligned with that government, or for failing to provide sufficient support to the AFRC/RUF. By his acts or omissions in relation, but not limited to these events, Charles Ghankay Taylor pursuant to Article 6.1 and, or alternatively, Article 6.3 of the Statute, is individually criminally responsible for the crimes alleged below:

Count 1: Acts of Terrorism, a violation of Article 3 common to the Geneva Conventions and of Additional Protocol II punishable under Article 3.d of the Statute; and

Count 2: Collective Punishments, a violation of Article 3 common to the Geneva Conventions and of Additional Protocol II, punishable under Article 3.b of the Statute.

Counts 3–5: Unlawful killings

33. Victims were routinely shot, hacked to death and burned to death. Unlawful killings included, but were not limited to, the following:

Bo District   34. Between 1 June 1997 and 30 June 1997, AFRC/RUF attacked Tikonko, Telu, Sembehun, Gerihun and Mamboma, unlawfully killing an unknown number of civilians;

Kenema District   35. Between about 25 May 1997 and about 19 February 1998, in locations including Kenema town, members of AFRC/RUF unlawfully killed an unknown number of civilians;

Kono District   36. About mid-February 1998, AFRC/RUF fleeing from Freetown arrived in Kono District. Between about 14 February 1998 and 30 June 1998, members of AFRC/RUF unlawfully killed several hundred civilians in various locations in Kono District, including Koidu, Tombodu, Foindu, Willifeh, Mortema and Biaya;

Bombali District   37. Between about 1 May 1998 and 31 July 1998, in locations including Karina, members of AFRC/RUF unlawfully killed an unknown number of civilians;

Freetown   38. Between 6 January 1999 and 31 January 1999, AFRC/RUF conducted armed attacks throughout the city of Freetown. These attacks included large scale unlawful killings of civilian men, women and children at locations throughout the city, including the State House, Parliament building, Connaught Hospital, and the Kissy, Fourah Bay, Upgun, Calaba Town and Tower Hill areas of the city.

By his acts or omissions in relation, but not limited to these events, Charles Ghankay Taylor pursuant to Article 6.1 and, or alternatively, Article 6.3 of the Statute, is individually criminally responsible for the crimes alleged below:

Count 3: Extermination, a crime against humanity, punishable under Article 2.b of the Statute;

In addition, or in the alternative:

Count 4: Murder, a crime against humanity, punishable under Article 2.a of the Statute;

In addition, or in the alternative:

Count 5: Violence to life, health and physical or mental well-being of persons, in particular murder, a violation of Article 3 common to the Geneva Conventions and of Additional Protocol II, punishable under Article 3.a of the Statute.

Counts 6–8: Sexual violence

39. Widespread sexual violence committed against civilian women and girls included brutal rapes, often by multiple rapists. Acts of sexual violence included, but were not limited to, the following:

Kono District   40. Between about 14 February 1998 and 30 June 1998, members of AFRC/RUF raped hundreds of women and girls at various locations throughout the District, including Koidu, Tombodu, Kissi-town (or Kissi Town), Foendor (or Foendu), Tomendeh, Fokoiya, Wondedu and AFRC/RUF camps such as 'Superman camp' and Kissi-town (or Kissi Town) camp. An unknown number of women and girls were abducted from various locations within the District and used as sex slaves;

Bombali District   41. Between about 1 May 1998 and 31 July 1998, members of AFRC/RUF raped an unknown number of women and girls in locations such as Mandaha. In addition, an unknown number of abducted women and girls were used as sex slaves;

Kailahun District   42. At all times relevant to this Indictment, an unknown number of women and girls in various locations in the District were subjected to sexual violence. Many of these victims were captured in other areas of the Republic of Sierra Leone, brought to AFRC/RUF camps in the District, and used as sex slaves;

Freetown   43. Between 6 January 1999 and 31 January 1999, members of AFRC/RUF raped hundreds of women and girls throughout the Freetown area, and abducted hundreds of women and girls and used them as sex slaves.

By his acts or omissions in relation, but not limited to these events, Charles Ghankay Taylor pursuant to Article 6.1 and, or alternatively, Article 6.3 of the Statute, is individually criminally responsible for the crimes alleged below:

Count 6: Rape, a crime against humanity, punishable under Article 2.g of the Statute; and

Count 7: Sexual slavery and any other form of sexual violence, a crime against humanity, punishable under Article 2.g of the Statute;

In addition, or in the alternative:

Count 8: Outrages upon personal dignity, a violation of Article 3 common to the Geneva Conventions and of Additional Protocol II, punishable under Article 3.e. of the Statute.

Counts 9–10: Physical violence

44. Widespread physical violence, including mutilations, was committed against civilians. Victims were often brought to a central location where mutilations were carried out. These acts of physical violence included, but were not limited to, the following:

Kono District   45. Between about 14 February 1998 and 30 June 1998, AFRC/RUF mutilated an unknown number of civilians in various locations in the District, including Tombodu, Kaima (or Kayima) and Wondedu. The mutilations included cutting off limbs and carving 'AFRC' and 'RUF' on the bodies of the civilians;

Freetown   46. Between 6 January 1999 and 31 January 1999, AFRC/RUF mutilated an unknown number of civilian men, women and children in various areas of Freetown, including the northern and eastern areas of the city, and the Kissy area, including the Kissy mental hospital. The mutilations included cutting off limbs.

By his acts or omissions in relation, but not limited to these events, Charles Ghankay Taylor, pursuant to Article 6.1 and, or alternatively, Article 6.3 of the Statute, is individually criminally responsible for the crimes alleged below:

Count 9: Violence to life, health and physical or mental well-being of persons, in particular cruel treatment, a violation of Article 3 common to the Geneva Conventions and of Additional Protocol II, punishable under Article 3.a of the Statute;

In addition, or in the alternative:

Count 10: Other inhumane acts, a crime against humanity, punishable under Article 2.i of the Statute.

Count 11: Use of child soldiers

47. At all times relevant to this Indictment, throughout the Republic of Sierra Leone, AFRC/RUF routinely conscripted, enlisted and/or used boys and girls under the age of 15 to participate in active hostilities. Many of these children were first abducted, then trained in AFRC/RUF camps in various locations throughout the country, and thereafter used as fighters.

By his acts or omissions in relation, but not limited to these events, Charles Ghankay Taylor, pursuant to Article 6.1 and, or alternatively, Article 6.3 of the Statute, is individually criminally responsible for the crimes alleged below:

Count 11: Conscripting or enlisting children under the age of 15 years into armed forces or groups, or using them to participate actively in hostilities, an other serious violation of international humanitarian law, punishable under Article 4.c of the Statute.

Count 12: Abductions and forced labour

48. At all times relevant to this Indictment, AFRC/RUF engaged in widespread and large scale abductions of civilians and use of civilians as forced labour. Forced labour included domestic labour and use as diamond miners. The abductions and forced labour included, but were not limited to, the following:

Kenema District   49. Between about 1 August 1997 and about 31 January 1998, AFRC/RUF forced an unknown number of civilians living in the District to mine for diamonds at Cyborg Pit in Tongo Field;

Kono District   50. Between about 14 February 1998 and 30 June 1998, AFRC/RUF forces abducted hundreds of civilian men, women and children, and took them to various locations outside the District, or to locations within the District such as AFRC/RUF camps, Tombodu, Koidu, Wondedu, Tomendeh. At these locations the civilians were used as forced labour, including domestic labour and as diamond miners in the Tombodu area;

Bombali District   51. Between about 1 May 1998 and 31 July 1998, in Bombali District, AFRC/RUF abducted an unknown number of civilians and used them as forced labour;

Kailahun District   52. At all times relevant to this Indictment, captured civilian men, women and children were brought to various locations within the District and used as forced labour;

Freetown   53. Between 6 January 1999 and 31 January 1999, in particular as the AFRC/RUF were being driven out of Freetown, the AFRC/RUF abducted hundreds of civilians, including a large number of children, from various areas within Freetown, including Peacock Farm and Calaba Town. These abducted civilians were used as forced labour.

By his acts or omissions in relation, but not limited to these events, Charles Ghankay Taylor, pursuant to Article 6.1 and, or alternatively, Article 6.3 of the Statute, is individually criminally responsible for the crimes alleged below:

Count 12: Enslavement, a crime against humannity, punishable under Article 2.c of the Statute.

Count 13: Looting and burning

54. At all times relevant to this Indictment, AFRC/RUF engaged in widespread unlawful taking and destruction by burning of civilian property. This looting and burning included, but was not limited to, the following:

Bo District   55. Between 1 June 1997 and 30 June 1997, AFRC/RUF forces looted and burned an unknown number of civilian houses in Telu, Sembehun, Mamboma and Tikonko;

Kono District   56. Between about 14 February 1998 and 30 June 1998, AFRC/RUF engaged in widespread looting and burning in various locations in the District, including Tombodu, Foindu and Yardu Sando, where virtually every home in the village was looted and burned;

Bombali District   57. Between 1 March 1998 and 30 June 1998, AFRC/RUF forces burned an unknown number of civilian buildings in locations such as Karina;

Freetown   58. Between 6 January 1999 and 31 January 1999, AFRC/RUF forces engaged in widespread looting and burning throughout Freetown. The majority of houses that were destroyed were in the areas of Kissy and eastern Freetown; other locations included the Fourah Bay, Upgun, State House and Pademba Road areas of the city.

By his acts or omissions in relation, but not limited to these events, Charles Ghankay Taylor, pursuant to Article 6.1 and, or alternatively, Article 6.3 of the Statute, is individually criminally responsible for the crimes alleged below:

Count 13: Pillage, a violation of Article 3 common to the Geneva Conventions and of Additional Protocol II, punishable under Article 3.f of the Statute.

Counts 14–17: Attacks on UNAMSIL personnel

59. Between about 15 April 2000 and about 15 September 2000, AFRC/RUF engaged in widespread attacks against UNAMSIL peacekeepers and humanitarian assistance workers within the Republic of Sierra Leone, including, but not limited to locations within Bombali, Kailahun, Kambia, Port Loko, and Kono Districts. These attacks included unlawful killing of UNAMSIL peacekeepers, and abducting hundreds of peacekeepers and humanitarian assistance workers who were then held hostage.

By his acts or omissions in relation, but not limited to these events, Charles Ghankay Taylor, pursuant to Article 6.1 and, or alternatively, Article 6.3 of the Statute, is individually criminally responsible for the crimes alleged below:

Count 14: Intentionally directing attacks against personnel involved in a humanitarian assistance or peacekeeping mission, an other serious violation of international humanitarian law, punishable under Article 4.b of the Statute;

In addition, or in the alternative:

Count 15: For the unlawful killings, Murder, a crime against humanity, punishable under Article 2.a of the Statute;

In addition, or in the alternative:

Count 16: Violence to life, health and physical or mental well-being of persons, in particular murder, a violation of Article 3 common to the Geneva Conventions and of Additional Protocol II, punishable under Article 3.a of the Statute;

In addition, or in the alternative:

Count 17: For the abductions and holding as hostage, Taking of hostages, a violation of Article 3 common to the Geneva Conventions and of Additional Protocol II, punishable under Article 3.c of the Statute.

APPENDIX B

Statement of Senator Patrick Leahy on the Indictment of Charles Taylor, 4 June 2003[34]

Mr President, I rise today to voice my strong support for the decision of the Special Court for Sierra Leone to indict Charles Taylor for 'bearing the greatest responsibility for war crimes, crimes against humanity, and serious violations of international humanitarian law in Sierra Leone'. I commend the Court's Prosecutor, David Crane, for taking this decisive action.

Since its inception, the Special Court has moved swiftly to indict key figures allegedly involved in some of the worst atrocities that occurred during the brutal civil war in Sierra Leone during the late 1990s. The Court has also made it a priority to emphasize outreach programs to further the reconciliation process and promote the rule of law throughout the country.

Despite important progress, we all know that the Court's work would be grossly deficient if those most responsible for these crimes were not brought to justice because they were too hard to catch, were high officials of a foreign government, or no longer resided inside of Sierra Leone. It would be like the United States deciding against pursuing the perpetrator of an act of terrorism on American soil, that killed or maimed thousands of individuals, because he left the country or was a high-ranking official in a foreign government.   That would be unacceptable.

That is precisely why Congress expressed its clear intent that the Special Court for Sierra Leone should pursue those most responsible, irrespective of where they currently reside.

In the report that accompanied the Senate version of the Fiscal Year 2002 Foreign Operations bill (Report 107-58), Congress stated in unambiguous terms: 'To build a lasting peace, the Committee believes that it is imperative for the international community to support a tribunal in order to bring to justice those responsible for war crimes and other atrocities in Sierra Leone, irrespective of where they currently reside.'

This statement was later endorsed by the Conference Report to the Fiscal Year 2002 Foreign Operations bill (Report 107-345), which put the House of Representatives on record on this issue as well.

Even before these reports were issued, Senators Feingold, Frist, McConnell and I wrote a letter to Secretary Powell, dated June 20, 2001, which stated: 'Because some of the individuals most responsible for the atrocities in Sierra Leone are no longer in the country, we believe it is imperative that the tribunal has the authority to prosecute culpable individuals – including senior Liberian officials – regardless of where they reside. This will prevent such persons from escaping justice simply by leaving the country.'

I can safely say that we had one individual especially in mind when we drafted that text: Charles Taylor. I was the principal author of the letter and two Congressional reports referenced above.

The involvement of Charles Taylor in the conflict in Sierra Leone is well documented and I will not go into great detail here. I will simply say that there is no doubt in my mind that he deserves to be brought to justice before the Special Court.

To its credit, the State Department took the advice of Congress. The State Department

---

34   Congressional Record, Senate, S7466-S7467, 5 June 2003.

successfully negotiated an agreement that established the Special Court for Sierra Leone and which did not contain geographic restrictions on the Prosecutor, allowing him to go after Charles Taylor.

Perhaps the Prosecutor for the Court, David Crane, best described the Special Court's mandate: 'My office was given an international mandate by the United Nations and the Republic of Sierra Leone to follow the evidence impartially wherever it leads.'

Today, acting on information that Charles Taylor was traveling to Ghana, the Special Court unsealed an indictment for Charles Taylor, originally approved March 7, 2003, and served the outstanding warrant for his arrest on Ghanaian authorities and transmitted the arrest warrant to Interpol.

Again, I commend the Prosecutor for taking this step. While I understand there are some, including in the Administration, who are concerned about the impact that this may have on the peace process now underway in West Africa, I agree with Mr Crane's comments on this sensitive issue: 'To ensure the legitimacy of these negotiations, it is imperative that the attendees know they are dealing with an indicted war criminal. These negotiations can still move forward, but they must do so without the involvement of this indictee. The evidence upon which this indictment was approved raises serious questions about Taylor's suitability to be a guarantor of any deal, let alone a peace agreement.'

Mr President, the Ghanaian Government needs to act immediately. It needs to uphold the basic tenants of international law, apprehend Charles Taylor and hold him until arrangements can be made to transfer him to the Court. In addition, the State Department needs to send an unequivocal message to Accra that action on this issue is urgently needed.

This may be the only chance that we get for years to bring Charles Taylor to justice. It is imperative that, in its most important moment thus far, the United States and Ghana do everything in their power to apprehend Charles Taylor. If this does not occur, the world will have missed a golden opportunity to bring to justice one of the world's most heinous war criminals and advance the cause of international justice.

In closing, I would like to read into the record Mr Crane's statement issued today that describes the situation concerning Charles Taylor:

Today, on behalf of the people of Sierra Leone and the international community, I announce the indictment of Charles Ghankay Taylor, also known as Charles Ghankay Macarthur Dapkpana Taylor.

The indictment accuses Taylor of 'bearing the greatest responsibility' for war crimes, crimes against humanity, and serious violations of international humanitarian law within the territory of Sierra Leone since 30 November 1996. The indictment was judicially approved on March 7th and until today, was sealed on my request to the Court.

My office was given an international mandate by the United Nations and the Republic of Sierra Leone to follow the evidence impartially wherever it leads. It has led us unequivocally to Taylor.

Upon learning that Taylor was travelling to Ghana, the Registrar of the Special Court served the outstanding warrant for his arrest on Ghanaian authorities and transmitted the arrest warrant to Interpol. This is the first time that his presence outside of Liberia has been publicly confirmed. The Registrar was doing his duty by carrying out the order of the Court.

Furthermore, the timing of this announcement was carefully considered in light of the important peace process begun this week. To ensure the legitimacy of these negotiations, it is imperative that the attendees know they are dealing with an indicted war criminal. These negotiations can still move forward, but they must do so without the involvement of this indictee. The evidence upon which this indictment was approved raises serious questions about Taylor's suitability to be a guarantor of any deal, let alone a peace agreement.

I am aware that many members of the international community have invested a great deal of energy in the current peace talks. I want to make it clear that in reaching my decision to make the indictment public, I have not consulted with any state. I am acting as an independent prosecutor and this decision was based solely on the law.

I also want to send a clear message to all factions fighting in Liberia that they must respect international humanitarian law. Commanders are under international legal obligation to prevent their members from violating the laws of war and committing crimes against humanity.

In accordance with Security Council Resolutions 1315, 1470, and 1478, now is the time for all nations to reinforce their commitments to international peace and security. West Africa will not know true peace until those behind the violence answer for their actions. This office now calls upon the international community to take decisive action to ensure that Taylor is brought to justice.'

18 Reflections on contemporary developments in international criminal justice

M. Cherif Bassiouni

International criminal justice is an idea whose time has come. Its constituencies within governments, intergovernmental organizations and international civil society have grown significantly in the last two decades. The establishment of the International Criminal Tribunal for the Former Yugoslavia (ICTY), the International Criminal Tribunal for Rwanda (ICTR), the International Criminal Court (ICC), and the mixed-model tribunals have contributed to that development by showing, *inter alia,* that fairness in process and justice-outcomes can be achieved.[1] More importantly, these institutions have shown, even with a limited number of cases, that accountability is on the rise and that impunity is no longer the norm.[2] Admittedly, severe constraints remain, but in view of the perennial resistance of *realpolitik* to the progress of international criminal justice, the results can be said to exceed expectations.[3]

The new era of international criminal justice started in 1992, when the United Nations Security Council re-engaged in international criminal law for the first time since the post-Second World War era by establishing the Commission of Experts to investigate violations of international humanitarian law in the then-ongoing conflict in the Former Yugoslavia.[4] That effort culminated in significant fashion with the establishment in 1998 of the ICC,[5] but

---

[1] For various articles on these institutions, see 3 INTERNATIONAL CRIMINAL LAW (M. Cherif Bassiouni ed., 3rd edn, 2008).

[2] See however, M. CHERIF BASSIOUNI, THE PURSUIT OF INTERNATIONAL CRIMINAL JUSTICE: A WORLD STUDY ON CONFLICTS, VICTIMIZATION AND POST-CONFLICT JUSTICE (2 vols., Intersentia: Brussels, Belgium, 2010) – (1961 pages), which shows that some 310 conflicts generated an estimated 100 million victims.

[3] M. Cherif Bassiouni, *Perspectives on International Criminal Justice*, 50 VA. J. INT'L L. 269–323 (2010); M. Cherif Bassiouni, *The Need for International Accountability*, in 3 INTERNATIONAL CRIMINAL LAW 3–28 (M. Cherif Bassiouni ed., 3rd edn, 2008); M. Cherif Bassiouni, *The Philosophy and Policy of International Criminal Justice*, in MAN'S INHUMANITY TO MAN: ESSAYS ON INTERNATIONAL LAW IN HONOUR OF ANTONIO CASSESE 65–126 (Lal Chand Vohrah *et al.* eds, 2003); M. Cherif Bassiouni, *The Future of International Criminal Justice*, 11 PACE INT'L L REV. 309 (1999); M. Cherif Bassiouni, *Combating Impunity for International Crimes*, 71 U COLO. L REV. 409 (2000).

[4] Security Council Res. 780, UN Doc. S/RES/780 (6 October 1992). This was followed by the establishment of the ICTY and the ICTR. Final Report of the United Nations Commission of Experts Established Pursuant to Security Council Resolution 780 (1992) S/1994/674, 27 May 1994; and Annexes I–XII of the Final Report S/1994/674/Add. 2 (Vol. 1) 31 May 1995. Available on the Internet at: http://law.depaul.edu/centers%5Finstitutes/ihrli/publications/yugoslavia.asp.

[5] Rome Statute of the International Criminal Court, 17 July 1998, 2187 UNTS 90; see also M. CHERIF BASSIOUNI, THE LEGISLATIVE HISTORY OF THE INTERNATIONAL CRIMINAL COURT (Transnational Publishers, Ardsley NY, 2005). The ICC is a treaty-based institution whose Statute is binding only upon its member states on the basis of complementarity of jurisdiction with national legal systems. See also M. Cherif Bassiouni, *The Future of the International Criminal Court: Quo Vadis?* 4 J INT'L CRIM. JUST. 421 (2006).

that Court is not a powerful supranational institution capable of single-handedly bringing justice to the world.

International criminal justice, in its current form, suffers from significant deficits in a number of areas. International tribunals standing alone are of questionable efficacy and frequently fail to engage with other post-conflict modalities.[6] As a result, these institutions often produce little impact on the communities they are meant to serve and in many cases create a historical record that is fragmented at best. The over-zealous promotion of international tribunals is pursued by many advocates of international criminal justice at the expense of other post-conflict mechanisms and of the indirect enforcement system of international criminal law.[7] This indirect system operates when international norms are enforced through domestic means, a process which strengthens national justice systems and which can lead to a more comprehensive and effective system of international criminal justice than can international tribunals. A broader perspective than the current narrow, focus on international tribunals is necessary in order to make the goals of international criminal justice become reality.

Generally, a complex and at times contradictory mixture of goals is involved in international and national prosecutions. Ostensibly, the principal goal is to prosecute individuals and establish their individual criminal responsibility. Frequently, there is also a broader goal of establishing a historic truth. The prosecution of Adolf Eichmann by Israeli courts, for example, was in large part an effort to establish, in open court, a historic record of the Holocaust.[8] Such a purpose was absent from the Al-Dujail trial of Saddam Hussein, which sought merely to establish personal criminal responsibility.[9] As a result of the varying goals pursued, cases before international criminal tribunals, cases before them will vary in length and costs. That variance has major implications for the duration of the proceedings and their costs.

Most of the inter-state cooperation in international criminal law is not about international criminal justice, namely international crimes,[10] but about inter-state cooperation in domestic criminal matters. This involves extradition, mutual legal assistance, transfer of sentences and sentenced persons, transfer of criminal proceedings, recognition of foreign penal judgments, freezing and seizing of assets, law enforcement intelligence sharing, and prosecutorial cooperation.[11] All of these areas also touch upon human rights issues.[12] More importantly, they are the essential methods by which states cooperate with each other and with international institutions in the enforcement of international criminal law.

The work of intergovernmental organizations and national criminal justice systems is largely separate from the human rights community's work supporting international criminal justice. The dividing line may well be based on the differences in the disciplines of domestic of criminal law, on the one hand, and international law, on the other. There are relatively few

---

6   THE CHICAGO PRINCIPLES ON POST-CONFLICT JUSTICE (International Human Rights Law Institute, 2001–2008).

7   See, for example, 2 INTERNATIONAL CRIMINAL LAW (M. Cherif Bassiouni ed., 3rd edn, 2008).

8   *Israel* v. *Eichmann*, Crim. Ct Jer. 40/61, [1961] ISR. DC 45(3), aff'd. *Israel* v. *Eichmann*, Crim. A. 336/61, [1962] Israel Supreme Ct 16 (2033). See also GIDEON HAUSNER, JUSTICE IN JERUSALEM (1968).

9   See Bassiouni and Hanna, note 20 *infra*; also see Landsman, note 13 *infra*.

10   M. CHERIF BASSIOUNI & EDWARD M. WISE, AUT DEDERE AUT JUDICARE: THE DUTY TO EXTRADITE OR PROSECUTE IN INTERNATIONAL LAW (1995).

11   *Supra* note 7.

12   This includes due process and specific rights of the accused in the criminal process (STEFAN TRECHSEL, HUMAN RIGHTS IN CRIMIONAL PROCEEDINGS (2005)).

experts in international criminal law who bridge the two disciplines, and that affects the quality of international criminal justice.

One of the shortcomings of international institutions, and a reason for this high cost, is the fact that each case is conducted separately from other cases arising out of the same situation. No process exists to assume as true the facts that have been found in previous proceedings. Thus, in each proceeding the parties must prove all the facts, even if certain ones have already been adjudicated. This results in a duplication of effort, wasting both time and resources. In each of these proceedings, different witnesses are called, different questions are asked, and a different record is established. Consequently, the proceedings of the ICTY, ICTR, ICC and mixed-model tribunals never produce a coherent story of a particular battle or event, let alone of a given conflict.

Although many expected that these trials would produce such a historical record, that expectation has not been fulfilled in practice.[13] This approach produces only slices of history, leaving the larger story of the conflict untold. The ICTY and ICTR, for example, have prosecuted different perpetrators whose crimes were committed in the same context. However, there was no mechanism for establishing the facts that applied to a specific battle or campaign in order that such a record can be used in different cases involving different defendants whose conduct was related to the same set of events.[14] Instead, the same facts are readjudicated in each individual case. This repetition not only increases the time and the costs required to conduct these prosecutions, it also increases the risk that in different cases the tribunal will come to different historical narratives regarding the same incident. The victims, their families and the rest of the world are left to wonder what really happened. This observation evidences the conclusion that international judicial institutions enforcing ICL cannot easily rely on domestic prosecutorial experiences. There are differences between these types of justice systems, if for no other reason than scale of what takes place in conflicts and the number of victims and perpetrators involved.

Post-conflict justice is meant to strengthen domestic stability, security and democracy following atrocities through the balancing of peace, justice and reconciliation goals with a view to achieve accountability and victim redress. These goals and the values and policies they embody require long-term, comprehensive plans that include holding individuals responsible for their crimes, creating a record of what happened so the victims and their families can heal and become the basis for future conflict-prevention. International prosecutions, in their present form, however, are structured in a way that they can only fulfil parts of these goals.

Notable at this stage in the history of international criminal law are the idealized perceptions and expectations of what international criminal courts and tribunals can accomplish which prevail within the international human rights community. This idealization and high expectations of international institutions, like the ICTY, ICTR, and ICC, whose jurisprudence, effectiveness, social impact and cost-efficiency give rise to questions, marginalizes other modalities of post-conflict justice which deserve more encouragement and support.[15]

---

13   See STEPHAN LANDSMAN, CRIMES OF THE HOLOCAUST: THE LAW CONFRONTS HARD CASES (2005), positing the proposition that criminal trials are designed to focus on the guilt or innocence of these trials' defendants, and that which goes in the records of a given case does not cover the entirety of a given conflict or even of a given situation.

14   The exception is in cases involving crimes of enterprise.

15   See International Human Rights Law Institute, The Chicago Principles of Post Conflict Justice, (2008).

Focusing on international criminal justice institutions, while neglecting the role and place of other post-conflict justice modalities,[16] evidences a narrow perspective which is detrimental to the overall goals of international criminal justice, namely prevention, protection and, yes, retribution.[17] Seldom does one see an assessment of the international and mixed-model tribunals in relations to such post-conflict justice modalities as truth commissions, truth-telling commissions, victim compensation and rehabilitation, memorialization, and education for prevention. Combined, these modalities are more likely to have a longer-lasting effect on the prevention of future conflicts than the selective prosecution of a few persons. All too often the more glittering appeal of international adjudicatory institutions substantially overshadows these other modalities, even though international prosecutions are only one component of post-conflict justice. More importantly, international prosecutions alone do not promote reconciliation between former enemies and seldom give the victim group a sense of historic and psychological closure. Precisely because every conflict is *sui generis*, each will require a different mix of post-conflict justice modalities to achieve peace and reconciliation and provide some closure to the victims.

The human rights community has been the principal champion of international criminal justice, particularly with respect to what in international criminal law is considered the 'direct enforcement method',[18] which has to do with international investigatory and adjudicatory bodies. But this community seems to focus more on international adjudicatory bodies than on other methods of post-conflict justice and, more importantly, it does so without any ascertainable method of analysis to assess the impact and outcomes of those bodies. What the human rights community and others have often ignored is that international criminal law is mostly enforced through the 'indirect enforcement method',[19] which happens at the level of national criminal justice systems. But the national criminal justice community is largely disconnected from its human rights counterpart working in the arena of international criminal justice, thus preventing synergies that could develop and enhance the effectiveness of international criminal justice.

A parallel path to that of international institutions should be the enhanced role of national criminal justice in both the domestic prosecution of international crimes and in greater inter-state cooperation concerning penal matters related to the investigation and prosecution of international crimes before national courts. The national path is likely to have more impact on peace and justice than the path of international and mixed-model judicial institutions. The former has certain inherent advantages because it builds upon the already established authority of national officials whose decisions have a direct domestic impact. Another clear advantage is that national institutions of criminal justice tend to be less bureaucratic and much less costly than international adjudicatory bodies. Suffice it to consider the limited impact on the

---

[16]   *Id.*

[17]   Anja Matwijkiw and Bronik Matwitkiw, *A Modern Perspective on International Criminal Law: Accountability as a Meta-Right*, in The Theory and Practice of International Criminal Law: Essays in Honor of M. Cherif Bassiouni (Leila Nadya Sadat aand Michael P. Scharf eds, 2008).

[18]   M. Cherif Bassiouni, Introduction To International Criminal Law 23–55, 259–332 (2003).

[19]   M. Cherif Bassiouni, *The Modalities of International Cooperation in Penal Matters*, in 2 International Criminal Law 3–34 (M. Cherif Bassiouni ed., 3rd edn, 2008).

victim groups before the ICTY and ICTR, consider only the ill-advised choices of The Hague for the ICTY and Arusha for the ICTR. The victims of both conflicts should have been able to witness or hear first-hand of the justice process that pertains to them, as opposed to having to learn of what happens through the international media. Can anyone seriously think that victims in the former Yugoslavia and Rwanda believe in this remote and distant form of justice and now feel closure? For sure not. More importantly, domestic prosecutions have a far more significant impact than their international counterparts.

Strengthening international criminal justice at the national level requires international support. Enhanced multilateral and bilateral cooperation in addressing terrorism, drug trafficking, organized crime, human smuggling and trafficking, money-laundering, corruption, financial frauds, cyber-crime and the like should not continue to operate in a separate compartment from cooperation in the field of international criminal justice relating to the three core crimes of genocide, crimes against humanity and war crimes.

Placing these international institutions at a remove from the people and conflicts concerned not only made them less accessible to what should have been their intended audiences, but also deprived the countries affected of a chance to strengthen their national judicial institutions. One can only imagine the hundreds, if not thousands, of indigenous persons who could have been employed by these tribunals over a period of 15 years. Professional cadres would have developed in far greater number, and would have accumulated professional experience potentially crucial to the support of the national legal systems. Last, but not least, over US$2 billion in resources would have been spent in these countries to the benefit of their economies.[20] We must not forget that the decision to locate each of these tribunals outside of the state whose conflict it was to address was based essentially on political and logistical considerations. The lack of effective national structures, legislation and trained personnel in the conflict states should be a matter of serious concern, but it has been largely ignored by the United Nations and organizations committed to the enhancement of international criminal justice.

The modalities of international cooperation in penal matters are also the foundation of the 'direct enforcement' of international criminal justice. That is why the ICC will only be as effective as the states' justice systems that will cooperate with it. The effectiveness of the ICC will largely depend on the willingness of states to cooperate with it, and on the ability of those states to carry out their obligations through their available national modalities.[21]

Even though lip-service is given to what the ICC Statute refers to as 'complementarity',[22] there is little implementation of the Statute's provisions at the national level. The ICC has not

---

[20]   *Ibid.* 6.

[21]   See Jakob Pinchon, *The Principle of Complementarity in the Cases of the Sudanese Nationals Ahmad Harun and Ali Kushayb Before the International Criminal Court*, 8 INT'L CRIM. L REV. 185 (2008).

[22]   ICC Statute, art. 17. See also M. CHERIF BASSIOUNI, II THE LEGISLATIVE HISTORY OF THE INTERNATIONAL CRIMINAL COURT: AN ARTICLE-BY-ARTICLE EVOLUTION OF THE STATUTE OF THE 1998 DIPLOMATIC CONFERENCE (2005); Sharon A. Williams and William A. Schabas, *Article 17: Issues of Admissibility*, in COMMENTARY ON THE ROME STATUTE OF THE INTERNATIONAL CRIMINAL COURT: OBSERVERS' NOTES, ARTICLE BY ARTICLE 605 (Otto Triftterer ed., 2008); Immi Tallgreen and Astrid Reising Coracini, *Article 20: Ne bis in idem*, in COMMENTARY ON THE ROME STATUTE OF THE INTERNATIONAL CRIMINAL COURT: OBSERVERS' NOTES, ARTICLE BY ARTICLE 669 (Otto Triftterer ed., 2008).

committed personnel and resources to strengthening the national justice systems of state-parties (let alone those of non-party states). Strengthening the capacity of those national systems is essential to achieve higher standards of international criminal justice. Experiences in post-conflict justice settings, particularly those that have given rise to international and mixed-model tribunals, as well as those in Iraq[23] and Afghanistan,[24] show that very little has been done to develop comprehensive justice reform plans, let alone to support sustainable transformative changes in these domestic justice systems. This should be a matter of much greater concern to the international community because it is hardly conceivable that international criminal justice can prevail in a given country while its national criminal justice system is ineffective.[25]

Most assessments of the ICTY, ICTR and mixed-model tribunals focus inordinately on the institutions themselves and the degree to which they are accepted by international civil society. But there is little empirical data as to the tangible deterrence results produced by international and mixed-model tribunals in conflict situations. The most positive assessments of these institutions derive essentially from Western sources, which generally fail to consider post-conflict mechanisms known to other cultures.[26] Justice is supposedly both the goal and the standard, but in all of the self-congratulatory and self-serving assessments of the international investigatory and adjudicatory institutions established post-1992, there is little or no mention of social-science impact measurement criteria on the effect of international and mixed-model tribunals concerning the perception of justice among the protagonists and victims of given conflicts. This is equally true of many laudatory revisionist views of the post-Second World War prosecutions. More importantly, there is at best only anecdotal data on the deterrent effect of such an institution's prosecutions and judgments regarding the conduct of protagonists in a single conflict, let alone any measurement of preventive impact on future conflicts.

---

[23]   See, for example, M. Cherif Bassiouni and Michael Wahid Hanna, *Ceding the High Ground: The Iraqi High Criminal Court Statute and the Trial of Saddam Hussein*, 39 CASE WEST. RES. J INT'L L 21 (2007).

[24]   See UN General Assembly, *Report of the Independent Expert on the Situation of Human Rights in Afghanistan*, UN Doc. A/59/370 (21 September 2004); UN ECOSOC, *Report of the Independent Expert on the Situation of Human Rights in Afghanistan*, UN Doc. E/CN.4/2005/122 (11 March 2005).

[25]   Two personal experiences are relevant. In Iraq, I chaired a group of 60 senior public officials, which included the Chief Justice, Minister of Justice, the Prosecutor General, and the Deputy Ministers of Interior and Defense. We worked for nine months to establish a comprehensive strategic plan for the reform of the Iraqi justice system. This was an extraordinary joint-Iraqi project based on consensus. But the key external political and economic players had no interest in it. So, we have two volumes (Arabic and English) describing the plan, but without implementation. In Afghanistan, after serving in 2004–2006 as the Independent Expert on Human Rights (whose mandate was not reviewed because of critical comments on the United States), I was asked to prepare a comprehensive strategic plan for the Afghan justice system to be submitted to the Donor Countries Conference of July 2007. The plan was completed with the buy-in of the Afghan stakeholders. As the Conference's rapporteur, I presented the plan, which was endorsed by the United Nations, European Union and 24 donor countries. But to date, it has yet to be implemented. Instead, each intergovernmental organization and each donor state prefers to act unilaterally and fund what they please, irrespective of the lack of synergies and counter-productive results. These are some of the realities that affect justice in post-conflict settings. More importantly, without viable national criminal justice systems, it is difficult to prosecute perpetrators of international crimes. Afghanistan and Iraq are examples of such occurrences.

[26]   See generally Erin Daly, *Between Punitive Reconstructive and Justice: The Gacaca Courts in Rwanda*, 34 N.Y.U. J. INT'L L. & POL. 355 (2002); William Schabas, *Genocide Trials and Gacaca Courts*, 3 J. INT'L CRIM. JUST. 879 (2005).

For sure, common sense and anecdotal data confirm the positive factors deriving from the establishment of the international and mixed-model tribunals of the last two decades.[27] However, the key issue of whether the international investigatory and adjudicatory bodies in question have produced deterrent and preventive effects is something that needs to be addressed; so far the issue has been ignored. The analysis needed to address this deficiency should include consideration of the following:

1. Has there been a general deterrence factor in the communities where conflicts have occurred?
2. Has there been a deterrence effect beyond these communities?
3. Has a sense of closure been achieved with respect to the victim community?
4. Has a sense of fairness been communicated to the community which has produced those who have been prosecuted?
5. Is it likely that these prosecutions will have a preventive effect as between these communities which have been in conflict?
6. What is the impact of individual prosecutions on the victims of the perpetrators who were prosecuted?
7. What is the impact of the prosecutions on the general community of victims in a particular conflict?
8. Do these prosecutions enhance the overall purpose of accountability, or do they simply highlight the fact that the new era of accountability is simply one of selectivity and symbolism?
9. In what ways have these institutions contributed to establishing a historic record, or a record of the victimization, or provided education for prevention?

The future of international criminal justice cannot be predicted, but some conjecture is appropriate here. International criminal justice is likely to progress along different, parallel, paths, and it will surely be influenced by certain world events. Sooner or later the need may arise, in the context of a post-conflict justice situation, for a unified international community to resort to the ICC and strongly support it. When that moment comes the ICC will acquire a new legitimacy and standing that could propel it into public consciousness as the unquestioned institution that its founders hoped for. Until then, however, the ICC is likely to remain the relatively weak and limited institution it is today, dependent on shifting international political consensus and vulnerable to critical appraisal from various parts of the international community.

Separate and apart from any substantive issues are those pertaining to costs and administration of international institutions. The economic costs associated with the ICTY/ICTR, as well as with the ICC, have raised concerns about whether it will be economically viable to pursue justice models such as these in the future. By 2008, the ICTY/ICTR costs exceeded US$2.2 billion, and they had cumulatively prosecuted 149 cases.[28] Admittedly, one should

---

27   Kathleen Claussen, *Up To The Bar? Designing the Hybrid Khymer Rouge Tribunal in Cambodia*, 33 YALE J. INT'L LAW (2008); David Cohen, 'Hybrid' Justice in East Timor, Sierra Leone, and Cambodia: 'Lessons Learned' and Prospects for the Future, 43 STAN. J. INT'L LAW 1 (2007).

28   As of 8 January 2009, the ICTY reported that 161 individuals had been indicted, with 116 proceedings concluded and proceedings against the remaining 45 ongoing. See www.icty.org. As of the same date, the ICTR reported indictments against 60 individuals. Of those, proceedings against 33 individuals had concluded, and proceedings against 27 individuals were ongoing. See www.ictr.org.

not put a price on justice, but these costs average US$10–15 million per case,[29] which is hardly acceptable. These costs are essentially due to the salary structure of the United Nations, its bureaucratic processes, and to the poor financial management of these institutions which have piled up investigatory and prosecutorial costs as well as judicial ones. The mixed models are, for all practical purposes, smaller and cheaper versions. They have generally received lesser resources, perhaps in part suffering the backlash from the costly experiences of the international tribunals. But the mixed model is not always cheaper. For example, the Extraordinary Chambers in the Courts of Cambodia is slated to spend US$180 million on prosecuting five accused, about US$36 million per accused.[30] The Court of Bosnia and Herzegovina, a much larger scale and longer term institution, spends about US$709,000 per accused, which is expected to be reduced to US$236,000 by 2010.[31] Not enough consideration has been given to the cost effectiveness and management effectiveness of these international institutions, which have been mired in UN bureaucracy. This is likely to affect the future credibility and effectiveness of the ICC, whose approximately US$130 million budget for 2009[32] is already under critical review. More importantly, this budget covers four cases and it could at best cover one more case in 2009–2010.

Lastly, there is one overarching observation that needs to be made. Amidst the enthusiasm and the forward momentum of international criminal justice, we must be mindful of the fact that *realpolitik* has not given up on its prerogatives. We still live in a world where political realism prevails and where state interests are considered by many policy-makers to be superior to commonly shared values. The forces of political realism have accepted the fact that they must coexist with the rising demand for international criminal justice. But they are not about to give up on curtailing and controlling it. The perennial struggle between *realpolitik* and international criminal justice continues,[33] and those who are committed to the latter must be on guard for the former. If not, international criminal justice, after emerging from the occasional or sporadic set of experiences after the Second World War[34] and progressing after the Yugoslavia and Rwanda conflicts,[35] may devolve into a permanent system with the characteristics of a 'Potemkin Village'.[36]

When this new era began in 1992, as chairman of the Commission to Investigate Violations of International Humanitarian Law in the Former Yugoslavia established by the Security Council, I experienced the limitations imposed by political realism on the pursuit of justice.[37] Then, in 2004–2006, as Independent Expert on Human Rights in Afghanistan, I

---

[29]   Rupert Skilbeck, *Funding Justice: The Price of War Crimes Trials*, 15 Hum. Rts Brief 6 (2008).

[30]   *Ibid.* 7.

[31]   *Ibid.* 8.

[32]   ICC Assembly of States Parties Resolution ICC-ASP/7/Res. 4 (21 November 2008).

[33]   M. Cherif Bassiouni, *The Perennial Conflict Between International Criminal Justice and Realpolitik*, 22 Ga. St. U L Rev. 541 (2006).

[34]   See M. Cherif Bassiouni, *International Criminal Investigations and Prosecutions from Versailles to Rwanda*, 3 International Criminal Law 31–65 (1999).

[35]   *Ibid.*

[36]   A 'Potemkin Village' refers to the illusion created by Russian Minister Grigori Aleksandrovich Potemkin, who in 1787 directed the construction of fake villages composed of hollow facades in Crimea to impress Empress Catherine II during her visit.

[37]   M. Cherif Bassiouni, in cooperation with Peter Manikas, The Law of the International

found that not much had changed. It took from 1998 to 2006 to have the UN General Assembly adopt a Resolution that embodies principles and guidelines on victim compensation, which I prepared in the first two years of the mandate.[38] The delay was mainly due to the fact that the principles included the duty to investigate and prosecute perpetrators of fundamental human rights violations and violations of international humanitarian law. Even so, the international criminal justice community was largely absent from the effort.

Things have improved, but the techniques of political realism are still working effectively. International institutions are not only controlled by various political mandates, they are even more effectively controlled by the use of bureaucracies and financial constraints. Suffice it to consider that the UN Security Council's referral of the Darfur situation to the ICC with the specific proviso that it would not give any financial resources to the ICC makes such a referral something pyrrhic. The ICC is in a vulnerable position without the financial and political support that would make its investigatory work in the Sudan possible.[39] Machiavelli would have been proud of this approach taken by the Security Council.

This political realism is in curious contrast to the idealized view of international criminal courts and tribunals which prevails within the international human rights community. A narrow focus on these institutions without providing for broader support and enforcement will lead to greater disappointment in the pursuit of international criminal justice. It will also detract from other important processes of transitional justice, including those which are to be carried out under domestic law. International criminal law is enforced mostly by national criminal justice systems, and this process should be encouraged and not bypassed for the benefit of international institutions. A broader and less politicized perspective is needed if the goals of international criminal justice are to become a reality. Even so, there are limits to what international criminal justice can achieve,[40] just as there are limits to deterrence at the national justice levels. Nevertheless, the need to develop measures of prevention and protection are becoming more imperative in light of the high level of human victimization occurring in various conflicts. This is reflected in the emerging concept of 'the Responsibility to Protect which has yet to become a reality'.[41]

CRIMINAL TRIBUNAL FOR THE FORMER YUGOSLAVIA (Ardsley, New York, Transnational Publishers, 1996).

[38] See M. Cherif Bassiouni, *Human Rights in Afghanistan*, UN Doc. A/59/370 (21 September 2004), UN Doc. E/CN.4/2005/122 (11 March 2005); and *The Rights to Restitution, Compensation and Rehabilitation for Victims of Grave Violations of Human Rights and Fundamental Freedoms*, UN Doc. E/CN.4/2000/62 (18 January 2000), UN Doc. E/CN.4/2005/L.48 (13 April 2005).

[39] *Prosecutor* v. *Omar Hassan Ahmad Al Bashir*, Case No. ICC-02/05-01/09-1, Indictment of Sudanese President Al-Bashir, 3 April 2009.

[40] See Payam Akhaven, *Beyond Impunity: Can International Criminal Justice Prevent Future Atrocities?*, 95 AM. J INT'L L 7 (2001); David Wippman, *Atrocities, Deterrence, and the Limits of International Justice*, 23 FORDHAM INT'L LJ 473 (1999).

[41] David Scheffer, *Atrocity Crimes, Framing the Responsibility to Protect*, 40 CASE W RES. J INT'L L 111 (2007–2008); *The Responsibility to Protect, Report of the International Commission on Intervention and State Sovereignty* (2001), available at www. http://www.iciss-ciise.gc.ca/report-en.asp. See also the various contributions contained in THE RESPONSIBILITY TO PROTECT: THE GLOBAL MORAL COMPACT OF THE 21ST CENTURY (Richard Cooper and Juliette Voinov Kohler eds, Palgrave Macmillan, (2008). This concept is based on the 2005 World Summit Outcome Declaration, General Assembly Res. A/Res/60/1, 24 October 2005.

General appendix: Rome Statute of the International Criminal Court

Adopted by the United Nations Diplomatic Conference of Plenipotentiaries on the Establishment of an International Criminal Court on 17 July 1998, entry into force: 1 July 2002, in accordance with article 126*

PREAMBLE

The States Parties to this Statute,

Conscious that all peoples are united by common bonds, their cultures pieced together in a shared heritage, and concerned that this delicate mosaic may be shattered at any time,

Mindful that during this century millions of children, women and men have been victims of unimaginable atrocities that deeply shock the conscience of humanity,

Recognizing that such grave crimes threaten the peace, security and well-being of the world,

Affirming that the most serious crimes of concern to the international community as a whole must not go unpunished and that their effective prosecution must be ensured by taking measures at the national level and by enhancing international cooperation,

Determined to put an end to impunity for the perpetrators of these crimes and thus to contribute to the prevention of such crimes,

Recalling that it is the duty of every State to exercise its criminal jurisdiction over those responsible for international crimes,

Reaffirming the Purposes and Principles of the Charter of the United Nations, and in particular that all States shall refrain from the threat or use of force against the territorial integrity or political independence of any State, or in any other manner inconsistent with the Purposes of the United Nations,

Emphasizing in this connection that nothing in this Statute shall be taken as authorizing any State Party to intervene in an armed conflict or in the internal affairs of any State,

Determined to these ends and for the sake of present and future generations, to establish an independent permanent International Criminal Court in relationship with the United Nations system, with jurisdiction over the most serious crimes of concern to the international community as a whole,

Emphasizing that the International Criminal Court established under this Statute shall be complementary to national criminal jurisdictions,

Resolved to guarantee lasting respect for and the enforcement of international justice,

Have agreed as follows:

---

* As corrected by the procès-verbaux of 10 November 1998, 12 July 1999, 30 November 1999, 8 May 2000, 17 January 2001 and 16 January 2002.

PART 1. ESTABLISHMENT OF THE COURT

Article 1

The Court
An International Criminal Court ('the Court') is hereby established. It shall be a permanent institution and shall have the power to exercise its jurisdiction over persons for the most serious crimes of international concern, as referred to in this Statute, and shall be complementary to national criminal jurisdictions. The jurisdiction and functioning of the Court shall be governed by the provisions of this Statute.

Article 2

Relationship of the Court with the United Nations
The Court shall be brought into relationship with the United Nations through an agreement to be approved by the Assembly of States Parties to this Statute and thereafter concluded by the President of the Court on its behalf.

Article 3

Seat of the Court
1. The seat of the Court shall be established at The Hague in the Netherlands ('the host State').
2. The Court shall enter into a headquarters agreement with the host State, to be approved by the Assembly of States Parties and thereafter concluded by the President of the Court on its behalf.
3. The Court may sit elsewhere, whenever it considers it desirable, as provided in this Statute.

Article 4

Legal status and powers of the Court
1. The Court shall have international legal personality. It shall also have such legal capacity as may be necessary for the exercise of its functions and the fulfilment of its purposes.
2. The Court may exercise its functions and powers, as provided in this Statute, on the territory of any State Party and, by special agreement, on the territory of any other State.

PART 2. JURISDICTION, ADMISSIBILITY AND APPLICABLE LAW

Article 5

Crimes within the jurisdiction of the Court
1. The jurisdiction of the Court shall be limited to the most serious crimes of concern to the international community as a whole. The Court has jurisdiction in accordance with this Statute with respect to the following crimes:

(a) The crime of genocide;
(b) Crimes against humanity;
(c) War crimes;
(d) The crime of aggression.

2. The Court shall exercise jurisdiction over the crime of aggression once a provision is adopted in accordance with articles 121 and 123 defining the crime and setting out the conditions under which the Court shall exercise jurisdiction with respect to this crime. Such a provision shall be consistent with the relevant provisions of the Charter of the United Nations.

Article 6

Genocide
For the purpose of this Statute, 'genocide' means any of the following acts committed with intent to destroy, in whole or in part, a national, ethnical, racial or religious group, as such:

(a) Killing members of the group;
(b) Causing serious bodily or mental harm to members of the group;
(c) Deliberately inflicting on the group conditions of life calculated to bring about its physical destruction in whole or in part;
(d) Imposing measures intended to prevent births within the group;
(e) Forcibly transferring children of the group to another group.

Article 7

Crimes against humanity
1. For the purpose of this Statute, 'crime against humanity' means any of the following acts when committed as part of a widespread or systematic attack directed against any civilian population, with knowledge of the attack:

(a) Murder;
(b) Extermination;
(c) Enslavement;
(d) Deportation or forcible transfer of population;
(e) Imprisonment or other severe deprivation of physical liberty in violation of fundamental rules of international law;
(f) Torture;
(g) Rape, sexual slavery, enforced prostitution, forced pregnancy, enforced sterilization, or any other form of sexual violence of comparable gravity;
(h) Persecution against any identifiable group or collectivity on political, racial, national, ethnic, cultural, religious, gender as defined in paragraph 3, or other grounds that are universally recognized as impermissible under international law, in connection with any act referred to in this paragraph or any crime within the jurisdiction of the Court;
(i) Enforced disappearance of persons;
(j) The crime of apartheid;
(k) Other inhumane acts of a similar character intentionally causing great suffering, or serious injury to body or to mental or physical health.

2. For the purpose of paragraph 1:

(a) 'Attack directed against any civilian population' means a course of conduct involving the multiple commission of acts referred to in paragraph 1 against any civilian population, pursuant to or in furtherance of a State or organizational policy to commit such attack;

(b) 'Extermination' includes the intentional infliction of conditions of life, inter alia the deprivation of access to food and medicine, calculated to bring about the destruction of part of a population;

(c) 'Enslavement' means the exercise of any or all of the powers attaching to the right of ownership over a person and includes the exercise of such power in the course of trafficking in persons, in particular women and children;

(d) 'Deportation or forcible transfer of population' means forced displacement of the persons concerned by expulsion or other coercive acts from the area in which they are lawfully present, without grounds permitted under international law;

(e) 'Torture' means the intentional infliction of severe pain or suffering, whether physical or mental, upon a person in the custody or under the control of the accused; except that torture shall not include pain or suffering arising only from, inherent in or incidental to, lawful sanctions;

(f) 'Forced pregnancy' means the unlawful confinement of a woman forcibly made pregnant, with the intent of affecting the ethnic composition of any population or carrying out other grave violations of international law. This definition shall not in any way be interpreted as affecting national laws relating to pregnancy;

(g) 'Persecution' means the intentional and severe deprivation of fundamental rights contrary to international law by reason of the identity of the group or collectivity;

(h) 'The crime of apartheid' means inhumane acts of a character similar to those referred to in paragraph 1, committed in the context of an institutionalized regime of systematic oppression and domination by one racial group over any other racial group or groups and committed with the intention of maintaining that regime;

(i) 'Enforced disappearance of persons' means the arrest, detention or abduction of persons by, or with the authorization, support or acquiescence of, a State or a political organization, followed by a refusal to acknowledge that deprivation of freedom or to give information on the fate or whereabouts of those persons, with the intention of removing them from the protection of the law for a prolonged period of time.

3. For the purpose of this Statute, it is understood that the term 'gender' refers to the two sexes, male and female, within the context of society. The term 'gender' does not indicate any meaning different from the above.

Article 8

War crimes
1. The Court shall have jurisdiction in respect of war crimes in particular when committed as part of a plan or policy or as part of a large-scale commission of such crimes.
2. For the purpose of this Statute, 'war crimes' means:

(a) Grave breaches of the Geneva Conventions of 12 August 1949, namely, any of the

following acts against persons or property protected under the provisions of the relevant Geneva Convention:
(i)   Wilful killing;
(ii)   Torture or inhuman treatment, including biological experiments;
(iii)   Wilfully causing great suffering, or serious injury to body or health;
(iv)   Extensive destruction and appropriation of property, not justified by military necessity and carried out unlawfully and wantonly;
(v)   Compelling a prisoner of war or other protected person to serve in the forces of a hostile Power;
(vi)   Wilfully depriving a prisoner of war or other protected person of the rights of fair and regular trial;
(vii)   Unlawful deportation or transfer or unlawful confinement;
(viii) Taking of hostages.
(b) Other serious violations of the laws and customs applicable in international armed conflict, within the established framework of international law, namely, any of the following acts:
(i)   Intentionally directing attacks against the civilian population as such or against individual civilians not taking direct part in hostilities;
(ii)   Intentionally directing attacks against civilian objects, that is, objects which are not military objectives;
(iii)   Intentionally directing attacks against personnel, installations, material, units or vehicles involved in a humanitarian assistance or peacekeeping mission in accordance with the Charter of the United Nations, as long as they are entitled to the protection given to civilians or civilian objects under the international law of armed conflict;
(iv)   Intentionally launching an attack in the knowledge that such attack will cause incidental loss of life or injury to civilians or damage to civilian objects or widespread, long-term and severe damage to the natural environment which would be clearly excessive in relation to the concrete and direct overall military advantage anticipated;
(v)   Attacking or bombarding, by whatever means, towns, villages, dwellings or buildings which are undefended and which are not military objectives;
(vi)   Killing or wounding a combatant who, having laid down his arms or having no longer means of defence, has surrendered at discretion;
(vii)   Making improper use of a flag of truce, of the flag or of the military insignia and uniform of the enemy or of the United Nations, as well as of the distinctive emblems of the Geneva Conventions, resulting in death or serious personal injury;
(viii) The transfer, directly or indirectly, by the Occupying Power of parts of its own civilian population into the territory it occupies, or the deportation or transfer of all or parts of the population of the occupied territory within or outside this territory;
(ix)   Intentionally directing attacks against buildings dedicated to religion, education, art, science or charitable purposes, historic monuments, hospitals and places where the sick and wounded are collected, provided they are not military objectives;

(x) Subjecting persons who are in the power of an adverse party to physical mutilation or to medical or scientific experiments of any kind which are neither justified by the medical, dental or hospital treatment of the person concerned nor carried out in his or her interest, and which cause death to or seriously endanger the health of such person or persons;

(xi) Killing or wounding treacherously individuals belonging to the hostile nation or army;

(xii) Declaring that no quarter will be given;

(xiii) Destroying or seizing the enemy's property unless such destruction or seizure be imperatively demanded by the necessities of war;

(xiv) Declaring abolished, suspended or inadmissible in a court of law the rights and actions of the nationals of the hostile party;

(xv) Compelling the nationals of the hostile party to take part in the operations of war directed against their own country, even if they were in the belligerent's service before the commencement of the war;

(xvi) Pillaging a town or place, even when taken by assault;

(xvii) Employing poison or poisoned weapons;

(xviii) Employing asphyxiating, poisonous or other gases, and all analogous liquids, materials or devices;

(xix) Employing bullets which expand or flatten easily in the human body, such as bullets with a hard envelope which does not entirely cover the core or is pierced with incisions;

(xx) Employing weapons, projectiles and material and methods of warfare which are of a nature to cause superfluous injury or unnecessary suffering or which are inherently indiscriminate in violation of the international law of armed conflict, provided that such weapons, projectiles and material and methods of warfare are the subject of a comprehensive prohibition and are included in an annex to this Statute, by an amendment in accordance with the relevant provisions set forth in articles 121 and 123;

(xxi) Committing outrages upon personal dignity, in particular humiliating and degrading treatment;

(xxii) Committing rape, sexual slavery, enforced prostitution, forced pregnancy, as defined in article 7, paragraph 2 (f), enforced sterilization, or any other form of sexual violence also constituting a grave breach of the Geneva Conventions;

(xxiii) Utilizing the presence of a civilian or other protected person to render certain points, areas or military forces immune from military operations;

(xxiv) Intentionally directing attacks against buildings, material, medical units and transport, and personnel using the distinctive emblems of the Geneva Conventions in conformity with international law;

(xxv) Intentionally using starvation of civilians as a method of warfare by depriving them of objects indispensable to their survival, including wilfully impeding relief supplies as provided for under the Geneva Conventions;

(xxvi) Conscripting or enlisting children under the age of fifteen years into the national armed forces or using them to participate actively in hostilities.

(c) In the case of an armed conflict not of an international character, serious violations of article 3 common to the four Geneva Conventions of 12 August 1949, namely, any of the following acts committed against persons taking no active part in the hostilities, including members of armed forces who have laid down their arms and those placed *hors de combat* by sickness, wounds, detention or any other cause:

(i)   Violence to life and person, in particular murder of all kinds, mutilation, cruel treatment and torture;

(ii)   Committing outrages upon personal dignity, in particular humiliating and degrading treatment;

(iii)   Taking of hostages;

(iv)   The passing of sentences and the carrying out of executions without previous judgement pronounced by a regularly constituted court, affording all judicial guarantees which are generally recognized as indispensable.

(d) Paragraph 2 (c) applies to armed conflicts not of an international character and thus does not apply to situations of internal disturbances and tensions, such as riots, isolated and sporadic acts of violence or other acts of a similar nature.

(e) Other serious violations of the laws and customs applicable in armed conflicts not of an international character, within the established framework of international law, namely, any of the following acts:

(i)   Intentionally directing attacks against the civilian population as such or against individual civilians not taking direct part in hostilities;

(ii)   Intentionally directing attacks against buildings, material, medical units and transport, and personnel using the distinctive emblems of the Geneva Conventions in conformity with international law;

(iii)   Intentionally directing attacks against personnel, installations, material, units or vehicles involved in a humanitarian assistance or peacekeeping mission in accordance with the Charter of the United Nations, as long as they are entitled to the protection given to civilians or civilian objects under the international law of armed conflict;

(iv)   Intentionally directing attacks against buildings dedicated to religion, education, art, science or charitable purposes, historic monuments, hospitals and places where the sick and wounded are collected, provided they are not military objectives;

(v)   Pillaging a town or place, even when taken by assault;

(vi)   Committing rape, sexual slavery, enforced prostitution, forced pregnancy, as defined in article 7, paragraph 2 (f), enforced sterilization, and any other form of sexual violence also constituting a serious violation of article 3 common to the four Geneva Conventions;

(vii)   Conscripting or enlisting children under the age of fifteen years into armed forces or groups or using them to participate actively in hostilities;

(viii) Ordering the displacement of the civilian population for reasons related to the conflict, unless the security of the civilians involved or imperative military reasons so demand;

(ix)   Killing or wounding treacherously a combatant adversary;

(x)   Declaring that no quarter will be given;

(xi)   Subjecting persons who are in the power of another party to the conflict to physical mutilation or to medical or scientific experiments of any kind which are neither justified by the medical, dental or hospital treatment of the person concerned nor carried out in his or her interest, and which cause death to or seriously endanger the health of such person or persons;

(xii)   Destroying or seizing the property of an adversary unless such destruction or seizure be imperatively demanded by the necessities of the conflict;

(f)   Paragraph 2 (e) applies to armed conflicts not of an international character and thus does not apply to situations of internal disturbances and tensions, such as riots, isolated and sporadic acts of violence or other acts of a similar nature. It applies to armed conflicts that take place in the territory of a State when there is protracted armed conflict between governmental authorities and organized armed groups or between such groups.

3. Nothing in paragraph 2 (c) and (e) shall affect the responsibility of a Government to maintain or re-establish law and order in the State or to defend the unity and territorial integrity of the State, by all legitimate means.

Article 9

Elements of Crimes

1. Elements of Crimes shall assist the Court in the interpretation and application of articles 6, 7 and 8. They shall be adopted by a two-thirds majority of the members of the Assembly of States Parties.

2. Amendments to the Elements of Crimes may be proposed by:

(a)   Any State Party;
(b)   The judges acting by an absolute majority;
(c)   The Prosecutor.

Such amendments shall be adopted by a two-thirds majority of the members of the Assembly of States Parties.

3. The Elements of Crimes and amendments thereto shall be consistent with this Statute.

Article 10

Nothing in this Part shall be interpreted as limiting or prejudicing in any way existing or developing rules of international law for purposes other than this Statute.

Article 11

Jurisdiction ratione temporis

1. The Court has jurisdiction only with respect to crimes committed after the entry into force of this Statute.

2. If a State becomes a Party to this Statute after its entry into force, the Court may exercise its jurisdiction only with respect to crimes committed after the entry into force of this Statute for that State, unless that State has made a declaration under article 12, paragraph 3.

Article 12

Preconditions to the exercise of jurisdiction
1. A State which becomes a Party to this Statute thereby accepts the jurisdiction of the Court with respect to the crimes referred to in article 5.
2. In the case of article 13, paragraph (a) or (c), the Court may exercise its jurisdiction if one or more of the following States are Parties to this Statute or have accepted the jurisdiction of the Court in accordance with paragraph 3:

(a) The State on the territory of which the conduct in question occurred or, if the crime was committed on board a vessel or aircraft, the State of registration of that vessel or aircraft;
(b) The State of which the person accused of the crime is a national.

3. If the acceptance of a State which is not a Party to this Statute is required under paragraph 2, that State may, by declaration lodged with the Registrar, accept the exercise of jurisdiction by the Court with respect to the crime in question. The accepting State shall cooperate with the Court without any delay or exception in accordance with Part 9.

Article 13

Exercise of jurisdiction
The Court may exercise its jurisdiction with respect to a crime referred to in article 5 in accordance with the provisions of this Statute if:

(a) A situation in which one or more of such crimes appears to have been committed is referred to the Prosecutor by a State Party in accordance with article 14;
(b) A situation in which one or more of such crimes appears to have been committed is referred to the Prosecutor by the Security Council acting under Chapter VII of the Charter of the United Nations; or
(c) The Prosecutor has initiated an investigation in respect of such a crime in accordance with article 15.

Article 14

Referral of a situation by a State Party
1. A State Party may refer to the Prosecutor a situation in which one or more crimes within the jurisdiction of the Court appear to have been committed requesting the Prosecutor to investigate the situation for the purpose of determining whether one or more specific persons should be charged with the commission of such crimes.
2. As far as possible, a referral shall specify the relevant circumstances and be accompanied by such supporting documentation as is available to the State referring the situation.

Article 15

Prosecutor
1. The Prosecutor may initiate investigations *proprio motu* on the basis of information on crimes within the jurisdiction of the Court.

2. The Prosecutor shall analyse the seriousness of the information received. For this purpose, he or she may seek additional information from States, organs of the United Nations, intergovernmental or non-governmental organizations, or other reliable sources that he or she deems appropriate, and may receive written or oral testimony at the seat of the Court.

3. If the Prosecutor concludes that there is a reasonable basis to proceed with an investigation, he or she shall submit to the Pre-Trial Chamber a request for authorization of an investigation, together with any supporting material collected. Victims may make representations to the Pre-Trial Chamber, in accordance with the Rules of Procedure and Evidence.

4. If the Pre-Trial Chamber, upon examination of the request and the supporting material, considers that there is a reasonable basis to proceed with an investigation, and that the case appears to fall within the jurisdiction of the Court, it shall authorize the commencement of the investigation, without prejudice to subsequent determinations by the Court with regard to the jurisdiction and admissibility of a case.

5. The refusal of the Pre-Trial Chamber to authorize the investigation shall not preclude the presentation of a subsequent request by the Prosecutor based on new facts or evidence regarding the same situation.

6. If, after the preliminary examination referred to in paragraphs 1 and 2, the Prosecutor concludes that the information provided does not constitute a reasonable basis for an investigation, he or she shall inform those who provided the information. This shall not preclude the Prosecutor from considering further information submitted to him or her regarding the same situation in the light of new facts or evidence.

Article 16

Deferral of investigation or prosecution
No investigation or prosecution may be commenced or proceeded with under this Statute for a period of 12 months after the Security Council, in a resolution adopted under Chapter VII of the Charter of the United Nations, has requested the Court to that effect; that request may be renewed by the Council under the same conditions.

Article 17

Issues of admissibility
1. Having regard to paragraph 10 of the Preamble and article 1, the Court shall determine that a case is inadmissible where:

(a) The case is being investigated or prosecuted by a State which has jurisdiction over it, unless the State is unwilling or unable genuinely to carry out the investigation or prosecution;

(b) The case has been investigated by a State which has jurisdiction over it and the State has decided not to prosecute the person concerned, unless the decision resulted from the unwillingness or inability of the State genuinely to prosecute;

(c) The person concerned has already been tried for conduct which is the subject of the complaint, and a trial by the Court is not permitted under article 20, paragraph 3;

(d) The case is not of sufficient gravity to justify further action by the Court.

2. In order to determine unwillingness in a particular case, the Court shall consider, having regard to the principles of due process recognized by international law, whether one or more of the following exist, as applicable:

(a) The proceedings were or are being undertaken or the national decision was made for the purpose of shielding the person concerned from criminal responsibility for crimes within the jurisdiction of the Court referred to in article 5;
(b) There has been an unjustified delay in the proceedings which in the circumstances is inconsistent with an intent to bring the person concerned to justice;
(c) The proceedings were not or are not being conducted independently or impartially, and they were or are being conducted in a manner which, in the circumstances, is inconsistent with an intent to bring the person concerned to justice.

3. In order to determine inability in a particular case, the Court shall consider whether, due to a total or substantial collapse or unavailability of its national judicial system, the State is unable to obtain the accused or the necessary evidence and testimony or otherwise unable to carry out its proceedings.

Article 18

Preliminary rulings regarding admissibility
1. When a situation has been referred to the Court pursuant to article 13 (a) and the Prosecutor has determined that there would be a reasonable basis to commence an investigation, or the Prosecutor initiates an investigation pursuant to articles 13 (c) and 15, the Prosecutor shall notify all States Parties and those States which, taking into account the information available, would normally exercise jurisdiction over the crimes concerned. The Prosecutor may notify such States on a confidential basis and, where the Prosecutor believes it necessary to protect persons, prevent destruction of evidence or prevent the absconding of persons, may limit the scope of the information provided to States.
2. Within one month of receipt of that notification, a State may inform the Court that it is investigating or has investigated its nationals or others within its jurisdiction with respect to criminal acts which may constitute crimes referred to in article 5 and which relate to the information provided in the notification to States. At the request of that State, the Prosecutor shall defer to the State's investigation of those persons unless the Pre-Trial Chamber, on the application of the Prosecutor, decides to authorize the investigation.
3. The Prosecutor's deferral to a State's investigation shall be open to review by the Prosecutor six months after the date of deferral or at any time when there has been a significant change of circumstances based on the State's unwillingness or inability genuinely to carry out the investigation.
4. The State concerned or the Prosecutor may appeal to the Appeals Chamber against a ruling of the Pre-Trial Chamber, in accordance with article 82. The appeal may be heard on an expedited basis.
5. When the Prosecutor has deferred an investigation in accordance with paragraph 2, the Prosecutor may request that the State concerned periodically inform the Prosecutor of the progress of its investigations and any subsequent prosecutions. States Parties shall respond to such requests without undue delay.

6. Pending a ruling by the Pre-Trial Chamber, or at any time when the Prosecutor has deferred an investigation under this article, the Prosecutor may, on an exceptional basis, seek authority from the Pre-Trial Chamber to pursue necessary investigative steps for the purpose of preserving evidence where there is a unique opportunity to obtain important evidence or there is a significant risk that such evidence may not be subsequently available.

7. A State which has challenged a ruling of the Pre-Trial Chamber under this article may challenge the admissibility of a case under article 19 on the grounds of additional significant facts or significant change of circumstances.

Article 19

Challenges to the jurisdiction of the Court or the admissibility of a case

1. The Court shall satisfy itself that it has jurisdiction in any case brought before it. The Court may, on its own motion, determine the admissibility of a case in accordance with article 17.

2. Challenges to the admissibility of a case on the grounds referred to in article 17 or challenges to the jurisdiction of the Court may be made by:

(a) An accused or a person for whom a warrant of arrest or a summons to appear has been issued under article 58;
(b) A State which has jurisdiction over a case, on the ground that it is investigating or prosecuting the case or has investigated or prosecuted; or
(c) A State from which acceptance of jurisdiction is required under article 12.

3. The Prosecutor may seek a ruling from the Court regarding a question of jurisdiction or admissibility. In proceedings with respect to jurisdiction or admissibility, those who have referred the situation under article 13, as well as victims, may also submit observations to the Court.

4. The admissibility of a case or the jurisdiction of the Court may be challenged only once by any person or State referred to in paragraph 2. The challenge shall take place prior to or at the commencement of the trial. In exceptional circumstances, the Court may grant leave for a challenge to be brought more than once or at a time later than the commencement of the trial. Challenges to the admissibility of a case, at the commencement of a trial, or subsequently with the leave of the Court, may be based only on article 17, paragraph 1 (c).

5. A State referred to in paragraph 2 (b) and (c) shall make a challenge at the earliest opportunity.

6. Prior to the confirmation of the charges, challenges to the admissibility of a case or challenges to the jurisdiction of the Court shall be referred to the Pre-Trial Chamber. After confirmation of the charges, they shall be referred to the Trial Chamber. Decisions with respect to jurisdiction or admissibility may be appealed to the Appeals Chamber in accordance with article 82.

7. If a challenge is made by a State referred to in paragraph 2 (b) or (c), the Prosecutor shall suspend the investigation until such time as the Court makes a determination in accordance with article 17.

8. Pending a ruling by the Court, the Prosecutor may seek authority from the Court:

(a) To pursue necessary investigative steps of the kind referred to in article 18, paragraph 6;
(b) To take a statement or testimony from a witness or complete the collection and exami-
     nation of evidence which had begun prior to the making of the challenge; and
(c) In cooperation with the relevant States, to prevent the absconding of persons in respect
     of whom the Prosecutor has already requested a warrant of arrest under article 58.

9. The making of a challenge shall not affect the validity of any act performed by the
Prosecutor or any order or warrant issued by the Court prior to the making of the challenge.

10. If the Court has decided that a case is inadmissible under article 17, the Prosecutor
may submit a request for a review of the decision when he or she is fully satisfied that new
facts have arisen which negate the basis on which the case had previously been found inadmissible under article 17.

11. If the Prosecutor, having regard to the matters referred to in article 17, defers an investigation, the Prosecutor may request that the relevant State make available to the Prosecutor
information on the proceedings. That information shall, at the request of the State concerned,
be confidential. If the Prosecutor thereafter decides to proceed with an investigation, he or she
shall notify the State to which deferral of the proceedings has taken place.

Article 20

Ne bis in idem

1. Except as provided in this Statute, no person shall be tried before the Court with respect
to conduct which formed the basis of crimes for which the person has been convicted or
acquitted by the Court.

2. No person shall be tried by another court for a crime referred to in article 5 for which
that person has already been convicted or acquitted by the Court.

3. No person who has been tried by another court for conduct also proscribed under article 6, 7 or 8 shall be tried by the Court with respect to the same conduct unless the proceedings in the other court:

(a) Were for the purpose of shielding the person concerned from criminal responsibility for
     crimes within the jurisdiction of the Court; or
(b) Otherwise were not conducted independently or impartially in accordance with the
     norms of due process recognized by international law and were conducted in a manner
     which, in the circumstances, was inconsistent with an intent to bring the person
     concerned to justice.

Article 21

Applicable law

1. The Court shall apply:

(a) In the first place, this Statute, Elements of Crimes and its Rules of Procedure and
     Evidence;
(b) In the second place, where appropriate, applicable treaties and the principles and rules of
     international law, including the established principles of the international law of armed
     conflict;

(c) Failing that, general principles of law derived by the Court from national laws of legal systems of the world including, as appropriate, the national laws of States that would normally exercise jurisdiction over the crime, provided that those principles are not inconsistent with this Statute and with international law and internationally recognized norms and standards.

2. The Court may apply principles and rules of law as interpreted in its previous decisions.

3. The application and interpretation of law pursuant to this article must be consistent with internationally recognized human rights, and be without any adverse distinction founded on grounds such as gender as defined in article 7, paragraph 3, age, race, colour, language, religion or belief, political or other opinion, national, ethnic or social origin, wealth, birth or other status.

PART 3. GENERAL PRINCIPLES OF CRIMINAL LAW

Article 22

Nullum crimen sine lege

1. A person shall not be criminally responsible under this Statute unless the conduct in question constitutes, at the time it takes place, a crime within the jurisdiction of the Court.

2. The definition of a crime shall be strictly construed and shall not be extended by analogy. In case of ambiguity, the definition shall be interpreted in favour of the person being investigated, prosecuted or convicted.

3. This article shall not affect the characterization of any conduct as criminal under international law independently of this Statute.

Article 23

Nulla poena sine lege

A person convicted by the Court may be punished only in accordance with this Statute.

Article 24

Non-retroactivity ratione personae

1. No person shall be criminally responsible under this Statute for conduct prior to the entry into force of the Statute.

2. In the event of a change in the law applicable to a given case prior to a final judgement, the law more favourable to the person being investigated, prosecuted or convicted shall apply.

Article 25

Individual criminal responsibility

1. The Court shall have jurisdiction over natural persons pursuant to this Statute.

2. A person who commits a crime within the jurisdiction of the Court shall be individually responsible and liable for punishment in accordance with this Statute.

3. In accordance with this Statute, a person shall be criminally responsible and liable for punishment for a crime within the jurisdiction of the Court if that person:

(a) Commits such a crime, whether as an individual, jointly with another or through another person, regardless of whether that other person is criminally responsible;
(b) Orders, solicits or induces the commission of such a crime which in fact occurs or is attempted;
(c) For the purpose of facilitating the commission of such a crime, aids, abets or otherwise assists in its commission or its attempted commission, including providing the means for its commission;
(d) In any other way contributes to the commission or attempted commission of such a crime by a group of persons acting with a common purpose. Such contribution shall be intentional and shall either:
  (i) Be made with the aim of furthering the criminal activity or criminal purpose of the group, where such activity or purpose involves the commission of a crime within the jurisdiction of the Court; or
  (ii) Be made in the knowledge of the intention of the group to commit the crime;
(e) In respect of the crime of genocide, directly and publicly incites others to commit genocide;
(f) Attempts to commit such a crime by taking action that commences its execution by means of a substantial step, but the crime does not occur because of circumstances independent of the person's intentions. However, a person who abandons the effort to commit the crime or otherwise prevents the completion of the crime shall not be liable for punishment under this Statute for the attempt to commit that crime if that person completely and voluntarily gave up the criminal purpose.

4. No provision in this Statute relating to individual criminal responsibility shall affect the responsibility of States under international law.

Article 26

Exclusion of jurisdiction over persons under eighteen
The Court shall have no jurisdiction over any person who was under the age of 18 at the time of the alleged commission of a crime.

Article 27

Irrelevance of official capacity
1. This Statute shall apply equally to all persons without any distinction based on official capacity. In particular, official capacity as a Head of State or Government, a member of a Government or parliament, an elected representative or a government official shall in no case exempt a person from criminal responsibility under this Statute, nor shall it, in and of itself, constitute a ground for reduction of sentence.

2. Immunities or special procedural rules which may attach to the official capacity of a person, whether under national or international law, shall not bar the Court from exercising its jurisdiction over such a person.

Article 28

Responsibility of commanders and other superiors
In addition to other grounds of criminal responsibility under this Statute for crimes within the jurisdiction of the Court:

(a) A military commander or person effectively acting as a military commander shall be criminally responsible for crimes within the jurisdiction of the Court committed by forces under his or her effective command and control, or effective authority and control as the case may be, as a result of his or her failure to exercise control properly over such forces, where:
   (i) That military commander or person either knew or, owing to the circumstances at the time, should have known that the forces were committing or about to commit such crimes; and
   (ii) That military commander or person failed to take all necessary and reasonable measures within his or her power to prevent or repress their commission or to submit the matter to the competent authorities for investigation and prosecution.
(b) With respect to superior and subordinate relationships not described in paragraph (a), a superior shall be criminally responsible for crimes within the jurisdiction of the Court committed by subordinates under his or her effective authority and control, as a result of his or her failure to exercise control properly over such subordinates, where:
   (i) The superior either knew, or consciously disregarded information which clearly indicated, that the subordinates were committing or about to commit such crimes;
   (ii) The crimes concerned activities that were within the effective responsibility and control of the superior; and
   (iii) The superior failed to take all necessary and reasonable measures within his or her power to prevent or repress their commission or to submit the matter to the competent authorities for investigation and prosecution.

Article 29

Non-applicability of statute of limitations
The crimes within the jurisdiction of the Court shall not be subject to any statute of limitations.

Article 30

Mental element
1. Unless otherwise provided, a person shall be criminally responsible and liable for punishment for a crime within the jurisdiction of the Court only if the material elements are committed with intent and knowledge.
2. For the purposes of this article, a person has intent where:

(a) In relation to conduct, that person means to engage in the conduct;
(b) In relation to a consequence, that person means to cause that consequence or is aware that it will occur in the ordinary course of events.

3. For the purposes of this article, 'knowledge' means awareness that a circumstance exists or a consequence will occur in the ordinary course of events. 'Know' and 'knowingly' shall be construed accordingly.

Article 31

Grounds for excluding criminal responsibility

1. In addition to other grounds for excluding criminal responsibility provided for in this Statute, a person shall not be criminally responsible if, at the time of that person's conduct:

(a)   The person suffers from a mental disease or defect that destroys that person's capacity to appreciate the unlawfulness or nature of his or her conduct, or capacity to control his or her conduct to conform to the requirements of law;

(b)   The person is in a state of intoxication that destroys that person's capacity to appreciate the unlawfulness or nature of his or her conduct, or capacity to control his or her conduct to conform to the requirements of law, unless the person has become voluntarily intoxicated under such circumstances that the person knew, or disregarded the risk, that, as a result of the intoxication, he or she was likely to engage in conduct constituting a crime within the jurisdiction of the Court;

(c)   The person acts reasonably to defend himself or herself or another person or, in the case of war crimes, property which is essential for the survival of the person or another person or property which is essential for accomplishing a military mission, against an imminent and unlawful use of force in a manner proportionate to the degree of danger to the person or the other person or property protected. The fact that the person was involved in a defensive operation conducted by forces shall not in itself constitute a ground for excluding criminal responsibility under this subparagraph;

(d)   The conduct which is alleged to constitute a crime within the jurisdiction of the Court has been caused by duress resulting from a threat of imminent death or of continuing or imminent serious bodily harm against that person or another person, and the person acts necessarily and reasonably to avoid this threat, provided that the person does not intend to cause a greater harm than the one sought to be avoided. Such a threat may either be:

(i)   Made by other persons; or

(ii)   Constituted by other circumstances beyond that person's control.

2. The Court shall determine the applicability of the grounds for excluding criminal responsibility provided for in this Statute to the case before it.

3. At trial, the Court may consider a ground for excluding criminal responsibility other than those referred to in paragraph 1 where such a ground is derived from applicable law as set forth in article 21. The procedures relating to the consideration of such a ground shall be provided for in the Rules of Procedure and Evidence.

Article 32

Mistake of fact or mistake of law

1. A mistake of fact shall be a ground for excluding criminal responsibility only if it negates the mental element required by the crime.

2. A mistake of law as to whether a particular type of conduct is a crime within the jurisdiction of the Court shall not be a ground for excluding criminal responsibility. A mistake of law may, however, be a ground for excluding criminal responsibility if it negates the mental element required by such a crime, or as provided for in article 33.

Article 33

Superior orders and prescription of law
1. The fact that a crime within the jurisdiction of the Court has been committed by a person pursuant to an order of a Government or of a superior, whether military or civilian, shall not relieve that person of criminal responsibility unless:

(a) The person was under a legal obligation to obey orders of the Government or the superior in question;
(b) The person did not know that the order was unlawful; and
(c) The order was not manifestly unlawful.

2. For the purposes of this article, orders to commit genocide or crimes against humanity are manifestly unlawful.

PART 4. COMPOSITION AND ADMINISTRATION OF THE COURT

Article 34

Organs of the Court
The Court shall be composed of the following organs:

(a) The Presidency;
(b) An Appeals Division, a Trial Division and a Pre-Trial Division;
(c) The Office of the Prosecutor;
(d) The Registry.

Article 35

Service of judges
1. All judges shall be elected as full-time members of the Court and shall be available to serve on that basis from the commencement of their terms of office.
2. The judges composing the Presidency shall serve on a full-time basis as soon as they are elected.
3. The Presidency may, on the basis of the workload of the Court and in consultation with its members, decide from time to time to what extent the remaining judges shall be required to serve on a full-time basis. Any such arrangement shall be without prejudice to the provisions of article 40.
4. The financial arrangements for judges not required to serve on a full-time basis shall be made in accordance with article 49.

Article 36

Qualifications, nomination and election of judges

1. Subject to the provisions of paragraph 2, there shall be 18 judges of the Court.

2. (a)   The Presidency, acting on behalf of the Court, may propose an increase in the number of judges specified in paragraph 1, indicating the reasons why this is considered necessary and appropriate. The Registrar shall promptly circulate any such proposal to all States Parties.

   (b)   Any such proposal shall then be considered at a meeting of the Assembly of States Parties to be convened in accordance with article 112. The proposal shall be considered adopted if approved at the meeting by a vote of two thirds of the members of the Assembly of States Parties and shall enter into force at such time as decided by the Assembly of States Parties.

   (c)   (i)   Once a proposal for an increase in the number of judges has been adopted under subparagraph (b), the election of the additional judgesshall take place at the next session of the Assembly of States Parties in accordance with paragraphs 3 to 8, and article 37, paragraph 2;

         (ii) Once a proposal for an increase in the number of judges has been adopted and brought into effect under subparagraphs (b) and (c) (i), it shall be open to the Presidency at any time thereafter, if the workload of the Court justifies it, to propose a reduction in the number of judges, provided that the number of judges shall not be reduced below that specified in paragraph 1. The proposal shall be dealt with in accordance with the procedure laid down in subparagraphs (a) and (b). In the event that the proposal is adopted, the number of judges shall be progressively decreased as the terms of office of serving judges expire, until the necessary number has been reached.

3. (a)   The judges shall be chosen from among persons of high moral character, impartiality and integrity who possess the qualifications required in their respective States for appointment to the highest judicial offices.

   (b)   Every candidate for election to the Court shall:
         (i)   Have established competence in criminal law and procedure, and the necessary relevant experience, whether as judge, prosecutor, advocate or in other similar capacity, in criminal proceedings; or
         (ii) Have established competence in relevant areas of international law such as international humanitarian law and the law of human rights, and extensive experience in a professional legal capacity which is of relevance to the judicial work of the Court;

   (c)   Every candidate for election to the Court shall have an excellent knowledge of and be fluent in at least one of the working languages of the Court.

4. (a)   Nominations of candidates for election to the Court may be made by any State Party to this Statute, and shall be made either:
         (i)   By the procedure for the nomination of candidates for appointment to the highest judicial offices in the State in question; or
         (ii) By the procedure provided for the nomination of candidates for the International Court of Justice in the Statute of that Court.

Nominations shall be accompanied by a statement in the necessary detail specifying how the candidate fulfils the requirements of paragraph 3.

(b)   Each State Party may put forward one candidate for any given election who need not necessarily be a national of that State Party but shall in any case be a national of a State Party.

(c)   The Assembly of States Parties may decide to establish, if appropriate, an Advisory Committee on nominations. In that event, the Committee's composition and mandate shall be established by the Assembly of States Parties.

5. For the purposes of the election, there shall be two lists of candidates:

List A containing the names of candidates with the qualifications specified in paragraph 3 (b) (i); and

List B containing the names of candidates with the qualifications specified in paragraph 3 (b) (ii).

A candidate with sufficient qualifications for both lists may choose on which list to appear. At the first election to the Court, at least nine judges shall be elected from list A and at least five judges from list B. Subsequent elections shall be so organized as to maintain the equivalent proportion on the Court of judges qualified on the two lists.

6. (a)   The judges shall be elected by secret ballot at a meeting of the Assembly of States Parties convened for that purpose under article 112. Subject to paragraph 7, the persons elected to the Court shall be the 18 candidates who obtain the highest number of votes and a two-thirds majority of the States Parties present and voting.

(b)   In the event that a sufficient number of judges is not elected on the first ballot, successive ballots shall be held in accordance with the procedures laid down in subparagraph (a) until the remaining places have been filled.

7. No two judges may be nationals of the same State. A person who, for the purposes of membership of the Court, could be regarded as a national of more than one State shall be deemed to be a national of the State in which that person ordinarily exercises civil and political rights.

8. (a)   The States Parties shall, in the selection of judges, take into account the need, within the membership of the Court, for:

(i)   The representation of the principal legal systems of the world;

(ii)   Equitable geographical representation; and

(iii) A fair representation of female and male judges.

(b)   States Parties shall also take into account the need to include judges with legal expertise on specific issues, including, but not limited to, violence against women or children.

9. (a)   Subject to subparagraph (b), judges shall hold office for a term of nine years and, subject to subparagraph (c) and to article 37, paragraph 2, shall not be eligible for re-election.

(b)   At the first election, one third of the judges elected shall be selected by lot to serve for a term of three years; one third of the judges elected shall be selected by lot to serve for a term of six years; and the remainder shall serve for a term of nine years.

(c)   A judge who is selected to serve for a term of three years under subparagraph (b) shall be eligible for re-election for a full term.

10. Notwithstanding paragraph 9, a judge assigned to a Trial or Appeals Chamber in accordance with article 39 shall continue in office to complete any trial or appeal the hearing of which has already commenced before that Chamber.

Article 37

Judicial vacancies

1. In the event of a vacancy, an election shall be held in accordance with article 36 to fill the vacancy.

2. A judge elected to fill a vacancy shall serve for the remainder of the predecessor's term and, if that period is three years or less, shall be eligible for re-election for a full term under article 36.

Article 38

The Presidency

1. The President and the First and Second Vice-Presidents shall be elected by an absolute majority of the judges. They shall each serve for a term of three years or until the end of their respective terms of office as judges, whichever expires earlier. They shall be eligible for re-election once.

2. The First Vice-President shall act in place of the President in the event that the President is unavailable or disqualified. The Second Vice-President shall act in place of the President in the event that both the President and the First Vice-President are unavailable or disqualified.

3. The President, together with the First and Second Vice-Presidents, shall constitute the Presidency, which shall be responsible for:

(a)   The proper administration of the Court, with the exception of the Office of the Prosecutor; and

(b)   The other functions conferred upon it in accordance with this Statute.

4. In discharging its responsibility under paragraph 3 (a), the Presidency shall coordinate with and seek the concurrence of the Prosecutor on all matters of mutual concern.

Article 39

Chambers

1. As soon as possible after the election of the judges, the Court shall organize itself into the divisions specified in article 34, paragraph (b). The Appeals Division shall be composed of the President and four other judges, the Trial Division of not less than six judges and the Pre-Trial Division of not less than six judges. The assignment of judges to divisions shall be based on the nature of the functions to be performed by each division and the qualifications

and experience of the judges elected to the Court, in such a way that each division shall contain an appropriate combination of expertise in criminal law and procedure and in international law. The Trial and Pre-Trial Divisions shall be composed predominantly of judges with criminal trial experience.

2. (a) The judicial functions of the Court shall be carried out in each division by Chambers.
   (b) (i) The Appeals Chamber shall be composed of all the judges of the Appeals Division;
       (ii) The functions of the Trial Chamber shall be carried out by three judges of the Trial Division;
       (iii) The functions of the Pre-Trial Chamber shall be carried out either by three judges of the Pre-Trial Division or by a single judge of that division in accordance with this Statute and the Rules of Procedure and Evidence;
   (c) Nothing in this paragraph shall preclude the simultaneous constitution of more than one Trial Chamber or Pre-Trial Chamber when the efficient management of the Court's workload so requires.

3. (a) Judges assigned to the Trial and Pre-Trial Divisions shall serve in those divisions for a period of three years, and thereafter until the completion of any case the hearing of which has already commenced in the division concerned.
   (b) Judges assigned to the Appeals Division shall serve in that division for their entire term of office.

4. Judges assigned to the Appeals Division shall serve only in that division. Nothing in this article shall, however, preclude the temporary attachment of judges from the Trial Division to the Pre-Trial Division or vice versa, if the Presidency considers that the efficient management of the Court's workload so requires, provided that under no circumstances shall a judge who has participated in the pre-trial phase of a case be eligible to sit on the Trial Chamber hearing that case.

Article 40

Independence of the judges

1. The judges shall be independent in the performance of their functions.

2. Judges shall not engage in any activity which is likely to interfere with their judicial functions or to affect confidence in their independence.

3. Judges required to serve on a full-time basis at the seat of the Court shall not engage in any other occupation of a professional nature.

4. Any question regarding the application of paragraphs 2 and 3 shall be decided by an absolute majority of the judges. Where any such question concerns an individual judge, that judge shall not take part in the decision.

Article 41

Excusing and disqualification of judges

1. The Presidency may, at the request of a judge, excuse that judge from the exercise of a function under this Statute, in accordance with the Rules of Procedure and Evidence.

2. (a)   A judge shall not participate in any case in which his or her impartiality might reasonably be doubted on any ground. A judge shall be disqualified from a case in accordance with this paragraph if, *inter alia*, that judge has previously been involved in any capacity in that case before the Court or in a related criminal case at the national level involving the person being investigated or prosecuted. A judge shall also be disqualified on such other grounds as may be provided for in the Rules of Procedure and Evidence.

(b)   The Prosecutor or the person being investigated or prosecuted may request the disqualification of a judge under this paragraph.

(c)   Any question as to the disqualification of a judge shall be decided by an absolute majority of the judges. The challenged judge shall be entitled to present his or her comments on the matter, but shall not take part in the decision.

Article 42

The Office of the Prosecutor

1. The Office of the Prosecutor shall act independently as a separate organ of the Court. It shall be responsible for receiving referrals and any substantiated information on crimes within the jurisdiction of the Court, for examining them and for conducting investigations and prosecutions before the Court. A member of the Office shall not seek or act on instructions from any external source.

2. The Office shall be headed by the Prosecutor. The Prosecutor shall have full authority over the management and administration of the Office, including the staff, facilities and other resources thereof. The Prosecutor shall be assisted by one or more Deputy Prosecutors, who shall be entitled to carry out any of the acts required of the Prosecutor under this Statute. The Prosecutor and the Deputy Prosecutors shall be of different nationalities. They shall serve on a full-time basis.

3. The Prosecutor and the Deputy Prosecutors shall be persons of high moral character, be highly competent in and have extensive practical experience in the prosecution or trial of criminal cases. They shall have an excellent knowledge of and be fluent in at least one of the working languages of the Court.

4. The Prosecutor shall be elected by secret ballot by an absolute majority of the members of the Assembly of States Parties. The Deputy Prosecutors shall be elected in the same way from a list of candidates provided by the Prosecutor. The Prosecutor shall nominate three candidates for each position of Deputy Prosecutor to be filled. Unless a shorter term is decided upon at the time of their election, the Prosecutor and the Deputy Prosecutors shall hold office for a term of nine years and shall not be eligible for re-election.

5. Neither the Prosecutor nor a Deputy Prosecutor shall engage in any activity which is likely to interfere with his or her prosecutorial functions or to affect confidence in his or her independence. They shall not engage in any other occupation of a professional nature.

6. The Presidency may excuse the Prosecutor or a Deputy Prosecutor, at his or her request, from acting in a particular case.

7. Neither the Prosecutor nor a Deputy Prosecutor shall participate in any matter in which their impartiality might reasonably be doubted on any ground. They shall be disqualified from a case in accordance with this paragraph if, *inter alia*, they have previously been involved in

any capacity in that case before the Court or in a related criminal case at the national level involving the person being investigated or prosecuted.

8. Any question as to the disqualification of the Prosecutor or a Deputy Prosecutor shall be decided by the Appeals Chamber.

(a) The person being investigated or prosecuted may at any time request the disqualification of the Prosecutor or a Deputy Prosecutor on the grounds set out in this article;
(b) The Prosecutor or the Deputy Prosecutor, as appropriate, shall be entitled to present his or her comments on the matter;

9. The Prosecutor shall appoint advisers with legal expertise on specific issues, including, but not limited to, sexual and gender violence and violence against children.

Article 43

The Registry
1. The Registry shall be responsible for the non-judicial aspects of the administration and servicing of the Court, without prejudice to the functions and powers of the Prosecutor in accordance with article 42.

2. The Registry shall be headed by the Registrar, who shall be the principal administrative officer of the Court. The Registrar shall exercise his or her functions under the authority of the President of the Court.

3. The Registrar and the Deputy Registrar shall be persons of high moral character, be highly competent and have an excellent knowledge of and be fluent in at least one of the working languages of the Court.

4. The judges shall elect the Registrar by an absolute majority by secret ballot, taking into account any recommendation by the Assembly of States Parties. If the need arises and upon the recommendation of the Registrar, the judges shall elect, in the same manner, a Deputy Registrar.

5. The Registrar shall hold office for a term of five years, shall be eligible for re-election once and shall serve on a full-time basis. The Deputy Registrar shall hold office for a term of five years or such shorter term as may be decided upon by an absolute majority of the judges, and may be elected on the basis that the Deputy Registrar shall be called upon to serve as required.

6. The Registrar shall set up a Victims and Witnesses Unit within the Registry. This Unit shall provide, in consultation with the Office of the Prosecutor, protective measures and security arrangements, counselling and other appropriate assistance for witnesses, victims who appear before the Court, and others who are at risk on account of testimony given by such witnesses. The Unit shall include staff with expertise in trauma, including trauma related to crimes of sexual violence.

Article 44

Staff
1. The Prosecutor and the Registrar shall appoint such qualified staff as may be required to their respective offices. In the case of the Prosecutor, this shall include the appointment of investigators.

2. In the employment of staff, the Prosecutor and the Registrar shall ensure the highest standards of efficiency, competency and integrity, and shall have regard, *mutatis mutandis*, to the criteria set forth in article 36, paragraph 8.

3. The Registrar, with the agreement of the Presidency and the Prosecutor, shall propose Staff Regulations which include the terms and conditions upon which the staff of the Court shall be appointed, remunerated and dismissed. The Staff Regulations shall be approved by the Assembly of States Parties.

4. The Court may, in exceptional circumstances, employ the expertise of gratis personnel offered by States Parties, intergovernmental organizations or non-governmental organizations to assist with the work of any of the organs of the Court. The Prosecutor may accept any such offer on behalf of the Office of the Prosecutor. Such gratis personnel shall be employed in accordance with guidelines to be established by the Assembly of States Parties.

Article 45

Solemn undertaking
Before taking up their respective duties under this Statute, the judges, the Prosecutor, the Deputy Prosecutors, the Registrar and the Deputy Registrar shall each make a solemn undertaking in open court to exercise his or her respective functions impartially and conscientiously.

Article 46

Removal from office
1. A judge, the Prosecutor, a Deputy Prosecutor, the Registrar or the Deputy Registrar shall be removed from office if a decision to this effect is made in accordance with paragraph 2, in cases where that person:

(a) Is found to have committed serious misconduct or a serious breach of his or her duties under this Statute, as provided for in the Rules of Procedure and Evidence; or
(b) Is unable to exercise the functions required by this Statute.

2. A decision as to the removal from office of a judge, the Prosecutor or a Deputy Prosecutor under paragraph 1 shall be made by the Assembly of States Parties, by secret ballot:

(a) In the case of a judge, by a two-thirds majority of the States Parties upon a recommendation adopted by a two-thirds majority of the other judges;
(b) In the case of the Prosecutor, by an absolute majority of the States Parties;
(c) In the case of a Deputy Prosecutor, by an absolute majority of the States Parties upon the recommendation of the Prosecutor.

3. A decision as to the removal from office of the Registrar or Deputy Registrar shall be made by an absolute majority of the judges.

4. A judge, Prosecutor, Deputy Prosecutor, Registrar or Deputy Registrar whose

conduct or ability to exercise the functions of the office as required by this Statute is challenged under this article shall have full opportunity to present and receive evidence and to make submissions in accordance with the Rules of Procedure and Evidence. The person in question shall not otherwise participate in the consideration of the matter.

Article 47

Disciplinary measures
A judge, Prosecutor, Deputy Prosecutor, Registrar or Deputy Registrar who has committed misconduct of a less serious nature than that set out in article 46, paragraph 1, shall be subject to disciplinary measures, in accordance with the Rules of Procedure and Evidence.

Article 48

Privileges and immunities
1. The Court shall enjoy in the territory of each State Party such privileges and immunities as are necessary for the fulfilment of its purposes.
2. The judges, the Prosecutor, the Deputy Prosecutors and the Registrar shall, when engaged on or with respect to the business of the Court, enjoy the same privileges and immunities as are accorded to heads of diplomatic missions and shall, after the expiry of their terms of office, continue to be accorded immunity from legal process of every kind in respect of words spoken or written and acts performed by them in their official capacity.
3. The Deputy Registrar, the staff of the Office of the Prosecutor and the staff of the Registry shall enjoy the privileges and immunities and facilities necessary for the performance of their functions, in accordance with the agreement on the privileges and immunities of the Court.
4. Counsel, experts, witnesses or any other person required to be present at the seat of the Court shall be accorded such treatment as is necessary for the proper functioning of the Court, in accordance with the agreement on the privileges and immunities of the Court.
5. The privileges and immunities of:

(a) A judge or the Prosecutor may be waived by an absolute majority of the judges;
(b) The Registrar may be waived by the Presidency;
(c) The Deputy Prosecutors and staff of the Office of the Prosecutor may be waived by the Prosecutor;
(d) The Deputy Registrar and staff of the Registry may be waived by the Registrar.

Article 49

Salaries, allowances and expenses
The judges, the Prosecutor, the Deputy Prosecutors, the Registrar and the Deputy Registrar shall receive such salaries, allowances and expenses as may be decided upon by the Assembly of States Parties. These salaries and allowances shall not be reduced during their terms of office.

Article 50

Official and working languages
1. The official languages of the Court shall be Arabic, Chinese, English, French, Russian and Spanish. The judgements of the Court, as well as other decisions resolving fundamental issues before the Court, shall be published in the official languages. The Presidency shall, in accordance with the criteria established by the Rules of Procedure and Evidence, determine which decisions may be considered as resolving fundamental issues for the purposes of this paragraph.
2. The working languages of the Court shall be English and French. The Rules of Procedure and Evidence shall determine the cases in which other official languages may be used as working languages.
3. At the request of any party to a proceeding or a State allowed to intervene in a proceeding, the Court shall authorize a language other than English or French to be used by such a party or State, provided that the Court considers such authorization to be adequately justified.

Article 51

Rules of Procedure and Evidence
1. The Rules of Procedure and Evidence shall enter into force upon adoption by a two-thirds majority of the members of the Assembly of States Parties.
2. Amendments to the Rules of Procedure and Evidence may be proposed by:

(a) Any State Party;
(b) The judges acting by an absolute majority; or
(c) The Prosecutor.

Such amendments shall enter into force upon adoption by a two-thirds majority of the members of the Assembly of States Parties.
3. After the adoption of the Rules of Procedure and Evidence, in urgent cases where the Rules do not provide for a specific situation before the Court, the judges may, by a two-thirds majority, draw up provisional Rules to be applied until adopted, amended or rejected at the next ordinary or special session of the Assembly of States Parties.
4. The Rules of Procedure and Evidence, amendments thereto and any provisional Rule shall be consistent with this Statute. Amendments to the Rules of Procedure and Evidence as well as provisional Rules shall not be applied retroactively to the detriment of the person who is being investigated or prosecuted or who has been convicted.
5. In the event of conflict between the Statute and the Rules of Procedure and Evidence, the Statute shall prevail.

Article 52

Regulations of the Court
1. The judges shall, in accordance with this Statute and the Rules of Procedure and Evidence, adopt, by an absolute majority, the Regulations of the Court necessary for its routine functioning.

2. The Prosecutor and the Registrar shall be consulted in the elaboration of the Regulations and any amendments thereto.

3. The Regulations and any amendments thereto shall take effect upon adoption unless otherwise decided by the judges. Immediately upon adoption, they shall be circulated to States Parties for comments. If within six months there are no objections from a majority of States Parties, they shall remain in force.

PART 5. INVESTIGATION AND PROSECUTION

Article 53

Initiation of an investigation

1. The Prosecutor shall, having evaluated the information made available to him or her, initiate an investigation unless he or she determines that there is no reasonable basis to proceed under this Statute. In deciding whether to initiate an investigation, the Prosecutor shall consider whether:

(a) The information available to the Prosecutor provides a reasonable basis to believe that a crime within the jurisdiction of the Court has been or is being committed;

(b) The case is or would be admissible under article 17; and

(c) Taking into account the gravity of the crime and the interests of victims, there are nonetheless substantial reasons to believe that an investigation would not serve the interests of justice.

If the Prosecutor determines that there is no reasonable basis to proceed and his or her determination is based solely on subparagraph (c) above, he or she shall inform the Pre-Trial Chamber.

2. If, upon investigation, the Prosecutor concludes that there is not a sufficient basis for a prosecution because:

(a) There is not a sufficient legal or factual basis to seek a warrant or summons under article 58;

(b) The case is inadmissible under article 17; or

(c) A prosecution is not in the interests of justice, taking into account all the circumstances, including the gravity of the crime, the interests of victims and the age or infirmity of the alleged perpetrator, and his or her role in the alleged crime;

The Prosecutor shall inform the Pre-Trial Chamber and the State making a referral under article 14 or the Security Council in a case under article 13, paragraph (b), of his or her conclusion and the reasons for the conclusion.

3. (a) At the request of the State making a referral under article 14 or the Security Council under article 13, paragraph (b), the Pre-Trial Chamber may review a decision of the Prosecutor under paragraph 1 or 2 not to proceed and may request the Prosecutor to reconsider that decision.

(b)   In addition, the Pre-Trial Chamber may, on its own initiative, review a decision of the Prosecutor not to proceed if it is based solely on paragraph 1 (c) or 2 (c). In such a case, the decision of the Prosecutor shall be effective only if confirmed by the Pre-Trial Chamber.

4. The Prosecutor may, at any time, reconsider a decision whether to initiate an investigation or prosecution based on new facts or information.

Article 54

Duties and powers of the Prosecutor with respect to investigations
1. The Prosecutor shall:

(a)   In order to establish the truth, extend the investigation to cover all facts and evidence relevant to an assessment of whether there is criminal responsibility under this Statute, and, in doing so, investigate incriminating and exonerating circumstances equally;
(b)   Take appropriate measures to ensure the effective investigation and prosecution of crimes within the jurisdiction of the Court, and in doing so, respect the interests and personal circumstances of victims and witnesses, including age, gender as defined in article 7, paragraph 3, and health, and take into account the nature of the crime, in particular where it involves sexual violence, gender violence or violence against children; and
(c)   Fully respect the rights of persons arising under this Statute.

2. The Prosecutor may conduct investigations on the territory of a State:

(a)   In accordance with the provisions of Part 9; or
(b)   As authorized by the Pre-Trial Chamber under article 57, paragraph 3 (d).

3. The Prosecutor may:

(a)   Collect and examine evidence;
(b)   Request the presence of and question persons being investigated, victims and witnesses;
(c)   Seek the cooperation of any State or intergovernmental organization or arrangement in accordance with its respective competence and/or mandate;
(d)   Enter into such arrangements or agreements, not inconsistent with this Statute, as may be necessary to facilitate the cooperation of a State, intergovernmental organization or person;
(e)   Agree not to disclose, at any stage of the proceedings, documents or information that the Prosecutor obtains on the condition of confidentiality and solely for the purpose of generating new evidence, unless the provider of the information consents; and
(f)   Take necessary measures, or request that necessary measures be taken, to ensure the confidentiality of information, the protection of any person or the preservation of evidence.

Article 55

Rights of persons during an investigation
1. In respect of an investigation under this Statute, a person:

(a) Shall not be compelled to incriminate himself or herself or to confess guilt;
(b) Shall not be subjected to any form of coercion, duress or threat, to torture or to any other form of cruel, inhuman or degrading treatment or punishment;
(c) Shall, if questioned in a language other than a language the person fully understands and speaks, have, free of any cost, the assistance of a competent interpreter and such translations as are necessary to meet the requirements of fairness; and
(d) Shall not be subjected to arbitrary arrest or detention, and shall not be deprived of his or her liberty except on such grounds and in accordance with such procedures as are established in this Statute.

2. Where there are grounds to believe that a person has committed a crime within the jurisdiction of the Court and that person is about to be questioned either by the Prosecutor, or by national authorities pursuant to a request made under Part 9, that person shall also have the following rights of which he or she shall be informed prior to being questioned:

(a) To be informed, prior to being questioned, that there are grounds to believe that he or she has committed a crime within the jurisdiction of the Court;
(b) To remain silent, without such silence being a consideration in the determination of guilt or innocence;
(c) To have legal assistance of the person's choosing, or, if the person does not have legal assistance, to have legal assistance assigned to him or her, in any case where the interests of justice so require, and without payment by the person in any such case if the person does not have sufficient means to pay for it; and
(d) To be questioned in the presence of counsel unless the person has voluntarily waived his or her right to counsel.

Article 56

Role of the Pre-Trial Chamber in relation to a unique investigative opportunity
1. (a) Where the Prosecutor considers an investigation to present a unique opportunity to take testimony or a statement from a witness or to examine, collect or test evidence, which may not be available subsequently for the purposes of a trial, the Prosecutor shall so inform the Pre-Trial Chamber.
   (b) In that case, the Pre-Trial Chamber may, upon request of the Prosecutor, take such measures as may be necessary to ensure the efficiency and integrity of the proceedings and, in particular, to protect the rights of the defence.
   (c) Unless the Pre-Trial Chamber orders otherwise, the Prosecutor shall provide the relevant information to the person who has been arrested or appeared in response to a summons in connection with the investigation referred to in subparagraph (a), in order that he or she may be heard on the matter.

2. The measures referred to in paragraph 1 (b) may include:

(a) Making recommendations or orders regarding procedures to be followed;
(b) Directing that a record be made of the proceedings;
(c) Appointing an expert to assist;

(d) Authorizing counsel for a person who has been arrested, or appeared before the Court in response to a summons, to participate, or where there has not yet been such an arrest or appearance or counsel has not been designated, appointing another counsel to attend and represent the interests of the defence;

(e) Naming one of its members or, if necessary, another available judge of the Pre-Trial or Trial Division to observe and make recommendations or orders regarding the collection and preservation of evidence and the questioning of persons;

(f) Taking such other action as may be necessary to collect or preserve evidence.

3. (a) Where the Prosecutor has not sought measures pursuant to this article but the Pre-Trial Chamber considers that such measures are required to preserve evidence that it deems would be essential for the defence at trial, it shall consult with the Prosecutor as to whether there is good reason for the Prosecutor's failure to request the measures. If upon consultation, the Pre-Trial Chamber concludes that the Prosecutor's failure to request such measures is unjustified, the Pre-Trial Chamber may take such measures on its own initiative.

(b) A decision of the Pre-Trial Chamber to act on its own initiative under this paragraph may be appealed by the Prosecutor. The appeal shall be heard on an expedited basis.

4. The admissibility of evidence preserved or collected for trial pursuant to this article, or the record thereof, shall be governed at trial by article 69, and given such weight as determined by the Trial Chamber.

Article 57

Functions and powers of the Pre-Trial Chamber

1. Unless otherwise provided in this Statute, the Pre-Trial Chamber shall exercise its functions in accordance with the provisions of this article.

2. (a) Orders or rulings of the Pre-Trial Chamber issued under articles 15, 18, 19, 54, paragraph 2, 61, paragraph 7, and 72 must be concurred in by a majority of its judges.

(b) In all other cases, a single judge of the Pre-Trial Chamber may exercise the functions provided for in this Statute, unless otherwise provided for in the Rules of Procedure and Evidence or by a majority of the Pre-Trial Chamber.

3. In addition to its other functions under this Statute, the Pre-Trial Chamber may:

(a) At the request of the Prosecutor, issue such orders and warrants as may be required for the purposes of an investigation;

(b) Upon the request of a person who has been arrested or has appeared pursuant to a summons under article 58, issue such orders, including measures such as those described in article 56, or seek such cooperation pursuant to Part 9 as may be necessary to assist the person in the preparation of his or her defence;

(c) Where necessary, provide for the protection and privacy of victims and witnesses, the preservation of evidence, the protection of persons who have been arrested or appeared in response to a summons, and the protection of national security information;

(d) Authorize the Prosecutor to take specific investigative steps within the territory of a State Party without having secured the cooperation of that State under Part 9 if, whenever possible having regard to the views of the State concerned, the Pre-Trial Chamber has determined in that case that the State is clearly unable to execute a request for cooperation due to the unavailability of any authority or any component of its judicial system competent to execute the request for cooperation under Part 9.

(e) Where a warrant of arrest or a summons has been issued under article 58, and having due regard to the strength of the evidence and the rights of the parties concerned, as provided for in this Statute and the Rules of Procedure and Evidence, seek the cooperation of States pursuant to article 93, paragraph 1 (k), to take protective measures for the purpose of forfeiture, in particular for the ultimate benefit of victims.

Article 58

Issuance by the Pre-Trial Chamber of a warrant of arrest or a summons to appear

1. At any time after the initiation of an investigation, the Pre-Trial Chamber shall, on the application of the Prosecutor, issue a warrant of arrest of a person if, having examined the application and the evidence or other information submitted by the Prosecutor, it is satisfied that:

(a) There are reasonable grounds to believe that the person has committed a crime within the jurisdiction of the Court; and

(b) The arrest of the person appears necessary:
   (i) To ensure the person's appearance at trial,
   (ii) To ensure that the person does not obstruct or endanger the investigation or the court proceedings, or
   (iii) Where applicable, to prevent the person from continuing with the commission of that crime or a related crime which is within the jurisdiction of the Court and which arises out of the same circumstances.

2. The application of the Prosecutor shall contain:

(a) The name of the person and any other relevant identifying information;

(b) A specific reference to the crimes within the jurisdiction of the Court which the person is alleged to have committed;

(c) A concise statement of the facts which are alleged to constitute those crimes;

(d) A summary of the evidence and any other information which establish reasonable grounds to believe that the person committed those crimes; and

(e) The reason why the Prosecutor believes that the arrest of the person is necessary.

3. The warrant of arrest shall contain:

(a) The name of the person and any other relevant identifying information;
(b) A specific reference to the crimes within the jurisdiction of the Court for which the person's arrest is sought; and
(c) A concise statement of the facts which are alleged to constitute those crimes.

4. The warrant of arrest shall remain in effect until otherwise ordered by the Court.

5. On the basis of the warrant of arrest, the Court may request the provisional arrest or the arrest and surrender of the person under Part 9.

6. The Prosecutor may request the Pre-Trial Chamber to amend the warrant of arrest by modifying or adding to the crimes specified therein. The Pre-Trial Chamber shall so amend the warrant if it is satisfied that there are reasonable grounds to believe that the person committed the modified or additional crimes.

7. As an alternative to seeking a warrant of arrest, the Prosecutor may submit an application requesting that the Pre-Trial Chamber issue a summons for the person to appear. If the Pre-Trial Chamber is satisfied that there are reasonable grounds to believe that the person committed the crime alleged and that a summons is sufficient to ensure the person's appearance, it shall issue the summons, with or without conditions restricting liberty (other than detention) if provided for by national law, for the person to appear. The summons shall contain:

(a) The name of the person and any other relevant identifying information;
(b) The specified date on which the person is to appear;
(c) A specific reference to the crimes within the jurisdiction of the Court which the person is alleged to have committed; and
(d) A concise statement of the facts which are alleged to constitute the crime.

The summons shall be served on the person.

Article 59

Arrest proceedings in the custodial State

1. A State Party which has received a request for provisional arrest or for arrest and surrender shall immediately take steps to arrest the person in question in accordance with its laws and the provisions of Part 9.

2. A person arrested shall be brought promptly before the competent judicial authority in the custodial State which shall determine, in accordance with the law of that State, that:

(a) The warrant applies to that person;
(b) The person has been arrested in accordance with the proper process; and
(c) The person's rights have been respected.

3. The person arrested shall have the right to apply to the competent authority in the custodial State for interim release pending surrender.

4. In reaching a decision on any such application, the competent authority in the custodial State shall consider whether, given the gravity of the alleged crimes, there are urgent and exceptional circumstances to justify interim release and whether necessary safeguards

exist to ensure that the custodial State can fulfil its duty to surrender the person to the Court. It shall not be open to the competent authority of the custodial State to consider whether the warrant of arrest was properly issued in accordance with article 58, paragraph 1 (a) and (b).

5. The Pre-Trial Chamber shall be notified of any request for interim release and shall make recommendations to the competent authority in the custodial State. The competent authority in the custodial State shall give full consideration to such recommendations, including any recommendations on measures to prevent the escape of the person, before rendering its decision.

6. If the person is granted interim release, the Pre-Trial Chamber may request periodic reports on the status of the interim release.

7. Once ordered to be surrendered by the custodial State, the person shall be delivered to the Court as soon as possible.

Article 60

Initial proceedings before the Court

1. Upon the surrender of the person to the Court, or the person's appearance before the Court voluntarily or pursuant to a summons, the Pre-Trial Chamber shall satisfy itself that the person has been informed of the crimes which he or she is alleged to have committed, and of his or her rights under this Statute, including the right to apply for interim release pending trial.

2. A person subject to a warrant of arrest may apply for interim release pending trial. If the Pre-Trial Chamber is satisfied that the conditions set forth in article 58, paragraph 1, are met, the person shall continue to be detained. If it is not so satisfied, the Pre-Trial Chamber shall release the person, with or without conditions.

3. The Pre-Trial Chamber shall periodically review its ruling on the release or detention of the person, and may do so at any time on the request of the Prosecutor or the person. Upon such review, it may modify its ruling as to detention, release or conditions of release, if it is satisfied that changed circumstances so require.

4. The Pre-Trial Chamber shall ensure that a person is not detained for an unreasonable period prior to trial due to inexcusable delay by the Prosecutor. If such delay occurs, the Court shall consider releasing the person, with or without conditions.

5. If necessary, the Pre-Trial Chamber may issue a warrant of arrest to secure the presence of a person who has been released.

Article 61

Confirmation of the charges before trial

1. Subject to the provisions of paragraph 2, within a reasonable time after the person's surrender or voluntary appearance before the Court, the Pre-Trial Chamber shall hold a hearing to confirm the charges on which the Prosecutor intends to seek trial. The hearing shall be held in the presence of the Prosecutor and the person charged, as well as his or her counsel.

2. The Pre-Trial Chamber may, upon request of the Prosecutor or on its own motion, hold a hearing in the absence of the person charged to confirm the charges on which the Prosecutor intends to seek trial when the person has:

(a) Waived his or her right to be present; or
(b) Fled or cannot be found and all reasonable steps have been taken to secure his or her appearance before the Court and to inform the person of the charges and that a hearing to confirm those charges will be held.

In that case, the person shall be represented by counsel where the Pre-Trial Chamber determines that it is in the interests of justice.

3. Within a reasonable time before the hearing, the person shall:

(a) Be provided with a copy of the document containing the charges on which the Prosecutor intends to bring the person to trial; and
(b) Be informed of the evidence on which the Prosecutor intends to rely at the hearing.

The Pre-Trial Chamber may issue orders regarding the disclosure of information for the purposes of the hearing.

4. Before the hearing, the Prosecutor may continue the investigation and may amend or withdraw any charges. The person shall be given reasonable notice before the hearing of any amendment to or withdrawal of charges. In case of a withdrawal of charges, the Prosecutor shall notify the Pre-Trial Chamber of the reasons for the withdrawal.

5. At the hearing, the Prosecutor shall support each charge with sufficient evidence to establish substantial grounds to believe that the person committed the crime charged. The Prosecutor may rely on documentary or summary evidence and need not call the witnesses expected to testify at the trial.

6. At the hearing, the person may:

(a) Object to the charges;
(b) Challenge the evidence presented by the Prosecutor; and
(c) Present evidence.

7. The Pre-Trial Chamber shall, on the basis of the hearing, determine whether there is sufficient evidence to establish substantial grounds to believe that the person committed each of the crimes charged. Based on its determination, the Pre-Trial Chamber shall:

(a) Confirm those charges in relation to which it has determined that there is sufficient evidence, and commit the person to a Trial Chamber for trial on the charges as confirmed;
(b) Decline to confirm those charges in relation to which it has determined that there is insufficient evidence;(c) Adjourn the hearing and request the Prosecutor to consider:
  (i)   Providing further evidence or conducting further investigation with respect to a particular charge; or
  (ii) Amending a charge because the evidence submitted appears to establish a different crime within the jurisdiction of the Court.

8. Where the Pre-Trial Chamber declines to confirm a charge, the Prosecutor shall not be precluded from subsequently requesting its confirmation if the request is supported by additional evidence.

9. After the charges are confirmed and before the trial has begun, the Prosecutor may, with the permission of the Pre-Trial Chamber and after notice to the accused, amend the charges. If the Prosecutor seeks to add additional charges or to substitute more serious charges, a hearing under this article to confirm those charges must be held. After commencement of the trial, the Prosecutor may, with the permission of the Trial Chamber, withdraw the charges.

10. Any warrant previously issued shall cease to have effect with respect to any charges which have not been confirmed by the Pre-Trial Chamber or which have been withdrawn by the Prosecutor.

11. Once the charges have been confirmed in accordance with this article, the Presidency shall constitute a Trial Chamber which, subject to paragraph 9 and to article 64, paragraph 4, shall be responsible for the conduct of subsequent proceedings and may exercise any function of the Pre-Trial Chamber that is relevant and capable of application in those proceedings.

PART 6. THE TRIAL

Article 62

Place of trial
Unless otherwise decided, the place of the trial shall be the seat of the Court.

Article 63

Trial in the presence of the accused
1. The accused shall be present during the trial.
2. If the accused, being present before the Court, continues to disrupt the trial, the Trial Chamber may remove the accused and shall make provision for him or her to observe the trial and instruct counsel from outside the courtroom, through the use of communications technology, if required. Such measures shall be taken only in exceptional circumstances after other reasonable alternatives have proved inadequate, and only for such duration as is strictly required.

Article 64

Functions and powers of the Trial Chamber
1. The functions and powers of the Trial Chamber set out in this article shall be exercised in accordance with this Statute and the Rules of Procedure and Evidence.
2. The Trial Chamber shall ensure that a trial is fair and expeditious and is conducted with full respect for the rights of the accused and due regard for the protection of victims and witnesses.
3. Upon assignment of a case for trial in accordance with this Statute, the Trial Chamber assigned to deal with the case shall:

(a) Confer with the parties and adopt such procedures as are necessary to facilitate the fair and expeditious conduct of the proceedings;

(b) Determine the language or languages to be used at trial; and
(c) Subject to any other relevant provisions of this Statute, provide for disclosure of documents or information not previously disclosed, sufficiently in advance of the commencement of the trial to enable adequate preparation for trial.

4. The Trial Chamber may, if necessary for its effective and fair functioning, refer preliminary issues to the Pre-Trial Chamber or, if necessary, to another available judge of the Pre-Trial Division.

5. Upon notice to the parties, the Trial Chamber may, as appropriate, direct that there be joinder or severance in respect of charges against more than one accused.

6. In performing its functions prior to trial or during the course of a trial, the Trial Chamber may, as necessary:

(a) Exercise any functions of the Pre-Trial Chamber referred to in article 61, paragraph 11;
(b) Require the attendance and testimony of witnesses and production of documents and other evidence by obtaining, if necessary, the assistance of States as provided in this Statute;
(c) Provide for the protection of confidential information;
(d) Order the production of evidence in addition to that already collected prior to the trial or presented during the trial by the parties;
(e) Provide for the protection of the accused, witnesses and victims; and
(f) Rule on any other relevant matters.

7. The trial shall be held in public. The Trial Chamber may, however, determine that special circumstances require that certain proceedings be in closed session for the purposes set forth in article 68, or to protect confidential or sensitive information to be given in evidence.

8. (a) At the commencement of the trial, the Trial Chamber shall have read to the accused the charges previously confirmed by the Pre-Trial Chamber. The Trial Chamber shall satisfy itself that the accused understands the nature of the charges. It shall afford him or her the opportunity to make an admission of guilt in accordance with article 65 or to plead not guilty.
   (b) At the trial, the presiding judge may give directions for the conduct of proceedings, including to ensure that they are conducted in a fair and impartial manner. Subject to any directions of the presiding judge, the parties may submit evidence in accordance with the provisions of this Statute.

9. The Trial Chamber shall have, *inter alia*, the power on application of a party or on its own motion to:

(a) Rule on the admissibility or relevance of evidence; and
(b) Take all necessary steps to maintain order in the course of a hearing.

10. The Trial Chamber shall ensure that a complete record of the trial, which accurately reflects the proceedings, is made and that it is maintained and preserved by the Registrar.

Article 65

Proceedings on an admission of guilt

1. Where the accused makes an admission of guilt pursuant to article 64, paragraph 8 (a), the Trial Chamber shall determine whether:

(a) The accused understands the nature and consequences of the admission of guilt;
(b) The admission is voluntarily made by the accused after sufficient consultation with defence counsel; and
(c) The admission of guilt is supported by the facts of the case that are contained in:
  (i) The charges brought by the Prosecutor and admitted by the accused;
  (ii) Any materials presented by the Prosecutor which supplement the charges and which the accused accepts; and
  (iii) Any other evidence, such as the testimony of witnesses, presented by the Prosecutor or the accused.

2. Where the Trial Chamber is satisfied that the matters referred to in paragraph 1 are established, it shall consider the admission of guilt, together with any additional evidence presented, as establishing all the essential facts that are required to prove the crime to which the admission of guilt relates, and may convict the accused of that crime.

3. Where the Trial Chamber is not satisfied that the matters referred to in paragraph 1 are established, it shall consider the admission of guilt as not having been made, in which case it shall order that the trial be continued under the ordinary trial procedures provided by this Statute and may remit the case to another Trial Chamber.

4. Where the Trial Chamber is of the opinion that a more complete presentation of the facts of the case is required in the interests of justice, in particular the interests of the victims, the Trial Chamber may:

(a) Request the Prosecutor to present additional evidence, including the testimony of witnesses; or
(b) Order that the trial be continued under the ordinary trial procedures provided by this Statute, in which case it shall consider the admission of guilt as not having been made and may remit the case to another Trial Chamber.

5. Any discussions between the Prosecutor and the defence regarding modification of the charges, the admission of guilt or the penalty to be imposed shall not be binding on the Court.

Article 66

Presumption of innocence

1. Everyone shall be presumed innocent until proved guilty before the Court in accordance with the applicable law.

2. The onus is on the Prosecutor to prove the guilt of the accused.

3. In order to convict the accused, the Court must be convinced of the guilt of the accused beyond reasonable doubt.

Article 67

Rights of the accused

1. In the determination of any charge, the accused shall be entitled to a public hearing, having regard to the provisions of this Statute, to a fair hearing conducted impartially, and to the following minimum guarantees, in full equality:

(a) To be informed promptly and in detail of the nature, cause and content of the charge, in a language which the accused fully understands and speaks;
(b) To have adequate time and facilities for the preparation of the defence and to communicate freely with counsel of the accused's choosing in confidence;
(c) To be tried without undue delay;
(d) Subject to article 63, paragraph 2, to be present at the trial, to conduct the defence in person or through legal assistance of the accused's choosing, to be informed, if the accused does not have legal assistance, of this right and to have legal assistance assigned by the Court in any case where the interests of justice so require, and without payment if the accused lacks sufficient means to pay for it;
(e) To examine, or have examined, the witnesses against him or her and to obtain the attendance and examination of witnesses on his or her behalf under the same conditions as witnesses against him or her. The accused shall also be entitled to raise defences and to present other evidence admissible under this Statute;
(f) To have, free of any cost, the assistance of a competent interpreter and such translations as are necessary to meet the requirements of fairness, if any of the proceedings of or documents presented to the Court are not in a language which the accused fully understands and speaks;
(g) Not to be compelled to testify or to confess guilt and to remain silent, without such silence being a consideration in the determination of guilt or innocence;
(h) To make an unsworn oral or written statement in his or her defence; and
(i) Not to have imposed on him or her any reversal of the burden of proof or any onus of rebuttal.

2. In addition to any other disclosure provided for in this Statute, the Prosecutor shall, as soon as practicable, disclose to the defence evidence in the Prosecutor's possession or control which he or she believes shows or tends to show the innocence of the accused, or to mitigate the guilt of the accused, or which may affect the credibility of prosecution evidence. In case of doubt as to the application of this paragraph, the Court shall decide.

Article 68

Protection of the victims and witnesses and their participation in the proceedings

1. The Court shall take appropriate measures to protect the safety, physical and psychological well-being, dignity and privacy of victims and witnesses. In so doing, the Court shall have regard to all relevant factors, including age, gender as defined in article 7, paragraph 3, and health, and the nature of the crime, in particular, but not limited to, where the crime involves sexual or gender violence or violence against children. The Prosecutor shall take such measures particularly during the investigation and prosecution of such crimes. These

measures shall not be prejudicial to or inconsistent with the rights of the accused and a fair and impartial trial.

2. As an exception to the principle of public hearings provided for in article 67, the Chambers of the Court may, to protect victims and witnesses or an accused, conduct any part of the proceedings *in camera* or allow the presentation of evidence by electronic or other special means. In particular, such measures shall be implemented in the case of a victim of sexual violence or a child who is a victim or a witness, unless otherwise ordered by the Court, having regard to all the circumstances, particularly the views of the victim or witness.

3. Where the personal interests of the victims are affected, the Court shall permit their views and concerns to be presented and considered at stages of the proceedings determined to be appropriate by the Court and in a manner which is not prejudicial to or inconsistent with the rights of the accused and a fair and impartial trial. Such views and concerns may be presented by the legal representatives of the victims where the Court considers it appropriate, in accordance with the Rules of Procedure and Evidence.

4. The Victims and Witnesses Unit may advise the Prosecutor and the Court on appropriate protective measures, security arrangements, counselling and assistance as referred to in article 43, paragraph 6.

5. Where the disclosure of evidence or information pursuant to this Statute may lead to the grave endangerment of the security of a witness or his or her family, the Prosecutor may, for the purposes of any proceedings conducted prior to the commencement of the trial, withhold such evidence or information and instead submit a summary thereof. Such measures shall be exercised in a manner which is not prejudicial to or inconsistent with the rights of the accused and a fair and impartial trial.

6. A State may make an application for necessary measures to be taken in respect of the protection of its servants or agents and the protection of confidential or sensitive information.

Article 69

Evidence

1. Before testifying, each witness shall, in accordance with the Rules of Procedure and Evidence, give an undertaking as to the truthfulness of the evidence to be given by that witness.

2. The testimony of a witness at trial shall be given in person, except to the extent provided by the measures set forth in article 68 or in the Rules of Procedure and Evidence. The Court may also permit the giving of *viva voce* (oral) or recorded testimony of a witness by means of video or audio technology, as well as the introduction of documents or written transcripts, subject to this Statute and in accordance with the Rules of Procedure and Evidence. These measures shall not be prejudicial to or inconsistent with the rights of the accused.

3. The parties may submit evidence relevant to the case, in accordance with article 64. The Court shall have the authority to request the submission of all evidence that it considers necessary for the determination of the truth.

4. The Court may rule on the relevance or admissibility of any evidence, taking into account, *inter alia*, the probative value of the evidence and any prejudice that such evidence may cause to a fair trial or to a fair evaluation of the testimony of a witness, in accordance with the Rules of Procedure and Evidence.

5. The Court shall respect and observe privileges on confidentiality as provided for in the Rules of Procedure and Evidence.

6. The Court shall not require proof of facts of common knowledge but may take judicial notice of them.

7. Evidence obtained by means of a violation of this Statute or internationally recognized human rights shall not be admissible if:

(a) The violation casts substantial doubt on the reliability of the evidence; or
(b) The admission of the evidence would be antithetical to and would seriously damage the integrity of the proceedings.

8. When deciding on the relevance or admissibility of evidence collected by a State, the Court shall not rule on the application of the State's national law.

Article 70

Offences against the administration of justice

1. The Court shall have jurisdiction over the following offences against its administration of justice when committed intentionally:

(a) Giving false testimony when under an obligation pursuant to article 69, paragraph 1, to tell the truth;
(b) Presenting evidence that the party knows is false or forged;
(c) Corruptly influencing a witness, obstructing or interfering with the attendance or testimony of a witness, retaliating against a witness for giving testimony or destroying, tampering with or interfering with the collection of evidence;
(d) Impeding, intimidating or corruptly influencing an official of the Court for the purpose of forcing or persuading the official not to perform, or to perform improperly, his or her duties;
(e) Retaliating against an official of the Court on account of duties performed by that or another official;
(f) Soliciting or accepting a bribe as an official of the Court in connection with his or her official duties.

2. The principles and procedures governing the Court's exercise of jurisdiction over offences under this article shall be those provided for in the Rules of Procedure and Evidence. The conditions for providing international cooperation to the Court with respect to its proceedings under this article shall be governed by the domestic laws of the requested State.

3. In the event of conviction, the Court may impose a term of imprisonment not exceeding five years, or a fine in accordance with the Rules of Procedure and Evidence, or both.

4. (a)   Each State Party shall extend its criminal laws penalizing offences against the integrity of its own investigative or judicial process to offences against the administration of justice referred to in this article, committed on its territory, or by one of its nationals;

(b)   Upon request by the Court, whenever it deems it proper, the State Party shall submit the case to its competent authorities for the purpose of prosecution. Those authorities shall treat such cases with diligence and devote sufficient resources to enable them to be conducted effectively.

Article 71

Sanctions for misconduct before the Court

1. The Court may sanction persons present before it who commit misconduct, including disruption of its proceedings or deliberate refusal to comply with its directions, by administrative measures other than imprisonment, such as temporary or permanent removal from the courtroom, a fine or other similar measures provided for in the Rules of Procedure and Evidence.

2. The procedures governing the imposition of the measures set forth in paragraph 1 shall be those provided for in the Rules of Procedure and Evidence.

Article 72

Protection of national security information

1. This article applies in any case where the disclosure of the information or documents of a State would, in the opinion of that State, prejudice its national security interests. Such cases include those falling within the scope of article 56, paragraphs 2 and 3, article 61, paragraph 3, article 64, paragraph 3, article 67, para-graph 2, article 68, paragraph 6, article 87, paragraph 6 and article 93, as well as cases arising at any other stage of the proceedings where such disclosure may be at issue.

2. This article shall also apply when a person who has been requested to give information or evidence has refused to do so or has referred the matter to the State on the ground that disclosure would prejudice the national security interests of a State and the State concerned confirms that it is of the opinion that disclosure would prejudice its national security interests.

3. Nothing in this article shall prejudice the requirements of confidentiality applicable under article 54, paragraph 3 (e) and (f), or the application of article 73.

4. If a State learns that information or documents of the State are being, or are likely to be, disclosed at any stage of the proceedings, and it is of the opinion that disclosure would prejudice its national security interests, that State shall have the right to intervene in order to obtain resolution of the issue in accordance with this article.

5. If, in the opinion of a State, disclosure of information would prejudice its national security interests, all reasonable steps will be taken by the State, acting in conjunction with the Prosecutor, the defence or the Pre-Trial Chamber or Trial Chamber, as the case may be, to seek to resolve the matter by cooperative means. Such steps may include:

(a) Modification or clarification of the request;
(b) A determination by the Court regarding the relevance of the information or evidence sought, or a determination as to whether the evidence, though relevant, could be or has been obtained from a source other than the requested State;
(c) Obtaining the information or evidence from a different source or in a different form; or
(d) Agreement on conditions under which the assistance could be provided including, among

other things, providing summaries or redactions, limitations on disclosure, use of *in camera* or *ex parte* proceedings, or other protective measures permissible under the Statute and the Rules of Procedure and Evidence.

6. Once all reasonable steps have been taken to resolve the matter through cooperative means, and if the State considers that there are no means or conditions under which the information or documents could be provided or disclosed without prejudice to its national security interests, it shall so notify the Prosecutor or the Court of the specific reasons for its decision, unless a specific description of the reasons would itself necessarily result in such prejudice to the State's national security interests.

7. Thereafter, if the Court determines that the evidence is relevant and necessary for the establishment of the guilt or innocence of the accused, the Court may undertake the following actions:

(a) Where disclosure of the information or document is sought pursuant to a request for cooperation under Part 9 or the circumstances described in paragraph 2, and the State has invoked the ground for refusal referred to in article 93, para-graph 4:

  (i)   The Court may, before making any conclusion referred to in subpara-graph 7 (a) (ii), request further consultations for the purpose of considering the State's representations, which may include, as appropriate, hearings *in camera* and *ex parte*;

  (ii) If the Court concludes that, by invoking the ground for refusal under article 93, paragraph 4, in the circumstances of the case, the requested State is not acting in accordance with its obligations under this Statute, the Court may refer the matter in accordance with article 87, paragraph 7, specifying the reasons for its conclusion; and

  (iii) The Court may make such inference in the trial of the accused as to the existence or non-existence of a fact, as may be appropriate in the circumstances; or

(b) In all other circumstances:

  (i)   Order disclosure; or

  (ii) To the extent it does not order disclosure, make such inference in the trial of the accused as to the existence or non-existence of a fact, as may be appropriate in the circumstances.

Article 73

Third-party information or documents

If a State Party is requested by the Court to provide a document or information in its custody, possession or control, which was disclosed to it in confidence by a State, intergovernmental organization or international organization, it shall seek the consent of the originator to disclose that document or information. If the originator is a State Party, it shall either consent to disclosure of the information or document or undertake to resolve the issue of disclosure with the Court, subject to the provisions of article 72. If the originator is not a State Party and refuses to consent to disclosure, the requested State shall inform the Court that it is unable to provide the document or information because of a pre-existing obligation of confidentiality to the originator.

Article 74

Requirements for the decision

1. All the judges of the Trial Chamber shall be present at each stage of the trial and throughout their deliberations. The Presidency may, on a case-by-case basis, designate, as available, one or more alternate judges to be present at each stage of the trial and to replace a member of the Trial Chamber if that member is unable to continue attending.

2. The Trial Chamber's decision shall be based on its evaluation of the evidence and the entire proceedings. The decision shall not exceed the facts and circumstances described in the charges and any amendments to the charges. The Court may base its decision only on evidence submitted and discussed before it at the trial.

3. The judges shall attempt to achieve unanimity in their decision, failing which the decision shall be taken by a majority of the judges.

4. The deliberations of the Trial Chamber shall remain secret.

5. The decision shall be in writing and shall contain a full and reasoned statement of the Trial Chamber's findings on the evidence and conclusions. The Trial Chamber shall issue one decision. When there is no unanimity, the Trial Chamber's decision shall contain the views of the majority and the minority. The decision or a summary thereof shall be delivered in open court.

Article 75

Reparations to victims

1. The Court shall establish principles relating to reparations to, or in respect of, victims, including restitution, compensation and rehabilitation. On this basis, in its decision the Court may, either upon request or on its own motion in exceptional circumstances, determine the scope and extent of any damage, loss and injury to, or in respect of, victims and will state the principles on which it is acting.

2. The Court may make an order directly against a convicted person specifying appropriate reparations to, or in respect of, victims, including restitution, compensation and rehabilitation.

Where appropriate, the Court may order that the award for reparations be made through the Trust Fund provided for in article 79.

3. Before making an order under this article, the Court may invite and shall take account of representations from or on behalf of the convicted person, victims, other interested persons or interested States.

4. In exercising its power under this article, the Court may, after a person is convicted of a crime within the jurisdiction of the Court, determine whether, in order to give effect to an order which it may make under this article, it is necessary to seek measures under article 93, paragraph 1.

5. A State Party shall give effect to a decision under this article as if the provisions of article 109 were applicable to this article.

6. Nothing in this article shall be interpreted as prejudicing the rights of victims under national or international law.

Article 76

Sentencing

1. In the event of a conviction, the Trial Chamber shall consider the appropriate sentence to be imposed and shall take into account the evidence presented and submissions made during the trial that are relevant to the sentence.

2. Except where article 65 applies and before the completion of the trial, the Trial Chamber may on its own motion and shall, at the request of the Prosecutor or the accused, hold a further hearing to hear any additional evidence or submissions relevant to the sentence, in accordance with the Rules of Procedure and Evidence.

3. Where paragraph 2 applies, any representations under article 75 shall be heard during the further hearing referred to in paragraph 2 and, if necessary, during any additional hearing.

4. The sentence shall be pronounced in public and, wherever possible, in the presence of the accused.

PART 7. PENALTIES

Article 77

Applicable penalties

1. Subject to article 110, the Court may impose one of the following penalties on a person convicted of a crime referred to in article 5 of this Statute:

(a) Imprisonment for a specified number of years, which may not exceed a maximum of 30 years; or
(b) A term of life imprisonment when justified by the extreme gravity of the crime and the individual circumstances of the convicted person.

2. In addition to imprisonment, the Court may order:

(a) A fine under the criteria provided for in the Rules of Procedure and Evidence;
(b) A forfeiture of proceeds, property and assets derived directly or indirectly from that crime, without prejudice to the rights of bona fide third parties.

Article 78

Determination of the sentence

1. In determining the sentence, the Court shall, in accordance with the Rules of Procedure and Evidence, take into account such factors as the gravity of the crime and the individual circumstances of the convicted person.

2. In imposing a sentence of imprisonment, the Court shall deduct the time, if any, previously spent in detention in accordance with an order of the Court. The Court may deduct any time otherwise spent in detention in connection with conduct underlying the crime.

3. When a person has been convicted of more than one crime, the Court shall pronounce

a sentence for each crime and a joint sentence specifying the total period of imprisonment. This period shall be no less than the highest individual sentence pronounced and shall not exceed 30 years imprisonment or a sentence of life imprisonment in conformity with article 77, paragraph 1 (b).

Article 79

Trust Fund
1. A Trust Fund shall be established by decision of the Assembly of States Parties for the benefit of victims of crimes within the jurisdiction of the Court, and of the families of such victims.
2. The Court may order money and other property collected through fines or forfeiture to be transferred, by order of the Court, to the Trust Fund.
3. The Trust Fund shall be managed according to criteria to be determined by the Assembly of States Parties.

Article 80

Non-prejudice to national application of penalties and national laws
Nothing in this Part affects the application by States of penalties prescribed by their national law, nor the law of States which do not provide for penalties prescribed in this Part.

PART 8. APPEAL AND REVISION

Article 81
Appeal against decision of acquittal or conviction or against sentence
1. A decision under article 74 may be appealed in accordance with the Rules of Procedure and Evidence as follows:

(a) The Prosecutor may make an appeal on any of the following grounds:
    (i)   Procedural error,
    (ii)   Error of fact, or
    (iii)   Error of law;
(b) The convicted person, or the Prosecutor on that person's behalf, may make an appeal on any of the following grounds:
    (i)   Procedural error,
    (ii)   Error of fact,
    (iii)   Error of law, or
    (iv)   Any other ground that affects the fairness or reliability of the proceedings or decision.
  2. (a)   A sentence may be appealed, in accordance with the Rules of Procedure and Evidence, by the Prosecutor or the convicted person on the ground of disproportion between the crime and the sentence;
    (b)   If on an appeal against sentence the Court considers that there are grounds on which the conviction might be set aside, wholly or in part, it may invite the

Prosecutor and the convicted person to submit grounds under article 81, paragraph 1 (a) or (b), and may render a decision on conviction in accordance with article 83;

(c)   The same procedure applies when the Court, on an appeal against conviction only, considers that there are grounds to reduce the sentence under para-graph 2 (a).

3. (a)   Unless the Trial Chamber orders otherwise, a convicted person shall remain in custody pending an appeal;

   (b)   When a convicted person's time in custody exceeds the sentence of imprisonment imposed, that person shall be released, except that if the Prosecutor is also appealing, the release may be subject to the conditions under subparagraph (c) below;

   (c)   In case of an acquittal, the accused shall be released immediately, subject to the following:

      (i)   Under exceptional circumstances, and having regard, *inter alia*, to the concrete risk of flight, the seriousness of the offence charged and the probability of success on appeal, the Trial Chamber, at the request of the Prosecutor, may maintain the detention of the person pending appeal;

      (ii)   A decision by the Trial Chamber under subparagraph (c) (i) may be appealed in accordance with the Rules of Procedure and Evidence.

4. Subject to the provisions of paragraph 3 (a) and (b), execution of the decision or sentence shall be suspended during the period allowed for appeal and for the duration of the appeal proceedings.

Article 82

Appeal against other decisions

1. Either party may appeal any of the following decisions in accordance with the Rules of Procedure and Evidence:

(a)   A decision with respect to jurisdiction or admissibility;

(b)   A decision granting or denying release of the person being investigated or prosecuted;

(c)   A decision of the Pre-Trial Chamber to act on its own initiative under article 56, paragraph 3;

(d)   A decision that involves an issue that would significantly affect the fair and expeditious conduct of the proceedings or the outcome of the trial, and for which, in the opinion of the Pre-Trial or Trial Chamber, an immediate resolution by the Appeals Chamber may materially advance the proceedings.

2. A decision of the Pre-Trial Chamber under article 57, paragraph 3 (d), may be appealed against by the State concerned or by the Prosecutor, with the leave of the Pre-Trial Chamber. The appeal shall be heard on an expedited basis.

3. An appeal shall not of itself have suspensive effect unless the Appeals Chamber so orders, upon request, in accordance with the Rules of Procedure and Evidence.

4. A legal representative of the victims, the convicted person or a bona fide owner of property adversely affected by an order under article 75 may appeal against the order for reparations, as provided in the Rules of Procedure and Evidence.

Article 83

Proceedings on appeal

1. For the purposes of proceedings under article 81 and this article, the Appeals Chamber shall have all the powers of the Trial Chamber.

2. If the Appeals Chamber finds that the proceedings appealed from were unfair in a way that affected the reliability of the decision or sentence, or that the decision or sentence appealed from was materially affected by error of fact or law or procedural error, it may:

(a) Reverse or amend the decision or sentence; or
(b) Order a new trial before a different Trial Chamber.

For these purposes, the Appeals Chamber may remand a factual issue to the original Trial Chamber for it to determine the issue and to report back accordingly, or may itself call evidence to determine the issue. When the decision or sentence has been appealed only by the person convicted, or the Prosecutor on that person's behalf, it cannot be amended to his or her detriment.

3. If in an appeal against sentence the Appeals Chamber finds that the sentence is disproportionate to the crime, it may vary the sentence in accordance with Part 7.

4. The judgement of the Appeals Chamber shall be taken by a majority of the judges and shall be delivered in open court. The judgement shall state the reasons on which it is based. When there is no unanimity, the judgement of the Appeals Chamber shall contain the views of the majority and the minority, but a judge may deliver a separate or dissenting opinion on a question of law.

5. The Appeals Chamber may deliver its judgement in the absence of the person acquitted or convicted.

Article 84

Revision of conviction or sentence

1. The convicted person or, after death, spouses, children, parents or one person alive at the time of the accused's death who has been given express written instructions from the accused to bring such a claim, or the Prosecutor on the person's behalf, may apply to the Appeals Chamber to revise the final judgement of conviction or sentence on the grounds that:

(a) New evidence has been discovered that:
   (i)   Was not available at the time of trial, and such unavailability was not wholly or partially attributable to the party making application; and
   (ii)   Is sufficiently important that had it been proved at trial it would have been likely to have resulted in a different verdict;
(b) It has been newly discovered that decisive evidence, taken into account at trial and upon which the conviction depends, was false, forged or falsified;
(c) One or more of the judges who participated in conviction or confirmation of the charges has committed, in that case, an act of serious misconduct or serious breach of duty of sufficient gravity to justify the removal of that judge or those judges from office under article 46.

2. The Appeals Chamber shall reject the application if it considers it to be unfounded. If it determines that the application is meritorious, it may, as appropriate:

(a) Reconvene the original Trial Chamber;
(b) Constitute a new Trial Chamber; or
(c) Retain jurisdiction over the matter,

with a view to, after hearing the parties in the manner set forth in the Rules of Procedure and Evidence, arriving at a determination on whether the judgement should be revised.

Article 85

Compensation to an arrested or convicted person
   1. Anyone who has been the victim of unlawful arrest or detention shall have an enforceable right to compensation.
   2. When a person has by a final decision been convicted of a criminal offence, and when subsequently his or her conviction has been reversed on the ground that a new or newly discovered fact shows conclusively that there has been a miscarriage of justice, the person who has suffered punishment as a result of such conviction shall be compensated according to law, unless it is proved that the non-disclosure of the unknown fact in time is wholly or partly attributable to him or her.
   3. In exceptional circumstances, where the Court finds conclusive facts showing that there has been a grave and manifest miscarriage of justice, it may in its discretion award compensation, according to the criteria provided in the Rules of Procedure and Evidence, to a person who has been released from detention following a final decision of acquittal or a termination of the proceedings for that reason.

PART 9. INTERNATIONAL COOPERATION AND JUDICIAL ASSISTANCE

Article 86

General obligation to cooperate
States Parties shall, in accordance with the provisions of this Statute, cooperate fully with the Court in its investigation and prosecution of crimes within the jurisdiction of the Court.

Article 87

Requests for cooperation: general provisions
   1. (a)   The Court shall have the authority to make requests to States Parties for cooperation. The requests shall be transmitted through the diplomatic channel or any other appropriate channel as may be designated by each State Party upon ratification, acceptance, approval or accession.
            Subsequent changes to the designation shall be made by each State Party in accordance with the Rules of Procedure and Evidence.

(b)   When appropriate, without prejudice to the provisions of subpara-graph (a), requests may also be transmitted through the International Criminal Police Organization or any appropriate regional organization.

2. Requests for cooperation and any documents supporting the request shall either be in or be accompanied by a translation into an official language of the requested State or one of the working languages of the Court, in accordance with the choice made by that State upon ratification, acceptance, approval or accession.
Subsequent changes to this choice shall be made in accordance with the Rules of Procedure and Evidence.

3. The requested State shall keep confidential a request for cooperation and any documents supporting the request, except to the extent that the disclosure is necessary for execution of the request.

4. In relation to any request for assistance presented under this Part, the Court may take such measures, including measures related to the protection of information, as may be necessary to ensure the safety or physical or psychological well-being of any victims, potential witnesses and their families. The Court may request that any information that is made available under this Part shall be provided and handled in a manner that protects the safety and physical or psychological well-being of any victims, potential witnesses and their families.

5. (a)   The Court may invite any State not party to this Statute to provide assistance under this Part on the basis of an ad hoc arrangement, an agreement with such State or any other appropriate basis.

(b)   Where a State not party to this Statute, which has entered into an ad hoc arrangement or an agreement with the Court, fails to cooperate with requests pursuant to any such arrangement or agreement, the Court may so inform the Assembly of States Parties or, where the Security Council referred the matter to the Court, the Security Council.

6. The Court may ask any intergovernmental organization to provide information or documents. The Court may also ask for other forms of cooperation and assistance which may be agreed upon with such an organization and which are in accordance with its competence or mandate.

7. Where a State Party fails to comply with a request to cooperate by the Court contrary to the provisions of this Statute, thereby preventing the Court from exercising its functions and powers under this Statute, the Court may make a finding to that effect and refer the matter to the Assembly of States Parties or, where the Security Council referred the matter to the Court, to the Security Council.

Article 88

Availability of procedures under national law

States Parties shall ensure that there are procedures available under their national law for all of the forms of cooperation which are specified under this Part.

Article 89

Surrender of persons to the Court

1. The Court may transmit a request for the arrest and surrender of a person, together with the material supporting the request outlined in article 91, to any State on the territory of which that person may be found and shall request the cooperation of that State in the arrest and surrender of such a person. States Parties shall, in accordance with the provisions of this Part and the procedure under their national law, comply with requests for arrest and surrender.

2. Where the person sought for surrender brings a challenge before a national court on the basis of the principle of *ne bis in idem* as provided in article 20, the requested State shall immediately consult with the Court to determine if there has been a relevant ruling on admissibility. If the case is admissible, the requested State shall proceed with the execution of the request. If an admissibility ruling is pending, the requested State may postpone the execution of the request for surrender of the person until the Court makes a determination on admissibility.

3. (a) A State Party shall authorize, in accordance with its national procedural law, transportation through its territory of a person being surrendered to the Court by another State, except where transit through that State would impede or delay the surrender.

   (b) A request by the Court for transit shall be transmitted in accordance with article 87. The request for transit shall contain:
   (i) A description of the person being transported;
   (ii) A brief statement of the facts of the case and their legal characterization; and
   (iii) The warrant for arrest and surrender;

   (c) A person being transported shall be detained in custody during the period of transit;

   (d) No authorization is required if the person is transported by air and no landing is scheduled on the territory of the transit State;

   (e) If an unscheduled landing occurs on the territory of the transit State, that State may require a request for transit from the Court as provided for in subparagraph (b). The transit State shall detain the person being transported until the request for transit is received and the transit is effected, provided that detention for purposes of this subparagraph may not be extended beyond 96 hours from the unscheduled landing unless the request is received within that time.

4. If the person sought is being proceeded against or is serving a sentence in the requested State for a crime different from that for which surrender to the Court is sought, the requested State, after making its decision to grant the request, shall consult with the Court.

Article 90

Competing requests

1. A State Party which receives a request from the Court for the surrender of a person

under article 89 shall, if it also receives a request from any other State for the extradition of the same person for the same conduct which forms the basis of the crime for which the Court seeks the person's surrender, notify the Court and the requesting State of that fact.

2. Where the requesting State is a State Party, the requested State shall give priority to the request from the Court if:

(a) The Court has, pursuant to article 18 or 19, made a determination that the case in respect of which surrender is sought is admissible and that determination takes into account the investigation or prosecution conducted by the requesting State in respect of its request for extradition; or

(b) The Court makes the determination described in subparagraph (a) pursuant to the requested State's notification under paragraph 1.

3. Where a determination under paragraph 2 (a) has not been made, the requested State may, at its discretion, pending the determination of the Court under paragraph 2 (b), proceed to deal with the request for extradition from the requesting State but shall not extradite the person until the Court has determined that the case is inadmissible. The Court's determination shall be made on an expedited basis.

4. If the requesting State is a State not Party to this Statute the requested State, if it is not under an international obligation to extradite the person to the requesting State, shall give priority to the request for surrender from the Court, if the Court has determined that the case is admissible.

5. Where a case under paragraph 4 has not been determined to be admissible by the Court, the requested State may, at its discretion, proceed to deal with the request for extradition from the requesting State.

6. In cases where paragraph 4 applies except that the requested State is under an existing international obligation to extradite the person to the requesting State not Party to this Statute, the requested State shall determine whether to surrender the person to the Court or extradite the person to the requesting State. In making its decision, the requested State shall consider all the relevant factors, including but not limited to:

(a) The respective dates of the requests;

(b) The interests of the requesting State including, where relevant, whether the crime was committed in its territory and the nationality of the victims and of the person sought; and

(c) The possibility of subsequent surrender between the Court and the requesting State.

7. Where a State Party which receives a request from the Court for the surrender of a person also receives a request from any State for the extradition of the same person for conduct other than that which constitutes the crime for which the Court seeks the person's surrender:

(a) The requested State shall, if it is not under an existing international obligation to extradite the person to the requesting State, give priority to the request from the Court;

(b) The requested State shall, if it is under an existing international obligation to extradite the person to the requesting State, determine whether to surrender the person to the Court or to extradite the person to the requesting State. In making its decision, the requested

State shall consider all the relevant factors, including but not limited to those set out in paragraph 6, but shall give special consideration to the relative nature and gravity of the conduct in question.

8. Where pursuant to a notification under this article, the Court has determined a case to be inadmissible, and subsequently extradition to the requesting State is refused, the requested State shall notify the Court of this decision.

Article 91

Contents of request for arrest and surrender

1. A request for arrest and surrender shall be made in writing. In urgent cases, a request may be made by any medium capable of delivering a written record, provided that the request shall be confirmed through the channel provided for in article 87, paragraph 1 (a).

2. In the case of a request for the arrest and surrender of a person for whom a warrant of arrest has been issued by the Pre-Trial Chamber under article 58, the request shall contain or be supported by:

(a) Information describing the person sought, sufficient to identify the person, and information as to that person's probable location;
(b) A copy of the warrant of arrest; and
(c) Such documents, statements or information as may be necessary to meet the requirements for the surrender process in the requested State, except that those requirements should not be more burdensome than those applicable to requests for extradition pursuant to treaties or arrangements between the requested State and other States and should, if possible, be less burdensome, taking into account the distinct nature of the Court.

3. In the case of a request for the arrest and surrender of a person already convicted, the request shall contain or be supported by:

(a) A copy of any warrant of arrest for that person;
(b) A copy of the judgement of conviction;
(c) Information to demonstrate that the person sought is the one referred to in the judgement of conviction; and
(d) If the person sought has been sentenced, a copy of the sentence imposed and, in the case of a sentence for imprisonment, a statement of any time already served and the time remaining to be served.

4. Upon the request of the Court, a State Party shall consult with the Court, either generally or with respect to a specific matter, regarding any requirements under its national law that may apply under paragraph 2 (c). During the consultations, the State Party shall advise the Court of the specific requirements of its national law.

Article 92

Provisional arrest

1. In urgent cases, the Court may request the provisional arrest of the person sought, pend-

ing presentation of the request for surrender and the documents supporting the request as specified in article 91.

2. The request for provisional arrest shall be made by any medium capable of delivering a written record and shall contain:

(a) Information describing the person sought, sufficient to identify the person, and information as to that person's probable location;

(b) A concise statement of the crimes for which the person's arrest is sought and of the facts which are alleged to constitute those crimes, including, where possible, the date and location of the crime;

(c) A statement of the existence of a warrant of arrest or a judgement of conviction against the person sought; and

(d) A statement that a request for surrender of the person sought will follow.

3. A person who is provisionally arrested may be released from custody if the requested State has not received the request for surrender and the documents supporting the request as specified in article 91 within the time limits specified in the Rules of Procedure and Evidence. However, the person may consent to surrender before the expiration of this period if permitted by the law of the requested State. In such a case, the requested State shall proceed to surrender the person to the Court as soon as possible.

4. The fact that the person sought has been released from custody pursuant to paragraph 3 shall not prejudice the subsequent arrest and surrender of that person if the request for surrender and the documents supporting the request are delivered at a later date.

Article 93

Other forms of cooperation

1. States Parties shall, in accordance with the provisions of this Part and under procedures of national law, comply with requests by the Court to provide the following assistance in relation to investigations or prosecutions:

(a) The identification and whereabouts of persons or the location of items;

(b) The taking of evidence, including testimony under oath, and the production of evidence, including expert opinions and reports necessary to the Court;

(c) The questioning of any person being investigated or prosecuted;

(d) The service of documents, including judicial documents;

(e) Facilitating the voluntary appearance of persons as witnesses or experts before the Court;

(f) The temporary transfer of persons as provided in paragraph 7;

(g) The examination of places or sites, including the exhumation and examination of grave sites;

(h) The execution of searches and seizures;

(i) The provision of records and documents, including official records and documents;

(j) The protection of victims and witnesses and the preservation of evidence;

(k) The identification, tracing and freezing or seizure of proceeds, property and assets and instrumentalities of crimes for the purpose of eventual forfeiture, without prejudice to the rights of bona fide third parties; and

(l)   Any other type of assistance which is not prohibited by the law of the requested State, with a view to facilitating the investigation and prosecution of crimes within the jurisdiction of the Court.

2. The Court shall have the authority to provide an assurance to a witness or an expert appearing before the Court that he or she will not be prosecuted, detained or subjected to any restriction of personal freedom by the Court in respect of any act or omission that preceded the departure of that person from the requested State.

3. Where execution of a particular measure of assistance detailed in a request presented under paragraph 1, is prohibited in the requested State on the basis of an existing fundamental legal principle of general application, the requested State shall promptly consult with the Court to try to resolve the matter. In the consultations, consideration should be given to whether the assistance can be rendered in another manner or subject to conditions. If after consultations the matter cannot be resolved, the Court shall modify the request as necessary.

4. In accordance with article 72, a State Party may deny a request for assistance, in whole or in part, only if the request concerns the production of any documents or disclosure of evidence which relates to its national security.

5. Before denying a request for assistance under paragraph 1 (l), the requested State shall consider whether the assistance can be provided subject to specified conditions, or whether the assistance can be provided at a later date or in an alternative manner, provided that if the Court or the Prosecutor accepts the assistance subject to conditions, the Court or the Prosecutor shall abide by them.

6. If a request for assistance is denied, the requested State Party shall promptly inform the Court or the Prosecutor of the reasons for such denial.

7. (a)   The Court may request the temporary transfer of a person in custody for purposes of identification or for obtaining testimony or other assistance. The person may be transferred if the following conditions are fulfilled:
(i)   The person freely gives his or her informed consent to the transfer; and
(ii) The requested State agrees to the transfer, subject to such conditions as that State and the Court may agree.

(b)   The person being transferred shall remain in custody. When the purposes of the transfer have been fulfilled, the Court shall return the person without delay to the requested State.

8. (a)   The Court shall ensure the confidentiality of documents and information, except as required for the investigation and proceedings described in the request.

(b)   The requested State may, when necessary, transmit documents or information to the Prosecutor on a confidential basis. The Prosecutor may then use them solely for the purpose of generating new evidence.

(c)   The requested State may, on its own motion or at the request of the Prosecutor, subsequently consent to the disclosure of such documents or information. They may then be used as evidence pursuant to the provisions of Parts 5 and 6 and in accordance with the Rules of Procedure and Evidence.

9. (a)(i)   In the event that a State Party receives competing requests, other than for surrender or extradition, from the Court and from another State pursuant to an international obligation, the State Party shall endeavour, in consultation with

the Court and the other State, to meet both requests, if necessary by postponing or attaching conditions to one or the other request.

(ii) Failing that, competing requests shall be resolved in accordance with the principles established in article 90.

(b) Where, however, the request from the Court concerns information, property or persons which are subject to the control of a third State or an international organization by virtue of an international agreement, the requested States shall so inform the Court and the Court shall direct its request to the third State or international organization.

10. (a) The Court may, upon request, cooperate with and provide assistance to a State Party conducting an investigation into or trial in respect of conduct which constitutes a crime within the jurisdiction of the Court or which constitutes a serious crime under the national law of the requesting State.

(b) (i) The assistance provided under subparagraph (a) shall include, *inter alia*:

a. The transmission of statements, documents or other types of evidence obtained in the course of an investigation or a trial conducted by the Court; and

b. The questioning of any person detained by order of the Court;

(ii) In the case of assistance under subparagraph (b) (i) a:

a. If the documents or other types of evidence have been obtained with the assistance of a State, such transmission shall require the consent of that State;

b. If the statements, documents or other types of evidence have been provided by a witness or expert, such transmission shall be subject to the provisions of article 68.

(c) The Court may, under the conditions set out in this paragraph, grant a request for assistance under this paragraph from a State which is not a Party to this Statute.

Article 94

Postponement of execution of a request in respect of ongoing investigation or prosecution

1. If the immediate execution of a request would interfere with an ongoing investigation or prosecution of a case different from that to which the request relates, the requested State may postpone the execution of the request for a period of time agreed upon with the Court. However, the postponement shall be no longer than is necessary to complete the relevant investigation or prosecution in the requested State. Before making a decision to postpone, the requested State should consider whether the assistance may be immediately provided subject to certain conditions.

2. If a decision to postpone is taken pursuant to paragraph 1, the Prosecutor may, however, seek measures to preserve evidence, pursuant to article 93, para-graph 1 (j).

Article 95

Postponement of execution of a request in respect of an admissibility challenge

Where there is an admissibility challenge under consideration by the Court pursuant to article

18 or 19, the requested State may postpone the execution of a request under this Part pending a determination by the Court, unless the Court has specifically ordered that the Prosecutor may pursue the collection of such evidence pursuant to article 18 or 19.

Article 96

Contents of request for other forms of assistance under article 93

1. A request for other forms of assistance referred to in article 93 shall be made in writing. In urgent cases, a request may be made by any medium capable of delivering a written record, provided that the request shall be confirmed through the channel provided for in article 87, paragraph 1 (a).

2. The request shall, as applicable, contain or be supported by the following:

(a) A concise statement of the purpose of the request and the assistance sought, including the legal basis and the grounds for the request;
(b) As much detailed information as possible about the location or identification of any person or place that must be found or identified in order for the assistance sought to be provided;
(c) A concise statement of the essential facts underlying the request;
(d) The reasons for and details of any procedure or requirement to be followed;
(e) Such information as may be required under the law of the requested State in order to execute the request; and
(f) Any other information relevant in order for the assistance sought to be provided.

3. Upon the request of the Court, a State Party shall consult with the Court, either generally or with respect to a specific matter, regarding any requirements under its national law that may apply under paragraph 2 (e). During the consultations, the State Party shall advise the Court of the specific requirements of its national law.

4. The provisions of this article shall, where applicable, also apply in respect of a request for assistance made to the Court.

Article 97

Consultations

Where a State Party receives a request under this Part in relation to which it identifies problems which may impede or prevent the execution of the request, that State shall consult with the Court without delay in order to resolve the matter. Such problems may include, *inter alia*:

(a) Insufficient information to execute the request;
(b) In the case of a request for surrender, the fact that despite best efforts, the person sought cannot be located or that the investigation conducted has determined that the person in the requested State is clearly not the person named in the warrant; or
(c) The fact that execution of the request in its current form would require the requested State to breach a pre-existing treaty obligation undertaken with respect to another State.

Article 98

Cooperation with respect to waiver of immunity and consent to surrender

1. The Court may not proceed with a request for surrender or assistance which would require the requested State to act inconsistently with its obligations under international law with respect to the State or diplomatic immunity of a person or property of a third State, unless the Court can first obtain the cooperation of that third State for the waiver of the immunity.

2. The Court may not proceed with a request for surrender which would require the requested State to act inconsistently with its obligations under international agreements pursuant to which the consent of a sending State is required to surrender a person of that State to the Court, unless the Court can first obtain the cooperation of the sending State for the giving of consent for the surrender.

Article 99

Execution of requests under articles 93 and 96

1. Requests for assistance shall be executed in accordance with the relevant procedure under the law of the requested State and, unless prohibited by such law, in the manner specified in the request, including following any procedure outlined therein or permitting persons specified in the request to be present at and assist in the execution process.

2. In the case of an urgent request, the documents or evidence produced in response shall, at the request of the Court, be sent urgently.

3. Replies from the requested State shall be transmitted in their original language and form.

4. Without prejudice to other articles in this Part, where it is necessary for the successful execution of a request which can be executed without any compulsory measures, including specifically the interview of or taking evidence from a person on a voluntary basis, including doing so without the presence of the authorities of the requested State Party if it is essential for the request to be executed, and the examination without modification of a public site or other public place, the Prosecutor may execute such request directly on the territory of a State as follows:

(a) When the State Party requested is a State on the territory of which the crime is alleged to have been committed, and there has been a determination of admissibility pursuant to article 18 or 19, the Prosecutor may directly execute such request following all possible consultations with the requested State Party;

(b) In other cases, the Prosecutor may execute such request following consultations with the requested State Party and subject to any reasonable conditions or concerns raised by that State Party. Where the requested State Party identifies problems with the execution of a request pursuant to this subparagraph it shall, without delay, consult with the Court to resolve the matter.

5. Provisions allowing a person heard or examined by the Court under article 72 to invoke restrictions designed to prevent disclosure of confidential information connected with national security shall also apply to the execution of requests for assistance under this article.

Article 100

Costs

1. The ordinary costs for execution of requests in the territory of the requested State shall be borne by that State, except for the following, which shall be borne by the Court:

(a) Costs associated with the travel and security of witnesses and experts or the transfer under article 93 of persons in custody;
(b) Costs of translation, interpretation and transcription;
(c) Travel and subsistence costs of the judges, the Prosecutor, the Deputy Prosecutors, the Registrar, the Deputy Registrar and staff of any organ of the Court;
(d) Costs of any expert opinion or report requested by the Court;
(e) Costs associated with the transport of a person being surrendered to the Court by a custodial State; and
(f) Following consultations, any extraordinary costs that may result from the execution of a request.

2. The provisions of paragraph 1 shall, as appropriate, apply to requests from States Parties to the Court. In that case, the Court shall bear the ordinary costs of execution.

Article 101

Rule of speciality

1. A person surrendered to the Court under this Statute shall not be proceeded against, punished or detained for any conduct committed prior to surrender, other than the conduct or course of conduct which forms the basis of the crimes for which that person has been surrendered.

2. The Court may request a waiver of the requirements of paragraph 1 from the State which surrendered the person to the Court and, if necessary, the Court shall provide additional information in accordance with article 91. States Parties shall have the authority to provide a waiver to the Court and should endeavour to do so.

Article 102

Use of terms

For the purposes of this Statute:

(a) 'surrender' means the delivering up of a person by a State to the Court, pursuant to this Statute.
(b) 'extradition' means the delivering up of a person by one State to another as provided by treaty, convention or national legislation.

PART 10. ENFORCEMENT

Article 103
Role of States in enforcement of sentences of imprisonment

1. (a) A sentence of imprisonment shall be served in a State designated by the Court from a list of States which have indicated to the Court their willingness to accept sentenced persons.

   (b) At the time of declaring its willingness to accept sentenced persons, a State may attach conditions to its acceptance as agreed by the Court and in accordance with this Part.

   (c) A State designated in a particular case shall promptly inform the Court whether it accepts the Court's designation.

2. (a) The State of enforcement shall notify the Court of any circumstances, including the exercise of any conditions agreed under paragraph 1, which could materially affect the terms or extent of the imprisonment. The Court shall be given at least 45 days' notice of any such known or foreseeable circumstances. During this period, the State of enforcement shall take no action that might prejudice its obligations under article 110.

   (b) Where the Court cannot agree to the circumstances referred to in subparagraph (a), it shall notify the State of enforcement and proceed in accordance with article 104, paragraph 1.

3. In exercising its discretion to make a designation under paragraph 1, the Court shall take into account the following:

(a) The principle that States Parties should share the responsibility for enforcing sentences of imprisonment, in accordance with principles of equitable distribution, as provided in the Rules of Procedure and Evidence;

(b) The application of widely accepted international treaty standards governing the treatment of prisoners;

(c) The views of the sentenced person;

(d) The nationality of the sentenced person;

(e) Such other factors regarding the circumstances of the crime or the person sentenced, or the effective enforcement of the sentence, as may be appropriate in designating the State of enforcement.

4. If no State is designated under paragraph 1, the sentence of imprisonment shall be served in a prison facility made available by the host State, in accordance with the conditions set out in the headquarters agreement referred to in article 3, paragraph 2. In such a case, the costs arising out of the enforcement of a sentence of imprisonment shall be borne by the Court.

Article 104

Change in designation of State of enforcement

1. The Court may, at any time, decide to transfer a sentenced person to a prison of another State.

2. A sentenced person may, at any time, apply to the Court to be transferred from the State of enforcement.

Article 105

Enforcement of the sentence

1. Subject to conditions which a State may have specified in accordance with article 103, paragraph 1 (b), the sentence of imprisonment shall be binding on the States Parties, which shall in no case modify it.

2. The Court alone shall have the right to decide any application for appeal and revision. The State of enforcement shall not impede the making of any such application by a sentenced person.

Article 106

Supervision of enforcement of sentences and conditions of imprisonment

1. The enforcement of a sentence of imprisonment shall be subject to the supervision of the Court and shall be consistent with widely accepted international treaty standards governing treatment of prisoners.

2. The conditions of imprisonment shall be governed by the law of the State of enforcement and shall be consistent with widely accepted international treaty standards governing treatment of prisoners; in no case shall such conditions be more or less favourable than those available to prisoners convicted of similar offences in the State of enforcement.

3. Communications between a sentenced person and the Court shall be unimpeded and confidential.

Article 107

Transfer of the person upon completion of sentence

1. Following completion of the sentence, a person who is not a national of the State of enforcement may, in accordance with the law of the State of enforcement, be transferred to a State which is obliged to receive him or her, or to another State which agrees to receive him or her, taking into account any wishes of the person to be transferred to that State, unless the State of enforcement authorizes the person to remain in its territory.

2. If no State bears the costs arising out of transferring the person to another State pursuant to paragraph 1, such costs shall be borne by the Court.

3. Subject to the provisions of article 108, the State of enforcement may also, in accordance with its national law, extradite or otherwise surrender the person to a State which has requested the extradition or surrender of the person for purposes of trial or enforcement of a sentence.

Article 108

Limitation on the prosecution or punishment of other offences

1. A sentenced person in the custody of the State of enforcement shall not be subject to prosecution or punishment or to extradition to a third State for any conduct engaged in prior

to that person's delivery to the State of enforcement, unless such prosecution, punishment or extradition has been approved by the Court at the request of the State of enforcement.

2. The Court shall decide the matter after having heard the views of the sentenced person.

3. Paragraph 1 shall cease to apply if the sentenced person remains voluntarily for more than 30 days in the territory of the State of enforcement after having served the full sentence imposed by the Court, or returns to the territory of that State after having left it.

Article 109

Enforcement of fines and forfeiture measures

1. States Parties shall give effect to fines or forfeitures ordered by the Court under Part 7, without prejudice to the rights of bona fide third parties, and in accordance with the procedure of their national law.

2. If a State Party is unable to give effect to an order for forfeiture, it shall take measures to recover the value of the proceeds, property or assets ordered by the Court to be forfeited, without prejudice to the rights of bona fide third parties.

3. Property, or the proceeds of the sale of real property or, where appropriate, the sale of other property, which is obtained by a State Party as a result of its enforcement of a judgement of the Court shall be transferred to the Court.

Article 110

Review by the Court concerning reduction of sentence

1. The State of enforcement shall not release the person before expiry of the sentence pronounced by the Court.

2. The Court alone shall have the right to decide any reduction of sentence, and shall rule on the matter after having heard the person.

3. When the person has served two thirds of the sentence, or 25 years in the case of life imprisonment, the Court shall review the sentence to determine whether it should be reduced. Such a review shall not be conducted before that time.

4. In its review under paragraph 3, the Court may reduce the sentence if it finds that one or more of the following factors are present:

(a) The early and continuing willingness of the person to cooperate with the Court in its investigations and prosecutions;

(b) The voluntary assistance of the person in enabling the enforcement of the judgements and orders of the Court in other cases, and in particular providing assistance in locating assets subject to orders of fine, forfeiture or reparation which may be used for the benefit of victims; or

(c) Other factors establishing a clear and significant change of circumstances sufficient to justify the reduction of sentence, as provided in the Rules of Procedure and Evidence.

5. If the Court determines in its initial review under paragraph 3 that it is not appropriate to reduce the sentence, it shall thereafter review the question of reduction of sentence at such intervals and applying such criteria as provided for in the Rules of Procedure and Evidence.

Article 111

Escape

If a convicted person escapes from custody and flees the State of enforcement, that State may, after consultation with the Court, request the person's surrender from the State in which the person is located pursuant to existing bilateral or multilateral arrangements, or may request that the Court seek the person's surrender, in accordance with Part 9. It may direct that the person be delivered to the State in which he or she was serving the sentence or to another State designated by the Court.

PART 11. ASSEMBLY OF STATES PARTIES

Article 112

Assembly of States Parties

1. An Assembly of States Parties to this Statute is hereby established. Each State Party shall have one representative in the Assembly who may be accompanied by alternates and advisers. Other States which have signed this Statute or the Final Act may be observers in the Assembly.

2. The Assembly shall:

(a) Consider and adopt, as appropriate, recommendations of the Preparatory Commission;
(b) Provide management oversight to the Presidency, the Prosecutor and the Registrar regarding the administration of the Court;
(c) Consider the reports and activities of the Bureau established under paragraph 3 and take appropriate action in regard thereto;
(d) Consider and decide the budget for the Court;
(e) Decide whether to alter, in accordance with article 36, the number of judges;
(f) Consider pursuant to article 87, paragraphs 5 and 7, any question relating to non-cooperation;
(g) Perform any other function consistent with this Statute or the Rules of Procedure and Evidence.
   3. (a)   The Assembly shall have a Bureau consisting of a President, two Vice-Presidents and 18 members elected by the Assembly for three-year terms.
     (b)   The Bureau shall have a representative character, taking into account, in particular, equitable geographical distribution and the adequate representation of the principal legal systems of the world.
     (c)   The Bureau shall meet as often as necessary, but at least once a year. It shall assist the Assembly in the discharge of its responsibilities.

4. The Assembly may establish such subsidiary bodies as may be necessary, including an independent oversight mechanism for inspection, evaluation and investigation of the Court, in order to enhance its efficiency and economy.

5. The President of the Court, the Prosecutor and the Registrar or their representatives may participate, as appropriate, in meetings of the Assembly and of the Bureau.

6. The Assembly shall meet at the seat of the Court or at the Headquarters of the United Nations once a year and, when circumstances so require, hold special sessions. Except as otherwise specified in this Statute, special sessions shall be convened by the Bureau on its own initiative or at the request of one third of the States Parties.

7. Each State Party shall have one vote. Every effort shall be made to reach decisions by consensus in the Assembly and in the Bureau. If consensus cannot be reached, except as otherwise provided in the Statute:

(a) Decisions on matters of substance must be approved by a two-thirds majority of those present and voting provided that an absolute majority of States Parties constitutes the quorum for voting;
(b) Decisions on matters of procedure shall be taken by a simple majority of States Parties present and voting.

8. A State Party which is in arrears in the payment of its financial contributions towards the costs of the Court shall have no vote in the Assembly and in the Bureau if the amount of its arrears equals or exceeds the amount of the contributions due from it for the preceding two full years. The Assembly may, nevertheless, permit such a State Party to vote in the Assembly and in the Bureau if it is satisfied that the failure to pay is due to conditions beyond the control of the State Party.

9. The Assembly shall adopt its own rules of procedure.

10. The official and working languages of the Assembly shall be those of the General Assembly of the United Nations.

PART 12. FINANCING

Article 113

Financial Regulations
Except as otherwise specifically provided, all financial matters related to the Court and the meetings of the Assembly of States Parties, including its Bureau and subsidiary bodies, shall be governed by this Statute and the Financial Regulations and Rules adopted by the Assembly of States Parties.

Article 114

Payment of expenses
Expenses of the Court and the Assembly of States Parties, including its Bureau and subsidiary bodies, shall be paid from the funds of the Court.

Article 115

Funds of the Court and of the Assembly of States Parties
The expenses of the Court and the Assembly of States Parties, including its Bureau and subsidiary bodies, as provided for in the budget decided by the Assembly of States Parties, shall be provided by the following sources:

(a) Assessed contributions made by States Parties;
(b) Funds provided by the United Nations, subject to the approval of the General Assembly, in particular in relation to the expenses incurred due to referrals by the Security Council.

Article 116

Voluntary contributions
Without prejudice to article 115, the Court may receive and utilize, as additional funds, voluntary contributions from Governments, international organizations, individuals, corporations and other entities, in accordance with relevant criteria adopted by the Assembly of States Parties.

Article 117

Assessment of contributions
The contributions of States Parties shall be assessed in accordance with an agreed scale of assessment, based on the scale adopted by the United Nations for its regular budget and adjusted in accordance with the principles on which that scale is based.

Article 118

Annual audit
The records, books and accounts of the Court, including its annual financial statements, shall be audited annually by an independent auditor.

PART 13. FINAL CLAUSES

Article 119

Settlement of disputes
1. Any dispute concerning the judicial functions of the Court shall be settled by the decision of the Court.
2. Any other dispute between two or more States Parties relating to the interpretation or application of this Statute which is not settled through negotiations within three months of their commencement shall be referred to the Assembly of States Parties. The Assembly may itself seek to settle the dispute or may make recommendations on further means of settlement of the dispute, including referral to the International Court of Justice in conformity with the Statute of that Court.

Article 120

Reservations
No reservations may be made to this Statute.

Article 121

Amendments

1. After the expiry of seven years from the entry into force of this Statute, any State Party may propose amendments thereto. The text of any proposed amendment shall be submitted to the Secretary-General of the United Nations, who shall promptly circulate it to all States Parties.

2. No sooner than three months from the date of notification, the Assembly of States Parties, at its next meeting, shall, by a majority of those present and voting, decide whether to take up the proposal. The Assembly may deal with the proposal directly or convene a Review Conference if the issue involved so warrants.

3. The adoption of an amendment at a meeting of the Assembly of States Parties or at a Review Conference on which consensus cannot be reached shall require a two-thirds majority of States Parties.

4. Except as provided in paragraph 5, an amendment shall enter into force for all States Parties one year after instruments of ratification or acceptance have been deposited with the Secretary-General of the United Nations by seven-eighths of them.

5. Any amendment to articles 5, 6, 7 and 8 of this Statute shall enter into force for those States Parties which have accepted the amendment one year after the deposit of their instruments of ratification or acceptance. In respect of a State Party which has not accepted the amendment, the Court shall not exercise its jurisdiction regarding a crime covered by the amendment when committed by that State Party's nationals or on its territory.

6. If an amendment has been accepted by seven-eighths of States Parties in accordance with paragraph 4, any State Party which has not accepted the amendment may withdraw from this Statute with immediate effect, notwithstanding article 127, paragraph 1, but subject to article 127, paragraph 2, by giving notice no later than one year after the entry into force of such amendment.

7. The Secretary-General of the United Nations shall circulate to all States Parties any amendment adopted at a meeting of the Assembly of States Parties or at a Review Conference.

Article 122

Amendments to provisions of an institutional nature

1. Amendments to provisions of this Statute which are of an exclusively institutional nature, namely, article 35, article 36, paragraphs 8 and 9, article 37, article 38, article 39, paragraphs 1 (first two sentences), 2 and 4, article 42, paragraphs 4 to 9, article 43, paragraphs 2 and 3, and articles 44, 46, 47 and 49, may be proposed at any time, notwithstanding article 121, paragraph 1, by any State Party. The text of any proposed amendment shall be submitted to the Secretary-General of the United Nations or such other person designated by the Assembly of States Parties who shall promptly circulate it to all States Parties and to others participating in the Assembly.

2. Amendments under this article on which consensus cannot be reached shall be adopted by the Assembly of States Parties or by a Review Conference, by a two-thirds majority of States Parties. Such amendments shall enter into force for all States Parties six months after their adoption by the Assembly or, as the case may be, by the Conference.

Article 123

Review of the Statute

1. Seven years after the entry into force of this Statute the Secretary-General of the United Nations shall convene a Review Conference to consider any amendments to this Statute. Such review may include, but is not limited to, the list of crimes contained in article 5. The Conference shall be open to those participating in the Assembly of States Parties and on the same conditions.

2. At any time thereafter, at the request of a State Party and for the purposes set out in paragraph 1, the Secretary-General of the United Nations shall, upon approval by a majority of States Parties, convene a Review Conference.

3. The provisions of article 121, paragraphs 3 to 7, shall apply to the adoption and entry into force of any amendment to the Statute considered at a Review Conference.

Article 124

Transitional Provision

Notwithstanding article 12, paragraphs 1 and 2, a State, on becoming a party to this Statute, may declare that, for a period of seven years after the entry into force of this Statute for the State concerned, it does not accept the jurisdiction of the Court with respect to the category of crimes referred to in article 8 when a crime is alleged to have been committed by its nationals or on its territory. A declaration under this article may be withdrawn at any time. The provisions of this article shall be reviewed at the Review Conference convened in accordance with article 123, paragraph 1.

Article 125

Signature, ratification, acceptance, approval or accession

1. This Statute shall be open for signature by all States in Rome, at the headquarters of the Food and Agriculture Organization of the United Nations, on 17 July 1998. Thereafter, it shall remain open for signature in Rome at the Ministry of Foreign Affairs of Italy until 17 October 1998. After that date, the Statute shall remain open for signature in New York, at United Nations Headquarters, until 31 December 2000.

2. This Statute is subject to ratification, acceptance or approval by signatory States. Instruments of ratification, acceptance or approval shall be deposited with the Secretary-General of the United Nations.

3. This Statute shall be open to accession by all States. Instruments of accession shall be deposited with the Secretary-General of the United Nations.

Article 126

Entry into force

1. This Statute shall enter into force on the first day of the month after the 60th day following the date of the deposit of the 60th instrument of ratification, acceptance, approval or accession with the Secretary-General of the United Nations.

2. For each State ratifying, accepting, approving or acceding to this Statute after the

deposit of the 60th instrument of ratification, acceptance, approval or accession, the Statute shall enter into force on the first day of the month after the 60th day following the deposit by such State of its instrument of ratification, acceptance, approval or accession.

Article 127

Withdrawal

1. A State Party may, by written notification addressed to the Secretary-General of the United Nations, withdraw from this Statute. The withdrawal shall take effect one year after the date of receipt of the notification, unless the notification specifies a later date.

2. A State shall not be discharged, by reason of its withdrawal, from the obligations arising from this Statute while it was a Party to the Statute, including any financial obligations which may have accrued. Its withdrawal shall not affect any cooperation with the Court in connection with criminal investigations and proceedings in relation to which the withdrawing State had a duty to cooperate and which were commenced prior to the date on which the withdrawal became effective, nor shall it prejudice in any way the continued consideration of any matter which was already under consideration by the Court prior to the date on which the withdrawal became effective.

Article 128

Authentic texts

The original of this Statute, of which the Arabic, Chinese, English, French, Russian and Spanish texts are equally authentic, shall be deposited with the Secretary-General of the United Nations, who shall send certified copies thereof to all States.

In witness whereof, the undersigned, being duly authorized thereto by their respective Governments, have signed this Statute.

Done at Rome, this 17th day of July 1998.

Special appendix: Resolutions adopted by the Review Conference of the Rome Statute, Kampala, Uganda, 31 May–11 June 2010[1]

Resolution RC/Res.1
Adopted at the 9th plenary meeting, on 8 June 2010, by consensus
Complementarity

Resolution RC/Res.2
Adopted at the 9th plenary meeting, on 8 June 2010, by consensus
The impact of the Rome Statute system on victims and affected communities

Resolution RC/Res.3
Adopted at the 9th plenary meeting, on 8 June 2010, by consensus
Strengthening the enforcement of sentences

Resolution RC/Res.4
Adopted at the 11th plenary meeting, on 10 June 2010, by consensus
Article 124

Resolution RC/Res.5
Adopted at the 12th plenary meeting, on 10 June 2010, by consensus
Amendments to article 8 of the Rome Statute

Resolution RC/Res.6
Adopted at the 13th plenary meeting, on 11 June 2010, by consensus
The Crime of Aggression

---

[1] These resolutions were passed as this book went to press. They are included here for the convenience of the reader. Source: http://www.icc-cpi.int/Menus/ASP/Resolutions/Sessions/2010+-+Review+Conference.htm [accessed August 10, 2010.]

RESOLUTION RC/RES.1

Adopted at the 9th plenary meeting, on 8 June 2010, by consensus

RC/Res.1
Complementarity

The Review Conference,
    Reaffirming its commitment to the Rome Statute of the International Criminal Court,
    Reaffirming its determination to combat impunity for the most serious crimes of international concern as referred to in the Rome Statute,
    Reaffirming further that the most serious crimes of concern to the international community as a whole must not go unpunished and that their effective prosecution must be ensured by taking measures at the national level and by enhancing international cooperation,
    Welcoming the efforts of the Court to investigate and prosecute those bearing responsibility for the most serious crimes of international concern,
    Stressing the need to achieve universality of the Statute as a means to end impunity and acknowledging that assistance to strengthen domestic capacity may have positive effects in this regard,
1.   *Recognizes* the primary responsibility of States to investigate and prosecute the most serious crimes of international concern;
2.   *Emphasizes* the principle of complementarity as laid down in the Rome Statute and stresses the obligations of States Parties flowing from the Rome Statute;
3.   *Recognizes* the need for additional measures at the national level as required and for the enhancement of international assistance to effectively prosecute perpetrators of the most serious crimes of concern to the international community;
4.   *Notes* the importance of States Parties taking effective domestic measures to implement the Rome Statute;
5.   *Recognizes* the desirability for States to assist each other in strengthening domestic capacity to ensure that investigations and prosecutions of serious crimes of international concern can take place at the national level;
6.   *Takes note* of the report of the Bureau on complementarity and its recommendations as a background paper for discussions at the Review Conference;
7.   *Welcomes* the fruitful discussions on the issue of complementarity held during the Review Conference;
8.   *Encourages* the Court, States Parties and other stakeholders, including international organizations and civil society to further explore ways in which to enhance the capacity of national jurisdictions to investigate and prosecute serious crimes of international concern as set out in the Report of the Bureau on complementarity, including its recommendations;
9.   *Requests* the Secretariat of the Assembly of States Parties, in accordance with resolution ICC-ASP/2/Res.3, and, within existing resources, to facilitate the exchange of information between the Court, States Parties and other stakeholders, including international organizations and civil society, aimed at strengthening domestic jurisdictions, and

requests the Secretariat of the Assembly of States Parties to report to the tenth session of the Assembly on progress in this regard;

10. *Requests* the Bureau to continue the dialogue with the Court and other stakeholders on the issue of complementarity and invites the Court to present to the Assembly at its tenth session, as appropriate, a report in this regard.

RESOLUTION RC/RES.2

Adopted at the 9th plenary meeting, on 8 June 2010, by consensus

RC/Res.2
The Impact of the Rome Statute System on Victims and Affected Communities

The Review Conference,

Recalling the Preamble of the Rome Statute which reminds that millions of children, women and men have been victims of unimaginable atrocities that deeply shock the conscience of humanity,

Reaffirming the importance of the Rome Statute to the victims and affected communities in ts determination to put an end to impunity for the perpetrators of the crime of genocide, crimes against humanity and war crimes, thus contributing to their prevention,

Recalling United Nations Security Council resolutions 1325, 1820, 1888 and 1889 on women, peace and security, as well as resolutions 1612 and 1882 on children in armed conflict, and in this context, underlining the need to address the specific needs of women and children as well as to put an end to impunity for sexual violence in conflict,

Further recalling, inter alia, the 1985 United Nations General Assembly Resolution 40/34 'Declaration of Basic Principles of Justice for Victims of Crime and Abuse of Power', and the 2005 United Nations General Assembly Resolution 60/147 'Basic Principles and Guidelines on the Right to a Remedy and Reparation for Victims of Gross Violations of International Human Rights Law and Serious Violations of International Humanitarian Law',

Recognizing that victims' right to equal and effective access to justice; protection and support; adequate and prompt reparation for harm suffered; and access to relevant information concerning violations and redress mechanisms are essential components of justice,

Emphasizing the importance of outreach to victims and affected communities in order to give effect to the unique mandate of the International Criminal Court towards victims,

1.   *Encourages* States to consider implementing those provisions of the Rome Statute relevant to victims/witnesses, where applicable, through national legislation or appropriate measures;

2.   *Further encourages* the Court, in dialogue with victims and affected communities, to continue to optimize the Court's strategic planning process, including the Court's Strategy in relation to victims, as well as its field presence in order to improve the way in which it addresses the concerns of victims and affected communities, paying special attention to the needs of women and children;

3.   *Underlines* the need to continue to optimize and adapt outreach activities, in light of different phases of the judicial cycle, and to encourage further efforts to ensure that victims and affected communities have access to accurate information about the Court, its mandate and activities, as well as about victims' rights under the Rome Statute, including their right to participate in judicial proceedings and claim for reparations;

4.   *Encourages* governments, communities and civil organizations at the national and local level to play an active role in sensitizing communities on the rights of victims in accordance with the Rome Statute in general and victims of sexual violence in particular: to speak against their marginalization and stigmatization, to assist them in their social reintegration process and in their participation in consultation, and to combat a culture of impunity for these crimes;

5. *Expresses its appreciation* to the Board of Directors of the Trust Fund for Victims for its continuing commitment towards easing the suffering of victims;

6. *Stresses* the importance of an ongoing dialogue between the Secretariat of the Trust Fund for Victims, the Court and States Parties, with a view to ensuring the transparency of the management of the Trust Fund and its Secretariat and further stresses the importance in this regard of regular exchanges with the international community, including donors and civil society, so as to promote the activities of the Trust Fund and contribute to its visibility;

7. *Calls upon* States Parties, international organizations, individuals, corporations and other entities to contribute to the Trust Fund for Victims to ensure that timely and adequate assistance and reparations can be provided to victims in accordance with the Rome Statute, and expresses its gratitude to those that have done so.

RESOLUTION RC/RES.3

Adopted at the 9th plenary meeting, on 8 June 2010, by consensus

RC/Res.3
Strengthening the Enforcement of Sentences

The Review Conference,

Recalling the Rome Statute of the International Criminal Court,

Conscious of the key role of States in the enforcement of the Court's sentences of imprisonment,

Recalling that the Court's sentences of imprisonment shall be served in prison facilities provided by States that have indicated their willingness to accept sentenced persons, in accordance with the Statute,

Mindful of the need for broader participation of States in the enforcement of sentences in order to allow for such enforcement in all relevant regions and sub regions and taking note of the unanimous view expressed by States Parties to this effect,

Emphasizing the need for enhanced international cooperation with a view to enabling more States to voluntarily accept sentenced persons on the basis of widely accepted international treaty standards governing the treatment of prisoners,

1.   *Calls upon States* to indicate to the Court their willingness to accept sentenced persons in accordance with the Statute;

2.   *Confirms* that a sentence of imprisonment may be served in a prison facility made available in the designated State through an international or regional organization, mechanism or agency;

3.   *Urges* States Parties and States that have indicated their willingness to accept sentenced persons, directly or through competent international organizations, to promote actively international cooperation at all levels, particularly at the regional and sub regional levels;

4.   *Requests* the Secretary-General of the United Nations to bring this resolution to the attention of all members of the United Nations, with a view to encouraging that the above objectives may be considered, as appropriate, in the relevant programmes of assistance of the orld Bank, the regional banks, the United Nations Development Programme, and other relevant multilateral and national agencies.

RESOLUTION RC/RES.4

Adopted at the 11th plenary meeting, on 10 June 2010, by consensus

RC/Res.4
Article 124

The Review Conference,

 Recognizing the need to ensure the integrity of the Rome Statute,

 Mindful of the importance of the universality of the founding instrument of the International Criminal Court,

 Recalling the transitional nature of article 124, as decided by the Rome Conference,

 Recalling that the Assembly of States Parties forwarded article 124 to the Review Conference for its possible deletion,

 Having reviewed the provisions of article 124 at the Review Conference in accordance with the Rome Statute,

 Decides to retain article 124 in its current form,

 Also decides to further review the provisions of article 124 during the fourteenth session of the Assembly of States Parties to the Rome Statute.

RESOLUTION RC/RES.5

Adopted at the 12th plenary meeting, on 10 June 2010, by consensus

RC/Res.5
Amendments to Article 8 of the Rome Statute

The Review Conference,

    Noting article 123, paragraph 1, of the Rome Statute of the International Criminal Court which requests the Secretary-General of the United Nations to convene a Review Conference to consider any amendments to the Statute seven years after its entry into force,

    Noting article 121, paragraph 5, of the Statute which states that any amendment to articles 5, 6, 7 and 8 of the Statute shall enter into force for those States Parties which have accepted the amendment one year after the deposit of their instruments of ratification or acceptance and that in respect of a State Party which has not accepted the amendment, the Court shall not exercise its jurisdiction regarding the crime covered by the amendment when committed by that State Party's nationals or on its territory, and confirming its understanding that in respect to this amendment the same principle that applies in respect of a State Party which has not accepted the amendment applies also in respect of States that are not parties to the Statute,

    Confirming that, in light of the provision of article 40, paragraph 5, of the Vienna Convention on the Law of Treaties, States that subsequently become States Parties to the Statute will be allowed to decide whether to accept the amendment contained in this resolution at the time of ratification, acceptance or approval of, or accession to the Statute,

    Noting article 9 of the Statute on the Elements of Crimes which states that such Elements shall assist the Court in the interpretation and application of the crimes within its jurisdiction,

    Taking due account of the fact that the crimes of employing poison or poisoned weapons; of employing asphyxiating, poisonous or other gases, and all analogous liquids, materials or devices; and of employing bullets which expand or flatten easily in the human body, such as bullets with a hard envelope which does not entirely cover the core or is pierced with incisions, already fall within the jurisdiction of the Court under article 8, paragraph 2 (b), as serious violations of the laws and customs applicable in international armed conflict,

    Noting the relevant elements of the crimes within the Elements of Crimes already adopted by the Assembly of States Parties on 9 September 2000,

    Considering that the abovementioned relevant elements of the crimes can also help in their interpretation and application in armed conflict not of an international character, in that inter alia they specify that the conduct took place in the context of and was associated with an armed conflict, which consequently confirm the exclusion from the Court's jurisdiction of law enforcement situations,

    Considering that the crimes proposed in article 8, paragraph 2 (e) (xiii) (employing poison or poisoned weapons) and in article 8, paragraph 2 (e) (xiv) (asphyxiating, poisonous or other gases, and all analogous liquids, materials and devices) are serious violations of the laws and customs applicable in armed conflict not of an international character, as reflected in customary international law,

    Considering that the crime proposed in article 8, paragraph 2 (e) (xv) (employing bullets which expand or flatten easily in the human body), is also a serious violation of the laws and customs applicable in armed conflict not of an international character, and understanding that the crime is committed only if the perpetrator employs the bullets to uselessly aggravate suffering or the wounding effect upon the target of such bullets, as reflected in customary international law,

1.   *Decides* to adopt the amendment to article 8, paragraph 2 (e), of the Rome Statute of the International Criminal Court contained in annex I to the present resolution, which is subject to ratification or acceptance and shall enter into force in accordance with article 121, paragraph 5, of the Statute;

2.   *Decides* to adopt the relevant elements to be added to the Elements of Crimes, as contained in annex II to the present resolution.

ANNEX I

Amendment to Article 8

Add to article 8, paragraph 2 (e), the following:

'(xiii) Employing poison or poisoned weapons;

(xiv) Employing asphyxiating, poisonous or other gases, and all analogous liquids, materials or devices;

(xv) Employing bullets which expand or flatten easily in the human body, such as bullets with a hard envelope which does not entirely cover the core or is pierced with incisions.'

ANNEX II

Elements of Crimes

Add the following elements to the Elements of Crimes:

Article 8 (2) (e) (xiii)
War crime of employing poison or poisoned weapons
Elements

1. The perpetrator employed a substance or a weapon that releases a substance as a result of its employment.

2. The substance was such that it causes death or serious damage to health in the ordinary course of events, through its toxic properties.

3. The conduct took place in the context of and was associated with an armed conflict not of an international character.

4. The perpetrator was aware of factual circumstances that established the existence of an armed conflict.

Article 8 (2) (e) (xiv)
War crime of employing prohibited gases, liquids, materials or devices
Elements

1. The perpetrator employed a gas or other analogous substance or device.
2. The gas, substance or device was such that it causes death or serious damage to health in the ordinary course of events, through its asphyxiating or toxic properties.[1]
3. The conduct took place in the context of and was associated with an armed conflict not of an international character.
4. The perpetrator was aware of factual circumstances that established the existence of an armed conflict.

Article 8 (2) (e) (xv)
War crime of employing prohibited bullets
Elements

1. The perpetrator employed certain bullets.
2. The bullets were such that their use violates the international law of armed conflict because they expand or flatten easily in the human body.
3. The perpetrator was aware that the nature of the bullets was such that their employment would uselessly aggravate suffering or the wounding effect.
4. The conduct took place in the context of and was associated with an armed conflict not of an international character.
5. The perpetrator was aware of factual circumstances that established the existence of an armed conflict.

---

[1] Nothing in this element shall be interpreted as limiting or prejudicing in any way existing or developing rules of international law with respect to the development, production, stockpiling and use of chemical weapons.

RESOLUTION RC/RES.6

Adopted at the 13th plenary meeting, on 11 June 2010, by consensus

RC/Res.6
The Crime of Aggression

The Review Conference,

 Recalling paragraph 1 of article 12 of the Rome Statute,

 Recalling paragraph 2 of article 5 of the Rome Statute,

 Recalling also paragraph 7 of resolution F, adopted by the United Nations Diplomatic Conference of Plenipotentiaries on the Establishment of an International Criminal Court on 17 July 1998,

 Recalling further resolution ICC-ASP/1/Res.1 on the continuity of work in respect of the crime of aggression, and *expressing its appreciation* to the Special Working Group on the Crime of Aggression for having elaborated proposals on a provision on the crime of aggression,

 Taking note of resolution ICC-ASP/8/Res.6, by which the Assembly of States Parties forwarded proposals on a provision on the crime of aggression to the Review Conference for its consideration,

 Resolved to activate the Court's jurisdiction over the crime of aggression as early as possible,

1. *Decides to adopt*, in accordance with article 5, paragraph 2, of the Rome Statute of the International Criminal Court (hereinafter: 'the Statute') the amendments to the Statute contained in annex I of the present resolution, which are subject to ratification or acceptance and shall enter into force in accordance with article 121, paragraph 5; and notes that any State Party may lodge a declaration referred to in article 15 bis prior to ratification or acceptance;

2. *Also decides* to adopt the amendments to the Elements of Crimes contained in annex II of the present resolution;

3. *Also decides* to adopt the understandings regarding the interpretation of the above-mentioned amendments contained in annex III of the present resolution;

4. *Further decides* to review the amendments on the crime of aggression seven years after the beginning of the Court's exercise of jurisdiction;

5. *Calls upon* all States Parties to ratify or accept the amendments contained in annex I.

ANNEX I

Amendments to the Rome Statute of the International Criminal Court on the Crime of Aggression

1. Article 5, paragraph 2, of the Statute is deleted.

2. The following text is inserted after article 8 of the Statute:

Article 8 *bis*
Crime of aggression
1. For the purpose of this Statute, 'crime of aggression' means the planning, preparation, initiation or execution, by a person in a position effectively to exercise control over or to direct the political or military action of a State, of an act of aggression which, by its character, gravity and scale, constitutes a manifest violation of the Charter of the United Nations.
2. For the purpose of paragraph 1, 'act of aggression' means the use of armed force by a State against the sovereignty, territorial integrity or political independence of another State, or in any other manner inconsistent with the Charter of the United Nations. Any of the following acts, regardless of a declaration of war, shall, in accordance with United Nations General Assembly resolution 3314 (XXIX) of 14 December 1974, qualify as an act of aggression:
a) The invasion or attack by the armed forces of a State of the territory of another State, or any military occupation, however temporary, resulting from such invasion or attack, or any annexation by the use of force of the territory of another State or part thereof;
b) Bombardment by the armed forces of a State against the territory of another State or the use of any weapons by a State against the territory of another State;
c) The blockade of the ports or coasts of a State by the armed forces of another State;
d) An attack by the armed forces of a State on the land, sea or air forces, or marine and air fleets of another State;
e) The use of armed forces of one State which are within the territory of another State with the agreement of the receiving State, in contravention of the conditions provided for in the agreement or any extension of their presence in such territory beyond the termination of the agreement;
f) The action of a State in allowing its territory, which it has placed at the disposal of another State, to be used by that other State for perpetrating an act of aggression against a third State;
g) The sending by or on behalf of a State of armed bands, groups, irregulars or mercenaries, which carry out acts of armed force against another State of such gravity as to amount to the acts listed above, or its substantial involvement therein.
3. The following text is inserted after article 15 of the Statute:

Article 15 *bis*
Exercise of jurisdiction over the crime of aggression
(State referral, *proprio motu)*
1. The Court may exercise jurisdiction over the crime of aggression in accordance with article 13, paragraphs (a) and (c), subject to the provisions of this article.
2. The Court may exercise jurisdiction only with respect to crimes of aggression committed one year after the ratification or acceptance of the amendments by thirty States Parties.
3. The Court shall exercise jurisdiction over the crime of aggression in accordance with this article, subject to a decision to be taken after 1 January 2017 by the same majority of States Parties as is required for the adoption of an amendment to the Statute.
4. The Court may, in accordance with article 12, exercise jurisdiction over a crime of aggression, arising from an act of aggression committed by a State Party, unless that State Party has previously declared that it does not accept such jurisdiction by lodging a declaration with the

Registrar. The withdrawal of such a declaration may be effected at any time and shall be considered by the State Party within three years.

5. In respect of a State that is not a party to this Statute, the Court shall not exercise its jurisdiction over the crime of aggression when committed by that State's nationals or on its territory.

6. Where the Prosecutor concludes that there is a reasonable basis to proceed with an investigation in respect of a crime of aggression, he or she shall first ascertain whether the Security Council has made a determination of an act of aggression committed by the State concerned. The Prosecutor shall notify the Secretary-General of the United Nations of the situation before the Court, including any relevant information and documents.

7. Where the Security Council has made such a determination, the Prosecutor may proceed with the investigation in respect of a crime of aggression.

8. Where no such determination is made within six months after the date of notification, the Prosecutor may proceed with the investigation in respect of a crime of aggression, provided that the Pre-Trial Division has authorized the commencement of the investigation in respect of a crime of aggression in accordance with the procedure contained in article 15, and the Security Council has not decided otherwise in accordance with article 16.

9. A determination of an act of aggression by an organ outside the Court shall be without prejudice to the Court's own findings under this Statute.

10. This article is without prejudice to the provisions relating to the exercise of jurisdiction with respect to other crimes referred to in article 5.

4. The following text is inserted after article 15 bis of the Statute:

Article 15 *ter*
Exercise of jurisdiction over the crime of aggression
(Security Council referral)

1. The Court may exercise jurisdiction over the crime of aggression in accordance with article 13, paragraph (b), subject to the provisions of this article.

2. The Court may exercise jurisdiction only with respect to crimes of aggression committed one year after the ratification or acceptance of the amendments by thirty States Parties.

3. The Court shall exercise jurisdiction over the crime of aggression in accordance with this article, subject to a decision to be taken after 1 January 2017 by the same majority of States Parties as is required for the adoption of an amendment to the Statute.

4. A determination of an act of aggression by an organ outside the Court shall be without prejudice to the Court's own findings under this Statute.

5. This article is without prejudice to the provisions relating to the exercise of jurisdiction with respect to other crimes referred to in article 5.

5. The following text is inserted after article 25, paragraph 3, of the Statute:

3 *bis*. In respect of the crime of aggression, the provisions of this article shall apply only to persons in a position effectively to exercise control over or to direct the political or military action of a State.

6. The first sentence of article 9, paragraph 1, of the Statute is replaced by the following sentence:

1. Elements of Crimes shall assist the Court in the interpretation and application of articles 6, 7, 8 and 8 bis.

7. The chapeau of article 20, paragraph 3, of the Statute is replaced by the following para-graph; the rest of the paragraph remains unchanged:

3. No person who has been tried by another court for conduct also proscribed under article 6, 7, 8 or 8 bis shall be tried by the Court with respect to the same conduct unless the proceedings in the other court:

ANNEX II

Amendments to the Elements of Crimes

Article 8 *bis*
Crime of aggression
Introduction

1. It is understood that any of the acts referred to in article 8 bis, paragraph 2, qualify as an act of aggression.
2. There is no requirement to prove that the perpetrator has made a legal evaluation as to whether the use of armed force was inconsistent with the Charter of the United Nations.
3. The term 'manifest' is an objective qualification.
4. There is no requirement to prove that the perpetrator has made a legal evaluation as to the 'manifest' nature of the violation of the Charter of the United Nations.

Elements

1. The perpetrator planned, prepared, initiated or executed an act of aggression.
2. The perpetrator was a person[1] in a position effectively to exercise control over or to direct the political or military action of the State which committed the act of aggression.
3. The act of aggression – the use of armed force by a State against the sovereignty, territorial integrity or political independence of another State, or in any other manner inconsistent with the Charter of the United Nations – was committed.
4. The perpetrator was aware of the factual circumstances that established that such a use of armed force was inconsistent with the Charter of the United Nations.
5. The act of aggression, by its character, gravity and scale, constituted a manifest violation of the Charter of the United Nations.
6. The perpetrator was aware of the factual circumstances that established such a manifest violation of the Charter of the United Nations.

---

[1] With respect to an act of aggression, more than one person may be in a position that meets these criteria.

ANNEX III

Understandings Regarding the Amendments to the Rome Statute of the International Criminal Court on the Crime of Aggression

Referrals by the Security Council

1. It is understood that the Court may exercise jurisdiction on the basis of a Security Council referral in accordance with article 13, paragraph (b), of the Statute only with respect to crimes of aggression committed after a decision in accordance with article 15 *ter*, paragraph 3, is taken, and one year after the ratification or acceptance of the amendments by thirty States Parties, whichever is later.

2. It is understood that the Court shall exercise jurisdiction over the crime of aggression on the basis of a Security Council referral in accordance with article 13, paragraph (b), of the Statute irrespective of whether the State concerned has accepted the Court's jurisdiction in this regard.

Jurisdiction *ratione temporis*

3. It is understood that in case of article 13, paragraph (a) or (c), the Court may exercise its jurisdiction only with respect to crimes of aggression committed after a decision in accordance with article 15 *bis*, paragraph 3, is taken, and one year after the ratification or acceptance of the amendments by thirty States Parties, whichever is later.

Domestic jurisdiction over the crime of aggression

4. It is understood that the amendments that address the definition of the act of aggression and the crime of aggression do so for the purpose of this Statute only. The amendments shall, in accordance with article 10 of the Rome Statute, not be interpreted as limiting or prejudicing in any way existing or developing rules of international law for purposes other than this Statute.

5. It is understood that the amendments shall not be interpreted as creating the right or obligation to exercise domestic jurisdiction with respect to an act of aggression committed by another State.

Other understandings

6. It is understood that aggression is the most serious and dangerous form of the illegal use of force; and that a determination whether an act of aggression has been committed requires consideration of all the circumstances of each particular case, including the gravity of the acts concerned and their consequences, in accordance with the Charter of the United Nations.

7. It is understood that in establishing whether an act of aggression constitutes a manifest violation of the Charter of the United Nations, the three components of character, gravity and scale must be sufficient to justify a 'manifest' determination. No one component can be significant enough to satisfy the manifest standard by itself.

Index